Max Weber and Democratic Politics

MAX WEBER &

DEMOCRATIC POLITICS

PETER BREINER

CORNELL UNIVERSITY PRESS

ITHACA AND LONDON

First published 1996 by Cornell University Press.

Printed in the United States of America

⊗ The paper in this book meets the minimum requirements
of the American National Standard for Information Sciences—
Permanence of Paper for Printed Library Materials, ANSI Z39.48-1984.

Library of Congress Cataloging-in-Publication Data

Breiner, Peter, b. 1947
    Max Weber and democratic politics / Peter Breiner.
        p.   cm.
    Includes bibliographical references and index.
    ISBN 0-8014-3147-6 (cloth : alk. paper)
    1. Weber, Max, 1864–1920—Contributions in political science.
2. Democracy.   3. Political ethics.   4. Political sociology.
I. Title.
JC263.W42B74   1996
306.2—dc20   96-31261

For Lizzie and Christiane

Contents

Preface

This book is a defense of a certain way of reading Max Weber. It interprets Weber as a theorist of political judgment, indeed as one of the few theorists of modern politics to have met the requirements of all good accounts of political judgment. A strong notion of political judgment should provide a map to navigate the unstable seas of politics, a guide to destinations we might reach and those we might not, and above all a rough assessment of the costs of reaching these destinations. Weber does all this and more.

Viewed under the concept of political judgment, Weber's ideal-types and typologies do not merely help us understand the meaning and consequences of the modern culture in which we are embedded or provide a comparative developmental history of different social formations within and outside of that culture. They also serve to construct the contexts, the logics, and the consequences that we will be exposed to in deciding on a course of social and political action. This feature of Weber's sociology is not hidden in his work. Weber recurrently emphasizes that sociology, especially an ideal-typical sociology of economics, culture, and politics, can help agents clarify the meaning of the fundamental ends that they seek and the necessary means and likely consequences of realizing them. He also emphasizes that no amount of sociological clarification can take away from the agent the ethical responsibility to exercise judgment and make fundamental choices of political projects. What remains obscure is precisely how Weber's abundant typologies and conceptual accounts of central matters of politics—such as power and legitimate domination, the development of the modern political party, state, and vocational politician, the tension between methodical discipline and charismatic leadership, and the power struggle endemic to the capitalist market—are operating to sharpen judgment and enhance responsible political choices.

In particular, there is a fundamental ambiguity in Weber's use of such accounts to establish the seemingly objective and subjective features of action. On the one hand, Weber uses his sociology to develop long-range, inexorable tendencies toward methodical rationalization; on the other, he uses it to underscore the uncertainty, contingency, and fortuitousness of all systematic political conduct. Weber deploys his typologies, especially in his magisterial but fragmentary *Economy and Society,* in both directions, intensifying objective causal forces at one moment and subjective contingency at another. By understanding Weber's combination and recombination of type-concepts as a mode of political judgment, I think it may be possible to make sense of one of the most elusive features about his work: its subjective stance toward the understanding of irresistible causal forces and its objective stance toward the sociological assessment of the subjective possibilities for action. More substantively, it will enable us to appreciate how at his best Weber provides us with the terms and concepts that we need in order to understand political situations in their full breadth—as constellations of power and domination manifested in parties, states, and forms of leadership, but also as broad convergences of cultural values, economic conduct, and political conduct, sometimes clashing and sometimes fusing to produce unexpected social formations. Even when well-known formations such as bureaucracy or rational capitalism are the outcome, Weber wants us to understand the role that unintended outcomes of social and political conduct play in producing them and what judgments about future action such development might imply.

But this book is more than an attempt to shift the angle on reading Weber from social science to political prudence. It also involves a critical engagement with him over the meaning his political prudence might have for participatory democrats. This latter purpose may seem curious. Weber was anything but a proponent of direct forms of democracy, and he saw the practical clarification provided by his political sociology and his political ethics as a firm chastening of all those who might entertain such a hope for modern politics. Yet, it is precisely his lack of sympathy for such a political project that makes him so important for those who might want to deepen democracy beyond routine party politics. There are several reasons for this.

First of all, his political sociological account of the logic of power and domination in general, and of the routine business of party politics in particular, sets the conditions that a realistic participatory democrat has to answer. If there is a possibility for deeper and more egalitarian participation, it will have to be found not by denying Weber's account of power and routine politics, but by teasing out the overlooked instrumental logics contained within it, as well as the fissures between its subjective construction and its objective claims.

Second, like participatory democrats, Weber argues that a central feature of both the economic and the political spheres is the separation of the means of power from those over whom it is exercised. Weber argues that the reappropriation of such means of power can at best be a tempo-rary phenomenon and in the main is unfeasible. It is a challenge to demo-crats to give some answer to this problem, especially in light of Weber's claim that such reappropriation collides with the unceasing power struggle that characterizes both economy and polity.

Third, Weber is concerned with a question that is at the heart of all theories of democracy: Who within the business of everyday politics is to exercise political judgment and responsibility? Weber thinks that citizens can be educated to accept certain political forms, but he does not think that collectivities can exercise the requisite responsibility to make ade-quate political judgments.

Fourth, and closely related, Weber provides a consequentialist account of political ethics that no participatory democrat can ignore. Weber places responsibility for the moral and practical paradoxes of deploying power for one's ultimate projects squarely in the hands of the vocational or leading politician. It is the job of the participatory democrat to show that participatory associations can practice such an ethic of responsibility. And it is an evasion to assume that participatory democracy will make this responsibility easier to bear by extirpating the paradoxes of power from political action.

Fifth, Weber complicates the choices of political forms in modern poli-tics by extending the conflict between routine competitive party politics and direct forms of democracy to include a third alternative, his famous plebiscitary leadership democracy. Weber shares many of the criticisms that participatory democrats level against routine professional politics. These include its tendency to dilute conflict over fundamental ends in favor of competition among sectional interests, the weak way in which it resists the transformation of politics into administration, and its propen-sity to substitute patronage for actual participation. To overcome these tendencies, Weber proposes a form of democracy, plebiscitary democracy, whose central feature is the testing of leadership and values through power struggle among charismatic leaders, rather than the democratization of state and economy through direct citizen involvement. A participatory democrat must have an answer to this model—or, at least, the logic of power that necessitates it—if the case for participatory politics is to be made adequately. Perhaps this answer lies not in another model but in a notion of participatory associations in constant and irresolvable conflict with the institutions of routine politics. In any case, such a politics will ignore Weber's sociologically informed political judgment and his political ethics only at its own peril.

The first three chapters of this book develop the foundations of and the tensions within Weber's account of a sociologically informed practical prudence. The first chapter revisits Weber's account of explanatory under-standing in the social sciences. Its purpose is to show how Weber's attempt to gain certainty in the midst of an interpretive view of social inquiry opens out both toward an objectified account of social practice (which critics have noted) as well as an intensely subjective one, which until recently has not been adequately appreciated. The next two chapters take up in turn the conflicting objective and subjective sides of Weber's notion of practical judgment.

The second chapter examines how Weber applies the notion of inter-pretive understanding to produce an objective account of practical politi-cal clarification distinct from the demands of partisan political argument. Here Weber claims against his own methodological perspectivism that his notion of sociology as *Wissenschaft* can interpret, and logically and instrumentally reconstruct, the meaning of fundamental political choices in the midst of irreconcilable value conflict.

The problems of this claim are revealed in the third chapter, which draws out the account of practical clarification of the previous chapter as it is applied to Weber's methodological and substantive criticism of mar-ginal utility theory in economics as a model of inquiry and guidance. Out of his criticism of this most lawlike of social sciences, he develops an account of practical clarification that emphasizes ambiguity, contingency, and the situation-bound nature of a sociologically informed political judg-ment. In a sense, these two chapters provide contradictory pictures of Weber's notion of practical judgment.

The fourth and fifth chapters lay bare the ways in which this fundamen-tal tension in Weber's account of sociological prudence is played out in his sociology of politics and his political ethics. In the fourth chapter, I discuss how Weber deploys the subjective-objective tensions in his ex-planatory understanding of the modern "business" of politics to open and restrict the possibilities for democracy.

In the fifth chapter, I show how Weber's famous political ethic of responsibility for the consequences of using power is one that all political actors should adhere to given the conditions under which political judg-ments have to be made; yet his deployment of this ethic against egalitarian democratic possibilities contains many of the problems already seen in his sociological account of politics. One can agree with his ethic and yet still want to ask how politically irresponsible citizens would hold vocational politicians to an ethic of responsibility.

The sixth chapter and last chapter looks backward and forward. First, it takes stock of the arguments Weber has provided and proposes two criticisms of his arguments against direct forms of democracy. These criticisms acknowledge his logic of power while finding within his subjective and objective notions of political judgment an entry for participatory democratic political alternatives that he rejects. Second, it draws out the implications of Weber's political ethics and sociologically informed prudence for strong participatory politics. In this chapter I provide an account of what participatory democratic theory and practice must look like if it is to meet up to Weber's demand for realism in the understanding of power and responsibility.

The idea for this book began quite a long time ago when I was awarded a German Academic Exchange Service Grant to study Weber's political writings in Germany. Since then, I have incurred some debts that I am pleased to acknowledge. Charles Drekmeier, Gabriel Almond, and Robert North read and commented on a very early version. Later on, Carole Pateman provided an encouraging reading. Tracy Strong, David Kettler, and Ron Jepperson gave me helpful advice on parts of the project as it developed. Two readers for Cornell University Press offered outstanding substantive and structural suggestions. My colleague Greg Nowell gave an acute reading of the manuscript. Special thanks go to my friend and colleague Jack Gunnell. Although he is a well-known critic of the practical pretensions of political theory, he has been an unfailing supporter of a project that in parts makes claim to precisely such pretensions. Our dialogue is an important part of this work. Thanks also go to Marty Edelman, who helped arrange some valuable free time for me to revise this book. My research assistant, Kevin Cameron, not only dutifully helped with references but also cheerfully allowed himself to be pressed into service as a discussion partner. Roger Haydon, my editor at Cornell, has been a wise and reassuring presence. My wife, Christiane von Buelow, kept reminding me that there is a difference between constructing schemes and engaging in interpretation. My daughter, Lizzie, both diverted me from this task and made me feel that something terribly important was going on at moments when I thought that finding a way through the logic of the Weberian world was next to hopeless. It is to Chris and Lizzie that this book is dedicated.

A condensed version of Chapter 3 was published as "The Political Logic of Economics and the Economic Logic of Modernity in Max Weber" in *Political Theory* 23 (1995): 25–47 (© 1995. Reprinted by permission of Sage Publications, Inc.). Portions of Chapter 6 are drawn from my article "Democratic Autonomy, Political Ethics, and Moral Luck," which appeared in *Political Theory* 17 (1989): 550–574 (© 1995. Reprinted by permission of Sage Publications, Inc.).

PETER BREINER

Albany, New York

Abbreviations of Max Weber's Works

The quality of the translations of Weber's work in English is rather uneven at best. I have therefore often made my own translations of passages cited from his work. To ensure accessibility, however, I have, where possible, cited the English edition along with the German one. Weber, as is well known, wrote in a difficult style, frequently qualifying and embellishing major claims within the same sentence. In translating him one is tempted to break into several sentences the many assertions often contained in one sentence. This is what many of his English translators have done. But this has the effect of frequently shifting Weber's emphasis, so that some marginal or peripheral qualification will be given the same or greater weight than some long-range tendency or outcome. What is worse, it may often leave the reader in the dark as to what the point of the sentence really is. To avoid this, I have tried where possible to keep the often packed sentences of Weber intact, even at the cost of awkwardness.

ES   *Economy and Society.* Translated and edited by Guenther Roth and Claus Wittich. Berkeley: University of California Press, 1978.

FMW   *From Max Weber.* Translated and edited by Hans Gerth and C. Wright Mills. New York: Oxford University Press, 1946.

GASS   *Gesammelte Aufsätze zur Soziologie und Sozialpolitik.* Edited by Marianne Weber. Tübingen: J. C. B. Mohr [Paul Siebeck], 1924.

GAW   *Gesammelte Aufsätze zur Wissenschaftslehre.* Edited by Johannes Winckelmann. 5th ed. Tübingen: J. C. B. Mohr [Paul Siebeck], 1982.

GPS   *Gesammelte politische Schriften.* 3d ed. Edited by Johannes Winckelmann. Tübingen: J. C. B. Mohr [Paul Siebeck], 1958.

Method   *The Methodology of the Social Sciences.* Translated and edited by Edward Shils and Henry Finch. New York: The Free Press, 1949.

MWG   *Max Weber Gesamtausgabe.* Edited by Horst Baier, M. Rainer Lepsius, Wolfgang Mommsen, Wolfgang Schluchter, and Johannes Winckelmann. Tübingen: J. C. B. Mohr [Paul Siebeck], 1984.

PE   *Die protestantische Ethik.* Vol. 1. Edited by Johannes Winckelmann. Hamburg: Siebenstern, 1975.

Abbreviations of Max Weber's Works

PESC   *The Protestant Ethic and the Spirit of Capitalism.* Translated by Talcott Parsons. New York: Scribner, 1958.

RK   *Roscher and Knies: The Logical Problems of Historical Economics.* Translated by Guy Oakes. New York: The Free Press, 1975.

WG   *Wirtschaft und Gesellschaft.* Edited by Johannes Winckelmann. 5th ed. Tübingen: J. C. B. Mohr [Paul Siebeck], 1972.

Zw   "Zwischenbetrachtung." In *MWG*, I: 19, edited by Helwig Schmidt-Glintzer. Tübingen: J. C. B. Mohr [Paul Siebeck], 1989.

Max Weber and Democratic Politics

Introduction

Max Weber's political vocabulary haunts our politics: the tension between vocational politics and bureaucracy; the fading of political responsibility; the reduction of politics to instrumental considerations and the detachment of fundamental ends from political practice; the functionalization of legitimacy and the consequent fact that politics has become the locus for the conflict among often irreconcilable cultural values; the fictional nature of democratic sovereignty when politics is hemmed in by parliaments, bureaucratic mass parties, and professional politicians; the difficulty of returning the means of production or administration to those caught within the division of labor. These are all fundamental features of politics in modern industrialized countries. An inquiry into any of these features quickly brings us back to Weber.

Yet, if we survey the interpreters of Weber's political argument we find that the precise location of his political theory is elusive. Some interpreters have seen it firmly located in his political sociology, especially that part devoted to his typology of domination.[1] Others have found it less in his sociological work on power and domination and more in his political writings that addressed contemporary issues. David Beetham, perhaps the most forceful proponent of this reading, has argued that Weber reserves a systematic treatment of issues such as class and class conflict, the political role of the administrative official, the limitations of bureaucracy, and the dynamics of politics as active power struggle only for his practical political writings.[2] More recently, some have found the heart of Weber's political theory to lie in his argument about competing cultural spheres imposing themselves on the individual who seeks to forge a coherent life plan. Politics thus becomes a particular, though by no means the exclusive, life sphere in which the conflict between subjective and objective culture

1. Reinhard Bendix, *Max Weber: An Intellectual Portrait* (New York: Doubleday Anchor, 1962).
2. David Beetham, *Max Weber and the Theory of Modern Politics* (Cambridge: Polity Press, 1985), pp. 252–253. Wolfgang Mommsen, *Max Weber und die deutsche Politik*, 2d ed (Tübingen: J. C. B. Mohr [Paul Siebeck], 1974), the major figure to press the case for Weber's partisan political writings as a clue to Weber's political commitments, especially to the nation state. But unlike Beetham, he sees Weber's political sociology and his political writings as complementary: both, he argues, have a common root in "the postulate of self-assertion and self-actualization of the personality in an administered world" (p. 446).

is fought out.[3] One commentator, Sheldon Wolin, has suggested that Weber's political theorizing is not to be found in his political sociology at all but, rather, in the act of founding a vocabulary for social science, one embued with political terms such as power, domination, legitimacy, state. According to Wolin, political theory in Weber is displaced onto methodology.[4] If we follow these commentators, "politics" in Weber seems to be everywhere and nowhere. It resides in his political sociology, in his practical political writings as opposed to his general sociology, in his account of modernist culture as opposed to his political sociology, and in his methodology as opposed to both his practical writings and his political sociology.

In this book, I suggest that a common locus for these disparate accounts of Weber's "true" political theory may be found if we read him as a theorist of practical political judgment or prudence.[5] In saying this, I want to align him with that strand of political thought that sees political knowledge as situation-bound advice on the means, ends, and logics of action to which political actors will be regularly exposed. For prudential political theorists, there can be general features of politics but no general "theory" of politics, because politics involves, in Aristotle's famous phrase, "things that could be otherwise." Politics involves judgment about possibility: What sort of political form can and should be realized, what sort of actions can and should be taken, what sort of public or sectional goals can and should be achieved, under a given set of conditions?

Of course, prudence or political judgment does not constitute one form

3. Wilhelm Hennis, in Max Weber: Essays in Reconstruction, trans. Keith Tribe (London: Allen & Unwin, 1988), and Lawrence Scaff, Fleeing the Iron Cage (Berkeley: University of California Press, 1989).

4. Sheldon Wolin, "Legitimation, Method, and the Politics of Theory," Political Theory, 9 (August 1981), 405–406.

5. A variety of commentators, many of whom sharply disagree with one another, have recognized that Weber's project is informed by an intention to use social science to provide practical self-clarification for social and political actors. See Wolfgang Mommsen, The Age of Bureaucracy (New York: Harper & Row, 1974), p. 5; Wolfgang Schluchter, "Value-Neutrality and the Ethic of Responsibility," in Guenther Roth and Wolfgang Schluchter, Max Weber's Vision of History (Berkeley: University of California Press, 1979); and more recently, "Beiträge zur Werttheorie: Gesinnungs und Verantwortungs Ethik: Probleme einer Unterscheidung," in Religion und Lebensführung, vol. 2 (Frankfurt: Suhrkamp, 1988). Wilhelm Hennis, "'A Science of Man': Max Weber and the Political Economy of the German Historical School," in Max Weber, trans. Tribe, pp. 108, 125. Hennis seeks to draw Weber back to the Aristotelian tradition of practical wisdom, arguing that Weber contributes a kind of Aristotelian ethical phronesis for the modern age, an age in which society has overwhelmed political community. Schluchter, by contrast, finds in Weber a pragmatic dialogue on fundamental goals with some strong similarities to that of Habermas. Except for Schluchter, few commentators up to now have sought to work out his account of practical clarification systematically, though Hennis promises to provide such an account in the future.

of political knowing. If Weber is to be understood as a contributor to political prudence, it is necessary to distinguish, at least tentatively, which kind he provides. Very roughly we can distinguish four kinds of political prudence: First, there is an Aristotelian prudence, or *phronesis,* that seeks to inform the translation of principles of good character into particular situations. This prudence, like political community itself, aims toward a life lived for its own sake, a life of internal excellences, and instead of informing the selection of means toward the realization of the virtues, it seeks to realize those states of character and actions that are constitutive of the good life. As Aristotle understands it, phronesis, or practical wisdom, is not self-sufficient. Its exercise requires a background judgment on the best form of polity achievable.

A second kind of prudence relies largely on custom and convention alone. Here judgment is exercised mostly by drawing appropriate conduct from conventional rules. And a change of policy must be implied by inherited understanding embedded in conventions and ancient constitutions. This notion has its roots in arguments for the ancient constitution of Fortescue, in Burke's defense of the social fabric as a continuous whole, and in the present in Michael Oakeshott's criticism of rational schemes of politics and his defense of judgment as drawing out "intimations."

A third kind of prudence, although defined more as practical reason, tests proposals for conventional political conduct against a generalization principle. This kind of prudence, represented by Rousseau and Kant and more recently by Habermas, seeks to overcome purely conventional, situation-bound, and partially interested judgments by testing their rationality and intelligibility according to the principle that they must make sense if applied to a whole community. This community could be one of equal active citizens agreeing to decide under a common will, human kind as such, or, as in the case of Habermas, a communicative community of rational linguistically competent agents constituting a public sphere.

A fourth tradition is represented by such thinkers as Thucydides, Machiavelli, and in modern times Maurice Merleau-Ponty and Antonio Gramsci. For these thinkers, political knowledge must provide foresight, although to put this foresight into practice, perceptive, energetic, and willful agents are needed. Even though such knowledge may provide generalizations about recurring cyclical tendencies or historical development, it will generally provide a panoply of historical situations and tentative generalizations that follow the vagaries and uncertainties of political action itself. Practical knowledge within this tradition, although not strictly utilitarian, is usually consequentialist. It tends to emphasize the paradoxical relation between fundamental political projects and consequences, and it often focuses on the contribution of power, as well as the limitations of our political foresight, toward producing such paradoxes. It also emphasizes the ways in which political judgment in practice often alters the very background conditions from whence it is derived, thus needing to incorporate its own tentativeness into the advice it gives. Not surprisingly, it is distrustful of philosophical attempts to find unchanging truths in political action or political arrangements. To be sure, "practical knowledge" of this kind does not reject attempts to find an ethics of politics; but it tends to shape political ethics to the changing necessities of political action.

Although Weber often frames his account of social scientific clarification of action in the Kantian categories of intrinsic ends and consequences, I am inclined to put his notion of prudence within the fourth tradition. Weber's prudence appears at two levels in his work. At an explicit level it is to be found in his claim that a broadly conceived political economy and an ideal-typical sociology can clarify for all actors the meaning and coherence of their ultimate commitments, the costs of deploying the necessary means to realize them, and the probabilities of success: "We can make clear to you the following: in this situation, you can in practice take this or that particular stand—for simplicity's sake please think of social phenomena as examples. If you take such and such a stand, then according scientific experience you have to apply such and such a means in order to carry it out practically. These means may be in themselves such that you believe you must reject them. Then one must simply choose between the end and the unavoidable means. Does the end [*Zweck*] "justify" ["*Heiligt*"] the means or not? The teacher can put this choice before you, more . . . he cannot do" (*GAW*, p. 607; *FMW*, p. 51). A sociologically informed prudence can do this by making clear not only the irrevocable features of political action such as power, domination, conflict, and uncertainty of outcome, but also the unique historical constellation of forces that deflect predictable outcomes in unforeseen ways. Here the ideal-types, such as those of monocratic bureaucracy, the modern political party, or the modern state, provide ways of constructing the configuration of forces within which political action may take place. Aside from reconstructing the pragmatic considerations facing an actor, sociological prudence can also present in ideal-typical ways the alternative formal ethical stances one might take toward political action. Weber's famous ethics of conviction and responsibility stand out here. Whatever substantive value commitments we may have, a formal ethics appropriate to our agency will require that we reconcile our innermost convictions with responsibility for the outcomes of deploying power on their behalf. But such a reconciliation in turn requires judgment, or *Augenmaß*, a sense of both situation and distance from self and of the various logics of power and domination one is contributing to or unleashing. A prudence so conceived will enhance the ambiguity of practical choice, Weber argues, rather than remove it from the agent.

At the less explicit level Weber's practical advice encompasses some of the central analyses of his political sociology: his attempt to reconcile understanding and explanation in social science, his critique of marginalist economics, his elaborate ideal-typical sociology of power and domination, his account of the origins and structure of modern politics as a business and vocation, and his examination, however unsystematic, of different state forms. Seen against the backdrop of his explicit account of practical advice, these various sociologies appear not merely as separate inquiries into the various logics of methodical social action, but also as contributions to a self-reflective clarification for individuals of the rationality guiding their social and political conduct. Thus, when in "Science as a Vocation" Weber describes his "scientific" task as providing both "knowledge of interrelated facts" and "self-clarification" on the meaning and consequences of our actions, I maintain that these two tasks are not separate but rather drive one another (*GAW*, p. 609; *FMW*, p. 152).

What links both of these levels and leads to an often fluid boundary line between them is a common concept of agency. This concept of agency understands us as at once capable of choosing first-person projects and of deliberating on the means and consequences of translating them into action: "Every serious reflection on the ultimate elements of meaningful human action is primarily tied to the categories of 'end' and 'means.' We want something concretely either 'for the sake of the value itself' or as a means of achieving something else which is more highly desired" (*GAW*, p. 149; *Method*, p. 52).

This awareness for Weber includes both the problem of having coherent first-person projects and commitments and the need to provide an assessment of the costs of acting upon them.[6] Although he is a thoroughgoing opponent of utilitarianism, Weber sees one of the tasks of ideal-typical constructs as showing the different costs of balancing agent-centered concerns for the integrity of one's projects with consequentialist considerations. Throughout both his partisan writings and his general sociology, Weber seeks to assess different potential commitments available to actors in a political context (socialism, direct democratic administration, rational capitalism, the nation, pacifism) against the logics of action undermining or contributing to their realization. Although he only makes the person-centered aspects explicit at certain select moments in his writings (e.g.,

6. I draw the concept of first-person projects and commitments from Bernard Williams, "A Critique of Utilitarianism," in J. J. C. Smart and Bernard Williams, *Utilitarianism For and Against* (Cambridge: Cambridge University Press, 1973), pp. 111–112, 116–117, 146.

on the economy of the East Elbian agricultural workers, vocational lectures, and in his methodological writings more than in *Economy and Society*), Weber is always interested in the social consequences of a model of society or a course of action for both the social formations they produce or reproduce *and* their effect on the agent. He puts this most dramatically in "Politics as a Vocation": "For everything that is striven for through *political* action, operating with violent means and following an ethic of responsibility, endangers 'the salvation of the soul.' If, however, one chases after the ultimate good in a war of beliefs, following a pure ethic of absolute ends, then the goals may be damaged and discredited for generations, because responsibility for the *consequences* are lacking and those diabolic forces which enter into play remain unknown to the actor. These [forces] are inexorable and produce consequences for his action and even for his inner self, to which he must helplessly submit, unless he perceives them" (*GPS*, p. 548; *FMW*, p. 126, Weber's emphasis). We need only note here that for Weber a perception of the "inexorable" sociological consequences one might unleash is necessary to avoid damage to one's own integrity as well as properly to assess the possibilities for realizing one's ultimate goals. Of course, Weber will often, especially in *Economy and Society*, put the emphasis more on the consequences for social formations than on agent-centered integrity, but his sociological claims are always encased in this duality of agency.

If we combine Weber's explicit and implicit accounts of prudential knowledge with his concept of agency, we discover three component parts to his political prudence: (1) a political sociology that can be read as a series of generalizations about the meaning and course of social and political action; (2) an explicit account of the requirements of social scientifically informed political prudence; and (3) an account of political ethics that is at once agent centered and consequentialist. The political ethics, which are largely formal, are given substance by the sociology. And they are linked together by his methodological account of the possibilities of social science in understanding and informing social practice.

Political Ethics, Political Prudence,
and Political Sociology

It is, indeed, one of the major strengths of Weber's political theory that he combines his political ethics—his ethics of responsibility and conviction—with a political sociology. The generalizations of his sociology provide both a context and a set of general maxims for political action. In doing so, Weber argues, a social scientific clarification of the meaning and consequences of political action will serve "moral forces" (*GAW*, p. 609;

FMW, p. 152). What he means by this is that it will inform responsible political agency, that is, it will help mold an agent who can exercise proper judgment in combining fundamental convictions and commitments with responsibility for the consequences of deploying political means to their realization. It is precisely the political sociology that gives this claim substance.

Weber's political sociology, especially the part that deals with the logic of power and domination and the emergence of politics as a profession and a calling, constructs the context in which his political ethics make sense. We need only recall that Weber always maintained that an ethic most suited to politics was an ethic demanding we be responsible for the "forseeable" outcomes of political action. A major part of this ethic is the demand that we be aware of the possibility that we might discredit our political projects without such responsibility. Therefore, in committing ourselves to fundamental political projects we also become responsible for judging properly whether they are feasible or not—and for that matter, if feasible, at what cost to other values. A political sociology is crucial for coming to such judgments. W. G. Runciman has put this matter most succinctly: "One of the things which Weber makes clear is how often it is feasibility which constitutes the crucial criterion by which a political argument may be settled; and it is such arguments which, if established, very often require the abandonment of a prescriptive political position."[7] Sociological evidence, including sociological generalizations, can often settle arguments over contending political positions by forcing political agents to ask what would happen if they were to pursue this goal within this context given the sociological tendencies their actions may play into.[8] Should the pursuit of a fundamental goal prove to be self-defeating, for Weber, this may prompt us to question the force of our original commitments or at least consider taking a new avenue to realize them. Even where such sociological tests of feasibility do not settle arguments but clarify fundamental differences, they force on us a more lucid account of precisely what it is that we actually stand for.

Both Weber's general sociology and his partisan political works are full of sociological generalizations that press such practical considerations on us. Some invoke a universal tendency like his famous argument that bureaucracy is the most efficient means of translating noninstrumental communal action into instrumental societal action or his closely connected claim that bureaucracy is inescapable once it is established (*WG*, pp. 569–

7. W. G. Runciman, "Sociological Evidence and Political Theory," in *Philosophy, Politics and Society,* 2d series, ed. Peter Laslett and W. G. Runciman, (Oxford: Basil Blackwell, 1962), p. 40.
8. Ibid., p. 45.

570; *ES*, p. 987). Others occupy a place between the historically contingent and universal account of rationalization, such as his claim that a self-
managed workplace does not undermine efficiency if efficiency is measured
merely by double-entry bookkeeping but will prove to be vulnerable when
measured by the need for capital accounting as a means of power struggle
within a capitalist market (*WG*, pp. 71–72, 77–78; *ES*, pp. 128–129,
137–138). The second assessment about the possibilities of achieving a
democratically run workplace modifies the first even as it undermines the
likelihood of in fact realizing this goal. But in either case, both generalizations constitute the kinds of logics that political actors are responsible for
knowing and taking into account when choosing a course of action.

A further aspect of this alignment of political theory with sociological
evidence deserves notice. Precisely because Weber's sociological generalizations are based on ideal-typical constructs, he avoids a problem that I
think inheres in the way modern moral philosophy assesses consequentialist notions of political responsibility. There is a tendency in modern
moral philosophy to test consequentialist arguments against our intuitions
about moral responsibility by invoking hypothetical cases. Often these
cases are bizarre, focusing on such things as life boats, killings of innocent
parties, unusual medical experiments, or odd contractual transactions.
Such odd examples are treated as if they could resolve ordinary cases of
moral or political choice when they frequently can do nothing of the kind.
The examples tend to be either underspecified or overly elaborate.[9] But
even when examples are not out of the ordinary, their construction tends
to be treated as unproblematic and distinct from the principles under
consideration. Often very good examples, such as the disaggregation of
decisions within a government bureaucracy or the private ownership of a
company-town, are treated as if they do not raise any theoretical problems
in themselves but merely for the principle at stake: In the first case the
assignment of political blame for failed policy; in the second the private
ownership of a firm.[10] But in making political judgments and in assigning
political responsibility, the examples we need are not merely instances of
principles or instances that might conflict with principles. Political principles, both those relating to fundamental projects and those relating to
consequences, depend on the political context in which they are meant to

9. For a good criticism of this tendency to use crazy cases in moral philosophy, see Robert
Goodin, *Political Theory and Public Policy* (Chicago: University of Chicago Press, 1982),
pp. 8–12.
10. For the first example, Dennis Thompson, *Political Ethics in Public Office* (Cambridge:
Harvard University Press, 1987), pp. 47, 48, 64; for the second, Michael Walzer, *Spheres
of Justice* (New York: Basic Books, 1981), pp. 291–303.

apply, and this context requires construction. This is what Weber supplies with his various ideal-types.

Weber's ideal-types and typologies, then, are not mere instances of social and political action. They are self-conscious constructs of the contexts in which social and political action takes place and the modes of action available in these contexts. Weber repeatedly emphasizes that ideal-types select the "distinctive" features of social constellations and that they register both the meaning and the consequences of acting through and within these forms. Thus, whether or not we focus on Weber's constructs of the logic of power and its tendency to routinize into forms of legitimate domination, his account of the modern business of politics—as embedded in the modern party, the modern state, the modern profession of politics— his accounts of the various forms of democracy, or his typological construct of the capitalist market as arena of power struggle, we are always faced with certain social and political logics that enable or constrain the realization of fundamental political goals. It is in these contexts that the tension between the moral integrity of political projects and the consequences of achieving them must be assessed for Weber. Moreover, these ideal-typical contexts are not seen as mere descriptions of reality but as self-conscious constructs from various value-laden points of view. The upshot of this approach is that Weber's sociological evidence relating to the problems of reconciling commitments with consequences is itself constructed from the vantage point of certain assessments of this relationship. If the meaning and consequences of political beliefs are susceptible to assessment by appeal to sociological evidence, Weber shows, sociological evidence is also susceptible to the interpretations of the meaning and consequences of social and political beliefs. It is precisely this (hermeneutic) self-consciousness about the construction of examples that is lacking in some of the more powerful tendencies of modern moral philosophy.

This said, there is also a distinctive danger in supporting or undermining political-ethical judgments by appealing to generalizations based on self-consciously constructed typologies and types. The danger is that in the construction and explanatory deployment of sociological typologies, criteria of what counts as feasible outcomes are often selected by what the interpreter finds to be a desirable state of affairs. A typology of ideal constructs always will select out one stream of meaningful action and its outcomes along with certain deflecting tendencies. It will thus contain a certain assessment of relevant consequences. In itself this is unavoidable. The problem occurs when the theorist has not argued for what she or he takes to be a desirable model or set of political goals but uses an inevitably one-sided typological construct to demonstrate them to be the only feasible ones compared to their competitors. Desirability criteria are collapsed into feasibility criteria. This tendency, I argue in this study, is pronounced in Weber. Using his sociological generalizations to demonstrate that some goal is not feasible because it conflicts with efficiency, leads to unintended results, or cannot survive the power struggle necessary for its realization, Weber will often be able to reject goals that he disagrees with as if his judgment were based on incontestable practical standards. Interestingly, Weber himself provides the grounds for criticizing this move. Not only does he demonstrate at times that practical standards are themselves in dispute, but more important, he also uses his political sociology to argue for the unfeasibility of political projects that he would reject on other grounds even if they were realizable. Again, the problem is not that Weber is not entitled to argue for the feasibility of some political projects as opposed to others based on sociological generalizations, but that his notions of feasibility and his rejection of rival criteria of feasibility are frequently cut to the size of his own fundamental commitments.

The Double Edge of Weber's Political Sociology: The
Objective and Subjective Logics of Methodical Action

The tension between feasibility and desirability in Weber raises a number of problems in the way his political sociology functions as a form of advice. I am concerned with two of them. The first revolves around the distinctive and often deliberate way in which Weber exploits the ambiguity over whether he is giving an impartial general account of the logic of methodical action or a subjective situation-bound account of the multiple logics that constitute the different terrains of action. The second revolves around the application of his political prudence to defend vocational politics against various forms of direct democracy. These two are related because Weber's exploitation of the ambiguity of subjective and objective logics in his work enables him to argue for vocational politics and against more direct forms of democracy by appealing to objective standards of feasibility while maintaining that commitment to either form is a matter of personal choice. In this way he is able to let feasibility criteria do the work of ethical justification for his model of personhood and politics.

As for the first problem, interpreters have had intense conflicts over the precise status of Weber's concept of rationalization. Discussion has centered specifically on whether Weber has a uniform developmental theory of the methodical rationalization of all spheres of life or whether he in fact was concerned with the way individuals can find an orderly direction for their lives in each distinctive life sphere. At the root of this debate is the controversial claim of Friedrich Tenbruck that although initially concentrating on a historical sociology of Western rationalism based on multiple forms of rationalization, Weber in his *Sociology of Religion* developed a universal evolutionary theory of rationalization based on the inner logic of ideas rather than material interests. This inner logic was embodied in the methodical economic ethics of religious ideas that in the West systematically deprived the world of magic: "Weber's important discovery . . . lay in the knowledge that rationalization in all its historical fragility was born from the compulsion of an inherent logic, which was situated in the irresistible drive towards the rationalization of religious ideas. Therefore, the process of rationalization is at heart an historico-religious process of disenchantment, and the stages and moments in the history of rationalization derive their unity from the process of disenchantment."[11] On this reading, Weber superimposed his account of disenchantment wrought by teleological modes of action on his prior account of the multiple forms of rationalization of conduct.

Critics have found this thesis inadequate because it creates an artificial split, textually as well as conceptually, between Weber's historical and his sociological writings. More important, they rightly maintain that it overlooks Weber's relentless attacks on evolutionary theories of history. However, among the critics of the Tenbruck thesis a protracted debate has raged in its own right. On the one side, Wolfgang Schluchter has maintained that Weber's work as a whole is concerned with rationalization but that any evolutionary account of the stages of rationality in his work must be subsumed under a "developmental comparative history" of rationalization in the West. This "developmental history" has two aspects: On the one hand it consists of a general account of rational social action and social order based largely on our inherent tendency to order our actions into methodical conduct; on the other, it consists of specific accounts of the way in which rationality is embodied in different cultures and within the variety of social orders in Western culture. For example, Weber, on Schluchter's reading, provides a general account of domination and the distinctive forms it may take; but he also compares the different

---

11. "The Problem of Thematic Unity in the Works of Max Weber" in *Reading Weber,* ed. Keith Tribe (London: Routledge, 1989), p. 56, a translation of Friedrich Tenbruck, "Das Werk Max Webers," *Kölner Zeitschrift für Soziologie* 27 (1975). In the prefatory remarks to the English edition, Tenbruck expresses regret that his own thesis contributed to the thinking that Weber had a uniform theory of rationalization. His interpretation meant to emphasize that teleological rationality for Weber was constantly deflected in irrational directions. The reason, however, why Tenbruck's thesis could unleash such a debate is that Weber himself, as I argue, moves among several versions of methodical rationalization, implying at times a uniform notion of rationalization, at other times a notion of multiple rationalizations subject to convergence or deflection, and at yet other times a contingent struggle among forces seeking to act systematically in the backdrop of either multiple forms of rationalization or one form alone.

historical configurations of domination to explain why it takes a more rational legal form in one case, a more traditional form in another.[12] Schluchter admits that Weber does not explicitly distinguish his general account from his developmental inquiries into rationalization. But he argues that for precisely this reason Weber's developmental history needs to be reconstructed in light of recent evolutionary theory such as that of Habermas.

Wilhelm Hennis, who represents the other side of this debate, rejects both the emphasis on rationalization and the attempt to improve on Weber. Hennis argues that the concept of rationalization is not at all central to Weber's theoretical project. On the contrary, he insists, the question that serves as the point of departure for Weber's whole corpus and to which all his particular empirical inquiries return, his *Fragestellung*, is "the fate of man" (or, more properly, the human personality as type) in the face of the competing spheres of life conduct that characterize modernity.[13] From his early inquiries into East Elbian rural labor, to his late sociology of domination, to his two vocational essays, Weber, according to Hennis, displays one overriding concern: how it might be possible for the subjective personality to develop and live an ethically coherent life given the objective and impersonal life orders to which the subject must adapt him/herself.[14] The origin of this "question" for Hennis is to be found in the historical comparison that Weber draws in his earliest work "Developmental Tendencies in the Situation of East Elbian Rural Laborers," "German Rural Laborers," and "The Rural Constitution of Labor." In these writings, Weber distinguishes between a period when the orders of life allow the cultivation of an ethical personality with obligations to others (usually occurring under traditional relations as in the case of the East Elbian rural aristocracy who on the basis of patriarchal relations to rural labor formed a "political aristocracy") and modernity where the different life orders such as the capitalist market or the bureaucratic state are so objectified that the subject can only attain personality by living up to their impersonal demands (pp. 70, 76–77, 100, 103). Thus Weber's special sociological inquiries into religion, economics, politics, and law are driven by his interest in the kind of personality, the type of human being that each of these life orders produce or prevent from appearing (pp. 55–56). On this reading, the rationalization process is not

12. Wolfgang Schluchter, *The Rise of Western Rationalism*, trans. Guenther Roth (Berkeley: University of California Press, 1981), pp. 5, 10.

13. Wilhelm Hennis, "Max Weber's Central Question" and "Max Weber's Theme: 'Personality and the Life Orders,'" in *Max Weber*, trans. Tribe.

14. Hennis, "Max Weber's Theme: Personality and Life Orders," p. 103.

simply embedded in a comparative developmental history but in the objective logics of each of the life orders of modernity (p. 98).

Not surprisingly, both of these positions find textual support in Weber.
From his earliest writings on, Weber speaks of his sociological inquiries
as providing *Entwicklungsgeschichte*, "developmental history," and he
most certainly speaks of the variety of conflicting values and value spheres
in which the person in modernity must seek to forge an intelligible life:
both the vocabulary of *Entwicklungsgeschichte* and the vocabulary of
Persöhnlichkeit, Lebensführung, and *Lebensordnung* are laced throughout his work. But further textual reference could hardly resolve this debate
because both interpreters in decidedly different ways claim to be eliciting
an underlying structure implicit in Weber's work. Schluchter explicitly
argues that he is providing a reconstruction of Weber's account of rationalization, and Hennis claims to reject any reconstruction in favor of an
"interpretive understanding" of Weber's underlying "theme" (pp. 68, 65).
The greatest difficulties appear precisely in these methodological claims.
Hennis's emphasis on eliciting Weber's "theme," or "central question,"
unnecessarily restricts the powerful insight he has gained in evoking
Weber's preoccupation with the subjective agent and the objective spheres
of life conduct. After all, to elicit an underlying theme or question in a
political or social theorist is hardly to have assessed the force of that
theorist's argument. Furthermore, it is unclear how thematic analysis
alone will register, let alone explain, those points in a work when the
argument provided may be at odds with the theme itself. This is precisely
what calls for reconstruction. However, Schluchter's reconstructive approach may also neglect a crucial feature of Weber's argument: its seemingly *deliberate* fragmentariness. Weber is fairly explicit about the reasons
why his plenitude of types are never synthesized into a whole historical
dynamic, why he might reject in Schluchter's terms a synthesis of evolutionary theory and comparative history. His ideal-types provide mere perspectives on the stream of historical events, and even when they are related
together into typologies they serve to intensify the distinctive features of
a particular dynamic of action rather than provide a synoptic evolutionary
account of rational social action as such (*GAW*, pp. 191–192; *Method,*
p. 91). In a sense, to have assembled these types into one scheme or matrix
would have inhibited their use in capturing a dynamic and multi-sided
processes of convergence and contingency in streams of conduct. Thus
the incompleteness of Weber's ideal-typical accounts of rationalization of
action is not merely the result of theoretical inadequacy. To have given
them systematic form and closure would have been to deny precisely their
heuristic purpose of analyzing historical situations.

Curiously, once we set the methodological conflict aside neither of these two positions is as far apart as they each claim to be, and Schluchter acknowledges this.[15] For they both identify an objective account of rationalization in Weber and a subjective and contingent one. They merely locate these accounts in different parts of Weber's argument. Schluchter claims that Weber's general conceptual account of rationalization is disaggregated into a number of specific developmental histories in which the course and outcome of rationalization are compared among the different spheres of society and between Western culture and cultures in which rationalization was deflected into traditional directions. Hennis claims that Weber's overall interest was in the breakdown of traditional personal relations in modernity so that each life order contained an inner rationalization that all persons seeking to act coherently within them would have to confront. The emphasis in the former interpretation is on an objective process of rationalization manifested in a variety of convergent (and occasionally divergent) historical developments. The emphasis on the latter is on subjective relations in modernity that unleash an objective rationalization of each order of life.

Now I would like to maintain that in substance, though not necessarily in method, both of these interpretations are correct about Weber even though they give a completely different priority to the place of rationalization in his theory. The reason why they could both be right yet conflict over the status of rationalization is that they each capture one side of a dichotomy that runs throughout Weber's work. On the one hand, Weber at various moments portrays the rationalization process as objective and inexorable. Agents unknowingly play into it because the rational process of methodically fitting means to ends is an unavoidable feature of human agency whatever other purposes it sets for itself. Here one stream of causality produces and reproduces, for example, monocratic bureaucracy, the modern state monopolizing the legitimate use of force, rational capitalism based on free labor and capital accounting, or the modern profession within the division of labor. The claim of Western culture to universality is in large part based on having raised this feature of agency to a fundamental cultural value and set it into motion above the heads of all social agents. On the other hand, Weber recurrently emphasizes the plurality of causes at work both on the subjective agent's conscious activity and in

15. See Wolfgang Schluchter, *Rationalism, Religion and Domination* (Berkeley: University of California Press, 1989), pp. 574–575. Schluchter cedes Hennis the claim that Weber was interested in the forging of the personality in the various modern spheres of life conduct, but he argues that Weber's inquiries into this matter took the form of a comparative developmental history of the various forms of rationalization. Not surprisingly, he denies Hennis's methodological claim that Weber's interest in this matter is a philosophical-anthropological one.

constituting any social relation. Thus an "understanding" of subjective action requires that we construct the variety of contingent logics that impinge on the agent's attempt to forge coherent and methodical conduct. Here the emphasis is on the contingency and uncertainty accompanying the appearance of a social formation such as rational capitalism or an agent such as the vocational politician. Modernity merely intensifies this multicausalism. For in modernity not only do the different value spheres such as religion, science, economics, politics, and aesthetics conflict with one another, but the variety of instrumental logics necessary to achieve the values of each sphere converge and collide with each other as well.

Many interpreters have noted Weber's tendency to argue for and practice a resolute multicausalism yet at times lapse into claims to be providing objective causal laws of social action. But they have usually explained this tendency away as an oversight on Weber's part. Discussing Weber's analysis of the bureaucratization of modern political parties, Schluchter remarks: "Weber always contextualized his statements concerning lawlike relationships by placing them in a constellational analysis and thus differentiating them in this way. This has to be taken into account if one intends to avoid oversimplifying his argument on the unavoidable bureaucratization of democratic organizations made in terms of the political parties in mass democracies." But he also notes:

Cognizance of technology as a "condition" and "limit" is not the same as a "technocratic" orientation. The latter arises only when certain technical means are hypostatized to a fundamental restrictive condition of all human action. This was, however, *inadvertently* done in some parts of Weber's analysis. Just the fact that he generally used rationalization and bureaucratization synonymously is already an indication of this. In some passages, the bureaucratic form of organization is exalted to the point where it becomes a principal instrument without which rational organization becomes impossible. Such a fixation is, however, untenable on the basis of Weber's very own premises. (my emphasis).[16]

Similarly, Wolfgang Mommsen remarks that Weber adhered to "a pluralistic model of societal change. Formal rationalization . . . could be but did not have to be the ultimate objective of the historical process." But he too notes that "*this is often obscured by Weber's own way of expressing himself*. . . . Even in the later writings there are residues of an objectivistic

16. Ibid., *Rationalism, Religion, and Domination*, pp. 380, 387.

use of language in regard to rationalization that give rise to misinterpretations" (my emphasis).[17]

This seeming contradiction at the heart of Weber's account of rationalization could be at least partially explained if we realize that his deviation from his stated interpretive perspectivism is not a mere oversight on his part but rather a strategy of argument, one that I think is driven by the prudential uses of his sociology. Weber, in fact, consciously plays with both positions, often claiming that he can provide an objective account of the consequences of any social action while also speaking of the multiplicity of values and causes impinging on social life. Weber never quite resolves this tension between his objectivist and intensely subjective account of the interpretation of social action. On the contrary, he often exploits it, sometimes claiming complete consistency between subjective and objective, at other times driving these two terms to extremes, and yet at other times, shuttling back and forth between them. Sometimes even, as in his famous essay on "Objectivity," he invokes a subjective and an objective account of rationalization in the very same sentence: "There are *no* out and out 'objectively' scientific analyses of cultural life or of 'social occurences' . . . *independent* of special 'one-sided' points of view from which they . . . are chosen, analyzed, and representationally classified as object of research [Forschungsobjeckt]" (*GAW*, p. 170). Here the phrase "independent of" allows us to slide in either direction.

This mobility of movement between subjective and objective—or, rather, between subjectively rooted objectivity and an agentless objectivity—allows Weber wide scope in providing a sociologically informed prudence. Focusing on the multiple logics of methodical conduct at work in a historical situation, he can stress the uncertainty and hard choices facing social and political actors. He can also stress the constantly shifting relations between converging tendencies and the possible outcomes that may ensue. He can, in particular, reveal the costs to one's own values as well as other equally important values when one acts in any one sphere of social and political life.

On the other hand, as commentators have noticed, Weber often singles out one strand of methodical social action, frequently selected from his typology of legitimate domination, such as the dependence of social action on obedience to formal-legal rationality, and raises it to the level of an irrevocable objective tendency of all social conduct. He then, sometimes digressively, measures various alternative outcomes against this tendency only to come to the conclusion that all social or political initiatives will

17. Wolfgang Mommsen, "Personal Conduct and Societal Change" in *Max Weber: Rationality and Modernity*, ed. Sam Whimster and Scott Lash (London: Allen & Unwin, 1987), pp. 40–41.

further contribute to it. For example, he claims that all attempts to realize substantive equality will inevitably further the rationalization of monocratic bureaucracy; or in turn he claims that once it is established, all political actors will be beholden to this form of domination. He then measures various substantive positions such as radical democracy, or socialism according to how they would fare in light of this tendency. But he often uses his account of inexorable logics more cunningly. Rather than simply showing how some political project or agent plays into a universal tendency that might efface it or lead to its opposite, he seeks to show the contingent conditions under which it may survive. But in this he is rather selective. At moments, he points to the frailty of some social or political model in the face of, say, the forces of legal rationalization or the demands of the struggle for power in order to examine the conditions under which it might be feasibly realized and sustained; at other times he will invoke an equally frail alternative only to demonstrate that the conditions under which it could be realized are marginal. In the latter case, the alternative is often one Weber would not support even if he could demonstrate its feasibility. Thus, as we shall see in Chapter 4, Weber argues that precisely because the logic that produces the vocational politician is so frail compared to logic that produces the modern state and modern political party, a political order must be created that nurtures such a figure. By contrast, as we will see in Chapter 5, he uses the same kind of argument against forms of direct democracy in local community or the workplace. Here he will argue that precisely because the logics sustaining direct forms of democracy are so frail compared to the logics producing state administration and the competitive political party, direct democratic forms will prove unfeasible except in the very short run or under extremely atypical conditions. Prudence therefore will dictate that politically responsible actors must be found within the confines of the logic of domination rather than in opposition to it. What this suggests is that Weber often invokes his objective stance to argue for the unfeasibility of political projects he disagrees with substantively. But it also suggests that he is at times willing to modify this stance to argue for projects he supports rather passionately, but whose survival is threatened, such as the need for vocational politics. In these moments, he invokes his multicausalism to examine the possible alternatives to some general law-like tendency. He now even is willing to fortify his assessment by comparing his favored political possibility with other alternatives he finds equally weak or weaker such as direct forms of democracy.

Of course, one could argue that precisely such modification is the sign of a sociologically flexible notion of practical prudence. Surely, political judgment requires that we know what is probable, the general tendencies social and political actors contribute to or play into, as well as what is possible, the contingent possibilities that can happen but are hardly fated to happen.[18] Weber is simply showing what is politically likely to occur— for example, the bureaucratization of modern parties and the modern state—and then measuring the possibility for different kinds of political actors and political models in light of these tendencies.[19] This is, indeed, what Weber is doing when he maintains the tension between his subjective multicausalism and his claims to describe objective tendencies. It is what he has in mind when he claims that he is merely providing subjectively rooted but impartial assessments of "the objective possibilities" for realizing political goals. The problems emerge when Weber collapses the possible into the probable and probable into the inevitable, especially when he does this in order to deny the feasibility of political projects that he finds to be disagreeable. Under these circumstances, Weber can withdraw a claim to realism from political projects he finds undesirable while extending that same claim to projects he believes should be furthered, even though both projects may merely be in the realm of the possible.

Weber deploys this strategy on many fronts.[20] What interests me here

18. I draw this distinction from Albert Hirschman, "In Defense of Possibilism," in *Rival Views of Market Society and Other Essays* (Cambridge: Harvard University Press, 1986).
19. A typical and very effective use of such analysis is to be found in his account of why the Socialist Party of Germany in Imperial Germany remained an ideological party, despite the general tendency of all mass parties to become bureaucratic and reject ideology for success within the state, and why it would eventually succumb to this tendency. See *GPS* pp. 540–543, 366. See also, Wolfgang Schluchter, *Rationalism, Religion and Domination*, pp. 377–383.
20. See Stephen Turner and Regis Factor, *Max Weber and the Dispute over Reason and Value* (London: Routledge, 1984), pp. 51–55, 58–59; Guenther Roth, "Weber's 'Political Failure,'" *Telos* 78 (Winter 1988–89) 136–139. Turner and Factor argue that Weber made a similar move in his struggles in the *Verein für Sozialpolitik* using the fact-value distinction to discredit partisan positions that he disagreed with, in particular those of Schmoller, while cloaking his own position in scientific objectivity. Similarly, Guenther Roth has argued that Weber's vocational essays as well as *Economy and Society* use objectivity to fight all the various agents that had frustrated his political projects for Germany, especially revolutionary students, literati, proponents of pessimistic philosophies of history, socialist leaders like Kurt Eisner: "Weber's return to single minded scholarship was not only an act of renunciation in an obvious sense but continuation of his political war by other means" (p. 145). Obviously, the argument to be presented here is sympathetic to the stance taken by Turner and Factor and Roth. But I also think that such a stance overstates the case. Even if Weber's claims to objectivity serve as a pretext to overcome political opponents, this says nothing about the validity of the actual theory provided, especially as a form of practical guidance. More substantively, it fails to distinguish the force of his explicit account of political judgment, the sociological types (and historical interpretations) that inform it, and his political ethics from the polemical uses to which this account is put. We need not buy into all of Weber's claims to objectivity or even agree with all Weber's substantive judgments to agree with his account of the role of sociology in providing practical clarification, his multicausal approach to political understanding, or his consequentialist notion of political responsibility. The diffi-

is the how he deploys it in his defense of vocational politics and his various accounts of democracy.

Weber and Democracy

In *Economy and Society,* in his vocational lectures, and in his partisan political writings, Weber directly challenges various schemes to extend active and in so far as is feasible direct and equal participation to citizens in modern political societies. But the thrust of his criticism, despite his many partisan writings on this matter, is not in defending or rejecting any particular constitutional state form for the principles it may embody. Rather, his account of democracy is framed firmly within his notion of scientific or scholarly clarification of politics: that is, it entails an ideal-typical analysis of different forms of democratic state over and against nondemocratic forms, the ways in which they function, and an account of the consequences of adopting one form or another for "the conditions of life" (*GAW*, 601).[21] Within such a frame, the question of democracy appears as a confrontation between vocational politics on the one side and both sectional party politics and direct democracy on the other. Forms of state, including his rather sketchy proposal for plebiscitary leadership democracy are seen largely as means of nurturing vocational politicians, that is, professional politicians with a higher calling both to politics and to fundamental commitments.

At the center of this confrontation, on my reading of Weber, is the development of modern politics into a day-to-day "business" with its own division of labor and professional demands. The logics underlying the development of the modern administrative state, the modern bureaucratic mass party, and the professional politician who lives off politics converge to produce politics as a *Betrieb,* as an autonomous methodical pursuit and as a business. In so far as the convergence of these three forms produce the context of modern politics, lay political actors become increasingly superfluous. Politics becomes the domain of professionals who in the case of party officials and parliamentarians live off politics but who to the degree that they are leaders committed to fundamental goals and programs as well as to taking responsibility for historical outcomes also live for politics.

---

culties in Weber's political theory, such as it is, I think are more fruitfully uncovered *within* his account of practical judgment than against it.

21. It is interesting to note that even where Weber claims not to be arguing about matters of practical-political judgment from a "scientific" vantage point, as in "Parliament and Democracy in a Reconstructed Germany," he still employs fundamental notions from his political sociology, as well as an ideal-typical account of bureaucracy and parliaments, to

The problem informing Weber's construction of modern politics is to find in the "business" side an actor who will be willing to pursue the struggle for power within the confines of the division of labor in party and state yet also seek to rise above it by turning professional commitment into a higher calling: this calling cannot just be an inner commitment to politics but must also include the ability through charismatic qualities to convince a party apparatus and mass following of this commitment. This actor is the vocational politician. This political agent transforms the functional features of politics into a higher moral commitment and in turn translates fundamental moral commitments into the functional demands of politics.

The appearance of this figure for Weber is ironic indeed. For the vocational politician is both an ideal-typical construct of Weber's sociological prudence and the agent meant to be guided by that prudence. She or he must therefore invent herself or himself from within the profession of politics itself. The vocational politician does this by combining insight into the sociological logics of politics with a political ethics of both conviction and responsibility. Toward this end, this agent must combine commitment to long-term concrete goals (a *Sache* as cause and *Sachlichkeit* as choosing a cause with factual possibility), responsibility for the means and consequences of using power to achieve these goals, and the judgment to know the variety of logics that will impinge on the exercise of his or her power. But the vocational politician has to do more than this: for he or she must know how to pursue power within the constraints imposed by the logic of the three legitimate forms of domination. In particular, this agent must know that the struggle for political power through and within the modern state and political party will be subject to a constant oscillation between the exercise of charismatic and formal-legal domination.

Weber's account of democracy follows from the need to find a form of state that cultivates vocational politicians with these qualities. Here he defines effectiveness as that form that selects out the vocational politician with leadership qualities as a type from the mere professional who lives off politics. From this vantage point, the first possibility, direct forms of democracy drops out from the start. Weber does not explicitly judge the feasibility of direct democratic forms on whether they cultivate vocational politicians because when they are functioning properly, all citizens are allowed to participate in deliberation and administration. They represent the denial of the need for vocational politicians. Weber's assessment there-

---

make his case for a strong parliament and plebiscitary executive (*GPS*, pp. 306, 320–323; *ES*, pp. 1381, 1394–1395).

fore depends on showing that if they want their laws to be carried out methodically, they have to designate some groups as administrators that in turn opens the way for the participation of notables who in turn usher in rebellion by the citizens and the formation of political parties. In effect, direct democracy is found wanting not because it denies vocational politics but because it cannot escape either the logic of administrative control or the power struggle among parties. Its denial of modern politics as a business does not immunize it against the logic of power and domination that frames this business.

Weber's second possibility, competitive party democracy, completely embodies the business of politics as a profession. Under this model parties viewed as the representatives of status groups and classes compete for office and in parliaments. Such parties are essentially machines whose task is to mobilize a mass electorate on behalf of professional party operatives who are seeking office. Here Weber rejects this model because it is too well adapted to the business side of politics. It produces professional politicians without a calling. That is, it weeds out politicians with responsibility, judgment, convictions, and charismatic leadership qualities.

The last alternative, leadership democracy, comes closest to cultivating professional politicians with vocational qualities, for it combines the business side of political parties and the administrative state with charismatic leadership. There is a double edge to the democratic claims of this model. As we will see, the authoritarian features of charisma are combined with democratic elections, turning elections into democratic plebiscites on the vocational qualities of political leaders but also rendering such elections unconditional acclamations of the leader's authority. Weber seeks to separate such elections from parliamentary ones, so that the sectional interests at work in parliaments do not find expression in the choice of political leaders.

Although presented as the most feasible form for the realization of vocational politics, the structure of plebiscitary leadership democracy offers nothing that guarantees that it will reach this goal. At best it encourages a struggle among charismatic individuals leading party machines, and through charisma it opens a narrow avenue through which responsible vocational politicians may possibly enter into political leadership. It should be fairly obvious that if the appearance of vocational politicians is a chancy occurrence within the modern organization of politics for Weber, plebiscitary politics increases these chances by only a small increment.

In this study, I want to argue that it is precisely in Weber's recommendation of this political model that the previously discussed ambiguities of his prudence and his political ethics come to the fore. In this model the inexorable tendencies toward bureaucratization of both state and modern mass party are assumed to be at work; yet against these tendencies a realm of subjective uncertainty is attained through the democratic process of selecting plebiscitary leaders. Now if Weber's ethic of responsibility requires that we be responsible for making adequate judgments about the consequences of exercising power toward fundamental goals, it is unclear whether plebiscitarian democracy will pass the test either as a model worth achieving or sustaining or as a state form within which this ethic is to be exercised. Much depends on whether we agree on the desirability and intrinsic worth of vocational politics against lay politics. Much also depends on whether we think that the risks attending this form of democracy are worth taking. Weber as I demonstrate in Chapter 5, seeks to convince us that the risk is worth taking. He does so by invoking the frailty of direct democratic forms against the inexorable logic of power struggle and formal legality, especially as this logic governs the business side of modern politics, by speaking about the inevitable stunting of mass political behavior by the demands of modern party machines, and finally by invoking the durability of a politics in which sectional interests in parliaments and the bureaucratic state monopolize all politics and so create a state form in which no political leaders take responsibility for political judgment. But these are arguments against other democratic alternatives, not arguments for plebiscitarian politics. More important, they manifest Weber's tendency to hypostatize the rationalization process or invoke the uncertainty of any one political tendency as it suits his purposes. At the end of the day, then, we are still left with an argument that an ethic of political responsibility for consequences can only be exercised in a state form that offers a chance of cultivating vocational politicians. But we are still not sure whether this proposal for plebescitary democracy itself accords with an ethic of political responsibility or happens to be in Weber's own terms a deeply felt and carefully thought-out conviction.

At the close of this work, I argue that once we look past Weber's strategies of making this judgment seem impartial, we can argue that his ethic of responsibility for the consequences of power can and must be exercised by both lay and professional political actors alike; and that if we accept this we may also notice a logic within Weber's own account of power that allows for an argument on the feasibility of direct forms of democracy. According to this logic, participatory forms engage in constant resistance to routine forms of domination and discipline, forcing proposals for greater equity on the political process without being able to overcome power once and for all. To be sure, this logic is one tendency, and hardly inexorable, but it allows us to connect an ethic of responsibility and a prudential claim to feasibility to one version of participant democratic arguments. This version of democracy does not view direct forms of participation as harmoniously integrated in the institutions of state and economy but, rather, as existing in constant tension with the logics of legitimate domination. This said, I also claim that unless participatory democratic theory takes into account the moral risks, the uncertainty of outcome, and the conflicting values and value spheres that impinge on political decisions, it will not live up to the demands of modern politics that Weber articulated so forcefully.

In arguing that there is a concept of strong direct democracy that might meet Weber's political-ethical test and at least open the possibility of meeting his practical sociological test as well, I am not discounting the power of Weber's sociological account of liberal democracy or the logics in which it entangles lay and vocational political actors alike; nor, for that matter, am I discounting the force of his ethic of political responsibility. If anything, I am acknowledging them both as the point of departure for any discussion about the possibility and desirability of forms of democracy that realize a political will grounded in the direct participation of equal citizens.[22] On this point I agree wholeheartedly with David Beetham who argues that, "Weber's thought . . . stands much more at the starting point than at the conclusion of a series of developments in the theory and practice of liberal democracy in the era of mass politics and bureaucratic organizations; it is much more as a precursor than as an 'epigone' that he should be understood."[23] It is only within his account of the logics of politics, economics, and culture that any more adequate alternative to Weber's own highly ambiguous account of liberal democracy is to be found.

A Note on Method

In developing the connection between Weber's sociologically informed political prudence and his theory of democracy—and the mutual interac-

22. Wilhelm Hennis and Lawrence Scaff have recently claimed that Weber did not consider the question of democracy to be part of his "central concerns." See Hennis, "Max Weber's Theme: Personality and Life Orders," p. 63; Scaff, *Fleeing the Iron Cage*, p. 154. For these two interpreters, Weber's central concern is with human coherence in the face of objectified spheres of life conduct of which politics is just one. I do not find these two sets of concerns mutually exclusive, especially given Weber's interest in finding the democratic model in which vocational political actors can flourish. Indeed, for Weber the dilemma of democracy is how to cultivate political actors who will be able to make hard choices given the conflicting values and instrumental logics endemic to modern culture in general and to the sphere of politics in particular. As we shall see, politics in the modern state is for Weber a nexus point for the conflict of values and value spheres. Thus his argument with routine party politics and various forms of direct democracy is in part about their failure to produce a type of person who can live up to the demands of this conflict.
23. Beetham, *Max Weber and the Theory of Modern Politics*, p. 7.

tion of the two concerns—I do not intend to provide a full account of either the variety of state forms proposed by Weber or the specific historical analyses he provides in his partisan political writings of forms of democracy, classes, and statuses. These matters have been admirably developed by Wolfgang Mommsen and David Beetham.[24] This book focuses more on the strategies Weber employs in arguing for or against various forms of politics. I am therefore interested in the tensions, the ambiguities, the fissures, the slippages and unmediated dualisms, the stylized examples, and the interpretive frames that are present in Weber's account of social scientific advice and his argument for vocational politics.

The point of pursuing these matters is not to catch Weber in contradiction for the sake of holding his argument up to a model of systematic consistency. This would violate my claim that he is providing a variety of judgments on social and political action. For in a situation-bound prudence it is the task of the reader (and actor) to assemble the parts according to the situation in need of analysis. To demand too unified a construct would be severely to limit the variety of situations to which the theory is applicable. Thus, the fragmentary nature of Weber's theory provides a way for the agent to assemble the different logics of action into a social constellation in light of his or her social or political location and of the historical and cultural situation under scrutiny. This, I think, is why Weber sees his ideal-type constructs as heuristic means toward the interpretation and explanation of social phenomena (GAW, p. 217). It is also why he distinguishes between methodology and practice. For Weber methodology must follow the practices it illuminates, not drive our understanding of them. Despite its reconstructive and critical intentions, this book tries to respect this quality of Weber's work.

On the other hand, I seek to reveal the points at which his account of the alternatives for democratic politics might be extended beyond those dictated by the demands of routine professional politics and vocational politics. And I think that these are to be found at the intersection between his tendency to objectify one strand of instrumental conduct above all others and his more common tendency to view the social and political world as constituted by a variety of strands of instrumental conduct converging toward and conflicting with one another. Between the way he forecloses political alternatives by emphasizing objective tendencies that render these alternatives self-defeating (for example, the tendency toward discipline in every sphere of life) or the subjective contingencies of political action that render them marginal or too frail to survive (for example, selectivity through power struggle), we may find logics of action that

24. Ibid. See also Mommsen, *Max Weber und die deutsche politik*.

Weber overlooks. This means that Weber's political judgments about the possibilities of democracy may not be wrong so much as overstated.[25] Perhaps, Weber could answer that this is not saying very much. Overstatement is unavoidable in rendering such judgments; for all ideal-typical constructs of social constellations are overstatements. Indeed, in interpreting forms of social and political action he is right. Yet, in matters of political judgment overstatement (and understatement) may be the source of the greatest practical errors. For not to judge a possibility rightly may mean foreclosing on worthy alternatives in advance and allowing the opportunity for their realization to pass; or it may mean recklessly pursuing worthy goals at a moment when to do so would discredit them practically. Weber, of course, knows this, and he knows the basic irony underlying both of these dangers that sometimes renders the very attempt to find the right equilibrium in political judgment itself a misjudgment: namely, as he suggests toward the end of "Politics as a Vocation," we may not achieve the possible in politics without sometimes pursuing what prospectively seemed impossible (*GPS*, p. 560; *FMW*, p. 128).

25. See Ira J. Cohen, "The Underemphasis on Democracy in Marx and Weber," in *A Weber-Marx Dialogue*, ed. Robert J. Antonio and Ronald Glassman (Lawrence: University Press of Kansas, 1985).

Social Science and the Interpretation of Means-End Rationality

Sociology . . . will mean for us a science which seeks the interpretive understanding [*deutend verstehen*] of social action and thereby gives a causal explanation of the way in which the action proceeds and the effects it produces.

—Max Weber, *Economy and Society*

Politics will mean for us the striving after a share of power or influencing the distribution of power, whether it be between states or between groups of people [*Menschengruppen*] included within a state.

—Max Weber, "Politics as a Vocation"

Critics of Weber's account of social science have often taken him to task for reducing all socially interpreted activity to instrumental rationality.[1] Sympathetic interpreters, in turn, have seen in his focus on the interpretation of the meaningful conduct of social agents a strong argument in favor of the subservience of explanation to the rules or everyday understandings under which actions are intelligible.[2] In a sense, both interpretations are correct. Weber indeed makes explanations of social phenomena depend on the interpretative understanding of the social relations being explained, but he also reduces this understanding to an account of meaningful social action that uses a kind of instrumental reason as its standard. Why does Weber make this move? What does he achieve in doing so?

In this chapter I try to answer both questions. Weber's account of the interpretive understanding of social and political relations is, I suggest, subtly caught between two conflicting imperatives. On the one hand, it must satisfy the demand that social inquiry be appropriate to its object; hence social inquiry must regard social action as meaningful activity and social relations as the outcome of our intentions and beliefs. On the other hand, it must satisfy the demand that it attain some measure of scientific certainty, or "objectivity," despite its reliance on interpretation of the subjective intentions of others; hence it must find some causal regularities

1. See Herbert Marcuse, "Industrialization and Capitalism in the Work of Max Weber," in *Negations: Essays in Critical Theory*, trans. Jeremy J. Shapriro (Boston: Beacon Press: 1968). 2. See Alfred Schutz, *The Phenomenology of the Social World* (Evanston, Ill.: Northwestern University Press, 1967), pp. 3–44; Peter Winch, *The Idea of a Social Science* (London: Routledge & Kegan Paul, 1958).

in explaining social relations and the activity that takes place under them. Framing both of these demands is the inescapable a priori condition for all social inquiry, namely, that the conceptual schemes we use to explain and interpret social action depend on our practical value interests. We consequently are always in danger of merely providing an interpretation of our own practical concerns when we interpret particular social relations. What I show is that Weber overcomes this dilemma only by steadily restricting his account of what counts as adequate interpretation of social action. From a general demand to reconstruct the intentional conduct of others, Weber reduces the goal of interpretation to a demand that we understand the rules under which we intend our actions; then to a demand that we understand the self-understood activity of others only to the degree to which they correspond to or deviate from rational motives of action; and finally to a demand that we identify rational motives primarily with instrumental motives for action. Thus Weber seems to attain objectivity and scientific reliability only through a rather narrow concept of the subjective interpretation of social relations, one that understands intentional conduct from the vantage point of instrumental conduct.

But this loss in interpretive richness in understanding intentional social conduct is compensated for by a gain in being able to explain the complex instrumental logics that are inseparable from social action. Thus Weber restricts the scope of interpretation of social conduct in order to include a feature of social and political action that resists the "thick description" he initially seems to be arguing for, namely, power. Furthermore, in linking interpretive understanding to conduct aimed at assessing the costs of different means to chosen ends, Weber has constructed an interpretive instrument peculiarly suited to a recurrent practical dilemma of the person seeking methodically to "rationalize" his or her social and political actions in a world in which action and power are inseparable: the well-known dilemma that self-understood conduct often plays into a logic of means whose consequences are at odds with or at least have an ironic relation to the intentional self-description of the agent. This attempt to link interpretation of social action to power and the ironic consequences of its use are part of Weber's major project (to be elucidated in the third chapter) of lifting economic rationality from purely maximizing conduct to a multiplicity of instrumental logics each dependent on the sphere in which they apply. This understanding of instrumental reason as differentiated according to life sphere and within each life sphere is only possible for Weber if we view instrumental conduct under the concept of *Verstehen*. For then we interpret the methodical organization of conduct toward self-imposed ends as totally dependent on the meaning context in which such reasoning occurs. Viewed in this way, Weber's loss in interpretive richness on the side of norms may be compensated for by an interpretive richness on the side of instrumental conduct. This allows Weber to examine the multiple ways in which an agent may face instrumental demands whether in politics or economics or religion and how these demands often conflict with one another as they impinge on an agent's life.

Practical Values and the
Presuppositions of Social Science

In his justly famous account of the meaning of "Objectivity" in the social sciences, Weber takes great pains to distinguish what he calls arguments "which appeal to our capacity and need for analytically ordering empirical reality and lay claim to validity as empirical truth" from arguments that either appeal to practical goals and cultural meaning or justify the validity of ethical norms (*GAW*, p. 155; *Method*, p. 58). Only the former are appropriate for "science." Having made this distinction, however, Weber proceeds to attack the claim that a nomological conception of the physical sciences can provide an adequate model for the conduct of social inquiry. One goal of the "cultural sciences," he points out is indeed to "explain" social phenomena. But prior to any explanation it may provide, its goal is to understand the interconnections and "the cultural significance" of the "surrounding reality of life in which we are placed in its characteristic particularity" (*GAW*, pp. 170–71; *Method*, p. 72). Social scientific investigation unavoidably finds its departure point in the attempt to discern the meaning of the particular culture in which we are located. Only then does it seek to explain that culture, for what we are trying to explain is why particular cultural forms have developed in this way and not in another. The empirical reality then that we are trying to "explain" through social inquiry is not raw data but the life forms of our "culture." Moreover, even within this reality only a finite portion is "significant" to us in the sense of being both important, that is, worthy of our attention, and meaningful:

> Now as soon as we attempt to reflect upon the way in which life confronts us in immediate concrete situations, it presents an infinite multiplicity of successively and coexisting emerging and disappearing events both "within" and "outside" ourselves. The absolute infinitude of this multiplicity is seen to remain undiminished even when our attention is focused on a single "object," for instance a concrete act of exchange, as soon as we seriously attempt an exhaustive description of all the individual components of this "individual phenomenon," to say nothing of explaining it causally. All the analysis of infinite reality which the finite mind can conduct rests on the tacit assumption that only a finite portion of this reality constitutes the

object of scientific investigation and that only it is "essential" [*Wesenswert*] in the sense of being "worth knowing" [*Wissenswert*]. (*GAW*, p. 171; *Method*, p. 72)

Our very sense of having analyzed the essential attributes of a phenomenon relies on a background assumption that these attributes are worth our attention. Hence, "we cannot discover ... what is meaningful to us by means of 'presuppositionless' investigation of empirical data. Rather, perception of its meaningfulness to us is the presupposition of its becoming an object of investigation" (*GAW*, p. 175; *Method*, p. 76). No causal law then, even one explaining why a particular cultural form such as economic exchange or patrimonial rule is this way and not otherwise, can provide criteria for the significance of this cultural form to us. Significance can only be conveyed by our ultimate conceptions of value: "The significance of a configuration [*Gestaltung*] of cultural phenomena and the basis [Grund] of this significance cannot ... be derived, grounded, and rendered intelligible by a system of analytical laws [*Gesetzesbegriffen*], no matter how perfect it may be, since the significance of cultural phenomena presupposes the relation of these phenomena to value ideas [*die Beziehung der Kulturerscheinungen auf Wertideen*]" (*GAW*, p. 175; *Method*, p. 76). This "relation of cultural phenomena" (or more precisely "cultural appearances") to "value ideas" becomes for Weber the decisive attribute that distinguishes the claim of social science to be a "*Wirklichkeitswissenschaft*," to be an empirical science, from that of the physical-nomological sciences. For value ideas become the presupposition for the "understanding," the intelligibility, and ultimately the causal explanation of social phenomena. They provide the horizon we draw around some particular aspect of social reality whose relations we are interested in knowing about; in this way, they define both the problem and the phenomena to be investigated (*GAW*, p. 175; *Method*, p. 76). Furthermore, within the vast multiplicity of causes working on any one event, value ideas enable us to delimit some set of causes that are significant in influencing the event being explained (*GAW*, pp. 177–78; *Method*, p. 78). Without some value interest that the event or social configuration affects, we lack any criteria to select relevant causes. Finally, value ideas delimit what count as relevant facts. As with causes, there are an infinite number of facts that can be brought to bear in describing or validating an interpretation of any cultural event of significance to us. Indeed, without some preconception of value significance we cannot even know what might count as a fact (*GAW*, p. 213; *Method*, p. 111). We thus rely on the horizon created by our conceptions of value to provide us with a "point of view" to discern facts of significance to the problem being investigated:

"all knowledge of cultural reality is always knowledge from a particular point of view [*Gesichtspunkt*]" (*GAW*, p. 181; *Method*, p. 81).

But what are these "value ideas" on which all meaning in social science depends? Weber is rarely explicit about their meaning, and perhaps logically he could not be because being the condition for intelligibility of human activity, they would be the conditions for their own definition.[3] That is, value ideas would depend on value ideas for their own intelligibility ad infinitum. But Weber does not in fact hold this position; for although he conceives of value ideas as a priori to all social understanding, he does not conceive them as abstract logical categories but, rather, as culturally embedded subjective motivations for action that often themselves are the object of social scientific inquiry. We can discern what they mean in the definition that opens his essay on "Value-Freedom": "*Wertungen*" are "practical evaluations of some manifestation subject to the influence of our actions which is understood as reprehensible or commendable" (*GAW*, p. 489; *Method*, p. 1) In "The Critique of Eduard Meyer," Weber describes them as the "particular concrete stance" one takes to an object in "its concrete individuality." The subjective source of this stance is a "thoroughly concrete, highly individual constituted and composed 'feeling' and 'preference'" (*GAW*, p. 252; *Method*, p. 150). They are conceptions we hold of the ultimate goodness or badness of particular contexts or consequences open to influence by our actions. These conceptions of value are particular both in their object and in their origin in the agent's will. Moreover, they are the regulative standards that constitute our worldviews, our ultimate concepts of culture. As such they are incessantly fought over because for Weber there is no objective grounding for value ideas, only perspectives on what we find to be valuable (*GAW*, p. 153; *Method*, p. 56). Still, *Wertideen* are derived from the very practical and ethical arguments that Weber initially insisted have nothing logically to do with the claims of social science to be empirical. They evidently have everything to do with these claims in so far as values provide us with the horizon for the intelligibility of social facts. And these value-embodied facts are themselves selected according to our value judgments. Weber says as much: "The concept of the 'social' . . . when taken in its general meaning provides no specific point of view from which the significance

3. Thomas Burger, *Max Weber's Theory of Concept Formation* (Durham: Duke University Press, 1987), points out that Weber is never very explicit about the relation between cultural value-ideas that are constitutive of historical and social phenomena relevant to us and value judgments through which we actively take a stance toward that value constituted data. Weber speaks of value ideas as general cultural values but also as informing value judgments that the inquirer makes outside of the role of scholarship (pp. 80–81). See also Guy Oakes, *Weber and Rickert* (Cambridge: MIT Press, 1988), pp. 23–24.

[*Bedeutung*] of particular elements of culture can be analyzed" (*GAW*, p. 166; *Method*, p. 69). Rather, "in the social sciences the stimulus to the posing of scientific problems is in actuality always given by practical questions, so that the mere acknowledgement of the existence of a scientific problem coincides personally with the particular directed will of human beings" (*GAW*, p. 158; *Method*, p. 61). In this sense, the knowledge-constituting interest of social science derived from our value ideas ("durch jene Wertideen bedingten Interesse") is ultimately the expression of a practical will: a conception of (cultural) value that we would seek to realize in action. It is our will that imposes significance on social phenomena in the form of knowledge-constituting "value ideas." In turn, it is this significance-imposing practical will that our "value ideas" describe.

But if the practical will, the will that wills actions judged by ultimate (cultural) ends, stands behind the *a priori* "value ideas" that constitute social phenomena for scientific inquiry, then Weber's own account of social science itself contains a particular conception of the relation between value ideas and practice. Our task then, is to ferret out this relation in Weber's most explicit account of his project, his account of "Verstehende Soziologie" in *Economy and Society*. With this in mind we turn to his concept of sociology as "Erklärendes-Verstehen."

The Rational "Understanding" of
Rationality and Irrationality

Weber's concept of "Verstehende Soziologie" in *Economy and Society* is usually seen as an attempt to synthesize two conflicting ways of studying society: the empathic understanding of cultural meaning characteristic of the *Geisteswissenschaften* and the nomological causal explanation of phenomena characteristic of the physical sciences. And indeed it is that.

But Weber uses this synthesis to subdue two more controversial conceptions of social science: a social science that provides us with practical norms of action, especially in ethical and political matters, and a social science that studies not action but external behavior and its effects on others. While rejecting both of these conceptions as inappropriate for a *Wirklichkeitswissenschaft*, a science of reality, Weber in fact incorporates them by linking the understanding of practical reasoning to causal consequences beyond the purview of the actor. In doing so, he prepares the groundwork for his own account of the sociological clarification of action under conditions of rationalization. It is the possibilities of action within rationalization that is being "understood" in his definition of sociology: "Sociology . . . will mean for us a science which seeks the interpretive understanding [*deutend verstehen*] of social action and thereby gives a causal explanation of the way in which the action proceeds and the effects it produces." (WG, p. 1; ES, p. 2)

In this definition, "understanding" through a kind of interpretive reconstruction of an agent's motives (based initially on either rational imputation or what Weber calls *nacherlebend Verstehen*, a kind of empathic reliving of the subjective experience of engaging in a particular mode of action) becomes the prerequisite for causally explaining why the action took the form it did and what its consequences were (WG, p. 2; ES, p. 5). At first glance, the reasoning behind this conjoining of two seemingly opposed modes of knowing should be obvious: one must first be able to describe what was intended in the performance of an action before one can explain why it took place. Otherwise it would be unclear what in fact one was explaining.

But there is a more fundamental and far-reaching reason for this move that has to do with the object of explanation. What we are trying to explain in social science according to Weber is not the contingent, external behavior of individuals, but "social action." "Action" is behavior to which agents attach "a subjective meaning." It is behavior that is intended, that has meaning and intelligibility in some context that we can identify. To explain the motivation for an action we must "understand" what the agent had in mind in doing it, that is, we must treat intentions as motivations for the behavior. And these intentions or meanings that move action are not discovered by the agent in some self-reflective vacuum. They are socially directed. Thus Weber defines "social action" as action whose "intended meaning [*gemeinten Sinn*] on the part of the agent or agents involves a relation to the behavior [*Verhalten*] of others and in the process of its performance is oriented to that relation." In other words, it consists in "one's own meaningful behavior [being] oriented to the behavior of another" (WG, p. 1; ES, p. 2; WG, p. 11; ES, p. 23). Social action, therefore, assumes that we draw the meaning of our own conduct from our expectations of the conduct of others as intentional agents.

The recurrent probability of such meaningful conduct, Weber maintains, is what we call a "social relation" (*soziale Beziehung*). We are not warranted to assume that a social relation is simply there, and we derive our intentions by performing some function within it. By the same token we are not entitled to assume that it is held together by "organic solidarity," as Durkheim argued. Rather, a social relation emerges out of the reciprocal disposition and orientation of a plurality of people who direct their conduct toward the same concept of subjective meaning (WG, p. 13; ES, p. 27). We identify a particular social relation by the recurrent orientation or meaning individuals give to a social activity. Thus a social relation could be a social form such as a state, a bureaucracy, or a competitive market; it could be a relational concept such as power or domination, community or society, struggle or solidarity, class or group; or it could be a value orientation such as legitimacy. Although they appear to us as stable interlocking complexes of intentions, Weber repeatedly emphasizes the contingency of all such social relations. They exist only so long as a particular kind of "meaningfully oriented social action" takes place. As soon as a plurality of persons ceases to direct their intended actions reciprocally toward one another in a particular way, the social relation dissolves.

This account of social action, despite its seeming emphasis on reciprocally shared meanings of social actors, rests on what appears to be a thoroughgoing methodological individualism, although it is not the methodical individualism that we associate with the reduction of social action to purely maximizing individual conduct: "For the 'Verstehende' interpretation of action via sociology, these structures [such as state, nation, association, family] are exclusively the processes and context of specific actions by individual human beings, since they alone are intelligible bearers of meaningful actions." (WG, p. 6; ES, pp. 12–13). Rejecting the intelligibility of collectivities acting meaningfully, Weber insists that expressions such as "state," "nation," or "family" are nothing more than "the outcome of the social actions of individuals." "Collective concepts" insofar as they refer to anything at all, exist only as "complexes of collective human action which govern the actions of individual men" (WG, p. 6; ES, pp. 12–13). They signify those social relations arising from, but ultimately controlling, reciprocally intended individual conduct. But what of the situation in which these same individuals seek to "govern" these complexes of human action described by collective concepts, say the state or an economic organization? Under these circumstances they are, indeed, acting under a collective concept. And in turn the collectivity is intending meaningful action. But this is an impossibility for Weber.

Instead, Weber firmly distinguishes social action, which describes the mutual orientation of individuals to the intentions of one another, from "behavior" (Verhalten), which is "accidental or conditioned" (WG, p. 6; ES, p. 13). Behavior is unintended and not mutually oriented. The understanding of its meaning is not part of its intelligibility to us. Weber illustrates this distinction with two revealing, if problematic, examples. In the first, he describes the accidental collision of two bicyclists as a typical piece of behavior. It was random, not intended. On the other hand, their attempt to avoid each other or the fight that ensues afterward is a typical piece of social action. Now this seems plausible. However, the activity of both bicyclists peddling down the road is most certainly a form of social action, because a crucial part of their activity was the mutual orientation by the agents toward the expectations of other agents engaged in the same activity. And this orientation rested on certain public rules and conventions regarding traffic that the two riders certainly were initially following.[4] The accident then, was simply a breakdown or misfire of social action, but that does not immediately make it behavior. To fail to perform a social action correctly is still to be oriented toward the intentions of others.

In the second example, Weber argues that the existence or formation of a "crowd" would not be an instance of social action, because the behavior of a crowd is merely reactive or imitative. The activity of a crowd, say even in a protest, is caused purely by random reaction of one member to another, not by *Sinnhaftbezogenes Handeln*. Here the problem is that Weber assumes that the activity of a crowd is not a set of meaningful actions oriented to others. There are many reasons why one might join a crowd—not the least of which is to act with others in order to display one's opposition to a policy, and this is certainly action mutually oriented toward others. But because Weber identifies "meaningful action" only with individual agents, he has to deny this rather obvious fact. The result is the rather odd conclusion that "social action" and collective mass action are unalterably opposed concepts. On this account, a popular protest against the actions of the state is not a form of social action, but the policy of the state that provoked this protest, or for that matter the exercise of police powers to repress it, falls under the concept of social action without any difficulty. In both these examples, Weber's methodological individualism restricts the purview of sociological understanding only to those social relations created by the interconnecting intentional actions of individuals. Actions oriented to conventional rules or taken by an assembled collectivity are judged not susceptible to sociological "understanding," only to explanation. The concept of "social action" in conjunction with the notion of "meaningfully oriented action" is subtly functioning here as a norm, designating which social activity deserves, so to speak, "understanding" and which merely causal explanation. Obviously, according to this norm, two of the most crucial public orientations toward intentional action, an orientation toward tacitly accepted rules of appropriate conduct and an orientation toward collectively determining these rules, are judged not to be part of intentional or meaningful action at all. *Sinnhaftorientiertes Handeln* can only be attributed to individuals. Having displaced both collective action and action under conventions to the category of "behavior" (albeit not successfully), Weber can now pose

---

4. This point is made by Anthony Giddens, "Max Weber on Interpretive Sociology," in *Studies in Social and Political Theory* (New York: Basic Books, 1977), p. 180.

the central problem informing his account of interpretive understanding: How do we describe the intended meanings of agents engaged in social action so that we attain an adequate causal explanation of their actions as well? After all we don't have access in some direct unmediated sense to the "meaningful" in social action in the form of raw data or brute facts. Weber's answer to this is to propose his concept of *erklärendes Verstehen*, which we will translate here as explanatory understanding.

"Understanding," as we have seen, is for Weber a prerequisite for explaining the form and consequences of social action. But there are two forms of "understanding," only one of which is directly relevant to social science. The first Weber calls direct understanding. This is the kind in which we understand the meaning of a rational proposition such as 2 x 2 = 4, or an emotion such as anger manifested in a facial expression, or the activity of chopping wood. In all these cases, Weber maintains, we perceive the meaning directly. No interpretation is necessary. But Weber is surely mistaken here. For neither the mathematical proposition, nor the expression of anger, nor the activity of chopping wood make the least sense without reference to the conventions that make them intelligible. We know these as a logical proposition or an expression of anger or a physical activity, because they are all part of publicly accessible conventions of mathematical reasoning or of expressing certain emotions or identifying an activity as chopping wood. Without knowing what anger means, or more properly, the rules of usage for the word *anger*, for example, we could not find a particular grimace to be an expression of anger.[5] In this sense, there is no direct understanding of meaning. What Weber calls direct understanding actually falls under a second kind of understanding, the one that Weber calls *erklärendes Verstehen*, or explanatory understanding.

Erklärendes Verstehen seeks to explain why a social action or social relation takes the form it does (and not some other form) by understanding "the meaning" (*Sinn*) or intention that social actors give to their actions (*WG*, p. 4; *ES*, p. 9). Thus, for example, we identify why an agent engages in the activity of writing down an equation by understanding the agent's intention in doing so, say, as a business or a technical calculation; similarly we identify why someone engages in the activity of chopping wood when we know that he or she is doing so to earn a wage or, alternatively, work off tension. In either case, the motive of a social action is explained when we describe what Weber calls the *Sinnzusammenhang* in which the action takes place: "All these [motives] are understandable complexes of meaning [*verständliche Sinnzusammenhänge*] whose under-

5. Ibid., pp. 181–82.

standing we regard as an explanation of the actual course of an action. For a science preoccupied with the meaning [*Sinn*] of action, explanation means no more than comprehension of the meaning complex in which on the basis of its subjectively intended meaning a present intelligible action belongs." (*WG*, p. 4; *ES*, p. 9).

Sinnzusammenhang has several possible meanings, all of which are implied in Weber's usage of the concept. It means at once, a complex of meanings, an interconnection of meanings, and a context of meaning. In any case, the term refers to the backdrop that lends intelligibility and meaning to social action. It is, as it were, the source of motives for social action: "A 'motive' is a complex of meanings [*Sinnzusammenhang*] which seems either to the agent or to the observer to provide meaningful 'grounds' for behaving a certain way" (*WG*, p. 5; *ES*, p. 10). Thus when we have described the *Sinnzusammenhang* in which an action has meaning—that is, the meaning complexes in which the intentions or motives of an individual action are intelligible and rational—we have also explained why the action took place and, indeed, why it is an action of this kind and not another.[6] It is the description of such *Sinnzusammenhänge* that Weber calls explanatory understanding of social action.

The problem that rises then is how do we go about describing a *Sinnzusammenhang*? Weber's answer is twofold: either we impute motives to agents in a particular historical situation, the particularities of the situation serving as the meaning context or, and this is the model for social science, we impute to agents a *Sinnzusammenhang* for their subjectively intended actions in the form of conceptually constructed pure types (*WG*, p. 1; *ES*, p. 4).

The Ideal Type: Uniqueness versus Generic Concepts

These ideal types are, as it were, imaginative reconstructions of the interrelated meanings that render a particular kind of social action intelligible or reasonable. They select out the characteristic features of a meaning context of an action according to the horizon created by the value ideas we bring to the inquiry and connect them into a logical construct (*GAW*, p.191; *Method*, p, 91). Consequently, they deliberately distort the characteristics of the meaning complexes of an action in the direction of coherence and particularity (*GAW*, p. 190; *Method*, p. 90). yet even if

---

6. Weber is adamant in maintaining that complete causal explanation of a social action is not an intelligible goal of social science. Even assuming that we were able to find the sufficient causes for some socially related human behavior, he argues, this would in no way alter the task of social science, which is "die Sinnhaft orientierten Handlungen deutend zu verstehen" (*WG*, p. 3).

they do not correspond to the variety of motives at work in any particular situation they still enable us to impute causes to individual or social actions. "One need not have been Caesar to understand Caesar," Weber reminds us (*WG*, p. 1; *ES*, p. 4).

Yet this raises the question of how adequate these imaginative analytical constructions are not just as interpretations of motives but as causal explanations. Do we achieve a degree of certainty (*Evidenz*) in understanding the motives of social action sufficient to provide a valid explanation of social action as well? Weber's answer to these questions is that explanatory understanding of meaningful (social) action can at best provide us with causal hypotheses of varying certainty (*WG*, p. 4; *ES*, p. 11). Often the same externally similar action can be taking place in radically different meaning contexts. Moreover, in the same context persons could be engaged in action derived from conflicting motives. Thus frequently no certainty in our interpretation of motives is attainable. Under these circumstances we must engage in a thought experiment in which we eliminate motives that we deem not to belong to a certain *Sinnzusammenhang* and then construct the probable cause of an action from what is left. In other words, we imaginatively project what an agent must have been doing by behaving in this way in this context. But even where we are more confident in identifying the meaning context of an action, an adequate explanation of social action consists in the claim that there is a "probability" of an action of certain kind taking place in a particular context (*WG*, p. 5; *ES*, p. 12). The most complete causal explanation of social action would, at best, establish a generalization to the effect that a certain observed internal or external event will be followed by (or occur simultaneously with) a certain other event according to a rule of probability that could be estimated in some way or other and that in the (rare) ideal case can be quantitatively measured (*WG*, p. 4; *ES*, p. 11). But because the contexts that provide us with subjective motives are ideal-type constructions, such generalizations remain hypothetical. It follows, then, that all explanations of meaningful action are estimations of probability whose certainty will vary with the types of motives we are trying to explain.

Weber singles out two levels of certainty (and reliability of evidence) as appropriate to explanatory understanding. The first applies to understanding the emotional complex of meaning (*Sinnzusammenhang*) in which an action takes place. Here we try to explain the motives for an action by "empathically reliving the experience" of acting in a certain way (*einfühlend nacherleben*). This entails that we project ourselves into the context of feelings an agent may have when acting in a particular context of social action. Thus we try to put ourselves in the place of someone orienting his actions toward others out of rage, pride, loyalty, jealously, or any combination of these feelings. Certainty and reliability of evidence are achieved "when an action and the complex of feelings experienced by the agent [are] completely relived in the imagination" (*WG*, p. 2; *ES*, p. 5). When, however, such completeness is achieved is itself a judgment on the part of the inquirer and will prove itself only in the (causal) adequacy of the imaginative ideal-type that ensues, that is, in the power of the ideal-type to predict the probable social actions of individual agents. The reliability of our empathic understanding is distinctively limited, Weber insists, by the range of emotional experience we ourselves have had.[7] The second level of certainty and evidence is far more reliable. This involves the reconstruction of the "rational" motives of an action. Here, imaginative projection is still necessary, but ostensibly the motives being understood are far more accessible—at least in a rationalized culture. Presumably we all intersubjectively agree on what counts as rational activity. With this form of causal understanding, certainty is achieved when "the intended complex of meanings" (*der gemeinte Sinnzusammenhang*) can be "intellectually," that is, rationally, understood "in its complete clarity" (*WG*, p. 2; *ES*, p. 5).

Now Weber seems to indicate initially that both of these kinds of *Evidenz* are necessary for an adequate causal explanation in a social science seeking the explanatory understanding of social action. But then, in a move decisive and indeed fateful for the direction of his whole sociology (and the very possibility of the sociological clarification of action as such), Weber argues that the highest degree of certainty will be achieved only when we can impute "rational" motives to an action within a social relation. And he restricts the meaning of "rationality" to one kind only, the rationality of calculating means to ends or justifying ends. All events and objects of social inquiry become "meaningful" only in a "relationship to human action," but human action now consists in regarding intentions "either as a means to some end or an end in itself" (*WG*, p. 3; *ES*, p. 7). Having identified the meaningful in action with the agent's orientation to means and ends, Weber then restricts this conception even more by identifying the rational intelligibility of action "with the instrumental calculation of means to desired ends" (*WG*, pp. 2–3; *ES*, p. 5). The consequences of this move is to reduce the interpretive understanding of meaning con-

---

7. Despite acknowledging the distinctive self-evidence of empathic understanding, Weber was extremely distrustful of the validity of intuitive projections into the experiences of another. For him intuitive understanding needs a more secure footing than direct re-living of the experience of others. Rejecting this Diltheyan conception of direct *Nacherleben*, Weber, borrowing from Husserl, argues that what is needed is "categorical intuition," rather than "perceptual intuition." Hence, his turn to the ideal type. This has been brought out by Kenneth Muse, "Edmund Husserl's Impact on Max Weber," *Sociological Inquiry* 51, no. 2, (1981).

texts so necessary for an adequate causal explanation of social action, to the discernment of axiomatic reasoning applied to the calculation of means to ends:

Rational intelligibility [*Rational verständlich*] which here means the possibility of achieving immediate and unambiguous intellectual grasp of meaning is to be found to the highest degree in those complexes of meaning [*Sinnzusammenhänge*] which are related to one another in the way in which logical or mathematical propositions are [i.e., axiomatically]. We understand the meaning of its meaning [*was es sinnhaft bedeutet*] quite unambiguously when someone states the proposition 2 x 2 = 4 or evaluates Pythagoras' Theorem in thought and argument, or when he completes a logical chain of reasoning in what is—according to our conventions of thought—the correct way. The same is true when someone in his actions derives from recognizably familiar empirical facts [*Erfahrungstatsachen*], the consequences which (according to our experience) clearly follow from the application of particular means. Every interpretation of such a rationally oriented purposive action [*Zweckhandelns*] attains the highest degree of certainty [*Evidenz*] in the understanding of the utilized means. (*WG*, p. 2; *ES*, p. 5)

The object of explanatory understanding becomes not social action in its variety of motives but, rather, those motives of social action consisting in the rational calculation of means to ends. This has a number of crucial implications for Weber's project of uniting causal adequacy and with adequacy of understanding in the study of social action.

First, Weber argues that we attain the highest degree of certainty in both our interpretive understanding and our explanations of social actions only to the degree to which we understand social action as an analog to axiomatic reasoning. This analogy is successfully made only when we are able to explain a social action or social relation either as an instance of logical deduction from a set of propositions or as an instance of a particularly correct calculation of means to ends, a calculation that takes into account the agreed-upon facts and the predictable consequences of an action. We will, therefore, achieve the greatest probability in our predictions in the degree to which we understand or interpret a social actor's motives for action as the logical deduction of the causally necessary means to attain a predictable consequence given a certain stock of facts (*GAW*, p. 127; *RK*, p. 186). As such, Weber's metholodogical individualism becomes especially crucial. The adequate interpretation of social action now means an understanding of the degree to which actors orient their conduct to one another on the basis of *rational instrumental calculations*. But this means that the attainment of certainty in interpretive sociology is highest when interpretive sociology selects out for understanding those social relations and those attributes of social relations that correspond to individual instrumental conduct. Hence the emphasis in Weber on bureaucracy, the rational state, the market economy, power, and domination.

Second, all social actions that are not or only partially motivated by strictly axiomatic reasoning applied to individual conduct can now be "explained" as "deviations" from what could have been expected had they been performed in a purely rational way (*bei rein rationalem Verhalten*) (*WG*, p. 3; *ES*, p. 6). Again we should note the slippage between instrumental rationality and rationality as such. This leads to the identification of all other motives susceptible to "understanding" with irrationality. Weber repeatedly emphasizes that such "deviant" motives cannot be understood with adequate certainty to explain social action based on them. Rather, our capacity to understand them within an intelligible context of meaning is purely contingent and coincidental. Success depends on the coincidence of our values with the values of the agents whose motivation we are trying to understand: "the more radically they diverge from our own ultimate values the more difficult it is for us to understand them by reliving them through an act of empathic imagination" (*WG*, p. 2; *ES*, p. 5–6). Thus, for example, a person who has no experience of religious zeal or, for that matter, of the rationalist zeal of a revolutionary, will have great difficulties reconstructing these motivations for social action. Weber, of course, rejects the imputation that his account of *erklärendes Verstehen* depends on a prejudgment in favor of "rationality"; but then he immediately reverses himself, arguing that an instrumentally rational frame is the only adequate "methodological means" to study behavior. Ultimately, the claim of *Verstehende* sociology to explanatory adequacy depends on the understanding of meaningful social action through the lens of *Zweckrationalität*. It is from this standpoint, or *Gesichtspunkt*, that his whole theory of social action is constructed.

The Theory of Social Action: Verstehen and Zweckrationalität

Weber's typology of social action is the linchpin of his whole *Verstehende* Sociology. It provides him with the foundations both for his explanatory understanding of motives in social action and for his practical clarification of the possibilities of social and political action within rationalized political society. Furthermore, as noted, it links *Erklären* and *Verstehen* by identifying subjectively meaningful action in social relations with instrumental reasoning. Without this typology, understanding and explanation go their separate ways. For Weber it thus forms the template through which the vast multiplicity of subjectively meaningful social actions can, at least provisionally, be causally explained and made intelligible.

Weber distinguishes four ideal typical forms in which individuals orient their conduct to one another: purposive rationality (*Zweckrationalität*), value rationality (*Wertrationalität*), affectual motives, and traditional motives. These forms are divided according to two axes: instrumental and intrinsic motives; and rational and irrational motives. Although he keeps them separate, Weber assimilates the latter division to the former with rather problematic consequences for his sociology.

A *zweckrational* orientation to social action, which I translate both as *goal-rational* and *purposively rational,* consists of action motivated by the calculation of means, ends, and subsidiary consequences. The agent whose actions fall under purposive-reason considers means in relation to desired or willed ends and ends in relation to the secondary consequences that follow from their achievement. Having calculated the subsidiary consequences of applying different means to achieve desired ends, the goal-rational agent also weighs the various ends in relation to one another (*WG*, p. 13; *ES*, p. 25). In saying this, we should avoid the common mistake of interpreting Weber as reducing all purposive reason purely to the calculation of the most efficient means to given ends. This, to be sure, is one form of purposive reason, which Weber later calls technical reasoning; however, purposive-reason also includes an assessment of the costs of reaching different ends in light of the means of achieving them. It thus involves weighing ends according to the differing costs of realizing, or at least trying to realize, them.

But such weighing of costs lacks any appeal to intrinsically worth values; for the end, whether intermediate or ultimate, is distinct from the means used to realize it. Rational deliberation cannot adjudicate between different conflicting ends. Beyond this, the purposively rational agent incorporates into his or her calculations of means an estimation of the probable behavior of others in the same social relation. The expectation of what others will do becomes a "condition," or "means," of success in rationally pursuing one's ends. Others must be treated as means of our designs or at least must be assumed to be acting in ways that can be understood through the calculation of effective causality. This is our orientation to others under *Zweckrationalität*.

Weber is quick to point out, however, that there is nothing intrinsically "objective" about such reasoning, as economists, in particular, seem to maintain. In fact, adherence to purposively rational standards of action, for example in economics, is strictly a subjective orientation to action. This is illustrated by the irreconcilable conflicts of interest between political groups and classes that take place in the modern state over the very question of whether or not instrumental economic reasoning such as free trade or the marginal calculation of profit will be imposed as a norm of social conduct (*GAW*, pp. 527–528; *Method*, pp. 36–37). Purposive reasoning is a particular subjective attitude toward the calculation of effective means. It cannot generate ultimate ends.

The source of ultimate ends is value rationality (*Wertrationalität*). All rational rejections of purposive rationality fall under this one category. This orientation toward social action consists of "the conscious belief in the unconditional intrinsic value . . . of a particular sort of individual behavior [*Sichverhalten*]." Value rationality claims to provide rational grounds for action but eschews *Zweckrationalität* as a criterion of reason. Instead, it provides us with a deontological standard of action: under value rationality a particular mode of conduct is judged to be worthy if it is done "purely for its own sake and independent of any criterion of success" (*WG*, p. 12; *ES*, pp. 24–25). Thus the agent orienting his or her conduct toward others purely according to value-rational motives, acts without consideration for "the foreseeable consequences" of his or her action. Rather, he or she acts out of the "conviction" that a particular standard of conduct is unconditionally demanded of him or her. The rational grounds for the choice of action are internal to the conviction itself. This is so whether one acts purely out of individual conviction or out of an appeal to a universal standard of reason. Thus value reason may include an appeal to natural law, individual conscience, or a Kantian categorical imperative. Indeed, it may even include nonmoral standards derived from art or science. What is important is the claim that one is acting according to unconditional laws or imperatives (*Geboten*) that determine our duties. As long as an agent acts out of the "belief" that a particular action is rationally demanded or fulfills an unconditional rational duty, his or her action will fall under value rationality (*WG*, p. 13; *ES*, p. 25).

But whether in fact these claims or beliefs are truly "rational" is not the province of a *Verstehende Soziologie*. Through *Verstehen* we can construct an ideal-type of a value-rational belief, but we cannot determine whether, in fact, value-rational motives measure up to an actual intrinsically rational standard. Sociology regards ethical standards of action as merely one kind of value-rational "belief" that ascribes the predicate "ethically good" to an action in the same way an aesthetic belief ascribes "beauty" to a work of art (*WG*, pp. 18–19; *ES*, p. 36). Interpretive understanding cannot judge the validity of this ascription. It can only reconstruct its meaning as a motive of social action.

Within the understanding of rational orientations to social action, value rationality forms the polar opposite to purposive reason. The former is intrinsic, the latter instrumental. But the other two orientations together form in turn a polar opposite to both rational motives for action. For in Weber's construct, they reside at the very boundaries of "meaningful," or intended, action. Both are "irrational" motives and thus function as limiting cases for the understanding (and subsequent explanation) of social action. Affectually motivated action is action moved by immediately present but fleeting emotional impulses and states of feeling. This motivation is nonreflective and reactive or imitative (WG, p. 12; ES, p. 25). A person acting purely according to such motives would not be able to give a rational account of his or her conduct. He or she would only be able to say that they felt a particular way at the time they acted. Weber's rather problematic characterization of collective activity falls under this category.

Traditional action is action moved by ingrained habit or custom (Gewohnheit). Not unlike affectual action but more continuous, traditional action is a "dull reaction to accustomed stimuli" (WG, p. 12; ES, p. 25). Although separate from value-rational action, traditional action can emerge from value-rational action once we no longer reflect on the intrinsic reasons of our conduct. Traditional action is value-reason become routine reactive behavior. The appeal to customary or publicly accessible conventions despite its value-rational implications falls under this category.

In this typology, affectual and traditional motives are marginal to the "explanatory understanding" of social action. From the vantage point of explanation, both motives intrude intermittently on value-and purposively rational action, reducing social action to raw behavior. Meaning is firmly attached to value-rational and purposively rational conduct. It is on this crucial distinction that Weber's whole sociology rotates, despite his extensive analysis of traditional modes of political domination.

Yet value reason also occupies an uncertain place in this typology. For one, all intrinsic values and modes of conduct are subsumed under this one category. Within the concept of value rationality, we are given no criteria interpretively to discern distinctions among the various values claiming to provide us with "rational" motives for action. This is especially problematic because for us to "understand" the rationality of a value, that is, why it is intrinsically compelling as a guide to conduct, requires that we understand not just its claims to validity but also the force of these claims, in particular against the claims of other values to inform conduct. One might even argue that the intelligibility of a value depends on our being, at least provisionally, convinced by its rational claims. But Weber cannot include this consideration into his typology. To do so would undermine one of the fundamental assumptions of his sociology of interpretive understanding: that the subjectively intended meaning of an action in an empirical science has nothing to do with determining the objectively right or metaphysically true meaning of social action (*WG*, pp. 1–2; *ES*, pp. 4–5). As a consequence, all values claiming rational validity as intrinsic ends are regarded as "beliefs." For example the ethical claim that an action is motivated by rationally grounded imperatives consists merely in a "belief" in their rational grounding. Of course, to treat the rational claims of most values as beliefs is to fail to understand them as values at all, because if they were mere beliefs, we would have no reason to follow them.

Second, and most important, Weber reduces value rationality to an irrational deviation from purposive rationality. Indeed, the more a particular value position claims not just rational grounding as an intrinsically compelling end but also unconditional adherence as an orientation to social action, the more irrational and unintelligible it becomes: "From the standpoint of purposive rationality . . . value rationality is always irrational, and indeed the more so, the more it elevates the value according to which action is to be oriented to an absolute value. For the less value rationality reflects upon the consequences, the more unconditionally its exclusively intrinsic value (such as pure conscience, beauty, absolute good, absolute obedience to duty) is taken into consideration" (*WG*, p. 13; *ES*, p. 26).

This means that the whole typology of social action—the very basis of Weber's claim to unify explanatory with interpretive understanding—is constructed from the perspective of purposive reason—indeed, a purposive reason purged of contingency and unpredictability, a purposive reason that reaches its greatest intelligibility in imitating axiomatic reasoning. This has a paradoxical consequence for Weber's theory. On the one hand, Weber insists that the rational claims of value conduct cannot be reduced to instrumental considerations. This is a condition of understanding them, and of even explaining the course of action motivated by them. On the other, *Zweckrationalität* has shifted from being the object of reconstructive understanding to being the *Wertidee*, the value idea, that frames understanding of social action. In other words, *Zweckrationalität* is turned into an intrinsic value, and value reason has become one more consideration in the deliberate calculation of means to ends and ends to consequences.

Although rejecting the premise that explanatory understanding of meaningful conduct in social action necessitates a judgment of the validity or rightness of a social relation, Weber has in fact set up a norm of practical conduct on his own. This norm consists, for one, in an equation between the understanding of rational conduct in a social relation and the calculation of means to ends and ends to consequences. It furthermore postulates that all rational claims to intrinsically worthy conduct are beliefs in rational ends. But given the constraints of action, they remain simply "beliefs," because they are unavoidably intrinsically irrational. Value-rational conduct is subject to purposive reason despite its claims not to be concerned with foreseeable consequences. Finally, this norm postulates that conduct according to customs or tacit rules and collective action is made up of purely causal reactions residing on the border of intelligibility. Because causal reactions are not "social actions" under Weber's overly restrictive definition, they are not subject to reconstructive understanding.

This norm of rational action permeates all of Weber's interpretive constructions of "meaningful" social relations; from the societalization and communalization of social action to association, struggle, power, domination, political organization, and the state. Indeed, Weber constructs a social and political world in which this norm of rationality underlies all action. Thus, the societalization (*Vergesellschaftung*) of social relations consists of a continuous attempt to reconcile action based on intrinsic duties with purposively rational action (*WG*, pp. 21–22; *ES*, pp. 40–41). The communalization of social relations (*Vergemeinschaftung*), by contrast, signifies a reduction of self-conscious, rational motives for action to affectual or traditional action, that is, action motivated by sentiment or momentary impulse. A community seeks to eliminate instrumental calculation and power struggle from its action orientation, but, in fact, Weber insists, it can never succeed at this as long as it seeks to mold a certain kind of member. A selection principle is required, and this entails struggle. Community, in this scheme, has only a contingent relation to politics. Political associations do, indeed, make communal claims, especially to their followers. But politics is characterized by its instrumental means: "Politics will mean for us the striving after a share of power or influencing the distribution of power, whether it be between states or between groups of people [*Menschengruppen*] included with a state" (*GPS*, p. 507; *GM*, p. 78). Because power and struggle are both defined as a social relation in which action is oriented to the imposition of one's will over resistance, politics is a constant struggle to impose one's will against the resistance of others (*WG*, p. 20, 28; *ES*, p. p. 38, 53). A successful power struggle will always issue in domination (*Herrschaft*), the chance that a command will be obeyed. The state, in turn, is the "result" of an effective power struggle, as it is that form of domination that can back up its claim to be obeyed with the legitimate deployment of force (*WG*, p. 29; *ES*, p. 5).

Therefore, mass collective action on the one hand, and conventional agreement on rules of usage on the other are marginal to "politics." They represent an intrusive element, the abandonment of the struggle between value reason and purposive reason in favor of purely reactive behavior motivated by unreflective feelings of solidarity or rage. To argue then that politics should or does reflect tacit commonly held norms of understanding or that it should realize full, direct mass participation on common questions, is to frame politics purely within categories of irrational action.

I explore the nexus between *Zweckrationalität* and Weber's claim to reconstruct and rationally clarify the context of social and political action in the following chapters. What is crucial here is that Weber uses this norm of purposive reason to reconstruct—or in his words, subjectively to "understand"—the very meaning of social and political rationality in the various spheres of conduct. It is ultimately on the basis of this reconstruction that Weber claims both explicitly in his methodological and political writings and implicitly in *Economy and Society* to clarify the rational possibilities for social and political action under the pressure of rationalization. In this sense the conjoining of *erklärendes Verstehen* to *Zweckrationalität* constitutes a norm of practical action that informs Weber's construction of the social and political world and from which he in turn finally derives both a concept of the role of sociology in clarifying action and an ethic appropriate to the purposively rational demands of politics. Not surprisingly, both his sociological account of the conditions of social and political action and his political ethic turn out to be imbued with the struggle between the demands of *Zweckrationalität* and the claims of *Wertrationalität*. He finds under the bush what he put there in the first place.

Having said this, however, I do not want to overlook the potential strength of Weber's attempt to combine *Zweckrationalität* with interpretative understanding. It is all too easy, as a number of interpreters have done, to see in Weber's purposively rational account of political and social action an aggressive intrumentalism that loses any interpretive understanding of normative order—indeed sacrifices interpretive understanding for the sake of empirical observation.[8] Although we might want to admit, as I have argued, that Weber's account of normative justification and conventional agreements is too thin, we should also recognize that he does not abandon subjective understanding, that is *Verstehen*, in his account of purposive reason. On the contrary, his interpretive understanding of instrumental action allows him to distinguish the fundamental differences in an agent's orientations to means and consequences in different spheres of endeavor and in different historical contexts. To cite just a few exam-

---

8. One recent example of this criticism is Jeffrey C. Alexander, *The Classical Attempt at Theoretical Synthesis: Max Weber* (Berkeley: University of California Press, 1983), pp. 76–77.

ples, Weber's *Verstehen* of purposive reason enables him to distinguish the instrumental demands of politics that require the deployment of power backed by force in the face of uncertain consequences from the instrumental demands of science whose drive toward predictability entails that discoveries are continuously superseded by new ones. It also allows him to distinguish both of these spheres of conduct from the instrumental demands of economic organization in which the requirement of marginal calculation of profit is in tension with the drive for disciplinary control over the division of labor in production and power within the market. All of these modern endeavors are contrasted with the instrumental demands of religions whose prophetic moment is embodied in systematic means of delivering salvation.[9] As for the multiple understanding of instrumentally purposive conduct in historical understanding, Weber's remarkable statement from *The Protestant Ethic* on the inadequacy of deriving capitalism from one mode of systematic conduct suffices:

> It might thus seem that the development of the spirit of capitalism is best understood as part of the development of rationalism as a whole, and could be deduced from the fundamental position of rationalism on the basic problems of life. . . . But any serious attempt to carry this thesis through makes it evident that such a simple way of putting the question will not work, simply because of the fact that the history of rationalism shows a development which by no means follows parallel lines in the various departments of life.
>
> In fact, one may—this simple proposition, which is often forgotten, should be placed at the beginning of every study which claims to deal with rationalism—rationalize life from fundamentally different points of view and in very different directions. (*PE*, pp. 64–69; *PESC*, pp. 76–79)

At its best, Weber's subjective reconstruction of the instrumental demands in different spheres of endeavor points to the variety of subjective

9. The work in which he presses this "interpretive understanding" of instrumental conduct to its fullest is the famous "Zwischenbetrachtung" translated in *FMW* as "Religious Rejections of the World and Their Directions." In this essay he underscores the tentativeness of interpreting social action under rational and teleological consistency: "the rationality, in the sense of logical or teleological 'consistency,' of an intellectual-theoretical or practical-ethical attitude has and always has had power over man, however limited and unstable this power is and always has been in the face of other forces of historical life" (*Zw*, p. 480, *FMW*, p. 324). Note the tension here between the power of deductive and instrumental reasoning over all social action and the instability of its influence in light of the total set of meanings, goals, and beliefs that social agents act under. Weber is always trying to keep an understanding of noninstrumental motives in tension with an understanding of instrumental reasoning, so that these two motives flow into each other, often playing the role of the other.

relations that agents may have in the calculation of means to ends. More-over, Weber can deploy, this reconstruction critically, as in his argument against those who would reduce all economic relations to economizing behavior under the principle of marginal utility. (*WG*, pp. 31–35; *ES*, pp. 65–68; see my Chapter 3). Here he insists, for example, that to reduce economic relations to combinations based on individual utility overlooks the power relation (*Verfügungsgewalt*) embodied in all production. The employee does not view the right to leave a job as the expression of free choice. And the capitalist combines the voluntary contract with striving for discipline and calculability in the work force. Superimposed on the subjective understanding of the modern rational contract is a rather un-equal power relation (*WG*, pp. 686–687; *ES*, p. 1156).

Aside from the critical possibilities contained in fusing *Vertehen* with instrumental action, Weber has potentially accomplished one more thing. He has, in principle at least, provided an instrument of the first order for analyzing the ways in which the subjective intentions of agents often contribute to and play into a causality that escapes their intentions. He can reconstruct how social relations come into being out of meaningful conduct yet, once formed, unavoidably impose instrumental considera-tions on the agent that define for him or her what he or she has done. Or to put the matter slightly differently, Weber can account for intentional meanings of actors, yet still account for the causal forces, as it were, flowing through them, producing outcomes that are paradoxical indeed. His constructs based on logical consistency and calculation can register the unintended social consequences that instrumental means produce as by-products of achieving predictability in the realization of goals.

The problem is that at times Weber identifies purposive reason with only *one* set of consequences, the increasing predictability and control effected through rational-legal domination. And although he is not incor-rect in pointing out that this is a significant outcome of instrumental action, he forgets at times that his description of how this comes about through subjective intentional conduct does not exhaust the variety of instrumental considerations and outcomes that social and political actors do and must face. The certainty attained through a rigid account of instru-mental conduct in these moments in his argument tends to devour, or at least displace, his claim to provide a *Verstehen* of rationality and rational conduct. In saying this, however, I would like to emphasize again that the problem in Weber's interpretive understanding of instrumental reason is not that he focuses on the instrumental features of meaningful conduct but, rather, that at times his account of the potential outcomes of instru-mental conduct is often too restrictive.

Why he often reduces his account in this way has a great deal to do with the different ways he uses his social science as a form of practical-political prudence. At times, he wants to emphasize against totalistic theories of history such as that of Marx that all developmental theories are partial perspectives on a multicausal reality and as such are mere heuristic constructs that develop one stream of instrumental conduct. In emphasizing the partiality of such constructs and their dependence on value-driven interpretations of meaning, he is able to argue that alternative judgments of social and political possibility follow once we have added other streams of conduct that deflect outcomes in a direction different from the one predicted. For example, class conflict as an integral part of rational capitalism might be deflected into the protection of status against outsiders. At other times, he wants to show that a particular practical project or mode of life is not feasible given some irresistible instrumental logic that will thwart its realization. For example, he argues against socialists that their attempt to expropriate the power of the state and hand it back to society will be thwarted by the inexorable dependence of all groups engaged in power struggle on hierarchical discipline. Thus he restricts or expands the range of instrumental logics at work on intentional conduct according the kind of judgment he wants the agent to make.

The Sociological Clarification of Action: Weberian Political Judgment

The political scientist may claim to know more . . . than many political agents; but his knowledge is not of a different kind, and there seems to be no reason to believe that the chances that he will be able to apply the inductively grounded maxims which he derives from his studies in the course of political action successfully are any higher than they are for any other political agent.
—Alasdair MacIntyre, "Is a Science of Comparative Politics Possible?"

The question of the appropriateness of the means for achieving a given end is undoubtedly accessible to scientific analysis.
—Max Weber, "Objectivity" in Social Science and Social Policy

When Weber argues for the "scientific" status of social science, he emphatically stresses its hermeneutic nature. We can predict the behavior of others only because we can understand the contexts in which their intentional behavior makes sense. And we can understand those contexts only because we ourselves are self-reflecting actors who orient our conduct toward others in an intelligible way. This is the point of departure for the sociological method of *erklärendes Verstehen*. By means of the ideal-type, this method enables us to attain a measure of explanatory reliability in an inquiry whose object is unavoidably the subjective understanding of human motive. But the features of social relations that we select in constructing ideal-types are chosen from the vantage point of our practical interests constituted by our fundamental values. This means that the regularities that we discover through sociology apply precisely to those social relations, such as the political association, in which our ultimate practical values, our ultimate *Wertideen* (value ideas) are most implicated. It would seem, then, that the explanatory interpretation of social action would be a preparation for clarifying for us the "meaning" of our own social and political actions, in particular those actions motivated by our most deeply held value ideas. *Verstehende Soziologie* then informs practical and political judgment in much the same way prudential knowledge had always done in political theory whether we are speaking of the ethical *phronesis* of Aristotle or the *prudenzia* of effective truth of Machiavelli.

In his methodological essays and his vocational lectures, Weber frequently stresses precisely this practical implication of his science. Social science has two functions: to provide "knowledge of interrelations among facts (*Erkenntnis tatsächlicher Zusammenhänge*" and to provide "self-clarification (*selbst Besinnung*)" for the individual agent. These two functions inform each other. Ideal-typical knowledge of factual contexts makes us increasingly self-conscious of the meaning and consequences of trying to realize our intentions in a terrain not of our choosing. In turn this increased self-consciousness of the meaning of pursuing our ends deepens our understanding of the features of social and political contexts. In this way science serves "'moral' forces" by making agents aware of the responsibilities of rationally pursuing their intentions (*GAW*, pp. 608, 609; *GM*, p. 152). Thus Weber seems to be aligning the interpretive aspect of his science with a kind of "moral" autonomy and personhood.

But Weber denies that *verstehende Soziologie* could or should justify the moral contexts or rules for the autonomous self it claims to enlighten: "We are of the opinion that it can never be the task of an empirical science to provide binding norms and ideals from which directives for practice can be derived" (*GAW*, p. 149; *Method*, p. 52). Science cannot rationally discern the appropriate ends or rules of practical action. Weber makes this point even more dramatically in "Science as a Vocation," his most remarkable account of the meaning of science not just as a method of inquiry but also as a life calling. What, he asks, is the meaning of science as a life calling? His answer, following Tolstoy, is that science is "meaning-less," because it does not answer the one question of importance to us: "What shall we do, and how shall we live?" And Weber adds, "the fact that science does not give an answer to this question is indisputable" (*GAW*, p. 598; *GM*, p. 143). Science cannot lend meaning either to our choices of action or to our choice of the kind of life (*Lebensführung*) that would set the context of our actions. Moreover, this limitation does not simply apply to *Wissenschaft* as the search for recurrent empirical laws of behavior but also to *Wissenschaft* conceived as the interpretive under-standing of social action.[1]

Why can a sociology based on *erklärendes Verstehen* not justify the

---

1. As has been frequently pointed out, *Wissenschaft* encompasses a conception of systematic knowing far broader than that of the natural or physical sciences. Unmodified, it may be translated as "discipline," "scholarship," or even "academic research," as well as, more specifically "science" as inquiry into causal regularities. Weber implies all of these meanings in his lecture "Wissenschaft als Beruf" and his essays on "Objectivity" and "Value-Freedom." In addition, Weber also uses the term to refer to the institution of science in specialized research organizations such as the university. In conjunction with the university, Weber argues for the distinctive authority of science in informing practical undertakings distinct from political partisanship. At the same time, much of his lecture attempts to show the inevitable contraction of the meaning of the term in the face of specialization and the division of labor.

very subjectively intended action it seeks to make intelligible? Weber advances two fundamental reasons for this, one cultural, one logical. In the first place, science's own claim to reason has contributed a most crucial part to undermining the very public background that once gave human action meaning. At one time, argues Weber, (relying on a construction imposed retrospectively from the vantage point of the modern nomological sciences) human beings regarded the world as governed by incalculable mysterious forces; with this understanding of the world, they sought to appeal to magical forces and a multiplicity of gods as a guide to conduct. For the Greeks, to cite the most significant example for the development of reason in the West, the world was still enchanted, magical; the multiplicity of gods supported common sacrifice and obedience to the law of the city (*GAW*, p. 604; *GM*, p. 148). Moreover, when Greek science, whose greatest practitioner was Socrates, provided a logical means to probe behind the claims of the multiple gods of the city, it did so not in order to control nature but to gain insight into "being," a being that was true and durable in the face of the contingent impulses and actions of human beings: "From this it appeared to follow that if one only had found the right concept of the beautiful, the good, or also perhaps, of courage, or of the soul—whatever—that one then also could grasp its true being. And this in turn, seemed to open the way for knowing and teaching how to act rightly in life, and above all as a citizen of the state. For the Hellenic man, whose thinking was political through and through, everything depended on this question. For these reasons, one engaged in science." (*GAW*, p. 596; *GM*, p. 141). In the backdrop of an enchanted world, science did not undermine a public context for action so much as provide it with stronger foundations by uncovering the meaning of right political action within the concept of being.

During the Renaissance, science supplemented the search for the right concept through the discovery of "the rational experiment," which provided "a means of reliably controlling experience" (*GAW*, p. 596; *GM*, p. 141. This new principle of research displaced the Greek inquiry into being, only to take over the function of providing a model of right action and the meaning of life. However, the means to "true nature" was now "art" rather than philosophy. Thus, science in the form of the experiment became the path both to true art and to true nature: "What did science mean to these men who stood at the threshold of modern times? To artistic experimenters of the type of Leonardo and the musical innovators, science meant the path to true art which meant for them at the same time the path to true nature. Art was to be raised to the rank of a science and this meant at the same time and above all that the artist was to be raised to the rank of doctor, socially and with reference to the meaning of his life."

(*GAW*, p. 597; *GM*, p. 143). But once science combines the concept and the experiment with the division of labor into special disciplines, it is able reliably to control both human beings and nature without eliciting anything about the meaning of the world. Having turned concept and experiment into a means detached from philosophy or art, science becomes the fundamental force in a process by which rational inquiry into the facts of the world and the discovery of right political action or true nature are irrevocably severed from one another. It is this that Weber in one of the great self-reflective acts of scientific naming labels the process of "intellectual rationalization." The process of "rationalization" entails the increased control and predictability both over human and physical phenomena through the application of reason. In all areas purposive-rational criteria of action supported by formal procedural rules become dominant. The peculiar contribution of science to this process of rationalization has been "intellectualization":

> The increasing intellectualization and rationalization do not therefore signify an increasing general knowledge of the conditions under which one lives. Rather it means . . . the knowledge or belief that if one only wished one could learn at any time; that, thus, there are in principle no mysterious, incalculable forces that come into play; that one rather, at least in principle, could master all things by calculation [*alle Dinge—im Prinzip—durch Berechnen beherrschen können*]. This however, signifies the demagification of the world [*die Entzauberung der Welt*]. One need no longer have recourse to magical means in order to master or implore the spirits as did the savage for whom such mysterious powers existed. Technical means and calculations perform this service. (*GAW*, p. 594; *FMW*, p. 139).

Science is not just a mode of thinking or a technique. It is a "belief" in the power of hypothetical reasoning to master any force we desire. That force may be nature or other human beings. But in either case, we believe that we can reduce their behavior to laws of causal efficacy: through calculation of cause, effect, and subsidiary consequences we can master all things. The problem is that once we believe that we in principle could master any natural force through the proper technical calculations, we have weak grounds for finding any particular value or end to be more compelling than any other. For unlike the Greeks, we are then deprived of any rational means to satisfy or propitiate the different gods, that is, for us, the multiplicity of values, that make claims on us. Furthermore, we divest ourselves of gods or ultimate ends that hold us in awe. By orienting our actions toward science, we have exchanged deployment of means to discern our duties and right conduct among a panoply of ends that were conflicting but authoritative in favor of technical control and predictability in achieving any ends we might choose. The result is that indications on how to live and act become a private matter: "The fate of our time is characterized by rationalization and intellectualization and above all the demagification of the world [*Entzauberung der Welt*]. Precisely the ultimate and most sublime values have retreated from public life [*Öffentlichkeit*] either into the transcendent realm of mystical life or the brotherliness of direct and personal human relations." (*GAW*, p. 612; *FMW*, p. 155).Thus, "the individual can only pursue his quest for salvation as an individual."[2]

As a result of this split between knowledge and the highest values that would guide conduct, we live in a culture that has a doubly paradoxical relation to its origins. Viewed from one perspective, our world appears to be the polar opposite of the one inhabited by the ancient Greeks for whom scientific knowledge promised to derive appropriate conduct from nature. However, viewed from another perspective, the present is, in fact, a pale reenactment of the Greek world for whom myth and civic conduct reenforced each other in the conflicting duties to the gods. "Today" we live, "as did the ancient world when it was not yet disenchanted of its gods and demons, but in a different sense: just as Hellenic man at times sacrificed to Aphrodite and other times to Apollo, and above all, as everyone sacrificed to the gods of his city, so we do so still today though disenchanted and denuded of the mythical but inwardly true plasticity of that conduct. And fate but most certainly not 'science' governs over these gods and their struggle [*Kampf*]." (*GAW*, p. 604; *FMW*, p. 148).

In our world, the gods appear as the many values that make claims on our conduct. But our actions no longer express an inner consistency of character. In turn, our determination as to which of these values should guide our conduct is not mediated by science, but contingency. In a world disenchanted by science, that is literally deprived of magical or incalculable forces, ideal ends of conduct war with one another for our attention, but we lack any form of knowledge, or for that matter, technique, to mediate among them. There is no universal reason to decide among ends or to rank them hierarchically. Indeed, Weber sees a rational mediation among values as an impossibility, because the logic of the process from enchanted polytheism to dis-enchanted, scientific polytheism entails that any claim to decide rationally among competing values can itself be only a way-station on the road to intellectual rationalization of conduct. All conduct is therefore reduced either to an act of choice or to a technical achievement: "All the natural sciences give us the answer to the question, what should we do if we wish to master life technically. But whether we

2. Max Weber, "The Social Psychology of World Religions," *FMW*, p. 282.

should or do wish to master it technically and whether it ultimately makes sense to do so—that they leave quite aside or posit for their own purposes." (*GAW*, pp. 509–600; *FMR*, p. 144).

Sociology in so far as it too is a *Wissenschaft* cannot give meaning to conduct. For as a *Wissenschaft*, it is itself both a product of rationalization and an agent of it. It "intellectually rationalizes" the very social phenomena that it seeks to interpret and explain. It seeks to control them and to make them predictable. And it measures them by their deviation from formal consistency and technical predictability. Thus even though it seeks to explain and reconstruct meaningful conduct, it is itself instrumental in emptying conduct of its meaning. The upshot of its complicity with "rationalization" is that it is condemned to trace the process by which rationally justified conduct loses meaning in the face of hypothetical calculation. To "understand" the process of intellectual rationalization from within is already to further it. Yet, science will typically claim that its own origins do not play any role in determining the validity of its concepts. Thus our second reason for its refusal to justify ultimate values or norms.

The second reason why social science cannot confer meaning on practical conduct rests on the specific logic of its claims. Statements of fact and statements of value are logically distinct. The latter cannot be derived from the former: "[for] the methodology of the empirical disciplines . . . the validity of a practical imperative as a norm [*die Geltung eines praktischen Imperativs als Norm*] on the one hand, and the truth value of an empirical proposition [*die Wahrheitsgeltung einer empirischen Tatsachenfeststellung*] on the other lie on absolutely heterogeneous levels of the problematic; and when one overlooks this and attempts to conflate both of these spheres, one takes leave of *the specific dignity* [*Dignität*] each has vis a vis the other"; (*GAW*, p. 501; *Method*, p. 12) (my emphasis).[3] For the sociologically informed political or social theorist this distinction means a binding imperative (*Forderung*) to separate strictly statements of facts and statements that evaluate these facts from an ethical standpoint:

> The researcher and teacher should [*solle*] keep unconditionally *separate* the establishment of empirical facts (including the "value oriented" conduct [*wertende Verhalten*] of empirical persons whom he is investigating) and *his* own practical evaluations i.e., the evaluative position by which he *judges*

3. "One can demand of [the teacher] only that he have the intellectual integrity [*intellektuele Rechtschaffenheit*] to see that factual statements, the determination of logical or mathematical relations, or the internal structure of cultural values on the one hand, and answering the question of the *value* of culture and its particular contents and in addition, the question of how one should act in the cultural community and the political association on the other, are both entirely *heterogeneous* problems (*GAW*, pp. 601–602; *FMW*, p. 146; Weber's emphasis).

those facts as satisfactory or unsatisfactory (including among those facts those "valuations" of empirical persons which have been made the objects of investigation). The reason for this is that we are dealing with completely heterogeneous problems. (*GAW*, p. 500; *Method*, p. 11; Weber's emphasis)

Imperatives indicating what we ought to do are logically distinct and therefore not derivable from factual statements about the world. This stricture applies not just to empirical statements about brute data but also to interpretive reconstructions of values in the form of ideal-types. Weber is quick to emphasize that our values are crucial in providing an horizon of understanding for the kinds of social relations that interpretive sociology seeks to explain. He also points out that the object of interpretive sociology is subjectively meaningful social action, not discrete pieces of datum. But he insists that from our "value-related" interpretations of social action we cannot derive "oughts" in the form of ethical imperatives (*WG*, pp. 1–2; *ES*, p. 45). Other oughts, as we will see momentarily, are not ruled out: "The 'objectivity' of social scientific knowledge depends . . . on the fact that although the empirical given is always aligned with those value ideas, which alone make it worth knowing [*Erkenntniswert*] and from which the meaning of the given is understood, it nevertheless never can be made the pedestal for the empirically impossible proof of its validity." (*GAW*, p. 213; *Method*, p. 111).

To argue that a particular value position (*Wertidee*) can be derived from our value-related understanding of social conduct is to deprive it of its "dignity" without gaining "objectivity" for it. Whenever we try to derive ethical stands from facts in social science, both our "understanding" of the facts (by which Weber means our reconstruction of the meaning of subjective action for the agents) and our claim truly to be pursuing an ethical end suffer (*GAW*, p. 602; *FMW*, p. 146). From this standpoint, Weber singles out two of the most fundamental strands of social and political theory for criticism, theories derived from natural right and theories that locate a telos in history. The first, which would undoubtedly include both Aristotle and Rousseau, derives what ought to be (*Seinsollende*) from what is existent (*Seinden*). The second, which includes Hegel and Marx, derives what ought to be from what is "irrevocably becoming" (*unvermeidlich Werdende* (*GAW*, p. 148; *Method*, pp. 51–52). Both, it would seem, "illegitimately" assume an ontological background from which political forms and political directives could be and, indeed are, derived. For Weber these backgrounds are at best prescriptive choices.

Now the argument for the logical heterogeneity of practical imperatives indicating what we ought to do and descriptive statements of what is the case has been subjected to some rather powerful criticism in large part inspired by the language philosophy of Wittgenstein and Austin.[4] But much of this criticism is directed against the empiricism of Hume; Weber is not an empiricist of this kind, because in large part his framing of the is-ought question is derived from Kant's distinction between the phenomenal and noumenal self. Consequently, he does not assume that we perceive a world of raw data that reduces our judgments of good to mere emotional preferences. Moreover, what he calls "facts" are intentional social actions embodied in ideal-typical constructions, and Weber insists that these constructs reflect our particular value standpoint. He is, therefore, not as susceptible to some of the most telling criticisms regarding the value-laden nature of empirical phenomena as some more simple empiricists.

The upshot of this is that Weber invokes the fact-value distinction in order to justify the autonomy of value judgments rather than to undermine them. This is indicated not just by Weber's distinction between practical "imperatives," or "demands" (*Forderungen*), and value-related empirical statements, but more significantly by his continuous intimation that this distinction itself is an "ought." We "ought" (*soll*) to adhere to the simple "demand" that "ought" and "is" are to be kept separate; because the "dignity" of both these spheres and the "intellectual integrity" (*intellektuelle Rechtschaffenheit*) of the theorist and teacher is at stake (*GAW*, pp. 501, 502, 601–602). To keep one's ethical judgments distinct from empirical social scientific statements is unconditionally required if we hope to preserve the dignity of both science and the scientist, on the one hand, and ethical judgment and the ethical individual on the other. What is being defended here is a certain concept of a person and the kind of ethics appropriate to a person.

Weber bypasses the whole question of whether it is, after all, possible to derive statements about what we ought to do from statements about the attributes of discrete things, of raw data. Instead, he seems to argue that even if we could derive oughts from empirical statements, we "ought" to refrain from doing so. For otherwise, both science and autonomous moral choice will lose their distinctive claims to validity, and we would lose an essential feature of the self.

The problem here is that despite his defense of personhood, Weber falls into a rather basic contradiction, although he seems to be quite aware of it (*GAW*, p. 599; *FMW*, p. 143). If the is-ought distinction is itself an ought, then it is in need of some prior justification. But that justification cannot come from the facts of the case, because then, we will have violated

4. For a good sample of this discussion, see *The Is-Ought Question*, ed. W. D. Hudson (New York: St. Martin's Press, 1969). For a collection of more recent contributions to this debate, see Geoffrey Sayre-McCord, *Essays on Moral Realism* (Ithaca: Cornell University Press, 1988).

the very distinction we are seeking to justify. It can, therefore, only come from a prescription, which is ultimately a choice for which no reason can be adduced. But if adherence to the fact-value distinction is merely a choice born of the belief in the integrity of both the spheres of empirical, causal statements and practical value judgments about such statements, why should the choice of *Wertfreiheit* as a value be any more compelling than any other value? Why for example, is the political right of Rousseau or the materialist concept of history not more compelling? To argue that these two political theories undermine the dignity of both science and practical judgment is to beg the question.[5] For the question of why the dignity of both spheres is worth maintaining has still not been adequately answered.

Weber could cede this point but then respond by arguing that we ought to keep practical value judgments and scientific statements distinct because of certain facts about the world that are unavoidable. On several occasions Weber does precisely that. A particularly striking instance is his continual invocation of John Stuart Mill to the effect that "if one proceeds from pure experience one arrives at polytheism"; and this entails "that the various value spheres of the world stand in irreconcilable conflict (*Kampf*) with one another (*GAW*, p. 603; *FMW*, p. 147)." Here Weber argues that if we canvass the various practical values for which we can adduce good reasons for adherence, we will be driven to the conclusion that there is no one overriding value whose reasons are more compelling than another, but that any decision we make will involve several conflicting practical imperatives each realizable but all compelling: "We are placed in various life spheres, each of which is governed by different laws" (*GPS*, p. 554; *FMW*, p. 123). Weber elaborates further on this claim in his increasingly significant "Zwischenbetrachtung." In this essay, Weber explicitly claims (although somewhat disingenuously) that he is not arguing for a particular philosophy of human conduct, but merely constructing ideal-typically the different spheres in which agents must forge

5. W. G. Runciman has defended Weber's distinction by arguing that even if he provides an inadequate account of moral reasoning, he is still right that no one standard of evaluation is ever required by the facts that social science discloses. *A Critique of Max Weber's Philosophy of Social Science* (Cambridge: Cambridge University Press, 1972). But Runciman overlooks the fact that explanatory frameworks in the social sciences not only imply certain evaluations but also cannot fail to contain certain conceptions of human needs, wants, and purposes. Furthermore, certain politics and policies are implied by explanatory frameworks. The upshot is that new factual considerations frequently require a revision of the framework's claim to connect a particular conception of politics to human purposes. This point has been made by Charles Taylor, "Neutrality in Political Science," in *Philosophy, Politics, and Society*, ed. Peter Laslett and W. G. Runciman (Oxford: Basil Blackwell, 1967), pp. 55–56.

some coherent life conduct (*Lebensführung*). It is a social and cultural fact that in modernity there is no one orderly life that we should pursue, but a number life spheres whose demands are objective and not influenced by the subject. Each of these spheres has its own logic of action (*Eigengesetzlichkeit*) to which we must submit. To focus on one sphere alone, the sphere of politics, we can only become political agents if we submit to the impartial demands of power, that is, reason of state. The value of politics is tied to the pragmatics of power and therefore any attempt to live a coherent life devoted to politics requires us methodically to order our conduct according to these pragmatic demands. However, once we do this, the logics of power turn back on our life plan, separating that plan from any substantive values and forcing us to accept on faith both the value of politics and any substantive values we might pursue through politics (*Zw*, pp. 480–481, 485, 490–492; *FMW*, pp. 323–324, 328, 333–335).

But is this merely a "fact" about modernity or a deep fact about all cultures? Although the narration appears to support the former view, the logic underlying the existence of polytheistic demands supports the latter. For the autonomization of each sphere of value and conduct in the culture of modernity merely makes explicit a fact about the relation among fundamental values and the empirical world that pertains generally whenever we seek to find some methodical conduct consistent with those values: "The destiny of our culture is however that we will *once again* become more clearly conscious [of the struggle among warring gods now depersonalized in different value spheres], after our eyes had been blinded for a millennium by the allegedly or presumably exclusive orientation towards the great fervor [*Pathos*] of the Christian ethic" (*GAW*, p. 605; *FMW*, p. 149; my emphasis). Under its claim to universality Christianity as an ethic of conduct served to hide from us a more basic fact about our cultural life: the basic plurality of forms of life conduct. But once this will to universality is stripped of its deistic associations and becomes a secular guide to inquiry about the world, it reveals its own partiality as a value, and in so doing reveals the factual plurality of forms of meaningful methodical conduct.[6] Thus an interpretive description of culture(s) supports the split between description and values.

6. Charles Turner, *Modernity and Politics in the Work of Max Weber* (New York: Routledge, 1992), pp. 92–93, rightly maintains that Weber is ambiguous about the status of the plurality of value spheres, sometimes arguing that it is a modern phenomenon, sometimes a universal feature of culture. But it would seem that even in the passages in which Weber attributes plurality to modernity, he implies that it was always already there in the logic of methodical, "teleological" conduct, although manifest in more personal and less impersonal ways in different historical periods. It is the impersonality of plurality that I think characterizes modernity for Weber.

This defense of "value freedom" relies in large part on a sociological account of the rationalization of all value spheres rather than on a logical distinction. The logical contradiction in this position still remains. Yet, it is also here where Weber is most persuasive, because he can argue that despite its logical problems, the insistence on value freedom is an appropriate response to a culture that has lost any public background from which conduct can be derived. In a culture characterized by intellectual rationalization, the only agreed-upon background is technical-purposive reason, and this form of reason is not attached to any ultimate values. In other words, in a disenchanted world, a world in which all phenomena can in principle be explained, we cannot expect to be able to derive ultimate value standpoints from our scientific understanding of that world. Moreover, this culture makes manifest a value pluralism rooted in the very logic of methodical action itself. So the only stance that corresponds to these "facts" is one that denies that we can derive practical value judgments from factual statements. A self-contradictory standpoint is the only logically consistent response to an incoherent institutional setting, that is, if unlike Marx one can see no possibility of changing it.

Weber's solution, then, to the contradictions of his second argument for the impossibility of scientific justification of the ultimate ends of practical conduct is to combine it with his first. The (sociological) analysis of scientific rationalization, although ostensibly distinct, rescues Weber's logical argument for the separation of facts and values from complete self-contradiction. Combined together, these arguments make up for the deficiencies (and ambiguities) of each argument taken singly.

Once Weber has firmly established the unconditional separation between the "scientific" understanding of social action and the justification of ultimate practical norms, he can begin to answer the question: In what sense can science, in particular a science based on *erklärendes Verstehen*, clarify practical action? Or as Weber puts it, not without paradox, "The only question that remains is the sense in which science gives 'no' answer [to the question of what we shall do and how we shall live], and whether or not science might yet be of some use to one who puts the question correctly" (*GAW*, p. 598; *FMW*, p. 143).

Weber's answer is that *verstehende* sociology can be used to clarify both sides of the fact-value dichotomy: first, it can be used to clarify value choices; second, it can disclose what is entailed in translating these choices into action. "The scientific treatment of value judgments may not just allow us to understand and empathetically analyze [*verstehen und nacherleben*] the desired ends and the ideals which underlie them; but it can above all teach a critical 'judgment' of them" (*GAW*, p. 151; *Method*, p. 54). In this clarification, the conjunction of sociological understanding with the explanation of action in terms of *Zweckrationalität* (purposive reason) and value rationality becomes decisive. The split between the two kinds of rational action forms the frame in which all practical action will be critically judged.

What I want to argue in the rest of this chapter is that Weber deploys his concept of purposive reason as a neutral critical standard against which all attempts to translate values into action are to be judged. For Weber this standard becomes both a means of defending a concept of individual moral freedom and personhood based on irreducible "choice" and a concept of action characterized by "power struggle." The result of this dichotomy for his account of the sociological clarification of action is not just an inadequate account of moral reasoning, as many critics have claimed, but also a problematic account of the practical instrumental necessities of action, something virtually all interpreters of Weber have overlooked. He opts, as it were, for a "scientific" clarification of action based on providing tendential laws of social action that will stand in tension with other parts of his work that are closer to a situation-bound political prudence. This other side of his notion of practical judgment is discussed when we examine his concept of political economy in Chapter 3; and the implications of the tension between both sides of his concept of judgment for politics is developed in Chapters 4 and 5 where Weber's restrictions on democratic participation flow directly out of his dichotomy between neutral practical clarification and subjectively irrational choice.

Value Choice and Value Conflict

Weber's claim to clarify our value choices relativizes all particular value positions while defending the significance of value choices in general. On the one hand, *verstehende Soziologie* can clarify an individual's own values and those of his opponents by empathically reconstructing what it means to hold a particular position. For this reconstruction the ideal-type is pressed into service in order to show the *distinctive* features of a position and what it means if that position is held coherently. Such ideal-typical constructs of subjective value positions enable us to "understand" what we "really mean" or what an opponent "really means" in holding an ultimate value position that informs action. That is, it discloses what we are "in fact" standing up for in being, let us say, a socialist, a pacifist, a nationalist, or a defender of the capitalist order. And it shows us what it would be like to hold subjectively an ultimate practical standpoint different from or opposed to our own. Such coherent reconstructions of differing value positions could in principle induce us to agree with a position other than our own. We could, so to speak, "understand it for the first time." But, as Weber puts it, to "understand is not to excuse." *Verstehen* does not entail agreement. So where such ideal-typical constructions of values do not produce agreement, they at least enable us to understand the precise points on which we cannot agree and the precise reasons why we disagree (*GAW*, p. 503; *Method*, p. 15).

Obviously, to show someone what he or she indeed stands for in taking a particular value position is no small matter, even if no standards to judge the validity of the position are provided. Knowledge of this kind does attain a kind of "objectivity" about what we hold and where we are opposed to one another—assuming, of course, that we agree on what the significant features are and what standard of coherence is being applied. At the same time, no normative ethic explicitly derives from the "truth" of such reconstructive understanding, and, in principle at least, all value positions are treated as equally subjective.

On the other hand, despite its tendency to relativize ultimate value positions, this subjective reconstruction enables Weber to defend the sphere of value choices as a whole. This defense arises out of a revision of Kant's conception of moral autonomy. Weber agrees with Kant that there is a radical disjuncture between is and ought based on a categorical split between the empirical world of phenomena and the will. The empirical world is causally determined. Thus, there is no rational way to ground norms based on empirical knowledge. If there are to be imperatives of what we ought to do at all, they must be an attribute of the will. But Weber rejects Kant's argument that reason can provide us with a universal objective moral law of the will that is binding on all rational beings. In particular, Weber does not accept Kant's categorical imperative that you should act only in accordance with that maxim through which you can at the same time will that it become a universal moral law.[7] Nor does he accept the postulate that our freedom inheres in willing according to such a rational law. There are no rational a priori conditions of the will in which our freedom resides, only "cultural values." It follows then that for Weber our freedom and autonomy inhere only in choosing ultimate values and in taking responsibility for the consequences of realizing these choices. A rational rule for justifying such choices is not available.[8]

Weber's rejection of an a priori universal law of the individual severely limits, if not undermines, Kant's conception of moral freedom. But Weber does this, paradoxically, in order to preserve the ethical meaning of Kan-

7. Immanuel Kant, *Foundations of the Metaphysics of Morals*, trans. Lewis White Beck (Indianapolis: Bobbs-Merrill, 1959), pp. 39, 59, 19. See *GAW*, pp. 505–506; *Method*, pp. 16–17.
8. See Richard Bernstein, *Beyond Objectivism and Relativism* (Philadelphia: University of Philadelphia Press, 1983), pp. 12–16.

tian autonomy from the instrumental demands of purposive reason. Kant argues that once we apply the formal universalization principle not just to conventional maxims of duty but also to itself, we logically arrive at a prior substantive maxim of conduct: "Act so that you treat humanity, whether in your own person or in that of another, always as an end and never as a means only."[9] To acknowledge another as a morally autonomous being capable of acting according to a rational law of the will is to refrain from treating him or her as an instrument to realize our end. To fail to do so is to deny the other the respect that is due him or her as a rational agent, as a "person." But Weber points out that when we canvass individual conduct taking into account not just our will but also our locatedness in meaningful social relations governed by causality, we discover that we are bound not by one but by two formal ethics, one corresponding to value rationality, and one corresponding to purposive rationality, not merely one based on value rationality alone. Thus, we are in continuous conflict between the demands of intrinsically worthy conduct and the demand we be responsible for the consequences of our actions (GAW, pp. 505–506; Method, p. 16). And no appeal to a priori presuppositions can solve this conflict. There are two spheres of conduct each with its own dignity. In the latter, in which instrumental considerations govern, to treat another as a means has its own substantive maxims that may conflict with those of intrinsic morals. Thus, to salvage the substance of Kant's imperative to respect the moral autonomy of the other, we will have to jettison the formal law that demands that it be a precept for all. And we must also include teleological means-ends reasoning as an essential part of our freedom: "we associate the strongest empirical 'feeling of freedom' with precisely those actions which we know ourselves to have accomplished rationally, i.e., in the absence of physical or psychic 'compulsion'; actions in which we 'pursue' a clearly conscious purpose by what to our knowledge are the most adequate means" (GAW, p. 226; Method, p. 124).

Once we sociologically "understand" the meaning of moral autonomy in a world in which value-rational claims conflict with instrumental claims and instrumental deliberations toward given ends conflict with one another, we are compelled to conclude that "the only appropriate metaphysics" of morals is not one based on an a priori rational law, but "an absolute polytheism" of values (GAW, pp. 507, 603; FMW, p. 147). Our autonomy as persons is then expressed by choosing among conflicting values, finding the most effective means of realizing them given the context, and taking responsibility for both the intended and unintended con-

9. Kant, Foundations of the Metaphysics of Morals, p. 47.

sequences that ensue: "the 'freer' . . . the 'action,' that is the less it is characterized as a 'natural occurrence,' the more the concept of the 'personality,' becomes relevant whose 'essence' is to be found in a constant and intrinsic relation to certain ultimate 'values,' and 'meanings' of life which are forged into purposes and thereby translated into rational-teleological action." (*GAW*, p. 132; *RK*, p. 192).

Interestingly, the teleological choice of means to ends alone is rarely what defines our personhood or autonomy.[10] Rather, it is the choice of ultimate values in the midst of conflict and without appeal to rational or empirical grounding that constitutes an essential attribute of our individual autonomy. Teleological rationality follows such choice or enters into the weighing of such choices or is necessarily connected to the translation of that choice into everyday conduct. But the choice of values is the one activity that unconditionally sets us off from submission to causal rationality, whether we choose those values alone or in conjunction with purposively rational criteria of action. This, Weber suggests, is the only form moral autonomy can take in a disenchanted age:

> The reason why I take every opportunity . . . to attack in such emphatic terms the jumbling of what ought to be from what exists is not that I underestimate the question of what ought to be. On the contrary, it is because I cannot bear it if problems of world-shaking importance—in a certain sense the most exalted problems that can move the human heart— are here changed into a technical-economic problem of production and the object of scholarly discussion. We know no scientifically demonstrable ideals. Certainly, in this age of subjectivistic culture, it is harder to try to derive them from one's heart. But we simply cannot promise a land of Cockaigne or a paved road there either in this world or the next, either in thought or in action. And it is the stigma of our human dignity that the peace of our soul cannot be as great as the peace of someone who dreams of such a land of milk and honey. (*GASS*, p. 420)[11]

We achieve "dignity" as human beings only when we individually derive our ideals from an irreducible private intuition regarding the aim of

---

10. In fact, Weber at times argues that although teleological reasoning on the means to attain logically entails that an actor exercise freedom of the will, it alone is not something agents identify with as part of their person. Rather, it is understood to be dictated by circumstance (e.g., the manufacturer choosing the most efficient economic means in the competitive struggle). See, *GAW*, p. 133; *RK*, p. 193. For this reason Weber argues in his political ethics that a mature agent will have to learn to identify with both the choice of fundamental values and the teleological logic and its outcomes, even though the latter often seems to be dictated by the logic of the value sphere in which action is taking place.

11. Quoted in Marianne Weber, *Max Weber: A Biography*, trans. and ed. Harry Zohn (New York: Wiley, 1975), p. 418.

our ethical conduct. Presumably Weber's response to the objection that justification requires some publicly accessible rules of appropriate conduct would be that to seek public justification is to fail to "understand" the meaning of an ideal in a society in which deductive consistency and purposive reason are the only public forms of reason.

Rejecting the adequacy of public or conventional rules of conduct, Weber goes on to argue that the typical moral situation is one in which we continually seek to choose our actions in light of an already chosen ultimate standpoint toward the world: "every single important action and ultimately life as a whole, if it is not to be permitted to run on as a natural event, but is instead to be consciously guided, is a series of ultimate decisions through which the soul—as in Plato—chooses its own fate, that is, the meaning of its activity and its existence." (*GAW*, p. 507; *Method*, p. 18).[12]

However for Weber this choice takes place not simply in a world in which there is a multiplicity of values and value positions (e.g., nationalism, socialism, pacifism, ethics of love) but in which these values are in intense and unremitting conflict with one another. It is this "fact" that sociological "understanding" of the variety of value positions reveals to us: "So long as life refers to itself and is understood from within itself [*in sich selbst beruht und aus sich selbst verstanden*], it knows only an unceasing struggle [*ewigen Kampf*] of these gods with one another. Or speaking nonfiguratively, it knows the irreconcilability and hence the inconclusiveness of the struggle over the ultimate possible standpoints toward life. Thus, the necessity to make a choice." (*GAW*, p. 608; *FMW*, p. 152; see also *GAW*, p. 603; *FMW*, p. 147). If we do not want to be submerged in "the shallowness of our routinized daily existence," we must recognize these constantly conflicting demands on our conduct in all significant moments of decision. We thus face two kinds of conflicts that demand decisions of us if we intend to rescue our personhood from dissolution into predictable submission to routine. Within the sphere of morality we are unavoidably confronted with conflicting ends, because for Weber all moral ends are realized only at the expense of others. Moreover, we lack any agreed-upon standard to rank conflicting moral ends hierarchically. Even in seeking to realize one ethical end such as justice, we find ourselves in an immediate struggle to determine its meanings (*GAW*, p. 504; *Method*, p. 15).

Furthermore, values are not conceptually the same as morals; for we

12. To cite Plato here as an example of individual value choice is most odd indeed, as for Plato true knowledge of the good compelled a choice for justice. Knowing was not separable from a condition of the soul. And so it is not choice but knowledge that defines the moments of our life.

attach "value" or "worth" to activities or ends in spheres that are often not necessarily judged by moral criteria at all, such as art or politics. These "value" spheres cross and interpenetrate. Each claims to provide criteria of worthy action for the other, the most obvious being the conflict between the political and the ethical sphere. Political action aims toward ethical ends but often employs means and has consequences that violate precisely those ends. In light of such conflicts, it is the task of any person who seeks to choose his actions consciously and knowingly, instead of merely reacting to the everyday, to decide which of these colliding value spheres is "god" and which "the devil," which good, and which evil (*GAW*, p. 507; *Method*, p. 18). An aesthetic good may turn out to be an ethical evil, and an ethical good may turn out to be a political evil, to say nothing of an ethical evil turning out to be a criterion of good at those moments when political and artistic good overlap. But as long as we seek to interpret life from within, Weber argues, the determination of which value sphere defines good action remains fundamentally a matter of individual choice.

Weber is quite aware that this expansion of moral autonomy from the Kantian universalization principle to choice among conflicting value spheres—indeed, to a decision as to which value sphere will authoritatively define the meaning of good action for the other—could be interpreted as a thoroughgoing value relativism. And this is precisely how it has been interpreted. For example, one commentator has suggested that "a political philosophy to Weber . . . is like a taste for ice cream. One can state one's taste and go away—there is no point in arguing."[13] But Weber would counter that to reduce his ethical argument to latter-day emotivism is a rather fundamental misunderstanding of the ethical reasons for his focus on choice. For what he is defending is nothing less than "the dignity of the personality," the very end that Kant sought to justify though his conception of moral autonomy. But unlike Kant's moral will this assertion is compatible with seeking the proper means to effectively realize that choice. Moreover Weber insists, it is only by subjectively positing certain values as objective and struggling to assert them against the tendency of everyday routine to relativize them, to reduce them to an instrumental means of something else, that an individual person achieves "objectivity" in his or her actions: "we regard precisely those inner elements of 'personality,' those highest and ultimate value judgments which determine our actions and give our life meaning and significance as something objectively valuable. We can espouse these values to be sure, only when they appear

13. W. G. Runciman, *Social Science and Political Theory* (Cambridge: Cambridge University Press, 1965), p. 156. Also see Alasdair MacIntyre, *After Virtue* (Notre Dame: University of Notre Dame Press, 1984), p. 26.

to us as valid, as flowing out of our highest values, and thus when they are developed in the struggle against the resistances life presents. Certainly the dignity of the 'personality' lies in the fact that for it there exist values to which it relates itself." (*GAW*, p. 152; *Method*, p. 55). In the context of rationalization, individual autonomy can be defended as an ultimate value only in the *Sichausleben*, the externalization of the individual's inner personality in the form of particular value choices on which he or she stakes his or her existence. In other words, we have dignity as persons who are the source of their own choices and actions only because we are able to posit certain values as objective and struggle for them in the context of conflicting value spheres. Thus, the very fact that social science can help us to "understand" value standpoints but not justify them becomes the condition for the *objective* justification of the dignity of the person who relates him-or herself to values, or more accurately, to value choices.

Social science as "science" preserves the objectivity of a realm in which individuals posit and rank value ideas purely subjectively, precisely by claiming not to provide rational criteria to make ultimate choices. In informing the choice of ultimate values, social science must confine itself to the interpretive reconstruction of the variety of interpenetrating values on which individuals act. It must, as is so often pointed out, be "value related" in its ideal types but remain "value free" in its claim to inform value choice.[14]

But there is a point where Weber's sociology of explanatory understanding does claim to attain a measure of objectivity, even neutrality, in directly informing action. And that is in clarifying what is entailed in translating ultimate or lesser values into action. To be sure, this clarification cannot justify ultimate values, but it can provide criteria for those seeking "concrete directives for practical political evaluations" (*GAW*, p. 508; *Method*, p. 18).

The Instrumental Clarification of Action:
Personal Projects and Instrumental Costs

The contribution of *verstehende* sociology to the translation of values into action is a central preoccupation of Weber both in his methodological

14. Talcott Parsons's contribution, "Value-freedom and Objectivity," in *Max Weber and Sociology Today*, ed. Otto Stammer (New York: Harper & Row, 1971), draws exactly the opposite conclusion from this defense of value freedom. Parsons argues that with this distinction, Weber prefigures the dissolution of liberalism, conservatism, and socialism and the coming of the "end of ideology" (p. 48). But if we take into account Weber's justification of value choice, we would have to conclude that, in fact, he prefigures the heightening of

and his political writings. Except for one very notable exception (the early "Antrittsrede"), Weber's solution to his problem remains remarkably consistent throughout all his works.[15] What interests me in his account of how science can inform value-oriented action is the way in which purposive reason is used as neutral arbiter between subjective choice on the one hand, and the practical demands indicated by subjectively constructed value-related social context in which we must act on the other. The result of his account is most ambiguous for the integrity of the autonomous value choice that Weber is ostensibly defending.

All "meaningful human conduct," argues Weber, is intelligible in terms of ends and means. We desire an end for its own, sake or we desire something as a means to an end that is more highly desired. The first motive of conduct corresponds to our value choices regarding what we ought to do. The second corresponds to the purposively rational considerations regarding what it is necessary to do to achieve a chosen end: "Scientific criticism" can directly clarify only the latter, although indirectly it can call into question the former (GAW, p. 149; Method, p. 52).

We must choose our ultimate values—science cannot help us here. But once we have done this, there are three fundamental ways in which science—still understood as interpretive sociology, can clarify for us what is entailed in translating our value standpoints into action. First, science can reduce an unreflectively accepted end, or a set of ends, to an internally consistent set of value axioms (GAW, p. 510; Method, p. 20; GAW, pp. 607–608; GM, p. 151). The highest values are made manifest and subsidiary goals are tested to see if they can be logically derived from them. In this way, the individual attains "self-clarification" (Selbstbesinnung) concerning the final axioms that underlie the content of his or her will. This "formal-logical" scrutiny of individually held value judgments adduces no empirical facts and relies on no interpretive reconstructions of value positions (GAW, p. 151; Method, p. 54), but it does aid the

the struggle among these ultimate value positions, as there would be no resolution among them other than the struggle for power.

15. See H. H. Brunn, Science, Values, and Politics in Max Weber's Methodology (Copenhagen: Munksgaard, 1972), p. 146. Brunn maintains that Weber's account of the translation of values into action seems far less important than his treatment of the relation of values to social inquiry, because it does not involve complicated methodological issues or introduce new concepts such as the ideal-type. But I think that Brunn overlooks Weber's own argument that his sociological clarification of practical evaluations is most useful in providing both new "value relations" to social reality, that is, new problems of social action to explain, and more accurate interpretations of value-directed action (GAW, p. 511; Method, p. 21; GAW, p. 512; Method, p. 22). It would follow, then, that an understanding of the meaning and the necessities of translating values into action is a presupposition for social and political inquiry that in turn would reflect back on our understanding of action. Weber does not draw this implication explicitly.

individual in two ways. First, it makes the individual aware of whether or not the immediate ends he or she holds follow consistently from his or her ultimate value axioms (e.g., whether amelioration of immediate workplace conditions or direct employee participation follows from a commitment to socialist equality). This assumes that these axioms can be discerned and are not simply imputed as consistent with a set of ends. Second, it enables the individual to see whether the ultimate value ideas that he or she holds are consistent with one another, (e.g., a commitment to the goal of socialism and a commitment to sustaining a particular national culture). Sometimes a particular practical stand can be consistently derived from several positions; sometimes only from one, but the reconciliation of several ultimate stands for Weber depends on the individual's own judgment (*GAW*, p. 608; *FMW*, p. 151). Following Onora 'O'Neil's account of Kantian notions of practical consistency, we can say that this form of clarification provides "conceptual consistency," because it tests whether an underlying intention pulls in opposite, and thus self-defeating directions.[16]

This reduction of value positions to logical or "conceptual" consistency may either compel an individual to deduce a different immediate end that is consistent with the now revealed ultimate value axiom or influence him or her to abandon the end for others more consistent with the ultimate value axiom. Or it may induce commitment to a different ultimate value once the axioms of an accepted value are shown to be inconsistent. All this assumes that the individual finds logical consistency to be itself a value, something Weber admits science cannot justify (*GAW*, p. 608; *FMW*, p. 151). Weber knows full well that such axiomatic clarification has no force at all unless it can be related to action.

Thus, the second way in which science can aid practical *Selbstbesinnung* (self-clarification) is by "determining" precisely which means are appropriate for the achievement of a proposed end. Moreover, it can calculate the "chances" of attaining a given end using each of the available means (*GAW*, pp. 149–150; *Method*, p. 53). In doing this, it sets before the individual at once the most likely effective means to a given end and the dilemma of whether the means are in some sense compatible with the end. Thus "social science" appears to take over the role that before Hobbes belonged to prudential political knowledge, which was to provide maxims of political necessity in the face of fortune. Indeed, for Weber, social science improves upon prior political prudence:

16. Onora O'Neil, "Consistency in Action," in *Constructions of Reasons* (Cambridge: Cambridge University Press, 1989), p. 89.

we can make clear to you the following: to the value problem [*Wertproblem*] that is at stake—for simplicity's sake please think of *social phenomena as examples*—you can in practice take this or that particular stand. If you take such and such a stand, then according to *scientific experience* you have to apply such and such a means in order to carry it out practically. These means may be in themselves such that you believe you must reject them. Then one must simply choose between the end and the unavoidable means. Does the end [Zweck] "justify" ["*Heiligt*"] the means or not? The teacher can put this choice before you, more . . . he cannot do. (*GAW*, p. 607; *GM*, p. 51; my emphasis)

As this passage indicates, science is now added to the vocabulary of prudence, "examples" and "experience," "ends and unavoidable means." Social science precisely in its claim to be "science" now must aid political judgment. It must show political actors what they have failed to comprehend when left to their own partisan judgments; it must clarify precisely what is at stake in taking political action, the necessary means, the logic of the end being pursued, and the unforeseen consequences. It is interesting to note that except for the words "science" or "scientific" in this passage, Weber is invoking the vocabulary of prudence: "example," "experience." What science adds to the understanding of the proper deployment of means and the assessment of possible ends in particular situations is not political or historical "experience" alone, but also impartial generalized typological knowledge of streams of conduct and their causes and consequences. Science cannot directly resolve the question of whether the ends justify the means, because this is a matter of choice. However, the third form of practical clarification can decisively influence the answer.

Science can determine "the factual consequences" of using a particular means to a proposed end. Certain means will produce certain foreseeable consequences directly compatible with the end being pursued, and these consequences in turn are accompanied by subsidiary consequences that are frequently both unforeseen and unwanted. This determination of consequences both intended and unintended enables the agent to weigh different possible means against each other according to whether the consequences of deploying them achieve or undermine the end (*GAW*, p. 150; *Method*, p. 53; *GAW*, p. 510; *Method*, p. 20; *GAW*, p. 539; *Method*, p. 35). Such weighing may be decisive in deciding whether a particularly intrinsically bad means is still compatible with the end aimed for. But the clarification of consequences may have an even more profound effect on practical decisions. The result of determining both the desirable and undesirable consequences of applying certain means to a given end, as well as the necessary means to do so, may very well compel the individual agent to revise his or her ultimate value axioms in the most fundamental way.

To begin with, scientific inquiry into the necessary means to attain an end may indirectly criticize the end. Such inquiry may indicate that there are no means available either in general or in the historical situation to realize the end no matter how consistent it is with certain ultimate value axioms. In that case, the end will be "practically meaningless," even though it is axiomatically consistent (*GAW*, pp. 149–150; *Method*, p. 151). Or it may turn out that the necessary means are such that they cannot be intrinsically justified despite the integrity with which the end was chosen or the intrinsic worth of the end (*GAW*, pp. 607, 608; *GM*, p. 51). In addition, we may become aware that even if our end is realizable, the consequences of realizing it no longer makes the end desirable. The consequences are simply too costly. Or even if the consequences are compatible with the end, we may realize that the subsidiary consequences that follow from what Weber calls "the interdependence of all events" undermine this compatibility.[17] These consequences may, then, have the effect of rendering our immediate end inconsistent with our value axioms, prompting us to adopt new value axioms and ends that we had not considered before. This in turn requires a new inquiry into the internal consistency of our ends and axioms. Once again, they must be subjected to scientific criticism to determine the best means to achieve them and the intended and subsidiary consequences following from that achievement (*GAW*, pp. 510–511; *Method*, p. 12).

Clearly these three forms of scientific criticism place numerous previously unforeseen decisions before the individual. Yet what is striking in the way they do this is that the process of clarification itself remains unaffected by its application to the kind of situation in which it is appropriate. One would expect of a consequentialist and means-driven concept of judgment to take into account the effect of its advice on the very social and political background conditions which it presupposes; that is, the advice it provides should explain whether or to what degree its translation into action would not just alter the both long-run and contingent features of a situation, but the background conditions and the law like tendencies from which the particular advice is drawn—a typical feature of prudential political judgment of the kind exercised by a Thucydides, a Machiavelli, or a Gramsci. Instead, "scientific" criticism retains a sovereign impartiality above the motives of the agent and the situations in which he or she seeks to translate those values into action. Once a value has been reduced to its most rationally consistent form, that is, to an "absolutely unambigu-

17. It is striking that Weber rarely mentions that the subsidiary consequences may be so desirable as to justify both the means and the immediate consequences. This possible relation between means and ends could vindicate some alternative models of politics that Weber declares too costly.

ous end," Weber argues, sociology can "understand" the necessary means to its realization. It can do so by reducing the end to a set of (counterfactual) propositions (e.g., in order to attain end *x, y* is the only effective means given condition *b*). These are merely inversions of causal propositions (e.g., *y* is caused by *x* under condition *b*) (*GAW*, pp. 535–536; *Method*, p. 45; *GAW*, p. 517; *Method*, p. 26). Such causal propositions can be incorporated into ideal-types that provide a model of the distinctive form that purposively rational action plays in this situation in achieving the end. The ideal-type is, then, used to measure the deflections from such pure accounts of instrumental conduct in a more complex reality. Presumably by means of other ideal-types it then explains how these deflections effect the realization of the end or ultimate value (*GAW*, p. 533; *Method*, p. 41). Of course, these deflections would have to include the subjective motives of the participants themselves, who may not be oriented toward pure *Zweckrationalität*. Such noninstrumental motives would then be used to explain the results that follow from failing to heed perfect purposive reason and thus would alter the perfect model. To deviate from clear purposive reason is itself treated as a purposively rational move.

In this way Weber can claim to provide a subjective understanding of the agent's intentions and of his or her situation while providing an impartial scientific criticism of practical undertakings. The ideal-type may be a subjective construction of social actions from the vantage point of the theorist's practical values. However, impartiality is maintained by reducing the relevant considerations of practical reason purely to axiomatic and teleological reasoning. The logic informing scientific criticism of practical action is not relative to the motives of the agent, only values are: "the logical analysis of an ideal according to its content and its ultimate axioms and the demonstration of the consequences which arise from pursuing it in a logical and practical way if successful must also be valid [for a Chinese]. At the same time, he can lack an 'ear' for our ethical imperatives. And [this is true] though he can and surely often will reject the ideal itself, and the concrete values that flow from it without thereby effecting the scientific worth of this intellectual analysis in the least" (*GAW*, pp. 155–156; *Method*, p. 58–59).

Weber assumes here that all possible rational people would acknowledge the truth of his deductive and purposively rational account of translating ideals into action.[18] These forms of reasoning correspond to human agency as such, and so, would be intelligible to an individual whatever

18. Richard Miller, "Reason and Commitment in the Social Sciences," *Philosophy and Public Affairs* 8, no. 3, pp. 247, 251.

his or her cultural presuppositions. A claim to the universality of reasoning on means and ends is not, he seems to be arguing, a cultural value—an assumption that in other places, in particular *The Protestant Ethic and the Spirit of Capitalism,* he explicitly questions. Like Kant, Weber might say that he is simply making manifest the rational considerations that inform all significant practical judgments. The three functions of scientific clarification of practical judgment retain their impartiality whatever the value at stake.

By the same token, however, scientific clarification cannot replace the decision of the individual as to the proper means in relation to ends any more than it can on the choice of ultimate value commitments. And Weber takes every opportunity to emphasize this "fact." Scientific criticism provides an answer to the question, "What will the pursuit of the desired end 'cost' in terms of the predictable injury to other [ultimate] values" held by the actor (*GAW*, p. 150; *Method*, p. 53). It can provide new "facts" that require a readjustment between ends and necessary means and goals and subsidiary consequences (*GAW*, p. 53; *Method*, p. 23). But it is unable to provide criteria to decide whether or not means and consequences should be readjusted or, alternatively, whether the cost is worth the price of achieving the end. As with the choice of ultimate value standpoints, whether or not to apply the results of Weber's "impartial" analysis of the consistency of ideals with means and ends must remain the choice of the willing individual:

> To apply the results of this analysis in the making of a decision . . . is no longer the task of science but rather the task of the willing person: he weighs and chooses from among the values involved according to his own conscience and his own personal Weltanschauung. Science can make him conscious that action and also, according to circumstances, inaction entail in their consequences the espousal of certain values and herewith—what is today so willingly overlooked—the rejection of certain others. The act of choice is his own responsibility. (*GAW*, p. 151; *Method*, p. 53)

Empirical social sciences cannot lift this responsibility from the individual and "should therefore not create the impression it can do so" (*GAW*, p. 508; *Method*, p. 19).

Weber illustrates this delicate nexus between the neutral scientific clarification of means (as well as value commitments) and the irreducibility of the individual's choice for or against certain values in light of the means required to realize them through the example of a revolutionary syndicalist and a follower of Realpolitik. Both the revolutionary syndicalist and the Realpolitiker presumably are arch enemies. Both hold the attainment of state power (*staatliche Machtinteressen*) as their ultimate end. But the supporter of Realpolitik would choose an absolutist state as his means, and the syndicalist would opt for a radical democratic constitution. Now a scientific clarification of means for the syndicalist and the Realpolitiker would be of the same kind, though different implications would be drawn for their respective positions. It would confront each with the question of whether or not he should give up the hope of realizing his ultimate end if "the clear cut developmental tendency" necessitates the use of ethically or otherwise dubious means, issues in personally abhorrent side consequences, or blunts the realization of the goal. The syndicalist may be made aware that his actions will not improve the class situations of the proletariat but, rather, buttress the forces of reaction (*GAW*, p. 512; *Method*, p. 23). But this in no way entails that the syndicalist must abandon his end. For the worth of syndicalism may lie not in its consequences (*Erfolgswert*) but in its conviction (*Gesinnungswert*). The syndicalist, in fact, cannot attain power through radical democracy. But in his actions on behalf of this end, he seeks to evoke in others and preserve in himself the feeling that his conviction is genuine and not mere bragging. Through his actions he preserves the idea of proletarian power through radical democracy as a conviction, even though sociological clarification demonstrates that it is not attainable in practice (*GAW*, p. 514; *Method*, p. 24). Science may demonstrate the goals of the syndicalist to be perfectly consistent precisely in the fact that no means can be found to realize it.

The supporter of Realpolitik, by contrast, assumes that he is not bound by convictions, only *Erfolgswert*, the value of success. Success for him means anything that enhances the state's power. He thus will adopt only those "convictions" that the developmental tendencies show will lead to immediate success. For him *Anpassung*, adaptation to trends, overrides any convictions he might hold. The scientific criticism of Realpolitik must therefore take on a different form from that of the syndicalist. For science seeks to detach itself from lending its authority to this principle. Science shows Realpolitik that its conception of its own scientific authority is woefully inadequate. Whether we should adapt our actions to "trends" is an ultimate value problem requiring choice in each political situation, not, as Realpolitik maintains, a principle of choice supported by science. To clarify the "trends" is not to endorse them. Moreover, the principle of adaptation to trends is not necessarily coextensive with what is politically successful: "in a sense, successful political action is always the 'art of the possible.' Nonetheless, the possible is often reached only by striving to attain the impossible that lies beyond it" (*GAW*, p. 514; *Method*, p. 24). The adaptation to the possible often obscures unforeseen possibilities in political action. Perhaps most important, the rejection of any ends beyond the power of the existent order makes it impossible to gauge what a success even consists in. By making *Erfolgswert*, the valorization of success, his ideal, the supporter of Realpolitik may fundamentally misunderstand political "realities." Thus scientific criticism will show that as an ultimate end Realpolitik should be abandoned.

This scientific criticism of Realpolitik and syndicalism is most ironic indeed. In the second case, the value position most akin to science, namely Realpolitik, is shown to be incoherent and unintelligible. To discern and adapt one's convictions to causally predictable trends is to turn into an ethic what can only be a preparation for one. In the first case, the value position most distant from purposive reason, syndicalism, is ethically vindicated as a consistent and coherent choice in the very midst of its unrealizability. Thus scientific criticism that embodies a neutral principle to judge successful political action rejects the one position that claims such neutrality while vindicating the other on the basis of its irreducibility as an individual choice based on conviction. In both cases, scientific clarification maintains an impartial standpoint separate from the ethical demands of either position.

For Weber the scientific clarification of the logical coherence of an end, the necessary means to attain it, and the inevitable consequences that will follow on such attainment must not be turned into a substantive ethic itself. It cannot claim to provide a rational or empirical procedure to judge the extent to which the necessary means or subsidiary consequences of pursuing an end either injure or justify that end. Nor can it arbitrate between or rank conflicting ends (*GAW*, p. 508; *Method*, p. 19). It can only prepare the individual to choose an action or a value position conjoined to a set of actions in the most lucid way possible. And part of this lucidity will surely include the likelihood that the practical necessities of realizing any end will regularly conflict with the axiological model to which it is connected.

But at this point the question arises; On what basis are we to weigh the choices presented to us by scientific clarification about what it means to translate our ultimate values into action if no rational means are available, to rank conflicting demands? Or to put the matter even more sharply, What does "deliberation" even mean if there is no kind of reason that is appropriate to deciding among ends? This is closely connected to the problem of the context in which deliberation occurs, because Weber is assuming that deliberation is taking place not, say in the public meeting of a political movement or political association, or even a parliamentary body but, rather, within the solitude of the individual "soul" seeking not to be overwhelmed by habituation to routine. Weber, to be sure, suggests that we deliberate in the backdrop of our "conscience" and personal Weltanschauung (*GAW*, p. 151; *Method*, p. 53). The problem here is that in the absence of the Kantian imperatives or of some other context-independent standard, an appeal to conscience does not yield any substantive decision, only an infinite regress by which the conscience must consult itself about the right decision that the conscience calls for. As for personal Weltanschauungen, some of the most fundamental of them like liberalism or socialism only make sense if holding them is not seen as a personal choice but, in fact, follows out of their interpretation of the social and political world in which we live and act.[19] Liberalism, to be sure, frequently denies this by basing its interpretation of society and politics on an abstract willing desiring, or contracting individual, and Weber's own formulation of subjective choice could be seen as an attempt to divest that individual of this abstract status. But it certainly does not ground itself merely on choice, but on an interpretation of the context in which the abstract individual is at home: in a system of formal rights, in the competitive market, in an interest association. In the case of socialism, in particular Marxism, the interpretation as it were chooses us depending on our own relation to class exploitation. And certainly in the case of socialism and radical democracy the choice to accept the "scientific" analysis of action flowing from these positions only makes sense by reference not to ourselves but to some concept that we have of a collective agent. It would seem that scientific clarification defends individual choice to deliberate on ultimate values and their realization, but at the cost of rendering this choice unintelligible for a wide variety of commitments. Except for one rather crucial sense, which I discuss at the very end, Weber's radical choice ineluctably leads to solipsism.

These considerations raise a further problem in Weber's account of scientific clarification Weber often conflates the integrity of an individual choice with the validity of the value chosen. This leads him at times to argue that a value standpoint must be respected simply because it is lucidly chosen, for example, the case of his syndicalist, while at other times, he argues that a lucid choice will entail awareness of precisely the points in which we find the positions of another to be practically invalid. What, then, is an adequate choice based on sociological clarification? Is it one that affirms individual autonomy based on the individual's responsibility for choosing values alone? That is, is it an adherence to "conceptual

19. Weber, to be sure, does not think that we live or develop our convictions in isolation from membership in social groups. On the contrary, he thinks that the modern period with its highly differentiated civil society has turned "the modern human being" into "an associational being [Vereinmensch] to a dreadful and unforeseen degree." From "the bowling club to the political party and to religious or the artistic or the literary sect" we belong to various groups (GASS, p. 442). But Weber does not see these as aiding reflective choice of commitments and their costs, but on the contrary as detracting from them. Hence the reference to the "fürchterlichen," dreadful, degree to which these associations have grown.

consistency" in one's choice of commitments? Or is it a choice based on both consistency in one's value choices and accepting the consequences of deploying the necessary means to their achievement? Or has Weber left the resolution of this question to the individual's success in imposing or at least defending that choice in the midst of a power struggle against those who are doing the same from opposing positions?

Individual Choice and/or Power Struggle

The answer to these questions is closely related to Weber's notion of personal autonomy. Weber seems to have identified individual autonomy with the willful choice of ultimate commitments in light of the often conflicting demands of logical consistency among values and teleological consistency in selecting the necessary means and consequences of realizing them. Scientific clarification thus becomes an education to a kind of rational freedom in which irrational choice is made responsible by being connected to axiological and teleological rationality (in the Kantian not the Aristotelian sense). This concept of freedom has three components: first it consists of our choosing and ranking ultimate ends not according to some rational standard, but according to some inner sense to which we are only privy once we make the choice; second, it consists of our testing an end for conceptual consistency and then rationally calculating the necessary means and subsidiary consequences of realizing an end; and finally it consists of taking responsibility for choosing or failing to choose a course of action based on that calculation. Freedom, therefore, consists in personally reconciling the tension between the demands of teleological and logical consistency in one's actions and choice of fundamental values. It thus depends on science or, more accurately, on a sociology whose concept of understanding is linked to an ideal-typical elucidation of purposive reason in social relations.[20] In numerous places Weber calls this concept of freedom will the ethic of responsibility.

With this concept of (nonrational) ethical freedom, the reduction of one's life activity to causality and adherence to convention has been arrested. Scientific clarification secures and completes the dignity of the willing responsible agent. No position can be discredited as long as the individual has chosen it in full clarity of the ultimate value it embodies and the means and consequences entailed in pursuing it. Of course, a position can be shown to be incoherent or not a position at all as in the case of Realpolitik. But scientific advice based on logical consistency and

20. See Karl Löwith, *Max Weber and Karl Marx*, trans. Hans Fantal (London: Allen & Unwin, 1982), pp. 45–47.

purposive reason cannot vitiate a genuine ultimate value choice, only make it more fully responsible.

This unification of science with the radically choosing individual enables Weber to find a new relation between a sociologically informed political theorizing and political practice. Specifically, Weber firmly distinguishes between the scientific clarification of politics and practical political positions arising out of action. Practical political positions are characterized by "partisanship," "rhetorical persuasion," and above all "struggle" (Kampf): "when one speaks in a popular assembly about democracy one does not hide one's personal standpoint; indeed to take a clearly recognizable partisan position there is one's damned duty and responsibility. The words that one uses, are not means of scientific analysis but means of winning over another to one's own position. They are not plowshares to loosen the soil of contemplative thinking but rather swords to be used against enemies: they are weapons [Kampfmittel]." (GAW, p. 60; FMW, p. 145). In political action, analysis is used merely as a means of prevailing over others in struggle. It is not neutral or objective and does not seek to understand perspicaciously the position of the opponent. On the contrary, political analysis is a direct means of persuasion, convincing the as-of-yet unconverted to one's partisan stance and above all preparing one's audience for a struggle against opposing positions.

By contrast, in "scientific analysis of political structures and party positions" one deploys concepts in such a way that even individuals of such divergent positions as a Catholic and a Freemason would agree to the same analysis. Instead of seeking to win over the listener, one turns the democratic forum itself into an object of analysis. One considers the various forms of democracy, analyzes the way in which they function, establishes the consequences that the adoption of each form has for the living conditions of those who must live under them, and compares these conditions with those of nondemocratic forms. "The goal of the analysis is to put the listener in the position to find the point when he can take a stand on it from his ultimate standpoint" (GAW, p. 601; FMW, p. 146). The goal is most definitely not to convince the listener of one's own personal standpoint as part of a struggle against opposing standpoints. Respect for the listener and presumably his or her capacity to evaluate and choose in accordance with his ultimate value axioms is paramount.

The basic assumption here is that as a political actor one is immediately implicated in partisan struggle; all analysis is used to promote one's own position. In the sociological clarification of political action, on the other hand, one allows the members of the audience to choose once their ultimate viewpoints are analyzed for logical coherence, for the necessary means to their realization, and for the consequences that follow once these means are applied. Agreement is attained not on values but on the objectivity of the ideal-typical analysis of action, an objectivity, however, that inheres in the process of concept construction itself, not in any correspondence between ideal-type and reality. A kind of individual moral autonomy, not partisan agreement, is enhanced by this process of analysis.

We would seem to have two basic attitudes toward political action: a scientific one that enhances individual freedom to choose the ultimate standpoints toward political action based on sociological "understanding"; and a directly "partisan" political one that emphasizes struggle and partisanship. But Weber attenuates this distinction drastically as soon as he characterizes the context of the choice that is enhanced through scientific clarification. For as seen, social science according to Weber is unable to validate ultimate value positions because the "different value orders of the world are in irreconcilable struggle [*Kampf*] with one another" (*GAW*, p. 603; *Method*, p. 147). Each of the different value spheres claims to guide us in our attempts to realize our ultimate value positions. But each of them also makes its own distinctive instrumental demands on our agency. In choosing to pursue the values of any one of these spheres, be it the political, the economic, the artistic, or the ethical, we must submit to the methodical logics of pursuing ends under those values as they clash with the logics of other life orders. It follows, then, that the scientific clarification of action is not merely clarification of the value-rational and the purposively rational aspects of conduct in preparation for autonomous individual choice but also a preparation to engage in a struggle to realize that choice. Indeed, for Weber the very definition of a significant value choice consists in the fact that its realization will injure or displace other equally valid (or invalid?) values: "The fate of an epoch which has eaten of the tree of knowledge is that it must know that we cannot read off the meaning of the world from the results of its analysis be it ever so perfect; it must be in a position to create this meaning itself; it must know that 'world views' can never be the products of increasing empirical knowledge, and that the highest ideals that move us are always formed only in the struggle with other ideals which are just as sacred to others as ours are to us." (*GAW*, p. 154; *Method*, p. 57).

Here Weber is refashioning one of Nietzsche's most crucial arguments. Until late modernity, argues Nietzsche, our will to power has been preoccupied with rhetorically sustaining the fiction that the meaning of our conduct could be derived from nature. But once knowledge is turned upon itself the will to power is revealed behind the will to truth. We must now learn to forge meanings without identifying too strongly with them: "When the morality of 'you ought not lie' has been rejected, 'The sense for truth' must legitimate itself before another forum—as means of main-

taining the human being, as will to power. Likewise our love of the beautiful is in this case the formative will. Both senses belong with one another;
the sense for the real is the means of getting power in one's hands in order
to form things according to our fancy. The joy [*Lust*] in forming and re-
forming—an original drive [*Urlust*]! We can only conceive [*begreifen*] a
world which we made [*gemacht*] ourselves.[21]

Unlike this dynamic, playful account of the pleasure in forging values
and imposing them on the world, Weber's draws the sober conclusion
that it is we who create values; we make them and impose them on the
world in a struggle with other values, that may be held with equal integrity. It is the will to prevail over the values of others that forms our
commitment and reveals what it is that we are committed to. The social
scientific elucidation of action only confirms this fact.

Weber's moderated Nietzschean argument, then, contains two conflicting attitudes toward individual choice of ultimate value standpoints *both*
supported by *verstehende soziologie*. On the one hand, we must learn to
"understand" subjectively, that is ideal-typically, the meaning of ultimate
values that conflict with ours. Each has different prospects of success, but
all still retain their integrity as convictions. Value choices should be regarded as valid as long as a person doing the choosing has done so lucidly
and with integrity. On the other hand, it is inadequate to regard value
choices as valid merely because we have chosen them. We can take our
individual value choices seriously only if we engage in a struggle to impose
them at the expense of the ultimate value judgments of others. And the
struggle to impose our will, even over the resistance of others in a social
relation, is precisely what Weber defines as power (*WG*, p. 28). Thus
power struggle is the "fate" of all serious pacifists, socialists, or champions
of capitalism. For most "social relations" in which we seek to translate
our ultimate values into action are characterized by *Kampf,* struggle, and
Auslese, selection:

> Conflict [*Kampf*] cannot be excluded from cultural life. One can change its
> means, its objects, even its bearers, but it cannot be eliminated. There can
> be instead of an external struggle of antagonistic persons for external ob-
> jects, an inner struggle of mutually loving persons for inner goods and
> therewith, instead of external compulsion an inner rape (precisely in the
> form of erotic or charitable devotion). Or it can take the form of a subjective
> conflict in the individual's own soul. It is always present and its influence
> is often the greatest when its course takes the form of indifferent or compla-

21. Friedrich Nietzsche, *Werke,* vol. III, ed. Karl Schlechta (Munich: Carl Hanser Verlag,
1969), p. 424, my translation.

cent passivity of self deception, or when it operates as selection [*Auslese*]. (*GAW*, p. 517; *Method*, pp. 26–27)

This means that despite Weber's distinction between science and practical politics, between *Wissenschaft* broadly conceived and political partisanship, the sociological clarification of political values and their translation into action will have as its object ultimate Weltanschauungen firmly located in some form of power struggle. As H. H. Brunn has acutely pointed out, Weber's argument that all sociological analysis of action assumes the inevitable conflict of ultimate values has its correlate in his characterization of politics as the continuous struggle between parties, groups, classes, and nations for power.[22] We can press this point even further. Politics for Weber is a nexus point for the conflict over values, because it is in this sphere as compared to the economic or the ethical ones that power is deployed to impose values on communities. And there is no value that has not at some point been made the object of politics (*WG*, pp. 514–515; *ES*, p. 902).

This link between value conflict and political conflict as one of the central locations for value conflict profoundly circumscribes Weber's recurrent emphasis on the solitary individual taking choices for ultimate practical values in a complete vacuum. Although Weber insists that the scientific clarification of political action leaves us to choose according to our conscience and Weltanschauung, he also is quite aware that we are socially located in making our choices and frequently choose out of class, status, or national interest. Moreover, he is equally adamant that this choice also takes place within a context of "general cultural values" and "conflicting world views." And these may or may not correspond to class interests. Whether they do or do not, "the distinctive social-political character of a problem is precisely that it cannot be resolved on the basis of merely technical considerations which assume already fixed ends, that regulative standards of value can and must be fought over, because the problem lies in the domain of universal cultural questions." (*GAW*, p. 153; *Method*, p. 56). The clarification of the teleological and axiomatic considerations regarding our ultimate political ends leaves us located in a political power struggle to realize our highest cultural values.

Once Weber has established that politics is the sphere in which ultimate cultural values are fought over and that the scientific or technical clarification of political action cannot suspend this struggle but only render the individual's awareness of his or her own role in it more perspicacious, Weber has irrevocably undermined his original defense of radical choice

22. H. H. Brunn, *Science, Values, and Politics in Max Weber's Methodology* (Copenhagen: Munksgaard, 1972), pp. 240–241, 249.

on the part of the responsible individual. The different ultimate value ideas under which we act do not derive their validity merely by lucidly being chosen but, rather, by prevailing in a struggle with other value ideas: "Every meaningful valuation of the will of another [*fremden Wollens*] can only be a *criticism* from standpoint of one's own 'Weltanschauung'; it can only be a *struggle* against another's ideals [*fremden Ideals*] from the standpoint of one's own" (*GAW*, p. 517; *Method*, p. 157; my emphasis).

This oft-quoted passage contains precisely the slippage from value choice based purely on the individual to value choice within power struggle. These two alternatives are suspended between the two words, "criticism" and "struggle." By putting the emphasis on "criticism," the passage emphasizes the hermeneutic fact that in criticizing the practical value standpoint of another we can find no neutral standpoint to appeal to. Rather, we draw our standards of criticism from our own fundamental theories of society and politics. To seek to get outside of this process is merely to hide from oneself this basic hermeneutic fact. It is no longer to be making a "meaningful" or "intelligible" criticism. However, once we put the emphasis on "struggle," the implication is that a meaningful evaluation or criticism of the ideals of another is always made from the vantage point of what will further one's own ideas in the inevitable struggle in which both of us are locked. The hermeneutic fact that we never get outside our own ultimate practical ideals in criticizing another's is framed within the statement that we never get outside of power struggle in criticizing the ideals of another. We move from a critical hermeneutic of *verstehen* to a critical hermeneutic of *verstehen* embedded in power.

Weber has put a subtle twist on John Stuart Mill's empirically grounded polytheism, which he cites so often. His argument that value ideas and value choices are irreducible once they are subjected to scientific criticism now gives way to an argument that individual choices only prove themselves to be valid in practice once they have survived a struggle to impose themselves against the claims of other ideas. Despite Weber's protestation that the sociological interpretation and criticism of individual value standpoints protect the integrity and autonomy of individual decision, he, in fact, solves the problem of determining the practical validity of choices through the concepts of *Kampf* (struggle) and *Auslese* (selection). He deploys these terms in particular against the claims of utilitarianism and other universal accounts of human welfare to reconcile or supersede conflicting value commitments in politics. The task of politics in dealing with the struggle over values is not to find some general concept of welfare, but to test (through power struggle) competing ultimate commitments and projects for the possibility of their realization, and perhaps more importantly, for the kind of human being these commitments embody

(*GPS*, p. 72).[23] This move has been put succinctly, if a bit too unquali-fiedly, by Wolfgang Mommsen: "Unrealistic value positions prove their lack of realism in political power struggle rather than through social scientific criticism."[24] It would be more accurate to say that unrealistic positions prove their lack of realism in political power struggle *and* through social scientific criticism. Weber has rendered ultimate value positions immune to sociological justification only to expose them to a social scientific criticism in which the instrumental necessities of politics are decisive. Central to this social scientific account of politics is the notion that politics involves the striving for power either for the prestige it brings or for the ends that it can realize (*GPS*, p. 507; *FMW*, p. 78). Social scientific criticism of politics therefore consists of understanding the prospects for success in realizing one's ultimate values within the logic of power (and as we will see, domination), not against it. As we saw with the syndicalist and the politician of Realpolitik, social scientific criticism tests to see how different ends will fare through an ideal-typical account of the available means of power struggle and the political forms that converge to produce routine politics. In short, social science, on Weber's account of political judgment, is not just "value related," it is also power related.

The Problems of Weber's Political Prudence

Weber's sociological clarification of practical action provides both a means of impartially evaluating the coherence and the likely success of translating values into action and a defense of the irreducible autonomy of the individual in selecting ultimate values. But, as seen, he provides two models of practically validating value choices. According to the first model, we validate a value simply by choosing it with lucidity and organizing our conduct around it. Social science can inform us about the value's logical coherence in light of its background assumptions and the necessary means and consequences of seeking to achieve it. According to the second model, there are no valid values as such, because all values are at war with each other. Thus we must similarly choose a value in light of its coherence and promise of success. But this in turn entails that we engage in a power struggle for its realization using the political means available.

23. "Politics is a tough business and he who desires to take on the responsibility of interven-ing in the spokes of the wheel of the political development of the homeland must have firm nerves and should not be too sentimental if he hopes to pursue earthly politics . . . above all he must be free of illusions and recognize one fundamental fact: the unavoidable, eternal struggle of human beings with other human beings as it in fact occurs," (*GPS*, p. 29).
24. Wolfgang Mommsen, *Max Weber und die deutsche Politik* (Tübingen: J. C. B. Mohr [Paul Siebeck], 1974), pp. 473–474.

In Weber's conceptualization of the political world these will include power, domination, and specifically violence and charismatic leadership. We demonstrate the practical validity of our value choice by defending it within political struggle. The second model follows out of the solipsistic implications of the first.

Much criticism has been leveled against Weber's sociological clarification of action, although not as much for his account of the role of sociology in providing advice but more for the relativism of his concept of value choice. Jürgen Habermas, for one, accuses Weber of being an incorrigible "decisionist," who in the name of value freedom restricts social science to a "cognitive interest" aimed exclusively at the production of technically useful knowledge.[25] By reducing value questions to individual self-assertion and imposition, Weber has undermined any possibility that "practical decision in a concrete situation [could] be adequately legitimated through reason."[26] The upshot of this, for Habermas, is that "political action cannot be rationally grounded; rather it realizes a decision between competing value orders and forces of belief which dispense with convincing arguments and before which binding arguments remain insufficient."[27] Habermas argues that Weber ignores the fact that the process of democratic legitimation through public discussion is a condition for the intelligibility of both technocratic and political decisions. He also overlooks the fact that within the communicative process of public discussion lies an a priori objective standard for legitimating political and practical decisions. Behind all speech there is a presupposition that discussion must be free of domination and that the best reasons appropriate to the sphere under discussion should prevail as the basis for agreement. Weber's decisionism flows out of the historical and structural restrictions on a legitimating public sphere.[28]

A similar criticism has been made by Alasdair MacIntyre. According to MacIntyre, Weber is not just a decisionist but an emotivist. Weber's argument that no one choice of values is more rational than any other and that all values are merely the expression of an irreducible feeling beyond reason puts him squarely within the moral philosophy of emotivism. But Weber goes further than emotivism by describing the context in which only instrumental relations would pertain, namely, bureaucracy.

25. Jürgen Habermas, "Discussion on Value Freedom and Objectivity," *Max Weber and Sociology Today* ed. Otto Stammer, p. 63.

26. Jürgen Habermas, "Verwissenschaftliche Politik und öffentliche Meinung," in *Technik und Wissenschaft als "Ideologie"* (Frankfurt: Suhrkamp, 1969), p. 121.

27. Ibid.

28. Ibid., pp 129–130. Habermas later made this argument the center of his critique of legitimation deficits in late capitalism in *Legitimation Crises,* trans. Thomas McCarthy (Boston: Beacon Press, 1975), pp. 35–36, 105–110.

Weber's conjoining of decisionism with purposive reason, on MacIntyre's interpretation, is the final stage in the dissolution of the Enlightenment project of grounding an impartial conception of moral reason within the individual.[29] What Weber denies, for MacIntyre, is the directedness of our actions and our lives, whose guidance can only be provided by a revised version of Aristotelian practical reason aimed at realizing the virtues internal to being human.

In many ways these criticisms form two of the most significant poles in the attempt to break out of Weber's dual model of practical prudence. Both of them are preoccupied with showing Weber's decisionism to be inadequate from the vantage point of a more comprehensive concept of moral reasoning. They also expect the social and political sciences to support this more adequate reasoning rather than merely providing an "understanding" of value possibilities and an axiomatic and technical criticism. The difficulty is that although both of these theorists level strong criticisms against Weber's account of value choice and value conflict, they leave his argument that social science can provide us with an impartial account of the instrumental necessities and consequences of political action virtually intact.

What I would like to do in conclusion, therefore, is to move in the opposite direction from this line of criticism. I would first like to discuss the problems of Weber's decisionism by showing precisely the kind of case where it might make sense. I would then like to show that Weber's account of the axiomatic and technical clarification of action is problematic not because it reduces all social and political choices to problems of consistency in one's goals or an account of the kind of means and consequences attending the realization of one's projects—surely such knowledge reveals a part of what even the best founded commitments are all about—but on the contrary, because it assumes a neutrality relative to agents and situations that is inadequate for the prudential knowledge needed for political action. But the irony of this is that Weber himself provides some of the very arguments that point to a more situation-bound prudence.

There are, indeed, problems with Weber's decisionism, and they permeate his whole political sociology. Habermas is particularly right about this. But in criticizing Weber one should, I think, distinguish a simple decisionism, in which he does not share, from a complex one, in which he does. A simple decisionism argues that all norms of human conduct are logically akin to decisions. Behind all norms lies an individual choice. There is no way to ground norms by either reference to empirical statements or a priori concepts. The problem with this position is that it as-

29. MacIntyre, *After Virtue*, pp. 26–34.

sumes that we can take up an attitude toward certain valuations without a subjective understanding of the norms and practices toward which we are taking up an attitude. A subjective *Verstehen* of the background for decisions is deemed unnecessary for a particular decision to make sense. However, Weber does not suffer directly from this problem, because he assiduously seeks to understand the subjective meaning of various values and meaning contexts in which action takes place—albeit often through the lens of purposive reason: "Empirical reality is 'culture' for us because and to the degree to which we relate it to our value ideas; it comprises those elements of reality which are rendered meaningful for us by this relation and only those elements." (*GAW*, p. 175; *Method*, p. 176). The facts of our culture, for Weber are only intelligible on account of their relation to our practical value interests.

However, it is from these value-constituted facts that Weber insists we cannot derive valid norms of conduct (*GAW*, p. 213; *Method*, p. 111). Once we "understand" various valuations in their multiplicity and their consequences in action, we still must commit ourselves to one of them without rational guidance. In this sense, Weber is a complex decisionist. The problem in Weber's position apart from the specific logical problems that I have already pointed out, is that he thinks that "decision" or "choice" is the fundamental concept of morality despite his recognition that decisions are only intelligible within subjectively understood and re-constructed contexts. Weber denies that these contexts can validate a decision; yet, in making the kinds of decisions that Weber regards as significant, we rely on these very contexts for a decision to be at all meaningful. Peter Winch has posed this problem most succinctly: "Decision is not the fundamental concept in morality. For a decision can only be made within the context of a meaningful way of life and a moral decision can only be made within the context of a morality. A morality cannot be based on decisions. What decisions are and what are not possible will depend on the morality within which the issues arise; and not any issue can arise in a given morality.[30] The simple point is that what constitutes an appropriate decision is not itself a decision. We do not choose the contexts in which our decisions make sense, and this is true not just for ethical choices but for all intentional conduct. As Wittgenstein has famously pointed out: "An intention is imbedded in its situation, human customs and institutions."[31]

Now Weber might respond that we cannot find objective grounding

30. Peter Winch, "Nature and Convention," in *Ethics and Action* (London: Routledge & Kegan Paul, 1972), pp. 54–55.
31. Ludwig Wittgenstein, *Philosophical Investigations*, 3d ed. (New York: Macmillan, 1958), p. 108.

for the contexts of decisions. But it is not clear that we need such grounding for many or most of the decisions that matter. Moreover, in pointing out that different contexts for decision conflict, especially in politics, Weber still is not completely right that therefore it is simply up to us to choose which of the contexts will provide a good decision and which an evil one. For it is not simply up to us to decide on the meaning of what is "good," even if good means different things in different contexts. When we use words such as good and bad properly, we are using them within a certain grammar according to certain rules of usage. If we judge an action or a condition to be unjust, or a person or a group to be uncourageous (as Weber frequently does), we also have to accept certain criteria of usage of the words *unjust* and *uncourageous*. There is evidence that would support these evaluations. One cannot choose the relevant evidence simply on whim: "Anyone who uses moral terms at all, whether to assert or deny a moral proposition must abide by the rules of their use, including the rules about what should count as evidence for or against the moral judgment concerned . . . a man cannot make his own personal decision about the considerations which are to count as evidence in morals."[32] In numerous instances we may make judgments of what ought to be simply by using certain moral terms correctly and giving evidence to support that we have used them correctly.

There is, however, a "context" in which Weber is right to point out that individual choice without clear guidance is required and that is one in which there are several conflicting but equally compelling claims about what is right to do. Peter Winch illustrates such a situation by reference to Vere in *Billy Budd* by Melville. Vere argues for Billy Budd's condemnation according to the naval code, even though he fully acknowledges that according to natural justice Billy Budd is innocent. Both oughts make universal claims in this situation. And after the decision is taken, both demands are still equally compelling. Here we have no external guide. And an appeal to convention will not help us out either; for it is precisely the proper context for the choice that is in doubt. To use Weber's terms, life must be interpreted out of itself. Or to put the matter in Winch's terms, "deciding what to do, in a situation like this, is itself a sort of finding out what is the right thing to do."[33] The decision itself becomes a way of finding out what one ought to do or have done in the circumstances in the sense that it becomes a way of discovering one's own moral dispositions. In other words, one comes to "understand" what one must do and what it is morally not possible to do in the circumstances at hand. It is

32. Phillipa Foot, *Virtues and Vices* (Berkeley: University of California Press, 1978), p. 107.
33. Peter Winch, "The Universalization of Moral Judgments," in *Ethics and Action*, pp. 164–165.

the kind of knowledge in which one realizes that this is the only thing he or she could have done in the situation. But somebody else in the same situation considering the very same arguments might conclude that the moral possibilities were different.[34]

Now Weber's clarification of practical standpoints and of the implications for translating them into action assumes that we are always confronted with a situation of this kind: that only a decision will enable us to discover the right choice because in choosing we will discover what we as individuals must do given equally compelling choices. But this finding out where one truly stands does not apply to all decisions of significance (except tautologically) but only to those in which an individual is forced to confront two or more equally justifiable ultimate claims. Weber assumes it does. And thus he stages all decisions against the background of the individual in a disenchanted world, as if the individual faces this world bereft of collective social and political ties to guide his or her decision. Weber in his political analysis constantly recognizes that we do enter action with precisely such ties, and it is out of our interest in struggling to further these ties that we need to know how our ends will fare given the necessary means and likely consequences of pursuing them.

This brings us to the second set of problems, those relating to Weber's purposively rational clarification of action. Underlying Weber's account of the scientific clarification of action is the assumption that *verstehende Soziologie* can attain objectivity and impartiality in analyzing the necessary means and the likely consequences once ends are clearly defined. This teleological clarification, Weber maintains, is possible because once we analyze social action according to purposively rational criteria, we will have merely provided the reverse of scientific nomological statements. The ideal-type will provide us with lawlike causal generalizations from which we can draw counterfactual predictions as to which means will be effective to attain a particular set of ends and which subsidiary consequences will follow from such attainment. The assumption is that Weber's revolutionary syndicalist and his supporter of Realpolitik would essentially agree to the same scientific analysis of the likelihood of success. The assessment is made from the same set of lawlike generalizations. In part, Weber can make this claim because his sociology will often abstract from its own multiplicity of purposively rational logics and focus exclusively on the inevitable rationalization of all value, emotional, or traditionally motivated actions into forms of domination informed by purposively-rational criteria of social action. The unforeseen consequences will rarely be that bureaucracy suddenly dissolves into radical democracy (this problem

34. Ibid., pp. 167–168.

awaits Chapters 4 and 5). A more significant reason for this claim is the assumption that counterfactual judgments of possibility are merely the inverse of categorical causal statements.

This is precisely where the problems arise. Judgments about possible outcomes of some action or series of actions are subjective or hypothetical conditionals and as such, are not verifiable, although they are perfectly intelligible. Their typical form is, if p then q, where p is not a fact or an event but a condition. A typical statement of this sort is the following: if a political actor is not willing to use power backed by force she or he will not achieve any fundamental goals in politics. Many such hypothetical conditional judgments can be replaced by general or particular causal statements. But frequently they are used in contexts where they cannot be, and more important, where we would not want them to be reduced in this way.[35] Historical, legal, and political judgments are of this kind. Such judgments are not ultimately decidable by reference to any general or specific causal law. Where this is the case, we seek plausible or reasonable judgments of possibility in light of the background conditions rather than true or false ones. Weber's claim to provide a scientific clarification of political commitments by revealing possible outcomes in light of certain necessary means are precisely "judgments" that cannot be reduced to general causal statements but, instead, are plausible inferences from general tendencies (for example, the tendency for policies under modern conditions of formal legality to be carried out through administration based on formal hierarchial discipline) and certain background conditions (that the political community is characterized by its right to carry out its commands with the sanction of force). Some of these judgments have a close affinity to empirical statements of causality; others are strong hunches about what might happen in light of similar situations. Curiously, Weber himself wrote one of the major defenses of the need for such counterfactual judgments in historical interpretation in his "Critique of Eduard Meyer" (GAW, pp. 266–290; Method, pp. 164–188). In it he defended the need for constructing objective possibilities in light of background conditions that themselves rest on interpretation. He also argued for the need for judgment in imputing relevant causes to a phenomenon, that is, historical explanations required adequacy in "causal imputation," but such adequacy rested on a judgment about the likelihood that a certain stream of events or structure could have branched off from those under consideration. Yet, his defense of scientific clarification claims to provide judgments that can be reduced to causal generalizations. This will have

---

35. In developing this criticism I have relied heavily on Stuart Hampshire, "Subjective Conditionals," in Freedom of Mind (Princeton: Princeton University Press 1971).

implications for his claim to provide objective and impartial accounts of means to ends that I will take up shortly.

A further problem, at least for politics, is that explanations of the motives for political action do not lend themselves to lawlike generalizations. It is perfectly reasonable to focus on means, ends, and subsidiary consequences, but to generalize their relationship into laws of causal necessity, even in the backdrop of interpretive understanding, provides only part of what is needed for political judgment. The reasons for this is that political agents face other political agents on the basis of open-ended maxims of conduct, not general laws of action. Which particular maxims regarding means and ends are applicable to a situation cannot be decided by some impartial general maxim. To know this requires experience and knowledge of the maxims of other agents. This insight derived from Machiavelli has been put extremely well by MacIntyre: "The difficulty in applying maxims is that the factors in the situation confronting the agent include the beliefs of every other agent about what each agent other than himself will do in applying maxims, including beliefs of every agent about what every other agent believes about his beliefs."[36] The problem, MacIntyre points out, is that to claim that lawlike regularities can be found by using sociology "would be to claim that we could understand what occurs in politics independently of the beliefs of the agents, for it would be to claim that beliefs do not play a causal role in political outcomes."[37] Weber, of course, is adamant that beliefs do play a causal role in social and political outcomes. But for all his emphasis on power in relation to conflicting values, he does not carry this insight to its conclusion: that political agents, especially those involved in the struggle for power, take the beliefs of other agents doing the same into account in their deliberations, thus altering the predictions one would make based on their initial beliefs.

The fact that beliefs about the beliefs of others play a most significant role in political outcomes implies one last problem with Weber's neutral clarification of action. The range of causes and effects one must take into account in order to calculate the necessary means to a given end and the necessary consequences that will follow from realizing or trying to realize it is not the same for different kinds of actors with different beliefs. To be sure, all of these actors may agree on certain general features of politics (e.g., its reliance on power, its potential influence on a whole community rather than a section of it). However, in deliberating on possible outcomes the socialist or the revolutionary syndicalist take into account a different

36. Alasdair MacIntyre, "Is a Science of Comparative Politics Possible?" in *Against the Self Images of the Age* (Notre Dame: University of Notre Dame Press, 1978), p. 274.
37. Ibid., p. 278.

range of relevant causes from those of the nationalist or the Realpolitiker. The causal influences and outcomes viewed as relevant to political judgment will vary depending on one's fundamental political commitments, and it is by no means clear that one could find some point outside of these positions from which all the relevant causes could be enumerated. Curiously, Weber in other places says precisely this:

> The number and type of causes which have influenced any given event are always infinite and there is nothing in the things themselves to set some of them apart as alone meriting attention. A chaos of "existential judgments" about countless individual events would be the only result of a serious attempt to analyze reality without presuppositions. And even this result is only seemingly possible, since every single perception discloses on closer examination an infinite number of constituent perceptions which can never be exhaustively expressed in a judgment. Order is brought into this chaos only on the condition that in every case, only a part of concrete reality is interesting and significant to us because only it is related to the cultural value ideas with which we approach reality. (GAW, pp. 177–178; Method, p. 178)

If Weber is right about this, then the socialist and the liberal, the syndicalist and the realistic politician may very well agree on the usefulness of the kind of social scientific account he provides—and still not agree on the necessary means to attain the end in view, to say nothing of the relevance of the ensuing subsidiary consequences. In other words they would see the practical necessities and relevant outcomes of the same situation extremely differently. Or alternatively, they would interpret the meaning of the same subsidiary consequence from different viewpoints. For example, a relevant subsidiary consequence of an election for a liberal would be that a conservative party now has enough votes to thwart reform. For a socialist the ability of the conservative party to thwart reform is a sign that a liberal politics of negotiation and compromise is self-defeating. More fundamentally, each of these actors would construct the situation differently and disagree as to the counterfactual possibilities for action.

Weber's claim to provide an "objective" sociological clarification of politics depends in the most fundamental of ways on the assumption that given the purposively-rational constraints on political action, there will be general agreement on the part of all parties at least to the relevant subsidiary consequences, of deploying certain means to ends flowing from their differing ultimate political standpoints. But if we follow Weber's own insight about the impossibility of giving an exhaustive description of all the causes relevant to a social relation, we must conclude against Weber that in Machiavelli's language what counts as an effective use of power will depend on whether one is the prince or one of the people. And in both cases, fortuna will play a far greater role than Weber allows.

The impossibility of gaining an impartial standpoint on the consequences of social and political action points to a fundamental asymmetry between Weber's account of the person who defines his or her identity through his or her choices of conduct and the sociological constructs that are meant to inform these choices. Weber time and again insists, as we have seen, that the significance of any explanation depends on our interpretation of the meaning of the activity explained; and this meaning is only available to us through ideal-typical constructs that themselves are constructed from the vantage point of the social scientist's fundamental cultural values. If this is so, then it follows that any "objective" account of the context in which meaningful action takes place and the consequences that follow from acting within these contexts will depend on the practical values of the theorist. This account therefore will be only one perspective on the causes underlying a set of meaningful actions—say, the attempt to realize a set of fundamental political goals. But then in what sense is such an account of closely connected ideal types impartial relative to the vast variety of stances one might take toward practical action? Given Weber's own interest in the fate of the person who takes personal responsibility for his or her fundamental choices, in what sense would his clarification of the relevant means and outcomes in a given stream of action be objective for the radical egalitarian who might have a different account of the person and pursue goals different from Weber's? Weber himself shows that given his account of value-relatedness of all ideal-types as well as his account of the person, there must be a fundamental lack of congruence between the practical partisanship of the individual and the social scientific account of his or her conduct unless the individual being informed agrees with the value that provides the vantage point for the ideal-types that are to render an impartial judgment on the consistency between values means and ends. Of course, there is one way out of this dilemma. Weber would have to claim that his own account of the person and of that person's moral responsibilities is impartial for all agents, and therefore, there is a fundamental set of values at the root of all ideal-typical accounts that render his practical clarification objective for all value-choosing agents. But then he would, so to speak, be separating partisanship from scholarship only to find a more authoritative means of making a partisan argument under the rubric of impartial social scientific clarification.

The Political Logic of Economics and the Economic Logic of Politics: Marginal Utility versus Prudential Political Economy

The explanation of everything by economic causes *alone* is never exhaustive in any sense whatsoever, in *any* sphere of cultural phenomena, not even in the economic sphere itself.
—Max Weber, "'Objectivity' in Social Science and Social Policy"

Weber's account of social science as a means of practical clarification for social and political actors was developed as a direct criticism of the original models of what we today call neoclassical economics. Weber claims logical and causal objectivity for ideal-typical constructs of historical and social contexts and potential courses of action, but this claim emerges precisely from an intensely subjective, multicausal, situationbound, and contingent account of political economy. Indeed, viewed through the prism of Weber's political economy, his claim to objectivity for his subjectively constructed ideal-types is meant to rival the claim to objectivity of the formal models of the new theories of marginal utility.[1] Thus many (though not all) of the criticisms that I have leveled against Weber's claim to provide an objective political prudence in the preceding chapter are already contained in his criticism and account of political economy. The subjective side of his notion of sociological advice is deployed against the claim of neoclassical economics to provide impartial models of rational behavior and efficiency.

Weber's methodological and sociological critique of marginal utility theory takes place in the aftermath of one of the most significant moments in the history of the social sciences, the late-nineteenth-century debate over the historical school of economics in Germany, when the proponents of marginal utility theory sought (to a large degree successfully) to replace historical and political accounts of economics with formal models built on simple postulates of maximizing behavior. The main proponent of

1. Weber's early awareness of marginal utility theory is to be found in his *Grundriss zu den Vorlesungen über Allgemeine ("theoretische") Nationalökonomie* (Tübingen: J. C. B. Mohr [Paul Siebeck] 1990), pp. 18, 19. But it is striking that the weight of his outline and reading list is on those economic theories that pull away from these models. Not only is historical economics and Marx's *Capital* well represented, but also the outline ends with contemporary theories of cooperatives, cartels, and unemployment.

this position, Carl Menger, although granting historical analysis its place, argued for the universal validity of maximizing models of social behavior. Max Weber sought to counter Menger by providing an account of political economy that refused to reduce social and political behavior to simple maximizing activity while maintaining that the methodical fitting of means to ends was a central feature of subjectively understood human action. In Weber's new political economy, maximizing conduct collides with a number of other logics that deflect or even disrupt the simple causality of marginal utility theory in which consumer behavior drives production. In particular, it collides with a logic of power and a logic of formal rationality. Once framed within these logics, the modern capitalist market looks remarkably similar to the realm of politics without being reducible to it.

In this chapter I trace Weber's methodological and substantive critique of the claim of marginal utility theory to be the authoritative model for political economy. I take issue with those commentators who maintain that Weber merely provides an interpretive understanding of a capitalist economy, that is, an account that reconstructs economic conduct from the viewpoint of the actors, while leaving the marginal utility theory of price intact. Against this claim, I show that despite some of his own assertions to the contrary, Weber's methodological critique prepares the grounds for a substantive account of a modern economy in which the struggle for power, formal rationality, and domination within the division of labor regularly overrides all but one of the assumptions of marginal utility theory, the claim that value is subjective. In this discussion, I am less interested in the historical course of the debate over the subjective theory of value, which has been amply documented, than in how Weber's contribution to it becomes the basis for a new form of political economy that is at once conceptual, theoretical, cultural, and historical. This political economy provides actors with advice on the "political" costs of economic action as well as the "economic" costs of political action in a world of conflicting spheres of life. Although Weber's alternative to marginal utility theory has none of the neat precision of its opponent, it offers the advantage that it presents a broader consequentialist notion of action, a fuller concept of personal agency, and a richer, more distinctive account of the varying contexts in which agents seek to translate cultural values into practice. Most significantly, it allows him to rescue the logic of politics from reduction to the logic of economics much as it allows him to rescue economics from the pure logic of marginal utility.

The irony is that some of the same passages quoted in the preceding chapter that appear to support Weber's claim to provide an impartial logical and causal account of practical clarification supports a multicausal and contingent notion of political judgment once they are framed within his account of political economy. This seemingly contradictory interpretation of Weber is possible because Weber himself seems to be operating with two notions of sociologically informed political judgment, one lawlike, the other situation-bound. The critical tension this dual notion of sociologically informed judgment creates for understanding politics is explored in the next chapter. For now I just note that Weber relentlessly undermines the claim of formal economics to find lawlike regularities while invoking such regularities as the inevitable tendency toward bureaucratization, the logic of discipline, and the necessity of party machines in assessing what is possible in the political sphere precisely where one would expect the greatest contingency.

The Claims of Marginal Utility Theory

I first review some of the major claims of marginal utility theory, especially as argued by Carl Menger and the first generation of the Austrian school. I am aware that the theory of marginal utility was not and is not a unified theory. The Austrian school, which influenced Weber so strongly, upheld the purity of deductive theories but was opposed to the reduction of economic behavior to pure mathematical models. Instead, it emphasized the qualitative judgments of economic actors and the uncertainty of outcomes. The strand of marginal utility theory inspired by Leon Walras and developed by Alfred Marshall, by contrast, emphasized formal mathematical models of perfect equilibrium based on a purely rational calculation of utility.[2] This difference is not of major relevance for my argument; Weber's "social economics" radically overthrows both the general principle of marginalism shared by all proponents of this approach and the Walrasian theory of price at equilibrium.

The first claim of marginal utility theory of concern to us is the famous postulate of scarcity. As Carl Menger put it, the goods to satisfy needs as well as the means of acquiring them are universally scarce.[3] Hence the value of any good will be measured by the importance of the want it satisfies. It is thus irrelevant how needs or wants are acquired. Given the universality of scarcity, economic activity can be detached from any social or cultural context.

The second, and perhaps most important, claim—indeed the claim on

2. Mark Blaug, *Economics in Retrospect*, 4th ed. (Cambridge: Cambridge University Press, 1985), pp. 296, 306. See also Robert J. Holton and Bryan Turner, "Max Weber, Austrian Economics and the New Right," in *Max Weber on Economy and Society* (London: Routledge, 1989).
3. Carl Menger, *Principles of Economics*, trans. James Dingwall and Bert Hoselitz (Glencoe, Ill.: Free Press, 1950), pp. 95–96.

which the theory of marginal utility seeks to ground itself as a nomological positive science—is the principle of "final utility" or "the equimarginal principle," sometimes also called the "principle of substitution." This principle claims that the value of any good or means to that good can be discovered not by its use but by considering which want we would be willing to sacrifice if we did not have that good in our possession.[4] Given a fixed quantity of goods or means to acquire them, such as money, we always distribute each unit until the gain of transferring one more increment of the good to one use equals the loss of withdrawing it from another.[5] Thus we attribute to a quantity of goods the value of the least desired increment. This is how we optimize the allocation of utilities. This principle becomes the definition of efficient and thereby optimal allocation of any set of goods that bring satisfaction or are means of bringing satisfaction. This principle of optimal allocation, as Mark Blaug has pointed out, was (and still is) applied to wider and wider contexts until it encompasses consumer spending, investment, interest, and virtually all social behavior.

A third claim translates the principle of final utility into economic practice: in a purely competitive market the price (and value) of all goods necessary for production is driven by the consumer's demand for utilities. As Menger argued, the value, that is, the marginal utility, of producer goods is determined causally by the prices consumers are willing to pay for consumer goods.[6] The result is that the producer (the entrepreneur or owner) optimizes his or her expenditures on factors of production according to the price determined by the optimization of the consumer. Thus the producer and the laborer are powerless before the marginal calculation of wants by the consumer—a claim indirectly about power and income that is never addressed.

A fourth claim underlies the last two: all individual marginal utility follows a law of diminishing return, that is, as the quantity of a good increases, the utility decreases by an increment of the additional good. Without this claim there would be no impetus to marginalize according the last desired increment.

Fifth, in a market driven by the principle that all consumers distribute their expenditures according to the last increment prior to a loss of utility

4. Eugen von Böhm-Bawerk, "The Austrian Economists," *Annals of the American Academy of Political and Social Science* (January 1891), p. 364.

5. Blaug, *Economics in Retrospect,* p. 297; George Stigler, "The Development of Utility Theory," *Essays in the History of Economics* (Chicago: University of Chicago Press, 1965), p. 83.

6. Blaug, *Economics in Retrospect,* p. 298; Maurice Dobb, *Theories of Value and Distribution since Adam Smith* (Cambridge: Cambridge University Press, 1973), pp. 170, 189.

and that producers in buying machinery and labor can only respond to this calculation of utility, there is in the long run no profits.[7] For if prices merely reflect the marginal utility of producers and consumers, then in the famous and puzzling conclusion of marginal utility theory, the marginal price will equal the marginal cost of any good.[8] Assuming a market in which entrepreneurs, workers, and consumers are all seeking to maximize their utility, it becomes difficult to explain the long-run creation of appropriated surpluses without imputing to producers or consumers some form of deviation from the pure notion of optimization. Thus Marshall sought to overcome this dilemma by arguing that profits are quasi-rents; that is, they are a kind of unearned interest resulting from the fact that in the short run, due possibly to some special advantage in location or efficiency, entrepreneurs gain a return above the price they were willing to sell in light of the full utility of producer goods.[9] In the long run such rents would disappear as the short term advantage was offset by a long-run equality of marginal costs and a marginal price.

Böhm-Bawerk sought to solve the problem by arguing that we tend to discount future utilities for present ones. For example, entrepreneurs tend to take out in profit what in the future would be used up in production costs. Both of these solutions merely beg the question: they explain deviations from utility maximization by hypothetically describing the various ways we might mistake our true utility. Why we either fail to assess utility properly or consciously deviate from our assessment of it quite obviously has causes outside of the model, which leads us to the sixth and last claim relevant for this discussion.

Marginal utility theory claims that for almost all intents and purposes an independent account of income distribution is unnecessary. Instead, it postulates a constant distribution of income so that subsequent distribution between rent, capital, and wages can be seen as a mere by-product of entrepreneurs covering their marginal costs while responding to consumer

7. This irony has been forcefully described in Joseph Schumpeter, *The Theory of Economic Development*, trans. Redvers Opie (Cambridge: Harvard University Press, 1955), pp. 29–31, 45–46.
8. See Dobb, *Theories of Value and Distribution*, pp. 205–206: "If assumptions of full static equilibrium are consistently adhered to, then production in the capital goods sector of the economy will tend to be enlarged until the output of these goods is severally adapted to the need for them; this need consisting of current replacement of existing (equilibrium) stock of machines, etc. in industries producing for the consumer (on a scale determined by final demand) and in the capital goods sector itself. With the supply of them fully adapted to the demand for them for purposes of current replacement, there will be no longer any ground for their prices to be above the (prime) cost of their own current replacement (or depreciation)."
9. See Blaug, *Economics in Retrospect*, pp. 370–376.

demand.[10] Equilibrium, the state of optimal efficiency, can thus be attained under a variety of different distributions. As a result, an explanation of access to the means of expressing utility (money and income) is held to be totally exogenous to the theory. This model sees no need to explain the demand for products or the causes for investment in general by reference to the distribution of the means of investment and consumption (i.e., wages, profits, and rents).[11] And in making the causes of income distribution exogenous, it renders potential social influences on income distribution exogenous as well. Among these influences we might include: the (asymmetrical) relations of power (and ownership) in a competitive economy, the differential motivations of participants that may incline them not to maximize utility across the full range of wants, and above all the contribution of the previous two influences to explaining the causes of profit—in particular, the way the drive for profits opens markets while providing a strong incentive for entrepreneurs to gain sufficient market power to dictate to employees the very conditions under which they ostensibly as consumers dictate their wants to entrepreneurs.[12]

In marginal utility theory the formal deductive method, resting as it does on the acceptance of the equimarginal principle as driving the law of supply and demand, is thus not easily separable from the substance of its account of an exchange economy. In a sense, to buy into the equimarginal principle is to buy into the formal method of its representation as well. Thus a methodological critique of its universal claims most likely also implies a different substantive account of political economy, no matter how much one would like to keep the two levels of criticism separate. Weber recognizes this. Thus his response to the methodology of marginal utility theory also opens a far-reaching substantive revision of its description of a modern capitalist economy.

The Weberian Response: Marginal Utility as Method

Weber's response to marginal utility theory is subtle. He approves of the pure formality of its "theoretical constructions," which "assist in the

10. Dobb, *Theories of Value and Distribution*, p. 171; Blaug, *Economics in Retrospect*, p. 298.
11. This is not to say that as the theory of marginal utility developed it did not try to explain demand in light of different income distributions. Indeed, a number of theorists discovered that if one did not assume the marginal utility of income (or money) to be constant but varied with the size of income, it did not necessarily follow that demand curves would slope downward or that the law of diminishing utility pertained. See George Stigler, "The Development of Utility Theory," in *Essays in the History of Economics* (Chicago: University of Chicago Press, 1965), pp. 136–138, 142–143, 155.
12. This problem is ably discussed in Randall Collins, "Weber and Schumpeter," in *Weberian Sociological Theory* (Cambridge: Cambridge University Press, 1986), pp. 122–

attainment of knowledge of reality," but he nonetheless rejects its claim to universality (*GAW*, p. 537; *Method*, p. 44). As is known, he sided with Menger against Schmoller in the famous "*Methodenstreit*" over the status of historical economics versus abstract deductive models. Menger had argued that history indeed had the task of seeking to understand all sides of a phenomenon but that theoretical economics reached precision as a science precisely because it derived certain conclusions deductively from a "one-sided" accentuation of self-interest.[13] Like chemistry or physics, economic theory did not have to correspond to all the relevant facts as long as it established deductive laws that under given conditions were always true.[14] Weber agreed, arguing that in order to create a model that seeks to discover "what form human action would take . . . were it to occur according to strict rationality" a definition of rationality as corresponding to unimpeded economic interest was an "indispensable methodological heuristic tool" of social inquiry. For Weber even the most resolutely historical inquiry into economic phenomena has to ask such hypothetical questions and initially factor out other logics (*GAW*, p. 536; *Method*, pp. 43–44). Following John Stuart Mill and the classical political economists, he maintains that to derive one stream of causality in explaining economic behavior necessarily requires the use of ceteris paribus clauses and abstraction from the full range of human motives. Weber also agrees with Menger that an irrevocable part of social agency is the necessity of deploying means effectively to achieve ultimate ends. "Every serious reflection on the ultimate elements of meaningful human action is primarily tied to the categories of 'end' and 'means.' We want something concretely either 'for the sake of the value itself' or of achieving something else which is more highly desired" (*GAW*, p. 149; *Method*, p. 52). Indeed, even action whose sole goal is to express certain values results from some calculation of the ways in which those values can be methodically realized in one's everyday conduct.

However, Weber argues, marginal utility theory often has refused to acknowledge its status as a mere ideal-type: that is, as a "one sided intensification *(Steigerung)* of one or a variety of points of view and through the synthesis of a great many diffuse, discrete, more or less present and occasionally absent individual phenomena which are arranged into those

---

124. A central point of Weber's critique of marginal utility theory is that he seems to accept its description as part of the definition of the criteria of economic conduct in a rational capitalist economy without assuming that there is any adequate methodological reason why the features it treats as exogenous should in fact be left out of the analysis.

13. Carl Menger, *Problems of Economics and Sociology* (Urbana: University of Illinois Press, 1963), p. 79, a translation of *Untersuchungen über die Methode der Sozialwissenschaften und der Politischeökonomie insbesondere* (Leipzig: Dunker under Humblot, 1883).

14. Menger, *Problems of Economics and Sociology*, pp. 86–87, 61–62.

one-sided points of view . . . formed into a unified analytical construct [*Gedankenbild*]" (*GAW*, p. 191; *Method*, p. 90). This construct, literally a "thought picture," selects from "traits in our culture which are *meaningful* in their *distinctiveness* (*in ihrer* Eigenart bedeutungsvolle *Züge unserer Kultur*) (*GAW*, pp. 191–92; *Method*, p. 91; Weber's emphasis). Here the crucial features of an ideal-type are its one-sidedness and its *Steigerung,* its intensification or accentuation of the characteristics of a phenomenon in its "distinctiveness" *(Eigenart).* "Distinctiveness" refers to those unique elements of our culture to which we give meaning. All this is opposed to generic models claiming to provide the general features of the phenomenon. We will note these words again at the very end in Weber's account of the role of political economy in providing practical advice. Thus in presenting "an ideal picture of events on the commodity market under conditions of a society organized on the principles of an exchange economy, free competition and rigorously rational conduct," marginal utility theory claims to provide the generic features of economies as such even though it is in fact providing an ideal construct emphasizing the "distinctive" characteristics of capitalist culture (*GAW*. p. 88; *Method*, pp. 87–88). It treats its account of economic behavior as if it rested on formal generic concepts rather than historically genetic ones. Thus, it falsely treats the market and the law of final utility as a reflection of nature and as regulated by natural laws of behavior (*GAW*, pp. 536–37; *Method*, p. 44). In doing so, marginal utility also forgets that it is reconstructing one aspect of "meaningful human action." Rather it takes a small subset of instrumental behavior, indeed a small subset of economic behavior, and generalizes it to all behavior, as if all means–ends conduct could be reduced to individual maximizing conduct. It thus confuses a general theory for its particular laws.

The laws of substitution of utilities or diminishing returns are distinctive perspectives on economic conduct. They could only be derivations from a general theory of how we select scarce means to satisfy needs if we could know the totality of historical causal relationships on which these laws are premised (*GAW*, p. 190; *Method*, p. 89). But we have no access to such a synoptic view. All we have is numerous ideal-types each emphasizing different distinctive traits of our culture (*GAW*, p. 192; *Method*, p. 91). Thus the deduction of behavior from certain axioms of self-interest and scarcity is not so much wrong as radically partial: it represents an *ideal-type* of a certain self-understanding of economic conduct rooted in subjectively understood meanings whose effects and origins require other constructs for intelligibility (*GAW*, pp. 190, 537; *Method*, pp. 89–90, 44). In the case of marginal utility theory, the postulate of maximizing agents each distributing the imputed value of the least desired item across the whole set of items and the market that ensues from their behavior is in fact one ideal-type providing a perspective on the distinctive features of "capitalist culture" (*GAW*, p. 192; *Method*, p. 91).[15] Weber's point is that the axiomatic deductions of marginal utility theory register, albeit unintentionally, one stream of "rational conduct" in a capitalist culture, but that stream is deflected by other streams of means–end conduct that this theory treats as exogenous. Even if means–ends calculations were a general feature of human action, the particular version of them proposed by marginal utility theory would not be.

To this criticism, of course, a proponent of utility theory could reply that all Weber is saying is that we should be aware of the interpretive context of our accounts of human motivation and social action and that such theoretical self-consciousness should prevent us from overstating our case. Joseph Schumpeter provides a typical statement of this position:

> it makes precious little difference to the practical work of a theorist whether Mr. Methodologist tells him that in investigating the conditions of profit maximization he is investigating "meant meanings" of an ideal type or that he is hunting for "laws" or "theorems" . . . Weber was not unwilling to declare that, so far as his almost complete ignorance of it enabled him to judge, he saw no objection of principle to what economic theorists actually did, though he disagreed with them on what they thought they were doing, that is on the epistemological interpretation of their procedure.[16]

But Weber is doing a great deal more than merely making economists aware of what they are really doing. He is shifting the very frame of political economy from one that derives all explanation from certain postulates about human behavior to one that emphasizes the *dependence* of

15. On the relation between the analytic constructs of marginal utility theory and the actual empirical course of economic conduct Weber argues the following: "The historical distinctiveness [*Eigenart*] of the capitalist epoch, and thereby also the significance of the theory of marginal utility (as of every theory of value) for the understanding of this epoch, rests on the fact that while the economic history of some epochs of the past was not unjustifiably designated as 'the history of noneconomizing,' the approach [*Annäherung*] of reality toward the theoretical propositions [of marginal utility theory] under present living conditions has been and will foreseeably continue to be a *constantly increasing* one in which fate entangles always wider strata of human beings. It is on this *cultural historical fact* . . . which the heuristic significance of marginal utility theory rests." Max Weber, "Die Grenznutzlehre und das 'psychophysische' Grundgesetz," *GAW*, p. 395. Clearly how people are entangled in conditions that demand economizing needs to be explained, but Weber implies that such explanations cannot be provided from within marginal utility theory itself, except perhaps tautologically. Also see, *Grundriss zu den Vorlesungen über Allgemeine ("theoretische") Nationalökonomie*, pp. 29–31.
16. Joseph Schumpeter, *History of Economic Analysis* (New York: Oxford University Press, 1954), p. 819.

all economic explanations on the interpretation of the social action and the cultural context from which they are derived, in this case rational capitalist culture. Once we recognize this dependence, that is, once we understand the postulates of thin theories of economic behavior such as marginal utility to be merely one perspective in an interpretive context, any causal nexus we derive from them could turn out to be drastically restricted in its scope or even altered. Thus we can gauge the force of the explanations of economic outcomes provided by a theory such as marginal utility only if we know precisely *what* it is that is being explained. The "what" here is how and to what degree a capitalist culture selects out and cultivates the very behavior that marginal utility postulates as universal.[17] But this in turn requires additional concepts emphasizing different aspects of the idea of capitalism that limit, deflect, or complement the causality produced by maximizing behavior.

For example, marginal utility theory can deduce an equilibrium state from the equimarginal principle, but it cannot explain the cultural (sociological and historical) conditions under which workers, capitalists, and consumers in general make the equimarginal principle the directive force of their behavior.[18] Why indeed would a consumer seek to maximize his or her satisfaction according to the last increment of utility, whereas the entrepreneur seeks to maximize the return on his or her investment and not consume all the profits? Why would the worker accept the discipline of the division of labor in exchange for a salary or wage based on the last increment an employer is willing to pay? All this is postulated but not explained, and it is not explained because the sense (or more precisely the social relations) in which social actors might find this meaningful— meaningful here also includes instrumental calculations—is not constructed. Were this context to be provided, the law of utility would appear to explain a great deal less than it claims to explain when it is derived from a mere set of postulates. In turn for the law of utility to explain what it claims to explain, both the conditions of consumer choice and of

17. Max Weber, "Die Grenznutzlehre und das 'psychophysische Grundgesetz,'" p. 393. Also see *PE*, p. 45, *PESC*, p. 55.
18. This is precisely what Weber seeks to provide in *The Protestant Ethic and the Spirit of Capitalism*, with his account of the concept of "calling." What strikes Weber in this work is that a purely instrumentally rational agent calculating utilities would never have become a capitalist, because that agent would have had no reason to defer immediate consumption endlessly for the sake of accumulation—or in the case of the worker, accept the wage as an incentive for increasing his or her labor. Only some "irrational" motive could have been at work, and this motive itself had to be cultivated by some commitment beyond rational accumulation. The Calvinist notion of calling is therefore not the "cause" of the rational accumulator so much as the form in which such an agent could be cultivated. Once such accumulators launch capitalism into existence, this system itself selects out such types on its own. See *PE*, pp. 44–46, 61–62, 66, 180; *PESC*, pp. 53–55, 61–62, 78, 172.

the selection of a particular quantity and mix of factors of production, the very features that it declares exogenous, have to be included as logics impinging on the logic of the maximization of utility.

Weber's methodological critique also sets him against the present-day instrumentalist notion that marginal utility is merely a set of hypotheses about economic behavior whose lack of realism is unimportant as long as it produces verifiable predictions.[19] Again the problem for Weber would not be the hypothetical nature of the theory—all ideal-types are hypothetical—but the unclarified nature of what is being predicted. What determines a price in the theory of marginal utility is not necessarily what determines price in a culture in which marginal analysis is a feature of economic calculation.

Weber's critique harkens back to the classical political economists. They argued that a theory based on simplified psychological assumptions of the kind that we are all rational calculators of subjective preferences or that our preferences follow a law of diminishing returns would lead to simplified predictions about events in the world. It would therefore have to be supplemented by accounts of disturbing causes, including noneconomic ones. The test of an economic theory, therefore, would be if it took enough disturbing causes into account to explain historical and present economic events.[20] For classical political economy, if the assumptions are true, say about some aspect of maximizing conduct, a proper deduction of consequences also is true; but the boundaries of that truth still have to be accounted for. Thus the test of a theory is *how applicable* it is to the thing being explained and what range of events it can explain, not merely its internal consistency.[21] What Weber adds to this approach is the claim that the premises of political economy themselves are ideal-typical intensifications of a culture in which these premises have meaning. The characteristics of that culture have to be accounted for.

Thus Weber's critique opens up the possibility of a political economy

19. The famous statement of this instrumentalist approach is Milton Friedman, "Essay on the Methodology of Positive Economics" in *Essays in Positive Economics* (Chicago: University of Chicago Press, 1953). In this essay Friedman argues that the assumptions of theories of economic behavior do not have to correspond to the beliefs or intentional activity of the economic agents being described, as long as the theory has predictive value. Yet, he also insists that the assumptions must specify the range of application of the theory. We would not for example want to apply a model of pure competition to an oligopolized industry. But if that is so, it is hard to see how we can avoid an account of the intentional contexts of economic activity if merely to make clear what in fact is being predicted.
20. John Stuart Mill, "On the Definition of Political Economy and the Method of 'Investigation Proper to It,'" in *Collected Works*, vol. 4, ed. J. M. Robson (Toronto: University of Toronto Press, 1976), pp. 323, 326–327, 330–332.
21. See Mark Blaug, *The Methodology of Economics* (Cambridge: Cambridge University Press, 1980), pp. 76–77, 81.

in which multiple logics represented by numerous ideal-types converge to produce a notion of economic conduct and in particular an "ideal picture" of an exchange economy based on the exchange of commodities, unrestricted competition, and rigorously rational conduct (*GAW*, p. 190; *Method*, p. 90). It also allows for a notion of political economy in which one is constantly conscious of alternatives to each form of economic activity labeled as rational or competitive. Weber, it seems, has prepared the grounds for arguing that the pure theory of price as an allocative mechanism has to be drastically altered if we are to recognize that it rests on an ideal-typical account of economic action based on genetic rather than generic concepts. Yet curiously Weber's own statements about his substantive account of economics appear to support the thesis that he is merely giving an interpretive account of economics as a form of social action while leaving the pure theory of price as valid in its own terms.

The Political Rationality of (Capitalist) Economies

Some interpreters who rely on Weber's own statements approving Menger's and Böhm-Bawerk's notions of utility have seen his ideal-typical sociological account of economic action in *Economy and Society* as merely the translation of "pure economic theory" into a sociological context (*WG*, p. 63; *ES*, pp. 115, 116).[22] On this reading, Weber leaves the theory of price intact and merely seeks to provide a supplementary sociological account of the social context for the "economizing" behavior imputed to agents by marginalist theory.[23] Weber's own statements of intention both in his essays on method and in *Economy and Society* appear to lend credence to such a reading. In the essay on "Objectivity in Social Science and Social Policy" Weber states that the *Archiv für Sozialwissenschaft und Sozialpolitik* will be devoted to "social economics" in all its breadth but not deal with "the discussion of technical-economic questions of prices and markets in the modern exchange economy" (*GAW*, p. 164; *Method*, p. 66).[24] *Economy and Society* represented Weber's contribution

---

22. At the outset of his account of economics in *Economy and Society* Weber claims that he will not provide an economic theory or economic explanations of money or price but merely translate concepts such as market, money, or price into "formal sociological categories." But in redefining the concepts he implies a drastic modification in economic theory as well.

23. See Werner J. Cahnman, "Weber and the Methodological Controversy in the Social Sciences," in *Sociology and History*, ed. Alvin Boskoff (New York: The Free Press, 1964), p. 114; Martin Albrow, *Max Weber's Construction of Social Theory* (Houndmills, England: Macmillan, 1980), p. 142; Joseph Schumpeter, *History of Economic Analysis*, p. 819.

24. It should, however, be pointed out that in the next sentence Weber states the concern of social economics to be "the present significance and the historical development of certain

to a series that he himself was editing devoted to "An Outline of Social Economics." Within that series Weber understood his assigned task as providing an "analysis of social orders and powers in relation to the economy," and he assigned Menger's most gifted student, von Wieser, the task of providing the volume on economic theory.[25] Moreover, at one point in this work he explicitly states that he is not providing an economic theory of his own, and at another he seems to accept the major claim on which marginal utility broke with classical political economy, that utility must be defined by subjective satisfaction, not use (WG, p. 34; ES, p. 69).

Yet, if I am correct about the thrust of Weber's methodological critique, we have reason to suspect that his sociological account of economies dramatically alters the scope and even the logic of marginal utility theory. This is indeed borne out. If we trace out both some of the concepts under which Weber understands economic action and his specific account of the dynamics of competitive (capitalist) economies, we discover an economic theory that directly conflicts with one based on formal deductive models derived from the equimarginal principle. In a move similar to but in several respects even more radical than Marx's, Weber renders all the features that this model treats as external and contingent (such as income distribution, power and ownership rights, the capacity to translate power into profit) as internal and necessary features of a competitive capitalist economy.[26] Having done this, he then treats all the features of such an econ-

---

interest constellations and conflicts of interest which have emerged through the dominant role of investment seeking capital [die führende Rolle des Verwertung suchenden Kapitals] in the economies of modern societies." This is precisely the framework that, if accepted as the ground for formal economic assumptions, fundamentally alters the reach of such laws as the marginal utility of a good to a consumer determining the marginal cost of producer goods.

25. Johannes Winkelman, "Introduction to the Fifth Edition of Economy and Society," WG, pp. xii–xiii; "Hayek on Von Wieser," in The Development of Economic Thought, ed. Henry Spiegel (New York: Wiley, 1952), p. 563.

26. When I say that Weber is more radical than Marx in the way he renders endogenous features that the pure theory of the market held to be exogenous to the explanation of a capitalist economy, I do not mean that his critical standpoint is more radical. Rather, I refer to the quite specific fact that Marx's model of the origins of capital in the worker's production of surplus value still assumes at least initially that the cost of labor and the prices for commodities is given—that capital cannot manipulate labor markets or markets for its products. Capital is relentlessly driven to extract more from labor out of the logic of valorization. Thus its right to own the means of production over and against the worker, its power over the division of labor, and its ability to distribute wages unequally are all means by which it satisfies this logic rather than overrides it. See Karl Marx, Capital, vol. 1, trans. Ben Fowkes (New York: Random House, 1977), chap. 11–12, 16–18. Weber, by contrast, claims that neither prices nor the cost of labor are constant once we introduce power and ownership rights, unequal income distribution, and the use of power for profit into an account of the market. Instead, he demonstrates that the ability of capital to manipulate the conditions of the market is the typical case.

omy, in particular the law of final utility, as contingent, as the unique confluence of a number of logics each of which could conceivably be absent. Needless to say, this account has a paradoxical relation to marginal utility theory. Although the law of utility appears to be a crucial motive for some agents in rational capitalist economy, hardly one of the major claims of marginal utility theory described above remains intact as an adequate description of economic conduct, save that utilities are means of satisfying subjective needs.

Weber's definition of "economic action" is broadly conceived. Indeed it stands closer to his general characterization of human action as always oriented either towards means, ends, or ends in light of means than to the law of utility. "Economic oriented action" then becomes "action . . . oriented toward the provision of utilities for the satisfaction of desires." And "rational economic action" becomes economically oriented action that involves "the peaceful exercise of means of control [*Verfügungs-gewalt*]" that is "purposively rational, that is deliberate" (*WG*, p. 31; *ES*, pp. 64–64). Thus "rational" economic conduct is *not* about finding the most "effective means" to a given end—that is, a matter of "technique" or "technology." Rather, "the economic" involves "the weighing of ends among one another and ends against their respective "costs" [*die Abwä-gung der Zwecke gegeneinander und gegen die 'Kosten'*]" (*WG*, p. 33; *ES*, pp. 66–67).[27] And cost cannot be understood under one metric. As with all values, once the costs have been laid out, there is no impartial standard of choice. Under this definition, the law of utility could only be one way, not *the* way, to compare ends in light of their cost. By the same token, a broad notion of the economic as weighing of ends in light of costs can be applied to a variety of economic situations, market or planned economies, because in a market economy we may weigh expenditures in light of money obtained, in a planned one in light of damage to other wants that are more urgent. Weber further stresses in this definition that rational economic action requires something that marginal utility treats as external to all economic behavior, *Verfügungsgewalt,* powers of disposition and control usually of labor, resources, or the means of production (*WG*, pp. 33–34; *ES*, p. 67). Whether we are talking about a modern market economy, a socialist economy, or a purely cooperative self-managed economy, the acquisition of needed utilities depends on some

27. In the sentence that follows the one cited, Weber states that from a sociological vantage point ends can be compared in light of their costs to the degree to which costs are *not* reducible to merely giving up one end in favor of a mere pressing one—the law of final utility. Here, as throughout this section, Weber is constantly holding open a concept of "the economic" that is connected not to mere preferences but, rather, to fundamental decisions of the will in light of equally pressing alternatives.

agents who hold power over labor and its tools and who can decide on their use. For example, a market exchange is as much over trading the means of power and domination in acquiring desired items as it is over goods. Thus through this category power becomes a central category of economic action.

Having set up his definition of rational economic action to include a broad conception of cost and a concept of transaction emphasizing exchange of powers as well as utilities, Weber is able to reconstruct the features of a modern rational economy not as the outgrowth of one principle of marginal substitution for the least desired good but as the confluence of several distinct instrumental logics—that is, logics of economic action—at times colliding with, at times complementing each other. The first logic is that of the "market." For Weber the market is not characterized simply by the coming together of self-interested agents "to barter, truck, and exchange" goods for money, as Adam Smith would have it. It is also characterized by the fact that it is a field in which individuals "struggle" with one another over price and market position. In other words, for Weber it is at once a mode of exchange and power struggle (WG, p. 43; ES, p. 82). Thus there are degrees of market freedom, but all markets involve restrictions on opportunities for exchange, whether through law, custom, or voluntary monopolies. Indeed, the market is seen here from the vantage point of different parties seeking to restrict the opportunities of others to gain utilities while keeping them open for oneself. Market restriction is the rule, not the exception.

The second logic, and the one most discussed in all of Weber's account, is the subjugation of all rational economic action to "formal rationality." Formal rationality extends to spheres outside the economic, to the legal, the political, even the religious, but in the economic sphere it means the most rational calculation attainable for the provision of utilities ("chances" to put goods to use to provide for wants), preferably in quantitative terms (WG, p. 44; ES, p. 85). For obvious reasons "money" becomes the means of achieving the highest level of formal rationality in the provisioning of goods because it allows for accounting, especially in estimating the available or prospective means of producing a good in light of market opportunities (WG, p. 45; ES, pp. 86–87). However, through the discovery of "capital accounting" it immediately becomes a means, perhaps more accurately *the means*, for effective struggle in the market, because it allows the firm to estimate the prospects for profit by comparing assets at the beginning and at the end of a venture. It allows, as it were, the entrepreneur continually to seek to predict the right deployment of capital for profit through the calculation of the probable risks involved (note again the need to choose among ends in light of costs, rather than technical means). But as such, Weber maintains, it is not oriented toward "marginal utility but profitability," by which he means that the logic of the entrepreneur calculating profit is fundamentally different from that of the consumer equalizing the cost of the least desired item across the whole of the goods she or he can obtain (*WG*, p. 49; *ES*, p. 92). The entrepreneur is competing with other entrepreneurs for control over producer goods, something the consumer cannot do, and so the consumer also does not have entry to the means of calculating the optimum use of capital. In short, capital accounting not only enhances the prediction of market opportunities, it also becomes the driving logic of struggle within the market, a struggle that is closed to the consumer:

> Capital accounting in its formally most rational shape thus presupposes the *battle of man with man*. And this in turn involves a further very specific condition. No economic system can directly translate subjective feelings of need into effective demand, that is into demand which is to be taken into account and satisfied through the production of goods. For whether or not a subjective want can be satisfied depends on the one hand, on its place in the scale of relative urgency; on the other hand, on the goods which are estimated to be actually or potentially available for its satisfaction. Satisfaction does not take place if the utilities needed are applied to immediate more urgent uses, or if they cannot be procured at all, or only by such sacrifices of labor and goods that future wants which are from a present point of view adjudged more urgent could not be satisfied. This is true of consumption in any kind of economic system including a communist one. (*WG*, p. 49; *ES*, p. 93; Weber's emphasis).

The struggle for power in a market intensified by capital accounting overrides the wishes of consumers and selects out which of them are to be satisfied.

But if capital accounting entails economic struggle between firms, then something else is required for maximum effectiveness both in struggle and in predicting one's future capital assets. Thus a third logic enters in, the division of labor and expropriation of the worker from the means of production in order to gain predictable output (*WG*, p. 62; *ES*. p. 114). Though workers could in principle, Weber argues, control this coordinated division of labor if technical efficiency were the only criterion, they must cede such control on economic grounds, that is, the economic evaluation of ends based on capital accounting. Only firms in which managers control and have disposition over labor and production are suited to the struggle for market opportunities (*WG*, pp. 77–78; *ES*. p. 137).

When we put these logics together as an account of rational capitalism—and of the challenge socialism would face—we get a picture of an economy that violates virtually every one of the strictures of marginal utility theory that we discussed. Formal rationality as the discovery of capital accounting and the competitive exchange market may be two distinct historical modes of action that happened to have come together in the West. But once these two contradictory logics coincide, they form an inextricable and mutually reinforcing relation that no economic actor can escape. Against this backdrop, the modern firm consists of a privately owned enterprise that is subject to two conflicting demands: it must achieve formal rationality through capital accounting, and it must at the same time struggle for market shares and opportunities for profit. This in turn entails strict discipline within the firm, especially over the division of labor, which includes separating the owner from the manager and all the employees from the means of production. It also requires that the firm be able to hire and fire at will (WG, pp. 72–73, ES, pp. 128–129). The owner, however, cannot consume the profits because the firm itself is a trustee of the banks that lend it capital (WG, p. 85; ES, p. 148; WG, p. 52; ES, p. 97). In turn, modern capitalism requires a market that consists of a struggle to conquer opportunities for profit (utilities) without necessarily the by-product of providing consumers with the best good at the lowest price (GAW, p. 528, Method, p. 36). Entrepreneurs are at once driven by the need to optimize profits and to secure power positions in the market, keeping it open for themselves but closed to others: "Capitalist interests are interested in the continuous extension of the free market up and until some of them succeed, either through the purchase of privileges from the political authority [politischen Gewalt] or exclusively through the power exerted by their capital [Kraft ihrer Kapitalmacht], in obtaining a monopoly for the sale of their products or the acquisition of their means of production, and in this way close the market for themselves alone" (WG, p. 384; ES, p. 638). Because in such a model capital goods are unequally distributed, the working classes—which Weber defines broadly to include clerical personnel as well as industrial workers—must comply with the "commands" (Anweisungen) of those who have capital goods (WG, p. 59; ES, p. 110).

Under this ideal-typical account both the second and the third claims of marginal utility theory are violated: It turns out that it is only at the "margins" that the equimarginal principle is operative or that utility calculations of the consumer drive capital investment. To be sure, profits depend on the "purchasing power" of consumers, and this demand for goods may very well follow the law of final utility. But this hardly entails, as marginal utility postulates, that marginal consumption directs production. On the contrary, "given the actual distribution of power [Machtlage], this is only true in a limited sense for the modern situation. To a large degree, even though the consumer has to be in a position to buy, his wants are 'awakened' and 'directed' by the entrepreneur" (*WG*, p. 49; *ES*, p. 92). Arguing along the lines later to be taken up by his co-worker Joseph Schumpeter, Weber insists that "from a sociological point of view . . . in a capitalist economy new wants are created and others are allowed to disappear and capitalist enterprises through their aggressive advertising policies exercise important influence on the demand function of consumers" (*WG*, p. 53; *ES*, pp. 99–100). Moreover, even to the degree to which producers respond to the demand of consumers, they are not responding to the last increment of utility of each consumer but only to the utilities of the last income *stratum* that has sufficient inclination and money to purchase the good. Expanding Marx's argument from production to the market itself, Weber argues that the asymmetry in the power over opportunities in the market is reflected in income distribution as well (*WG*, p. 59; *ES*, p. 108).[28] Thus the distribution of income can hardly be regarded as exogenous to the explanation of economic action.

But what of the consumers who have adequate income? Here the underpinning of the law of utility, the law of decreasing utility, offers an inadequate description of the relation of the buyer to the goods provided. In his essay, "Marginal Utility Theory and the Law of Psychophysics," Weber points out that the famous law of diminishing utility as a psychological law is fundamentally flawed. For many items, among them Tiffany vases, toilet paper, and classical editions, the acquisition of each additional item does not lead to a decline but in fact an increase in utility. For others utility is constant, yet for others it is occasional. Thus demand curves may slope positively, be discontinuous, or go downward depending on the item and the consumer's conscious needs.[29] In any case, economics deals with subjective need, not psychological states, and its generalizations are about rational conduct to attain a variety of values under scarcity and thus cannot be reduced to one covering law.

If consumers do not develop their preferences independently of supply, it follows that prices are not a simple response to demand but, rather, a register of power in controlling utilities and market opportunities in the struggle that defines the market: "Money prices are the product of contests of interests and of compromises, they thus result from power constel-

28. Weber points out that although in marginal utility theory, profitability depends on the price a consumer is willing to pay in light of the marginal utility of money in relation to his or her income, this condition can only be met if there are consumers with enough money to outbid others for the product. Hence, distribution of income is not exogenous but, rather, determines the direction in which goods may be produced (*WG*, p. 50, *ES*, pp. 93–94).
29. Max Weber, "Die Grenznutzlehre und das 'psychophysische Grundgesetz,'" pp. 388–389.

lations. Money is not a mere 'voucher for unspecified utilities' which could be altered at will without any fundamental effect on the character of the price system as a struggle of man against man. 'Money' is rather, primarily a weapon in this struggle and prices are the prize of the struggle [*Kampf-mittel und Kampfpreis*]; they are instruments of calculation only as estimated quantifications of relative chances in this struggle of interests." (*WG*, p. 58; *ES*, p. 108). Just as personal ownership of troops was once the means of struggle for the feudal lord, so now money, presumably in the form of capital to purchase labor and machinery, is the means of struggle for the capitalist. As both the medium of capital accounting and of the struggle for power over the market, money enables the capitalist to override the law of final utility. The successful capitalist is able to extract profits when the law of utility would predict that in the next cycle they would be absorbed by marginal costs of production. The implication of this Nietzschean interpretation of capitalism superimposed on Marx is that if an entrepreneur must respond directly to the utility calculations of consumers, this is a sign of weakness in the power struggle that constitutes the rational capitalist market. Given the asymmetries in the power relationships in the market both the consumer and employee must accept the outcome of this process rather than dictate their demands to it. That is, the consumer must take the price that successful entrepreneurs on the market give them; the worker must take the job opportunities available within the division of labor: "It is the most elemental economic fact that the way in which the disposition over material property is distributed among a plurality of people meeting competitively in the market for the purpose of exchange alone creates specific life chances. The mode of distribution, in accord with the law of marginal utility, excludes the non-wealthy from competing for highly valued goods; it favors owners and, in fact, gives them a monopoly to acquire such goods." (*WG*, 531; *ES*, 927).

Interestingly, Weber's construct of a modern political economy makes no claim that this is a desirable state of affairs or even that it is fully rational. On the contrary, he directly states that this clash between formal rationality and power struggle in the market is accompanied by substantive irrationality at every turn. For it registers very little about the want satisfactions of most of the participants in this market (*WG*, p. 59; *ES*, pp. 108–109). Yet, he maintains that any alternative that might want to bring substantive rationality to the economic sphere, be it a planned socialist economy or a self-managed market economy, must be able not simply to counter the claims of market efficiency based on the law of final utility—these he thinks can be countered—but also the parasitic logics of formal rationality and power within the market and the division of labor that characterize "rational" capitalism. Ironically, recent defenses of socialism have been based on its meeting the criteria of marginal utility to the neglect of the problem of formal rationality and power.[30]

A New Political Economy? Marginal Utility versus the Economic Logic of Modernity

Weber's conclusion about the practical justifications for capitalism and socialism derives from his specific account of political economy based on translating the marginalist theory of price into the logics of action unleashed by the practical self-understanding of economic actors under market conditions. This political economy in the more restricted sense of the term tells you what it means to be an economic actor once you enter the economic sphere, the roles available, the logics you will be subjected to, the fate or at least problems of alternative economic arrangements. However, behind Weber's specific analysis of a rational capitalist economy as I read it stands a broad notion of political economy whose relevance extends well beyond the economic sphere.

The principle undergirding this new political economy is already contained in Weber's broad notion of "the economic" as not reducible to a "technical decision" about the most effective means to given ends, but as consisting in "the comparison of ends" in light of the cost of procuring them (WG, pp. 32, 33; ES, pp. 66–67). In his essay "The Meaning of Value-Freedom" Weber makes this notion of economics clearer by distinguishing between two kinds of practical advice that political economy can provide, one relying on purely "technical correctness," the other on "subjective rationality." The first kind is based on economic theory in its restricted sense as pure hypothetical deductions from simplified postulates. Here economic theory can tell us that to attain a given technical end such as the optimal distribution of some good, a certain determinate means or a combination of means will be the only appropriate one(s) and will be accompanied by a certain determinate set of subsidiary consequences. Under this kind of reasoning maxims are merely inverted causal sequences; therefore the "rationality" of different means can be unambiguously evaluated because they differ according to some common metric

---

30. For an emblematic example of this move, see John Roemer, "Should Marxists Be Interested in Exploitation," *Philosophy and Public Affairs* 4, no. 1 (Winter 1985), *A General Theory of Exploitation and Class* (Cambridge: Harvard University Press, 1982); and most recently *A Future for Socialism* (Cambridge: Harvard University Press, 1994). Ironically, Roemer's attempt to show that Pareto optimal cases can be deduced in which unequal ownership over production assets does not necessarily entail exploitation defined as unequal exchange for labor leads to the Weberian conclusion that domination follows a separate logic from capitalism.

of efficiency such as the quantity of output or the certainty and speed with which a given end may be attained. Because these assessments are based on formal generic models, the social structure and the economic goals are held constant. But, Weber argues, "the fictions of pure economics, which are useful for theoretical purposes, cannot . . . be made the foundation for practical evaluations of real concrete circumstances *(die Grundlage von praktischen Wertungen realer Tatbestände)*" (*GAW,* p. 529; *Method,* p. 37). In most circumstances evaluation is ambiguous: without an impartial standard of evaluation purposes are in conflict, and social structure results from the confluence of a number of contingent logics. Here a second kind of practical evaluation, one that is not susceptible to economic analysis in the strict sense, is necessary. This mode of evaluation takes value conflict as given. More importantly, it sets against the rational agent evaluating the range of desired goods against the least desired increment an agent who simultaneously organizes his or her life around commitments to fundamental values and seeks the instrumental means of realizing them. Against this backdrop it tries to assess the costs of translating into practice those values with which we identify as part of our life projects. This assessment includes an account of how the social structures in the sphere in which we are acting dictate the instrumental means available to realize our ultimate ends, as well as the by-products that ensue from deploying these means. But such an assessment can be accomplished only if we first reduce ideal-typically the vast array of values that subjects identify with to first axioms of conduct, revealing their "subjective rationality," the sense in which a subject might take them up as the first premise of his or her conduct. Then we must construct the "objective rationality," the instrumentally rational means that the subject must adopt if he or she is methodically to realize that axiom in practice (*GAW,* p. 530; *Method,* p. 38). This latter function of political economy allows the agent to assess "the chances" of reaching a particular goal and in this way to decide whether in the given historical circumstances and social conditions his or her commitment to this goal is still meaningful practically as well as subjectively. It also allows for an inventory of some of the consequences both desirable and undesirable that would accompany its realization so that the agent might have a provisional answer to the question: "what is the 'cost' of achieving these desired ends in the form of the predictable injury to other values?" (*GAW,* pp. 149–150; *Method,* p. 53). In this subject-centered notion of political economy "ambiguity" of evaluation is not to be extirpated but rather by means of the ideal-type to be heightened:

> once we pass beyond these considerations [of technical evaluation in the economic sphere], we are face to face with the confusion of an infinite

multiplicity of possible evaluations which can only be overcome through reduction to their ultimate axioms. For—to mention only one—behind the particular "action" stands the human being. For him or her, the intensification [*Steigerung*] of the subjective rationality and the *objective technical* "correctness" of action as such can beyond a certain threshold—yes, quite generally from certain standpoints—be a threat to goods of the greatest (ethical and religious) importance (*GAW*, p. 530; *Method*, p. 38).

Once again, Weber invokes the ideal-type as a means of *Steigerung*, intensifying, accentuating, emphasizing the distinctive and contingent features of social action. However, here the intensifying function of the ideal-type becomes the means by which political economy can evaluate both the subjective and objective costs of acting under the logic of modernity— a logic in which different spheres of life conduct—the economic, the ethical, the scientific, the artistic, the political—represent different and competing values to which we might commit ourselves and demand a variety of conflicting logics of action.[31] According to this new political economy, generalizations about means–end behavior must be understood not through formal models claiming to derive causal outcomes of a wide variety of behavior from a few simple postulates about equalizing the utility (or cost) of the least desired good across the whole range of them but, rather, through ideal-types that collect the *distinctive* features of conduct in different kinds of economic contexts. More important, this new political economy tries to understand the meaning and the logic of means–end conduct in each sphere of social life. Rather than assuming a uniform means–end rationality in all spheres of life, it must reconstruct the distinctive logics of methodically fitting means to ends pertaining to each life sphere. Thus the sphere of economics has a different means–ends logic from that of science, and science a different one from that of religion, religion a different one from that of ethics, and politics a different one from all of them. Moreover, Weber shows that within each of these spheres of social life different logics of instrumental reason conflict with each other, so that even in economics the logic of domination in coordinating the division of labor may at once further and hinder the logic of maximizing profit.

31. This notion of competing value spheres as the signal characteristic of modernity is developed in *Zw.* Wilhelm Hennis, "Max Weber's Theme: 'Personality and the Life Orders,'" *Max Weber: Essays in Reconstruction,* trans. Keith Tribe (London: Allen Unwin, 1988), has argued that the struggle of the personality to live a coherent life in the face of conflicting life orders in modernity is the central "theme" that all of Weber's work continually elaborates on and returns to. Obviously, there is a parallel between Weber's subjective and technical forms of practical clarification and the subjective agent facing the competing objectified logics of each life order.

What this means for the analysis of politics and political action should be fairly obvious. Simply put, it allows Weber to rescue the understanding of politics from models based on economic utility without having to deny the instrumental features of political action. It enables him to argue that political action follows its own instrumental logic rather than one of preference maximization—a logic of power and domination in which actors are seeking to appropriate, some even to expropriate, the legitimate means of domination backed by force embedded in the state in order to achieve fundamental ends (*GPS*, pp. 505, 510–513; *FMW*, pp. 77, 85–87.

Paradoxically, it also allows him to argue that although economics may limit political action, economic conduct frequently has a strong "elective affinity" to politics precisely because it is inseparable from a logic of power and domination in tension with the demands of formal rationality. But this affinity does not mean that economic activity is itself a form of politics. Although one is tempted to treat Weber's account of the capitalist economy as "a political process" in which "not supply and demand, but political maneuvering and power within the business community itself become the central concepts,"[32] there are at least two fundamental differences between the capitalist economy and the sphere of modern politics. First, power and domination in politics are legitimately backed up with the sanction of force, whereas in economics conflict is putatively peaceful, although by no means uncoercive. Second and more important, politics is the domain in which the full variety of ultimate values is struggled over, whereas economic conduct consists largely of struggle over utilities.[33]

These two characteristics enable Weber to explain why political action is so full of "hard choices" in a way that economic action is not. Political actors face a world where not only fundamental values (relative to different spheres of conduct) but also multiple logics of means and ends conflict and converge. The actor perceives only some of these logics, and of those perceived only some are in his or her control. Reconstructing these logics, we discover that the projects of political actors may collide not only with the maximizing logic of economic actors seeking power over the market

32. Collins, "Weber and Schumpeter," pp. 118–119.
33. "Every rational 'politics' makes use of an economic orientation in the choice of *means* and every politics can serve the interest of economic *ends*" (*WG*, p. 32, *ES*, p. 65). Note in this passage how at first Weber uses "economic" in the broad sense of calculating the costs of using socially available means in light of chosen values; only in the second part of the sentence does he use "economic" in the restricted sense of the struggle for "utilities." Obviously, politics is informed by a broad economics of action in the use of power, although one class of the ends it may deploy power toward consists of economic ones. Even in the latter case, Weber wants to insist that economic ends are not separable from power or formal rationality and it is a matter of circumstance whether political intervention clashes with the logics of economics or not.

but also with the logic of bureaucracy, which undermines this economic logic. To overcome both of these logics the political actor may have to mobilize masses of citizens under party machines. This in turn may require personal charismatic qualities that she or he may have in part or not at all.

Thus against the model of marginal utility theory, Weber provides an argument for a model of a "political economy" that gives us an enlarged notion of the costs and benefits of political action and thereby restores the "political" element to the term. For it reconstructs the multiple logics of instrumental activity in every sphere of life conduct and seeks to give some tentative generalizations about when they collide. However, these generalizations can be assessed only in light of the costs to the actual substantive values that we pursue in political action, rather than some formal matrix of preference ranking. If Weber is right, then, that the test, for example, of the feasibility of an industrial capitalist economy as opposed to a planned or self-managed socialist economy relies on understanding the means and ends of economic conduct in terms not reducible to marginal utility, it should be all the more true that an assessment of fundamental "political" projects requires an "economics" of politics beyond what economic models based on marginal utility can provide. To put the matter in terms relevant to contemporary debate about the "economic approach," if Weber is correct in saying that marginal utility theory and models derived from it provide an inadequate description of the logic of economic conduct, it follows that it is all the more inadequate as a description of the logic of political action.[34]

Schumpeter's Criticism

Commentators have responded to this notion of political economy by arguing that what Weber provides is sociology, not economics. Once again, it is Schumpeter who puts the matter most forcefully: "[Weber] was above all a sociologist. He was only indirectly a political economist, even though he was a sociologist inclined primarily to economic matters. His interest in economics does not focus on the *mechanisms of economic life described by economic theory;* nor on the historical and real phenomena as such, but rather on the course of historical types in their *social and*

34. Amartya Sen draws a similar conclusion about the application of maximization models derived from welfare economics to other areas of social life: "The thing about this 'economic imperialism,' as it sometimes is called is not that these tools don't apply very well outside of economics. The trouble is that they don't apply very well inside of economics either . . . they are narrow and do not have much predictive and explanatory power even in economics." In *Economics and Sociology,* ed. Richard Swedberg (Princeton: Princeton University Press, 1990), pp. 264–265.

psychological plenitude" (my emphasis).[35] At the heart of this remark is the claim that Weber is not an economist because he lacks parsimony: he fails to derive "mechanisms" of economic behavior from simple premises and instead overwhelms us with his "plenitude" of ideal-types and sequences of social action described by these types. Instead of providing us with clear determinate mechanisms underlying social conduct as does economics with its law of economizing, Weber leaves us with a plethora of types and generalizations whose relation to one another is indeterminate.

But once his economics is seen in conjunction with his notion of practical political judgement, this defect emerges precisely as a virtue. Weber's plenitude of types allows the agent to put together the relations among forms of economic action according to the kind of political society in which that economy is embedded. In this way he or she may assess the meaning and cost of a social activity from one historical situation to the next and from one sphere of action to the next. The derivation of mechanisms of cost and price from simple assumptions may capture one relevant causal mechanism at work in social life but alone it cannot provide what Weber's types and generalizations in their sprawling multiplicity can: a set of concepts and generalizations that allow us to come to plausible judgments about possible political and economic futures that are fundamentally undecidable by reference to clear determinate law like statements. He therefore provides the concepts with which the scope and relevance of the law like deductive mechanisms of economics can be judged.

In conclusion, then, Weber's own account of economics as I read it is more than just a translation of marginal utility into the vocabulary of sociology as many interpreters have claimed. It is in fact more than a mere attempt to provide an economic sociology that emphasizes formal rationality and power rather than the law of final utility. Above all, it is a reinterpretation of economic action from the vantage point of a political economy whose task is to provide practical clarification for actors seeking a clear knowledge of their own agency. This account of practical clarification rejects utilitarianism in favor of emphasizing the ambiguity of all significant choices involving a judgment of consequences.[36] And from the

35. Joseph Schumpeter, "Max Weber's Werk," in *Max Weber zum Gedächtnis,* ed. Rene König and Johannes Wincklemann (Cologne: Westdeutscher Verlag, 1985), p. 69.
36. One of the few interpretations to appreciate this aspect of Weber's political economy is Wilhelm Hennis, "'A Science of Man': Max Weber and the Political Economy of the German Historical School," in *Max Weber: Essays in Reconstruction,* trans. Keith Tribe, pp. 108, 120. Hennis views Weber's critique of marginal utility less as a compromise position between the historical school and the position of Menger than an echo of positions already taken by historical political economists like Knies. However, Weber is seen to have covered

vantage point of a new political economy, it is a defense of politics (and for that matter, economics) against those tendencies that would reduce it to simple maximizing behavior.

Epilogue

In the preceding argument I have emphasized the link between Weber's analysis of the contingent logics converging to produce a rational capitalist market and his broad account of a political economy that employs rationality to intensify the ambiguities of action in all life spheres. But this is only one side of Weber's strategy. As seen in Chapter 2, the other side consists of a claim to transform the very subjectivity of our value-related perspectives on social reality into an objective account of the causal tendencies and concrete possibilities inherent in historical reality.

What enables Weber to move in both directions? The answer lies in a kind of "gestalt" created by the constellations of meaning produced by his ideal types. Viewed retrospectively the various ideal typical modes of action converge to produce a historical form like rational capitalism that is inescapable and durable. Each ideal-typical element mutually reenforces the other. Viewed prospectively, the same constellation can appear as a mere convergence of contingent modes of action whose entwinement is fortuitous and could fall apart or be deflected in another direction by some unforeseen action. A similar interpretive switch occurs in his typology of domination, though in a different sense. In this case, the various typologies of inducing belief in the legitimacy of one's commands are at moments portrayed as fluid, each conceivably turning into one another. At other moments, however, the movement from one to another follows an irresistible sequence from the most personal to the most impersonal forms of discipline. Weber exploits this Gestalt switch between objective and subjective as he sees fit, producing judgments that hold open the contingency, say of the capitalist economy, and judgments that see it as enclosed in a mutually reinforcing logic that no one can escape.

When we examine Weber's sociology of politics and his political ethics, we find both of these sides of his account of scientific clarification on display. Sometimes Weber will intensify the contingency of both the formation of modern politics and its logic of action. He does this by empha-

---

his tracks for polemical purposes. The one difficulty with Hennis's interpretation is that he emphasizes thematic similarity rather than similarity in the strategy of argument. One might thus agree that Weber displays a kind of "anxiety of influence" toward his mentor Knies, and one might still want to argue that the *substance* rather than the themes of Weber's notion of political economy are a marked departure from that of the historical school.

sizing the fluidity through which his ideal-types of power and domination can turn into one another or by providing a comparative developmental history of modern professional politics or by suggesting the variety of forms that groups may organize to further their economic interests on the terrain of politics. But just as often Weber's scientific clarification of politics will veer away from this emphasis on contingency and toward a claim to have found impartial lawlike generalizations about the processes of social action that are irresistible, especially to those who hope to overcome the need for domination in economic and political life. Quite surprisingly, we will find that although Weber often abstractly asserts the contingency of politics and its outcomes, he surrounds his substantive analysis with objective logics that dictate, as it were, the direction and consequences of all political action.

This may not seem problematic. Indeed it may be the sign of a well-balanced social and political theory. After all, the convergence of different logics of methodical instrumental conduct may unleash a relentless logic like that of the capitalist market that in turn defines and entangles all agents.[37] The same may be true of politics. A good social theory ought to understand how subjective self-understood actions may unleash streams of activity beyond the control of the actors. By the same token, such a theory should understand how such streams of action may be dictated by logics of power beneath the cognizance of the participants.

However, Weber does not neatly balance these concerns. On the contrary, in his sociological analysis of politics, he often abruptly preempts the very emphasis on contingency that bulks so large in his account of economics. Instead of an account based on convergent developments and contingent constellations of power, he invokes a variety of tendential laws, such as the process of political expropriation or the tendency toward bureaucratization, and treats them as if they were immutable and irreversible. This is especially odd, considering that politics, precisely because it is a locus of conflicting values and involves the deployment of power over society at large, should be even more exposed to contingency than the economic sphere. Why Weber sometimes emphasizes the uncertain and contingent aspects of politics while at other times framing it within relentless laws rooted in the logic of power and domination is explored in the following chapters. At times this alternation seems to derive from a perfectly sensible attempt to combine the contingent with the recurrent features of politics. At times, however, it creates a fundamental problem in his account of political advice—one that unjustifiably restricts the set of

---

37. For a most persuasive argument that this describes Weber's mature theory of capitalism, see Randall Collins, "Weber's Last Theory of Capitalism."

feasible political alternatives in modern politics. In tension with both of these interpretations we will also discover that Weber at times uses the claim of objective impartial laws rhetorically to claim the unfeasibility of political projects he disagrees with. I am especially concerned with how he deploys this shuttle between the subjective and objective features of politics in providing prudential and political-ethical advice on the possibilities for democracy. The problems Weber raises by doing so opens up the possibility of arguing for forms of democracy that he rejects without abandoning his justified emphasis on prudential justification of political goals according to the instrumental conditions of their realization.

The Reason of Modern Politics: Politics as a Business, Politics as a Vocation

Since politics is always made by a small number of persons . . .
—Max Weber, "Parliament and Government in a Reconstructed Germany"

There is a flawed logic in a doctrine which denies large sectors of the population effective participation in the decision-making process on the ground that their demands are likely to be "extremist" and then seizes on their lack of restraint as proof of rightness of their exclusion.
—M. I. Finley, *Democracy Ancient and Modern*

Weber's application of his sociologically informed prudence to analyze the origins, the logics, the institutions of modern politics, and the necessary means and probable consequences of political action displays both the strengths and the difficulties of his approach. On the one hand, his account of politics demonstrates his broad concept of political economy at its height. The various logics that come to constitute modern politics are developed within the larger frame of his interrelated logics of domination. Alternative forms of political rule are constantly kept in sight. The costs of acting on this terrain both to the self and its projects are often alluded to, and the whole account is viewed in light of the ambiguous choices facing the professional politician with a calling for politics. On the other hand, Weber's sociological prudence of politics also displays his tendency to argue that subjective constructs of meaning can, through the ideal-type, provide not just strong and plausible judgments but also objective accounts of the necessary means and probable consequences of political action. From an apparently contingent account of the various tendencies producing the conditions of modern politics, Weber often slips into arguing that the position of the vocational politician (the professional politician with a calling) and the irresistible, as well as contingent, forces that he faces constitute the objective vantage point from which all political action is to be understood and explained. The model of political judgment that is to inform all potential political actors of the meaning and consequences of their actions from their point of view, from within their role and ultimate commitments in the sphere of politics, becomes identical with the judgments made by the professional politician with a calling. The professional politician with a calling becomes a medium, as it were, through which Weber's account of the person is to be realized and tested. Thus his conclusion about the set of feasible political alternatives in modern politics depends largely on our agreement both with his claim to impartiality in his account of the logic(s) of politics he presents and with his claim to impartiality in his account of the person facing these logics.

In this chapter I argue that Weber makes precisely such a claim to impartiality, especially in his most comprehensive account of political ethics and the origins of modern politics, "Politics as a Vocation." Relying on this essay, as well as on his partisan political writings and his political sociology in *Economy and Society*, I show that Weber's claim to provide an impartial account of "effective" and "feasible" alternatives for political action is valid only if we accept his concept of the person as an impartial account of agency as well. I further show that Weber circumvents having to provide an argument in favor of this ethical concept of personhood by employing his political sociology as the neutral arbiter of contending substantive political projects. I also argue that Weber's concentration on the leading or vocational politician as the only figure within politics to translate his notion of scientifically informed political judgment into a world of power struggle and value choice is not just the conclusion of his social science applied to politics but also informs that application. I finally argue that Weber's account of the vocational politician and the political model he chooses as the only feasible one for cultivating such a figure replicates in a large part his *Verstehen* of social action according to which both publicly accessible conventions or norms of conduct and collectively directed social action, in particular mass political action, are characterized by irrationality, unintelligibility, and emotional reactiveness. This marginalization of public agreement on norms and of mass political action is a crucial element of Weber's "understanding" of modern politics. It is the underside of Weber's distinctive "political education" to leadership and citizenship that demands that we recognize the irreconcilable split between irrational individual choice and the responsibility for political power.[1]

"Understanding" Politics

Political theory does not describe and explain independent objects incapable of self-reflection or of understanding their own behavior. It describes social and political practices constituted by the self-understanding of the

---

1. For an argument that Weber's political corpus is driven by the desire to provide political education both to leaders and citizens of the nation, see Lawrence Scaff, "Max Weber's Politics and Political Education," *American Political Science Review*, 61, no. 1 (1973), 128–141.

participating social and political actors themselves.[2] It thus seeks to clarify the meaning that political actors themselves attribute to political action, the means they use, the standards they apply, and the ends they aim to achieve. This task of understanding has typically involved an attempt to canvass what we mean when speaking of something as "political" or describing ourselves as engaged in "political action." Such inquiry has invariably been a preparation for reconstructing the meaning of political association and for providing an account of the kind of political action appropriate to it. To describe a political association is to describe the intentions we can pursue within it—which ends appropriately belong to politics, which means are appropriate to realize them, and which ends are self-defeating or even unattainable. In this sense, political theory is prudential, providing both an account of the ends we might pursue politically and the effective or ethically appropriate means to attain them. Weber's use of a sociology of explanatory understanding to provide practical political advice seems very much within the notion of understanding at the center of canonical political theory.

At the same time, the purpose of such *Verstehen* of politics is not merely to provide advice on political means and ends, but also to discover the ends and the kinds of actions that are "internal" to the meaning of political action itself.[3] Political theory regards certain ends such as justice, the common good, or even security as part of the meaning of politics. They are regarded as logical attributes of the concept of politics so that we cannot be said to be engaging fully in politics without seeking to realize these ends. However, political theorists have disagreed on the meaning of these ends or at least on how we would want to rank them.

For Aristotle the ends internal to "politics" were virtue and justice. These ends were constitutive of the life of a flourishing political community. In turn, political action was a praxis, not a techne: it was a form of action whose end was the doing itself, not the deployment of means to external ends. Justice and virtue were the constitutive ends of "politics," not ends of which public political deliberation was merely a means." For Rousseau the highest internal good of "politics" was individual self-determination, "moral liberty," a good that could only be realized through participation in determining the general will of a political community. The internal goods of politics, therefore, were identical with the internal goods of the general will. The goods contained within the general will consisted of equality and the common good. Hence, part of what it meant

---

2. See Charles Taylor, "Social Theory as Practice," in *Philosophy and the Human Sciences, Collected Papers*, vol. 2 (Cambridge: Cambridge University Press, 1985), pp. 93, 101.
3. I am borrowing the concept of "an internal good" from Alasdair MacIntyre, *After Virtue* (Notre Dame: University of Notre Dame Press, 1984), pp. 187–189).

to participate in the general will was to seek decisions promoting the good of the republic and equality among its citizens. The virtue of the citizens would be a by-product effect of such participation.

In both these cases the instrumental aspects of political action were subservient to the internal goods of politics. And "politics" always had the logical attribute of dealing with things that were common, public, and civic.[4] This priority was reversed by Machiavelli, for whom all intrinsic goods had to be judged according to their effectiveness in maintaining the state and attaining glorious memory. But even for him "il commune utile" and civic "libertà" were internal attributes of "il vivere civile," the political community. By urging the "use" of moral ends as a political means, Machiavelli sought to provide advice on how liberty could be most effectively maintained in a republic. The new prince who is nothing more than the effects of the means he deploys becomes Machiavelli's instrument for founding a civic life where none existed before. And the founded republic has to learn to protect the internal goods of politics by recourse to the instrumental means of princes.[5]

Viewed against this background, Weber seems to follow Aristotle and Rousseau by founding his social and political theorizing on a reconstructive understanding of social and political action. At the same time he takes into account Machiavelli's reversal of the priority between the internal goods of politics and the instrumental necessities of realizing them. Like Machiavelli, he understands politics in light of the instrumental demands of political action and the consequences that ensue in applying the means of politics in a methodical and deliberate manner. However, his understanding of social and political action presses well beyond Machiavelli's account of political prudence. Whereas Machiavelli still maintains the communal and civic meaning of "il vivere civile e liberá," a free and civic community, in the midst of his resolute consequentialism, Weber detaches the calculation of means to ends in politics from the discernment

---

4. See Hannah Arendt, *The Human Condition* (Chicago: University of Chicago Press, 1958), pp. 50–58. For an attempt to combine Weber's and Arendt's diametrically opposed conceptions of "politics," see W. G. Runciman, *Social Science and Political Theory* (Cambridge: Cambridge University Press, 1965), p. 41. Runciman argues that "the political" entails "both the coercive and the public," but the question is not whether one or the other is more strongly connected to the concept of "politics" but rather the degree to which the striving for power and domination and participation in public deliberation and decision are in conflict with one another, to say nothing of what happens to the "logic of concepts" when power has priority over public.

5. Niccolo Machiavelli, *The Prince*, chap. 9, 15–19, 21; *The Discourses on the First Ten Books on Livy*, Book 1. See J. H. Whitfield, "On Machiavelli's Use of Ordini," *Italian Studies* (1955); "The Politics of Machiavelli," *Modern Language Review* 50 (1955) J. G. A. Pocock, *The Machiavellian Moment* (Princeton: Princeton University Press, 1976), chap. 3, 6, 7.

of ends internal to (or constitutive of) political practice or political association. With this reversal politics loses its "public" and communal attributes. Neither its internal practices nor its instrumental deployment of power is any longer intrinsically connected to realizing anything that we might call public goods. To see this we must once again consider his typology of social action, if ever so briefly.

Let us recall that one of the central features of Weber's typology of "meaningful social action" is that it is constructed from the vantage point of *Zweckrationalität*, that is, the weighing of given ends in light of the means and consequences of their realization. This is so despite the clear distinction made between the rational calculation of means to ends and the rationality of intrinsic values. All values, all ultimate ends are subsumed under one category. It is simply assumed that ends gain their validity by being chosen. From within the sociological understanding of values and value spheres there is no criteria of rationality to distinguish the validity of different ends. Although Weber seems to be arguing that there are intrinsic reasons for adhering to particular values, the choice of values themselves is irrational; and the more consciously one seeks to guide one's social conduct, one's orientation toward the activity of others, on the basis of values alone, the more irrational one becomes (*WG*, p. 13, *ES*, pp. 4–5. The choice of values is equated with irrationality, and the pursuit of ends through rational means–ends calculations becomes the only standard whose claim to reason is not an arbitrary choice. It is coextensive with rational social action itself. Thus for an individual, a choice of action under value reason is always subject to the means–ends necessities of purposive rationality, even if he or she rejects purposive reason as a criterion of deliberative choice. The individual who seeks to perform actions that are intrinsically worthy will not be able to escape the chains of cause and effect that are always at work in any social action.

If this is so for value reason, collective action and appeals to commonly accepted standards reach some extreme point of irrationality. In this scheme collective action, especially collective action based on shared values, is reactive, unreflective, and subject purely to emotional stimuli. There can be no claim to translate collective action into purposively rational conduct except when especially gifted agents channel traditional or affectually reactive behavior toward ultimate ends. Thus, purposive reason and value reason are in constant tension, and both are in constant danger of being overwhelmed by traditional and effectual motives for action. Yet, behind all social action lurks purposive reason. Only against the standard of purposive reason does social action become intelligible, susceptible to ideal-typical "understanding" and "explanation."

Once Weber applies his typology to the explanatory understanding of political action, the nexus between understanding the meaning of "the political" and adducing its internal goods is broken. It is not simply that the intrinsic goods of politics are rendered subservient to the instrumental necessities of politics—this is what Machiavelli did for the sake of "effective" republican liberty. The very claim that there are any intrinsic goods of politics is undermined:

> As a separate structure a "political" community . . . exists only then and insofar as the community is not merely an "economic community" [Wirtschaftgemeinschaft], that is possesses directives [Ordnungen] ordering matters other than the directly economic disposition of goods and services. *The particular content which the communal action aims at beyond the forcible domination of territory and inhabitants is conceptually irrelevant.* It may vary greatly according to whether we are dealing with a "robber state," "a welfare state," a "constitutional state" [Rechtstaat]. or a "culture state." Owing to the drastic nature of its means of control, the political association is particularly capable of arrogating to itself all the possible values toward which associational conduct [Verbandshandelns] might be oriented; and there is, in fact, nothing in this world which was not at one time or another an object of communal action on the part of political associations [Gemeinschaftshandelns politischer Verbände]. (WG, p. 514–15; ES, p. 903; my emphasis; see WG, p. 30; GPS, p. 506).[6]

The reason for this disjuncture between political community and its ends lies in the fact that the concepts of "politics" and "political association" now fall under purposively rational action. In turn what defines our "understanding" of politics is the distinctive purposive rationality appropriate to it in contrast to the purposive rationality of other spheres such as economics. The values pursued in politics are arbitrary, subject to choice, but the means deployed to realize them stay roughly the same from one political association to another. Thus we cannot, argues Weber, understand "the meaning of political action" by determining the "kind of politics one should pursue," that is, the particular content one should give to one's political action" (GPS, p. 505, FMW, p. 77). Sociologically considered, by which Weber means understood ideal-typically through his typology of social action, politics and the state can only be defined by the "means" peculiar to them.

6. By speaking of political "community," which under his definitions applies to a "social relation" resting on "subjective feelings of belonging on the part of the participants" (WG, p. 21), Weber is stressing that even a political association (Verband) based on emotional or traditional loyalties has no ends internal to it. If this is so for a political association based on communal ties, it will be all the more so for the modern bureaucratic state. In this sense, even the concept of "nation" is contingently related to the modern state, although Weber frequently treats this concept as if this were not the case.

Thus political association *(politischer Verband)* is reduced to one particular, though decisive, means: "An association based on domination [*Herrschaftsverband*] shall be called a political association [*politischer Verband*], insofar as its existence and the validity of its orders [*Ordnungen*] within a given geographical area are continually guaranteed through the application and threat of physical force on the part of its administrative staff." (*WG*, p. 29; *ES*, p. 54). Likewise, the state is defined as "that human community that (successfully) claims the monopoly of the legitimate use of physical force within a particular territory—territory is one of its characteristics" (*GPS*, p. 506; *FMW*, p. 78). The state merely arrogates the right to use physical force as a monopoly. What sets a political association apart from all other associations therefore is not its substantive claim to legitimacy or the validity of its directives, to say nothing of its internal relation to things common, public, participatory, but the fact that it is a form of legal administrative domination over a territory that can back up its claim to be obeyed by using coercion and force. An association may claim legitimacy on the basis of some value-rational end; but for Weber it does not become a political association until it organizes an administrative staff and seeks to back up its orders by using force. Common membership and public goals alone are insufficient to claim political status. Village communities, guild associations, or even workers' councils, Weber argues, are not truly political until they claim a legitimate right to back up their decision by using force or strive to appropriate or redistribute a government's political power (*WG*. p. 29; *ES*, p. 54–55). This means that one of the main tasks of the state is to prevent such associations from becoming fully "political"; this containment of the attempts of associations to become "political" becomes one the decisive reasons for the state's monopoly of the means of coercing obedience to its administrative domination. An association that claims a legitimate monopoly of force will probably be subject to instant repression on the part of the state, for it will be threatening the very attribute that distinguishes the rule of the state from that of all other associations. Thus we can presume that the state is in a constant struggle to prevent *politische Verbände* from forming within its territory that seek to expropriate its claim to coordinate actions with the sanction of force.

It should hardly be surprising, then, that politics should mean "the striving after a share of power or influencing the distribution of power, whether it be between states or between groups of people [*Menschengruppen*] included within a state" (*GPS*, p. 506; *FMW*, p. 78). To say that a question or a decision is "political" is not to say that it concerns things public, but rather that it concerns the distribution, maintenance, or transfer of power within the state or between states (*GPS*, p. 506; *FMW*, p. 78).

Hence value-rational motives have only a contingent relation to politics: "The person who pursues politics strives for power, power either as a means toward other ends, (ideal or egotistical)—or power for its own sake" (GPS, p. 507; FMW, p. 78). Power itself may become the intrinsic value of politics, albeit one that denies all intrinsic values. Or it may become the means to achieve values chosen by individual political actors. In either case, politics, not unlike Hobbes's state of nature, demands a constant striving for means to impose one's will over others.

If politics entails the striving for power, for Weber, it also entails two other attributes: "Kampf," struggle or conflict, and "Auslese," competitive selection. Struggle (Kampf) as Weber defines it is coextensive with power: it refers to a "social relationship" in which action is oriented toward the intention of imposing (Durchsetzung) one's own will against the resistance of others (WG, pp. 20–22; ES, pp. 38–39). The peaceful attempt to impose one's will over others within a social relationship in which others orient their conduct by the same motive is "competition" (Konkurrenz). But when struggle takes place not merely over desired opportunities but also over life or chances of survival of individuals, then we must speak of "selection," or Auslese (WG, p. 21; ES, p. 39). In this sense "selection" is latent in any struggle (Kampf), peaceful or not; for every struggle and competition selects out those persons with the personal qualities necessary for victory. As Weber describes them, these qualities are typically the qualities we associate with kinds of political actors: they could be "physical force" or "unscrupulous cunning," intellectual power or skill at demagogy, loyalty to superiors or to the masses; they could also be originality in discovering new courses of action or adaptability to changing circumstances. Whatever the case, social order, be it primarily oriented toward traditional, value-rational, or purposively rational motives, requires Auslese and struggle. Politics contains both of these characteristics: "The essence of politics . . . is struggle [Kampf], the recruitment of allies and of a voluntary following; for "everything and everyone that participates in the goods of the power state [Machtstaat] is implicated in the necessity of the pragmatics of power that govern all political history." This characterization entails "the unavoidability of a power struggle [Machtkrieges]" (GAW, p. 349; GPS, p. 145). Thus as long as politics is characterized by a struggle for power, it will also be characterized by competition, which in turn is always regulated by a process of selection.

While the state, then, is characterized as a form of administrative domination that can legitimately back up obedience to it by force, politics is identified with the struggle for power within the state, that is, within areas not yet governed by a staff and administrative hierarchy. Although confining politics to the state, Weber is careful not to identify the striving for power, *Macht,* with the state's domination, its (administrative) *Herrschaft.*[7] Politics is exclusively concerned with *Macht,* not Herrschaft. Herrschaft, or domination, "is the probability that a command with a given specific content will be obeyed by a given group of persons," but "power [*Macht*] is the probability that one actor within a social relationship will be in a position to carry out his own will despite resistance regardless of the basis on which this probability rests" (*WG,* pp. 28–29; *ES,* p. 53).[8] Politics, then, will be distinctly concerned with those qualities of a person and circumstance that make it possible for an actor to impose his or her will on a situation, rather than to have commands fulfilled through simple obedience. It thus encompasses a whole constellation of means whose effective use is not generalizable. *Herrschaft* within the state, on the other hand, is a kind of power that is strictly limited to those organizations in which personal commands are sent down a hierarchy and strictly obeyed. Power, therefore, despite its strictly instrumental definition, holds open the possibility that the freedom exercised in choosing ultimate purposes and seeking to find the proper means to realize them could be translated into politics: "the distinctive social-political character of a problem is precisely that it cannot be resolved on the basis of merely technical considerations which assume already fixed ends, that regulative standards of value can and must be fought over, because the problem lies in the domain of universal cultural questions" (*GAW,* p. 153).[9] Politics then becomes the struggle over the realization of ultimate values, some of

7. In keeping with recent practice, I have usually chosen to define *Herrschaft* as domination, rather than rule or authority. This usage seems most appropriate, because the distinctive attribute of *Herrschaft* under Weber's definition is the resistanceless acceptance of commands, not the acknowledgment of any particular right or "authority" to rule. For example, if a people obey out of threat of physical punishment, this certainly is the exercise of domination, although this could take place where a government has lost all "authority." This would all be more problematic if Weber did not define *Herrschaft* instrumentally but as having certain ends internal to it.

8. For a rather unsatisfying attempt to connect Weber's concept of politics to the tradition of political theory by arguing that *Herrschaft,* not power, is the means that is characteristic of all political forms, see Manfred Hättich, "Der Begriff des Politischen bei Max Weber," *Politische Vierteljahresschrift,* no. 8 (1967), 44–47. The problem with Hättich's "correction" of Weber is that even though the political association exercises domination, this cannot be its defining characteristic even within Weber's purposively rational frame, because it is precisely the routine domination of the state bureaucracy that threatens all "politics" as Weber conceives it. If domination were the defining characteristic of the concept of politics, then bureaucratic *Herrschaft* could never undermine "politics" as a power struggle, and as struggle over ultimate values.

9. This passage would seem to modify substantially Weber's instrumental definition of politics. For politics is now identified with the struggle over ultimate values using political means, not merely with the use of power backed by legitimate force. But we should remember that Weber's notion of purposive reason also includes the weighing of values in light of the means that they require.

which might even deny the split between *Zweckrationalität* and *Wertratio-nalität*. It would become the activity, as it were, in which agents and groups test competing claims to the meaning of culture against each other and against the costs of using the means of power to impose their values on the state.

But this notion of politics as the striving for power in the service of cultural struggle, although not ruled out, is severely restricted by the purposive reason governing the maintenance of *Herrschaft*, or domination, in the state. What it is possible to achieve in politics will always be limited by the need at once to deploy and to oppose legitimate forms of domination consisting of staffs to which large numbers of human beings submit *(fügen)* (*GPS*, p. 507; *FMW*, p. 78): "Every organized domination [*Herrschaftsbetrieb*], which calls for continuous administration, requires on the one hand, the conditioning of human action towards those masters who claim to be bearers of legitimate power, and on the other hand, by means of this obedience, the control over those material goods which in a given case are necessary for the imposition of physical force. This consists of control over the personal administrative staff and the material means of administration," (*GPS*, p. 508; *FMW*, p. 80). It is thus within the constraints of organized domination—the need for a staff and the material and physical means to back up that staff's authority—that power can be united to values in politics both in the struggle for power itself and in stabilizing one's gains. We must therefore consider Weber's analysis of legitimate domination as the logic to which all actors have to submit if they are to lead followers into the political struggle.

Between Bureaucratic Domination and Charisma

Herrschaft for Weber is not attainable simply through coercion. It requires a minimum of willful obedience on the part of those who are to accept commands. This willingness or interest in obedience constitutes the legitimation for a particular form of domination (*WG*, p. 122; *ES*, p. 212). However, just as with the definition of political association and politics, the forms of "legitimate domination" are "understood" ideal-typically from the vantage point of *Zweckrationalität*, not value reason. Thus, although legitimate forms of domination are distinguished by the grounds on which obedience is attained, the validity of those grounds for obeying is not the basis for understanding "legitimacy." All that matters for legitimacy is that commands and the form of domination in which those commands are given are "believed" to be valid. "Legitimacy" is therefore a means of attaining obedience to commands whatever their validity and whatever the motives of the individuals who submit to them:

every form of domination "seeks to evoke and cultivate the belief in its 'legitimacy'" (*WG*, p. 122; *ES*, p. 213).

It is on the basis of the different "beliefs" in the "validity" of a command structure that Weber constructs his famous typology of the three pure types of legitimate domination. Thus rational-legal domination rests on a belief in the impersonal legality of enacted rules and of the right of those called upon to enforce those rules. Traditional domination rests on the "everyday" belief *(Alltagsglauben)* in the sanctity of traditionally valid rules and in those who enforce them. And charismatic domination is based on the "extraordinary" *(ausseralltäglichen)* devotion to a person on account of his or her piety, heroism, or exemplariness and the norms "revealed" or "ordained" by him or her (*WG*, p. 124; *ES*, p. 215). Each of these forms of domination is graded from the most impersonal to the most personal and from the most formally predictable to the most unpredictable, but on both of these scales traditional domination combines a certain element of personal devotion with routine command. Although extremely crucial for understanding the formation, as well as the dynamic aspect of modern forms of political domination, it is less crucial to understanding the limits of modern politics. Hence, I focus at first almost exclusively on the polar opposites of charismatic and rational-legal domination. Only when I examine the dynamic that produces modern politics as an autonomous pursuit and a business will I add traditional domination to the discussion.

In its purest form, rational-legal domination is realized in bureaucratic administration. Its typical characteristics according to Weber's construction bespeak at once the complete organization of domination on the basis of purposively rational criteria of predictability and the loss of the moral autonomy associated with value reason. Thus, all business is carried out according to explicit formal "rules"; offices are distributed according to a division of labor in which each person is allotted a specified sphere of competence and coercive power; offices are also organized in a hierarchy and according to a chain of command; disposition of the rules of office are technical and require specialized training to apply them; officials have no proprietary right to offices; administrative acts are carried out according to written rules, and all communications are based on written documents; and every decision is made on the basis of explicit reasons based on written rules. Nevertheless, the facts and the reasons for bureaucratic decisions are kept secret. Most important, members of the administrative staff are separated from the means of administration much as the worker is from the process of production. The result of this separation based on formal rules is that officials treat all cases impersonally, that is, they ignore the particularities of the case, refusing any emotional or empathic involvement (*WG*, pp. 125–130; *WG*, pp. 551–556).

Whereas other forms of domination legitimate their commands on the basis of some substantive end or personal relationship, bureaucratic domination legitimates its commands purely on its claim to have appropriated control through formal rules. These formal rules in turn are beyond the control of those who apply them. They designate the division of labor, the hierarchy, and the particular arrangement of offices. The very fact that they are written indicates that they are not open to "discussion," either by those who apply them or by those on whom they are imposed. The only discretion is in their application. The result is that the administrator's separation from control over the formation of the rules is directly reproduced in the relation between the bureaucracy and its clients. In both cases, rules are treated as impersonal, deducible from a previously established code that has no substantive justification. In both cases, the personal judgment of the administrator or client plays no role in either the decision rendered or the command carried out.

In this sense bureaucratic domination embodies *Zweckrationalität* as formal principle of legitimate obedience for both its staff and its clients, because the legitimacy of bureaucracy depends on a belief, whether it lives up to that belief or not, that it carries out commands and creates order in the most impartial and rationally predictable way possible. In other words, the instrumental definition of legitimacy as merely a means of gaining predictable submission to commands becomes the explicit principle on which bureaucracy claims legitimacy. Thus, bureaucracy functions something like an efficient machine to produce obedience to commands and is thus available to whichever master is able to control it. Viewed this way, bureaucratic domination is at the root of all legitimate order as Weber defines it, because all legitimate order whatever its claim to be obeyed is merely trying to attain submission to its staff in the most efficient manner possible. Bureaucratic domination is the prototype of all forms of domination, and legitimacy is simply the unavoidable tool to attain this end.

However, the development of bureaucratic domination as a distinct form unencumbered by traditional domination occurs only in the West:

> a rational, systematic, and specialized pursuit of science, with trained and specialized personnel, has only existed in the West in a sense at all approaching its present dominant place in our culture. Above all this is true of the trained official [*den Fachbeamten*], the pillar of both the modern state and the economic life of the West. Only suggestions of him are to be found [but] nowhere were they in any sense so constitutive of the social

order as in the Occident. Of course, the "official," even the specialized official within the division of labor is a very old occurrence in the most diverse of cultures. But no country and no age has known, in the same sense as the modern Occident, the absolute and complete channeling of our entire existence, of the fundamental political, technical, and economic foundations of our being, into the shell of a technically trained organization of officials, the technical, commercial, and above all juristically trained state officials as the bearers of the most important everyday functions (*PE*, p. 11; *PESC*, pp. 15–16).

One need only note here that what is unique in the West is not merely the organization of administration according rational legal rules, but the selection process in which that organization produces a new human type: the trained official, der Fachbeamter. It is the appearance of this type in all spheres along with our dependency on him in the ordering of our everyday life that signals something new.

What are the causes of this development? First, the imposition of bureaucratic domination and the rule of the professional administrator is a most crucial part of the development of "rationalism" in general. There is a logic in rational social action itself whereby the world and society become increasingly more predictable, more susceptible to control, more formalized, more reducible to rational means–ends calculation. This logic, which Weber labels "rationalization," involves the steady abandonment of customary or affectual motives for action in favor of calculations of interest or of rational adherence to values:

An essential component of the rationalization of actions is the replacement of inner acquiescence to lived custom by the deliberate adaptation to situations based on interest. To be sure, this process does not exhaust the concept of the rationalization of action. For beyond this, this process of rationalization can proceed positively in the direction of conscious rationalization of values [*Wertrationalisierung*], but also negatively at the expense of both custom and affectual action; and finally also in favor of a value-skeptical purely purposively-rational form of action at the expense of action bound by value rationality (*WG*, pp. 15–16; *ES*, p. 30).

Implied in this dynamic is the tendency both for values to be justified by an appeal to good reasons rather than custom or feeling and for value rationality to give way to purposive rationality once values have been severed from affectual or customary motives. In the later case values lose all rational grounding or are reduced to expressions of interest. Bureaucratic domination is the realization of this dynamic in the social and political order, because it is the ultimate perfection of purposive-reason applied to social action. It is not simply that the reciprocal orientation of members and clients of bureaucracy is based on the deduction of the most efficient means to attain technical ends. More important, through its formal rules based on rationally deducible reasons bureaucracy is the most efficient means to impose predictable behavior on society:

> according to all experience, the monocratic-bureaucratic administration based on written documents is from a purely technical point of view capable of attaining the highest degree of efficiency in precision; continuity; discipline; stringency and reliability, that is, calculability [*Berechenbarkeit*] for its rulers and all those interested parties acting in relation to it; intensity and scope of its efficiency, and formally universal applicability of all its tasks: it is in all these meanings the most formally rational form of exercising domination attainable. (*WG*. p. 128; *ES*, p. 222).

No other form of domination can exercise domination with such comprehensiveness, intensity, and predictability. Consequently, Weber points out, the development of every modern association *(Verband)*, whether state, party, economic enterprise, or interest group, is coextensive with the development of bureaucratic administration. To secure its own existence in the absence of custom, an association must adopt rational-legal forms of control, even though to do so will usually undermine its substantive goals and relations of personal dependence that were the very basis for its existence.

The second reason for the distinctive proliferation of bureaucratic organization as the typical form of domination in the West lies in the supremacy of that great bearer of instrumental reasoning, of the rationalization of economic action, rational capitalism. Capitalism, as Weber points out, is not opposed to bureaucracy; on the contrary, it develops it and furthers it. Indeed, it could not do without it. Capitalism requires bureaucracy because it seeks a stable, disciplined work force and calculable administrative decisions. In addition, the capitalist market requires that business be discharged with precision, continuity, and efficiency. Above all, bureaucratic domination of the enterprise is a requisite of survival in accumulating profits because the market is not merely a set of voluntary contracts but also a struggle for power and market share. It is a means of gaining positional power and assuring market opportunities will be closed to competitors (*WG*, p. 129; *ES*, p. 223; see my Chapter 3).

A third reason seems distinctly opposed to the capitalist deployment of bureaucracy for the sake of calculability and control over labor and the securing of market share, namely, the historical movement to level economic and political privilege and introduce democratic equality. However, in opposing economic and social inequality, democratic movements are subject to that peculiar double dynamic of rationalization whereby the rational appeal to substantive values requires rational calculation for success. For Weber every democratic impulse to reduce domination *(Herrschaft)* demands equality of rights and guarantees against the arbitrary use of power. It therefore appeals to substantive, not formal justice. However, because this concept of justice demands to be applied to all equally, it requires a rational-legal form of domination regulated by principles of formal rationality *(WG,* pp. 565–566, 567; *ES,* pp. 979–980, 983–984). The upshot of this is that each attempt to equalize privilege opens up new ground for bureaucratic intervention, not merely because of the technical efficiency of bureaucracy but also because of its formal and impersonal equality in exercising domination. Traditional honorary status unequally distributed gives way to formal rules applied to all equally. Ultimately, the successful expansion of bureaucracy under the pressure of this "passive democratization," as Weber calls it, rests on the fact that it is able to control vast numbers of individuals equally. Hence, it always accompanies "mass democracy" *(WG,* p. 130; *ES,* p. 225; *WG,* p. 567; *ES,* p. 983).

Finally, bureaucracy accompanies the development of the modern state in the West. In the early modern period, presumably through a kind of selection process, state power *(Staatsgewalten)* accumulated in the hands of those princes who ruthlessly took the course of administrative bureaucratization to secure their power *(WG,* p. 560; *ES,* p. 971). This involved a process in which the prince actively expropriated from the private holders of administrative power their means of administrative control, in particular their source of revenue and their military forces. These means of administration became his own private property. In doing this, he centralized administrative domination under his own command. But this newly won power was in turn expropriated by the administrative staff that he selected to carry out his commands. This staff became increasingly technically specialized in deploying the means to carry out his commands, while the prince was increasingly forced into the position of a political dilettante. Yet as the staff itself acquired an increasingly complex hierarchy and division of labor, especially under the pressure of new state functions, it too became separated from the means of administration. The administration of the state now came to resemble the ideal-type of rational monocratic bureaucratic domination *(GPS,* pp. 510–513, 518). The upshot of this development is that "the longer the modern large state *(Grossstaat)* is simply dependent upon a bureaucratic basis, and the more technically this is so, and the larger that state is, and above all the more that state is or will become a great power *(ein Grossmachtstaat),* the more unconditional such bureaucratic dependency will be" *(WG,* p. 560; *ES,* p. 971).

Although the first impulses toward bureaucratization of the state came from the related necessities of maintaining armies and ensuring sound public finances, the major impulse for the modern state has come from the increasingly varied claims made on the state administration due to what Weber calls the "complexity of modern culture." The state has become responsible for seeing to it that a basic standard of living is maintained, which in turn depends on the bureaucratic provision of increasingly changing life needs. In particular, the state has become responsible for police protection and social welfare policy ("*sozialpolitischen" Aufgaben*), the latter being instituted because of either pressure or ideological or power political reasons (*WG*, p. 561; *ES*, p. 973). In all of these areas in which human wants arising from social relations demand satisfaction, the state is required to introduce bureaucratic domination to maintain its own political *Herrschaft*.

These four convergent causes for the distinctive development in the West of monocratic bureaucracy legitimated by formal reason have an ironic consequence for politics. All social and political initiatives based on fundamental values, in particular those seeking to realize some conception of social and political freedom combined with equality, unavoidably play into the furtherance of monocratic bureaucracy. Every attempt to engage in rational social action, that is, action that is effective as well as substantively legitimate, requires the expansion of bureaucratic *Herrschaft*. Of course, the force of Weber's argument depends on the imposition of his ideal-type of bureaucratic domination on to all of the individual events just described. They are then deemed to be intelligible only insofar as they express the attempt to attain rational control, that is, rational control is identified at the outset with bureaucratic domination. Then all political societies in the West that failed to develop rational bureaucracy are judged to be deviations from the general drift of these multiple rationalizations. The assumption is that idiosyncratic causes were operative rather than a counter-tendency with its own logic of success. To cite just one example, Weber points out that the Roman and the English states became power-states of the first rank, although they were ruled by notables and failed to develop fully rational state bureaucracies. He explains this deviation by arguing that in these states the structure of state power molded a homogenous and unified culture resistant to bureaucratic rationalization (*WG*, pp. 560–561; *ES*, p. 972). This mode of explanation surely begs the question. For the unity of Roman or British social structure as a cause of the small number of tasks taken up by state administration is defined by the fact that rational bureaucracy was unable to penetrate it. It is on the basis of this kind of circular argument that Weber often argues that all roads lead to bureaucratic domination, that this constitutes "the fate" of politics in the West, and above all that "the progress of bureaucratic mechanism is irresistible" (*GASS*, p. 413).

Once introduced, Weber argues, bureaucratic *Herrschaft* becomes inescapable. No other form of domination generates as much power in the specific sense in which Weber defines the term as the capacity to impose one's will in a social relation, even over the resistance of others. Its apparent efficiency generates an instrument of power for whoever rules it that can subdue all competitors not similarly organized:

> Once fully established, bureaucracy belongs among those social structures that are hardest to destroy. Bureaucracy is the specific means of transforming "communal action" into rationally ordered "social action." As an instrument for "the societalization [*Vergesellschaftung*] of relations of domination [*Herrschaftsbeziehungen*], bureaucracy was and is a *means of power of the first rank for the one who controls the bureaucratic apparatus*. For under otherwise equal conditions, systematically ordered and directed "social action" is superior to every resistance through "mass action" or "communal" action. Where bureaucratization of administration has been completely introduced, there has been created practically an indestructible form of relations of domination (*WG*, pp. 569–70; *ES*, p. 987; my emphasis).

Why is bureaucratic *Herrschaft* so indestructible for Weber? Why is it so resistant to all mass or communal action? Here Weber appeals to a variety of purely instrumental grounds. First, there is no other way to carry out the multiplicity of tasks monocratic bureaucracy performs. Through its division of labor and specialization of offices according to function, it can simply carry out more tasks with a greater deployment of technical skill than, say, directly democratic administration. Thus bureaucracy can be eliminated in societies with large populations only if their members are willing to accept the neglect of a whole host of social and political tasks on which they depend (*WG*, pp. 548, 561; *ES*, pp. 951, 972).

Second, bureaucracy provides continuity of control that no other form of political rule can provide. Combining the specialization with habitual discipline, it increasingly becomes the *Grundlage aller Ordnung*, the foundation of all order, against which all other forms of political rule appear improvised and temporary (*WG*, p. 570; *ES*, p. 988; *WG*, p. 128; *ES*, p. 223). Finally and most important, for Weber, bureaucracy is superior to all other forms of *Herrschaft* in its mobilization of *Fachwissen* and *Tatsachenerkenntnis*, specialized knowledge and knowledge of the facts, within its field of purview. No other form of social organization is able to mobilize so much expertise and factual knowledge and to deploy it so comprehensively to solve any social problem that might arise. Indeed, what bureaucracy exercises is not simply control through formal rules but also a kind of *rationalen Wissensherrschaft,* a rational domination through knowledge. Weber admits that this domination through knowledge rests partly on official secrecy, which would raise the question of how much it indeed rests on specialization and how much simply on depriving its clients of needed information, a point Weber does not address (*WG,* 129; *ES,* p. 225). In place of such questioning, Weber simply points to the fact that all "mass organizations," by which he means all movements for democratic control and social equality, have succumbed to the formal rationality of bureaucracy in much the same way that they have succumbed to machine production (*WG,* 129; *ES,* p. 225).[10] Bureaucratic domination was the price they had to pay for having their goals implemented with uniformity and rational efficiency. To the degree that they sought a methodical realization of their goals, this was their fate.

The problem with this "fate," this *"Unentrinnbarkeit der bureaukratischen rationalen Wissensherrschaft,"* is that the triumph of rationality is accompanied by a complete loss of power for all those who work within it or are subject to it. With this loss of power comes a virtually complete loss of self-determining freedom. Moral autonomy, even in Weber's reduced understanding of it as choosing values and taking responsibility for the effects of acting on them, and bureaucratic claims to legitimacy are incompatible: "The more bureaucracy is 'dehumanized,' the more completely it succeeds in eliminating from official business love, hatred, and all purely personal irrational, emotional elements which escape calculation." The incapacity of bureaucracy to take particular values into account, because they are not reducible to instrumental social action or impersonal rules becomes, as it were, "its special virtue" (*WG,* p. 563; *ES,* p. 975). It attains predictability and imposes predictable behavior on society at the cost of satisfying those ends we may deem most important. Indeed, it treats all values as irrational emotional reactions separated from the "facts." "Facts," according to the rational understanding of subjectively meaningful action constituting bureaucracy as a "social relation," are coextensive with the predictable behavior achievable through domination according to specialized expertise and formal rules.

This aspect of rational bureaucracy poses for Weber the central dilemma for "politics": "How can one possibly save any remnants [*Reste*] of 'individualist' freedom of movement [*Bewegungsfreiheit*] in any sense?" And how can the influence of the bureaucratic stratum be checked so that democracy in a limited sense will be possible? Ultimately, who will take

10. For some reason the English translator chose to translate *Massenverbänden* as "large-scale organization," which obscures the contrast in this passage between mass organizations or associations and formal rational domination.

political responsibility for acting on "conviction" (*GPS*, pp. 333–334; *ES*, p. 1403)? Weber's answer is not to discover a collective agency that might deepen democracy or oppose bureaucratic expansion. Agency of this kind, he insists, can only open up new areas for bureaucratic expansion. It is only "remnants" of freedom that we can preserve at best. Bureaucratic domination can only be countered—and individual freedom preserved—by a different kind of "legitimate domination," namely, charismatic domination.

Charismatic domination *(Herrschaft)* constitutes the polar opposite of bureaucratic domination. It is a catch-all concept for all nonroutine forms of domination that rely exclusively on personal loyalty. Unlike traditional or rational-legal domination, charisma is a form of domination that rejects everyday routine obedience. In particular, it seeks to respond to those demands and needs that the economic everyday is unable to meet or indeed most likely marginalizes. Typically, it makes demands that everyday routine cannot satisfy. Thus, it arises at times of crises in traditional or rational-legal domination, usually in response to the depersonalization of routine domination.

Charisma refers to those qualities of individual leaders that are not reducible to rational causal explanation, that is, to reconstruction under criteria of *Zweckrationalität*. Unlike the person who exercises command by dint of formal office, "natural leaders" "are thought" to possess "gifts of body and spirit" considered to be "supernatural" (*WG*, p. 654; *ES*, pp. 1111–1112). Often these "gifts" are considered part of the leaders' divine mission. On the basis of these imputed qualities, charismatic leaders are able to inspire faith or blind support in their following. As usual Weber is careful to withhold judgment on the validity of the leader's claim to deserve support. What is crucial to him is that these personal qualities are the basis of a leader's support and that such leaders are able to "prove themselves as charismatically gifted within the beliefs of their adherents" (*WG*, p. 654; *ES*, p. 1112). The leader is able effectively to deploy belief in his or her personal qualities in order to exercise domination over the followers and convince them of his or her mission. This is what counts "sociologically" for Weber.

Yet, if he is "successful," the charismatic leader insists that his followers support his mission out of unconditional "duty," not out of voluntary consent. In turn this duty requires that they submit to his commands on account of his extraordinary personal attributes, not merely because he occupies a particular office (*WG*, p. 665; *ES*, p. 1113). In order to make this claim, the charismatic leader must display "self-imposed inner determination and inner limits," extraordinary powers, preferably supernatural or superhuman, and "divine grace and god-like heroic strength" (*WG*, pp.

654–657; *ES*, pp. 1112–1117). The legitimacy of charismatic domination depends, then, ultimately on the unusual inner discipline of the leader and his capacity to represent himself as inspired by some supra-individual end.

In this sense, charismatic domination gains its distinctive definition by rejecting all the typical attributes of bureaucratic domination. A charismatic leader does not occupy a formal office with a career, salary, and expert training based on the separation of the office holder from the means of command. Instead, he or she demands obedience on the basis of internal qualities and of his or her mission. There is no separation between office and means of command. The charismatic leader sets the attributes and limits of domination on his or her own. Furthermore, charismatic domination rejects abstract legal codes and formal adjudication. Justice is revealed through the person of the leader. Finally, charismatic domination rejects all methodical economic conduct or purposively rational modes of deriving an income. Charismatic leaders live *in* the world, not *from* it. Hence, they often ask for financial support from followers or seek to live a simple life whose economic requirements are minimal (*WG*, pp. 655–657; *ES*, pp. 1111–1115).

This economic rejection is part of a general rejection of all attempts to order everyday life and individual contact along purposively rational lines. The charismatic leader gains devotion from his following precisely because he represents "the extraordinary and the unheard of, what is foreign to all rule and all tradition." In the place of traditional rules based on habit and formal-legal rules rationally deduced from abstract concepts of right, the charismatic figure introduces new values or inverts the customary hierarchies of old ones: "Charismatic domination conducts itself in a revolutionary manner revaluing all values [*alles umwertend*] and in a sovereign manner breaking with all traditional or rational norms." The emblematic figure of this revolutionary revaluation is the prophet who announces, "It is written . . . but I say unto you," (*WG*, p. 657; *ES*, p. 1115). In this sense, unlike other forms of *Herrschaft* the commands to be obeyed by the following are not already prescribed but in fact created or transmitted by the charismatic hero. He or she recognizes the values guiding the daily lives of followers—his or her words are acknowledged as a new text.

By introducing new values or revaluing old ones, charismatic domination counters in a most revolutionary way the revolutionizing effects of bureaucratic rationalization in splitting values from the organization of daily life. Bureaucratic rationalization reorders daily life through technical means "'*von aussen*' *her*," from without. It does not do this directly but first reconstitutes material conditions and social orders according to formal reason; it then "displaces the conditions of adaptation [*Anpassungsbedingungen*]," forcing human beings to adapt to the conditions of formal reason and eventually to orient all their conduct on the basis of means–ends calculations. Inner motive does not matter. Charisma, by contrast, rests on the "belief" in "revelation and heroes." The follower is secure in "the emotional conviction as to the importance and the value of a manifestation be it religious, ethical, artistic, scientific, political or another kind." Thus, charisma consists in a belief that "revolutionizes human beings 'from within' [*von innen hearaus*] and seeks to form material conditions and social orders according to its revolutionary will" (*WG*, p. 658; *ES*, p. 1116). It changes the inner disposition of the followers to "submit to that which has never been [*das noch nie Dagewesene*] and is absolutely unprecedented." Its power, then, is to will new values and ways of life into existence by changing the inner motives of a group, a class, or a nation and then to organize material conditions around this new orientation toward social action. It is on these grounds that Weber calls charisma "the specifically 'creative' revolutionary force of history" (*WG*, p. 658; *ES*, p. 1117).

There is something quite ironic in this reduction of all revolutionary revaluations to charismatic leadership. As Weber conceptualizes it, charismatic domination precisely in its rejection of instrumental reasoning is the one "instrumental means" that can counter the formalization of instrumental reasoning in bureaucratic domination. Moreover, it is the one means by which the split between purposive reasoning based on means–ends calculations and value reason based on the "belief" in intrinsic values is overcome—indeed, one could say, reversed, as it is the one means of creating a revolutionary revaluation of values and forcing instrumental considerations to follow. But paradoxically, this reversal of rationalism is precisely the source of its intense instability. On the one hand, the charismatic leader's claim to "legitimacy" depends on his personal strength and capacity rather than codes, statutes, or customs. He rejects any external impersonal claims to be obeyed. He must therefore incessantly—one might even say obsessively—demonstrate his strength and capacity by overcoming various challenges posed by external circumstances. He must constantly perform miracles or heroic deeds. On the other hand, those who submit to his authority expect to "fare well," not just be dazzled by his extraordinary accomplishments; and so the charismatic individual must constantly demonstrate to his following that submission to him will bring a felicitous life, good fortune, or well-being. He must, in short, demonstrate some relation between his extraordinary capacities and beneficial "effects" in everyday life (*WG*, p. 656; *ES*, p. 1114). This requirement becomes the impulse for the "routinization [*Veralltäglichung*] of charisma," the submission of charisma to the demands of the everyday.

The problem that charismatic domination faces is that if it hopes to be more than a transitory phenomenon, it must give itself an everyday form. This entails that charisma alter its antieconomic and antipurposively rational character, because a charismatic movement must seek to embody material interests as well as the ideal interests of its followers in an ongoing community. They must be able to live from as well as for the charismatic movement. This is especially true of the disciples, the administrative staff, the party workers of the leader who will begin to appropriate their offices in the form of fixed statuses or positions. Hence, the personal qualities of the charismatic leader—his extraordinary capacities and the values he professes—come to be translated into everyday means of domination, that, is either in traditional or rational legal forms of *Herrschaft*. The result of this is that charisma at the very moment of its success is immediately subject to the demands of purposive reason, that is, the need for predictable command and obedience: "Charisma is a phenomenon typical of prophetic movements or of expansive political movements in their early stages. But as soon as domination is well established, and, above all else, as soon as control over large masses of people exists, it gives way to the forces of everyday routine" (*WG*, pp. 146–147; *ES*, p. 252). For this reason, Weber argues, "in its pure form charismatic domination may be said to exist only in its moment of inception" (*WG*, p. 142; *ES*, p. 246). As soon as we identify charismatic forms of leadership as "charismatic," we have begun to explain the phenomenon, reduced it to an instrumentality, made it disappear.

In a rather fundamental sense, then, the value creating power of charisma over and against bureaucratic domination is only evident retrospectively from the vantage point of the prophetic moment lost in the wake of its adaptation to the instrumental necessities of predictable everyday order. Like value reason, charismatic domination depends for its intelligibility on its opposition to bureaucratic rationalization. It is the one ephemeral moment of rupture in the process of rationalization when values are created and imposed; yet conceptually, it is completely defined by its binary relation to rational-legal domination.

This typology of legitimate domination has some rather profound consequences for Weber's analysis of the possibility of translating moral autonomy into politics, particularly in explaining the consequences of different available avenues of resisting bureaucratic domination and the reduction of politics to negotiation and bargaining. First, Weber's concept of moral autonomy and personhood based on individually positing values, selecting means to realize them, and taking responsibility for the consequences that ensue are subsumed under the concept of charismatic domination.[11]

11. See Wolfgang Mommsen, "Universalgeschichtliches und politisches Denken," in *Max Weber: Gesellschaft, Politik und Geschichte* (Frankfurt am Main: Suhrkamp, 1974), pp.

Only the person who has the instrumental capacity to "use" his or her personal qualities to gain a mass following will be in a position to exercise moral autonomy as Weber defines it, because only such a person will have escaped from everyday obedience to commands and have generated a form of legitimate domination that can resist the depersonalization of rational-legal domination. Obviously, this does not apply to the followers who have exchanged one form of resistanceless obedience for another.

Second, individually posited values can be connected to the struggle for political power, the struggle to impose one's will even over the resistance of others by using political means, only within the frame of action created by charismatic domination and rational-legal domination. Where bureaucratic domination has become the "dominant" means of political rule, only charismatic leadership combined with bureaucratic domination will generate sufficient "power" to set values and impose them on political society.

Third, the conjoining of individual autonomy with charismatic leadership backed by bureaucratic *Herrschaft,* excludes any possibility of "effective" mass political activity under the concept of self-determining freedom. The charismatic leader organizes the emotional motives of the "masses" toward value-rational ends. Under this conceptualization, the masses are only capable of obedience to his or her personal commands. They can neither posit ends of their own nor develop a political will to realize them. This exclusion is of crucial importance to the discussion of modern professional politics that follows.

Fourth, the appearance of moral autonomy in politics, even under Weber's highly restrictive definition, is utterly fortuitous, because charismatic domination decays into everyday domination at the very moment it successfully organizes a mass following. The irreducibility of choice under value reason then is identified with that one irreducible incipient moment of charisma before it gives way to rational legal forms of command. Value reason is thus tied to the tenuous possibility of charisma in modern politics.

Curiously, as many a commentator has puzzled over, Weber's first run at his typology of legitimate domination includes legitimation according to the belief in the intrinsic worth of a value; moreover, in his discussion of the sociology of law formal rationality in law is constantly contrasted with substantive law based on value rationality (*WG,* p. 19; *ES,* p. 33; *WG,* pp. 496–507; *ES,* pp. 865–867).[12] Clearly Weber recognizes that

---

134–135. Mommsen reduces Weber's concept of political freedom to a maxim: "the greatest possible freedom through the greatest possible domination" (p. 138).

12. For the debate over the disappearance of value rationality in Weber's typology of domination, see Martin Barker, "Kant as a Problem for Weber," *British Journal of Sociology* 31,

what we normally define as the meaning of substantive legitimacy cannot be ignored. But why does it then drop out of his scheme considering that it is fairly clear that legitimation according to substantive notions of justice or rights needs to be understood? It would be easy enough to explain this by pointing to Weber's argument that formal reason undermines all substantive reason in the very attempt to realize it. Surely this is not wrong, but it does not explain the relation between domination and power so central to Weber's account of politics as struggle, *Kampf,* and selection, *Auslese.* I would suggest that there may be a reason for Weber to leave this notion of legitimacy out that has more to do with his concept of politics and its contingencies than simply with his account of rationalization. This reason has to do with the origins of politics in traditional domination.

Politics as it emerges out of traditional domination arises as a struggle to appropriate the means of power. In this struggle value reason—legitimation by consent to a principle deemed to be intrinsically rational— represents a weak source of support against opponents even after personal ownership of political means of power has given way to a struggle for these means in the modern state. Value-rational legitimations for obedience are not irrelevant in this scheme, but they operate not as a source of grounds to overcome conflict but as instruments for gaining supporters in the struggle among contending parties, classes, and statuses. So they are subservient to, as well as intensified within, the conflicts that take place within the three-part scheme Weber chooses to use. For Weber the inescapable struggle for political power—to gain supporters by means of belief in legitimation and resources to implement one's projects—drives the need for various forms of domination. In politics fundamental values may be what defines the differences between political agents and their goals, but within the struggle itself legitimation based on voluntary adherence to substantive values can neither survive the struggle nor for that matter succeed within it.

From these considerations, it should be clear that for Weber politics is indeed a struggle for power in which ultimate values are at stake. But because the power to impose those values in the modern state can only be generated within the logic of charismatic and bureaucratic domination, politics as struggle *(Kampf))* "selects out" *(Auslese)* only those values that can be harnessed to and realized through some *Herrschaftsform* based on subordination and discipline. Thus, "politics" excludes, from the outset,

no. 2 (June 1980), 225–245; Gert Müller, "The Notion of Rationality in the Work of Max Weber," *Archives Européennes de Sociologie* 20 (1970) 141–171; and Adrian Weights, "Weber and 'Legitimate Domination': A theoretical critique of Weber's conceptualisation of 'relations of domination,'" *Economy and Society* 7 (February 1978), 56–73.

seemingly purely on grounds of feasibility, any possibility of realizing a concept of freedom as direct public participation in the common matters of political society. At best it can preserve some remnant of *"individuelle Bewegungsfreiheit"* (individual freedom of movement). It can do this only through the agency of the charismatic leader. Once charismatic leadership has become the only way of preserving some remnant of "individual freedom of movement" against the formal rationality of bureaucracy, the problem for Weber is to seek some means by which charismatic leadership can develop and assert itself given the rationalization of modern politics into a *Betrieb*, an organization or undertaking with its own purposively rational laws. Within the modern bureaucratic state, the only bearer of charismatic leadership will be the professional politician with a "calling."

The Expropriation of the Political Expropriators:
The Berufspolitiker as Agent of Ultimate Values
and Responsible Political Choices

Weber's sociological analysis of the "meaning" of being a political actor in the modern state and the ethical dilemmas that this entails rests on his analysis of "the development of modern politics into a 'Betrieb' which provides schooling in the struggle for power and its methods" (*GPS*, p. 519; *FMW*, p. 90; *GPS*, pp. 508, 545). Indeed, Weber's renowned lecture, "Politics as a Vocation," is in fact two interconnected essays: one devoted to the distinctive personal commitments required by the political sphere; the other to the demands of politics as a *Betrieb*. Weber's central concern in this essay—and perhaps in his political sociology in general—is to reconstruct the meaning of the higher calling for politics within the *Betrieb* of politics. We can measure the degree to which politics has undergone the process of rationalization by investigating the degree to which it has been "organized" into a *Betrieb*. It is the *Betrieb* of politics that generates the possible roles that an individual may pursue in politics both as a profession and as an ethical calling (*GPS*, pp. 514–515; *FMW*, p. 114).

In German the word *Betrieb* has numerous meanings. It can mean an organization, an enterprise, a firm, a factory, a pursuit, or an organized or disciplined activity. It can also be used pejoratively to describe the reduction of all significant social activity to mere "business" or "organization" and to a mechanically organized activity that runs on its own momentum, free of all human intervention. In describing politics as a *Betrieb*, Weber wants to exploit all of these meanings.

Modern politics has developed into a *Betrieb*, an autonomous as well as a disciplined activity that cannot be pursued occasionally with any success (*GPS*, pp. 514–515; *FMW*, p. 85). When one "engages in politics" in general, one *"treibt Politik"* (GPS, p. 512).[13] But at present one can only "pursue" the activity of politics within an "organization," that like the economic enterprise, is devoted solely to the disciplined and specialized activity of politics. This *Betrieb* of politics, this organized and disciplined pursuit of political power is characterized by an elaborate division of labor. It is this division of labor that determines the roles open for "the politically talented and which could give them a satisfying political task" (GPS, pp. 545; FMW, p. 114; GPS, p. 513; FMW, p. 84). However, what prevents the political actor from finding a satisfying task is precisely the transformation of politics into routine business, into an organization devoid of substantive goals.

This suggests the most significant way in which Weber exploits the term *Betrieb*. One can speak of the political *Betrieb* in the same sense as one can speak of a capitalist *Betrieb*, or firm. Weber's analysis of the rationalization of modern politics rests in large part on this economic usage of the term. Marx had argued in his famous account of "Primitive Accumulation" in *Capital* that fully developed capitalism was only able to create a free unencumbered "laborer" selling his or her labor power to capital by repeating within its own dynamic expansion its historical origin in the separation of the worker from the ownership of productive means:

> The capital-relation presupposes a complete separation between the workers and the ownership conditions for the realization of their labour. *As soon as capitalist production stands on its own feet, it not only maintains this separation, but reproduces it on a constantly extending scale.* The process, therefore, which creates the capital-relation can be nothing other than the process which divorces the worker from the ownership of the conditions of his own labour; it is a process which operates two transformations, whereby the social means of subsistence and production are turned into capital, and the immediate producers are turned into wage-labourers (my emphasis).[14]

Borrowing heavily from Marx, Weber draws a direct parallel between the origins of modern capitalism in the expropriation of the means of production from the worker and small producer and the origins of modern politics in a similar process of political "expropriation" of the means of power and domination from those who deploy them. And like Marx—and this is not often noticed—Weber also sees the internal dynamic of the modern

---

13. "Man kann 'Politik treiben'—also die Macht—Verteilung zwischen und innerhalb politischer Gebilde zu beeinflussen trachten" (GPS, p. 512).
14. Karl Marx, *Capital*, vol. 1, trans. Ben Fowkes (New York: Random House, 1976), p. 874.

political enterprise as continually recapitulating in wider and wider spheres the "traditional" (Marx calls it "original," [*ursprünglich*]) process in which political means are separated piece by piece from personal ownership.

For Weber the modern bureaucratic state, the modern political party, and above all the modern professional politician are all the direct or indirect outcome of a "process of political expropriation" [*politischen Enteignungsprozess*] whose distinctive characteristic is the separation of the *means* of political administration and power from the politician, the official, and the citizen. This separation has its origin in traditional forms of domination, in particular patrimonial forms. The first professional politician, the prince, initiates this expropriation of political means from the private possessors of financial and military power, only to be himself displaced by his staff that has now become expert in deploying these means; the staff in turn has these means expropriated from it by the central administration that it creates to execute its orders; however, the central administration, though forming a status of its own, is no longer subject to any one individual but to the one institution that can back up its *Herrschaft* with force, the state:

> The whole process is a complete parallel to the development of the capitalist enterprise [*des kapitalistischen Betriebs*] through gradual expropriation of the independent producers. In the end, we see that in the modern state control over the total means of political organization [*die gesamten politischen Betriebsmittel*] in fact comes together under a single head. No single official personally owns the money he pays out or the building, stores, tools, and war machines he controls. In the contemporary "state"—and this is essential for the concept of the state—the "separation" of the administrative staff, of the administrative officials, and of the workers from the material means of administrative organization is completed (*GPS*, pp. 510–511; *FMW*, p. 82; see also *GPS*, pp. 511, 512–513, 518; *FMW*, pp. 83, 84, 89, 295).

This means that apart from any substantive goals a political actor might pursue, the goal of all modern politics will be to gain at least partial control over the state, to become in Weber's words its "master." Only at the pinnacle of the state does one have the full complement of means through which political power can be exercised; only through the offices at the commanding heights of the state does one gain control over the financial, military, and bureaucratic means of imposing one's will regardless of the resistance of others.

If the limits of political action are defined by the extremes of rational-legal and charismatic domination it is the logic of traditional domination that contains the origin of modern politics. Indeed, the political struggle to expropriate the owners of political means of action that defines traditional domination is never overcome even under modern conditions. On the contrary, modern political actors are condemned to play out this struggle again and again, resorting at one moment to rational-legal domination, at another to charismatic domination, to break the hold of this logic. "Politics" then becomes an unceasing and perhaps ultimately self-defeating striving to overcome the distinctive characteristic of the organized business of politics: the separation of the agent from the means of power. It is unceasing because instead of overthrowing its origin in the prince's struggle for appropriation and expropriation of the means of power, it merely internalizes it as its defining feature: "Social action, especially organized action, will be spoken of as 'political oriented' if it aims at exerting influence on the government of a political organization [*die Leitung eines politischen Verbandes*], especially on appropriation, expropriation, redistribution, or allocation of the powers of government" (*WG*, p. 29; *ES*, p. 54). It is self-defeating because one gains control over the means of power embedded in the state only to surrender them back to the state once one's substantive goals have been achieved. In the modern *politischer Verband* legitimated by rational-legal domination the means of power belong to the state, not the office holder.

The modern political party develops according to an instrumental logic directly parallel to this expropriation of the means of power by the state. Only the modern party takes its form as a response to mass democracy rather than to the centralization of power over territory. When the political party merely represents a severely restricted constituency, it can afford the leadership of notables—avocationary politicians who rule the local party personally. However, with the introduction of mass suffrage, the party has to become an efficient machine to bring in votes over a vast territory. For mere political survival the parties must now employ officials who live off the party, organizing local party organizations and deploying party finances to deliver the mass vote (*GPS*, pp. 532–536). The upshot of this deliberate organization of the mass electorate is that the party official, like the state bureaucrat, is separated from the means of party administration, especially the financial ones. He or she organizes campaigns but neither leads the party nor makes party policy (*GPS*, pp. 532–533; *FMW*, pp. 103–104). In turn, the followers of the party are themselves separated from the party's administrative apparatus. Yet there is one crucial difference between the modern party and the state. Unlike the modern state the modern party cannot claim the legitimate right to back up its commands by using violence. For this it must capture the state through the "peaceful" battle of elections.

Both of these expropriations of the means of power are accompanied by a development that Weber alludes to in the passage just cited, the separation of the citizen from the means of power both in party and in state. Indeed, a fundamental question this development poses for Weber is whether the process by which the state has expropriated the means of political power can be reversed and whether society can re-expropriate these means for its own determination.[15] Referring to the German Revolution of 1918, Weber remarks, "Here the most modern development begins, and we see with our own eyes the attempt to inaugurate the expropriation of this expropriator of political means [i.e., the state] and therewith of political power" (*GPS*, pp. 510–511; *FMW*, p. 82). Can the members of the modern state reverse the rationalization of the political *Betrieb*, expropriate the state's means of domination and power, and "pursue" politics directly and democratically? Although admitting such control over the political staff and material goods has temporarily been attained through the workers and soldiers' councils, and although this new political form has been legitimated by popular sovereignty, not rational-legal authority, Weber's answer to the question is resolute and unconditional: such a reappropriation of power in any durable sense is impossible. The separation of the worker and citizen from the means of domination and power is not merely a necessity of private capitalist ownership that can be abolished once capitalist control over production is overthrown; it is not even exclusively the result of increasing bureaucratization. It is above all a result of a general process in which all actors are separated from the means of action because of the necessity of disciplined coordination over the division of labor:

Everywhere the same thing: the means of control [*Betriebsmittel*] within the factory, the state administration, the military, and the university institute

---

15. Wilhelm Hennis, "Max Weber's Theme: 'Personality and Life Orders,'" in *Max Weber: Essays in Reconstruction*, trans. Keith Tribe (London: Allen & Unwin, 1988), p. 63, argues that Weber "did not consider the question of democracy to be 'central.'" Apart from the question of how much is gained by determining one "central theme," this claim overlooks the fact that Weber constantly invokes the impossibility of reversing the political expropriation process against radically egalitarian positions that argue for the opposite. From his account on bureaucracy to his two vocational lectures to his writing on "Parliament and Democracy in a Reconstructed Germany," Weber reiterates this central "fact" about modern politics and economy as the basis for asking the question, Who will take responsibility for historical consequences given the separation of all social actors from the means of their activity? His answer, the vocational politician, draws its force precisely from this sociological fact. This matter aside, I doubt it is mere coincidence that when in "Science as a Vocation" he seeks to illustrate the difference between social scientific clarification of political action and partisan persuasion, he uses the example of democracy to make his point (*GAW, p.* 60, *FMW,* p. 145.

is, by means of a bureaucratically sub-divided human apparatus, concentrated in the hands of the one who rules that apparatus. This is in part determined purely technically, by the kind of means of production [*Betriebsmittel*]: machines, protection, etc.; in part, however, it is determined simply by the greater efficiency of this kind of coordination of human beings through the development of "discipline," military, administrative, workplace, and organizational discipline. In any case, it is a major error to hold that this separation of the worker from the organized means [of power] is purely characteristic of the economy and ultimately the *private* economy. (author's emphasis)[16]

Against the backdrop of this seemingly irresistible process, Weber sees the striving for democratic political expropriation of political or economic means not merely as unfeasible, but also as a threat to his concept of individual autonomy and personhood equal to the threat posed by the reduction of politics to bureaucratic domination. For Weber the distinctive "business" of politics cannot be reversed; it can only be countered, and there is only one agent within the modern political *Betrieb* who is able to offset the separation of the means of power from their executors both in the state and the modern party, the *Berufspolitiker*, "the vocational politician," the professional politician with a calling for politics who is also a "leading politician."

This figure appears in modern politics largely out of a historical logic that runs counter to the political expropriation process. But unlike the other two logics, which historically seem to reinforce one another, the logic that produces the vocational politician in Weber's narrative is hardly relentless. On the contrary, it converges fortuitously and intermittently with the expropriation process that produces the state and the party, and not unlike charisma it is constantly threatened with extinction. As we shall see shortly, Weber is so concerned with the frailty of this historical logic over and against the mutually supporting logics of the bureaucratic political party and the bureaucratic state that he seeks to find a political form in which it might be nurtured and strengthened.

The vocational politician, a distinctive figure of the West, appears in the Greek city-state in the form of the demagogue, the charismatic democratic leader who moved the assembly of citizens to action not by dint of his office but by his words. Here the figure of Pericles, the equal among equals, is paramount (*GPS*, p. 525). The logic that would cultivate this type of person is subsequently interrupted, and a new kind of political figure appears historically, the renaissance prince who owns the means of

16. Max Weber, "Der Sozialismus," in *Max Weber: Gesamtausgabe*, vol. 1/15, ed. Wolfgang Mommsen (Tübingen: J. C. B. Mohr [Paul Siebeck], 1985), pp. 608–609.

power as his private possession and uses it to capture cities and regions. This figure contributes a crucial feature to the ideal-type of the vocational politician, namely the person who is devoted exclusively to the expropriation of the means of power. The demagogue does not reemerge until the democratization of the modern political party and the parliament. This democratization, driven as we have seen by universal suffrage, allows for the cultivation of the modern demagogic leader who by dint of his personality leads the party and its mass following to success in elections and subsequently to a kind of dictatorship over parliament (*GPS*, pp. 535, 537). He rules through the "exploitation of mass emotionality" while struggling to appropriate for his own projects the means of power—finances, military power, administrative domination—from his opponents in the state.

Only through him can individual value-giving autonomy be linked to the struggle for power through which ultimate values are made general for all of political society; and only through the creation of political institutions in which he can flourish can the value-creating power of charisma be introduced into politics. In short, it is only through the vocational politician that individual autonomy and responsible personhood can be introduced effectively into politics and that the struggle to test fundamental values can take place. Why is this so? Weber's answer involves a blending of his concept of personhood with the functional necessities of the modern political enterprise.

First, the struggle for power in the modern state can only be carried on with skill and consistency by the *Berufspolitiker*, the professional politician who "lives off" politics as well as derives "the inner meaning of his life" from it (*GPS*, p. 513; *FMW*, p. 84). Not every member of a modern state can devote his or her full time to politics, because unlike the citizens of the Greek polis who were released from the toils of work to attend the assemblies, the majority of citizens in the modern state must make their living in large-scale economic organizations structured according to bureaucratic domination (*GPS*, p. 514; *FMW*, p. 85). Their means of livelihood depends on their dispossession from the means of administration and production.

Second, and closely related, few are disposed to commit themselves to politics as the "ideal" justification for their lives. Only a certain kind of individual derives his or her sense of identity from the possession of political power and the use of that power in the service of a cause (*GPS*, p. 514; *FMW*, p. 85). This person is the politician with a "calling," or *Beruf*. The concept of *Beruf* in German means both calling in the vocational sense of an inner *Ruf*, or voice that tells the individual to commit himself or herself to a particular disciplined way of life and profession in the sense of technical specialty for which one is trained and receives both status and salary. The word *profession* contains within it the modern meaning of the trained specialization and the older meaning of professing a particular faith that justifies one's life. But there is a dilemma, of course, in this concept's unification of the ideal and the functional. In its original meaning the inner voice had to come from God; but where there is no certainty that such a voice exists or in any case is the true voice of God, one can only demonstrate one's calling through the external effects one produces on the world as a result of one's devotion to a cause or profession. These personal effects must elicit from others the acknowledgment of one's inner calling.[17] Thus its link to charisma. The original meaning of "politics as a calling" then has its roots in the personal charisma of the leader who understands himself and is taken by others as the "innerly 'called' leader of human beings," one who is obeyed purely because others believe in him (*GPS*, p. 508; *ES*, p. 79). A politician with a true *Beruf* therefore must combine the technical skill of the professional and the charismatic moment that justifies a life's commitment to one's "calling" for politics. It is only in having a calling in the second sense that the professional politician can be a bearer of values and take responsibility for acting on them. The politician with a "calling" combines technical skill in the struggle for power, in using political means to impose his will over the resistance of others, with a commitment to ultimate values: he "lives for his cause and 'strives for his work' [*lebt seiner Sache und 'trachtet nach seinem Werk'*]" (*GPS*, p. 508; *ES*, p. 79). For Weber few have a calling for "politics" in this sense.

Third, only the professional politician with a calling can harness and direct the central means of entering the struggle for power in the modern state, the party organization, or "machine." Only here does he receive a training in the struggle for power; and only in the leadership of the party is his calling in the sense of inner charisma tested. As the leader of the party, he does not engage in its normal operations. The continuous work of the party is done by the professional politicians without a calling, the party operatives or officials who live off politics and are organized ac-

17. In this sense, vocation obviously has its roots in a religious notion well before Calvinism—one need only think of Augustine's struggle with his own doubts. But this notion involved worldly retreat. In trying to give an explanation of the modern use of the concept, Weber points to the success of Calvinism in turning the doubt engendered by vocational commitment into a methodical reconstitution of economic life from one of acquisition and consumption to one of saving and investment. Vocational politics for Weber is to have a similar effect. The doubt engendered by one's genuine commitment to politics as an ideal must be allayed by continuous testing of one's leadership qualities and one's efficacy in prevailing both in power struggle and against routine bureaucracy. Compare *PE*, pp. 128–129, 187–188; *PESC*, pp. 111–112, 180–181; with *GPS*, p. 560; *FMW*, 128.

cording to bureaucratic discipline. Instead, the *Berufspolitiker* through his charismatic qualities, in particular through his use of demagogy, takes the leadership of this machine and overcomes the distrust and resentment of the operatives by mobilizing the masses behind it. The party becomes the system of *Herrschaft* through which the charismatic political leader leads the "masses" in electoral campaigns and parliamentary battles much like the commander of an army (*GPS*, p. 535; *FMW*, p. 107). He becomes in Weber's vivid description of Gladstone, "the dictator of the battlefield of elections," using the support of the masses as a Caesarist plebiscite on his personal rule (*GPS*, p. 535; *FMW*, p. 106). The result of this "plebescitarian leadership of parties" is "the 'soullessness' [*Entseelung*] of the following, their intellectual proletarianization" (*GPS*, p. 544; *FMW*, p. 113). The "masses" can only follow blindly, enthralled by the charismatic demagogy of the political leader, while obeying the commands of the party. Mobilized only by their emotional response to the leader, they are simply asked to react, not to make choices (*WG*, p. 167; *ES*, p. 285).

Although Weber admits that we can act as "occasional politicians" when we vote, applaud a speech or protest in a political assembly, or even give a political speech, (*GPS*, p. 513). Weber also insists that the functional demands governing all political associations larger than small political communities necessitate that they be ruled by a select group of people who make politics their profession:

In all in some way extensive political associations [*politische Verbänden*], that is, those which go beyond the sphere and range of tasks of small rural Cantons with periodic elections for the holders of power, the business of politics [*der politische Betrieb*] is *necessarily* [my emphasis] *only the business of those who have a special interest in it [Interessentenbetrieb]* [Weber's emphasis]. In other words, a relatively small number of men who are primarily interested in political life, in sharing political power, provide themselves with a following through free recruitment, present themselves or their protegés as candidates for elections, collect financial means, and go out campaigning for votes. It is unimaginable how in large associations elections could practically come about at all without this form of organization [*ohne diesen Betrieb*]. In practice this means the division of citizens with the right to vote into politically active and politically passive elements. And since this difference rests on *voluntary choice [Freiwilligkeit]* [my emphasis], it cannot be abolished through measures like obligatory voting or "occupation" status group representation, or similar proposals that are expressly or actually directed against this state of affairs and the rule of professional politicians [*die Herrschaft der Berufspolitiker*]. The leadership and following as active element of free recruitment are necessary elements in the life of the party as are the following and through it the passive electorate for the election of the leader (*GPS*, pp. 528–529; *FMW*, p. 99).

Modern (democratic) politics demands that there be a split between politically active and politically passive citizens. Weber seems to give two complementary arguments here in favor of this split. The first rests on a seeming empirical observation about the functional conditions for democracy in modernity: given the large numbers that constitute modern political associations compared with local forms of democracy, it is absolutely necessary that only a small portion of the electorate devote themselves to everyday politics. Neither election campaigns nor public office can sustain a continuous participation of all citizens. Happily, this corresponds to a second claim, that only a few citizens actually prove to be interested in the business of politics both as profession and vocation. Thus citizens voluntarily choose what turns out to be a functional necessity of contemporary democratic politics. Now in principle there should be nothing problematic here. It would seem that it is in the nature of most citizens not to pursue a sense of personhood in politics. And modern politics selects out those who are so inclined.

But let us note the use of the words *voluntary* and *necessary* in this passage. Although initially basing his claim on functional necessity, Weber suddenly tells us that the members of the passive electorate "freely choose" to be routine followers of leaders and party machines, *as if this followed* from his previous descriptions of functional necessity ("And since . . ."). Then, having informed us that all attempts to involve ordinary people in politics will fail because political passivity is voluntarily chosen, he once again reiterates the necessity of leaders, party followers, and a passive electorate for the vitality of political associations with competing leadership parties.

That mass political passivity may be necessary to that kind of party politics in no way entails that it is chosen voluntarily, especially if the citizens do not have any other option available. Submission to functional necessity on the part of citizens is here reframed as voluntary choice. Weber's argument in this case for the *"Herrschaft der Berufspolitiker,"* in fact, is made entirely from the self-justifying vantage point of the Berufspolitiker himself. The voluntary choice of the citizens does not enter into the rule of vocational politicians at all: "It is not the politically passive 'mass' which produces the political leader, but the political leader who recruits a following and wins the mass through 'demagogy.' This is so under even the most democratic political arrangements. Therefore it is the opposite question that is more immediate: do the parties in a fully developed mass democracy permit the rise of men with real leadership qualities?" (*GPS*, p. 389). Without a machine, to organize the passive electorate, a leader with the charismatic gifts for politics simply cannot enter the struggle to influence or shift the distribution of power in the modern state, and it is the role of parties to allow such leaders to flourish, not to represent or organize a popular will (*WG*, p. 666; *ES*, p. 1128). Thus it remains unclear in what sense the general passivity of the electorate is voluntarily chosen in the same sense that an individual actor chooses vocational politics.

By inserting an argument about voluntary submission derived from his concept of personal autonomy into his political sociology, Weber in effect preempts any search for other instrumental means of politics that could democratically reverse the political expropriation process. Weber's slippage between acquiescence to causality and willful choice now appears as an empirical description of the functional conditions of modern politics alone. Through this functional description Weber places the full burden of responsible politics on the vocational politician alone.

Thus, fourth, the professional politician using his demagogic skills to lead a political machine with a mass following in a struggle for power in the state is indispensable to prevent the dissolution of all government into the routine domination of administrative officials carrying out commands according to rational-legal authority. Although the administrative official acts according to impersonal formal rules, rejecting any personal responsibility for his actions, the politician insofar as he lives up to his calling must take "the exclusive personal responsibility for what he does which he cannot and must not reject or transfer;" for his task is "to be partisan, to fight, to be passionate" (*GPS*, p. 524; *FMW*, p. 95).

The force of the "cannot" *(kann nicht)* and "must not" *(darf night)* in this passage rests on the distinctive double identification of the *Berufspolitker* with both ultimate values and the struggle for power. Unlike the administrator (and the party operative), who is duty-bound to carry out directives, even if he thinks they are wrong, the politician with a calling is firmly immersed in a struggle to shift power in his favor within the state. He thus must make compromises, sacrificing less important to more important ends. His duty, then, is to uphold his "cause" *(Sache)* while struggling to use the means of power and *Herrschaft* effectively to realize it; unlike the civil servant he is not required to obey orders whether they are false or true (*GPS*, p. 335; *ES*, p. 1404). This duty to calling, in turn, arises from Weber's ultimate reliance on the professional politician to set the ultimate values that bureaucratic administration is duty-bound to carry out. The formal rules and the division of office by competence characteristic of monocratic bureaucracy require only predictability and orderly submission. Political problems, it is assumed, can be dealt with once they are subdivided into various tasks and are assigned to various administrators according to technical competence. But bureaucracy cannot set substantive goals for the state or the political *Verband:* "To posit political goals is not a technical matter, and the professional civil servant purely as such should not determine politics" (*GPS*, p. 354; *ES*, p. 1419). To rank and impose goals on political society is the ultimate responsibility of the politician, and it is only in so doing that he sets an adequate *Gegengewicht*, a counterweight, to *Beamtenherrschaft*, the rule of officials (*GPS*, p. 351; *ES*, p. 1417). It is to this end that he is to deploy his charisma, especially in the form of demagogic capacity.

The *Berufspolitiker* thus embodies the concrete translation of value rationality into the distinctive purposively rational logics of power and domination in politics. He personally chooses values and seeks to lead both machine and masses to impose them on society. But his success depends on his personal charisma. As Mommsen has pointed out, for Weber it is "not the concrete setting of goals as such that decides the outcome of an election, but rather the personal-charismatic qualification of the leader-candidate." The masses and the machine are devoted to him personally, but he alone is responsible for choosing and fighting for his value ideas.[18] As a consequence, the power he generates by means of his charisma, even for the sake of chosen ultimate ends, is subject to immediate adaptation to everyday forms of rational-legal domination, because even success in the struggle for power both against opponents and against the tendency of bureaucracy to resist all personal values will dissipate into *Herrschaft*, routine formal domination, considering that implementation requires continuous submission from those it defeats. Thus, the political leader's responsibility to posit goals and struggle for them is constantly being undermined: by the mass following that supports him merely on account of his individual demagogic qualities and not on account of the rationality of the values he upholds; and by the continuous restrictions on his field of activity, whether because of power struggles within parliaments or election campaigns or because of his reliance on bureaucratic administration for the implementation of his goals: "As domination congeals into a permanent structure, charisma recedes as a creative force and erupts only in short-lived mass emotions with unpredictable effect during elections and similar occasions" (*WG*, p. 679; *ES*, p. 1147). In modern politics, the opportunities to impose values and take responsibility for the consequences of implementing them are few and far between. Only one who is willing to devote himself or herself to the hard and frustrating task of constantly waiting for the opportunity to press his or her goals past the resistance of office-seeking party officials, opposing parties, and conservative civil servants, only that person has a calling for politics beyond its professional demands.

18. Mommsen, "Universalgeschichtliches und politisches Denken," pp. 136–137.

Fifth, despite engagement in the peaceful use of power on the battlefield of elections, only the political actor who is committed to politics as a profession can deal with the fact that she or he will be responsible for the problem of "dirty hands." Even the contest for power through "peaceful" elections and parliamentary battles is a veiled representation of the power that every political association claims to monopolize legitimately: "the decisive means of politics is violence" (*GPS*, p. 556; *FMW*, p. 124). The very fact that we use the language of war to describe peaceful political struggle indicates the politician's complicity with the threat of force in his or her day-to-day activity. Behind all attempts of the professional politician to impose willed ends on others and to redistribute power in the state is the threat of physical force. Hence, in seeking to wield power at all, every "politician" contracts with violence as a potential means. Minimally, every politician engages in coercion. To seek and avoid this is to opt out of politics. For Weber most people would rather opt out of such complicity.

With complicity in and responsibility for "dirty hands" comes a final and perhaps most important reason for entrusting the vocational politician with our fate: only the vocational politician as a type combines passionate commitment to a cause and responsibility for consequences of pursuing that cause using power backed by force. This combination of conflicting qualities is held together by the exercise of "political judgment," or *Augenmass* (*GPS*, p. 546; *FMW*, p. 115). In a sense, this ability to exercise judgment in combining the conflicting demands of upholding one's ultimate project and taking responsibility for exercising power on its behalf defines the vocational politician as such. But it also deflects this figure toward an abstract type who stands as an ideal of action above and beyond the sociological context of his appearance: he becomes, as it were, the very embodiment of sociologically informed political judgment. The judgment he exercises is not just a distance from self and a sense of concrete circumstances, although it is that to be sure; but it is also the ability to exercise the very sociological and economic assessments that Weber suggests can be provided by his social science. Replicating the reasoning of social science, the vocational politician measures the distance between fundamental goals, the means necessary to realize them, and the immediate consequences and by-products of deploying those means to intermediate goals. This politician then exercises a kind of perception in applying this reasoning to concrete historical circumstances.

Here responsibility and judgment become closely connected. The vocational politician emerges as a figure who takes inner responsibility for a judgment about the uses of power that only he or she makes.[19] Given

19. Michael Walzer, "Political Action: The Problem of Dirty Hands," *Philosophy and Public Affairs*, no. 2 (1973), 177.

either our commitment to other vocations or more likely our dull submission to the division of labor, Weber seems to be arguing, we are delivered up to the judgments of vocational politicians. And we suffer the fate that their judgments unleash or contribute to. But there is no other choice. Unless we entrust political responsibility to such a figure, Weber argues, distinctively "political judgment" will be exercised by no one in the discipline and business of modern politics.

There is in this and the preceding arguments a kind of prudential blackmail. Weber demonstrates the necessity of the vocational actor as the agent of political judgment by demonstrating the frailty of his or her appearance. Externally, Weber demonstrates, the logics that converge to produce this type are weak compared to those of the bureaucratic state and political party. Internally, we are told, the qualities constituting such a figure, namely, passionate commitment to a cause, responsibility for power, and the judgment to combine the two, are in constant danger of descending into the vain pursuit of power or the moral self-indulgence of absolute righteousness. Like Machiavelli's prince, this figure is a type whose appearance is fortuitous and whose agency is constituted by the very theory of political judgment that is intended to advise him.

Therefore, one would expect a search for a more durable source of political responsibility and judgment. But Weber forecloses on such an inquiry through his functional demonstration that power cannot be entrusted to anyone else because of the irreversibility of the modern expropriation of power from its agents. This conclusion leads Weber into an inquiry into the state forms in which vocational politicians might arise and be fortified. His question now becomes how best to order the modern state so that vocational politicians—politicians who will be able to maintain firm commitments, yet temper them with judgment and a sense of responsibility for the influence of the business side on political outcomes—will be selected out and flourish.

Political Leadership and the
"Feasible" Forms of Democracy

In seeking a solution Weber rejects the concept of democratic government based on popular will as a fiction;[20] instead he argues that once the masses are included in politics, the (democratic) state can take only two forms: "There is, however, only the choice between leader democracy with a machine, and leaderless democracy, the rule of professional politicians

---

20. Max Weber, "Letter to Michels," quoted in Wolfgang Mommsen, *Max Weber und die deutsche Politik* (Tübingen: J. C. B. Mohr [Paul Siebeck], 1974), p. 392.

without a calling [*Berufspolitiker ohne Beruf*], i.e., without the inner charismatic qualities that make a leader" (*GPS*, p. 544; *FMW*, p. 113).

Leaderless democracy with a machine corresponds, I think, to what has today been called, originally by its partisans, and later by its critics, "the elitist theory of democracy."[21] Under this conception of politics, elites who are merely professional politicians or political "entrepreneurs" compete with one another for a share of power. They view the party apparatus and the party program as a means for mobilizing the multitude but see no need to fight for convictions (*GPS*, p. 538). Their goal is to attain office. The professional politician who is skilled at party organization assumes that as long as he or she is successful in attaining office, setting goals and taking responsibility for them is unnecessary. Indeed, politicians who set goals and fight for them are seen as divisive and destabilizing.

Weber is fully aware that this form of politics is what typically characterizes the modern state, but unlike his close follower, the great synthesizer of elitist democratic theory, Joseph Schumpeter, he relentlessly opposes it. Schumpeter argues that competitive party democracy is a "political method" through which leaders are to be selected out through competition. But the justification for such selection is essentially a corollary argument to the one that he gives for dynamic predatory capitalism: the competition between parties is justified by its unintended effect of producing good policies much as the striving for profit has the unintended effect of increasing production. The procedure produces good results by regulating competition and providing incentives for leaders to compete for votes.[22]

21. See C. B. Macpherson, *The Life and Times of Liberal Democracy* (Oxford: Oxford University Press, 1980). Ironically Weber, especially through his influence on Michels and later Schumpeter, contributed to the very elite theory from which he is so desperately trying to escape through the concept of the *Berufspolitiker*. For his influence on Michels, see Lawrence Scaff, "Max Weber and Robert Michels," *American Journal of Sociology* 86, no. 6 (1981), 1269–1285. For Schumpeter's influential argument for democracy as a "political method for arriving at political decisions in which individuals acquire power to decide by means of competitive struggle for the people's vote," see Joseph Schumpeter, *Capitalism, Socialism, and Democracy* (New York: Harper & Row, 1962), pp. 269–283. Borrowing heavily from Weber, Schumpeter sees the competition of elites for popular acclamation through elections as a means for leaders to articulate policy about which the electorate is uninformed. But unlike Weber he attaches no particular substantive concept of personal autonomy to this notion of leadership. For him such competition parallels the drive toward innovation and the constant refinement of efficiency of an imperfectly competitive market. One might even say that for Schumpeter, the political method of competition among politicians for the people's vote retains an element of the creative selection that unlike Weber he sees on the wane in the economy.

22. "The social meaning or function of parliamentary activity is no doubt to turn out legislation, and in part administrative measures. But in order to understand *how* democratic politics serves this social end, we must start from the competitive struggle for power and

Weber sees political competition without the vocational and charismatic element as thoroughly inadequate. He calls it "a mockery of the principle of democracy in the interests of parliamentary horse trading" and an "impotent surrender to cliques" (GPS, p. 418). Reducing politics purely to a competition between party operatives who have become candidates for office, this "leaderless democracy" with a machine closes politics to the politically talented by not providing such individuals with "a satisfying political task" (GPS, p. 545; GM, p. 114). Unless a Caesaristic element is present in the liberal parliamentary state, he insists, the leader who sets goals for the state and struggles for them will be driven out of politics. But it should be fairly clear that the tense balance between parliaments, parties, and charismatic vocational politicians under a principle of popular sovereignty that is at once a fiction and an active exercise of popular recall cannot be engineered.

What are the possibilities then given the extremely weak logic that produces vocational politicians in the full sense of the word? In the period prior to (and virtually up and until) the total collapse of the Reich in 1918, Weber argued that a strong monarch combined with a strong parliament was the most effective form of state over and against limited constitutional republics. The advantage, however, as Wolfgang Mommsen has pointed out, was functional: The monarch would represent a stable charismatic element in the state, providing a stronger foundation for mass obedience than could be provided by impersonal formal legality; the monarch would also serve as a useful barrier to ambitious and talented individuals seeking executive power, channeling their political strivings into parliamentary leadership.[23] But once it became clear that monarchy was doomed, Weber shifted his functional concerns to the objective possibilities within democratic state forms. Here he discovered the inadequacies of relying on party (and interest group) competition to test fundamental political projects and cultivate skill of political leadership.

The only objective possibility within the modern democratic state to overcome the tendency to reduce politics to negotiating and bargaining is what Weber in his famous, albeit sketchy, formulation calls "plebiscitary

---

office and realize that the social function is fulfilled, as it were incidentally—in the same sense as production is incidental to the making of profits." Joseph Schumpeter, *Capitalism, Socialism, and Democracy*, p. 282. For Weber there are few such happy by-products of "democratic" politics: the unintended effects of using political power for fundamental values is usually the dissipation of political energy and the struggle for power into various forms of (bureaucratic) discipline legitimated by rational-legal domination and the discrediting of the goal for subsequent generations. If there are worthwhile unintended consequences, they only emerge in the pursuit of ends in which struggle and conflict are inherent features, such as "the nation," and the commitment to vocation itself.

23. Mommsen, *Max Weber und die deutsche Politik*, pp. 311–314.

leadership democracy." There is a double edge to this political form in Weber: On the one hand, it represents the transformation and reinterpretation of the authoritarian personal legitimacy of the charismatic leader into an anti-authoritarian direction. As such, the principle of legitimacy undergirding charismatic domination of the plebiscitary leader becomes increasingly based on a formal process of recognition by "the people" through "election" in the double sense of the word. "The ruler becomes the freely elected leader," and the masses make or break that leader, as it were. Charisma now becomes strictly dependent on democratic sovereignty (WG, pp. 155–156; ES, pp. 267–268).

On the other hand, Weber treats this principle as a fiction hiding its authoritarian origins: "'Plebiscitary democracy'—the most important type of leadership democracy [Führerdemokratie]—is in its genuine sense a kind of charismatic domination which conceals itself under the form of legitimacy which is derived from the will of the ruled and only sustained by them. . . . Standing opposed to plebiscitary leadership democracy as a type . . . are the types of leaderless democracy which are characterized by the striving after the minimization of domination of man over man," (WG. pp. 156–157; ES, pp. 268–269).

To explain how it could be both deflection of charisma toward popular sovereignty and concealment of personal domination, we could perhaps see this form as occupying a tenuous position in what for Weber is a power struggle among fundamentally opposed political forms: that is, between routine politics based on party competition and non-leader–centered direct radical democracy, as referred to in the passage just quoted. Only plebiscitary democracy transcends the routine business side of professional politics under conditions of modern mass politics without trying to overthrow it like radical democracy (and socialism) in the name of ending domination once and for all. It introduces the struggle between party and administrative discipline and the offsetting discipline of charismatic leadership into a political framework that has the rudiments of parliamentary democracy.

This concept of "democracy" is distinguished neither by popular participation in the rule of the state nor by party competition but, rather, by the numerous opportunities it affords for selecting out (Auslese) leaders with the sufficient demagogic qualities to gain the faith of the masses. In "Parliament and Democracy in a Reconstructed Germany" Weber argues that parliaments can play this role by serving not primarily as bodies to articulate political issues but as Auslesestätte, selection or proving grounds for leaders with a "great political power instincts" and "highly developed leadership qualities" (GPS, p. 341; ES, p. 1409). Parliaments also allow the development of political expertise, especially through the committee system while checking the authoritarian claims of leaders. Yet parliaments alone also undermine the selection of talented leaders for they tend to become bodies for the representation of particular sectional interests, occupational, religious, class interests, not of the interests of the state as a whole. Weber then argues that it is the political parties that must serve as the true proving grounds for democratic leaders. For the leader of the political party uses elections as plebiscites in which he seeks a "profession of faith" in his "calling." This "Caesaristic principle" becomes the unavoidable attribute of democratic politics, as elections become struggles between leaders seeking popular acclamation to their unimpeded rule of the state (*GPS,* pp. 393–394; *ES,* pp. 1451–1452).

For Weber the competition between demagogues seeking public acclaim is the price we must pay for having a democratic politics in which great cultural values are fought for and realized. Election (and parliamentary struggle) become the way in which the charismatic individuals test their charisma, demonstrate their magical power, in the "demagicified" context of the rational "organization" of politics. The alternative is the reduction of politics to a "business." And this in turn means a struggle of status groups and classes organized into party machines seeking office and patronage.

Either mass election campaigns and parliaments become means for leaders to deploy their demagogic qualities to organize and lead a party machine with a "mass" following toward ultimate ends articulated by the leaders themselves, or they will become means for professional politicians without any ultimate convictions to gain office and influence. Therefore, Weber argues vigorously for the introduction of direct popular election for president into the Weimar constitution. Invoking every argument at his disposal Weber insists that such direct election would at once enhance popular sovereignty—indeed, it would truly realize the dictatorship of the proletariat—and overcome the inadequacy of parliament as a "proving ground *(Auslesestätte)*" for political leaders (*GPS,* p. 498–501; *GPS,* p. 544). Obviously the latter outcome is the one that interests Weber, but popular election becomes the means of testing leaders. In principle, the members of the mass electorate, like the members of the ancient public assembly, sit in judgment of the leader holding out "the noose and the gallows" for any leader who fails to act in the interests of the state. But Weber denies that such popular judgment could be exercised through any other means than mass elections. The vote is the way in which the masses subordinate themselves under a leader chosen by themselves, *"die Unterordnung unter selbstgewählte Führer"* (*GPS,* p. 501). The ultimate goal of such direct choice of leaders is, it seems, to turn the whole state into a "proving ground" for the selection of leaders. In such a state, both parties and parliaments are forced out of their preoccupation with bargaining and individual interest and instead become instruments for training leaders with strong value commitments.

This solution to the problem of rationalization of the political *Betrieb* has been subject to much critical discussion especially in light of its apparent authoritarian overtones.[24] Typically, the debate among interpreters has centered on whether or not Weber has rejected the concept of natural rights and voluntary consent as the foundation of the modern state. Weber, indeed, seems to be arguing that only through the introduction of the Caesarist principle into liberal democracy can the value-creating power of charisma be sufficiently strengthened to offset the depersonalizing effects of bureaucracy and the intrusion of sectional interests through competing party apparatuses. But to criticize him for ignoring liberal rights may miss the point. Rather than criticize Weber for illiberalism, it might be more apposite to argue that Weber is in fact revealing the sociological underpinnings of the liberal state based on rights. In this state form formal constitutional legality cannot solve—indeed it may exacerbate—the problem that political conflict rotates largely around partial interests and negotiated compromises at the cost of clearly articulated fundamental goals. At the practical level he is arguing that the only way to offset the self-defeating aspects of routine party and interest-group competition is through a plebiscitary actor who overrides the stalemate or sectional preoccupations of parliamentary institutions. Viewed this way, it becomes incumbent upon the critic to find a more adequate way to insert substantive ends and political responsibility into routine politics.

Some interpreters defend Weber's proposal by arguing that he sought to defend individual rights or limited government through a properly designed state. His purposively rational understanding of legitimacy and political forms is thus seen as way of realizing individual rights in a time when an appeal to rights no longer has a universal foundation.[25]

This interpretation has much to recommend it, because it draws a parallel between the internal constraints on the vocational actor and the balance between leadership, parliament, and electorate in his model. However, it focuses on only one side of Weber's dualistic account of plebiscitarian democracy, the one that speaks of its democratizing effects on charisma. It does not take into account the other side of Weber's concept,

---

24. Wolfgang Mommsen, "Zum Begriff der plebiszitären Führerdemokratie," in *Max Weber: Gesellschaft, Politik und Geschichte*, pp. 46–47, 69.
25. See David Beetham, *Max Weber and the Theory of Modern Politics* (Cambridge: Basil Blackwell, 1985), p. 113; Stephen P. Turner and Regis A. Factor, *Max Weber and the Dispute over Reason and Value* (London: Routledge & Kepan Paul, 1984), pp. 71, 73; and Robert Eden, *Political Leadership and Nihilism* (Tampa: University of South Florida Press, 1983).

in which the fusion of substantive values with the struggle for power of the charismatic leader with a vocational sense is linked to a fundamental distrust of mass democracy, a distrust nurtured by his concept of personhood. For Weber political leadership has always been achieved against democratic equality, all the more so under democratic conditions: "However since the great political decisions, and especially in a democracy are unavoidably made by a few men, mass democracy has bought its success since Pericles' time with major concessions to the Caesarist principle of selecting out leaders [*Führerauslese*]" (*GPS*, p. 394; *ES*, p. 1451). Democracy is of interest to Weber depending on whether it permits the rise of individuals with leadership qualities. Even though Weber saw parliamentary democracy as the means for producing such leadership, there is nothing in this form of politics that expresses the values that Weber finds intrinsically desirable. It is not just Gladstone, the great parliamentary leader, that is Weber's model here but also Pericles, who often without formal office led the ecclesia by sheer dint of his demagogy, his speech to the demos of Athens (*GPS*, p. 525; *FMW*, p. 96). In making Pericles the model of the original plebiscitary leader, Weber conveniently ignores Diodotus' Periclean defense of the necessity of free public discussion in democracy against that demagogue of resentment, Kleon:

> The good citizen ought to triumph not by frightening his opponents but by beating them fairly in argument; and a wise city without over-distinguishing its best advisers, will nevertheless not deprive them of their due, and far from punishing an unlucky counsellor will not even regard him as disgraced. In this way, successful orators would be least tempted to sacrifice their convictions to popularity, in the hope of still higher honors and unsuccessful speakers to resort to the same popular arts in order to win over the multitude.[26]

Thus, increased democratic deliberation, based on rewarding good political judgment, is the only solution for dangers inherent in the reliance of democracy on leadership, for it harnesses the contest among ambitious leaders to the necessity of giving good public advice. It also encourages leaders to maintain convictions that require tough choices by allowing them to continue to convince the public even when their recommendations have led to harsh results.

Weber's defense of plebiscitary democracy depends on arguing precisely the reverse of this Periclean defense of direct democracy.[27] For Weber

26. Thucydides, *The Peloponnesian War* (New York: Random House, 1982), pp. 176–177.
27. This model also heightens the very dangers that Diodotus points to when he argues against a democratic politics that encourages citizens to "get even" with political leaders whose political judgment met with bad luck: For it is precisely this desire to get even after

democracy is fundamentally a means of developing leadership that will be able to use its demagogic qualities to mobilize the masses for the struggle to impose values over the resistance of other leaders doing the same. And it is the punishment of the masses that unsuccessful leaders have to face, a punishment born of rage rather than deliberative judgment.[28] It is this model of democratic politics that corresponds to Weber's identification of politics with power struggle.

The assumption here is that the mass of men and women in the state lack any personhood at all:" they are "soulless," "intellectually" and "psychologically proletarianized," unable to will values or take responsibility for the consequences of realizing them.[29] But this leads us to ask whether this is due to the inexorable rationalization of modern politics into a profession and a business or to Weber's fusion of democracy with his aristocratic account of personhood. Or perhaps, whether the construction of the rationalization of modern politics and Weber's attempt to counter its destructive tendencies through plebescitarian democracy are both refracted through his notion of the person who combines a life organized around values with a life organized around the instrumental paradoxes of realizing values. If we combine his account of the vocational politician as ideal embodiment of political judgment with his instrumental account of state, party, and modern democracy, the last reason would seem most persuasive.

Whatever the case, it is unclear why the plebiscitary leader who takes his political calling seriously represents a more adequate *purposively rational* alternative to the rationalization of politics than does the democratization of the business side of politics; for central features of the political business such as large numbers, the division of political labor in party and state, and the constant preoccupation with appropriating political power should cut down plebiscitary leaders just as relentlessly as they do leaders coming from direct democratic forms of power. By encouraging political struggle among charismatic individuals leading party machines, plebiscitary leadership democracy at best opens a narrow avenue through

---

the fact that allows for leaders to play toward what people would like to hear in lieu of presenting them with the hard choices they must make as deliberating members of the polity.
28. It is this assumption of popular vengeance that Weber has in mind in his oft-quoted discussion with Ludendorff: "In democracy the people elect a leader in whom they have confidence. Then the elected leader says: 'Shut up and obey me.' People and parties may no longer meddle in what he does. . . . Afterwards the people can sit in judgment. If the leader has made mistakes—to the gallows with him." Quoted in Marianne Weber, *Max Weber,* trans. and ed. Harry Zohn (New Brunswick, N.J.: Transaction Books, 1988), p. 653.
29. For Weber a condition of the "plebiscitarian leadership of parties" is "the 'soullessness' [*"Entseelung"*] of the following, their intellectual proletarianization" (*GPS,* p. 544; *FMW,* p. 113).

which responsible vocational politicians might enter into political leadership. If the appearance of truly vocational politicians is a rare occurrence within the modern organization of politics for Weber, plebiscitary politics increases that likelihood by only a small increment. That increment is the difference between the general appearance of charisma in politics and the distinctive form that it takes in the vocational political actor—a minute amount indeed.

All this might give us reason to suspect that what leads Weber to this "leap of faith" in plebiscitarian politics is more than just his search for a historical solution to the failures of any force, party, or class within the German political conjuncture to take responsibility for the leadership of the nation, though one would not want to discount this motivation. A stronger reason for the endorsement of this form can be found in an argument that Weber saw plebiscitarian leadership as the only way to overcome both bureaucracy and, more important, a concern on the part of ordinary people and parties purely with economic rationality, with "bread and butter issues" as David Beetham has so ably argued.[30] According to this reading, plebiscitarian leaders embody a way of saving politics as a higher calling by injecting into routine politics struggle over fundamental issues affecting the life of the nation. Surely this is true. However, the very language with which Weber defends plebiscitary politics points to an even more fundamental reason for endorsing this model of democracy, one that does not depend on historical circumstance. For example, in his inaugural lecture he speaks of saving political leadership and politics from mere eudaimonistic concerns, from mere striving for personal satisfaction (*GP*, pp. 12, 14). Much later he insists that if the working class restricts its organized activity to merely enhancing its economic well-being rather than to organizing its own political leadership its collective consciousness would remain *banausic*, mechanical and technically repetitive and would lose any will toward "upward striving" (*GASS*, p. 405).[31] Over and over again the failure to develop "political" leadership with a will to set ends for the state and struggle for them is contrasted with everyday routine, with the loss of that striving through and above the routine that makes for a *person*. Thus plebiscitary politics becomes a means through which some actors escape the dull, technical repetition of the division of labor and cultivate their personhood, although not by escaping the demands of everyday routine but, rather, by taking responsibility for its contribution to all action. And through them, it becomes a way for a nation to be something more than a geographic collection of

30. Beetham, *Max Weber and the Theory of Modern Politics*, p. 226.
31. Cited in ibid., p. 222. See also *GPS*, pp. 487–488.

statuses, classes, and parties each seeking their well-being. That a political model should be judged not only by its adaptation to the instrumental demands of everyday routine alone but also by the kind of person it cultivates is for Weber a perfectly consistent position, as he remarks in one of his most famous statements on this matter: "Every type of ordering of social relations whatever its form, must, if one wants to *evaluate* it [*bewerten*], be ultimately examined according to the human type to which it affords optimal chances to gain superiority [*herrschen*] by means of external or inner (motivational) selection procedures" (*GAW*, p. 517; *Method*, p. 27). But if this is true, our agreement with his constitutional response to the business of politics and its demands depends not simply on whether we agree with his account of the feasible alternatives to routine politics but also on whether we agree with his equation of unique personal nobility with the vocational politician. That there may be something problematic both in the account of what is instrumentally feasible in modern politics and the type of person it selects out may become clear when we turn to Weber's political ethics.

Political Ethics and the Fear of Mass Politics: The Partial Uses of Impartiality

How much resignation will you still have to put up with? Such concepts as "will of the people," genuine will of the people, have long since ceased to exist for me; they are fictitious. All ideas aimed at abolishing the dominance of men over men are "Utopian."
—Max Weber, "Letter to Michels"

If politics must be understood independently of its goals, then it follows that an ethic of politics must also be independent of any substantive political commitments. Is there such an ethic? What is "the *ethos* of politics as a 'cause' [*Sache*]?" This is the question Weber poses in his closing discussion of political ethics in "Politics as a Vocation."[1] But he quickly subsumes this question, which applies to all political actors, ordinary citizens and vocational political actors alike, under another more specific and more restrictive question, that seems to be addressed exclusively to one kind of political actor, the vocational political actor: Is there an ethic to guide a political actor with a "calling" for politics that takes into account the sociological constraints imposed on political action by the political *Betrieb* and yet remains intelligible to all self-reflective political actors whatever their substantive political commitments? (*GPS*, p. 548; *FMW*, p. 117).[2] Weber's answer to both questions is his justly famous construc-

1. From the manuscript of Weber's notes for the lecture, it appears that the discussion of the inner meaning of "vocation" and of political ethics constituted the core of "Politics as a Vocation" as a lecture. Weber's sociology of the origin of modern politics with its analysis of the multiple strands of development that together constitute the modern *Betrieb* of politics was put together separately and interpolated into the lecture as it was delivered. See "Editorial Note," "Politics as a Vocation," in *MWG*, vol. 17, pp. 125–126, 128. This helps explain a curious theoretical tension in this work between an analysis of politics based on the convergence of multiple contingent instrumental logics and a political ethical argument that often invokes for polemical purposes a uniform sociological logic based on the inexorable movement of all social action toward bureaucratization and routine discipline. The tension between these two accounts informs my analysis of Weber's political ethics. I show that Weber's political ethics opens out in two directions. In the first, Weber aligns his political ethics of responsibility with a sociological logic of contingent convergent tendencies such as the development of the state, political party, and the professional politician. In the second, he aligns it with a unilinear logic of ends and means in which power backed by force irresistibly leads to disciplined routine.
2. In introducing the political-ethical question in his lecture Weber first poses it as the problem of finding "the *ethos* of politics as 'cause' [*Sache*]." That is, what ethic corresponds strictly to the conditions of politics or what ethic goes hand in hand with a commitment to

tion of two ideal-types of ethics: an ethic of conviction *(Gesinnungsethik)* and an ethic of responsibility *(Verantwortungsethik)*. Each of these ethics represents an ideal-type of a general ethical orientation toward political action corresponding to his distinction between "motivations" based on value reason and those based on purposive reason. As such both ethics represent an attempt to understand impartially two different ways in which political actors might justify their political projects and the actions they undertake to realize these projects.

But they are also meant to do more than this. They also represent the translation of Weber's dual concept of personhood into politics. Weber, we should recall, develops a notion of the person whose defining feature is a will with no ultimate rational guidance on the choice of fundamental ends. Rationality is exercised only in the choice of means and the weighing of consequences. As persons we are constantly suspended between choosing ultimate values on the basis of inner conviction and taking responsibility for rationally choosing the most effective means of realizing them *(GAW, pp.* 132, 226). The intuition that we have a self—and are not merely reacting to inner causality—expresses itself in our willing of values. But we display our reason in understanding the causally effective means of achieving our will. Personhood and the autonomy that goes with it are thus most paradoxical indeed, for our sense of self is found in irrational willing, but our relation to the world as agents is found only through the reduction of all willing to causal efficacy. Thus the self is constantly threatened with disappearing into the chains of causality unleashed by the very means of translating that self into action. Weber's two ethics thus consist in a disaggregation of the principle components of his concept of the person into will and causal efficacy. Weber only reunites these two ethics under a concept of the person as political actor once he has tested each of them individually for its appropriateness to the distinctive demands of the political *Betrieb.* He claims that an understanding of the (purposively rational) "consequences" of adopting one or another ethic or a combination of the two ethics can serve as a guide to the ethical

---

politics? But Weber immediately ties this inquiry to *Beruf*, the concept of calling and profession: "What calling [*Beruf*] within the total ethical economy of life conduct [*Gesamtökonomie der Lebensführung*] can [politics] in itself fulfill independent of its goals?" Similarly, at the very beginning of the lecture Weber announces that he will address the question of "the meaning of political action within the totality of life conduct [*Lebensführung*]." Once again, he collapses this general question of the role of politics in the distribution of the agent's everyday life activity into the more specific question of *Beruf*, "what politics as a vocation [*Beruf*] is and can mean" *(GPS,* p. 505; *GM,* p. 77). It is precisely Weber's claim that the first set of questions is necessarily linked to the second (or more precisely that an answer to the second question fully answers the first) that I want to question here.

demands of politics. But more important, this understanding reveals what it means to have selfhood in politics.

I argue that it is precisely the strength of this strategy of testing his two ethics against the sociological conditions of their application that also is its weakness. Clearly, in constructing these two ethics as impartial ideal-types and in seeking a reconciliation between them in light of both his concept of the person and his notion of the sociological demands of politics, Weber gives us an account of political responsibility that would be difficult to reject without rejecting some of the most persistent features of politics itself. In arguing for a political ethic in which convictions should be and inescapably are subject to consequences rooted in the sociological and economic logics of politics, he is strengthening the meaning of his political ethics through a political sociology of power; by the same token, he is giving greater meaning to his political sociology as a reconstructive understanding of the conditions for political action by drawing out the ethical implications of acting within the sociological constraints of politics. Surely, it would be a decisive ethical criticism of a political project if the empirical consequences of realizing it proved to be sociologically self-defeating or if they were fundamentally, rather than temporarily, inconsistent with the original goal.

Yet, Weber often uses his sociology of vocational and antivocational politics to avoid making a direct argument about those substantive values that he finds compatible and those that he finds incompatible with his formal account of political ethics. Instead he draws judgments about responsible political projects by claiming merely to assess their costs according to an impartial sociological account of the means and consequence of political action under modern conditions. Thus he very neatly finesses having to argue with substantive political projects he disagrees with, either by labeling them as convictions cut off from an appreciation of the consequences of deploying power on their behalf, or by claiming they do not fully meet up to an impartial ethic of political responsibility for consequences. At the same time, certain favored substantive positions pass his test of political responsibility with flying colors. He often lets, so to speak, his sociology do the hard work of political-ethical argument rather than justify the political commitments underlying his reconciliation of the two ethics of conviction and responsibility. This gives us reason to agree with his political ethics and his notion of political responsibility in general, while rejecting the particular way in which he applies this ethics to all projects at odds with his own substantive values, especially those projects concerned with extending democratic equality to ordinary nonprofessional actors.

The Two Ethics: Political Ethics and Moral Risk

The "ethic of conviction" is the perfect translation of value rationality, or what we are apt to call deontological commitments, into political terms. It insists that we need not be cognizant of the consequences of an action but only of the "intention" or "conviction" motivating it. If an intrinsically good conviction leads to bad results, then it reflects the world's failure to live up to the conviction, not the actor's failure of practical judgment (*GPS*, p. 552; *FMW*, p. 121). Although acting purely out of political conviction requires passionate devotion to a fundamental end, there is a form of rationality appropriate to it, what we might call "conceptual consistency," according to which the intentions constituting a political conviction must not be contradictory.[3] Acting purely under an ethic of conviction, then, the agent seeks to live in complete consistency with his or her ultimate values. Actions are regarded as expressions of these values. For the conviction politician the action comes off if it expresses those features of a value that make commitment to it intrinsically worthy.

Thus the *Gesinnungsethiker* does not feel obliged to acknowledge the responsibilities that political power imposes on political actors. Rather, the political actor whose maxims of action fall under this formal ethic is responsible only for keeping a good intention or cause alive, even in the face of inevitable failure. The typical (though not only) *Gesinnungsethiker* for Weber is the revolutionary syndicalist whose sense of the injustice wrought by economic and political expropriation of the workers from production motivates him or her to set an example by trying to organize militant mass resistance to domination. Failure or subsequent repression are irrelevant considerations (*GAW*, p. 513; *Method*, p. 23). Ultimately for Weber the political actor motivated by an ethic of conviction ignores the prudential lessons of the sociology of power struggle and domination governing modern politics: in particular she or he fails to view politics under the colliding logics of rationalization that force all actors to replay the continuous struggle for appropriation of the means of power at the origin of all politics. For the politician of conviction, only pure political will matters.

3. I draw this term from Onora O'Neil, "Consistency in Action," in *Constructions of Reason* (Cambridge: Cambridge University Press, 1989), p. 89. Weber expresses the same notion in his account of sociological self-clarification when he speaks of the social scientist

From the viewpoint of judging action according to success, then, the ethic of conviction appears irrational. Every conviction pursued for its own sake, no matter how internally consistent, is subject to purposively rational considerations. For Weber the ethic of conviction is in fact a deviation from an ethic of responsibility in much the same way that value reason is a deviation from purposive reason. It fails to account for the necessity of rationally calculating means to ends and ends to subsidiary consequences; indeed it rejects any assessment of means in light of ends, a concept so central to Weber's prudence: "The ethic of conviction must apparently go to pieces on the problem of the justification of means by ends. And as a matter of fact, logically it has only the possibility of repudiating all action that employs ethically dangerous means" (*GPS*, p. 553; *FMW*, p. 122).

On purely logical grounds, Weber is arguing, an ethic of conviction should in and of itself have no place in politics at all, because it forgoes the justification to which any rational political ethic must submit, namely, a justification of means in light of the ends pursued. Political action always requires ethically dangerous, or at least ethically risky, means. Politics inevitably involves moral risk.

Politics can only be adequately understood under purposively rational action, because political action is inseparable from "power" in the instrumental sense of trying get some agent to carry out one's designs. Means must be calculated according to their success in imposing one's will over the resistance of others; the distribution of power in the state (i.e., the probability of imposing one's will) must be shifted in one's favor. This may entail mobilizing masses of people under bureaucratic machines, systematic compulsion, and in the extreme case violence. No inner conviction or ultimate value on which a person or a community base their integrity can remain unscathed when political means are deployed on their behalf.

The only ethic that corresponds to the particular purposive reason appropriate to political action in the modern state is an ethic of responsibility, an ethic Weber initially intended to call an "ethic of power [*Machtethik*]"[4] because it largely encompasses responsibility for the consequences of using political power. This ethic of responsibility requires the political actor "to give an account of the foreseeable results of [his] actions" (*GPS*, p. 552; *FMW*, p. 120; *GAW*, p. 505; *Method*, p. 16). We may justify our political commitments according to intrinsic goods we hope to realize, but the prescription for any political action taken in their

---

as being able to provide actors with an account of the axiomatic consistency of their values. See Chapter 2.

4. Wolfgang Mommsen, *Max Weber und die deutsche Politik*, 2d ed. (Tübingen: J. C. B. Mohr [Paul Siebeck], 1974), p. 149.

name is always justified by consequences.[5] And it is the consequences of our political actions that justify or discredit our political projects. But what foreseeable consequences are relevant and why indeed only "foreseeable" ones? Weber gives a threefold answer to this question: a general description of the existential conditions faced by all truly "political" actors rooted in a conceptual account of politics and personhood; a particular account of the sociological conditions in which responsible political action must take place—this account includes the multiple logics that intervene in modern politics; and an example-driven account of contemporary political action drawn from the unique historical moment in which he is writing. In the last account the examples Weber chooses are meant to instantiate the logic of his sociology, which in turn is meant to instantiate the general existential account of politics. However, despite Weber's explicit claims to the contrary the examples drive both the sociological and the general account of an ethic of political consequences, rendering it far less impartial than it may at first seem.

Let us look first at Weber's general answer. Instead of expecting others to live up to the highest ends, or assuming human beings can live up to their best capacities, the "responsible political actor" must take "account of precisely the average deficiencies of people" (GPS, p. 552; FMW, p. 121). In light of this assessment he must scale down his ends to those that can be realized in effective reality. He should not forget that he can be responsible for the consequences of expecting too much from people in trying to realize his political projects. Curiously, Weber rarely indicates that a political actor could be responsible for the consequences of expecting too little as well. For example, opportunities for gaining a space for democratic decision or for reversing the political expropriation process could be lost precisely by underestimating the political capacity of others.

More important, the responsible political actor must be aware that in political action there is frequently an ironic relation between intentions (convictions) and consequences: "The final result of political action . . . stands in a completely inadequate and often paradoxical relation to its original meaning" (GPS, p. 547; FMW, p. 117). Weber is arguing that it is precisely the "paradoxes" of political intention and political consequences that determine the "foreseeable" results for which we are responsible. What he has particularly in mind here are the paradoxes produced on the one hand by the inescapability of power struggle in politics and on the other by the rationalization of politics into an autonomous *Betrieb*, or business.

---

5. See Dennis Thompson, *Political Ethics and Public Office* (Cambridge: Harvard University Press, 1987), pp. 5–6.

Specifically, "politics operates with very special means, namely, power backed by violence" (*GPS*, p. 550; *FMW*, p. 119). Given this particular attribute of political means, neither generosity, nor love, nor truthfulness, nor above all coercion-free social relations or absolute justice can be directly realized through political action (*GPS*, pp. 550–551; *FMW*, pp. 119–120). Indeed, and here Weber is echoing Machiavelli, the pursuit of these ethical qualities through politics often results in the realization of their opposite: "He who lets himself in for politics, that is, for power and force as means, contracts with diabolical powers and for his action it is not true that good can follow only from good and evil only from evil, but that often the opposite is true" (*GPS*, p. 554; *FMW*, p. 123). Power backed by violence undermines the simple translation of ideals into effective political action on their behalf. By the same token, good ends can frequently be attained in politics only by using morally questionable means: "No ethics in the world can dodge the fact that in numerous instances the attainment of "good" ends is bound to the fact that one must be willing to pay the price of using morally dubious means or at least dangerous ones—and facing the possibility or even probability of more evil subsidiary consequences" (*GPS*, p. 552; *FMW*, 121).

Furthermore, the attempt to introduce substantive values into politics is subject to the logic of domination *(Herrschaft)* that governs all social action.[6] All ultimate values that are successfully imposed on state and society gain their initial impulse from movements organized according to charismatic domination. But under modern conditions the struggle for these values requires the mobilization of masses of people under bureaucratically organized political parties, and the implementation of values always depends on administrative staffs organized and legitimated according to rational-legal domination. This sociology of domination entails that all attempts to impose new values on political society expand the purview of impersonal administration both in the sphere in which power is fought for and into spheres where it is routinely exercised. Precisely because they depend on charismatic individuals, power struggles over values immediately dissipate into a rational-legal *Herrschaft* that rejects all considerations of substantive value.

An ethic of responsibility requires the political actor to be fully aware of these costs of pursing any end through politics and to take full responsibility for any outcomes that may ensue. It is precisely this willingness to

6. "In an extraordinary number of cases, it is domination and the way it has been exercised that allowed a rational societalization to arise out of an amorphous communal action. And where this is not the case, it is nevertheless the structure of domination and its unfolding which form a communal action and decisively determine its clear directedness toward a 'goal'" (*WG*, p. 541; *ES*, p. 941).

take on political responsibility that constitutes the distinctive recognition we give to political actors, even when we fundamentally disagree with their substantive goals: "The honor of the political leader and the statesman is . . . precisely the exclusive *personal* responsibility for what he does, a responsibility which he cannot and must not refuse or transfer" (*GPS*, p. 524; *FMW*, p. 95). "The business of politics" may not entail a particular substantive ethic but "also in politics there is a certain minimal sense of shame and dignity which cannot be violated without punishment" (*GPS*, p. 247). Here Weber is implying that, given the ironic nature of political action, the political person must not just be responsible for calculating the necessary means to ends but is also de facto responsible for any public outcomes, both foreseen and unforseen, that result. Moral notions of good and bad may not be directly translatable into politics, but there is a certain dignity or shamefulness in an actor's stance toward the outcomes of political action and its costs apart from such notions. To avoid responsibility for hard choices or unpleasant outcomes, especially out of commitment to pure moral principles, is to demonstrate not high-mindedness but dishonor and shame (*GPS*, pp. 550–551; *FMW*, pp. 118–119). (Weber's example is the actor who follows the Sermon on the Mount and abjures violence when she or he encounters it.) Weber's point is that we do not reward political actors for their principled stances alone, but also for facing up to the hard choices that need to be made in translating such stances into practice by using political means.

The upshot is that the ethic of responsibility contains, as it were, a dual responsibility corresponding to the demands of Weber's sociological clarification of action. First, the political actor must correctly calculate the kinds of power necessary to achieve his or her fundamental projects, taking account of the desired results and the unwanted subsidiary consequences that will ensue in general and in the particular historical situation. Here the axiomatic reconstruction of values, the analysis of these values into constitutive intentions, and the teleological deduction of consequences become the forms of reasoning appropriate for political judgment.[7] Second, she or he must decide without relying on any ethical or

---

7. See Wolfgang Schluchter, "Value-Neutrality and the Ethic of Responsibility" in *Max Weber's Vision of History*, ed. Guenther Roth and Wolfgang Schluchter (Berkeley: University of California Press, 1979). Schluchter seeks to show that if we combine Weber's technical clarification of action with his ethic of responsibility we have a standard by which to judge the ethical adequacy of political projects. Thus Weber's ethic of responsibility is not "decisionist" as Habermas has claimed. Rather, if we read the ethic of responsibility in conjunction with Weber's concept of scientific clarification, Weber provides a "dialogical" justification of political standpoints (p. 90). The technical clarification of means and consequences under an ethic of responsibility also includes a dialogue about ends and therefore belongs under the category of what Habermas following Dewey called a "pragmatic" model

prudential guidance whether the goal being pursued is worth the consequences of using the particular economy of power and violence necessary
to achieve it. Weber insists that as long as the goal is self-consistent, there
are no impartial criteria ultimately available to decide whether the cost
of achieving the goal is worth it given the constraints of politics: "From
no ethics in the world can it be concluded when and to what extent
the ethically good purpose 'justifies' the ethically dangerous means and
subsidiary consequences" (GPS, p. 552; FMW, p. 121). The agent must
simply be as lucid about the consequences of applying political means as
possible, remaining always aware that unknown causes may enter, and
then take responsibility for the choice whatever the outcome.

In dividing responsible political decision in this way, Weber, I think, is
pointing to the inescapable fact that political conduct is subject to "moral
luck."[8] This means that no matter how good the reasons that we can
adduce for our ultimate political projects are, the justification for political
actions taken on their behalf will ultimately rest on "luck," that is, on
the contribution of fate or chance to the outcome of our actions. Justification for our political actions ultimately depends on the consequences that
they unleash, and these consequences are regularly beyond our control.
This means that whatever our initial justification for political action in
terms of the projects we are trying to achieve, justification is retrospective.
We find out whether we have vindicated our political intentions or projects only after the relevant consequences have occurred. Only then can
we say that our initial reasons for deploying power in a certain way with
a cost to other values is correct and our project is what we claimed it
was. (See Chapter 6 for a more extensive account of the relation between
moral luck and political justification.)

---

of political choice. On this account, only the ethic of conviction is purely monological and
decisionist. Schluchter is right to say that Weber's technical clarification also involves an
assessment about the risks and costs of realizing our fundamental ends in modern culture
and thereby implies a standard of ethical adequacy. But he overlooks Weber's firm insistence
that both the technical clarification and the ethic of responsibility merely intensify the individual's self-awareness of irreducible choice and its risks. No model of dialogue could overcome this problem for Weber. Of course, this does not mean that an argument could not be
made that Weber's political ethics and technical clarification should be shaped into a dialogical account of political judgment.

8. I draw this term from Bernard Williams, "Moral Luck," in Moral Luck (Cambridge:
Cambridge University Press, 1981). I also have profited greatly from the response by Thomas
Nagel to this essay also called "Moral Luck" in Mortal Questions (Cambridge: Cambridge
University Press, 1979). Williams focuses on the "internal" luck of being a certain kind of
person that is only proven in light of the consequences of one's actions. Nagel insists that
this is only one of the kinds of luck that play a role in justifying our actions and perhaps
not even the most significant kind. External circumstances are even more significant. Nagel's
account is more compatible with the demands of politics where third-person judgments of
political actors are far more important than first-person ones.

Viewed in this way the ethic of (political) responsibility imposes a far more demanding concept of responsibility than an ethic that merely tries to keep a conviction alive. For that matter, it demands a greater responsibility than the ordinary conception that we are responsible for those consequences that we could have brought about voluntarily.[9] Thus, political actors are in Robert Goodin's words "strictly liable" for the outcomes of their actions, even if fortune or logics beyond the control of the actor contributed to the result. Political actors are entrusted to make judgments and decisions for the good of the public in the midst of risks and dangers. Because they get praised for success even if it occurs fortuitously, they also get blamed for failures that so occur.[10] In Weber's account of politics as not aiming to any internal ultimate goal, this liability is intensified because political actors are "strictly liable" for the impersonal logics they may set in motion or contribute to and for the conflicts between the different values and value spheres that political action inevitably affects. Political actors act at a point where these logics and values collide.

If this is so, commitment to an ethic of responsibility endangers a coherent self, for as political actors we incur praise and blame for a self that events beyond our control (the historical situation, our given inner qualities of character, and unforeseen circumstances) impose on us. In this sense the ethic of responsibility is not so much an imperative demanding that one ought to account for the foreseeable consequences of one's political actions as a phenomenological description of the responsibility one, in fact, *does* incur when one takes the role of a political actor: "Whoever wants to engage in politics at all, and especially in politics as a vocation [*Politik als Beruf betreiben*], has to become conscious of these ethical paradoxes and his responsibility for *what may become of himself* under the pressure of these paradoxes" (*GPS*, p. 557; *GM*, p. 125; my emphasis;

9. This is the position that Dennis Thompson takes in *Political Ethics in Public Office* (Cambridge: Harvard University Press, 1987), pp. 47, 48, 64. Thompson criticizes Weber's ethic of responsibility (p. 41) for providing a notion of personal responsibility that evades moral culpability. Too many agents share in the implementation of policies. Moreover, politicians can take responsibility ritualistically. Thus we should restrict political responsibility to the moral culpability adhering to those actions that an agent voluntarily brought about. The problem here is that political culpability is not identical with moral culpability. Even in the most democratic polity, we might approve of an agent's political actions while still admitting that they involve a moral cost. By the same token, we might want to hold an agent responsible for political failure even if the outcome was out of his or her control. In any case, we often hold political actors responsible for failures of political judgment even when they acted under moral principles.
10. Robert Goodin, "Review of Dennis Thompson, *Political Ethics and Public Office,*" *Political Theory* 16 (November 1988), 665–666. A similar argument is made in Michael Walzer, "Political Action: The Problem of 'Dirty Hands,'" *Philosophy and Public Affairs*, no. 2 (1973), 179–180.

see also *GPS*, pp. 55–57). As political actors we experience ourselves as acting toward goals that are not just chosen by us but also are meaningful intentions of others. We subjectively identify with our political intentions and projects. They define our (political) self. However, the consequences of using power backed by force in a history whose direction is ambiguous and often paradoxical frequently violate the intentions underlying our political projects and severely blunt our subsidiary goals. They thereby impose on us an identity in which we cannot recognize ourselves, even though we are utterly responsible for it. Power unleashes effects that we cannot often foresee or control but that define what we actually did and who we are for others, in particular those for whom and with whom we act politically. Although we often cannot subjectively identify with the self that political action imposes on us, we are responsible for that self nonetheless.[11]

Does this mean that Weber's political ethic is "consequentialist?" It does, but as seen in previous chapters, not in the utilitarian sense of appealing to an impartial ranking of preferences or a general balance of overall happiness. Rather, his ethic might correspond to what we may call a "situated consequentialism." For Weber there is no utilitarian way to rank consequences, because what we are comparing when we compare consequences in politics are situations.[12] Depending on how we describe a situation, we may pick different consequences as relevant and judge the consequences of a political act to be good or bad, beneficial or harmful in light of the fundamental convictions that we bring to the situation. For Weber causal sequences and outcomes are intelligible to us only from horizons of meaning that are themselves constructed from the vantage point of our ultimate practical values.

The description of political situations in light of their consequences is the job of historical investigation and of the ideal-type (*GAW*, pp. 178–179; *Method*, pp. 178–179). Whether a general recurrent causal sequence adheres to a particular value-inflected context of meaningful action is largely a contingent matter. How the two connect is for Weber a matter of judgment (*GAW*, pp. 176, 180; *Method*, pp. 77, 80).

At the same time, one would not want to press this point too far with Weber. In keeping with his constant shuttle between the subjective and objective standpoint, Weber also claims that his ideal-typical reconstruction of the everyday business of politics provides us with an *objective* account of which political consequences are relevant from one situation

11. Maurice Merleau-Ponty, *Humanism and Terror*, trans. John O'Neill (Boston: Beacon Press, 1969), p. 43.
12. See Frederick Schick, "Under Which Descriptions?," in *Utilitarianism and Beyond*, ed. Bernard Williams and Armatya Sen (Cambridge: Cambridge University Press, 1982), p. 254.

to the next, at least within the modern state. Moreover, as we will see shortly, Weber most certainly does assume a consensus on what constitutes harmful or self-defeating consequences. The result is that, despite his emphasis on the situated nature of political consequences, Weber leaves a number of distinctions unanalyzed that will allow us to call into question his claim to have provided an impartial assessment of the political consequences for which we are foreseeably responsible.

In particular, it is not merely that descriptions of situations select out the consequences that will be relevant in justifying our actions, but that most events, certainly political ones, can fall under a variety of descriptions each of which will highlight or give priority to different consequences. Even more problematic for an objective description is that it is often difficult to disentangle what constitutes an action from its consequences.[13] Depending on how we understand a situation, we can either understand a feature of someone's action as a part of the overall intention being described or as a result of some intentional conduct; it may in short be part of the stream of action or be understood as distinct from it. Thus sometimes we say that an actor is responsible for an action as if it were a "consequence" of his or her deliberative activity, and at other moments we understand "consequence" to be merely an outcome unleashed by a deliberated action. What we become responsible for under an ethic of political responsibility for foreseeable consequences becomes quite ambiguous indeed.

Consider an example, which Weber himself cites. In the midst of World War I during the Zimmerwald debates (1915–16) in Switzerland, both Lenin and Trotsky claimed that the carnage of prolonging the war was a price to be paid for bringing revolution to Russia. Weber's judgment of this stance was severe. Weber commenting in the aftermath of World War I on the Russian revolution thinks that the consequences of this position, even for a historical materialist, would be an abortive revolution that would never realize socialism given the lack of a bourgeois economy in Russia; it would thus lead to a needless continuation of the war (*GPS*, pp. 552–553). A revolutionary socialist, he insisted, "could" (meaning "should") logically reject this means as unjustifiable if, at worst, a dictatorial regime with a precapitalist economy, or at best, a somewhat modernized bourgeois economy were the tawdry result. Curiously, one of the revolutionary socialists Weber most despised, Rosa Luxemburg, assessed the consequences of World War I for revolutionary goals in a way similar to Weber and yet drew a wholly different set of conclusions about the relation between the direct and subsidiary consequence of this event and

13. Brian Barry, *Political Argument* (London: Routledge & Kegan Paul, 1965), p. 182.

the political means that these consequences implied.[14] In her famous "Junius Pamphlet" and her own theses on Zimmerwald, Luxemburg argued that the war was a disaster for the Left in Europe and would set it back many years rather than bring it closer to success.[15] She did not think that Russia could jump over bourgeois society to a socialism built on democracy either. She therefore opposed the war relentlessly and rejected any calculation to the effect that it was worth prolonging even if it produced revolutionary consequences: "The present World War, whether it brings victory or defeat for anyone, can only mean the defeat of Socialism and democracy."[16] From this initial judgment of the war's consequences for the left, she drew a number of foreseeable subsidiary consequences as well. The war had discredited any legitimate nationalism because it had occurred as the result of elites seeking opportunities for capital realization. Furthermore, the war would strengthen militarism in its aftermath, thus sharpening economic and political rivalries. This in turn would set the precondition for new wars—a point on which she was prescient, to say the least.[17] Therefore, for Rosa Luxemburg political responsibility for foreseeable consequences in this case required a complete rejection of nationalism, an international coordination of socialist parties, and a continuous attempt to encourage class conflict even against overwhelming forces that were mobilizing the working classes for war. From the same initial assessment of the direct consequences of the war for the Left as that of Weber, Rosa Luxemburg drew completely opposite conclusions as to responsible action and this in large part because from the vantage point of a socialism combined with democracy she discovered a different set of (historically) relevant subsidiary consequences than did Weber. Despite the seeming impartiality with which Weber and Luxemburg assess the political consequences of prolonging the war, each of these figures views the same event under different descriptions, gives priority to different consequences, draws completely opposite conclusions about the use of political means, and understands his or her historical responsibility for the consequences of using those means in opposite ways in light of these

14. Max Weber's contempt for Rosa Luxemburg (as well as for Karl Liebknecht) is documented in Mommsen, *Max Weber und die deutsche Politik*, p. 328. Weber's rather ungenerous attitude toward her, including his remarks implying that she deserved her ignominious death, is striking given her own struggle to unite her socialist convictions with political responsibility for foreseeable consequences. Weber's remarkable cultivation of his dialogue with Lukács, with whom he disagreed fundamentally on the goal of revolution, compared with his hatred of Rosa Luxemburg deserves an examination in its own right. A great deal would be revealed, I suspect, about his political ethics through such a comparison.
15. Peter Nettl, *Rosa Luxemburg* (London: Oxford University Press, 1969), p. 39.
16. Quoted in ibid., p. 393.
17. Ibid.

different descriptions. All of this may give us pause to question the claim that we can be impartial about the consequences that a political actor may be responsible for. The point I want to emphasize here is simply that Weber's ethic of responsibility assumes that political consequences, especially subsidiary consequences, cannot be separated from political situations. If this is so, the "foreseeable" consequences of political action depend on the description under which we understand the action to be taking place.

Weber has provided us with a rather convincing account of the political responsibility we cannot escape if we intend to translate our ultimate commitments into politics. He is indeed right that a general ethic of political responsibility requires us to take into account the paradoxical relations between value commitments and the rational necessities of politics. Justification of our political actions most certainly depends on luck—largely because we cannot control the descriptions under which our actions are understood and because the kind of political responsibility political actors incur is one of strict liability: political actors cannot claim that outcomes they contributed to were out of their control, and hence they are not responsible for them. Responsibility for the consequences of political action therefore may very well entail a discontinuous self, precisely what an ethic of conviction seeks to prevent.

But Weber is not satisfied to provide us with a general political ethic that takes into account "the entwinement" of political consequences in "the ethical irrationality of the world" (*GAW*, p. 595; *Method*, p. 16). He also deploys his political ethics against a whole host of political projects that reject the demands of professional politics: Acosmic religions that urge the individual to turn the other cheek or turn away from the goods of this world and militant pacifists who assume that good means produce good results are both skewered for escaping into pure convictions and refusing to take responsibility for the pragmatics of power (*GPS*, pp. 538–539; *FMW*, pp. 118–119). Yet neither of these two ethical projects poses quite the challenge of the one he singles out for sustained attack: radical and socialist democracy. The reason for this is partly that acosmic religions and pacifism reject either political engagement outright or the specific use of power backed by force. Moreover, neither of them seeks to overturn the political and economic expropriation process that has left most individuals of the modern state dispossessed from the means of domination and power. This is clearly not the case for radical democracy, socialism, or revolutionary syndicalism, all of which Weber attacks interchangeably. The democratic socialist or radical democrat accepts the need to use power backed by force but assumes that the masses are more than merely the passive followers of leaders with party machines. He or she also maintains that the political expropriation process can be at least in part reversed. It is the acceptance of politics as power struggle along with the possibility of introducing a self-governing society on the part of the radical democrat and socialist revolutionary that earns Weber's particular attention—and criticism. Here we see that Weber frequently loses his sensitivity to the multiple descriptions under which political actions can be understood. In place of a sociology of multiple convergent descriptions he starts to treat the logic of bureaucratization, discipline, and mass passivity as unilinear and unconditional.

Political Ethics and the
Critique of Egalitarian Politics

Socialist and radical democrats, argues Weber, claim to accept the necessities of political power; yet they do not meet up to an ethic of political responsibility, for they fail to recognize that their claim to realism, in fact, consists merely in a "conviction" detached from effective political action.[18] They assume that their ultimate commitment justifies the morally questionable means and the possible side effects of realizing it. And they assume that their goal of radical self-determining democracy and the expropriation of the means of power by society can be realized practically, that domination can be abolished or at least minimized. In brief they propose that just as domination can be given an effective social embodiment so too can self-determining freedom. But any political actor who out of conviction seeks to introduce a self-determining political society must realize, Weber insists, that "everything that is striven for through political action operating with violent means and following an ethic of responsibility endangers 'the salvation of the soul'" and may discredit the goal for generations. In a letter to Otto Neurath written in 1919, Weber makes clear that what he has in mind is socialism: "I . . . regard the plans for a 'planned economy' to be a dilettantish *objectively absolutely irresponsible* craziness . . . which can discredit 'socialism' for a hundred years and throw everything that could be *at the moment* into a stupid

18. In a letter to Michels, in a rather questionable move, Weber shifts the revolutionary syndicalist's reliance on the mass strike from an ethic of success that looks to results to what he calls a "religion of conviction": "'the strike ethic'? Yes my dear friend but at the end of your article you state: Every strike is justified because it is one step on the way to the future goal . . . this is however an ethic of success [*Erfolgsethik*]; the means are 'justified' because the hoped-for result [*Erfolg*] is 'just.' While syndicalism is in fact . . . a religion of conviction, whose rightness also pertains [even] if there is no future goal which will be 'achieved,' and even if it is scientifically established that there is no way of realizing it." Quoted in H. H. Brunn, *Science, Values, and Politics in Max Weber's Methodology* (Copenhagen: Munskgaard, 1972), p. 155 (my translation).

reaction" (Weber's emphasis).[19] Only the capitalist entrepreneur can re-build and sustain a modern economy.

Behind this historical assessment of the fundamental political choices of the epoch stands Weber's typology of legitimate domination, impartial relative to the variety of political communities that exist (*GPS*, pp. 507–508). For Weber the struggle for political power, which is the struggle for means to impose one's will within a social relation over the resistance of others, goes on within contexts framed by the forms of legitimate domination: forms of obedience based on belief in purely charismatic personal qualities, in traditional status and patronage, or in legality become the primary means for political actors to engage in this struggle and impose their will once success is attained. What drives this logic is the way in which legitimate domination, whatever its form, produces "discipline"—the habitual and unconditional obedience to commands (*WG*, pp. 681–687). Charismatic obedience based on belief in the purely personal qualities of an individual can produce in its everyday form either traditional statuses of routine personal dependence or rational obedience to formal rules and their executors, because each of these forms takes over the discipline forged by the charismatic individual. By the same token, "discipline" can become detached from any form of personal obedience, whether traditional or charismatic, and invest all forms of social organization (*WG*, p. 687). As we have seen in the previous chapter, it is not its ability to impose methodical routine alone that threatens to defeat any attempt to reverse the expropriation of power in the economy or the state, but its use as means in the inevitable and unresolvable struggle for power in both of these realms.

Forms of legitimate domination intermingle and converge. But the outcome of all of these forms, discipline, frames both routine and extraordinary politics. The revolutionary leader merely imitates for extraordinary politics what the plebiscitary leader does within routine party politics. The plebiscitary leader stands above parliament, bringing the parliamentary party, the party operatives, and the mass following behind him. His leadership is only successful through the bind obedience of the following, a robbing of their will. The revolutionary must do the same to succeed against the state. The goal is fought for through the exertions of the

19. Quoted in Mommsen, *Max Weber und die deutsche Politik*, p. 332. He voiced similar sentiments to Georg Lukács in 1920. For Weber there were two fundamental historical choices for the reconstruction of Germany in the aftermath of the German revolution: either the socialization of production and the introduction of a worker council republic or the reliance on entrepreneurial investment. Only the latter in conjunction with a plebiscitary model of government and an elected parliament met his standard of political responsibility for consequences in light of what was possible. See Mommsen, pp. 320–321.

masses, who, Weber argues, must be organized by leaders under a political machine that "intellectually proletarianizes" its following (GPS, p. 544; FMW, p. 113). If successful, this following will now be organized under the routine Herrschaft of "political Philistines and banausic technicians": "This development completes itself especially quickly precisely in a struggle over faith, because it is led and inspired by genuine leaders, that is, prophets of revolution. For here as with every leader's apparatus, one of the conditions of success is the emptying of ideas of all content [Entleerung] and the reduction of everything to matters of fact [Versachlichung], the psychological 'proletarianization' in the interests of 'discipline'" (GPS, p. 557; FMW, p. 125). The logic of rational political action consists ineluctably in an oscillation between leaders imposing their will on the state through bureaucratically organized mass followings and the routine execution of that will through forms of rational-legal domination, both forms of domination requiring blind obedience, and in the last instance when obedience fails, violence. Mass revolution for a self-determining society does not break out of this process; it only accelerates it.

It is for the outcomes of this logic of personality and discipline investing both plebiscitary and revolutionary attempts to transcend routine politics that we are responsible under Weber's political ethic. Indeed, the warning to heed the costs it exacts on all political goals constitutes perhaps the centerpiece of Weber's political advice.

Beyond this logic that radical democratic movements simply accept in part (i.e., the need for power struggle), Weber argues the agents of democratic self-determination are only capable of reactive, affectual behavior, not value-rational or purposively rational action. In contrast to the cool-headedness of responsible political actors, "the masses" act out of emotional motives, in particular rage, jealousy, resentment: "the relatively greater susceptibility of the propertyless masses who struggle in everyday conflict for existence to emotional motives in politics, i.e., to passions and momentary impressions of a sensational kind" can only be offset by well-off political leaders who lead democratic parties and at the same time uphold convictions (GPS, p. 275). Thus there is another great danger apart from the reduction of politics to interest group behavior or from the absorption of all politics into bureaucratic administration: the "emotional motives" of the mass: "The political danger of mass democracy to the state lies first and foremost in the possibility of the strong predominance of emotional elements in politics. The 'mass' as such (irrespective of the social strata which it comprises in any given case) 'thinks only as far as the day after tomorrow.' For it is, as every experience teaches, always exposed directly to purely emotional and irrational influence" (GPS, pp. 403–404; ES, p. 1459; Weber's emphasis).

With this account of mass behavior, it is not surprising that when class struggle breaks out in mass democracy, it will be moved not by justice or a desire for collective autonomy but by feelings of resentment and desires for revenge against those who govern. The revolutionary leader organizes this resentment and vengefulness under a party machine, but he or she cannot transform it into conscious self-direction. Such a leader therefore cannot possibly act responsibly, because in order to be successful he or she must satisfy these motives both in his apparatus and in his mass following: "Under conditions of the modern class struggle, the internal premiums consist of the satisfying hatred and the craving for revenge; above all resentment and the need for pseudo-ethical self-righteousness: the opponents must be slandered and accused of heresy. The external rewards are adventure, victory, booty, power, and spoils" (*GPS*, p. 556; *FMW*, p. 125). The result is that the leader cannot realize the putative goal of the revolution, the eradication of injustice and the introduction of collective self-determination, because he or she must submit to "the predominantly base [*gemein*] ethical motives of action of his following" (*GPS*, p. 556; *FMW*, p. 125). At best such a leader can momentarily restrain these motives by dint of his or her personality.

Weber, here, following Nietzsche, identifies collective self-determining freedom as an expression of resentment rather than as an alternative to it. Radical democracy or socialist democracy are both foreclosed because there is no form of collective self-determining freedom that can be separated from desires of envy, jealousy, and ultimately rage against "responsible" political leaders, that is, leaders with ascetic self-discipline and the value-giving power of a calling. On the contrary, the whole notion of realizing popular political freedom is merely a legitimation for desires born of resentment toward all that rules, dominates, creates, and imposes responsible order. The masses cannot, given Weber's phenomenological reconstruction of their motives, act willfully; they can only react emotionally, and the more they collect together publicly, the more reactive they become: "As for irrational 'mass instincts,' they govern politics only where masses are tightly compressed and exert pressure" (*GPS*, pp. 286–287). Normally, conduct by large collections of people is not to be understood as meaningful social action at all: "It is not proposed in the present sense to call action 'social' when it is merely a result of the effect on the individual of the existence of a crowd as such and the action is not oriented to the fact on the level of meaning" (*WG*, p. 11; *ES*, p. 23).[20]

But even if mass collectivities could engage in meaningful social action,

---

20. As we saw in Chapter 1, Weber denies that the activity of an individual in a crowd or a crowd itself engages in "meaningful social action."

and consciously will their actions in directly democratic political institutions, Weber argues, collective self-determination would not be feasible. For although direct democracy can be made plausible as a rational value, and as such be empirically realized for short moments, it cannot be translated into the purposively rational demands of *Herrschaft* in the modern state: "The system of so-called direct democracy [*unmittelbare Demokratie*] is technically only possible in a small state (Canton). In every mass state, democracy leads to bureaucratic administration, and without parliament [it leads] to pure administrative domination" (*GPS*, p. 289).[21]

Even in a small state or political association, direct democracy is extremely unstable. It assumes that everyone is in principle equally qualified to conduct public affairs and that the scope of the power to command can be kept to a minimum. In order to realize these principles, all questions of importance to the community must be decided by an assembly of the citizens while the administration, which itself must be rotated, merely carries out the assembly's commands. The decay of this "domination-free unmediated democracy" *(herrschaftsfreie unmittelbare Demokratie)*, however, sets in as soon as some aspect of the execution of public business is given over to a technically qualified professional administrator *(fachmässige Berufsbeamter)*, because doing so provides an opening for bureaucratization. When the administration becomes distinct from the assembly a series of offices is created that is not susceptible to democratic recall or decision. The execution of policies now depends on technical expertise that is kept hidden from the scrutiny of the assembly. Moreover, even within the assembly there is a tendency for political decisions to fall into the hands of "honoratiores" (notables), those citizens who on account of their wealth (though not necessarily their political capacity) can devote themselves full-time to politics. In that case, the inequalities created provide an impulse for those alienated from power to form parties in order to recover democratic administration. But once the disfranchised people form parties as a means to struggle for democratic power against the

21. See J. J. R. Thomas, "Weber and Direct Democracy," *British Journal of Sociology* 35, no. 2 (June 1984), 216–240, for a very helpful discussion of Weber's account of direct democracy. In his article he seeks to show that Weber does indeed have a well-worked-out discussion of direct democracy that is at once instrumental and practical. But Thomas admits that Weber understands this form to be feasible only when technical expertise and simplicity of roles can be maintained. For a contrasting argument that claims that Weber has an insufficient appreciation of the openings to direct democracy provided by Western procedural democracy, see Ira J. Cohen, "The Underemphasis on Democracy in Marx and Weber," in *A Weber–Marx Dialogue*, ed. Robert J. Antonio and Ronald Glassman (Lawrence: University Press of Kansas, 1985). Cohen argues that Weber's universal postulates of the inevitability of the principles of selection and domination incline him to overstate the case for the impediments to direct democratic participation.

notables, the notables organize parties in their defense and participation turns into submission to the hierarchical domination typical of party organization (*WG*, pp. 169–171, 545–548; *ES*, pp. 289–292, 948–952): "With the appearance of the power struggle of parties, 'direct democratic administration' loses its character as containing 'domination' only in an incipient form [*die 'Herrschaft' nur im Keim enthaltenden Charakter*]. For every authentic party is a structure that struggles for domination in the specific sense and therefore is burdened with the tendency, however hidden, to organize its internal structure according to an explicit chain of command [*ausgeprägt herrschaftlich*]" (*WG*, p. 548; *ES*, p. 951). The small polity in which citizens participate directly through reliance on technical expertise and well-born notables can no longer contain the logics of traditional domination in the case of the notables and rational-legal domination in the case of the magistrate—logics that Weber assumes to be operating in all methodical social action. Such a polity unleashes the struggle for power among parties and for control over the administration. In other words, direct democratic institutions always already contain *in potentia* the model of politics that eventually organizes vast populations under modern competing bureaucratic parties. This outcome is a function of a selection process by which only those forms of political organization survive that can adapt themselves to the logic of power struggle and stable domination.

But even though local forms of direct democratic administration succumb to the unavoidable struggle of parties for power, what about the workplace itself, where the employees have been expropriated from control over the division of labor? Here Weber's answer is more subtle. It is not always noticed that for Weber a cooperatively self-managed workplace does not necessarily undermine efficiency if efficiency is measured merely by double-entry bookkeeping. As long the self-managed firm is not under pressure to struggle for profit, income and costs must simply balance and workers need simply produce to cover costs. What undermines the existence of this form of control over the productive means is the need for the technical optimization of labor power demanded by formal rationality. Formal rationality, which means predictable optimization of profit, and thereby predictability in production, collides with the tendency of cooperatively managed firms to impose substantively rational standards on the distribution of work and production. Formal rationality is resisted in cooperatively managed firms, Weber argues, because of the resistance to technical innovations that might threaten job security. But none of this would in itself undermine the feasibility of worker self-management if it were not for the fact that formal rationality in the workplace is how the greatest precision in capital accounting and success in the power struggle that characterizes the market are achieved (*WG*, pp. 71–72, 77–79, *ES*, pp. 128–129, 137–140).[22] Just as the inexorable power struggle over interests and values dictates the eventual organization of parties in directly democratic political communities, so too the inexorable power struggle for market position dictates the dissolution of any cooperative enterprise into one with strict managerial control over the division of labor. Although this parallel would seem to rest largely on the existence of a capitalist market economy, a democratically organized socialist economy would also engender power struggles by associations of workers over the amount to be reinvested and the distribution of desirable jobs and working conditions (*WG*, pp. 118–119; *ES*, pp. 202–204). Thus models of democratic control over the division of labor cannot be immunized against having to engage in a power struggle for survival whether in a capitalist market or a planned socialist society. In either case, they will collide with the demands of formal rationality and discipline.

That direct democratic associations in economy or locality could themselves become effective instruments for the struggle for power in opposition to hierarchical parties and state bureaucracy is not a possibility for Weber either, for they would have no way to rationalize their gains into some form of methodical everyday order, unless they were to rely on routine forms of domination. The worker and soldier councils of the German revolution, for example, seem to be an exception to this, as they did, indeed, succeed temporarily to wrest power away from the state; but they were able to do so, Weber insists, only because they had arms, were led by charismatic leaders, and made use of the technical skill of the old state bureaucracy to execute their orders (*WG*, p. 155; *ES*, p. 265).[23] Their directly democratic form of organization had nothing to do with their success in expropriating the state's power. For Weber such attempts to translate direct democracy into modern politics simply undermine parliaments and professional politicians, the only agents that can offset the penetration of bureaucracy into all areas of life. They would thus be politically "irresponsible."

Weber's judgment of the worker's councils as irresponsible is of course not just part of his general argument for the political-ethical inadequacy of the attempt to combine socialism with democracy. It is also intended as a direct comment on the revolutionary moment of 1918–19 during which Weber wrote some of his most mature and systematic political

22. For a discussion of the relation of capital accounting to Weber's notion of the market as a power struggle to gain market share, see Chapter 3.
23. Of course this argument comes close to begging the question because he seems to be identifying success with the deployment of charismatic and bureaucratic domination whatever the political form.

argument, brilliantly summarized in "Politics as a Vocation." Weber directly accuses the Bolsheviks and the German Spartacists of ignoring the ethical demands of political action in the modern state. The organized violence they directed against the state could not be justified by the actual consequences of trying to achieve socialism: were they to succeed, he insists, they would both achieve *"the same result"* [Weber's emphasis], namely a military dictatorship. And as for the worker's councils of the Russian and German revolutions, only "dilettantism distinguishes the rule of the work and soldier's councils from and arbitrary powerholder of the old regime" (*GPS*, p. 550; *FMW*, p. 119). Turning to the professional politicians of revolution, Weber, as we have already seen in a different context, invokes the Trotsky of the Zimmerwald conference who argued that the continuation of World War I was justified if it brought revolution to Russia and the rest of Europe in its aftermath. But, Weber argues, the cost in human lives and economic dislocation is too high for the "modest result" of such a calculation: namely, a modernized bourgeois economy. Even if one were a solid scientific socialist "one could reject a purpose that demanded such means" (*GPS*, pp. 552–553; *FMW*, pp. 121–122. See also "Der Sozialismus," *GPS*, pp. 630–632). Weber concludes that the Zimmerwald choice is the paradigm case for all revolutionary socialists: a clear understanding of the political-ethical problem of revolution entails a disproportion between the violent means and violent circumstances necessary to bring about revolution and the end which will be disappointing, inadequate, and not even socialist.

Now there is something odd about Weber's deployment of these examples to support his ethic of political responsibility. According to his account of social scientific clarification of action, he is only entitled to show the inconsistency between revolutionary means and ends and the consequences that would follow in trying to stabilize a successful mass revolution; but he cannot scientifically assess whether the choice of revolutionary action or the attempt to realize socialism is politically justified. No systematic form of knowledge has the warrant to take this choice from the individual.[24] Yet, Weber assumes that once these particular historical examples are refracted through his political sociology and his formal ethic of political responsibility, all rational individuals would agree on good or bad, justifiable and unjustifiable political consequences. He even indicates

24. "Every particular new fact can likewise have the consequence that the readjustment between end and unavoidable means and between desired goal and unavoidable subsidiary consequences must be undertaken anew. But whether this readjustment *should* take place and which practical conclusions *should* be drawn from it is not only not a question of an empirical science, but in general not a question of any science whatever its form" (*GAW*, p. 513, *Method*, p. 23).

that such rational agreement could serve as the basis for determining which political projects are justifiable and which are not. Without such an assumption, he would never be able to maintain that the striving to combine socialism with democracy is a politically irresponsible goal for all self-reflecting individuals, but only an irresponsible goal from the more restricted vantage point of the *Berufspolitiker,* the vocational politician. Once he has conceded this, his ethic of political responsibility becomes detached from his particular deployment of it against the attempt to reverse the political expropriation process.

Now what is the nature of this assumed agreement? To answer this question we have to make explicit a number of hidden assumptions rooted in Weber's account of the scientific clarification of practical political action. On the most explicit level, Weber assumes that we would all find the political consequences of pursuing socialism or radical decentralization of power to be self-defeating because the goal is unattainable; or, which amounts to the same thing, if attainable would have side effects that would undermine any claim to have ended domination, especially the side effect of bureaucratic centralization of both state and economy rendering the political expropriation process at once uniform and complete. On a slightly less explicit level, Weber assumes that we would all agree that if these consequences are indeed the inevitable outcome of "political trends," then the cost of using force as a political means to the *personal integrity* of the participants could not be justified. Despite our individual projects presumably we all agree that sacrificing those with whom we have solidarity is to show no respect for their integrity and we would have to have very good reasons indeed to override this respect.

This leads us to the least explicit and perhaps for this reason most important assumption of Weber's ethical-political assessment. Weber assumes that the political outcome of pursuing socialism is undesirable, not merely because it negates its own stated goal of ending domination in the economic and political sphere (i.e., is self-defeating), but because it negates a concept of autonomy and personhood based on the individual who finds values, in Weber's vivid phrase, within "his own breast" and takes full responsibility for deploying means to realize them. Weber's political sociology, as we have already seen, relentlessly seeks to show the ways in which the solitary autonomous individual, who wills and fights for values in a world where fundamental values clash, is hindered on the one side by sectional interests using political parties to advance their partial claims and on the other by the bureaucratic consequences of deploying power in the modern state. This concept of the individual is part and parcel of a more general concept of personhood. According to this notion, personhood is attained only by an agent who can live with discontinuity in the self and in the world. Both are in constant conflict. The world is governed by conflicting spheres of life conduct each with its own ends and logic of reaching them. The self is constantly caught between willing fundamental ends and willing the means to struggle for them. Such an individual seeks to choose values by relying on his or her will alone. Yet he or she knows that the realization of that will in action will be subject to a causality that turns all will into contingent outcomes. Only a rare individual can continually seek to transcend the everyday routine that turns all our acts into reactive causal behavior, yet also live up to its demands. Such an individual, Weber insists, would be given virtually no room to flourish under socialism (GPS, pp. 332–333).

Once we take into account Weber's notion of personal autonomy, it follows that he necessarily has to regard socialism and radical egalitarianism as irresponsible political goals whether or not they could be given a directly democratic political form. To put the matter differently, even if it were possible to show that political means could be found to realize a directly democratic form of socialism, Weber would have to condemn it as a violation of his concept of the autonomous person. This means that Weber's assumption that we all would agree on the bad consequences of pursing and achieving socialism, rests ultimately on a prior assumption that we all share his concept of autonomy and personhood, that his account of personhood is impartial relative to any substantive position, quite part from whether or not we agree with the consequentialist judgment he draws from his account of political rationalization.[25]

Obviously, if our concept of autonomy extended to broad collectivities, we could in principle still agree with his first assessment that within the confines of the political Betrieb the pursuit of this goal will ultimately prove to be self-defeating. We could also agree with his second assessment that the cost of achieving such autonomy is too high in the situation he describes since the very groups that would eventually enjoy collective autonomy would be sacrificed in the act of achieving it. But we might also have reason to question whether the political sociology on which both of these assessments are based did not itself select out tendencies, situations, and consequences from the vantage point of Weber's rather distinctive concept of personal autonomy. Such a sociology would surely be relevant to but not necessarily decisive for a political sociology and political ethics informed by a collective concept of autonomy. Or to put the matter more bluntly, we may have good reason to suspect that the

25. Weber never systematically defends this concept of the autonomous person against rival concepts. Instead, he allows the intelligibility of his concept to emerge both as the background of his notion of understanding and within the background of his notion of a world of constant struggle among value spheres.

political sociology from which Weber draws his political-ethical judgments may depend for its explanatory force on our prior acceptance of his will-centered concept of individual freedom. In that case, much of our prior agreement with Weber's assessment of the political consequences of socialism and direct democracy depends on our clear rejection of a collective concept of autonomy in favor of a concept in which only a unique individual can hold together personal responsibility and the dissipation of all will into the causal nexus surrounding our (political) acts.

The Odd Reconciliation between
Convictions and Responsibility

It is in light of this sociological assessment of the costs of direct democracy and socialism to his concept of what counts as a person that we should read Weber's famous reconciliation of his political ethic of responsibility with his ethic of pure conviction:

> it is immensely moving when a *mature* human being—no matter whether old or young in years—who really and with heart and soul feels this responsibility for the consequences and acts according to an ethic of responsibility at some point says: "Here I stand, I can do no other." This is something humanly genuine and moving. . . . In so far as this is true, an ethic of conviction and an ethic of responsibility are not absolute contrasts but rather supplements which only together constitute the genuine human being who *can* have "the calling for politics" ["ein Beruf zur Politik"] (*GPS*, p. 559; *FMW*, p. 127).

There is a fundamental ambiguity in this passage: "at some point" a political actor who makes an ethic of responsibility for consequences the guiding maxim of both feeling and will chooses to stand by an unconditional conviction. But we are left in the dark as to when this point has been reached.[26] We might want to read this passage broadly in keeping with Weber's notion that choice is necessary as a process of discovering what we are inclined to do, what reasons have greatest priority for us when we have equally reasonable alternatives. (See Chapter 2 for a discussion of this notion of choice in Weber.) One such reading may go like this: A political agent who fully realizes that in politics unlike social life we are *strictly liable* for the consequences of our actions and that the multiple logics impinging on the struggle for the means of state power may often produce costly by-products (or even prevent the realization of

26. This point is beautifully brought out in Walzer, "Political Action: The Problem of Dirty Hands," p. 177.

one's goals) will reach a point when to defer his or her ultimate convictions for present compromises is to abandon those convictions outright. At this point, Weber seems to be saying, we do not choose the conviction under which we discover constitutive goals of political action so much as reaffirm a previously held conviction so that the subsidiary goals we are seeking still make sense.

An equally broad reading might understand this passage to be saying that *before* we commit ourself to any political project we must become aware of the subjective and the objective costs of our choice. An intense awareness of this split between inner responsibility to one's person-defining political projects and outer responsibility for the consequences of using power to realize them is precisely a preparation for the political actor finally to translate conviction into action. In the process of deliberating on all the consequences of his actions—the ironic relation between means and ultimate ends, the conditions of gaining a mass following given modern political organization, the need for the deployment of physical force, or at least backing one's claim to legitimacy with physical force, and the inevitable cycle of charisma, power, domination, and discipline— a political actor will eventually reach a point when he will have to choose a "cause" *(Sache)* as his own. Precisely because it is governed by the ironies of political action, political power requires some ultimate end so as not to result in "empty and meaningless effects" *(GPS*, p. 548; *FMW, pp.* 116–117). Moreover, without this "belief" in a cause, the political agent who strives for and deploys power will not be able to maintain some sense of identification with his or her political actions in the midst of effects that define him or her quite apart from his or her will or intentions. It is only through an individual commitment to some ultimate value along with a fully transparent knowledge of the likelihood of its compromise or failure on account of the ironic necessities of power and domination that an individual political actor can discover a "calling" for politics beyond the professionalism of the political *Betrieb*.

Yet, in the sociological context in which Weber sets this reconciliation, the very opposite conclusion follows for a political agent with strong egalitarian convictions. This suggests a third reading. It is precisely by realizing the impossibility of uniting mass politics and self-determining freedom, of embodying direct democracy in social and political institutions, Weber seems to argue, that we can finally reconcile an ethic of conviction with an ethic of responsibility and prove our calling for politics. The political actor who is responsible for the consequences of political action accepts the necessity of *not* pursuing ideals that seek to realize a self-determining freedom beyond the logic of power struggle and domination in the state in order not to discredit such ideals for the future. In this way both the ethic of conviction and the ethic of responsibility receive their proper acknowledgement and come to complement each other. The conviction is maintained within, but responsibility for power and its results demands that we do not act on the conviction for fear of unleashing the diabolical powers of violence and rationalization (*GPS*, p. 558; *FMW*, p. 126).

Political Commitments and
the Ethic of Responsibility

Once the translation of certain radically egalitarian political commitments like radical or socialist democracy into effective political action are shown to be politically irresponsible, the question arises, What value choices could be translated into politics according to the ethic of responsibility?

As I read him, Weber gives two answers to this question. The first is the commitment to the "calling" of politics itself both as a specialized skill in the struggle for power and as an inner voice that is only confirmed by the possession of a charismatic gift for leadership. This commitment involves submitting oneself to all the requirements of professional politics, including the need to prove one's capacity to lead a political machine in the struggle to impose ends upon the state, all this for the sake of defending the concept of autonomous personhood as positing and fighting for individual values against the depersonalization of bureaucracy and the imputed "reactiveness" of the "masses."

Only the full-time professional politician who strives to be a charismatic leader of a political machine or parliamentary party can in fact reconcile conviction with the calculation of means, ends, and ironic subsidiary consequences; for only he can take responsibility for his political actions or, more accurately, for political action as such. The party operatives resentfully follow only as long as success is promised; the administrator is interested only in the adherence to rules of technical implementation. Above all, the "masses" remain an amorphous aggregation, becoming political agents only as followers of a leader and his machine. The masses, being "soulless" can never calculate the relation of means to ends and ends to subsidiary consequences in the struggle to alter the distribution of power in the state; nor can they take responsibility for the outcome of any power struggle for ultimate ideals. This, according to Weber, only individuals can do, to wit the individual professional politician responsible to the demands of his "calling." For the mass of citizens of a modern state, the split between value rationality and purposive rationality, between conviction and responsibility for consequences, still prevails. Popular self-determining freedom is a value whose realization according to the political rationality of power and domination is an impossibility, or as in the case of the German workers councils a fortuitous event. For the masses and the classes and groups for whom dispossession from the means of power is their defining characteristic, *Herrschaft* is an effect. Self-determining freedom realized in a direct democratic practice must remain a value separated from fact. In the name of defending the possibility of struggling for convictions in politics and of taking responsibility for the power-political consequences of doing so the individual with a commitment to politics as a *Beruf* will have to accept this split as an irreducible condition of all politics. Otherwise, he will not be responsible for the foreseeable consequences of choosing the calling of professional politics as a value.

But there is a double edge to this commitment. On the one hand, the commitment to politics as one's cause *(Sache)* is a way of overcoming the discontinuity of self that attends the split between one's highest value choices and the dulling political means that undermine them. The choice for the political calling provides the ordinary political actor with some end to identify continually with through bad and good fortune. On the other hand, to commit oneself to politics as an end of life (as a *Lebensführung*) is to commit oneself to forces that threaten the continuity of self from all sides: the paradoxes of means and ends, the need to identify with irreconcilable conflicting values, the irrationality of the world as a source of justification for political goals. Commitment to politics as a way of overcoming discontinuity of self in politics is to commit oneself simultaneously to the very forces that threaten the continuity of the self. Hence this value is only a partial solution to the demands of the ethic of responsibility. A more solid value is necessary. And Weber proposes one.

The second value that one can responsibly translate into politics is itself perfectly compatible with the commitment to the political calling but does not change its substance over time: this is Weber's own well-known substantive commitment to nationalism and the nation-state, especially against the strivings of socialism and radical democracy. I have no desire to recapitulate the controversies surrounding the status of this value in Weber. What interests me here is the way in which Weber's political ethics is able to lend, as it were, this partisan position a measure of impartiality much as it robbed egalitarian arguments of the same claim. Already in his Freiburg Inaugural Lecture of 1895 Weber proposed this end as the one substantive value that could be reconciled with the claims of political science to impartiality: "the science of substantive political economy is a *political* science. It is a servant of politics, not the day to day politics of the ruling individuals and classes, but rather the enduring power interests of the nation" (GPS, p. 14). It was the articulation of this end that he thought was being undermined by the encroachment of bureaucracy on political leadership, as well as the reduction of politics to economic bargaining (GASS, pp. 98–99). As Mommsen rightly has pointed out, it was this end that was most compatible with a concept of power as the struggle over values.[27] The reason why the commitment to the nation-state can reconcile both the ethic of responsibility and conviction is that it is the one ideal that is not injured when power backed by violence is deployed on its behalf. Moreover, its pursuit at once unifies the four types of social action into an integrated whole; traditional, affectual, and value-rational beliefs no longer conflict with the instrumental power of the state but in fact support it: "Time and time again, the concept of 'nation' refers us to its relation to political 'power.' And apparently the notion of 'national'—if it is something unified at all—is then a specific type of pathos which links a human group which shares a common language, or religion or common customs, or communal fate to the idea of an already existing or longed-for political form of power organization. And the more 'power' is emphasized the more specific this link is" (WG, p. 244, ES, p. 398). Purely emotional commitment to the nation as a value and as a traditional habituation to common language, religion, or custom continually entails an enhancement of the state's power. Thus when we expose this commitment to the paradoxes of political power in history, we in fact vindicate it instead of discrediting it for generations, as was the case with socialism.

Perhaps most significant, this ideal is not injured if its pursuit violates personal morality or in Weber's words "the salvation of the soul."[28] On the contrary, it is the one value in which the individual who chooses it puts, in the words of Machiavelli, one's city or patria above the salvation of one's soul and submits to "the genius or demon of politics":

Time and again, the papal interdict was placed upon Florence and at the time it meant a far more massive power for men and the salvation of their soul than (to speak with Fichte) the "cool approbation" of the Kantian ethical judgment. The burgher, however, fought the church-state and it was with reference to such situations that Machiavelli in a beautiful passage, if I am not mistaken, of the History of Florence, has one of his heroes praise those citizens who deemed the greatness of their native city [Vaterstadt] higher than the salvation of their souls. If one says "the future of socialism" or "international peace," instead of native city or "fatherland" (which at

27. Mommsen, Max Weber und die deutsche Politik, p. 67.
28. "A nation forgives damage to its interests, but not damage to its honor" (GPS, p. 549; GM, p. 118).

present may not be an unambiguous value to everyone), then you have the problem as it now stands (*GPS*, pp. 557–558; *FMW*, p. 126).[29]

What Weber is suggesting in this passage is that we engage in a practical thought experiment, a thought experiment in which commitment to the nation or political community becomes the paradigm case of a value that can pass the test of responsibility for consequences much as the commitment to socialism becomes the paradigm case of precisely the opposite.[30] To know whether a value can be responsibly pursued given the purposively rational demands of political action, one must try hypothetically to commit the whole political community to it as if it were the one unconditional value for which any sacrifice were justified. One would then have to decide personally if one was willing to accept the injuries to the (inner) ethical world that political means on behalf of that value would entail. Weber is making a wager that we would find the price to our inner sense of ethical integrity worth paying for the enhancement of the political community based on the value of the nation but that we would not find it to be so for the values of socialism or world peace. The basis for this wager is that these ideals, unlike commitment to the nation, are not adapted to a world

29. Interestingly, in *The Protestant Ethic and the Spirit of Capitalism*, he also invokes this passage. However, here he contrasts the "proud worldliness" of Machiavelli's Florentine citizen with the Puritan's obsessive concern with salvation (*PE*, p. 125, *PESC*, p. 107). The concept of vocation with its "impersonal" demand that we methodically transform the world for God's glory is set against the virtue of the citizen who happily puts the civic good above individual salvation. In "Politics as a Vocation," the Florentine citizen represents the demands that vocational politics imposes on our substantive commitments. This difference of usage can be partly accounted for by the sociological narrative of both works. In the aftermath of the Calvinist creation of the worldly calling, the noble commitment to the good of the political community can only be realized within the political calling. But this still leaves us with the figure of the Florentine on both sides of the narrative—against calling and for political commitment to the common good and for calling and the commitment to the common good. Perhaps Weber's earlier usage of the Machiavelli example points to a much more ambiguous relation of the concept of calling or vocation to the ethic of responsibility than appears to be the case in "Politics as a Vocation." The Florentine citizen who puts his city above his own salvation represents a kind of political leader and citizen who combines passionate commitment and political responsibility without necessarily being devoted to the business side of politics. There is in this figure a kind of political actor who approaches the risks of politics with a clear sense of loyalty to others and a fearless sense of adventure beyond conventional morals. This figure is harnessed to the concept of the political calling in the passage from "Politics as a Vocation" to create an impersonal test that only a few actors and few substantive political commitments can pass.

30. In the historical context, Weber was very likely aware of the parallel he was drawing. One need only look at Rosa Luxemburg's attempt to connect the standard of political effectiveness in the socialist movement to an ideal of internationalism to see the persistence of the national metaphor: "The fatherland of all proletarians is the Socialist International and the defense of it must take priority over everything else." Quoted in Nettl, *Rosa Luxemburg*, p. 394.

in which the struggle for power and the conflict among deeply held values is unceasing. By linking the nation as value to the noncontingent fact of power struggle, Weber has raised commitment to the patria into an impartial maxim almost equal to the ethic of responsibility itself.

Interestingly enough, Weber does not mention that the speaker in Machiavelli's example is addressing republican citizens and that it is their full participation in the political life of the city that entails their unconditional military engagement on behalf of the patria. He subtly allows the *Vaterstadt* to become later in the passage *Vaterland,* as if his thought experiment would be the same in both contexts.

This link between the formal ethic of responsibility and the substantive end of nationalism should be only a contingent one. The example of commitment to the nation should be a mere instance of the application of the ethic of responsibility and its sociological content to a historically situated value. However, like the example of the Zimmerwald conference, which is meant to teach a negative lesson about the incommensurability between the costs and benefits of using revolutionary means to attain socialism, the example of the Florentine citizen becomes paradigmatic of the kind of situation where the ethic of responsibility can be vindicated. Both examples drive the reconciliation of the two ethics: namely, that the ethic of conviction and the ethic of responsibility together supplement each other only in a political actor for whom the calling for politics entails the abandonment of any link between responsible political action and collective self-determining freedom through popular political participation.[31] The nation becomes the single overarching value under which individual moral autonomy and the cultivation of the person can be practically realized given the demands of politics.[32] Submission to the nation and its

31. This is not to say that Weber rejected all socialist parties as politically irresponsible. But the criterion for responsibility was the degree to which their demands were reconcilable with the demands of the nation-state. For example, in his essay on "Socialism" he argued that workers "will always become socialist in some sense or other . . . the only question is whether this socialism will be of such kind that it is acceptable from the standpoint of the interests of the state." "Der Sozialismus," *MWG,* vol. 15, p. 633.

32. It is precisely this commitment to the nation that, according to Guenther Roth, prevented Weber from extending his ethic of responsibility to independent socialists such as Kurt Eisner. Eisner who as president of the Bavarian worker-council republic and as one of the prime movers behind the release of the documents revealing German guilt in World War I was seen by Weber as the typical conviction politician lacking in political honor or responsibility for power. For Roth, the nascent Weimar Republic would have had a chance of success only if democratic liberals such as Weber had reconciled themselves with independent socialist such as Eisner—especially on the topic of German war guilt. Only under such a reconciliation would Weber as political actor have lived up to his own ethic of political responsibility for historical consequences by tying the fate of this ethic to the republic itself. Thus for Roth, "it is on this concrete historical level, not on the level of ideational filiation, that we (Winter 1988–1989), can speak of liberal failure." Günther Roth, "Weber's Political

demands becomes a discipline that gives freedom a content. In turn the individual political leader with charismatic gifts sets ends for the nation to fulfill. He, as it were, provides the nation with a calling, with a substantive end beyond the negotiated compromises of routine politics and the formal bureaucratic division of labor that characterizes all social relations. In so doing, he exercises individual moral autonomy and thereby achieves an ideal of personhood of which most members of a state are deemed to be incapable.

Against the backdrop of this vindication of the nation as object of sentiment linked to the commitment to politics as an intrinsic value and profession, we can finally understand Weber's famous reconciliation between his two ethics; for it is precisely by realizing the impossibility of reversing the political expropriation process and democratically reappropriating the means of power—and by the same token by seeking to transcend the grinding business of politics within the constraints of the profession of politics—that we can finally discover those convictions that are reconcilable with an ethic of responsibility for the political consequences of using power to achieve one's goals: in this case commitment to vocational politics under the substantive commitment to the nation.

Apart from whether we find the nation to be our overriding substantive commitment, there is obviously something very compelling about Weber's solution to the translation of moral autonomy and personhood into political ethics, because it preserves a residue of the autonomous self while still subjecting it to responsibility for political consequences influenced by the rational logic(s) of politics. But there is also something very problematic here. It all too neatly shuffles undesired political positions (such as a socialist or a radical democracy) into the catch-all category of *pure* convictions cut off from "political realities," while linking convictions corresponding to desired political positions to an ethic of responsibility.[33] The ideal professional politician with a calling is in this way shielded from criticism, and all positions that question "vocational politics," in particular those claiming to find democratic forms for the exercise of collective

---

Failure," *Telos* pp. 143–145. Although this historical account tracks with the conceptual account given here—Weber indeed often withdrew his political ethic of responsibility from partisan positions he disagreed with, especially those representing a rejection of nationalism and an embrace of radical forms of democratic involvement—Roth overstates his point by seeing Weber's political failure purely as a failure of historical judgment blinded by his nationalism. It is not his nationalism alone that leads to the problems in political judgment but his aristocratic notion of who could take political responsibility for the nation even within democratic forms, a notion deeply rooted in his theoretical account of the agent presupposed by his prudential clarification.

33. This point has been made by David Beetham, *Max Weber and the Theory of Modern Politics* (Oxford: Basil Blackwell, 1985), p. 175.

autonomy, are shown to be self-defeating by a sociological clarification of politics that makes the rather questionable claim to be an objective account of *all* relevant political consequences. The *Berufspolitiker* emerges as the only realistic agent capable of taking responsibility for the "consequences" of translating convictions into politics. He embodies Weber's definition of personal autonomy personhood and protects it against the rationalization of political "organization" into party machines and bureaucracy.

This claim to "realism" is questionable. After all, we have seen in the preceding chapter that the appearance of the vocational politician in the full sense—who combines long-range devotion to a cause with responsibility for consequences and political judgment—is fortuitous to say the least. If either durability or the ability to survive the power struggle endemic to politics is the standard of feasibility under which practical political ideals are to be judged according to an ethic of responsibility, then vocational politics embodied in plebiscitary forms of democracy is just as vulnerable as are direct forms of democracy. Indeed, what is durable in modern politics is precisely the routine forms that for Weber threaten responsible political judgment, the modern state and the bureaucratic party. The question then in judging fundamental political projects under an ethic of responsibility is which models one finds worth nurturing against the tendencies in modern politics that undermine them. Feasibility, a concern for the means and consequences of action, is relative to this choice. Thus Weber's political ethic of responsibility may be convincing, but the political sociology that gives this ethic content may be problematic indeed if taken as a full and impartial account of the possibilities for combining personhood with participation in modern politics.

Conclusion

At the beginning of this chapter we noted that Weber elides the general question of determining the formal political ethics appropriate to both ordinary and vocational political actors with the specific question of the appropriate political ethics for a political actor with a calling for politics. What we have seen is that Weber thinks that an answer to the second question automatically provides an answer to the first question as well, because the agent entering politics can only achieve full personality under the vocational demands of professional politics. Furthermore, only the vocational politician can reconcile conviction with responsibility for the consequences of using power and the moral risks this entails. The avocationary political actors who express their "will" through balloting, applauding, or protesting in a political meeting or for that matter delivering "political" speeches are deemed capable of partisanship, but not of taking responsibility for the paradoxical outcomes that are produced by the logics of political expropriation and its routinization.

What I hope to have shown here is that Weber's answer to the second question regarding the ethics of the vocational politician does not exhaust the first and more general question regarding the political ethics of both vocationary and avocationary actors. We can, after all, agree with Weber that as long as politics involves the deployment of power in an instrumental sense, whatever other kinds of power it also entails, and as long as politics remains a nexus of conflicting values, and finally as long as the multiple logics at work on political action produce practical paradoxes that impose ethical paradoxes, the appropriate ethic of politics is an ethic of strict responsibility for consequences. But it does not follow except tautologically that ordinary citizens are incapable of living up to the demands of such an ethic. Weber himself admits this implicitly in his general account of the ethic of responsibility: If the vocational politician, insofar as she or he is living up to the dual role of professional politician and called leader, must be held to strict accountability for the consequences of using political means, surely someone must do so. Presumably it is Weber's "occasional politicians" who hold the political actor accountable for his or her decisions. If this is true, they must understand a great deal more about the ethic of responsibility than Weber credits them with. It seems that Weber's political ethical argument practically requires that numerous loci for deliberation and participation should be provided; surely the ethic of responsibility can only become fully operative if lay citizens are given the opportunity to acquire the knowledge to apply it properly. This they can do only by practicing political responsibility themselves. (After all, Weber himself maintains that responsibility and judgment in choosing ultimate commitments in light of the foreseeable means of achieving them is something the agent cannot delegate.) Thus the answer to the second question of what ethics are proper to the vocational politician depends on an answer to the first question on "the 'ethos' of politics as a cause" for *all* actors. That answer may still include Weber's two ethics combined in an agent exercising political judgment; however, that agent has to be cultivated through strong democratic participation. Unless numerous loci for democratic political participation can be feasibly realized, it is unclear how we can vindicate an ethic of political responsibility for consequences either as the ethic for all political actors or for the vocational politician alone.

Weberian Political Ethics, Moral Luck, and The Problems of Participatory Democracy

> The idea of a value that lies beyond all luck is an illusion, and political aims cannot continue to draw convictions from it.
>
> —Bernard Williams, *Ethics and the Limits of Philosophy*

Weber views radical democracy in its socialist or communal form as naive, confining, and hopelessly ill-adapted to the complexities of a modern state and society. Above all, he sees it at odds with individual political responsibility for the consequences of power. This chapter attempts to vindicate radical democracy from the Weberian critique. It does this, however, by incorporating Weber's emphasis on the ironic and risk-laden outcomes of political action into the radical democratic argument. This account rests on our critique of Weber's all too restrictive political consequentialism, but also argues for a substantial revision of three of the standard claims of radical democracy in light of Weber's sociological prudence and ethic of political responsibility: The first claim is that participation in politics in common with others is an intrinsically worthy activity. The second is that democratic participation has priority over other intrinsically worthy practices because only as direct democratic participants do we identify with our distinctly human capacity for self-legislation and public judgment. The third claim is that participation in democratic political forms is self-reinforcing and thus solves many of the problems flowing from the unforeseeable consequences of using power. Without abandoning these claims outright, I argue that the autonomy and responsibility for public outcomes afforded by participation goes hand in hand with the intensification of a distinctive aspect of moral conduct that renders the justification of many of our autonomous decisions contingent and fortuitous, namely, *moral luck*. Moral luck refers to the fact that despite our intuitive sense that moral judgments must be applied to actions that we control, that fall under the purview of our autonomy, we regularly judge the conduct of others to be good or bad according to consequences that cannot be predicted with any certainty. Fate and fortune contribute mightily to the justification of our conduct.[1] With luck, of course, comes irony;

---

1. I draw this term from Bernard Williams, "Moral Luck," in *Moral Luck* (Cambridge: Cambridge University Press, 1981). I also have profited greatly from the response to this

and direct democratic politics is intensively subject to the ironies of intention and consequences that come with the exercise of power. Thus if we democratize political power to small communities of participants in production and locality, we will at the same time intensify the political responsibility for both intended and unintended consequences of our public decisions, especially for the public good. This is an inescapable part of the freedom that radical democracy realizes.

This aspect of participant democracy has been neglected by radical democrats and has opened this political practice to recurrent attack by instrumentalist and consequentialist critics since Weber. Such critics argue that strong democracy cannot deal with the fortuitous and ironic consequences of exercising political power. Power struggle is not to be abolished; nor is the reliance of people on methodical domination over the division of labor. They further argue that citizens of radical democratic political associations are neither capable nor willing to take political responsibility for the outcomes of their decisions. Presumably, if I can show that it is possible to insert such participation within rather than beyond the logics of power described by Weber, and further that it is possible to combine radical democracy with an ethic of responsibility for ironic or fortuitous consequences, I will have come some distance to answering the Weberian criticism of radical democracy.

This discussion has two parts. In the first part I revisit some of the critical comments I have made about Weber's notion of political judgment and its application to his account of democracy. I do so in order to draw out two significant tensions in his theory of power and in his account of sociological advice that have until now been implicit in my argument. Each of these tensions will provide an opening for my later argument for radical democratic political responsibility. They do not so much refute Weber as hold him to the partiality that he himself insisted was an inescapable feature of historical and political judgments based on a social science of explanatory understanding.

In the second part of this discussion I combine Weber's argument for a political ethic of responsibility and Rousseau's argument for popular sovereignty. Here I show precisely how a Rousseauist argument for democratic self-legislation inescapably requires a Weberian argument for a political ethic of consequences, an ethic that takes account of the inseparability of politics from moral luck. I maintain this position despite Weber's resolute rejection of direct democracy and Rousseau's rather explicit attempts to separate politics from moral luck for the sake of popular

---

essay by Thomas Nagel also called "Moral Luck," in *Mortal Questions* (Cambridge: Cambridge University Press, 1979).

sovereignty. I then show how recent arguments for radical democracy
have accepted Rousseau's arguments without acknowledging his strategies
for warding off the influence of fortuitous consequences on political decisions. By avoiding Rousseau's strategies, I maintain these recent democratic arguments need a political ethic of responsibility for ironic
consequences even more than did Rousseau; for in these theories there
are structural as well as conceptual reasons for adopting such an ethic
that have a great deal to with the attempt to insert radical democracy
into the very economic and political conditions so acutely analyzed by
Weber. I finally end by suggesting a concept of direct participant democracy that takes moral luck and political irony into account—one, that is,
that accepts Weber's ethic of political responsibility without subscribing
to his conclusions about the desirability or possibility of direct democratic
forms of politics.

The Critique of Weber Revisited

At the end of the preceding chapter, I argued that Weber's formal ethic
of responsibility for the consequences of deploying distinctively political
means on behalf of self-chosen ends is one that no self-reflecting political
actor could ignore. After all, it describes rather accurately the responsibility we do incur when we seek to use power to realize our political commitments. However, Weber's assumption that only an individual political
actor with a calling can live up to the demands of this ethic is most
problematic. Even when we apply the ethic of responsibility to a vocational political actor we assume a citizenry capable of holding that actor
accountable. If this is so, the only solution to a public's lack of responsibility for the consequences of public decisions is to make available the opportunity to develop such responsibility. Here extended participation both
within communities and the process of production are strong candidates
for providing such political education.

The Sociological Grounds for
Limiting Political Responsibility

Weber counters this claim by appealing to a series of political judgments derived from his sociological reconstruction of politics. Within a
modern bureaucratic state with a parliament and political parties, the
public always consists of a "psychologically proletarianized" mass who
can do nothing but be passive followers of bureaucratic parties and plebiscitary leaders. Thus unless avenues for talented individuals with a vocational commitment to politics are opened within professional politics

itself, there will be no agent able or willing to take political responsibility. But this begs the question. Why are the mass of citizens of a modern state unable to take political responsibility? For Weber to be right, he would have to show that in a nonatomized setting the citizens of a political order would also be unable to take political responsibility. He would have to show why a public that participates directly under a common will cannot take responsibility for the effects of its decisions, even those with ironic outcomes.

Weber tries to show just that by arguing that mass politics can only be a politics of resentment and reactiveness. According to him, all desires for social and political self-determining freedom on the part of the masses are mere expressions of repressed rage and the desire for revenge, the very definition of resentment. Only an individual with the self-discipline of a vocation can avoid such reactiveness and take responsible political action. Once again, though, this argument fails to ask why mass politics has become a politics of resentment, if this is indeed an accurate description of modern politics. Under the rationalized business of politics, the masses can only "react" when they are discontented as a result of mistaken policies of leader or the bureaucratic dispossession from the means of power. If the great mass of members of a modern state are allowed to give periodic acclamation to leaders of party machines while experiencing in their work life the dispossession from the material means of production and administration, it is hardly surprising that mass politics would be a politics of repressed rage and displaced blame. There are two solutions to this dilemma, only one of which Weber sees as feasible. One can seek to resist the dispossession from the means of power wrought by bureaucratic *Herrschaft* that makes resentment the only possible response to failed politics. But this entails organizing a collective agent capable of using power to struggle for the introduction of self-determining institutions for direct democratic participation. Through the introduction of such institutions, indeed even through the struggle for them, reactive politics can be transformed into active will. But Weber does not accept a distinction between collective self-determination and resentment, so he must opt for an alternative solution, namely, to further plebiscitary leadership democracy as a means of channeling mass resentment toward goals beneficial to the nation at large. In this model charismatic leaders direct mass resentment against opponents, bureaucracy, and even the party apparatus itself in order to generate the support necessary to impose their ends on the state.[2] It is the leading politician who transforms resentment into the

2. This point has been made by Robert Eden, *Political Leadership and Nihilism* (Tampa: University of South Florida Press, 1983), pp. 196–197.

affirmative pursuit of public goals and renders judgments on the policies for the polity at large.

The practical problem with this solution is that it assumes that resentment can be controlled and will not turn on plebiscitary democracy itself, on its leaders and its institutions, when they fail to deliver the material and psychic rewards that are promised. Logically the problem is that it tautologically defines all attempts of the masses to break with repressed rage and reactiveness and to strive for institutions of collective self-determination as expressions of resentment. Thus it withdraws the ethic of responsibility from precisely those attempts to achieve political forms that seek to overcome the conditions that breed resentment politics. The ethic of responsibility, then, in the name of preserving "politics" and the responsible pursuit of political ends requires the containment of the very collective initiatives that might extend the meaning of responsible politics. We are once again back at our original argument.

But Weber argues that we have no other alternative but to reject of attempts to find a locus for self-determining participation within modern mass politics, because viewed from the vantage point of power, both democratic forms of socialism and radical democracy are self-defeating projects. All attempts to introduce self-determining institutions into either economy or state lead to increased bureaucratic domination or short-lived democratic forms that will not survive the power struggle endemic to politics. Although direct democracy can exist on occasion there is no way it can carry on a successful power struggle against bureaucratic parties or bureaucratic states; and even if it were to hold its own in such a struggle it could not be routinized into an everyday form of *Herrschaft* either in the modern state or in the modern firm. This is the heart of Weber's sociological argument for the impossibility of direct forms of democracy. It cannot and should not be dismissed lightly.

Feasibility and Power

At its core, this argument about feasibility does not rest on the conditions necessary for modern politics alone but, rather, on Weber's account of the relation between power *(Macht)* and domination *(Herrschaft)*. Weber's ideal-typical construction of the modern business of politics and its feasible forms—the bureaucratic state and party and the modern vocational politician—merely manifests, perhaps intensifies, a more basic logic inherent in power and domination itself. Let us recall that Weber defines power as "the probability that one actor within a social relationship will be in a position to carry out his own will despite resistance regardless of the basis on which this probability rests" (*WG*, pp. 28–29, 542; 531; *ES*, pp. 53, 942, 926). Domination becomes a kind of power characterized by the fact that a command will be accepted without resistance, and legitimate domination is the likelihood that a command will be accepted as valid without resistance (WG, pp. 548–549; ES, pp. 952–954). Weber claims that power does not need to be exercised as legitimate domination but may arise from strategic position as, for example, an economic monopoly over a portion of the market. But to gain continuity and reliability of command, Weber argues, legitimate forms of domination are necessary. Legitimacy ensures that a command will be carried out by those to whom it is given (WG, pp. 122–124; ES, pp. 212–216).

Once power is defined this way, a curious dynamic follows. All successful attempts to exercise power in the broad sense of using available means to impose one's will over resistance either lead to positionally exercised domination, which must be imposed again and again, or give way to forms of "domination" whereby one's will is obeyed without resistance because the command is taken as valid according to custom, formal rules, or purely personal qualities. As such power tends to run out into "legitimate" forms of domination and in turn tends to be recovered by mobilizing some form of legitimate domination against the routine forms in which power has previously dissipated.

When Weber applies this logic of power and domination to direct democracy, it appears as an extremely weak and unstable *Herrschaftsform;* it is a form of domination or rule that has difficulty maintaining itself as a form through which power is exercised. Direct democracy assumes that all major public decisions are made in assemblies of equally qualified participants. But for Weber the very exercise of power by the democratic assembly in deliberating, deciding, and giving commands to an administration signals its decay as well. For unless the citizens themselves carry out the commands of the assembly, their methodical implementation will be given to an administrator who in turn can claim independent legitimate acceptance of his or her commands. When successful, the power to impose commands over resistance becomes dependent on an independent specialized body that can claim obedience on the basis of rules whose validity is separate from the assembly itself. The assembly still retains power, but increasingly the administration can exercise commands independently of it. This makes the assembly vulnerable to factions that increase their power to impose their will by organizing themselves on the same lines as the administration, thus turning the assembly into a power struggle among parties. Rather than restraining routine domination, the direct democratic exercise of power disappears altogether (WG, pp. 169–171, 545–548; ES, pp. 289–292, 948–952; WG, p. 548; ES, p. 951). The bureaucratic organization of legitimate domination in administration and parties merely exacerbates an internal dynamic in the logic of power and legitimate domination itself.

Let us now extrapolate this dynamic of power and domination to a simple hypothetical case of the exercise of democratic power without a strictly institutional form. Assume that a mass movement occupies government buildings through mass demonstrations and by dint of numbers forces upon the state a more equal distribution of welfare benefits. Here power is being exercised in Weber's sense of imposing one's will over resistance, but the problem arises once success has been attained. This democratic movement is now faced with three ways of securing its gains. It must carry this demand out itself, in which case it must be able to empower itself to carry out its own commands, that is, the participants must become administrators. Or it must rely on the administration of the state to carry out the program because only the state administration can count on its commands being accepted as legitimate and valid. Or if it cannot rely on the state administration to exercise legitimate domination on its behalf or in turn does not accept the state's commands as valid, it must continually exercise power to see to it that in fact the command is carried out as envisioned. In this last sense, democratic sovereignty must be united with the practice of exerting constant power against the state as legitimate domination.[3]

In his analysis of the failures of direct democratic forms of politics to take on a durable form, Weber invokes the first and second problem. Here Weber's feasibility arguments are indeed telling for any democrat. Over the long run it would indeed be difficult for participants to be both sovereign exercisers of power and routine implementers of policy—quite apart from the added question of specialization. Furthermore, a reliance on routine legitimate domination continually erodes the scope of power belonging to a democratic assembly. Yet, such dependence is inescapable if a democratic assembly wants its will imposed methodically, with continuity and reliability. But Weber almost completely neglects the third response to the dynamic of power and domination. This third response entails that the direct democratic forms of participation not merely exercise power routinely over the legitimate forms of domination that carry out its commands, but like the protest movement, also exercise a continuous resistance and pressure on the administrative body. By so doing the directly democratic bodies must have an institutional legitimacy, but like a protest movement they must be in constant conflict with the state, seeking to exercise their power over the resistance of the state to carrying out their

3. This notion of a creative tension between full-time rulers and democratic political association bears some resemblance to that proposed by Machiavelli in *The Discourses on Livy.* See especially Book 1, chap. 4.

commands as originally envisioned. This possibility for democracy is compatible with Weber's logic of power and domination, but it does not entail the complete extinction of the power exercised by democratic assemblies. It does, however, assume a tension between forms of direct participation as legitimate forms of democratic will and these same forms as pressing their power against the power of parties, state, and bureaucracy, but it makes no assumption that this tension can always be maintained either.

Weber's argument that direct democracy will only prove effective if it is able to stabilize into a routine functional form of *Herrschaft* is to frame the whole problem all too restrictively, for it presupposes that participatory forms of politics must become exclusively routine forms of legitimate domination. But direct democracy need not, like bureaucracy, be frozen into a routine model of rule. Indeed, as we have just seen it cannot maintain itself if forced to meet up to this standard alone, because it is not exclusively a "form of domination" *(Herrschaftsform)* or even of administration. Rather, it falls among those models of political action that are not realized once and for all but that must be constantly fought for. Direct democracy is a means through which self-determining freedom is constantly fought for in resistance to both the parties and their leaders and the bureaucracies of state and economy. It is the possibility that direct democracy may *require* forms of domination but not *be* a "form of domination" *(Herrschaftsform)* and that democratic self-rule may the "consequence," perhaps more accurately the by-product, of continuous resistance to forms of rational-legal domination that Weber's sociology of *Herrschaft* is unable to understand.

When applied to politics as an impartial logic, Weber's sociology of legitimate *Herrschaft* defines the conditions of political success in such a way that even deviations from the typology of charisma, bureaucratic administration, and traditional domination must be explained in its terms. All conditions of success or failure in politics are defined either by the degree to which they further charismatic leadership within the modern *Betrieb* of politics or by the degree to which they further rational-legal domination. Traditional domination becomes the middle term of this account of consequences, because it consists of routine personal relationships of authority based on custom while allowing, as it were, the arbitrary decision of the ruler to hand out customary emoluments, prebends, or sinecures. Thus when deployed to analyze the emergence of the modern business of politics, traditional domination is used to measure the degree to which patronage or personal dependency prevent formal legal office or the modern party machine from emerging.

This means that all rival standards of success or "effectiveness" are screened out.[4] Thus, in our oft-mentioned example, the German worker's councils according to Weber were successful because of their reliance on their expropriation of military force, the charisma of their leaders, and their dependence on the surviving state bureaucracy (*WG*, p. 155; *ES*, p. 265). Let us grant Weber this point. But we must also add that this practical criticism is not as devastating as it may seem, especially in the historical context to which it refers. For despite the tendency of liberals such as Weber, parliamentary socialists, and revolutionary socialists to pose the problem of the new order in Germany as an irreconcilable choice between a parliamentary or a worker-council republic, the majority of members of the councils understood the institution to be an intermediate form of participation subsisting side by side with parliament and parties. The issue for them was not their reliance on the state or socialist party, but whether they should seek to be an integral part of a new republic supplementing the system of representation or should pursue their own interests in tension with both parties and the state—our second and third response to the dynamic of power and domination. It was precisely the tendency of parliaments to represent sectional interests and do their business behind the scenes, as Weber feared, that prompted both theorists and members of the work councils to argue for this form of participation. Thus they embodied freedom in a form of mass participation whose criteria of political success could not be "understood" merely under the purposively rational demands of domination. They realized, if only momentarily, collective self-determining freedom as a "consequence" of one form of the struggle for power. They combined self-rule with the purposive reason of power in the midst of a struggle with parliamentary institutions and the state

---

4. This also applies to his argument for discipline within the division of labor. Indeed, along with his account of power struggle, his concept of the irreversibility of the political expropriation process rests on an account of the hierarchical division of labor. Weber argues that a hierarchical and disciplinary organization of the division of labor is the only way for us to apply modern techniques and to elicit formally rational efficiency in performing the various social tasks on which we have become so dependent, be they production of goods, state administration, knowledge production, or the application of force. Yet Weber himself argues that the division of labor is a power relation in which the very definition of efficiency is relentlessly fought over. What determines standards of efficiency is itself rooted in particular social relations. Indeed, as seen, the hierarchical control over the division of labor is for Weber largely driven by the need of economic or political organizations to prevail in a power struggle with other forms. This means that there is no objective standard of efficiency that corresponds to a particular formal division of tasks, but several standards over which those who perform the tasks and those who impose them are in constant conflict. These standards correspond to different conceptions of property, need, and relevant social goals. What is at stake then in such conflicts is precisely how much and what kind of control is necessary to perform a social task. This critique is developed in Dietrich Reuschemeyer, *Power and the Division of Labor* (Stanford: Stanford University Press, 1986), pp. 36–53.

administration.[5] As seen, Weber almost admits this point but then insists that such expropriation of power cannot be transferred to the means of production: "[In the German revolution of 1918] the leaders ... have attained control over the political staff and the apparatus of material goods and they deduce their legitimacy—no matter with what right from the will of the governed. Whether the leaders, on the basis of this *at least apparent success,* can rightfully entertain the hope of also carrying through the expropriation within the capitalist enterprises is a different question" (*GPS,* p. 511; *FMW,* p. 82; my emphasis). His typology simply cannot register effects of politics that do not strengthen charisma, bureaucracy, or traditional domination or that are not part of the process of expropriation of political power from its personal bearers.

The Problematic Claim to Impartiality
and the Problem of Circularity

This example, points to the most fundamental problem in Weber's unification of sociology with political ethics mentioned in the preceding chapter: namely, Weber bases his political-ethical argument for the meaning of responsible politics on the assumption that his political sociology can provide an *impartial* assessment of the consequences of political action in the modern state. In light of his account of economics, this is ironic indeed. As we saw, in his account of economics and his criticism of the claim of marginal utility theory to find impartial deductive laws of individual behavior, Weber demonstrated that the modern capitalist market is driven by a number of *contingent* logics—formally rational capital accounting, power struggle for market position, and the disciplined division of labor—that do not congeal into one law of "economizing." The precise relation among these logics, Weber demonstrated, is not reducible to any one deductive scheme. Rather, the determination of the precise relation among them depends on judgment or what Weber at times calls "historical imputation." Weber's own "judgment" as to the relation of these terms was that under modern capitalism firms are constantly striving to override the equimariginal principle and usually succeed in doing so. In any case, the outcome of this struggle is not measurable by the theory of price or the law of utility.

5. For a view that these institutions were not a mere vanguard with a disciplined party apparatus that legitimated itself by an appeal to popular sovereignty as Weber would claim, see Hans Manfred Bock, *Geschichte des "linken Radikalismus"* (Frankfurt: Suhrkamp, 1976), pp. 74–164; Ulrich Kluge, *Die Deutsche Revolution, 1918–1919* (Frankfurt: Suhrkamp, 1985), pp. 54–138; and Dieter Schneider and Rudolf Kuda, *Arbeiterräte in der Novemberrevolution* (Frankfurt: Suhrkamp, 1973).

Now one would have expected that this account of economics would have been the model for his account of politics as well. Surely, given the variety of ends pursued using political means and the variety of ways in which one can exercise political power, the contingent logics at work on modern politics would be even greater than in economics. But curiously Weber draws this conclusion only to preempt it by invoking impartial laws of political action derived from his sociology of domination. To be sure, in his account of the development of modern politics into a business in "Politics as a Vocation" or in his criticism of the autonomous status of bureaucracy as a political force or in his account of classes, status groups, and parties in *Economy and Society*, and "Parliament and Democracy in a Reconstructed Germany" Weber provides an analysis of politics as the contingent convergence of multiple logics of methodical activity along the lines of his account of modern economic order. Here traditional forms of domination seem ironically to contain modern forms of political domination that are released only through the unique convergence of several instrumental logics: the political expropriation of the private bearers of power, the democratization of political parties, and the frail recovery of the classical demagogue within the vocational politician. However, when assessing political responsibility, Weber arrests this emphasis on the contingent and multiple instrumental logics at work in politics by invoking his typology of domination as a continuous and cyclical logic underlying all political action. Indeed, Weber claims that by applying both his typology of social action and his typology of legitimacy to the understanding of politics, he has provided an impartial—indeed scientific—explanation of the necessary means and unavoidable consequences of engaging in political action in the modern state. From this "scientific" reconstruction of the coordinates of politics he derives the conditions for the application of his ethics of responsibility and conviction and their ultimate reconciliation.

The problem here is that his typology of legitimate forms of domination and his account of the rationalization of modern politics (to say nothing of his general typology of social action) are constructed from the vantage point of the very ethic that they are meant to instantiate. The link here is Weber's concept of the person. The person who combines value choice with responsibility for means and outcomes is precisely vindicated as the only feasible and appropriate response to the demands of routine politics. But the sociology from which this judgment is derived assumes this same notion of the person as the a priori condition of its construction.

Is this a vicious or a hermeneutic circle? Let us assume that Weber has provided a hermeneutic of political action. Then, the formal ethic of politics will deepen our understanding of the relevant attributes that constitute the ideal-typical constructs of the political sociology, and the political sociology will reveal the various implications of applying the formal political ethic. But the problem is that Weber uses his political concepts and *Herrschaft* sociology as a neutral construct of the "facts" of politics, a construct that provides us with the possibility of foreseeing the means, ends, and subsidiary consequences of political action above and beyond this circle. The more he presses his argument for the impartiality of his typology of domination and the tendential movement of charisma to bureaucracy, the closer Weber moves toward a purely circular relation between his political ethic and the sociology that is meant to give it content.[6]

What Weber has demonstrated against himself is that his sociological clarification of political ethics is not scientific and impartial but prudential and situation-bound. He supports such a reading in his own methodological writings, when he argues that there are no exhaustive causal explanations for we discern relevant causes from our own practical value standpoint. If he is correct about this, then, opposing positions will select different relevant causes in determining means, ends, and subsidiary consequences.

Thus, the radical democrat and democratic socialist may have to take into account certain inescapable means and conditions of politics—here Weber is on strong ground indeed—and yet be responsible for a different stream of action and set of consequences under the ethic of responsibility than is the vocational politician devoted to the nation. Weber's *Herrschaftssoziologie* is not a neutral construct that can serve as an arbiter between the contending political convictions striving to realize themselves in a struggle for power. Rather, it is one very powerful construct that assumes from the outset that political action and domination are inseparable and that only the individual can take responsibility for the consequences of realizing fundamental ends in light of this fact. But if from a different perspective collective political freedom can also be an "effect"

6. Wolfgang Mommsen acutely points out that Weber altered the role of his typology of the three pure types of legitimate domination between 1913 and 1920. Initially it was presented as a historical construction meant to illuminate the distinctive features of modernity. In 1916–17 it was still seen as directional, but it was emphasized that the various types could appear in a variety of historical settings in different periods. Subsequently the typology, especially charisma, was viewed as a universal set of types. See Wolfgang Mommsen, "Personal Conduct and Societal Change," in *Max Weber, Rationality, and Modernity*, ed. Sam Whimster, and Scott Lash (London: Allen Unwin, 1987), p. 46. Ironically the universal claim for the typology did not necessarily entail that it be a basis for objective tendential laws any more than the historical application entailed the contingent convergence of these types. On the contrary, Weber used these types at times to signal a universal historical trend, at other times a universal logic of action, and still at other times a contingent convergence of certain unique logics of domination, for example, charisma and bureaucracy in the modern party.

of political action, albeit one that can never be successful should it routinize into a *Herrschaftsform*, then Weber's judgments on the irresponsibility of direct democracy can be called into question. It is this simple point that could break the sociological fate that ties us to vocational politicians as the only agents in modern politics capable of achieving self-determining freedom and of "taking responsibility for history."

Therefore, his critique of direct democracy as an irresponsible goal of politics will be as much a function of the perspective *(Gesichtspunkt)* from which he constructs his ideal-typical account of power and domination in modern politics (i.e., his ideal of personhood), as it is of the failures of direct democracy to prove its effectiveness according to a political ethic of responsibility.

By the same token, however, if the argument for direct public participation in political life is to have any force, it will have to take into account Weber's perspective on the ironic relation between pursuing our highest ends in politics and their implementation through forms of domination. It will have to show that this paradox of political action is, indeed, just one perspective and that from a different perspective, one of the ironic outcomes of political action can be the realization of public freedom as well as domination.

This, however, requires a prudence of modern politics that seeks the instrumental logics deflecting away from the logic of legitimate domination, a prudence that although not denying the validity of his logic of legitimate domination, remains aware of the partiality of the Weberian claim to have objectively shown us the relevant means, ends, and consequences of political action on the terrain of the modern organization of politics. With a few notable exceptions, later social and political theorists who have sought to break out of Weber's rational clarification of modern politics have been hesitant to exploit this major fissure that runs right through the center of his theory. Rather than challenge his claims to have "objectively" and impartiality mapped out the "foreseeable consequences" of political action within modern politics, they cede Weber this point and choose instead to expand the noninstrumental sphere of social action.[7] The upshot of this argumentative strategy is to come up with a "public" foundation for political and social agreement while neglecting to develop the concept of political prudence or foresight that will inform and sustain a more thorough democratic politics. If we are to conceive of a form of democratic politics that does not psychically proletarianize the vast majority of citizens, yet still incorporates what is valid in Weber's

7. Jürgen Habermas, *Theory of Communicative Action*, vol. 1, trans. Thomas McCarthy (Boston: Beacon Press, 1981), pp. 1–141; Charles Taylor, *Hegel* (Cambridge: Cambridge University Press, 1975), pp. 540–542.

political ethics and his political sociology, it is necessary to provide an account of a democratic political prudence that maps out the consequences that "responsible" democratic actors have to take into account. One starting point is Weber's ethic of political responsibility.

Despite the previous criticism of the partiality of Weber's sociologically informed prudence, Weber is right that political action is uniquely subject to a consequentialist ethic of political responsibility and that our acceptance of this claim will affect our concept of personal and collective autonomy in significant ways. We should recall that along with his emphasis on the responsibility of all political actors for the "foreseeable" paradoxes of using power to attain their ends, Weber also insists that politics is inseparable from moral risk: "No ethics in the world can dodge the fact that in numerous instances the attainment of "good" ends is bound to the fact that one must be willing to pay the price of using morally dubious means or at least dangerous ones—and facing the possibility or even probability of evil subsidiary consequences (*GPS*, p. 552; *FMW*, p. 121). In keeping with his rejection of both utilitarianism and pure Kantianism, Weber also rejects any notion that there is some impartial ethic that can provide a standard to weigh the worth of the ultimate goal against the by-products of using power, including force and domination, to achieve the goal. Despite the absence of any such ethic, we are still, Weber argues, responsible for the self we become under the influence of the these practical and moral paradoxes of politics (*GPS*, p. 557; *FMW*, p. 125; *GPS*, pp. 55–57). What Weber is pointing to in his ethic of political responsibility, as noted in Chapter 5, is that political action is uniquely subject to "moral luck." At this point it would be appropriate to go a bit deeper into the meaning of moral luck and its relation to politics.

Moral Luck and Political Action

Moral luck is the notion that a strong concept of moral autonomy cannot immunize us from the role personal and external contingencies play in justifying or discrediting our conduct. It thus includes in our assessment of an action the contribution of fate or chance to its outcome. To be sure, our concepts of autonomy, both personal and collective, depend on an intuition that we have a capacity to will actions for ourselves by means of our own reason and that this capacity is not an incidental feature of our agency. Indeed, it is an essential feature of our concept of human dignity and worth. But without denying this, the concept of moral luck points to the radical incompleteness of such conceptions. It points to the fact that if we apply moral assessment only to those actions or features of an action which are under our control, we will lose most of the moral assessments we commonly make, because most of them are applied to *what we do*, not merely to what is under our control.[8] Therefore, in addition to those features of our conduct that directly flow from our will, we must include those features that we do not control but that contribute to the success or failure of our actions: the situation in which we act, our attributes of character, prior influences on our behavior, and above all the unintended consequences of our actions.

Moral luck therefore compels us to reinterpret the meaning of personal identity and responsibility. A full concept of free agency demands that we take responsibility for the unintentional aspects of our actions—even the aspects that we foreseeably cannot intend.[9] Detachment from these features entails a loss of identity, not its preservation, because it leaves us with a disembodied will detached from the world in which we act and take responsibility. Yet, our reliance on the world to gain identity as agents is paradoxical. For our identification with the unintentional causes we have contributed to, or the feelings and capacities that are beyond the control of our will, or the circumstances in which we act but do not create, threatens to dissolve the self into events beyond its control. Thus moral luck means that we will have to take responsibility for a self we have brought about through our actions, yet one we have difficulties identifying with: the dilemma is that we must incur the risk of identifying the fortuitous outcomes of our actions as our own or face detachment from the world.

This dilemma has a crucial implication for the way in which we justify our actions. For whatever our practical reason dictates we ought do, the justification of our actions is retrospective. It depends on antecedent circumstances outside the control of our will: the outcome, the qualities of character we discover we have, the situation that defines our role and influences the consequences of what we did.[10] For politics this means that our initial prospective justifications for political action in terms of the projects we are trying to achieve will prove inadequate: despite strong reasons for undertaking a political project, justification will be retrospective. We find out whether we have vindicated our political intentions or projects only after the relevant consequences have occurred. Only then can we say that our initial reasons for deploying power in a certain way with a cost to other values is correct and that our project is what we claimed it was, say, the realization of equality, the overcoming of domination, the concrete realization of the common good.

If our justifications for political action tend to be retrospective descrip-

---

8. Nagel, "Moral Luck," p. 26.
9. Williams, "Moral Luck," p. 29.
10. Nagel, "Moral Luck," p. 33–35.

tions, then politics imposes a far more demanding concept of responsibility for the self than a theory of will-centered autonomy. For as political actors we incur praise and blame for a self that events beyond our control impose upon us. Power unleashes effects that we often cannot foresee. In politics we cannot know all the causes at work on the political means we deploy to reach our goals. We cannot take into account the reaction of all other political actors to our policy. Most important, power affects and alters the very context in which our political actions are interpreted, often lending our actions a meaning quite different from the one that motivated them in the first place. The consequences of deploying the means of power define what we actually did and who we are for others. Political action imposes on us a self we cannot often identify with; nevertheless, we are responsible for that self.

This problem of responsibility for self has particularly dogged theories of direct democratic participation, because the claim to equalize power through participation has always rested on the communitarian claim that only by making decisions in common do we identify with the part of our self that is essentially human or essentially self-legislating. This has also meant putting democratic participation beyond luck. The emblematic theorist of this move is Rousseau, to whom participatory theorists still turn for guidance.

Jean-Jacques Rousseau:
Radical Republicanism beyond Luck

Rousseau's justification of a radical democratic sovereign depends on seducing calculating self-interested individuals in liberal society into a bargain, one in which they will lose their individual interest by submitting themselves to a general will that they create and in which they become voting members. Through the creation of a political association based on a general will, Rousseau argues, we come to recover our human essence as beings capable of legislating for ourselves and taking moral responsibility for our conduct. From this new vantage point we come to see the instrumental calculating self that made the original bargain as having a thoroughly misconceived concept of its interest. For our interest now lies in achieving moral freedom under a general will.

But why can the general will realize our essence in a way that a contract merely guaranteeing our right to maximize our utility does not? The reason for this, according to Rousseau, is that the structure of the general will as the common will of a voting assembly enables each individual member simultaneously to legislate moral laws to himself or herself as she or he is legislating to all members. This is possible because under the political body created by this contract, the political sovereign is related to the state as an active moral will is related to the passive body, that is, it gives it general commands. By the same token the citizens participating in the sovereign are identical with the subjects who submit to the laws of the state.[11]They too gain an identity between their moral will that commands and the body that obeys. But this identity between individual moral will and body can only be maintained if the citizen remains identical with the subject, and this in turn depends on an identity between sovereign and the state. Should the legislative sovereign—the general will—be separated from the subjects who obey the laws, moral freedom, or "autonomy," the very purpose of this republic, will be destroyed: "The essence of the political body lies in the union of freedom and obedience so that the words 'subject' and 'sovereign' are identical correlatives, the meaning of which is brought together in the single word 'citizen.'"[12]

It is therefore the business of the members of the sovereign to pass laws that at once express and maintain moral autonomy, that is, maintain the identity between citizen and sovereign. This is accomplished only if the citizens are steadily at work asking what the general will (or the common good) demands, debating proposed answers to this question, expressing these answers in laws, and voting to accept or reject these laws on the basis of a majority vote (p. 147). Rousseau points out that as a practical matter the size of the majority required for any law can vary according to the gravity of the decision on the one hand, and the need for a quick decision on the other (p. 154). What is crucial in public deliberation is to pose the question correctly. If the question for debate asks merely what the majority prefers, that is, whether the majority approves the law or rejects it, then public decision is reduced to the aggregated private interest of citizens and the decision taken is not an expression of moral autonomy. Only if the debate consists of an interrogation into which law corresponds to the general will, into whether this proposal is "advantageous to the state," will the decision taken be an expression of moral autonomy, and hence the right one (pp. 154, 151).

Rousseau thinks that such a dialogical process of deliberation, of questioning the meaning of the general will in public, has the consequence of leading to laws beneficial to the state as a whole. However, he regards this as a by-product of the internal goods that are coextensive with civic participation. The central good of participation does not consist in the fact that beneficial laws result from it—after all, finding laws beneficial

11. Jean-Jacques Rousseau, *The Social Contract,* trans. Maurice Cranston (Harmondsworth: Penguin, 1968), pp. 61–62.
12. Ibid., p. 138. Rousseau's point here is that as long as we remain citizens we avoid submission to events within and outside of us beyond our control.

to each individual in a state might be accomplished equally well by a technically adept aristocracy or monarch—but, rather, that the citizens themselves legislate general laws for the whole community. In this way citizens become not just autonomous, that is, self-legislating, but moral and not just moral, but morally responsible. They develop duties to one another freely incurred; they regulate their desires by their reason; they develop a sense of egalitarian justice over inegalitarian private interest; above all they develop a principle of right for all public matters (pp. 64–65). Once again, for Rousseau, the good that accrues to citizens through participation in the general will is internal and transformative, not private and consequentialist.[13] The "utility" of this concept of political right consists in the education of citizens to identify the act of legislating the general will with the regulation of their own individual conduct according to a moral will.

Indeed, according to Rousseau's conception of the general will, we are protected from all significant ironies and paradoxes of political action that expose the justifications of our pubic decisions under an impartial common will to moral risk. Public decisions under the general will should not rely for their ultimate justification on the luck of who we are, of prior influences, of unforeseen consequences, of local circumstances. If in our deliberation as citizens we unwaveringly ask the question, What will lead to the common good?, rather than, What policy leads to my net utility as an individual, we will be immunized from moral luck. Our responsibility is to find generalizable laws and will them for the whole community; but this responsibility does not extend to the effects of implementing the law. On the contrary, in deliberating as citizens we commit ourselves only to concern ourselves with finding public goods and remaining blind, as it were, to the particular consequences or technical means employed in putting this general policy into practice.

Yet, Rousseau is acutely aware that the preservation of moral autonomy under the general will, both as a foundation for right and as the basis for utility, is extremely fragile. Therefore he adopts a number of strategies to strengthen the popular sovereign against intrusion by the paradoxical consequences of fortune and fate. I discuss two of them briefly. The first strategy Rousseau adopts is to distinguish the general will from the will of all. The general will is always a simple statement about what counts as the public good at this moment. It is never mistaken, he insists, if we assume that in every public discussion of the sovereign about the general will, there is an answer that corresponds to the public

13. Carole Pateman, *The Problem of Political Obligation* (Berkeley: University of California Press, 1985), pp. 154, 156.

good but that we as citizens do not always discern it.[14] It cannot be undermined by the consequences of imposing the general laws that express it because it is a logical attribute, not a by-product of our autonomy. The will of all, by contrast, is the aggregation of all the individual preferences of the members of a polity. As has been shown repeatedly, first by Rousseau's own contemporaries and more recently by Kenneth Arrow, the aggregation of individual preference orderings does not translate into a social preference ordering that all individuals would accept as theirs.[15] Numerous unintended paradoxes ensue from this, perhaps the most important being that pure majority voting based on the private interest of each voter fails to produce a public interest. In light of this dilemma Rousseau insists that if we rely on the will of all, agreement on the public good will consist only of what is left over when all the individual preferences have canceled one another out: It will consist of those matters for which no one has a private preference. All unintended fortuitous outcomes of public decisions, especially those in which our individual interest fails to be registered, inhere for Rousseau in majority decisions expressing the will of all. These paradoxes are overcome as soon as we subscribe to the general will.

A second strategy focuses on the implementation of the general will. Here, Rousseau separates the general will of the sovereign from the government. The government is responsible for translating the general laws of the sovereign into a particular will that takes into account the local circumstances, the particular interest affected, and the problems of effectively applying the law to all citizens equally (p. 103). The sovereign assembly must elect the magistrates of the government and exercise sufficient power over it to prevent it from becoming detached from the general will and aiming purely at the satisfaction of private interests. This it can do by assembling frequently and if need be by sacrificing the government and constituting a new one (p. 106). However, governments have a tendency to develop a "corporate will" of their own in the very process of effectively adapting general laws to particular circumstances. If this will separates from the sovereign, citizens no longer exercise autonomy: The body is no longer subject to the will; the subject of the laws is no longer identical to the citizen that makes them; and the members of the political association begin "to live outside of themselves."[16] If, however, the supremacy of the popular sovereign over the government can be maintained,

14. Rousseau, *The Social Contract*, pp. 72, 150–151.
15. Kenneth Arrow, *Social Choice and Individual Values*, 2d ed. (New Haven: Yale University Press, 1963).
16. Jean-Jacques Rousseau, *The First and Second Discourses*, trans. Roger Masters and Judith Masters (New York: St. Martin's Press, 1964), p. 179.

the government can protect the public deliberations of the general will from the intrusion of private interests with its numerous attendant paradoxes. It also protects the popular sovereign from the uncontrollable and fortuitous effects of translating laws into practice. Above all, its magistrates can be held responsible for all harmful effects, both preventable and unpreventable, of translating the general will into a particular will. In other words, government can be made responsible for moral luck, for the paradoxes of deploying power, leaving the general will a pure expression of public good. Thus, the people, the morally autonomous citizens of the state, become responsible only for the decisions that they control. Despite their freedom to deliberate on and choose general laws, fortune plays no role in the justification of their public decisions. The members maintain the continuity of communal self against the threats of private interest and the contingencies of exercising effective political power.

It would seem, then, that the citizens of Rousseau's popular sovereign do not need Weber's political ethic of consequences, because they never have to suffer the problem of "dirty hands." Such an ethic would most likely only be needed by the elected magistrates of the government. However, this neat separation between citizen and magistrate is not as unproblematic as Rousseau makes it appear. Under this arrangement, the citizens of the popular sovereign are not merely protected, but also *isolated* from the subsidiary consequences of their decisions. Without an ethic of responsibility for external consequences to supplement an ethic of the common good, they may pay a very high price indeed for their splendid isolation. To be sure, they experience the *internal* consequences of political decisions, the political education to autonomous choice, to generalizing interest, to communal obligation, but they do not directly experience the particular external effects of translating their decisions into practice. The danger here is that by taking responsibility only for the decisions under their control, only for that part of a policy informed by the general will, they discover the external consequences of their decisions only with the onset of the breakdown of the general will itself. Unseen effects may erode the relation between citizen and subject, between moral will and body, and once this erosion is complete the citizen no longer possesses the autonomy to reverse it. If we accept Rousseau's argument, then, we are lead to the ironic conclusion that a political association based on popular sovereignty can preserve the moral autonomy of the citizens as legislators and subjects of general laws, their self-identity as human beings, only by denying them an education to the external consequences of their decisions. (This is underscored by Rousseau's suggestion that citizens should only be allowed to meet with one another in the assembly to avoid the emergence of private factions).[17] The alternative is that they communally experience the discontinuity of self that typically accompanies the identification of what we did with the features of our actions beyond our control. Then, indeed, democratic self-legislating autonomy will need an ethic of moral luck.

The Defense of Strong Democracy

Surprisingly, many recent theorists of participatory democracy have ignored the problem of finding such an ethic. Indeed, although they have largely adopted Rousseau's argument that participation can be made relatively immune from moral risk, they have more often than not ignored his strategies for ensuring such immunity. Consequently, they have opened themselves to elitist critics of various kinds who argue that they have an insufficient account of the ironies of political action, ironies, as we have seen, for which Rousseau has provided some answers. There are at least two significant reasons for this neglect. One is that the recent debate over the nature of democracy has been polarized between two concepts of democracy that in fact are parasitic on one another: a developmental and an instrumental concept. Radical democratic forms of participation have been aligned with intrinsic justifications based on the educative effects of democracy, whereas elitist competitive party conceptions have been aligned with instrumental concepts of democratic arrangements. Thus the latter could claim to be more effective in ensuring individual welfare, and the former could claim to realize the intrinsic goods of autonomy.[18] This has left no room to argue for participatory democracy as both an enlargement of moral autonomy and a deepening of responsibility for *external* public consequences of decisions, bad or good.

A second reason for this neglect has to do with the social location in which radical democratic theorists expect to realize direct participation. Ironically, participatory democrats argue that Rousseauist participation

---

17. Rousseau, *The Social Contract*, p. 73.
18. For useful discussion of the relative claims of both models to intrinsic and instrumental justifications, see David Miller, "The Competitive Model of Democracy," in *Democratic Theory and Practice*, ed. Graeme Duncan (Cambridge: Cambridge University Press, 1983). Although Miller avoids the typical alignment of competitive party democracy with instrumental and radical democratic with intrinsic justifications, he unfortunately identifies instrumental effectiveness exclusively with market satisfaction, against which by definition radical democracy will not match up. His proposal to combine both models is promising, but it is unclear why radical democracy has no instrumental benefits of its own that are not translatable into the concept of market benefit. On his argument direct forms of participation improve the market efficiency in aggregating preferences provided by mass political parties competing for votes.

can be realized at the very social locations that Rousseau identified with the particular will, namely, local governmental administration and economic production. This should have made present-day proponents of radical democracy particularly receptive to an ethic of political consequences. But it has not done so because they have not yet fully worked out a relation between the participants' adherence to a Rousseauist concept of a common good and the particular effects of democratic decisions in economic organization and local administration. This has given recent radical democratic arguments their distinctive shape—at once emphasizing the educative effects of self-legislation, yet filling the content of that legislation with what Rousseau would call the corporate or particular will.

Recent theorists of radical or participatory democracy essentially follow Rousseau's justification for popular sovereignty. Like Rousseau they maintain that we need moral autonomy to be self-respecting human beings and live self-respecting human lives. Moral autonomy, they argue, can only be realized through the direct participation of equal citizens in decisions affecting the whole community. We can only become self-legislating when we have the resources to do so; and only by decentralizing the means of decision to small units in which we directly participate will we put these means into our hands.[19] More important, we need some standard of right to act in a morally autonomous way. For an egalitarian community, this standard can only be provided by a concept of a common good that we at once create and impose on ourselves. If we all are assumed to be capable of autonomy there is no justification for a differential good relative to moral capacity. Finally, the act of participation is not simply a means to moral autonomy but also a means that is itself the emergence of the end. We gain the capacity for self-legislation by continually participating in it. Thus the goods of participatory democracy emerge out of the process of participation itself. No instrumental justification for participation will do. Thus, according to a recent definition, "strong democracy" is "politics in the participatory mode where conflict is resolved in the absence of independent grounds . . . through the participatory process of ongoing, proximate self-legislation and the creation of a political community capable of transforming dependent private individuals into free citizens and partial private interests into public good."[20] According to this

19. For a recent debate over the meaning of political equality in decentralized forms of direct democracy, see Philip Green and Robert Dahl, "What Is Political Equality," *Dissent* (Summer 1979), 351–368. In this debate Dahl finds a purely procedural model of participant democracy that has the peculiar attribute of not entailing any egalitarian content to political decisions.

20. Benjamin Barber, *Strong Democracy* (Berkeley: University of California Press, 1986), p. 132.

definition of democracy, not even prior agreement on the common good is assumed; rather it emerges out of public discussion about what we want to legislate to the community at large. Thus in contrast to Rousseau no fundamental act of precommitment to the general will is necessary to prevent the dissolution of participatory politics into private interest.[21] The dialogical process of deliberation on conflicting claims to the common good is seen as self-sustaining.

More than even Rousseau, present-day participatory democrats view the activity of politics as not just deciding in common but also speaking in common. Speech under radical democracy is not about private interests but common matters. All participants must have the opportunity to speak; for it is in this activity that we learn to reason about public matters and translate our reasonings into action. One might even say, with Hannah Arendt, that the main activity of citizens participating directly in the public is public speech.[22] It is this activity of proposing and debating in which we discover the interests we have in common. It is also through speech that we exercise power in radical democracy.

But this does not mean that anything may be said. There is an internal standard that governs all deliberations: All arguments must be framed not in terms of what I or we want, what I or we prefer, but in terms of what would be good for the community as a whole.[23] The most persuasive argument would then be the one that shows which proposal would most benefit the community. This in turn entails a principle of equality according to which all decisions should benefit and burden all citizens equally.[24] To propose a policy advantageous to some sectional interest would be inappropriate for public discussion.

Yet to realize this standard of public decision-making in practice, participatory democrats have had to confront Weber's multiple expropriation process. This has meant adapting Rousseau's argument for popular sovereignty under the general will for the purpose of democratizing those areas of society that Rousseau viewed as distinctly characterized by a corporate will translating itself into a particular will—the contexts that are particularly prone to ironic outcomes. To be specific, most radical democrats have sought to introduce democracy into local administration and the workplace. The upshot has been that most recent radical democratic theo-

---

21. Pateman, *The Problem of Political Obligation*, p. 154, stands out for recognizing that political obligation in modern participatory association depends on the creation of a general will through an explicit act of promising.
22. Hannah Arendt, *The Human Condition* (Chicago: University of Chicago Press, 1958), pp. 25–27, 50–52.
23. Barber, *Strong Democracy*, pp. 200–201.
24. Pateman, *The Problem of Political Obligation*, pp. 155–156, 187.

ries advance a model of participatory politics that has a paradoxical relation between its ends and its means structured into its institutional form—
and this aside from the paradoxes of political action characteristic of all
direct democratic political action. This has meant that the content of the
general will in such contexts as workers' control over production or local
democracy consists of decisions beneficial to the corporate will or the
particular interests of the institution. Thus the intrinsic good of legislating
the common will in the workplace or the locality is in constant tension
with debate over the details of self-administration and implementation,
even if the issue is, for example, the investment policy of the firm or the
maintenance of the integrity of the locality. Under the putative general
will, debate fluctuates between sustaining the corporate will of the city
or firm and satisfying the particular interests of its members.[25]

The response of radical democratic theory to this problem has been to
follow the lead of de Tocqueville and to recast it into an argument favoring
participatory democracy.[26] Two arguments have been made. First, it is
argued that direct participation in locality and in industry provides citizens with both the social preconditions and the political capacities to
make judgments on the national level. In industry, Carole Pateman points
out, participation in matters such as work coordination, selecting managers, deciding on investment policy not only creates a form of substantive
equality for the worker, but also develops a feeling of political efficacy
and political skill that carries over to judgments on the national level. By
exercising power in the plant with others, the individual worker is able
to generalize from the experience of exercising authority in the plant to
the exercise of authority in governmental structures.[27] This leads directly
to the second argument. It is argued that the consequences of decision
making at the level of the workplace and in local communities tend to

25. See Barber, *Strong Democracy*, pp. 200–201, who argues that competition to advance
and define common ends is an integral feature of strong democratic participation. For a
contrasting examination of some of the dilemmas of overcoming a concept of political
participation based on adversarial pursuit of private interest in favor of a unitary concept
of direct democracy, see Jane Mansbridge, *Beyond Adversary Democracy* (Chicago: University of Chicago Press, 1983).
26. See Alexis de Tocqueville, *Democracy in America*, trans. George Lawrence (New York:
Doubleday, 1969), p. 511. "It is difficult to force a man out of himself and take an interest
in affairs of the whole state, for he has little understanding of the way in which the fate of
the state can influence his own lot. But if it is a question of taking a road past his property,
he sees at once that this small public matter has a bearing on his greatest private interests
and there is no need to point out to him the close connection between his private project
and the general interest." The best recent version of this argument is still Carole Pateman,
Participation and Democratic Theory (Cambridge: Cambridge University Press, 1970), pp.
24–25, 50.
27. Pateman, *Participation and Democratic Theory*, pp. 43, 47, 50.

reinforce the individual's capacity for autonomy, his or her capacity to legislate general ends for himself or herself. In turn, to insist that such participation must also lead to efficiency of (productive) output is to fail to understand the fundamental justification for democratic participation: namely, that it is an education to human autonomy. Thus, Cohen and Rogers argue that a "principle of democratic legitimacy" can "freely acknowledge that as people shift among different types of work and spend time debating the problems facing a particular workplace and the relationship between the workplace and the democratic order, there may in fact be some loss of potential output (even if total output were growing). If there were such a loss, by conventional criteria, workplace democracy could be regarded as 'inefficient,' but that is because those criteria apply only to losses or gains in material output, and not to losses or gains in human autonomy."[28] Pateman argues that "the justification for the democratic system in the participatory theory of democracy rests primarily on the human results that accrue from the participatory process. One might characterize the participatory model as one where maximum input (participation) is required and where output includes not just policies (decisions) but also the development of social and political capacities, so that there is 'feedback' from output to input."[29] Here the output consists of the continuous development of "political efficacy" and "political competence" and political responsibility.[30]

Now such arguments do not deny that the justification of autonomous decisions taken by direct democratic forms in the workplace or locality depend on their consequences; but they assume that the fundamental standard by which to judge democratic consequences is the reinforcement of the capacities for self-legislating freedom itself. This rests on a further assumption that is fundamental to all recent participatory theory: that a properly organized participatory democratic order, one that provides sufficient scope for deliberation and decision making, can contain the consequences of democratic decisions so that they will foster the transformation of the participants into morally autonomous agents.

This justification for participatory democracy under Weberian conditions is persuasive in its own terms but significantly incomplete. It is incomplete in a number of senses. First, it defines the relevant consequences of direct participation too narrowly, including only those that directly reinforce the transformation of the participant's capacities for legislating common ends to himself or herself. Thus the participant is not

28. Joshua Cohen and Joel Rogers, *On Democracy* (Harmondsworth: Penguin, 1983), p. 164.
29. Pateman, *Participation and Democratic Theory*, p. 43.
30. Ibid., p. 46.

responsible for reconciling the tension between the more instrumental particular effects of decisions, the by-products of implementation of policy or a technique, with the more developmental ones. It is simply assumed that one can always bring instrumental consequences into line with developmental ones or in the worst case, that one can safely sacrifice the latter to the former.

Second, it assumes that as we become more skilled at making political decisions at the local plant or community level, for example by equalizing benefits or burdens while maintaining efficiency, we automatically become more capable of achieving a moral autonomy that has the common good as its standard. There may very well be a paradoxical relation here, one in which we discover that we become skilled in promoting the corporate will of our community or plant only at the expense of the common good of the political society. Or alternatively, it may turn out that we can only be effective in promoting the common good as a guide to our democratic choices if we inhibit our skill at local politics. In this case a simple inclination toward finding the common good is necessary rather than political sophistication.

Third and most important, it could very well be that the educative effects of direct political participation, especially for the realization of autonomy, cannot be attained as a deliberate goal of politics. Given the ways in which political participation enhances the contingency of political outcomes, radical democratic goals such as autonomy, community, and development of capacities for practical judgment may turn out to be the by-products of common decision-making rather than explicit goals. And the more we make them the explicit object of political decisions, the more their realization eludes us.[31] In making this last point, I am not denying that direct local participation educates our capacity for positing public ends and legislating them to ourselves. However, whether or not we achieve these goods in democratic politics often depends on our not intending them as objects of political deliberation and decision. I am also saying that this irony is particularly structured into the contexts in which participatory democracy seeks to reappropriate the means of power. In brief, without Rousseau's strategies of containment, and perhaps even with them, the practice of democratic autonomy inspired by him requires

31. See Jon Elster, *Sour Grapes* (Cambridge: Cambridge University Press, 1985), pp. 91–100. Elster argues that the goods of democratic participation, such as dignity, political education, and solidarity, cannot be achieved as intentional goals but only emerge as by-products of decision making to solve concrete instrumental political problems. Although I agree that this is frequently the case, what such an argument overlooks is the reverse irony—that often the pursuit of ideals of dignity, political autonomy, and solidarity, may have the unintended instrumental result of capturing a space where democratic activity governed by the previous irony can take place.

a political ethic of moral luck, a political ethic of responsibility for political paradoxes.

Radical Democracy and Freedom as Participation in Moral Risk

What does direct participant democracy look like from the vantage point of a political ethics of moral luck? In a sense it does not change so much as we notice certain neglected features about it. It is still true that we can only realize the intrinsic good of autonomy if we bring the political means that once belonged to disciplinary regimes and formal chains of command under the power of directly democratic institutions. The good realized through participation in deciding both particular problems of administration and general policy is still our distinctive capacity collectively to prescribe ends that we obey and to do so on the basis of our reasoned deliberations. But we must now recognize that it is inadequate to argue, as do Rousseau and present-day theorists of participatory democracy, that participation under a self-created general will entails that we are primarily responsible for those political decisions that are under our control. For both sociological reasons and reasons intrinsic to the process of participation itself, participatory citizens are responsible for the foreseeable and unforseen consequences of the power they exercise. Indeed the very process of participation renders them intensively responsible for such consequences. For radical democratic decisions depend on public discussion rather than on a purely impartial standard of the common good, and the freedom of such discussions consists precisely in our inability to predict their outcome, that is, to predict what decision will finally be taken and whether it in fact will correspond to the common good.[32] Merely to be responsible for the decisions taken is to be responsible for events whose course is not predictable beforehand. Furthermore, the power exercised in making democratic decisions—a power that is exercised in the process of discussion and deliberation itself—is only efficacious because decisions that were previously routine have now become contingent. Radical democracy reverses Weber's expropriation process only at the price of predictability, a price I believe to be worth paying; but the democratic side of this bargain entails that luck plays an increased role in whether decisions happen to be good ones or not. Once we decentralize power in corporate institutions, there simply is no sociological possibility to make citizens responsible only for that aspect of decisions that are under their control unless, of course, we want to sacrifice the common good for the corporate good of the democratic unit. The risks

32. This has been emphasized by Hannah Arendt, *The Human Condition*, pp. 232–236.

of public decisions are part of direct participation, and so the luck of success or failure will justify the decisions participatory citizens legislate to themselves. Yet even in arguing for a strong connection between moral luck and the democratic autonomy of participatory political associations, we can still "foresee" certain determinate ironies, much as Weber could for his vocational political actor.

Let me suggest a few of the kinds of political irony to which radical democracy might regularly be subjected. The first we might call ironies of control. This set of ironies arises from the tension between the need for regular implementation of policies and the need to prevent autonomy from being eroded through the bureaucratic expropriation of political means. Any decision taken by a participatory community at the workplace or at the level of local administration will presumably always have at least two goals corresponding to the inextricable connection of autonomy to outcomes we contribute to but do not control. On the one hand it seeks to preserve the goods that arise from the process of collective decision making, in particular autonomy, solidarity, and egalitarian justice. On the other, it seeks to have policies imposed with reliability and reasonable coordination. The problem is that the effects of coordination tend to erode the sphere of decisions we leave open to collective deliberation. So the goal of all public decisions is to uncover means of carrying out decisions that will increase democratic control rather than diminish it.[33] But we cannot predict with certainty whether democratic decisions will have this outcome because increased democracy would introduce increased scope for a kind of deliberation that is only intelligible if it is not engineered. Thus time and again democratic decisions within participant democracies consist of a gamble that the control that is necessary for execution will provide for the needs of their members without eroding communal autonomy. Indeed, one might view radical democratic decision-making as necessary precisely because it probes the different causal effects of control and their meaning for autonomy. Such "inquiry" has not usually been possible in liberal capitalist society.

A second set of ironies we might call ironies of equity. These concern the fact that redistributions for the sake of equality most frequently take away from some for the benefit of others, even if general equality is achieved. Although this is indeed an outgrowth of substantive equality, that is, an equality that seeks to create the preconditions for autonomy, the participants often times have to deny themselves the nondemocratic Aristotelian claim of unequal distribution for unequal contribution in

33. For an attempt to view democratic decisions in this "more or less" way, see Frank Cunningham, *Democratic Theory and Socialism* (Cambridge: Cambridge University Press, 1987), pp. 25–35.

favor of promoting numerous equalities so that all will share the developmental possibilities of participation.

A third variety of ironies we may call ironies of coercion. Radical democracy gambles that it can drive violence out of history and with it the state as a monopoly of legitimate violence. Yet if the previous two ironies always persist, the need to apply coercion will persist as well, although now under truly democratic control. In particular, coercion may be necessary in resisting the tendency within each sphere of activity toward the expropriation of the means of power that attends control and coordination. It may also be necessary to reestablish equity when unforeseen outcomes of democratic decisions strengthen the power or privileges of certain sectional interests at the expense of the polity.

A fourth set we may call ironies of political invention. This is perhaps the most nebulous of the ironies of radical democracy, for these political ironies result from the unpredictable political inventiveness that may be released with the political capacities that radical democracy may mobilize. Participant democracies may discover solutions to public problems that surpass normal moral terms of civic virtue or common good or just distribution. Yet, these will still be seen as expressions of a general will that democratic citizens impose upon themselves. After all, social and political invention may very well be a result of simplifying political virtue. Thus Rousseau's attack on the corrupting effect of social sophistication on the political judgment of citizens under the general will may be a strategy of releasing political ingenuity rather than repressing it.[34]

A final set of ironies we might call ironies of resistance. This set may be the most important of all. Radical democracy as argued previously, may never be a settled institutional form, but it will very likely always exist within a "state" as an institution that coordinates social powers over a territorial space.[35] Such coordination always works against the will to legislate public decisions through local units. Hence participant democratic political association in the workplace and in the community usually make decisions in resistance to the claims of the state to monopolize the means of power, to say nothing of the claims of the institutions in which it is locally realized. Thus some of the decisions it makes will be decisions on how most effectively to preserve its power to legislate for itself against the constant tendency for the state to expropriate political means for itself. Indeed, it may be here that the argument becomes especially relevant that the internal ends of autonomy, the cultivation of the common good,

---

34. Rousseau, The Social Contract, pp. 149–150.
35. I derive this notion of the state from Michael Mann, "The Autonomous Powers of the State," in States, War, and Capitalism (Oxford: Basil Blackwell, 1988), pp. 17, 29.

self-respect as an egalitarian member of a community, the cultivation of public judgment are not goals we can achieve by directly aiming at them. For these goods may only emerge as by-products of seeking to preserve and expand the powers of radical democratic forms of politics. In other words, the very goods of radical democracy may in fact be only achievable as ironic effects of trying to act as effectively as possible in making specific instrumental decisions about the preservation of local power against the coordinating claims of the state. This may be the final and perhaps most important irony connecting radical democratic politics to a political ethic of moral luck.

These ironies leave us with still one nagging question. How far does the responsibility of citizens extend in participatory associations, because surely citizens cannot be responsible for each and every outcome of their decisions, however remote or unforeseen? To answer this question adequately would require a separate inquiry, but a few tentative remarks are in order. Clearly citizens of participatory associations are responsible for the injuries to the common good of society, solidarity, and substantive equality brought about by self-aggrandizing corporate decisions, even if this emerged out of an attempt to bring equity to the workplace or locality. They are responsible for the longer-range outcomes of decisions seeking to ensure substantive equality in respect, in distribution of social and political resources, in sharing of benefits and burdens—this would be especially the case if such decisions were to discourage necessary contributions to the common good. Furthermore, if many of the goods of participation do indeed emerge out of a tension between participatory associations and the claims of the state a certain instrumental deployment of power will be necessary that may very well violate the dignity that all citizens deserve. Thus participant citizens will be responsible for the by-products of deploying coercive means to maintain their autonomy, especially if the by-product is a mixed outcome, the preservation of the will of the political association and a loss of social solidarity. As for leaders, obviously democratically chosen leaders would have to take greater responsibility than participating citizens for consequences of the kind just mentioned. But in a true participant democracy, it is difficult for citizens to cast full blame on an individual leader as they themselves have directly chosen him or her and willfully and after some deliberation delegated to him or her responsibility for the paradoxes of political action. Unlike Weber's model in which the professional politician takes full responsibility for foreseeable ironic outcomes because the mass is deemed incapable of willing political ends and taking responsibility for their realization, the participant democratic model assumes that responsibility between democratic citizens and leaders is shared. Obviously there are numerous tensions here that we cannot resolve abstractly.

Conclusion

Is the notion of democratic autonomy as moral risk and political irony worth achieving? It is, I think, if democratic autonomy itself is still regarded intrinsically worthy, because to link the intrinsic concept of democracy to one that includes political irony does not discredit the former so much as provide a more adequate account of the conditions for its attainment. Surely, when we connect the freedom of democratic self-legislation to political irony we face a far more difficult and demanding freedom than radical democrats have typically insisted on, for to deliberate and choose public policies in common becomes not just the realization of autonomy and community, but also a necessary education to ambiguity of outcome and constant political struggle against routinized domination. This may, however, be the only public freedom available to those who hope to reverse the Weberian political expropriation process and recover democratic autonomy. One last irony: Even if I am correct on this point, it may still be true that the democratic freedom to participate in moral risk with others can only be realized if we pursue a model of democracy that promises to extirpate such risk from politics once and for all. After all, without Rousseau's account of moral autonomy under the general will we may find neither a motivation nor an intelligible justification for pursuing strong democracy at all. It is this double irony that continually draws us back to Rousseau's model for guidance on the meaning of radical democracy despite the sobering power of Weber's consequentialist ethic of political responsibility.

Index

Kat Gordon was born in London in 1984. She attended Camden School for Girls, read English at Somerville College, Oxford, and received a distinction in her Creative Writing Master's from Royal Holloway. In between, Kat has been a gymnastics coach, a theatre usher, a piano accompanist, a nanny, a researcher, and worked at *Time Out*. She has spent a lot of time travelling, primarily in Africa. Kat lives in London with her boyfriend and their terrifying cat, Maggie.

THE ARTIFICIAL ANATOMY
OF PARKS

At twenty-one, Tallulah Park lives alone in a grimy bedsit, where a strange damp smell causes her to wake up wheezing. When she finds out her estranged father has had a heart attack and arranges to visit him, she isn't looking forward to seeing her relatives again. Years before, she was being tossed around her difficult family: a world of sniping aunts, precocious cousins, emigrant pianists and lots of gin, all presided over by an unconventional grandmother. But no one was answering Tallie's questions: why did Aunt Vivienne loathe Tallie's mother? Who was Uncle Jack, and why would no one talk about him? And why was everyone making excuses for her absent father? As Tallie grows up, she learns the hard way that in the end, the worst betrayals are those we inflict on ourselves. . .

KAT GORDON

---◆---

THE ARTIFICIAL ANATOMY OF PARKS

Complete and Unabridged

CHARNWOOD
Leicester

First published in Great Britain in 2015 by
Legend Press Ltd
London

First Charnwood Edition
published 2016
by arrangement with
Legend Press Ltd
London

A catalogue record for this book is available
from the British Library.

ISBN 978–1–4448–2779–8

Published by
F. A. Thorpe (Publishing)
Anstey, Leicestershire

Set by Words & Graphics Ltd.
Anstey, Leicestershire
Printed and bound in Great Britain by
T. J. International Ltd., Padstow, Cornwall

This book is printed on acid-free paper

This book is dedicated to
Janet and Alex Gordon,
and to Tom Feltham, with thanks.

PART ONE

Heart

1

It's nine o'clock in the morning when the phone call comes through.

'Miss Park?'

'Yes?'

'This is Marylebone Heart Hospital. I'm afraid your father has had a heart attack.'

For a moment I don't understand. I'm still in bed, under the covers, head and one arm out in the open.

'He was brought in here at six this morning. We'll be moving him to coronary care shortly, where you'll be able to visit him. He's still under, though.'

'Right.' I feel I should say more. 'Please let me know if there's any change in his condition.'

'Of course.'

I hang up.

I lie back in my bed. My brain feels like it's out of sync with the rest of me. I try to think about the last time I spoke to my father; it was five years ago. I can see him before me, white-faced, the nurse's arm around his chest as she propelled him out of the room. I wonder whether this heart attack was already lurking offstage, biding its time. I know that heart problems can build up over a long period, treacherous plaque mushrooming on the inner walls of the coronary artery. When I was a baby, my father gave me a plastic simulacrum of a

3

heart to play with. It was meant for medical students, but I used it to chew on when my teeth were coming through.

Years later, when I was alone in the house on rainy afternoons, I would read his medical journals. I became obsessed with the heart, its unpredictability. I can still recite the facts: . . . *damage to the heart restricts the flow of oxygenated blood usually pumped out of the left ventricle. This causes left ventricular failure and fluid accumulation in the lungs; it's at this point that the sufferer will feel a shortness of breath. Patients may also feel weak, light-headed, nauseous; experience sweating and palpitations. Approximately half of all heart-attack patients have experienced warning symptoms such as chest pain at some point prior to the actual attack.*

My ears are ringing now. I plug them with my fingers, trying to push the sound back into my brain. I can't imagine how it must feel, the realisation that your heart is failing you, when for so many years you forgot that it was even there, ticking away like a little death-clock. All my muscles start to curl up just thinking about it. I couldn't have stopped it, I tell myself, but there's a heavy feeling in the room, like when you're a kid and you've done something bad and you're waiting to be found out.

I drag myself out of bed to throw up in the sink that stands in the corner of the bedroom. My hands shake when I run the taps to clear away the mess. I cross the room to the window. *We don't swim in your toilet, so don't piss in our*

4

pool — my cousin, Starr, taped that sign to the glass.

I force the window open and stick my head out into the fresh air. Below me a cyclist screeches to a stop, drops his bike and runs into the building two doors down, his hair slick with sweat. The traffic is heavy and the air is already thick and sultry. Shop workers stand in their doorways, fanning themselves. Behind them, JXL curls out of the radio — the remix of Elvis Presley's 'A Little Less Conversation'. It's been number one in the charts for a month this summer. It's 2002, the year of the King's big comeback.

I feel sick again; I haven't been in a hospital for five years either.

My flat is in a converted Victorian house on Essex Road, N1. It's supposed to be a prestigious postcode, but the ground floor of our building and the one next door is taken up with a funeral parlour, hence the cheap rent. They do transporting, embalming, flower arrangements, the works. When I first moved in I was freaked by all the coffins I saw being carried in and out, but now I'm used to it. Below me is another flat, I share a toilet on the half-landing with him. Mine is the attic — two medium-sized rooms, a bedroom with sink, a kitchen with shower. It's not much — it's peeling and yellow and recently there's been a strange damp smell that sometimes means I wake up wheezing. I took it because it was close to work, and I have a weakness for badly-fitting wooden floorboards and windowpanes that let in cold air. I blame my grandmother.

5

Now, though, for the first time since I moved in five months ago, I wish the place felt more like home.

I pad into the kitchen and fill the kettle, checking my reflection in my cracked, bear-shaped hand mirror while it boils. My hair is dirty and there's yesterday's makeup smeared around my face; I don't necessarily want to go to the hospital, but I can imagine what my grandmother would say if I turned up like this — 'The poor man's got a weak heart, do you want him to die of fright?'

I shower, scrubbing myself hard. I drink a coffee while it's steaming and sort through the post, drumming my fingers on the kitchen table, impatient for the caffeine to kick in.

My uniform is draped across the back of a chair, waiting to be put on. It's a tight turquoise-and-purple mini-dress like waitresses used to wear in American diners in the fifties. My name is stitched into it over the left breast, so male customers can gawp at my chest and get away with it.

Maybe I should let my boss know about my situation, but the more time that passes, the more I feel I don't have to go and sit by my father's bedside — there's a reason we haven't kept in touch.

I get dressed in the kitchen, trying to iron out the creases with my hands. I can hear the golf coming in waves through the paper-thin wall separating me from my neighbour. I wonder what my mother would say to try to convince me to go, although if she were here we probably wouldn't be in this mess in the first place. She was always able to talk me out of being angry when I was younger. She'd say something like, 'This is the only point in your life you can go to the post office in a Batgirl outfit. Don't waste it on getting upset.'

She was the one who bought me the Batgirl outfit too, a reward for being brave after I fell out of a tree in our garden when I was five. I don't remember the fall; I remember my father picking me up off the lawn and carrying me inside. He laid me down on the sofa and started prodding me gently. I was completely still, but I winced when he took my head in his hands and examined my eyebrow. I could feel something warm start to meander down my face, and when I blinked my eyelashes felt sticky.

'You're bleeding a bit,' he told me. 'Do you know how bleeding happens?'

'How?'

'It means you've severed tiny blood vessels near the surface of the skin. When you do that, the blood comes out of the body, and we call that loss 'bleeding'.'

'Okay,' I said.

'Good girl,' he said, and helped me up.

'Is it serious?' my mother asked.

'She'll need stitches, but she'll be fine.'

We sat in the hospital waiting room for an hour; the bright lights and squeaky plastic floor and coughing patients made me shrink back into my chair. My mother held my hand the whole time. On the way home she rode in the back with me, showing me all her scars.

7

'This one is from my first cat,' she said, showing me a white line running down the inside of her right arm. 'And this one is from chickenpox.' She pointed to a circle next to her left eye.

'You obviously ignored your doctor and scratched it,' my father said, from the front seat.

'If only I'd known you back then, Edward,' my mother said.

She was smiling. I looked at my father's eyes in the rear-view mirror and saw the skin crease around them, like he was smiling too.

'What's that one?' I asked, putting my finger on the little cross on her chin.

'That was from when your mother was saving the world,' my father said.

'I fell over at a CND demonstration,' she said, 'and cut myself. It was when you were a tiny baby, and I was going to take you along in a sling, like in those photos I showed you, but thank God I didn't, or I might have squashed you.'

'Where was I?' I asked.

'At home with Daddy,' she said. 'It was the first time I was away from you.'

'Yes,' my father said. 'I seem to remember you cried all night.'

★　★　★

I'm feeling the caffeine buzz now — my heart is pumping a little too fast and my ears are choked up with its clamouring. *Lub-dub, lub-dub.* I wonder if I'm going to throw up again.

8

My mobile rings, it's Starr. 'Thank God you picked up, have you heard?'

'Yeah, the hospital just called.'

'Are you there?'

I light a cigarette. 'Not yet.'

'Are you on your way?'

'Not yet.'

'Hon, what are you waiting for?'

I make my hand into a fist, and consider it. Roughly speaking, it is the size of my heart; my father taught me that. 'I have to call work.'

'So call them.'

'I will.'

'When?'

'Now.'

'This is a really big fucking deal. You're the only one he has left, apart from Mum and Aunt G . . . You *have* to go.'

I pretend not to hear her. 'Where *are* you? It's a really bad line.'

'I'm in Spain, remember, with Riccardo. I wish I could fly back but we're in the middle of fucking nowhere — flights once every ten days or something, and we've just missed one. Give Uncle Edward my love.'

'Alright.'

'You are *going*, aren't you?'

'Get off my back, Starr. I don't know yet. It's not like we're that close, is it?'

I hang up. I'm not ready to face my past quite yet, no matter how bad Starr makes me feel.

I sit on the edge of the bed, working up the will to put on my socks and shoes — black flats that won't pinch after an eight-hour shift. My

9

feet have always been big with knobbly toes, like monkeys'. When I was a kid I used them to pick things up and carry them around — pens, rubber bands, coins. I wonder if my father remembers it.

If he dies now . . .

I pick up the phone again and call my boss to tell him I won't be in today. 'It's a family emergency,' I say.

'You can't expect me to believe that,' he says. 'That's the oldest trick in the book.'

'Well this time it's true.'

He makes a disgusted noise down the receiver. 'I see right through you, missy,' he says. 'You've got a hangover again.'

I start to say something, but he cuts me off. 'I don't really care. If you're not in usual time on Wednesday, you can forget about coming in for good.'

I bang the telephone down. If I had the guts or the money I'd quit in a flash.

'And do what?' Starr asked me once. I pretended I hadn't thought about it.

So work isn't an obstacle anymore. I don't want to see my father, but I can't pretend I don't know about it. If I hadn't picked up the phone this morning, I could get on with my daily routine. But I did pick up the phone. 'You were raised to know the right thing to do,' my grandmother would say. 'If you don't go now, it'll be because of your own pig-headedness.'

'You win,' I tell her. 'But I'm only going for you.'

I throw on some non-work clothes and grab

10

my cigarettes, keys, and phone and leave the flat, locking the door behind me. I walk to Islington Green, running the last few yards to catch the number 30 pulling in at the stop. It's only when I'm on it that I realise my aunts might be at the hospital too. The doors are still open, and I almost get off again, but something inside me puts its foot down — no more wavering. My grandmother's influence again, probably. I sit by the window and watch as the bus sails past sunbathers on the green, then Pizza Express and William Hill and the new Thai restaurant, with potted bamboo and stone buddhas outside. Pedestrians amble alongside us in the heat, flip-flops slapping against the pavement, and Brazilian flags still hang from second and third-floor flat windows, mementoes of their fifth World Cup win back in June.

I don't want to see any of them — my place among the family was always a little uncertain — but especially not Aunt Vivienne. She's my father's younger sister, Starr's mum, and I remember her being tall and glamorous and fierce. When I knew her, she had short, dark hair that licked each ear. 'To look like Cyd Charisse,' she said. In 1974 and 1975, a twenty-two-year-old Vivienne had appeared, scantily clad, in several films with titles like: *Vampira*, *The Arabian Nights* and *Supervixens*.

She might not show up though — she has a bad track record of attending funerals at least. And as far as I could tell, when I was a kid, Aunt Vivienne didn't seem to notice my father much; maybe they haven't seen each other recently either. Starr said, once, that after I left my father basically turned into a recluse, but Starr exaggerates.

* * *

When we were children I thought Starr was the coolest person I knew. She wore glitter eye-shadow that suited her name, and could balance whole stacks of books on her head while walking round the living-room. Sometimes we'd visit them in their Primrose Hill flat and she would show us. She said that Aunt Vivienne made her practise every night so she'd have the right posture for modelling or acting.

'You know, I went a whole year without buying myself a single drink,' Aunt Vivienne said once, smoking a cigarette and crossing her legs. '*Everyone* took me out to dinner. I went along with it of course, but I knew they just wanted to see if I'd get my tits out.'

Me and Starr, playing quietly under the kitchen table, giggled to ourselves at the t-word.

'You should have come with me sometimes, Evie,' Aunt Vivienne said to my mother. 'You're very cute, you know. Not exactly right for the roles I got, but you could definitely have played a young country *ingénue*. That would have been right up your street, wouldn't it?'

Under the table I saw my mother's hands tighten in her lap.

'Right,' Aunt Vivienne said, her face appearing suddenly. 'Get out you two. Don't think I don't know you're snooping around down there.'

12

We crawled out and I went to stand next to my mother. Aunt Vivienne watched me. I watched her back. Aunt Vivienne never dressed the same as other women on the street — she looked more like the people from black and white films — and now she was wearing white trousers that flared at the bottom, and a white silk shirt. I could see through her top to her purple bra, and I wondered if she still needed to show people her tits.

My mother was wearing her red tea dress and her blonde hair big and wavy. When she'd come down for breakfast that morning my father had pretended to think she was Farrah Fawcett, although I thought she was much prettier. She put her arm around me and buried her face in my hair, speaking into it. 'What are you up to?'

'Playing with dolls.'

'That sounds nice,' she said, and nuzzled my ear.

Starr was standing near the door. Aunt Vivienne crushed her cigarette out in the saucer in front of her and turned in her seat. 'Starr, go to your room. And take your cousin with you. Can't I ever have an adult conversation around here?'

'Come on,' Starr said when we were in the hallway. 'Let's go to Mum's bedroom and try on makeup.'

'Okay,' I said. I thought Starr was very brave after the way Aunt Vivienne had just looked at her.

Aunt Vivienne had a whole row of lipsticks and pots of cream and brushes.

'The blusher's in here,' Starr said, pulling open the top drawer of the dresser. She was wearing shiny silver leggings with gold spots on them, and a pink t-shirt with two elephants kissing. I stuck my hands in the pockets of my denim shorts and wished I looked as exciting as her.

'Oh, it's the left one.' Starr struggled to close the open drawer. 'Help me.'

We tried pushing it together.

'You have to jiggle it,' Starr said. 'Quietly, or she'll hear us.' She mimed drawing a line across her throat. I giggled.

'There's something stuck at the back,' Starr said, reaching into the drawer and pulling out sheets of writing paper, bills and photos. 'Take these. We have to shove everything down.'

I looked at the photo on the top of the stack Starr had given me. It looked like a birthday shot; there was cake on a table in the front and, standing slightly behind it, Aunt Vivienne and my mother, wearing party hats. My mother had an arm around Vivienne's waist. There was another face in the frame as well, all blurry. It looked like a man with dark hair, no one I'd ever seen before. Both my mother and Aunt Vivienne were looking at him, and Aunt Vivienne was reaching out a hand like she was trying to catch hold of his arm.

'Who's that?'

'Where?'

'Here.'

We heard someone go into the bathroom next door and water running.

14

'Give them to me,' Starr said, grabbing the stack and piling it back in the drawer. We scuttled out of Aunt Vivienne's bedroom and into Starr's. My mother put her head around the door as soon as we'd sat down. Her eyes looked red around the rims, like she had a cold.

'It's time to go, Tallie,' she said.

Starr gave me a look and put her finger on her lips. We giggled again.

*　*　*

I get off at Harley Street and make my way through Marylebone, past women with expensive hair drinking coffee, down wide, sunlit streets with 'doctor' written in front of the parking spaces, and quiet pockets of residential mews and small, peaceful parks. After the grey and brown of my road, it feels like the whole area has been splashed in colour — red brick, green trees and silver Mercedes. I wonder if I'll run into Toby; he used to live nearby, although I think he was closer to Edgware Road.

A young mother comes into view with a toddler in tow. She's carrying too many bags and feeding bottles and a ball under one arm. The toddler is red-faced, and one tug away from a screaming fit. The woman looks tearful. I look away.

My mother — Evelyn — was wonderful with children, everyone said so. She used to stop and coo at babies whenever we went for walks together and they always smiled at her. She used to bake proper cakes for my birthdays, elaborate

15

ones in the shapes of cartoon characters, with buttercream icing, and she would stay up all night sewing costumes for me when I was invited to fancy-dress parties. She could do lots of different voices when she was reading stories aloud at bed-time. She smelled like vanilla, and sang low and sweetly.

I have all these memories at least. She's there in my head. It's in the real world that I've lost her — I haven't smelt her perfume since I was ten, or seen the strands of hair that used to build up in her hairbrush. I can't remember how it felt to touch her when she was still warm and soft from a bath. And what was she like when she wasn't with me? What was she like as a person? I think about my mother all the time.

2

My father isn't in Coronary Care. When I ask at Reception I'm told he's been moved to Floor One. My father's worked here at the heart hospital all my life and I know what's on Floor One: Intensive Care.

'I'm afraid the heart attack, and the heart rhythm he went into, were very severe,' a pretty nurse is telling me. 'He had to be anaesthetised to let it recover.'

Nurse Slattery, her badge says. She's very gentle with me, but she doesn't smile. I used to want to be a nurse. I wonder how I'd break the news if it was me in her place, if I could be as calm.

'Thanks.'

'He's still under. You can sit with him if you want.'

I make it to the doorway of his ward before I feel my chest begin to tighten. I pull up short and flex and unflex my fingers; they feel cold, like all the blood has rushed elsewhere. I tuck them into my armpits. It's okay, I tell myself. No one even knows you're here. You can go home without explaining yourself to anyone. My feet start to move instinctively, I'm halfway down the corridor in the other direction when I hear someone calling my name. I lift my face up to see Gillian, my father's older sister, coming out of the lift.

I stop. She hurries up to me and puts her bags on the floor — she's been to Harvey Nichols — and kisses me on both cheeks. She smells of lavender, she's wearing navy linen trousers and a stripy top and her hair in a tight, blonde bun, just as I remember it.

Her eyes are shiny, like she's holding back tears. 'How are you, darling?'

'I'm fine.'

'I went to call you earlier,' she says. 'But then I realised I don't have a number for you. I didn't even know if you were in the country — I was so worried no one would be able to reach you. How long has it been? Five years?'

She's skirting the issue, letting me know my disappearance has been noticed, but not asking for a reason.

'The hospital called me,' I say.

Now that I think about it, I realise Starr must have given them my number. My father certainly doesn't have it.

She hasn't taken her eyes off my face yet. 'Have you seen him?'

'No.'

'Come on then.'

We walk to my father's room and Aunt Gillian goes straight in. I hover, half-in, half-out.

'Edward,' I hear her say. She sounds choked.

My father looks terrible. His whole face is grey. I didn't know people could be this colour and still be alive. I look away, at the floor; there are scuff marks by the bed, as if it's been moved rapidly at some point.

'He's unconscious,' I say.

Aunt Gillian is stroking his hair.

'They had to anaesthetise him to let his heart recover,' I say. 'They'll probably keep him under for a while.'

'Yes,' she says. 'They said on the phone they'd done a PCI.' She looks at me, then back down to my father. 'We sound like pretty cold fish, don't we?'

'We sound like him,' I say. My father is a heart surgeon, and when I was a little girl this terminology was as familiar to me as my nursery rhymes. Perhaps even more so — I can't remember anything beyond the second line of 'Oranges and Lemons'.

It's when Aunt Gillian turns to face me that I realise I'm humming the tune. 'Sorry,' I say. I come and stand beside my aunt.

'Don't be,' she says. 'You're under a lot of stress.' She guides me into a bedside chair. It's almost too close to my father to bear. I can smell his aftershave, dark and woody, mingling with antiseptic and rubber. He must have already finished his morning routine when he had the heart attack; he always got up early. I find myself looking at his ear, checking for the tell-tale crease, Frank's sign, named after Dr Sanders T. Frank. Frank's sign is a diagonal earlobe crease, extending from the hard pointy bit at the front, covering the ear-hole, across the lobe to the rear edge of the visible part of the ear. Growing up, I was fascinated by the idea that this little rumple of skin could anticipate heart disease. You find it especially on elderly people. My father doesn't have it.

19

'He's still so young,' Aunt Gillian says, like she's reading my mind.

She's kind of right. He's fifty-four, but he looks much older than I remember — maybe it's the illness. He's the same, but he's changed. His hair seems finer, and I can see a dusting of grey in the blond, like the time my mother's camera had metal shavings on the lens and everything came out speckled with silver. There are a few hairs that have started to creep out of his ears and nose. His moustache and eyebrows are bushier, too, and there's a deeper 'V' at the cleft between neck and collarbone, where he must have lost weight. His hands are lying palm-down on either side of his body, but even at rest they're wrinkled. He's not wearing an oxygen mask — part of me wishes his face was covered up more.

I'm here now, Dad. I didn't want to see you again, but I came anyway. So now what?

Someone taps at the door and comes in. It's the pretty nurse from before. I watch as she takes my father's pulse and examines his respiratory pattern. She opens his eyelids one after the other, and looks at his pupils. Then she turns his head from side to side, keeping the eyelids open.

'What does that show?' I ask.

'We call it the doll's eye test,' she says, laying his head gently back down on the pillow. 'If the eyes move in the opposite direction to the rotation of the head, it means his brainstem is intact.'

'Like a doll,' Aunt Gillian says, vaguely. I can tell the presence of someone official is making

20

her feel better; she's stopped fidgeting and she's watching the nurse like she's going to perform some kind of miracle.

'Exactly,' the nurse says, smiling encouragingly. 'He's doing really well. He should be out of here in no time at all.'

By which point I'll be long gone.

'The doctor's already seen him today, but he's around if you have any questions?'

'We're fine,' I say. There's nothing quite like a man in a position of care and responsibility to set my teeth on edge, actually, Nurse.

She straightens his pillow, writes a few sentences on her clipboard and leaves, her shoes squeaking on the floor.

'They're very good here,' Aunt Gillian says.

'Yeah,' I say.

★   ★   ★

When I was six I was in a ballet performance, dancing the part of a flower girl in something our ballet teacher had written herself. My mother had stitched pink and gold flowers onto my wraparound skirt, but I was in a bad mood because I wanted to wear a tutu, like the older girls, or carry a basket, like Jennifer Allen. I was already jealous of Jennifer Allen because this was 1987, and my favourite TV character, even more than Batgirl, was Penny, Inspector Gadget's niece, who also had blonde hair that her mother tied up in pigtails.

'Look at that pout,' my mother said, helping me into my tights.

21

'You have what is called a 'readable face', Tallie,' my father said. He tapped my nose and I tried to hide a smile. 'Shall we go?'

My mother straightened up. 'Let me just get my camera.'

The phone rang while we were waiting for her; I could hear my father put on his doctor's voice, and got a heavy feeling in my tummy.

My mother came downstairs. 'Where's Daddy?'

He came back into the kitchen with his doctor's bag. He always said that he could run a hospital from his bag, and usually I loved it, loved the instruments he took out to show me. 'I'm afraid I've got to go see a patient around the corner, Tallulah, so I might not be back in time for the show. I'm sorry — I did want to see you.'

'Mummies *and* Daddies are supposed to come,' I told him, sticking my lower lip out.

My father shook his head. 'I have to go. It's very sad, she's the same age as you but she's been extremely ill. Maybe I can bring you a treat home instead.'

I could feel my face get hot, like it did whenever my father talked to me about other little children who needed him.

'Never mind,' my mother said. 'You can come to the next show.'

'There isn't going to *be* another show,' I said. 'Belinda said so.'

'Who's Belinda?'

'The ballet teacher,' my mother said. 'Come on, we're going to be late if we don't hurry.'

My father was asleep in front of the TV when

22

we got home. We tiptoed past the open door and into the kitchen. My mother made me baked beans and potato smiley faces, and I ate in my ballet costume. I never wanted to take it off.

'You'll have to get undressed to have a bath,' my mother said, picking bits of fluff out of my hair.

'I don't want a bath.'

'Ever again?'

'Never ever.'

'What if you start to smell?'

I chewed a smiley face. 'I won't.'

'Well in that case, there's nothing to worry about,' my mother said. She pointed to my plate.

'I'm hungry.'

'So?'

'Will you let me eat something of yours?'

'Like what?' I asked, giggling; I knew what was coming.

'Like . . . *this* finger.' She opened her mouth and grabbed my hand, lifting it up towards her face.

'No,' I squealed. 'You can't eat that.'

'No? What about your elbow?' She cupped her hand underneath my elbow and put her teeth very lightly on it, pretending to chew. It tickled and I laughed, trying to wriggle away.

'Hello girls.' My father appeared in the doorway. 'How was it?'

'She was a star,' my mother said. 'How was your patient?'

'Absolutely fine.'

'Good.'

He yawned. He must have forgotten my treat,

I thought, and I looked at the table rather than at him. He'd forgotten to get me a treat when he missed my birthday party at the swimming pool as well, when I'd had chickenpox, when I'd been singing at the school summer fair, and when I'd been left at school for two hours because my mother was at the dentist and he was meant to be picking me up. The teacher in charge of the afterschool playgroup was very nice and let me eat toast and jam with her in the office, while all the other children took turns on the scooters outside. But even she was worried when it was five-thirty and he still wasn't there. She'd locked up and stood outside with me, checking her watch, and I couldn't stop the hot tears from spilling out.

'Would you like a cup of tea?' my mother asked.

'Yes, that would be nice.'

My mother closed the door of the living-room after taking my father his cup, so we wouldn't disturb him, and we read together in the kitchen.

'Are all Daddies always tired?'

'Only if they work too hard,' she said

'Does Daddy work too hard?'

My mother stroked my hair. 'He works very hard,' she said. 'But he's very important. And he's trying to look after me and you.'

'I can look after you,' I told her, because she looked sad. 'When Daddy's working.'

'I think it's meant to be the other way around,' she said, and kissed my forehead.

★   ★   ★

'Goodness,' Aunt Gillian sighs, bringing me back to the present.

This tightness of chest, this hotness behind my eyes, is exactly the way I remember it from another hospital vigil. I can't tell if the aching feeling inside is for now, or for that memory. 'Do you think we can open a window?' I ask Aunt Gillian.

It's a perfect day outside. Late summer, brilliant blue sky. We're far enough away from Marylebone High Street that the traffic is muffled, but we know that life is going on out there. There's a jug of water — presumably for relatives — on a table at the end of the bed, and ripples sparkle in it whenever we stir. I feel like this moment is made of glass.

'Perhaps we should wait and ask someone,' Aunt Gillian says. She pulls another chair up alongside the bed and starts stroking my father's hair again.

We sit in silence.

Silence never bothered me. There are people in the café who have to talk all the time, but I was an only child with a busy parent. My mother and I developed our own sign-language for those mornings when he was trying to rest. The days got longer, and I spent more time outside: climbing, building, jumping. My mother would open the door that led to the garden and sit down in the kitchen, I would wrap my legs around the tree branch, one finger drawing a circle in the air — 'I'm going to roll over and hang upside down.'

I could bear being upside down for two

minutes. I liked the feel of the rough bark digging into my legs as I gripped the branch, liked stretching my fingers out towards the ground, liked feeling the strain of my stomach muscles as I pulled myself back upright. My mother would press her hand to her cheek and open her mouth in a perfect 'O' — 'I'm impressed,' — then press her hand to her heart — 'I love you'.

Aunt Gillian is talking — she seems to be trying a different tack. 'You must come round to the new house,' she's saying. 'We're still in Knightsbridge, but a smaller place now. We moved after Georgia got married. Of course, you didn't come to the wedding . . . ' She fixes me with another wet-eyed stare. 'She would have loved it if you were there — we all would have.'

'I'm sorry,' I say, feeling like someone's punched me in the gut. I didn't know cousin Georgia had got married, she's only twenty-two as well. Starr can't possibly have forgotten to tell me. Maybe she thought I'd be jealous since I couldn't even manage a secondary-school crush on Toby without screwing it up. I try to push all thoughts of him away.

Apparently the groom is much older than Georgia, but very rich and very nice. I nod fuzzily. The dizziness has returned and I'm starting to get hungry.

'Are you alright, love?' Gillian puts her hand on my arm. 'You look faint.'

'I haven't eaten today,' I say.

She beams. 'I was just about to meet Paul at

the steakhouse.' Paul is her third husband. 'Why don't you come and join us? It'll take your mind off things.' She glances away from my father, who's so still he could be made of wax. Aunt Gillian is a great believer in minds being elsewhere.

Lunch with Gillian and Paul will probably be a disaster, I think, but I really want a steak now. I allow myself to be hustled to the restaurant, where Paul greets me without mentioning that we've never met. He might not be able to tell one cousin from another — Paul is Gillian's oldest husband yet. He looks and smells like leather. 'I see the stock market's taken another nosedive,' he says.

We don't mention my father. We talk about Paul's indigestion and their upcoming holiday in Majorca. Paul shows me a wad of Euros, fanning them out so I can admire them properly. I remember the fuss everyone made last year about introducing a single European currency; the notes don't seem particularly complicated to me. 'You wouldn't believe the difference it's made,' Paul says. 'Bloody pesetas, and francs and lira — that was the bloody worst.'

'Paul travels a lot,' Aunt Gillian says.

I eat my steak quickly. Gillian is drinking red wine and she's a little flushed by the time we finish. Paul makes his excuses after the main course, although I think I see him eyeing the cheese selection wistfully. Aunt Gillian always puts her husbands on a strict no-dairy regime.

'No rest for the wicked, eh?' he says.

'You must be very busy then,' I say. He

guffaws, but Gillian gives me a look.

After Paul leaves she brings up Georgia's wedding again. 'She looked so beautiful you know,' she says. 'We bought this *beautiful* ivory-coloured gown. And a cream, diamond-studded crown.'

'Sounds nice.'

Gillian fishes in her handbag. 'I have some photos. You must see them, since you couldn't be there. Now where are they?' She rummages some more, then makes a little triumphant sound and pulls out a pocket-sized, leather-bound photo album. I lean in, and feel my eyes pop. Cousin Georgia has changed since I last saw her. She used to be chubby and placid. Aunt Gillian said it was the result of quitting her swimming training, but we all knew it was because Georgia ate hunks of butter by themselves.

The Georgia in the photos before me is slim and fresh, with large brown eyes and a vibrantly scarlet shade of lipstick. I think she looks beautiful. Beautiful and lost.

'You two look so alike now, dear,' Aunt Gillian is saying. 'One would think you were sisters.' She's always had active hands when she talks, and now she flutters them in my direction. She's slightly drunk though, and her glass of wine gets knocked over and starts to bleed onto the album. 'Oh,' she says. 'Oh, how *silly* of me.' She fusses with napkins, mopping the wine from the photo of Georgia (alone with her bouquet in a garden setting), and makes faces of distress. She is berating herself, under her breath and very fast. Instinctively I put my hand on her arm. She stops muttering and mopping and looks up; we're both surprised. I take my hand away.

'Well,' she says. 'Well, I think I'm going to have dessert. Perhaps the sticky toffee pudding. How about you, Tallulah?'

3

In the beginning, you are two separate entities — spermatozoon, and ovum. When the two cells come together, the ovum is fertilised. You (fertilised-egg-you) leave the fallopian tube, pass through the utero-tubal junction and embed yourself into the endometrium — the lining of the uterus. You need nourishment, sustenance, and foetus-you does not take in oxygen or nutrients the same way you will outside the womb; your lungs remain unused for the gestation period. Instead you get everything you need from the placenta and the umbilical cord. During pregnancy, your mother's heart rate will increase by as much as twenty percent to produce thirty to fifty percent more blood flow for you. This blood is carried from the placenta by the umbilical vein, which connects with veins within you. Oxygenated blood is collected in the left atrium of your heart; from here it flows into the left ventricle, is pumped through the aorta and travels around your body. Some of this blood will return to the placenta, where waste products such as carbon dioxide will leave you and enter your mother's circulation. This is part of what is called the 'communication' between foetus and mother.

Even before I was born, therefore, my mother's heart and mine were working for the same purpose.

Like me, my mother had been an only child, and sometimes she worried I would get lonely.

'Were *you* lonely?' I asked her.

'Not always.' She was mending my dungarees as I stood in them, kneeling in front of me, holding up buttons to see which was the right one. I was wearing a short-sleeved check shirt underneath the dungarees, my favourite shirt from the age of seven to ten. She had a flowery dress on, and she was wearing her tortoiseshell reading glasses for the first time, which must have made it 1989. 'It would still have been nice to have a little sister, or a brother to run around with.'

'What about your mum and dad? Did you play with them?'

She held up a big pearly button with brown rings around the holes. 'What about this one? Do you like it?'

'Yes.'

'They were quite old when they had me,' she said, biting off the thread. 'They used to call me their little surprise.'

'And you didn't have *any* other family?'

'No. And my parents died when I was sixteen, so then I was an orphan.'

She'd made a mistake, I thought — orphans were children, like Annie, or Sophie in *The BFG*.

'Hold still,' she said. 'You'll get stabbed if you keep on wriggling.'

'Are you lonely now?'

'Not now,' she said. 'I have you and Daddy now, don't I?'

'When did you meet Daddy?'

'When I was twenty-one.'

'How did you meet?'

'At an ice-rink.' She patted my bottom. 'There — all sewn on.'

'I want to hear about you and Daddy.'

My mother started packing her sewing kit away. 'I was there with a friend,' she said. 'And she fell over. She couldn't get up, and then your father suddenly appeared and said he was a doctor. It was all very romantic.'

I went and stood on her feet and she walked us across the room, wrapping her arms around me to keep me upright.

'What was wrong with your friend?' I asked.

'He said her ankle was twisted, so we sat in the bar for the rest of the night with him and his friend.' She kissed the top of my head. 'He had a moustache back then, and a big hat, and I thought he looked like a blond Omar Sharif.'

'Who's that?'

'An actor I used to have a crush on.'

'What happened to your friend?'

'She ended up going out with the other boy,' my mother said. 'And then she moved back to Wales and we lost touch.'

'And you and Daddy got married?'

'Not straight away.'

'But you stayed together forever?'

She smiled, but she lifted me off her feet and started tidying up, shuffling my drawings together. 'That's nice,' she said, turning the top one to me. 'Is it Snow White and the seven dwarves?'

'It's me and my cousins,' I said. 'I wrote it at the bottom.'

'I see it now.'

'Anyway, *I'm* not lonely,' I said. 'I've got Starr and Georgia.'

'And Michael and James.'

Because my mother was so worried about me being lonely we saw a lot of my cousins. We all lived in London, but usually, when the weather got hot, we would visit our grandmother out in Shropshire.

Our grandmother was terrifying — she towered over us, all bones and dark eyes. Her fingertips were yellow after years of smoking and she smelled like lavender with an undercurrent of mushrooms. She walked four miles every day; she didn't believe in being ill. She never spoke to us, unless it was to tell us off, and she cleared her throat all the time, making a sound like 'hruh'. If she wasn't there, James said, going to hers would be great. I agreed, the house seemed like a castle to me, with a gardener and a cook, a lake, and stables — although, sadly for us grandchildren, no horses. My grandfather had been the rider and within a week of his death, she'd sold them all off to the farmer two fields away.

Most of the house, my mother told me, had been built in the Victorian period, but little extensions had been added over the years so that from the outside it looked like a puzzle with the pieces jammed together in any order. There was a long, tree-lined drive leading up to it that twisted and turned and suddenly opened out onto a clearing and the house and a silver glint of the lake in the garden beyond. The windows on the ground floor were the biggest, at least three times as tall as me; the first floor windows led on to a little balcony that ran along the front of the house and the second floor windows were small, where the ceilings were lower. The outside of the house was a pale yellow colour, like it was made of sand, and the roof was covered with grey tiles.

There was an older wing, made of small, grey stones, to the left of the house. It slanted upwards like a church, and it was the only part of the original Tudor house left after a fire destroyed the building in the nineteenth century. My grandmother had a painting of the house in flames that she hung in the entrance hall. When I was older, I asked her why she kept it; she said it was a reminder that our family had been through disaster and come out the other side.

The Tudor wing was where I slept, in a yellow room that faced the walled garden at the side of the house. I was separated from the others by a short, uneven corridor, and a thick, wooden-beamed doorway. My parents' room was just beyond the doorway; it was rear-facing with a view of the lake, but I liked my sloping ceiling, and the latticed window high up in the wall. I had to climb onto a chair to see out of it, which was forbidden because the chairs at my grandmother's were all at least a hundred years old, or so she said.

One visit we were having milk and malt-loaf in the kitchen when a rabbit limped up and collapsed against the open French door. Its eyes were glassy and it had red all over its fur, like something had taken great bites out of it. Aunt Gillian shrieked when she saw it.

Michael stooped to pick it up. 'It's hurt,' he said.

'Michael, *don't touch it*,' Aunt Gillian said. 'Get the gardener,' but my grandmother snorted and strode over.

'Let me see that,' she said, and Michael held it out to her. She looked it over quickly then put her hands on it and twisted the neck until we all heard the snap.

'Foxes,' she said. 'Or dogs. Nothing else we could do.' She took the body and went out into the garden. Next to me, I heard Georgia whimper softly, and Michael turned away from us, white-faced.

That night I had a nightmare about a ghost being in the room with me, and stumbled down the corridor to my mother. My father steered me back to my own bed and tucked me in again. 'There are no such things as ghosts,' he said, but he sat at the end of my bed until I fell asleep again.

We spent most of our time by the lake, seeing who could skim stones furthest across the water, launching paper sailing boats that Michael taught us to make, or eating cold chicken or cheese and pickle sandwiches that we had to sneak from the kitchen. The grown-ups stayed indoors, playing cards and arguing, especially

Aunt Gillian and Aunt Vivienne. My father usually sat apart from the others, reading a newspaper. Sometimes he'd save the cartoons for me, especially ones about Alex, the businessman in a pinstripe suit and his friend Clive and wife, Penny. I wasn't always sure I understood what was going on, but I liked how hopeless Clive was.

Our grandmother sat apart too, watching everyone from her special armchair. There was another, matching armchair that Starr told us had been our grandfather's while he was alive, but no one ever sat in it. The grown-ups never talked about our grandfather either. Michael, who was eleven at that point, said our family was a matriarchal society, like elephants, and men weren't important, although one time when me and Georgia were on a food raid we heard Aunt Vivienne and our grandmother in the hallway fighting about one. They didn't mention his name, and Aunt Vivienne seemed pretty angry by the end.

'You just want me to be a fucking doormat, say please and thank you and kiss their feet.'

'No one forces you to come down and see everyone, Vivienne.'

'And look what happens when I'm not here.'

There was a pause.

'I know you're strong, my girl, but sometimes circumstances are stronger.'

'Don't be ridiculous, Mother. Just because *you* failed to stop it doesn't mean it was inevitable.'

There was another pause, then, 'You're a cold person and no mistake,' my grandmother said, and her voice was even more terrifying than normal.

We heard footsteps start in our direction. Georgia, her hand deep in the biscuit tin, looked at me with widened eyes. We slipped out of the kitchen and back to the others. Without agreeing on it, neither of us said anything about the conversation.

★　★　★

At four a.m. I give up trying to sleep and drag my duvet into the kitchen to watch TV. I'm addicted to it in the way my mother was to afternoon plays. She used to talk about the characters as if they were real. I used to come home from school and find her in the kitchen with the radio on, eyes wide and hands paused mid-action: chopping a tomato, scrubbing the table, feeding the cat. I guess she liked the company. My mother didn't work. She'd been a waitress, like me, when she met my father at the ice-rink.

Later that morning my eyeballs feel like someone's pushing them back into their sockets. Aunt Gillian calls me as I'm sweeping up china shards from a bowl I smashed in the kitchen.

'Paul's gone to Glyndebourne,' she says. 'To see *The Magic Flute*. I don't like Mozart all that much, although I know you're not meant to say that. *Madame Butterfly* is really more my cup of tea.'

'Aunt Gillian . . .'

'Anyway,' she continues. 'I just thought it

might be nice if you could come and keep me company for the day. Maybe we could go to the hospital together. That's if you don't have any plans? You're not working, are you?'

'No,' I say, before I can stop myself.

'Oh good, maybe Georgia will join us. I doubt Vivienne will.' She sniffs.

I meet Aunt Gillian at the bus stop by Hyde Park Corner; she's brought two teas and more photo albums.

We sit at the front of the top deck.

'Let's see which one this is,' Aunt Gillian says, bringing out another slim black volume, with 'Memories' written in gold calligraphy on the bottom left corner. I cradle my cup in my hands, blowing on the liquid to cool it down. She licks her thumb and opens to the first page — I'm surprised to see a black and white photograph of Aunt Vivienne as a young girl. She's wearing a knitted jumper dress, long socks pulled up to her knees and t-bar sandals. Her hair is in two bunches on either side of her head, which is tilted away from the camera, though her eyes are definitely on it. She's laughing at something.

'She loved that dress,' Aunt Gillian says. 'The sixties died for Vivienne the day it unravelled past repair.'

'I didn't think you two were close,' I say.

Aunt Gillian's leaning over me, looking down at the photo and shaking her head. 'She always was a hoity-toity little madam. Just like you when you were younger.' She smiles at me. I'm not sure how to respond, so I take a sip of my tea.

'Do you remember my second husband, George?'

I remember George, a wheezy red-head who used to squeeze all the girl cousins inappropriately, until Starr complained. Aunt Gillian and Aunt Vivienne didn't speak to each other for a year after that. The last I heard of him, he was going to prison, although I'm not completely sure what for.

'He used to say you were going to grow up to be a real handful,' Aunt Gillian tells me. 'You certainly used to drive us all to distraction with that mangy old cat you carried around.'

She's talking about Mr Tickles.

A week after my sixth Christmas, I found a cat in our garden. It had half an ear and one eye and clumps of fur missing; I wanted to adopt it straight away.

My mother was washing up when I ran in and tugged at her skirt. 'There's a cat in the garden,' I said breathlessly. 'But I think he's hurt.'

'Tallie,' my mother sighed. 'Are you sure he's hurt? Is he just lying down?'

The week before I had dragged her over to see a squirrel who walked funny, who was walking fine by the time she got there. And I was always scared that pigeons would get run over — they didn't seem to have ears to hear the cars coming. If I saw a pigeon in the road I would chase it off, flapping my arms at it.

'No, really hurt,' I said. 'Can we help him, pleeeease?'

My mother was resistant at first to bringing an animal indoors, but she gave in when I showed her the frost on his coat.

'Can I name him?' I asked as my father wiped his wounds and sprayed them with antiseptic.

'What would you name him?' my father asked.

'Mr Tickles.'

'That's a good choice.' My father shone his penlight in Mr Tickles' ears and down his throat. 'He seems pretty healthy, all things considered. Although we should probably take him to a vet.'

'Don't get her hopes up, Edward,' my mother said. She put her hands on my shoulders. 'Tallie, this is someone else's kitty. See, he has a collar. We'll have to advertise in case anyone wants him back.'

'But he ran away.'

'Cats run away a lot,' my mother said. 'Don't get too attached to him. I don't want you to be upset about it if someone gets in touch.'

We advertised in the local paper. I spent a month in fear every time the telephone rang, but no one came forward to claim him. It wasn't that surprising — the cat ate like a horse and smelt like an onion. From that moment on, wherever I went, Mr Tickles came too.

* * *

Aunt Gillian is looking out of the window at the road ahead of us. I think I see water welling up in her eyes.

'We never really know what we have until it's gone, Tallulah,' she says.

My father is no longer under anaesthetic, but the rhythm of his heart hasn't stabilised yet, and

40

they want to keep him in Intensive Care.

He's asleep when we enter, his face still the colour of papier-mâché. Aunt Gillian and I pull chairs up next to the bed. She starts talking to him in a low voice. After a few minutes I realise she's singing. Some song I don't know — from their childhood, probably. I feel ridiculous, like I'm an imposter.

I think about what she said on the bus. I wonder who she was talking about. John, her first husband? George, my grandparents? Not my father, anyway, he's not gone yet. I catch myself trying to imagine my life without him; it's hard to see how it would be different, when we haven't spoken in so long. I can't see it being like when my mother died — if my father stopped breathing now, I don't think I would even cry.

'What was that?' I ask Gillian when she's finished.

'It's something our French nanny used to sing to get him to sleep,' Aunt Gillian says, waving her hands. 'It was from the region of France she grew up in.'

'It was from France, period,' a voice from the doorway says. 'So it's probably all about adultery and fine wines.'

Aunt Vivienne enters the room. She's wearing a black suit; the jacket is fitted and the skirt is pencil-style. Her hair is shoulder-length and chestnut-coloured — a dye job, but a good one. I tried to describe her to Toby once, but now I think I might have underplayed her old-Hollywood magnetism.

'Vivienne,' Aunt Gillian says icily.

41

'Gillian,' Aunt Vivienne drawls, eyebrow raised. 'And *Tallulah*. The prodigal daughter returns.' Maybe it's a good thing he never got to know my family, I think.

I can feel Aunt Gillian fuming next to me. 'Why the hell are you dressed for a funeral?' she snaps.

I slip out while they're arguing and find a nearby nurse. She's not best pleased; she rushes in and I can hear her scolding from outside the room, 'This is an *intensive care* unit. If you two want to continue whatever this fight is, then you're going to have to go outside to do it.'

One of the aunts murmurs something.

'If you're finished, then you can stay. But one more word from you, and I'll have you out so fast, don't think I'm afraid of you' — that must be to Aunt Vivienne — 'I have a duty to my patients you know.'

I lean against the wall in the corridor. I've hardly smoked all day and my body is screaming for some nicotine. I close my eyes and concentrate on the buzz. While I still did ballet all the spinning made me feel dizzy and sick. I learnt to turn my focus inwards, and then I could shrink the dizziness to a tiny, manageable lump inside me. I try to do that now, but it's been a while. When I open my eyes I have to blink twice. I can see someone far off down the hall being very still — they look familiar. It takes me a few moments to realise it's my reflection. 'You're cracking up,' I say out loud, and a passing nurse gives me an odd look.

I walk to the lift and push the button, but it

takes too long, so I find the stairs and jump down them two at a time.

Outside, I light my cigarette, disconcerted to see my hands shaking. I tell myself to get a grip, smoke two cigarettes in quick succession and go back inside.

It doesn't seem real, being here for any reason other than waiting for my father to finish his shift. My mother used to bring me after tea-time on a Thursday. She had a friend who ran an old book-binding shop and we'd go there for biscuits and orange squash first, then walk the ten minutes to the hospital, sometimes with my mother's friend, too. Her name was Vicky; she had dark, curly hair and lots of rings on her fingers. She was the only person who ever babysat me, and only once — my parents can't have gone out much. I guess most families have the grandparents around to help out with things like that, but my grandmother lived too far away, and her husband had died of a heart attack when my father was thirty-one. Not — as Starr once informed me — because my granny poisoned him, but because he drank like a fish right up until the day he keeled over.

I was jealous of other kids at primary school, who had all their grandparents left. My best friend Kathy lived next door to hers; she used to go across the front lawn every afternoon to have tea while her granny plaited her hair. When I was young, I thought my grandmother was so different to Kathy's granny, and to all grannies in books and TV shows, that she almost didn't count. It was my mother who first let me see my grandmother as a real person — not a figure of authority — on a fruit-picking trip.

My mother used to make all our jams and marmalades herself. She said her own mother had started doing it during the war years when there was rationing, and then she'd taught her daughter. Now she was going to continue the tradition by teaching me. I had a special stool to stand on, so I could reach the counter where all the fruits and glass jars were lined up neatly, freshly washed. I wasn't allowed to use the knife, so I stirred the pulpy messes in their pans. Every so often I would lick my finger then stick it in the bag of sugar.

In 1990 — the year I turned nine — we had an unusually late autumn that was still sunny in October, so my mother and I went blackberry picking. 'They'll be extra big and juicy,' she told me. 'It'll be nice to choose the best ones for ourselves, won't it?'

I waited impatiently in the hallway while my mother searched for the pails.

'You have to wrap up nice and warm for me,' she said, when she finally appeared. 'I don't want you to catch a cold.'

'I don't want to wear my scarf,' I grumbled. 'It's scratchy.'

'Hmmm.' My mother considered me for a moment, turned around and walked towards her bedroom. She came back holding her pink cashmere jumper, my favourite of hers. 'What if you put this on underneath the scarf and coat?' she asked. 'Then if the scarf feels scratchy you can just concentrate on how the jumper feels instead.'

I stroked the cashmere. It was unbearably soft and feminine. 'Okay,' I said. She slipped it on over my outstretched arms and pulled it down; it felt like cream being poured over me. I rubbed my face with the sleeve. My mother handed me my coat and scarf and watched as I buttoned up. I was still wearing my red duffel coat with the hood from when I was seven. Back then I used to like to think I was Little Red Riding Hood. My mother would pretend to be the wolf and jump out of bed at me. Now that I was upstairs at school with the oldest kids, we didn't play that game anymore.

'Where are we going?' I wanted to know.

'Richmond Park woods.'

We walked hand in hand. The air was cold enough to turn my nose and feet numb.

'How come I can see differently out of each eye?' I asked. We were swinging our linked arms for warmth. My mother carried the pails in her other hand.

'What's the difference?' she asked.

'Things look more colourful out of my right eye than my left.'

'Really?'

'Yes. And when I look at something then shut my left eye and look at it out of my right, then it looks the same, but when I shut my right eye and look at it out of my left then it moves a little bit, like I've moved my head, but I haven't.'

'Well,' my mother said. 'That means your right eye is stronger than your left.'

45

I thought about that for a while. 'Does everyone have a stronger eye?'

'No,' my mother said. 'Not everyone.'

'Is it good to have a stronger eye?'

My mother squeezed my hand. 'There's nothing wrong with it,' she said. 'Your aunt Vivienne is short-sighted in one eye, even though she won't wear glasses. And your grandmother is blind in one eye.'

'How come?'

'Something happened to her.'

'What?'

My mother paused. 'Someone hit her,' she said eventually. 'On the left side of her face. Her cornea was damaged and she never saw out of that eye again.'

'What's a cornea?'

'It's the part of your eye that you can see.'

'Who hit her?'

My mother stopped walking and put our pails down. She took her hand back from mine and rubbed it against her cheek, not looking at me. I waited for a minute, then asked her again.

'Your grandfather,' she said, still not looking at me.

I tried to grasp this idea. 'Why did he hit her?'

'They fought a lot. And your grandfather grew up in a time when it was accepted that a man might hit his wife. He could be very respectable on the street, but what happened behind closed doors was his business.'

'Oh.'

She picked up the pails and we tramped on. The woods smelt like earth and cold air. The

46

leaves underfoot weren't crunchy anymore, but stuck to the ground.

'Why did Grandma stay with him?'

My mother smiled at me. We stopped by a blackberry shrub and she picked some blackberries. She put one in her mouth. 'Open up.'

I opened my mouth obediently. She gently placed a berry on my tongue. I brought my teeth down and the juice was sweet, just right. Not like some blackberries, where it was so sharp it made my mouth sting.

My mother was picking more blackberries and tossing them into her pail. 'I don't know,' she said. 'I imagine it's because there was nowhere for her to go. Things were harder for women back in the 1950s. And she loved him.' She turned away then.

'How can you love someone who hits you?'

'Sometimes people are drawn to each other because they're both damaged by something that has happened to them,' she said. 'And sometimes, if you're damaged, then you can't see past it, and then you hurt the other person, or you expect the other person to hurt you.'

'I don't understand what you just said,' I said.

She sighed. 'Sweetheart. It's absolutely wrong to hit someone, and most people know that. But sometimes you can love someone so much that even when you know they're wrong, even when they hurt you, you still go on loving them.' She placed a pail in front of me.

'That's stupid,' I said. 'If someone hit me, I would stop loving them.' I kicked my pail. It tipped over and rolled away.

47

My mother cupped my face in her hands. 'It's not always simple,' she said. 'But you're clever and brave, and I'm so thankful for that. Every day.' She kissed me on the forehead.

'Now go pick up your pail.'

★ ★ ★

I buy a coffee from the café by the entrance and find a place to sit in one of the chairs that line the hallway.

Maybe I took in what she was saying more than I realised. Maybe I've even used it as an excuse.

If I had to describe myself, 'damaged' would probably make top of the list, and look at me now — best friend gone, a family of strangers and a dead-end job.

I rip off the top of the sugar packet with my teeth; my mother used to make a tear in the middle, my father opened them like a bag of crisps, but I use my teeth.

I tip the sugar into the liquid. I've forgotten to pick up a wooden stirrer, so I wait for it to cool then use my finger. No one gives me a second glance here — hospitals are like train stations, or hotels without the complimentary toiletries, an endless round of people turning up, staying, moving on. Everyone blends into the background unless they do something drastic. Or maybe I'm particularly good at being inconspicuous.

Maybe I never really tried to make my life any better because I assumed this was my lot. I wouldn't be the first Park to do that.

★ ★ ★

I didn't see my grandmother until the following Easter. It was 1991 and I'd just had my tenth birthday. My parents decided to celebrate with the whole family in Shropshire; it was dark by the time we set out and I had a blanket to cover my legs. Mr Tickles was purring in his cage next to me. I watched the houses become fewer and farther between, until the only light came from lampposts along the central reservation, and occasional cars overtaking us. My mother peeled an orange and handed back the segments for me to eat. I fell asleep in the backseat, a Roald Dahl tape playing on the car stereo.

The next morning I woke up in my bed at my grandmother's. I didn't remember arriving the previous night. I shuffled along the corridor and down the stairs. My cousins were all in the kitchen, eating cereal.

'Tallie,' Georgia said, when she saw me standing in the doorway. 'We're having an Easter egg hunt.' She patted the chair next to her. 'Can we be on a team together?'

My mother and the gardener were responsible for the hunt, with paper clues scattered around the house and garden and a prize at the end of the trail. The prize was a pillowcase full of miniature chocolate eggs that we were supposed to divide equally between us, but later that afternoon James was sick, which made me think he'd managed to sneak more than everyone else.

I hadn't run into my grandmother much by that point, but on Easter Sunday I was made to

49

take her a plate of hot cross buns that the cook had baked. She was asleep in the living-room, or at least I thought she was. It was a warm day so she'd rolled up the sleeves of her jumper, and her hands were clasped across her stomach; I noticed how the skin on her arms was still smooth like a younger woman's, and see-through, but her face was wrinkled like an old apple, especially around the mouth. She had a mole on her cheek, and I strained to see if there were hairs growing out of it, but I couldn't find any.

I lingered for a moment after balancing the plate on her knee, watching her breathing in and out. Her teeth made a sucking sound. I wondered if they were false, although my mother hadn't mentioned that on our fruit-picking trip. I tried to remember what her eye looked like, but I'd never been brave enough to look her directly in the face.

At the door to the living-room I turned around and caught her sitting bolt upright, her eyes wide open and looking at me. I fled.

The grown-ups were arguing less than usual that weekend and, apart from my grandmother, we all ate together in the garden every night. Uncle George and my father carried the kitchen table outside and my mother strung lanterns up on the roof of the porch. The cook made potato salads, meat pies, and meringues, and put dishes of butter out with ice cubes nestled among the yellow pats to stop them from melting. A cake with candles was brought out for me and everyone sang happy birthday. Afterwards, Aunt

Vivienne said how Aunt Gillian had always been the loudest singer, even if she was the most tone-deaf. Uncle George bellowed with laughter. Aunt Gillian's face flushed, but she just said, 'I suppose you're right, Viv.'

My mother put us to bed that night. Georgia and Starr brought their mattresses into my room and she read us a bedtime story. After she'd gone, Starr and I talked while Georgia snored gently in between us.

'You know I'm going to a new school soon, right?' she said.

'Yeah — I heard your mum say.'

'She's enrolled me in a boarding school — all the Parks went to it, she says.'

'Where is it?'

'Not that far from here.'

'Are you going to come and see Grandma by yourself?'

Starr shuddered. 'No way. She probably eats children when no one's watching.'

I giggled.

'Where are you going to secondary?'

'I don't know,' I said. 'I haven't even finished Year Five. But I just want to go wherever my friends go.'

'Oh,' Starr said. 'Well, you should think about boarding school. You get to be away from your parents — it's really grown up.'

'I don't want to be away from my parents,' I said.

Starr rolled over. 'Yeah, I guess not,' she said. 'Anyway, I'm tired. Night night, Tallie.'

'Don't let the bedbugs bite.'

Starr snorted softly. 'You can't say that when you go to secondary,' she said.

* * *

The next day after breakfast my grandmother suggested we go for a picnic. None of us grandchildren said anything.

'That'll be nice, won't it?' my mother said, smiling at me over the rim of her mug.

'We'll go to the field at the back of the garden,' my grandmother said. 'They've got horses — we can take them apples.'

I looked at Michael, who raised and dropped his shoulders slightly.

'If we can pat the horses,' I said.

Starr came and stood in front of me when I was putting my wellies on.

'I'm not coming,' she said; she looked fed up. 'Picnics are boring anyway.'

'They're not,' I said. I knew Starr didn't think they were either, and I was going to ask if she was okay, but then my mother called for me to help her pack the picnic basket.

Outside, my grandmother led the way and carried the blanket. She wore old people's clothes — a long tweed skirt and an old, cream woollen jumper whose arms she kept rolling up — but she walked very quickly and upright. Michael tramped behind her, a cricket bat under one arm. After him was Georgia, limping because of blue jelly shoes that were too small for her. She was wearing split-coloured cycling shorts — one leg lime green, the other hot pink

— that I'd seen once in C&A. My father had refused to buy them; he said I'd thank him when I was older.

Behind Georgia and Michael, James carried the apples and sugar for the horses. My mother and I were at the back, holding the basket between us. I let it bang against my legs, not caring if it hurt because my mother seemed so happy. She had her hair up in a ponytail and it rose from side to side like a swing-boat when she turned her face to smile at me. She looked young and beautiful, I thought, and was I proud of her.

'What a lovely day,' she said.

'What's Starr doing?'

'I think your aunt wanted some alone time with her,' my mother said.

'Why?'

'Well . . . '

'Dad said she just didn't want Starr spending time with Grandma,' James said, keeping his voice low so our grandmother couldn't hear.

'I'm sure that's not true, James,' my mother murmured, but she didn't finish answering me.

We reached the wooden fence at the bottom of the garden. My grandmother swung her legs over the top and landed on the grass on the other side, then took the cricket things Michael was handing over. He jumped up to sit on the fence and held his arms out to Georgia, who let herself be picked up and dropped lightly into the field. Michael stood up, balancing on the top rung.

'Michael,' my mother said. 'Are you sure it's safe to do that?'

'I'm on the gymnastics team,' he said, and

walked to the nearest post and back without wobbling. He looked so confident and grown up that I stared at him; he was actually quite handsome, I thought, and then I was embarrassed to be noticing my cousin that way.

James looked annoyed. 'I can do that too,' he said. 'You don't have to be on the gymnastics team to be able to walk.'

'Bet you can't do *this*,' Michael said, and somersaulted backwards off the fence. He landed off balance and had to take a step forward to stop himself from falling. 'I learnt that last week.'

'I'm sure it comes in handy,' my grandmother said, raising an eyebrow.

'You're so *clever*, Mike,' Georgia said, and Michael grinned. For a moment, I was jealous of how close she was to him, then James started climbing onto the top of the fence and my mother dropped the picnic basket and put her hand out to stop him.

'James, please,' she said. 'I wouldn't be able to face your mum if you got hurt.'

'Michael did it,' James said.

'Yeah, but I know what I'm doing,' Michael said. 'You'll probably break your neck.'

'No I won't.'

'Gymnastics is certainly less important than saving your neck,' my grandmother said. 'James, Tallulah and Evelyn, if you wouldn't mind climbing over the usual way.'

James looked furious, but he climbed down carefully, and my mother and I joined everyone else, handing the basket to Georgia while we were trying to get over.

'I *can* do a somersault,' James muttered, on the other side. 'I've done one before.'

My grandmother pinned him down with what I assumed was her good eye, and he turned a funny colour. When she started leading the way again, he hung back, looking sullen. Georgia tried to take his hand, but he shoved her away.

'Get lost, podgy,' he said.

'That's not very nice, James,' my mother said.

'It's Dad's nickname for me,' Georgia said; her eyes were full of tears, and I prayed she wouldn't blink. Everyone knew once you blinked you were definitely going to cry.

'Do you want me to help you with the basket?' I asked her. 'We can carry it like me and Mummy did.'

'Yes, thank you,' Georgia said. She smiled again and I felt ashamed of being jealous of her before.

'Thank you, darling,' my mother said.

'Is anyone actually coming?' my grandmother called to us.

The field was mostly muddy; eventually my grandmother stopped and beckoned me and Georgia over to a dry patch. 'Unpack that here,' she said.

We took the basket to the blanket, which she'd already laid out, and opened it. There were salmon-paste sandwiches, salad, jacket potatoes in their skins, Petits Filous, slices of cold chicken, Ribena and leftover cake from my birthday dinner.

We all tucked in. My mother shifted to make room for James on the blanket when he reached us, but he took a sandwich and went and sat facing away from everyone.

My grandmother asked Michael, loudly, what he was doing at the moment. He was going into fourth year, and he reeled off a list of subjects he'd be studying, mostly languages. 'You must have got that ability from your father's side,' she said, and he went quiet.

My mother broke the silence, saying school seemed like a long time ago to her; she'd stopped going when her parents passed away, which she said was a shame, as it was something else she lost. She sipped her wine and smiled at Michael, who was still being quiet.

My grandmother turned to Georgia who was still in primary, like me. 'And what would you like to do?'

Georgia thought about it for a moment. 'I'd like to be Mary in the Nativity play,' she said. 'Last time I was only a shepherd.'

I thought my mother and grandmother were trying to hide smiles. I was hoping they wouldn't get around to asking me, but my grandmother swivelled her head in my direction.

'And you, Tallulah?'

'I'm the same year as Georgia.'

'And would you like to be Mary?'

'No,' I said. 'I'd rather be a Wise Man and wear a beard.'

'I see,' my grandmother said.

My mother pulled me onto her lap and hugged me.

After we'd finished all the food, Michael tried to teach me and Georgia how to play cricket.

56

Georgia was supposed to catch the ball when I hit it with the cricket bat, and throw it back to Michael, but she wasn't very good and spent most of her time trying to find it, instead. Michael said he wanted to practise his bowling, and threw the ball too fast for me to see it, until I threatened to throw it back at his head.

'Sorry,' he said. 'I'm not used to playing with little kids.'

'Oh, you're so *grown up*,' I said.

'Do you want me to teach you properly, or do you want to play a sissy game?'

'Forget it,' I said, dropping the bat. 'Cricket's boring anyway.'

I made my way back to the picnic blanket and flopped down onto my belly. My mother and grandmother were sitting at the other end. I watched them over the hill of my forearms, screwing my eyes up so it looked like they were closed and I wasn't spying.

My grandmother looked very serious. 'Nothing to forgive . . . ' she said.

My mother put her glass down. I caught the last bit of her sentence, ' . . . hard on you.'

'I can't blame her,' my grandmother said. 'We saw him through different eyes.'

My mother turned away as she was speaking, and the next thing I heard was my grandmother saying, 'Whatever you do, Evelyn, don't blame yourself.'

I felt something cold land on my neck and jumped up, yelling and brushing it off. James was laughing evilly, and when I looked at my fingers they were covered in slime. A fat, grey slug was curled up on the blanket where I'd just been.

'Your face,' James said. 'You were so scared.'

'Was not.'

'Were too.'

'Was not.'

'That's enough, children,' my grandmother said.

'Were too,' James said under his breath, and looked smug.

Later, we walked over to the corner of the field where the horses were grazing. My mother placed apple segments and sugar lumps on our palms, and taught us to feed them, keeping our hands flat and still. The horses' mouths tickled when they took the food and I squirmed inside, but didn't move, because my grandmother was watching me closely.

'Good girl,' she said.

4

'Excuse me.'

I look up at the man in front of me; he has dirty silver hair and an even dirtier dark-green fleece. His shoes squeak on the hospital floor as he takes another step closer. Above us, a neon light flickers, on-then-off-then-on. All the lights along this corridor buzz quietly.

'Excuse me,' he says again, 'have you seen Marilyn?'

'No,' I say. 'Sorry.'

His eyes look milky. 'She went to see her sister last week,' he says. Spit is forming at one corner of his mouth. 'I'm getting worried because she hasn't called — she always calls to say goodnight to Jane.' He wipes a hand across his face.

A middle-aged woman hurries down the corridor towards us. 'Dad,' she says; she has lipstick on her two front teeth. 'You can't go wandering off like that.' She takes her father's hand and he looks at her blankly.

'Are you Jane?' I ask.

'Has he been bothering you?' She shakes her father gently by the shoulder. He's looking off into space now.

'Jane's ten,' he says.

'He's looking for your mum.'

The woman rolls hers eyes. 'She died about ten years ago,' she says, kneeling down to tie her father's shoelace. 'We all miss Mum, don't we, Dad?'

'She's got lovely black hair,' he says.

'Oh for crying out loud,' the woman says. She's still kneeling in front of her father, and she takes his hand again and clasps it between her own. 'What are we going to do with you?'

He looks down at her and smiles uncertainly. 'Have you seen Marilyn?' he asks.

'Come on, Dad,' she says. 'Let's take you home.'

'You need any help?' I ask.

'No thanks,' she says. 'Sorry for bothering you.'

I watch them walk towards the exit; he's leaning on her shoulder. That'll never be us, will it, Dad? I wonder what Jane's father was like when she was growing up, for her to be so dedicated now.

You're absent from so many of my memories. I guess that's how I would have characterised you as a father, at least in the beginning. But if that's all you'd been, I'd probably have been okay with it. Plenty of doctors' children never see their parents, after all.

★   ★   ★

It was May of the same year when the dark-haired man turned up. It was one of those weekend mornings where my father hadn't come home from work yet, and my mother made me waffles. She always made waffles in the spring, she said they reminded her of breakfast in Paris,

60

where it was sunny enough to eat outdoors. She'd gone once, with a friend for a weekend, and it had stuck in her mind. That morning she sat across from me at the kitchen table and sipped coffee while I ate.

'I want to try some coffee,' I said.

My mother raised her eyebrows and smiled at me.

'Please,' I wheedled.

'Coffee's very bitter,' my mother said. 'And strong.'

'But I'm strong too.'

She pushed her mug towards me, handle-first. The first swallow was horrible. I blew on the liquid and pretended I was waiting for it to cool down. The doorbell rang. I jumped up to get it, my mother smiling as I ran out the kitchen.

The man at the door had very long eyelashes. He was wearing a t-shirt and jeans. My father never wore jeans, neither did any of the other men who came to the house.

'Hi there,' the man said.

'Hi,' I said.

The man was staring at me. I noticed one of my socks needed straightening. 'Are your mummy and daddy home, Tallulah?' He was talking to the top of my head.

I ran back to the kitchen. My mother had taken the coffee back while I was gone.

'It's for you,' I said.

She was in the hallway before I realised what was bothering me — he knew my name.

My mother stopped smiling when she reached the door.

'Evie,' the man said, grinning. Something about him reminded me of next door's wolfhound.

My mother stood in the doorway. She kept the door open with one hand on the latch; I hid behind her and saw her knuckles go white. 'What are you doing here?' she asked.

The man laughed, but it didn't sound like he found anything funny. 'Come on, Evie,' he said. 'It's pretty cold out here.'

My mother hesitated, then stood back to let him in. He stepped past her and stopped on the doormat, stamping his boots. 'You're looking good,' he said.

Her cheeks went pink. The man leant over to give her a kiss, but at the last minute she turned her head and he got a mouthful of hair.

I caught my mother's hand as she shut the door. 'Who's he?' I whispered.

'I'm your Uncle Jack,' the man said, looking straight at my mother. She always said my whispering voice needed more practice. He crouched down in front of me. 'Aren't I, Evie?'

'Yes,' my mother answered. She squeezed my hand hard. I remembered where I'd seen the man's face before — in the photo at Aunt Vivienne's house.

We all heard the key at the same moment. When my father walked through the door he found us frozen in our positions in the hallway.

I'd never seen my father go pale before.

'Eddie,' — the man came forward to give my father a hug — 'it's been too long.'

They embraced quickly. It was over before I

could goggle at the sight of my father hugging another man.

My father hung up his coat very carefully, as he always did. 'Evelyn, could I have a word with you in the kitchen?'

My mother was twisting her ring. 'Of course. Jack, could you wait here?'

Uncle Jack held up his hands and laughed again. 'No problem, guys. I'll just get acquainted with this one here.'

'Tallulah has homework to do,' my father said. 'Tallulah — upstairs, now.'

I climbed upstairs and walked along the corridor. When I heard my parents go into the kitchen and shut the door, I walked back and sat on the top step. Uncle Jack was leaning against the wall, scowling. He didn't see me at first, and when he did he blew his cheeks out and stuck his hands in his pockets. He didn't say anything.

'I don't like you very much,' I said.

★   ★   ★

Uncle Jack only came three or four times after that first visit, but the house always felt uneasy when he was there. He would go to my father's study with him and talk; they always closed the door. Once my father came out unexpectedly and caught me trying to listen in. 'What were you doing?' he asked, frowning.

I thought he probably knew what I was doing. 'I was trying to hear what you were saying,' I said. I didn't know what to do with my hands, so I started scratching my head.

'Evelyn,' my father called. My mother came out of the kitchen, wiping her hands on her skirt. Uncle Jack appeared behind my father.

'Perhaps you could find something for Tallulah to do,' my father said to my mother. 'Then she wouldn't have to eavesdrop to amuse herself.'

'Edward,' my mother said. 'That's hardly fair.'

He stared down at me again. 'Do you have some sort of parasitic problem, Tallulah?'

'No.' I dropped my hands down by my side, wondering why my father was clearly so irritated with me.

He turned and ushered Uncle Jack back into the study. I saw a smile on Uncle Jack's face, and I thought I heard him say: 'Well at least you've brought *her* up to be honest, Eddie.'

The next time Uncle Jack came to the house my mother turned off the cartoons I was watching and handed me an apron.

I didn't need a stool anymore. I stirred the jam with one hand and held a wineglass of water in the other, imagining I was Keith Floyd, and we were cooking on a fishing boat, like in his show. Mr Tickles was nudging at my feet. 'Why does Uncle Jack have to come round?' I asked my mother.

She was taking the stones out of the plums. 'He's your father's brother, Tallie.' She kept her eyes on what her hands were doing.

'Is he really Daddy's brother?'

'Of course he is.'

Uncle Jack didn't look like my father, I thought. My father was blond and heavy and blinked a lot. Uncle Jack was tall and dark and looked like he never blinked, even though his eyes were always moving.

'He doesn't act like a brother,' I said. 'Or an uncle. He never even brings me presents.'

My mother looked sideways at me and smiled.

'Other peoples' uncles bring them presents,' I pressed. 'Charlotte's uncle buys her fudge, and she brings it into school. It's pretty good fudge.'

'Do you want to take some of this jam into school?' my mother asked.

Mr Tickles meowed in front of his empty bowl.

'No.' I turned back to the jam.

'Okay then,' she said.

Mr Tickles made the rattling sound that passed for purring with him. I picked him up and hugged him.

'I've already fed him twice,' my mother warned. 'Don't be fooled.'

'He can smell food,' I said. 'He doesn't want to miss out.'

My mother picked up a plum and waved it in his face. 'Trust me,' she said. 'You don't want this.'

Mr Tickles eyed it eagerly.

My mother took a step back and put the plum down. 'I think he might just eat it anyway,' she said. 'This cat . . . '

I scratched his ear. 'It's just because it smells so good,' I said.

'It does,' Uncle Jack said from the doorway. 'Plums always remind me of you, Evie.'

I dropped Mr Tickles, who let out a yowl and

left the room. My mother put a hand up to her face.

'Don't worry,' Uncle Jack said to me. 'I'm just returning my glass.'

He walked around the table to the sink and put his glass down in it. When he walked back to the door he went the other way around; we had to squeeze together to let him past.

'See you later,' he said to us. 'Maybe I can have some of that jam when you've made it.' He was looking at me, but my mother answered.

'Sorry, Jack, I'm only making enough for the three of us.'

His smile slipped for a moment, then he shrugged and winked at me as he left.

⋆　⋆　⋆

'I've been sent to find you,' Aunt Vivienne says, appearing before me in the hallway. 'Gillian would have come, but she's staying with our comatose brother, in case he wakes up and suddenly needs mothering.' She peels off her leather gloves; I wonder why she's kept them on until now. Probably in protest against the dingy, neglected air that seems to choke the building.

I gesture to the chair opposite me. She sits down.

'So you all but dropped off the family radar,' she says. 'What exactly have you been doing with yourself these past five years?'

'Nothing much,' I say warily.

She arches an eyebrow again; it must be her trademark. 'Darling, I do hate the way your generation seems to cultivate inactivity and boredom as if they're virtues,' she says.

I blow my cheeks out. Aunt Gillian is probably right when she says that Vivienne could do with being taken down a peg or two. 'Speaking for my generation,' I say. 'I think we prefer to call it *ennui.*'

Aunt Vivienne inclines her head slightly in my direction. 'I'm glad you haven't turned out so *nice*,' she says. 'I was afraid you would. Your mother was the nicest person I've ever met.' She wrinkles her nose.

'Fortunately,' I say, 'the Park genes seem to have overcompensated slightly.'

Aunt Vivienne appraises me again, and takes a hipflask from her handbag. 'Fancy an Irish coffee?'

I push my cup towards her. She gives me a generous splash of whisky and stops a male orderly walking by to order a coffee.

He's confused. 'We don't have table service here, Madam,' he says. 'But there's a café just over there . . . '

'I'm sorry,' I say. 'It's okay, I'll get it. Aunt Vivienne, I'll get it.'

The orderly smiles gratefully at me and leaves.

'Thank you, darling,' Aunt Vivienne says. She settles back further into her chair. 'That's very sweet of you.'

The café is small and smells like antiseptic and new paint. The boy on the till recognises me from my last order and tries to make conversation. 'Caffeine addict, huh?'

I think of saying that this one isn't for me, but

it's easier just to force a smile.

'I can spot a fellow coffee fiend a mile away,' he says, ringing up two pounds fifty on his till. 'I drink at least twenty cups a day.'

'Mmm,' I say. He's got blond facial hair, little tufts growing in patches on his chin and up his jawline. I wonder if Toby has a beard now — it would be dark if he did, like his hair. I think it would suit him.

The boy's still talking. 'I probably should be dead by now,' he says, 'the amount of junk I put into my body.'

'Sensitive,' I say. 'For someone who works in a hospital.'

His mouth drops open and his face flushes red. 'Shit, no, I didn't mean — I'm sorry, I hope I haven't offended you.'

'Forget it,' I say. I hand him a five pound note.

He scrabbles for change. 'No, really. I didn't think . . . '

'It's fine,' I say.

Vivienne's right — I'm not as nice as my mother. Or Georgia. I inwardly curse my cousin for not keeping her promise to Aunt Gillian and showing up. Georgia used to remind me of my mother, all soft and sweet-tempered. I couldn't be as good as her if I tried.

I bring Aunt Vivienne her coffee; she doesn't say thank you. We sit, not talking, looking at each other from time to time. I notice she has a scar, a very small one, slinking down her neck.

'This is the part people complain about I suppose — the waiting,' Aunt Vivienne says, breaking into my thoughts. 'I always wondered what could be worse than hearing bad news.'

I shrug and inspect my coffee cup. 'Maybe the anticipation is the worst part,' I say.

'How polite,' Aunt Vivienne says coolly. 'Do you really believe that?' She cocks her head at me. I think how if they were birds, Aunt Vivienne would be an eagle. Aunt Gillian would be a hen.

'I can't speak from experience,' I say. 'Everyone I know has died suddenly.'

I look at the ceiling, away from her. At least she's not trying to hug me.

'You remind me of him, you know,' she says.

I'm still, blinking at the ceiling, not saying anything.

'I'm talking about your father.'

I'm careful with my next words. 'I wouldn't have said we were anything alike.'

'Well, in what way are you different?'

I think of my father's love of silence, the careful way he buttered my toast when my mother was too ill to make breakfast. I think of how he changed after Uncle Jack turned up, his slight frown and his closed doors and his closed face; I think of the cards from grateful patients and families every Christmas. I shrug again. I don't think he ever opened up enough for me to know who he is, even before he stopped liking me.

'I'm going to find a bathroom,' Aunt Vivienne says. 'I'm sure it'll be as depressing as the rest of this place, but needs must.'

I down my drink when she's gone; the alcohol leaves a tickling feeling in my throat. I wonder what my father told them. I'm sure he made it all out to be my fault. Knowing he's in the building with me makes me feel light-headed. He could wake up at any moment and Aunt Gillian would bring me forward, expecting us to hold hands. I rub my temples, but that seems to make my eyesight bad. Tiny black spots are creeping in from the far corners of both eyes.

I need to get outside, away from my family, especially my father. I start walking towards the exit. If the roles were reversed, would anyone be there waiting at my side? Would my father? I dig my nails into the palms of my hands. Probably, just so he could let me know what a failure I was when I woke up.

I push my way out of the hospital into the heat and walk far enough away that I don't recognise the streets around me anymore.

'Screw him,' I yell.

A couple, arms linked, hurry their steps to get away from me. I hear them giggling when they think they're at a safe distance. I'm officially a crazy person.

When I start running I don't stop; I don't look back.

★   ★   ★

Summer 1991 was languid, the hottest I could remember. Everywhere on the news people spoke of hosepipe bans, and ice-cream trucks running out of supplies, and pub gardens filling up, even during the daytime. We lazed in the garden on picnic rugs, or sat indoors in swimsuits with the curtains drawn. My mother made lemonade and I got browner and browner. Mr Tickles paused in his quest to eat everything in sight, and stretched out in the cool at the bottom of the stairs, where my father tripped over him all the time.

I was about to start my last year at primary school, and try-outs for the swimming team were that September. When we went up to my grandmother's, I spent most of my time in the lake with my cousins. It was also an excuse to avoid the grown-ups, which was something I wanted to do more than usual because on the second day of the visit, Uncle Jack had joined us.

We were all snoozing in the garden after lunch when we heard the doorbell. Aunt Gillian got up to answer it, strolling indoors with her giant, floppy sunhat in one hand.

A moment later we heard her scream.

'What the blazes?' Uncle George sat up.

Uncle Jack's voice wafted out to us. 'Calm down, Gilly — didn't Eddie tell you I was back?'

The grown-ups all turned to look at my father, then Aunt Vivienne jumped up and ran across the lawn and the porch, banging the kitchen door open in her rush to get to the figures inside. '*Jack*,' she screamed. 'Is that you?'

They reappeared, Aunt Vivienne clutching Uncle Jack and Aunt Gillian walking behind them, looking bewildered. Aunt Vivienne was white, with red spots on her cheeks. 'Mother, Jack's here,' she said loudly.

My grandmother pursed her lips. 'So I see,' she said.

'How's my favourite girl?' Uncle Jack asked,

71

breaking away from Aunt Vivienne and taking long strides towards his mother. Us grandchildren watched with open mouths as Uncle Jack reached her and suddenly hesitated — maybe he was put off by her expression.

Our grandmother let her gaze travel over him. 'Still alive,' she said finally, and turned her cheek up to be kissed. Uncle Jack leant down and gave her a quick peck, and I thought I saw his shoulders drop, like he'd been tensed up for something.

'Who *is* that?' James hissed.

'It's Uncle Jack,' I said, pleased to know something the others didn't.

'Who's Uncle Jack?'

'He's Dad's brother, and your mum's, and yours.'

'Where's he been?' Georgia asked.

'Dunno,' I said.

'Bloody hell,' Uncle George said to my father. 'You could have warned us, Edward.'

'I didn't know we were to be having the pleasure,' my father said, his face expressionless.

'Jack never said anything,' my mother said.

Aunt Vivienne wheeled around. 'So *you* knew as well?' she demanded.

Aunt Gillian had been standing to one side, silently, and now she stepped forwards. 'Children — this is your Uncle Jack — he's been travelling and now he's home,' she said. She smiled brightly. 'Isn't that fun?'

'Why has no one ever talked about him before?' Michael asked.

'Haven't we?' Aunt Gillian said.

72

'I know him,' Michael said.

Aunt Gillian shook her head. 'No, Michael, you don't.'

'I do,' he said. 'I remember him. He used to live with Starr and Aunt Vivienne. And . . . '

'With *me*?' Starr asked.

'Michael, it *doesn't matter*,' Aunt Gillian said. 'Why don't you all have a quick swim — it's getting very hot out here.'

We started to move off and Aunt Gillian beckoned to Michael. 'A quick word,' she said. I thought I saw him give me a funny look before he followed her.

The atmosphere was strained for the rest of the visit. The first night, over pre-dinner drinks on the terrace, Aunt Gillian mentioned a party their neighbours were throwing because Nelson Mandela had been elected head of the ABC, or some other letters I couldn't hear properly. 'They're artists, of course,' she said. 'But it sounds fun — they know some terribly important people.'

'I'm not going,' Uncle George said. 'The man's a terrorist.'

'I didn't know you were such a friend to ex-cons, Gilly,' Uncle Jack said.

All the grown-ups went quiet, and Aunt Vivienne got angry with Aunt Gillian for some reason. I waited until we went in for dinner, then complained about Uncle Jack to my mother, saying that he was always around, until she told me to stop it, looking sad although I couldn't tell why.

I concentrated on the swimming instead.

Georgia and the boys were already strong swimmers, but Starr had never been in the water because of her asthma. Sometimes, watching her, I wanted a cool blue inhaler of my own. Aunt Vivienne had bought her a white bikini, and she lay on her towel on the jetty, squealing whenever the boys splashed her.

'Come in with us, Starr,' Georgia said once. 'It's nice.'

'No thanks,' Starr said. She wore her sunglasses on the end of her nose, so she could look at us over the top of the lenses.

'But won't you be lonely out here while we're all having fun?' Georgia asked.

'You can't *have* fun with boys,' Starr said, sitting up. 'Not at this age anyway.'

Term hadn't even started, but ever since Starr had been accepted at the boarding school, she'd been putting on airs. Georgia and I knew about the school, everyone did; kids there were famous for smoking, and for kissing before they were twelve. Whatever Starr was talking about, she probably knew more than us, or would do soon.

'What do you mean?' I asked. I hugged my knees to my chest, so did Georgia. Starr sat with her legs curling away from her, her body turned in our direction. I thought how flat her stomach looked like that, especially next to Georgia's rolls of flesh.

'Well,' she said, lowering her voice. 'Boys have this thing called *sperm*. It's like, swimming around in their bodies . . . '

'Where in their bodies?' I asked.

'In their blood, or something,' Starr said,

74

annoyed. 'I wasn't listening in class. And it gives them these *urges*, which make them act funny in front of girls. That's why they pull girls' hair, and want to take your clothes off and stuff.'

'Are you talking about . . . ' Georgia started, her eyes round.

'*Sex*,' Starr said in a stage whisper.

Georgia's eyes got rounder. I thought it sounded stupid.

'So Michael and James want to take our clothes off?' I asked. Georgia looked unhappy with this idea.

'No, they don't, because we're family,' Starr said. 'But all other boys do.'

'I think that's bullshit,' I said. It was the first time I'd used that word, although I'd heard Uncle Jack say it. It seemed grown up enough for this conversation. 'No one wants to have sex now, we're too young, and it's too . . . ' I searched for the right feeling, 'disgusting.'

Starr rolled her eyes at me. 'Not everyone's as much of a baby as you, Tallulah,' she said, draping herself back over the towel.

'Ten's not a baby.'

Georgia drew her breath in sharply. 'Starr, have you *had sex*?' she asked.

'I shouldn't say.'

'Oh *come on*,' I said. 'You haven't had sex.'

Michael and James appeared behind us, dripping water all over the jetty and laughing. 'Of course she hasn't had sex,' Michael hooted. 'Look at her, she doesn't even have any tits. Who'd have her?'

Starr got up, haughtily, and started walking

back towards the house. 'I'm going to find your mother, Michael,' she called over her shoulder.

Michael shrugged and grinned at us. 'Stuck-up little princess,' he said.

'Yeah, as if anyone's gonna want to have sex with *any* of you,' James said. 'You all look about seven.'

I kicked him hard in the shin, he let out a shriek and started hopping around. Michael laughed so hard he stopped breathing.

'I don't want to grow up,' Georgia said softly. 'Mummy said I'm going to have to wear a bra, and bleed and stuff.'

I wrapped my arms around my chest and glared at James, who was inspecting his shin. 'I don't wanna grow up either,' I said. 'You're older and you suck.'

'Whatever,' he said. 'Bet you can't do a dive bomb. Bet you're a crybaby — you look like one.'

There was no way I was going to let the boys win. I sprinted down the jetty and launched myself into the air. I was going too fast. I didn't have time to bring both knees up into a tuck. One leg was still extended when I hit the water. The force of it brought my head forward, just as my knee jerked upwards. I opened my mouth to shout and swallowed water. I swallowed again and again, trying to get rid of the water in my mouth, my throat, until everything started to go red and I felt like someone was squeezing my chest. My body suddenly remembered how to swim and I climbed to the surface. The other three pulled me out of the lake. I could feel blood trickling down from my nose where the collision had taken place.

Georgia wanted to call for a grown-up. Michael and James hovered around me, inspecting the damage. 'Does it hurt?' Michael was asking. 'You smacked it pretty hard.' He patted me on the back, the only physical contact he allowed since his voice had dropped. Standing next to him, I noticed how tall he was now, and how a faint line of hair kissed his upper lip.

'Oh, Tallie,' Georgia said. She looked like she was going to cry.

'Does it feel broken?' James asked. 'Can I touch it?'

'It's fine,' I said. I touched it gingerly and felt a sharp pain. 'It doesn't hurt. I'm just going to wash it.'

I set off back to the house at a trot. I wanted to find my mother, but she wasn't reading in her bedroom where I'd last seen her. I checked the time — the grown-ups would be having tea in the front room now.

I heard a snatch of the conversation as I opened the door. 'For God's sake, Vivienne,' Aunt Gillian was saying. '*She* wasn't the one who broke your . . . '

'She did what she always did — nothing.'

'I am *here*,' my grandmother said. She nodded her head in my direction. 'As is Tallulah.'

They all turned at the same time towards me. I cupped my hand over my nose so they couldn't see the blood.

'Yes, Tallie?' my father said. He was balancing a teacup on one knee, and, as usual these days, he looked annoyed.

'Where's Mummy?' I asked.

'I can't hear you,' he said. 'Don't you know not to talk with your hand over your mouth? Come in properly, take your hand away and ask the question.'

She obviously wasn't there. I moved my hand but ducked my head. 'What were you saying just now? What got broken?'

Aunt Vivienne was closest to me. I'd felt her eyes on me and now I looked at her properly. Her face was tense. Something passed over it quickly when she caught my gaze. 'Edward, darling, you're too uptight,' she said. 'Tallulah, I saw your mother go towards the rose garden, if that's who you were looking for.'

I bobbed out gratefully and closed the door. As it shut I heard Aunt Vivienne say, 'Tallulah is really quite pretty, Edward. You shouldn't let her run wild like that. Comb her hair once in a while, put her in a dress.'

'Her mother does all that,' my father said tersely.

'Well I think the problem is that she *doesn't* do all that,' Aunt Vivienne said. 'When I was in the flicks I had to look ravishing *every day*.'

'You haven't been in a film for well over a decade,' Aunt Gillian said.

'And you should really watch out for Georgia, you know, Gilly. She looks like she'll get your acne.'

Aunt Vivienne laughed. No one else did. I hung around, hoping for some more comments on my appearance. I'd always felt too dark and

78

skinny to be pretty. I wanted to look more like my mother: blonde and soft and round, with big green eyes. Not my brownish ones, under eyebrows that Starr said looked like caterpillars.

The aunts started arguing; it wasn't about me anymore, so I ran off.

The rose garden was inside the walled garden to the west of the house, separated from it by a gravelled pathway. I decided to wash my face before I went to find my mother. The blood had dried now, and the skin underneath felt raw and tight.

My bathroom was at the end of the corridor, all cold white squares. The toilet had an old-fashioned cistern high above the bowl, and a chain flush. When I was younger, I hadn't been able to reach the chain unless I climbed onto the toilet, which didn't have a lid, and several times I'd nearly fallen in.

I splashed my face now with cold water — the only kind we got at the house other than for two hours in the morning — and scrubbed it with an old, rough towel. My skin still felt raw, but at least I was all the same colour again.

Out of the lake, I'd been feeling colder and colder so I sprinted back to my room to put some clothes on. I found an old pair of ripped jeans and a yellow Aerosmith t-shirt. I was still in my Steve Tyler stage; I'd fallen in love with him on Top of the Pops and had made my mother buy me the *Pump* LP the day it came out. I would put it on in my room, draw the curtains and dance in my knickers and vest, practising my spinning and strutting. Sometimes she joined in, but she always said they'd gone downhill since the seventies.

Voices had been floating up towards me as I was getting dressed, but it was only when I was buttoning my flies that I started to pay attention to what they were saying, and who they belonged to. Uncle Jack and my mother were beneath my window in the rose garden. My mother was angry. She was shouting at Uncle Jack, and she never shouted. I dragged a chair over, as quietly as I could, and stood on it, fingers hooked into the diamonds of the lattice. They must have been just inside the garden, behind the high walls, because I couldn't see them.

'Don't you *dare* say anything,' my mother was saying. 'I won't — I *won't* let you come between us, you hear me?'

Uncle Jack said something in reply, quieter. I couldn't hear the words but his voice reminded me of the time the piano tuner had come to service the baby grand. I'd watched as he opened up the lid, and seen all the wires stretched out. 'Be careful there girly,' he'd said. 'If one of these snaps, it could take your arm off — they go right through the bone.'

I shivered.

'How can you say that?' my mother said. 'You're not being fair, Jack. Do you think I don't feel guilty?'

Her voice made me feel hot and cold at the same time.

'But you managed to make quite a comfortable little nest for yourself, didn't you?' Uncle Jack said, louder now. 'He probably couldn't believe his luck when you went back to him. Edward's not strong. He always did drool over you.' His voice dropped again. 'You took advantage of my brother, Evie, of both of us. That's not what nice girls do.'

I was digging my fingers into the metal. There was a slap and an intake of breath then I heard the stones on the gravel walkway scattering and what sounded like two people struggling.

'Viv was right to warn me about you, Evie.'

'Get off.'

More gravel scattered. I ducked instinctively.

'Tea was served an hour ago, you two,' another voice said loudly. It was Aunt Vivienne. I could hear her now, walking down the path between the house and the garden walls. I imagined her entering the garden, looking at my mother and Uncle Jack, that half-smile on her face.

'Tallulah's been looking for you, Evelyn,' she said. 'I told her you might be here, but it doesn't look like she's found you.'

My mother said something I couldn't catch. I heard quick steps leaving the garden.

There was a silence from below. I pictured the other two facing each other, not blinking.

'You should leave it alone, Jacky boy,' Aunt Vivienne said finally. 'She's not your type, good little soul that she is.'

Uncle Jack laughed colourlessly and said: 'Poor Evie.'

'I sent the girl out here after you two — I thought it'd be a nice surprise for her.'

'Catty, Viv. You always did try to make trouble where there wasn't any.'

'That wasn't quite the impression I got, darling.'

'You know what I mean.'

'Well, I can't help it. I can't *stand* how faultless she thinks she is.'

'I need someone with a bit more edge then?' Uncle Jack asked.

'Exactly,' Aunt Vivienne said. I heard the scratch of a match being lit and a deep breath.

'Someone dark and depraved like you?'

'You're perverted,' Aunt Vivienne said evenly. 'Let go of my wrist, my darling.'

Uncle Jack laughed again, but he must have let go of Aunt Vivienne. I heard him sigh. 'How can you even bear to be here?'

'It's my house too.'

'Doesn't it give you nightmares?'

'No.'

'I can't stand it,' Uncle Jack said. 'All this tea and politeness. And the bloody people — even the kid.'

There was a pause. My lungs and throat felt like they were filling up with stale air. I'd stopped breathing.

'Don't let it get to you, Jack.'

'Don't be stupid, Viv,' Uncle Jack said. 'This is my *life*.'

'Yes it is,' Aunt Vivienne said. 'So fuck them. Now come inside and have tea. Gillian's such a bitch these days, I need an ally.'

Their voices passed beneath my window, then were gone.

I climbed down from the chair as quietly as I could. I heard footsteps coming up the stairs; my mother was calling me. I opened the door and walked to the top of the staircase.

'There you are,' she said, as if nothing had happened. 'The boys said you'd hurt yourself. Do you want me to take a look?'

I shook my head. My mother watched me for a moment, then stretched her hand out. 'Tallie,' she started to say. 'If anything's wrong, you know we can talk . . . '

'I'm fine,' I mumbled.

I slipped past her and took the stairs two at a time, passing Starr at the bottom, who screwed up her face in disgust as I went by. 'You know, Tallulah, you're going to have to start acting like a girl sometime,' she said.

I made the V sign at her back and carried on running.

I sat inside a bush at the back of the garden with my knees drawn up to my chest, wishing I had Mr Tickles with me. I closed my eyes and imagined I could feel his wet nose wiping itself on my skin, his small furry head butting into me and pushing at my arms, trying to get past them and into my lap. This had been the first time I wasn't allowed to bring him to my grandmother's — my mother said he was too old for long journeys.

When I thought about my mother I got a knotted feeling in my stomach.

It was Georgia who found me. I was lying on my side, my knees still hugged against my ribcage.

'Tallie?' she said. I could see her anxious eyes peering in at me. 'Tallie, are you alright?

Everyone's been calling you for hours.'

I crawled out of the bush and wiped myself down. Above us, the sun was sliding down a pink, waxy sky. We walked back to the house. My father was standing in the doorway frowning at me. 'Dinner's cold,' he said.

'Sorry.'

'Go and wash,' he said. 'We're going to eat in five minutes, whether you're down or not.'

Georgia came upstairs with me and laid out some clothes while I was washing. She sat on my bed and watched me get dressed, playing with her plait; it was nice to have the company. I wanted to be nice to her back, but I was full of my mother and Uncle Jack, and I could only think of one thing to say. 'Your hair is really pretty.'

'Thank you,' Georgia said, going pink.

Dinner was almost silent. Aunt Vivienne ate with an amused expression on her face. Uncle Jack drummed his fingers on the table. Starr asked me why I looked so pale and I said I had stomach ache.

'We can go home tomorrow if you're still not feeling well,' my mother said. I could feel her trying to catch my attention, but I wouldn't look at her.

'Maybe it's the weather,' Aunt Gillian said brightly. 'It's still unbearably hot, isn't it?'

My father said nothing.

★　★　★

The next day I have seventeen missed calls listed on my phone. I go to work like nothing's

84

happened. My boss still thinks the heart attack was an excuse — he narrows his eyes at me and asks if I've recovered, overly polite; I don't bother to try to correct him.

The café is small — there's space for ten tables and, at the far end of the room, a formica counter, with a cheap, plastic register, a tips jar and a basket of paper napkins. Behind the counter is the serving hatch to the kitchen, and above that, our menu, with pictures of the meal options, in case someone hasn't had a Full English Breakfast before, and wants to know what it is.

The walls are dirty off-white, with a green tile frieze running around them. The floor is lino, made to look like parquet. I don't know who thought that would be a good idea. As soon as I get in, my boss puts me on mopping duties with one of the other waitresses. It's nine a.m., so I've got about fifteen minutes before the second shift of regulars start to traipse in. I grip the handle harder than usual as I'm mopping, trying to concentrate on what's in front of me now, forget the last few days. I'm good at clearing my mind. I have these little tricks I developed after my mother died, trying to escape the strangeness that remained long after that day.

'Stop dawdling,' my boss says.

He's leaning against the counter, inspecting me. He's got a big mole on his chin that he sometimes covers with a plaster, and hair sprouting out of his ears. He wears the same colour scheme every day: off-white wife-beater, dark trousers, brown shoes. I wouldn't be surprised if they were actually the same clothes; he's the tightest person I know.

I finish mopping and collect my notepad. The café gets busy soon, and I'm on my feet all day except for a half-hour break at two, where I drink a carton of orange juice in the alley running alongside the building and smoke a couple of cigarettes. I take the second one slower, gradually building a haze around my head. Through it I watch a teenage boy run for the bus; he drops his MiniDisc player and I'm about to go pick it up for him when Sean, one of the chefs, comes out and sneaks a few puffs of my cigarette while I'm distracted.

'I'm giving up,' he says.

'So give up.'

'Get out of bed the wrong side this morning?' He passes it back. 'Not that there's a right side in that dump you live in, Maggie.' He started calling me that after Princess Margaret died earlier this year and I cried at her obituary. I was mostly crying because I felt like her life had been wasted, but he said, 'I didn't know you were such a monarchist,' and brought me a packet of tissues when the Queen Mother died seven weeks later.

He reaches over and wraps his hand around one of my shoulders now, digging his fingers in to massage me. I've slept with him a few times, nothing too emotional; he's a fun person to have around, but he's no Toby. I let him knead me for a moment or two then shrug him off. 'My dump's fine,' I say.

'It's uninhabitable.'

'You've got health and safety on the brain.'

He grins at me. 'Good,' he says. He pulls me in towards him and kisses my neck. I stand there, enjoying being blank for a while, then I reach up and bite his earlobe, gently.

'Crazy,' he says, laughing down at me.

'Break's over,' my boss calls to me. 'Get your arse back in here now — they're waiting for you on table four.'

'See you around,' I say to Sean. I go back to waiting tables, wiping surfaces, yawning, blocking out my thoughts.

I clock off at five p.m., and check the rota on the wall: in again tomorrow.

'Shit,' one of the other waitresses grumbles, 'always work.'

I pull a sympathetic face. Right now, though, I'd rather be at work than back at the hospital.

Another two waitresses arrive to take our place, and for a moment there's a babble of other languages, gossip exchanged — tongues clicking and shocked exclamations as jackets are taken off or shrugged on. Five of the waitresses live together in a freezing cold flat by Old Street roundabout. I went back there once after a late-night shift; all I remember is a bottle of vodka and a lot of empty takeaway cartons. The next morning I woke up with a killer hangover and near frostbite.

'Bye,' I say to the knot of voices and shiny, dark hair.

'Tomorrow,' someone says back, and I leave through the kitchen.

Back at home, I shower and take an aspirin.

My fridge is cold and empty — like the flat — except for some coffee, milk, a few cans of beer, half a tin of baked beans, some squashed clementines and a Peperami stick. I pick at the cold beans and wash them down with milk.

I turn on the TV and watch the news for a while. The average price for a property in England and Wales has topped a hundred grand, a blonde reporter is saying, although properties in London are expected to cost double the national figure soon.

In the bedroom, my phone starts ringing; it's shrill and impatient. I let it go to voicemail. The news moves on to a grim forecast about pensions. I switch off the TV and wash up, taking my time over it, until there're no more distractions left. I might as well get this over with, I tell myself, and go to the bedroom to listen to the answer-machine message.

It's Aunt Gillian.

'Tallulah,' she says. 'I just wondered what happened to you yesterday. Vivienne said she came back from the bathroom and you'd disappeared. And I didn't see you at the hospital today, so thought I should give you a call. Let me know, dear.'

I delete the message.

I turn the radio on for some background noise. Maybe the heart attack will change him, I think, reveal a softer side.

I run my finger along an invisible line in the air in front of me and recite out loud, 'The prognosis post myocardial infarction will be influenced by a number of factors. If a

88

mechanical complication such as papillary muscle or myocardial free wall rupture occurs, prognosis is considerably worsened.'

Maybe my father will die, after all.

The phone rings again, shocking me into banging my elbow against the wall. I see Aunt Gillian's number flickering on and off the screen in luminescent green. Seven-thirty. I try to work out what time of day it is in the hospital schedule — end of daytime visiting hours, probably.

She doesn't leave another message. Nothing's happened, then. I rub my eyes, and my throbbing elbow. If only everything could stay exactly the same, in stasis. I know it can't though. I pull on some clean socks and shoes; if my past is catching up with me, I might as well find the one person from it I really want to see.

★   ★   ★

We left the next morning. Uncle Jack hadn't been at breakfast, and I'd heard murmurs that his bed hadn't been slept in. Aunt Vivienne said loudly that he'd earned the right to have a little fun and my mother went pale. I clattered my spoon against my cereal bowl, saying I wanted to leave right away, hoping home would feel safer.

As we reached the gate at the end of the drive I saw a flash of dark. I turned around to look properly, straining against the seatbelt. Uncle Jack was standing just off the road, hands clasped behind his head, watching our car disappear.

The weather was still hot when we returned

89

home from my grandmother's; tempers were even hotter. My parents barely spoke to each other, although my father must have said something to my mother about my appearance, because she started to sit me down after breakfast with a brush in her hand and a determined look on her face, but, however smooth and knot-free she got it, the next morning it would always be as matted as a bird's nest. She was gentle with me, but the tangles pulled at my scalp like burning little needles. Most of the time I would give in to the ordeal, but once I jerked my head away and stamped my foot, yelling in pure frustration, until she smacked my thigh with the back of the brush, something she'd never done before.

The smack stung for a few seconds; a red mark appeared then slowly faded. I stopped yelling and looked at the floor, playing with my sleeve. I could see my mother out of the corner of my eye, she looked exhausted. I went to her and laid my head on the cool of her shoulder; she wrapped her arms around me and kissed my face. I felt tears building behind my eyelids. 'Do you have to brush it?' I asked. 'It hurts.'

'No, sweetheart,' my mother said into my hair. 'We don't have to brush it. We'll braid it before bed, then it shouldn't be so bad.'

She gave me another kiss, then a pat on the bottom. 'Go and play now, while I clear up the breakfast things.'

'Can I go see Kathy?'

'Kathy's on holiday in France, remember?'

'Do you want to play cards then?'

'Not right now, Tallie.'

I went outside. Mr Tickles wouldn't join me so I tramped up and down the lawn for hours, trying not to think too much about what I'd heard at my grandmother's and dragging a stick behind me to make little channels in the grass. When my father came home and caught me I thought he would tell me off, but he just asked where my mother was.

'In bed.'

'How long has she been in there?'

'Since she cleared up the breakfast things.'

'Is that true, Tallulah?'

'*Yes* — I've been bored all day.'

'Well, another few hours won't kill you,' my father said, and went indoors.

He came back downstairs before dinner and told me I had to be less of a nuisance for my mother from now until the end of the holidays.

'*I'm* not a nuisance,' I said.

I went to find my mother. She was making the beds — something she normally did in the morning.

'Am I really a nuisance?'

I had to repeat myself, louder, before she looked over at me.

'Of course not,' she said. 'But I've been having headaches for a few days now, Tallie. I might have to lie down from time to time and you'll have to entertain yourself.'

'Can I watch TV?'

'Ask your father,' she said, not really looking at me. She still seemed tired, even after her lie-down.

'Was that you bellowing upstairs?' my father asked when I went down.

'I was trying to get Mummy's attention.'

My father opened his mouth like he was going to say something, then closed it again. I played with my fingernails, trying to scrape out the dirt from the garden. 'What's wrong with Mummy?'

'Nothing,' my father said, but he didn't look at me either.

'Where's your bag?' I asked. 'Maybe we could take her temperature.'

'The bag isn't a toy, Tallulah.'

'But . . . '

'There's nothing in the bag for your mother, and I don't want you messing around with it.'

He went into his study and banged the door shut. I wanted to shout after him that I wouldn't mess around but he wouldn't believe me. Recently my father seemed to have forgotten that I'd stopped being an annoying baby. He'd always been away lots with work, but now he didn't want to spend time with me even when he was around.

Georgia came over to play the next afternoon and we built a den at the back of the garden, in the pine tree. We draped blankets over branches until there was a small, enclosed section at the foot of the trunk, just high enough for us to sit upright, and long enough for us to lie down. I dragged up the stack of shelves that were in the cellar, waiting for my mother to make them into a bookcase, and we laid them down as a floor.

'How shall we decorate it?' I asked Georgia, because she was the guest.

'With flowers,' she said. 'And ribbons.'

We went around the garden pulling up daisies and buttercups and some of the more withered-looking roses and spent an hour or so winding them around the trunk and branches.

'Shall I make us a fire?' I suggested.

'How would you do that?'

'I don't really know,' I said. 'But the Famous Five managed it, and they seem kind of stupid.'

'I'm not cold anyway,' Georgia said. 'Let's play shopping — I'll be the shopkeeper.'

She got really into it and hunted out some tins from our cellar to stack in the corner of the den.

'These peaches are really good, madam,' she said.

'Can I have two?'

'That's twenty pence.'

By the time she left I'd bought tins of kidney beans, tomato soup, alphabetti-spaghetti, macaroni cheese and pineapple chunks.

'What did you need my tins for?' my mother asked.

'Pretending to be at the shops,' I said.

'You girls are going to love being grown-ups,' she said.

I entertained myself for the next few days, reading *Alice in Wonderland*. I liked to lie on my front on the lawn, my vest rolled up so I could feel the cold tickle of the grass on my stomach, my head cupped in one hand, one arm across the pages. Mr Tickles liked to lie on the book. Occasionally my mother would appear and ask me about the story.

'She's at the tea party,' I said. 'There's a

mouse in the teapot.'

'With the Mad Hatter and the March Hare?'

'Yes.'

'Good,' she said, and went away again.

That was the day my father came home early in the afternoon. I'd given up reading and I was sitting cross-legged on the floor in front of the TV when I heard his footsteps, and his key in the door. I turned *Danger Mouse* off quickly; my father didn't like me to watch too much TV.

He came into the living-room, slower than usual. 'Where's your mother, Tallulah?' he asked.

'She's lying down upstairs again,' I told him.

He put his hands over his face, almost like he'd forgotten I was there.

'Do you want me to wake her up?' I said. I thought if I asked him questions, maybe he would be distracted enough not to notice where I was.

He didn't seem to have heard me, so I repeated the question. My father took his hands away from his face and looked at me. His face seemed tired and old, older than he'd looked this morning. Something terrible must have happened, I thought, and I felt very sorry for him.

'Don't stare, Tallulah.' He looked away. 'Your Uncle Jack's disappeared, I'm afraid.'

'Oh.' But isn't that a good thing?

'I'd better go and tell your mother.'

5

The passage is open, but a sign on the reinforced metal door warns it's about to be closed for the night. I loiter on the stone steps that lead down to the triangular courtyard, one hand on the black rail, the other jammed into my pocket.

I've come to see Toby — Starr said he works here — but now I can feel my flight instinct kicking in. It's been five years since I saw him, too.

Daylight is purpling, and behind several windows there are lights on, spilling gold into the evening. To my left is the row of houses I've just walked past and a gravel path; in front of me are railings enclosing Gray's Inn lawn, the metal poles completely hidden by pink climbing roses and greenery. On the right is a white building with a few ornate balconies and venetian blinds down over most of the windows. His building is through an archway on the right. I looked it up a week or so ago, maybe I was already planning on finding him back then. I think about him nearly every day. I've tried to imagine how he would react to my boss, some of the odder customers. If something funny happens, it gives me a hollow feeling that I can't share it with him. If something bad happens — but that's why I'm here. I know he'll understand.

I stare at the grey, uneven paving slabs on the courtyard floor, then at my feet. If someone comes out and sees me here like this, there's no chance I won't look out of place. I inspect my outfit: black jeans with holes in the knees, white vest with polka dots and bright orange cardigan. I don't know why I didn't take the time to put on something nicer, smear on some eyeliner and rouge.

I guess the logical thing to do would be to go to his building, buzz on the door, or wait outside to see if he comes out. I could be waiting for a long time, though, or he could come out with someone else, not want to talk. After all, we didn't just lose touch gradually. I left pretty abruptly.

Or he might have forgotten me. Maybe I've built up our relationship in my head. Maybe he never felt the same way. Maybe it's weird I think about him so much.

I hear footsteps, and talking; I resist the urge to hide. A man and a woman come around the corner. They're both in smart suits, carrying briefcases, and both have shiny brown hair; I wonder if they're related. Or maybe they're dating.

They see me and smile. Or, at least, the man smiles, the woman looks like she's sizing me up.

'Working late?' he asks.

Tell them you're looking for a friend.

'Yeah,' I say.

'You're not the first,' he says. He climbs the steps to stand in front of me and gestures at the door. 'After you.'

'Thanks,' I mumble.

They follow me out into the road I was just

on. I could ask them now if they know Toby. I don't know how many people work in the Inn, they probably won't have heard of him.

'Have a nice evening,' the man says.

'You too,' I say, but he's already turning to the woman and asking how she's getting home.

I walk the long way around to get to the tube, making sure I don't bump into those two again. I feel like an idiot, standing on the escalator as it takes me underground. What was the point in coming all this way, then?

I wonder if Toby still has his shy smile, if he's developed a slouch from sitting in front of a computer all day. Maybe he was never as good-looking as I thought; there weren't many guys to compare him to.

A gust of warm air hits me at Highbury & Islington, even though it's evening. I walk home quickly, my bag strap's rubbing against my neck and my feet hurt and I'm tired. I let myself in. My phone rings again, I check I'm not missing a call from Starr. If she was around, I wouldn't have gone to see Toby. I just need someone to talk to, I tell myself, but I know it's bullshit. Toby's the only person I've ever even *thought* of opening up to about my father.

At around eleven o'clock I go over to the open window and lean out. The sky is velvet-black and close with the heat. A cat prowls among the rubbish bins. A few drunk guys stagger past, one of them wraps himself around a lamppost and pretends to feel it up. His friends think it's hilarious. I pull my head back inside and draw the curtains.

★ ★ ★

'Why *did* Uncle Jack leave?' I asked Aunt Gillian, a week after the news reached us. We were helping get her house ready for my mother's birthday party.

'He probably had to,' Aunt Gillian said, mysteriously.

'Why?'

'I don't know. He could have been mixed up in things.'

'What things?'

'Things — ' Aunt Gillian said. She flapped her hands at me. 'This isn't the time, Tallulah.'

'What things?'

'Could you find your mother in the kitchen?' she asked. 'Her birthday cake needs dusting with icing sugar. I forgot to do it before.'

Aunt Vivienne was setting up folding chairs next to us in the living-room. Georgia told me that she and Gillian had been fighting over having my mother's birthday party at Gillian's, and not at our house. Aunt Vivienne said Gillian was a control freak; Gillian said she was only trying to help out. When I thought about it, I couldn't remember ever having a party for my mother. Usually we went to the cinema, and she and my father had a glass of wine when he got back from work. She didn't like to make a fuss, she said. And her birthday was in August, which meant that most people were on holiday anyway. Georgia also told me that my father had said this was a special occasion, to try to get her out of herself, but neither of us were

98

sure exactly what that meant.

'What cake is it?' I asked.

'It's Victoria Sponge,' Aunt Gillian said, looking down at a list in her hand.

'My mum hates Victoria Sponge.'

Vivienne opened another folding chair, a little too forcefully. 'See that, Gillian?' she said. 'You don't always get it right.'

Starr and Georgia, who had been polishing the cutlery, looked up, interested. Aunt Vivienne and Aunt Gillian were facing off above my head, hands on hips. Aunt Vivienne was wearing a tight-fitting black cocktail dress, with a long green ribbon tied around her bun. Aunt Gillian was wearing white trousers and a mustard-coloured sweater, and her face looked pink and hot.

'Well, I'm sorry, Tallulah, but most people don't,' Aunt Gillian said, ignoring Vivienne's comment. 'Most people love chocolate cake, but hate lemon. Or love lemon but hate carrot. Victoria Sponge is a compromise.'

Outside, we could hear the whooping from James and Michael as they tried to bat a cricket ball into an open, upstairs window. They'd been excused from setting up because they were boys and would only get in the way.

'My mum hates it,' I said again.

'It's Evelyn's fucking party, and she doesn't like Victoria fucking Sponge,' Aunt Vivienne said. Starr looked embarrassed.

'I don't see why *you're* getting so involved, Vivienne,' Aunt Gillian said. 'Maybe you should just go outside for a bit. Have some air.'

99

'Are you afraid I'll make a scene, Gilly?'

'I just don't know why you're getting so upset,' Aunt Gillian said.

'Of course I'm upset,' Aunt Vivienne hissed. 'Jack's missing. You need to fucking react, Gillian, he's your brother too, I mean . . . ' She tailed off, and smoothed her hair back from her face.

'Mum?' Starr said.

Aunt Vivienne swept out of the room.

The room got calmer after she left. Aunt Gillian shrugged her shoulders. 'Perhaps it's best if you just help with the cake now, pet,' she said.

I nearly ran into my father in the hallway. He was carrying a newspaper and looked like he was trying to escape. 'Don't run indoors, Tallulah,' he said automatically.

'Sorry,' I said, trying to look responsible. Since Uncle Jack, I'd been careful not to get on my father's bad side, although I rarely succeeded. I carried on past him, walking quickly but carefully.

My mother was sitting in the kitchen, fresh coffee in front of her. She was wearing jeans and a cream top and that made me feel uneasy, because normally my mother dressed up for parties. She was tapping her wedding ring against the mug, making a dull clinking sound; that seemed unlike her too. I shook my head. This was my first grown-up birthday celebration, and so far it was shaping up to be a pretty strange afternoon.

'Aunt Gillian says you have to do the icing sugar,' I said, pointing at the cake in front of her.

My mother turned her face towards me. She had bright red spots on her cheeks, but besides these I'd never seen her face so grey. She took my hand with both of hers, and cupped it underneath her chin, kissing it absent-mindedly. I shifted my weight from one foot to the other. My mother held my hand loosely, her fingers hot from the coffee. A ladybird dropped from its flight path onto her shoulder and we watched it together with interest.

'Shall I get a leaf to put it on?' I asked her after a while.

She didn't act like she'd heard me, but when I made a move to go she pulled me in towards her and squeezed me hard. She nibbled on my ear, like she used to do when I was little. I let her, even though bending down made my back ache.

'I love you, Tallie,' she said. 'Everything's going to be alright.'

On my way back to the living-room I stopped short; Aunt Vivienne was blocking the hallway, standing in front of the coat rack. As I was about to turn and tiptoe in the other direction, she reached out and took the sleeve of my mother's jacket in between her fingers, stroking it. She made a weird half-moan, half-whisper noise in her throat, which sounded like '*Jack*', then stood perfectly still, looking like she was in pain.

'Aunt Vivienne?' I said.

She wheeled around. 'Were you spying on me?'

'No.'

'Yes you were. How long have you been standing there?'

'I dunno.'

'Bloody child,' she said, then walked out of the front door.

The hours slipped by. People arrived, mostly strangers; they stopped to talk to me, and to eat the food that my mother and Aunt Gillian had laid out. I ate too; I was starving. Despite the fuss I'd made, Aunt Gillian's Victoria Sponge was perfect: warm, soft and buttery, with just a hint of lemon.

Halfway through the party, I took a cup of orange squash and drew myself into a corner. I flipped open a folding chair and sat down, crossing my legs on the seat until I remembered I was wearing a dress and was probably exposing my knickers.

The dress itself was bothering me, all lace and stiff underskirt. Aunt Gillian had loaned me one of Georgia's. She'd also jammed me into a pair of Georgia's tight, polished shoes and they were making my feet hot. I envied Starr on the other side of the room, barefoot and in black stirrup leggings and a crop top. Even if Aunt Vivienne was crazy, she chose cool clothes for her daughter. I wanted to scream and rip mine off, but I sat quietly and sipped my juice. As I was draining the last drop, the front doorbell rang.

'I'll get it,' Aunt Gillian called. She shimmied over the floor, air-kissing guests as she passed them. I caught Starr's eye across the room — she made a face and I grinned.

I heard the front door opening and then my grandmother's voice. 'Gillian, I found someone to chauffeur me, so I didn't need a taxi after all.'

102

Then my grandmother appeared in the doorway, with a giant man I'd never seen before. Aunt Gillian was right behind them, looking flustered. 'You didn't tell me you were bringing anyone, Mother.'

'It's not a date, if that's what you're worried about,' my grandmother said. She saw me and nodded in my direction. I gave her a shy wave.

'Mother . . .'

'Be quiet, Gillian,' my grandmother said, and strode over to my mother. 'Happy birthday, Evelyn.'

'Thank you,' my mother said.

'I brought you an old friend.'

'Thank you,' my mother said again, but I saw her shake a little.

Out of the corner of my eye, I saw Starr signalling me to follow her outside. I wanted to watch what was happening at the other end of the room, but she looked desperate.

'Have you seen my mum?' she hissed at me, when we were in the hallway.

'Not since before the party.'

'Crap. She'll flip if she misses him.'

'Misses who?'

'That new guy, who came in with Grandma.'

'Who is he?'

'I can't remember his name, but he came to the flat once before. She was talking about him the other day. Can you help me find her?'

'Okay.'

I spent five minutes walking around the house and garden but I couldn't see Aunt Vivienne. I came back and sat on the doorstep, and after a moment, the giant came out and sat down next to me. 'Howdy,' the giant said.

'Hey,' I said.

He had long grey-streaked hair and he was wearing dirty brown boots. When he smiled I noticed that a few of his teeth were black. 'You must be Tallulah,' he said. 'I'm Malkie.' He put his hand out — a huge paw, with rough patches of yellow skin at the base and tip of each finger. I gave him my hand and he shook it solemnly. We let go and sat in silence. Malkie smelled like bonfire smoke. I liked just sitting and breathing him in.

'I haven't seen you around before,' he said after a while. His voice was low, and soft, and when he said 'round', it sounded more like '*roond*'.

'I've never seen you either,' I said.

'I've been looking out (*oot*) for you, though. Jacky used to talk about you, and I wanted to see for myself.'

'See what?' I asked.

Malkie looked down at me, smiling. 'You, sugar.'

I stared at him.

'He seemed pretty taken with you,' he said after a while. He crossed one leg over the other, letting the raised ankle rest on his knee. 'I guess everyone should get to know their nieces.'

I continued staring.

'Well?' Malkie said. He smiled encouragingly.

'I only saw him a couple of times,' I said. 'I don't really know him.'

Malkie pulled a cigarette packet from his suit

pocket. 'Jacky isn't always good with people.'

The sun came out and flooded the garden with light. Malkie leaned back and sucked sincerely on his cigarette. I took off my shoes and socks and stretched out my legs. Ivy and purple wisteria curled up the trellis on the front of the house, and filled my nose with the smell of summer. Aunt Gillian had placed a doormat in front of the doorstep. It was brown, with curly writing spelling out 'come in' to the visitor.

'Have you seen Uncle Jack?' I asked Malkie.

'Nope,' he said, flicking some ash to the ground. 'From what I hear no one's seen him for a few weeks. Your aunt's pretty mad about that.'

'You mean Vivienne?'

He nodded and grinned. 'She's a handful that one.'

'Why's he disappeared?'

'Jacky was always pretty much a law unto himself.' Malkie looked away and dragged on his cigarette again. 'How's your mom enjoying her party? I haven't had much of a chance to speak to her.'

'Do you know her as well?'

'Yeah, from a while back. Nice lady, your mom.'

'No shit,' I said.

Malkie gave me a sideways look, but didn't say anything. I warmed to him even more. 'How do you know her?'

'Me, your Uncle Jacky and Vivienne were all friends first and then Vivienne introduced us to Evie — your mom.'

'And you were good friends?'

'Pretty good, yeah.'

'What about my grandma?'

'I have a lot of respect for your grandmother too.'

'How did you know Aunt Vivienne and Uncle Jack?'

'Jacky was right about one thing — you ask a lot of questions.'

I was silent for a moment. 'Are you annoyed?'

'By you? Course not.'

I sighed loudly, hoping to convey the depth of my feeling. '*I'm* annoyed,' I said. 'No one cares about me. I'm sick of it.' I picked up a stone and threw it at Aunt Gillian's driveway, then curled my toes on the ground, gathering more ammunition into my feet.

'I see.' Malkie stubbed out his cigarette. 'Well, when I'm feeling frustrated I like to listen to music.'

'Like what?'

'Classical, mostly.'

'Boring.' My father had a huge collection of classical tapes — all music and no words.

Malkie looked back at me, resting his chin on his shoulder. 'Chopin's 'Funeral March',' he said after a pause. He grinned again. 'They played it at JFK's funeral.'

'Who's that?'

He shook his head. 'Don't you know any history?' he teased. 'Kennedy was the President of the USA. Before your time, of course.'

'Oh,' I said, trying to look like I knew what he was talking about.

'Jeez,' Malkie said, rubbing his neck. 'You never really know how old you are 'til everyone you've heard of is dead.' He looked away.

'How old *are* you?'

Malkie grinned again. 'I try not to think about that,' he said. 'How old are you?'

'Ten.' I scratched at a bite on my leg. 'How does it go?' I asked, 'The Kennedy song.'

'If I had a piano, I'd pick it out for you.'

'You play the piano?' I was surprised. Malkie's hands didn't look like they could do anything delicate.

He pretended to swipe at me. 'Yes I can play the piano, little lady,' he said.

I stood up. 'There's a music room downstairs,' I said. 'We can go down, no one will be there, and it's soundproofed.' Aunt Gillian wanted her kids to be musical, but she didn't necessarily want to hear it.

I led Malkie back into the house, carrying my socks and shoes in my hands. Malkie followed on his tiptoes along the parquet floor.

He whistled when he saw the piano, a black Steinway Grand. I pulled up the stool from the corner for him; it didn't seem like Georgia and James had been practising too hard.

Malkie sat down and ran his fingers lightly over the keys. I sat cross-legged on the wooden floor, my shoes and socks abandoned, my heart thumping in my chest. Malkie started to play. He closed his eyes and swayed slightly, rocking backwards and swelling forwards with the movement of the music. I drew my legs up and buried my face into my knees, using them to

107

squeeze my eyes shut too. I had never played the piano, or heard anyone who was any good play in front of me, and it made me feel the closeness of the room, and the humming of my body and the air around us.

'That was so sad,' I said, when the piece was over.

'Yeah,' he agreed.

I looked down at my feet, my eyes welling up. Malkie must have seen them, because he swung his legs around and faced me. 'You can let it all out, doll, I don't mind.'

It was just as well — the tears were already spilling out onto my dress. Malkie gathered me up in his arms and sat me down in his lap. I was too big to sit like that with my mother, but I felt almost lost inside Malkie's giant hug. I waited until my shoulders had stopped heaving before I spoke.

'It's my mum's birthday and she's sad,' I said.

'I'm sorry, doll. Do you know why she's sad?'

'No. But she got worse after Uncle Jack went away,' I said. I sniffed and wiped snot off my face. Malkie offered me his sleeve.

'Is that so?'

'Yeah,' I said. 'But I know they're not friends anymore. I heard them arguing and my mum said Jack wasn't being fair, and Uncle Jack said she took advantage of my dad.'

'Oh?'

'Why would he say that?'

Malkie looked uneasy. 'I dunno,' he muttered.

I punched my leg in frustration. 'I don't like Uncle Jack,' I said. '*I'm* not sad about him going away. I just want my mum to be normal, like before.'

'Sometimes people are sad, doll. You just have to let it run its course.'

'So do nothing?'

'Yep.'

'That's stupid.'

'Well that's my advice,' he said. 'You can take it or leave it.'

'I'm gonna leave it.'

Malkie chuckled. 'You know your own mind, at least,' he said.

Aunt Gillian swooped down on us when we emerged from the music room. 'Tallie,' she cried. 'We've all been so worried about you.'

'I was just downstairs with Malkie,' I said, pulling my arm out of her grip. 'He was playing the piano for me.'

'You play the piano?' Aunt Gillian looked a little taken aback. My face burned.

Malkie inclined his head at her, and gave me a wink.

'Well, it was very nice of you to show Tallie,' Aunt Gillian said. 'But really, none of us knew where she was. Everyone's very upset.'

'Who's upset?' I asked.

She ignored me. 'Evelyn's . . . not strong at the moment,' she said to Malkie. 'And the children . . . '

James strutted out of the kitchen with the largest sandwich I'd ever seen. 'Hi, Dolly,' he said to me, spraying crumbs everywhere.

Aunt Gillian looked a little put out. 'Dolly?'

'Dolly Parton,' James said. He dug me in the

109

ribs with his elbow, then remembered the last time and quickly sidestepped away. 'It's a joke, Mum. 'Cos she's got no *tits*.'

'James,' Aunt Gillian said, looking shocked. 'I can't believe I just heard that word come out of your mouth.'

'Yeah, shut up, idiot,' I said. I refrained from kicking him; I didn't want Malkie to see me lose my cool.

'I'm sorry, Gillian,' Malkie said. 'I didn't mean to cause any trouble.'

'Well in that case you shouldn't be here at all,' Uncle George said, suddenly behind Aunt Gillian and James and putting his hands on their shoulders.

Malkie narrowed his eyes. 'I don't see how it's any of your business.'

'It's my *house*, sonny. And I don't appreciate old skeletons forcing their way out of locked closets.'

'Matilda invited me.'

'Well, no one else wants you here.'

'Why can't Malkie stay?' I said.

The sunlight falling through the hall window glinted off Uncle George's glasses, hiding his eyes. 'Because, Tallulah,' he said slowly. 'Your aunt and I don't welcome thieves and drug addicts into our house. Especially not crack-heads who ruin people's lives. Why don't you just run on back to Canada, where you belong.'

Malkie's bellow was like no sound I'd ever heard a human make. James' mouth fell open and Aunt Gillian whimpered. Turning towards

Malkie, I saw him ball his hand into a fist and start advancing on Uncle George, then, 'Mr Jones,' my father said, appearing from the kitchen. I realised he must have been standing just out of sight, listening to our conversation. Malkie stopped and my father gestured towards the front door. 'If you wouldn't mind stepping outside.'

'Malkie,' Aunt Gillian said, her voice trembling. 'Malkie, please — we're just trying to think of the children.'

Malkie glared at Uncle George and followed my father outside. Uncle George faced Aunt Gillian, wiping his forehead. 'Did you see that?' he asked. 'He was going to *hit me!*'

Aunt Gillian put her hand on his arm and shook her head quickly. She looked at me and James, then at someone behind us. I turned to see Michael with a strange expression on his face.

'Tallulah, James, you two run off and play now,' she said. 'Michael, can you make sure they stay upstairs for a bit?'

'We don't need looking after,' James grumbled, but he followed his older brother and so did I.

Upstairs, James shut his bedroom door behind us, muffling the buzz of the party downstairs. We sat on the floor, leaning against his bed. Michael stood at the window, kicking his heels against the wall.

'Why was your dad hiding in the kitchen?' James said.

'Why was *your* dad so mean?'

'He's not our dad,' Michael said, without looking at me.

I was surprised. Uncle George was Aunt Gillian's second husband, but my cousins never talked about it. Uncle John, Gillian's first husband, had died when I was one, and I'd never questioned how the children would feel about his replacement.

'Your stepdad then,' I said. 'What he said was horrible.' I hadn't understood what he'd meant exactly, but I'd caught the tone. 'What's a crack-head?'

Michael was ignoring us, fiddling with the cord that tied the curtain back, so I turned to James who shrugged. I felt angry. Malkie had been nice to me. I didn't understand why everyone was being rude to him.

'He called Malkie a thief, but he wasn't stealing — I was with him, he didn't touch anything.'

'George doesn't like Uncle Jack or his friends,' Michael said.

'Why?'

'He's a bad influence,' James said. 'Jack always has problems and we always have to pick up the pieces.'

Michael snorted. 'You're just repeating George word for word.'

'What problems does Uncle Jack have?' I asked.

James gave me a funny look. 'You can't actually be as thick as you seem,' he said pityingly.

I went to kick him, but he scrambled out of the way.

'Stop it, kids,' Michael said, but I saw his grin.

112

I lay down; James stayed where he was, looking down at me. 'You know, Tallie, if you don't change your behaviour, you're going to end up like Jack,' he said.

'Like how?' I asked.

James muttered something under his breath.

'I can't hear you,' I said. 'But you better not be calling me names.'

'Don't say anything,' Michael warned from across the room.

'I won't. Tallie's too much of a baby, anyway, and she'd just tell her mum.'

'I wouldn't,' I said. 'I don't tell her everything.'

I was annoyed — I really didn't know anything about Uncle Jack, like I'd told Malkie, and no one seemed to want to tell me, either. Even James knew something.

'I'm bored of babysitting,' Michael said after a while. 'I'm going downstairs. Tallie, if he's annoying you have my permission to thump him.'

'You can't give permission for that,' James yelled.

'I'm your older brother — I can do what I want,' Michael said. He walked over to us and cuffed James around the head. 'Like that.'

James tried to throw a punch but Michael blocked it easily and cuffed him again.

'Get lost,' James shouted after the closed door, then turned to me. 'I can beat him.'

'In your dreams,' I said. 'So tell me about Uncle Jack.'

'He was in prison.'

'You're *lying*.'

'Am not,' James said, inspecting his nails.

'When was he in prison?'

'Until this year.'

'What was he in for?'

James looked shifty. 'I think drugs,' he said.

'You don't know.'

'I do — Dad said he was into drugs, so it must be drugs, right?'

My mouth felt dry. I thought of my mother at the kitchen table, ring finger clinking against her coffee mug, and wondered if she knew about Uncle Jack being in prison, and why she'd never told me if she did.

'He was selling drugs to people.' James's voice was starting to make me feel sick. 'You do that, you go to prison — it's as simple as that, and anyone who says different is just a hippy.'

'Stop it.'

'I can say whatever I want.'

'My mum says it's society's fault if someone becomes a criminal.'

James smirked. 'That's just more proof she's going mental.'

'What?'

'Everyone's been talking about it. They say your mum's cracking up.'

I felt my stomach rush towards the floor. 'Don't say that about my mum.'

'Why not?'

'Shut up.'

'I'm just telling you what they're saying.'

I kicked his bed. 'Don't talk about my mum like that.' My voice was high and James started to look worried.

'Sorry, Tallie,' he said. 'I didn't think *you'd* go mental.' He came over and tried to touch my arm. I scratched his face.

'Leave me *alone*,' I yelled.

He backed away from me. 'Sorry,' he said again, looking even more frightened. He paused. 'Can we make up?'

I stood there, waiting, until I could breathe again.

'Tallie,' James whispered after a moment. 'You won't say anything to anyone, will you?'

I wiped my eyes with the back of my hand, then my nose. He looked really scared and for a second I thought about telling.

'Tallie?'

'I'm not a grass.'

James looked relieved. 'Friends, okay?'

'Fine.'

We went downstairs. Aunt Gillian shrieked when she saw the scratch on James' face, which was bleeding a little. 'James. What happened to you?' she asked, mopping at him with a tissue.

James looked guilty again, and a little sick at the sight of the blood.

'I scratched him,' I said. 'We were fighting.'

'*Tallulah*.' Aunt Gillian straightened up and looked disapprovingly at me. 'You've been *very* naughty today. Going off with strangers, and now *fighting*.'

Uncle George, who was skulking behind her, muttered something like: 'Blood will out.'

I stared at him with what I hoped looked like hate. If Malkie could have come in just then and smashed Uncle George in half I would have

115

clapped. I tried to imagine it happening. I imagined the piano wire snapping and taking Uncle George's head off, blood pouring from his neck and his body crumpling to the floor. I imagined kicking his head as it rolled towards me, or jumping on it until it was a pulpy mess beneath my feet.

'Believe me, young lady, you have no reason to be smirking like that,' Aunt Gillian said.

I went home in disgrace.

6

'You're late,' my boss says when I turn up for the early-morning shift the next day.

'I know,' I say. I'm already annoyed with myself for bottling out of finding Toby, and now I'm working my least favourite shift: six a.m. until two p.m., with a half-hour for lunch. I'll have to deal with the truckers and builders in the morning, the vulgar comments and the blatant sexism, and the local office workers around midday, sexist in a subtler way. On the whole I prefer the builders.

I take the plates Sean is holding out to me, push my way through the kitchen doors and put them down in front of the two men on table three.

'Lovely,' one of them says. He's got a scar running diagonally across his face, dissecting his mouth so it looks like he's talking out of one side of it.

'This isn't ours,' the other one says. He's got a tattoo of a bluebird on his neck.

I check the order again — it's for table eight. 'Okay,' I say, scooping the plates back up.

'I don't mind,' the first one says. 'I'm fucking starving.'

'I'll bring yours out soon,' I say, and deliver the plates to the right table. Table eight don't say anything; they don't look up from their newspapers.

117

'Any sauces?' I ask. 'Ketchup, mayonnaise, mustard?'

One of them grunts, probably a no. I go back behind the counter and refill the coffee pot. The bell goes off by the serving hatch and I take the plates out to table four, then table five, then table three.

'About bloody time,' the first guy says.

'Don't mind him,' the other one says, winking. When I turn around I feel a sting on my arse. I look back and he's leering at me. I pick up his fork and bend down towards him.

'If you do that again,' I say, 'I'll put this through your hand.'

'Fucking hell.'

'Calm down — he's only playing around,' the first one says.

'I'm not,' I say. I put the fork back on the table and give him my best Aunt Vivienne smile.

My boss is standing behind the counter; he beckons me over. 'What the fuck's going on?' he hisses.

'Nothing.'

'What were you doing with his fork?'

'Nothing.'

'Where's my ketchup?' the guy from table eight yells.

'Pull yourself together,' my boss says. 'I dunno what your problem is today, but it better fucking disappear.'

I take the ketchup over and settle the bill for tables four and five; I refill coffee mugs for table two and take table six's order. I clear surfaces and dry the cutlery that's just come out of the dishwasher with a teatowel. One of the guys on table three makes a signal with his hand and I take their bill over.

'Sorry about before,' the first guy says. 'He was only playing though, sweetheart.'

'Eight pounds ten,' I say.

'We don't wanna make any trouble — we come here all the time.'

'You shouldn't eat so much fried food,' I say. 'It's bad for your heart.'

'I know, I know,' he says. 'But the fags'll probably kill me first.'

I take the tenner he's holding out and dig in the pockets of my apron for some change.

'Keep it, love.'

'Thanks,' I say, trying for a real smile this time.

I wipe the table down after them. I think about my father, and how healthily he ate, compared to this lot. Salads and fresh fruit juices, muesli for breakfast. It went downhill a little after my mother died; maybe he stopped altogether after I was out of the picture. Maybe he spent the last five years gorging himself. Toby used to be able to get through two dinners a night.

I vaguely hear the bell from the kitchen, but it doesn't register until my boss shouts my name across the café. 'Are you bloody deaf?'

All the workers are laughing. I carry the plates over to table six. I try to avoid looking anyone in the eye. Halfway across the room I stumble and the contents of one of the plates slops all over the floor. My boss is fuming when I get back behind the counter. 'That's

119

coming out of your wages.'

'I know.'

'Go and clean it up.'

I get the mop and some cheap blue kitchen roll and clean it up as best as I can. I take the new plate over when it's ready and put it down in front of the guy. 'Sorry,' I say. 'Any sauces?'

'Let's not risk it, eh?' he says.

I try to rinse the mop out. My boss stands over me, watching. 'I mean it, young lady. Don't think there isn't a queue of girls waiting to take your place. Fuck up again and you're out.'

I think about the nurses pottering around my father the other day, wonder whether they enjoy their work. Maybe I'm being naïve, and no one does what they really want to do; maybe the nurses are all frustrated pop stars. I take the dirty dishes from table three into the kitchen and start loading the dishwasher.

★ ★ ★

Sunday night after the party I lay awake for longer than usual, long enough to hear my parents come to bed, halfway through a conversation I didn't understand.

'So he actually accepted it?' my mother asked.

'Yes,' my father said. 'Why?'

'I just thought . . . '

'Thought what, Evelyn?'

'I thought it was going to get better.'

'This *is* better. Surely you understood what a strain it was, the whole situation?'

'Of course, Edward. I was under the same strain.'

'I'm glad to hear it.'

'Excuse me?'

'Sometimes I got the impression that you welcomed . . . Never mind.'

'What were you going to say?'

'It doesn't matter.'

'*I* didn't know he was going to turn up.'

'Hmm.'

'How could I? He stopped speaking to me ten years ago.'

'That's exactly my point.'

'Edward.'

'Yes?'

'Aren't you tired of all this?'

I heard the bedsprings creak, like someone had sat down, and then my father's voice, 'Of course.'

I didn't understand what 'all this' was, but it sounded serious. I thought about Uncle Jack standing in my grandmother's garden, watching us leave, and shook my head immediately, trying to make the picture go away.

'If Vivienne's giving you a hard time . . . ' my father said.

'No more than usual.'

He sounded impatient. 'Why do you insist on dwelling on it then?'

'Don't be like that, Edward. What do you want me to do? Where are you *going*?'

'Out.'

On Monday my mother didn't get out of bed. My father had gone to work early so I made porridge for myself. It was a little burnt, but I scraped the top off and fed it to Mr Tickles. I took some to my mother on a tray. I picked some orange flowers from the garden and took them up too. I couldn't find a vase, so I washed out a milk bottle and put them in that. My mother hadn't opened the curtains. I left the tray just inside the room, next to the door.

My father came home late that night, so I ran my bath and made myself and my mother a ham sandwich for dinner. He was working early the next morning too. I had an apple for breakfast.

I didn't run myself a bath that night. I watched TV until I heard my father's key in the lock. There was something exciting about running upstairs before he could see me and pretending to be asleep when he stopped at my door, although I was fully dressed beneath the sheets, trying to make my breathing come slow.

On Wednesday my father came home early. I was sitting in the kitchen when he walked in. I hadn't washed for two days and Mr Tickles was licking peanut butter off my fingers.

Aunt Gillian moved in on Thursday morning.

My father called at lunchtime; I knew he'd want to talk to Gillian, but I beat her to the phone.

'Where are you?' I asked him.

'I'm busy at the hospital,' he said. 'Can you put your aunt on the phone?'

'Why can't you take time off? Why does Aunt Gillian have to . . . ' I didn't want to sound too rude. 'Who's looking after Georgia?'

'Tallulah, I'm due in surgery in five minutes.

Gillian's going to take good care of you, don't worry, now let me speak to her.'

I passed Aunt Gillian the phone and stomped upstairs.

Before Aunt Gillian arrived, I'd been cleaning up after myself, opening my parents' curtains and arranging things in their room, trying to make it seem as if my mother was getting up from time to time. With Aunt Gillian there I couldn't. Instead, I kept watch at the bottom of the stairs in case the bedroom door opened.

Aunt Gillian appeared next to me once, with lemonade and buttery biscuits.

'Tallie, does your mother — does she *look after* herself at the moment?' she asked, hovering over me.

I turned to face her. She lowered the plate and I took a biscuit.

'I mean, is she eating, and washing?'

'She's just tired,' I said, biting into the biscuit. 'She eats and washes.' I didn't know whether she was washing, but she'd left most of the porridge and sandwiches I'd taken her.

'Oh, good,' Aunt Gillian said. She looked relieved. 'Your father didn't really leave any instructions about that. Oh, you know he's had to go to a conference?' She lowered the biscuit plate again, and handed me the lemonade.

I nodded, though I hadn't known.

'And how are you?'

I shrugged.

'It must be difficult, your mother being — *tired.*'

I shrugged again. Aunt Gillian hovered for a

123

moment then left. 'Just give me a shout if there's anything you need,' she said.

The next day, when Aunt Gillian was on the phone, I carried a sponge and a cake of soap upstairs to my mother's room. I could hear Aunt Gillian tutting below us. 'George, you can't *imagine* what it's like here,' she said. Then: 'Yes. I mean, I can see how it got too much for him. You know how busy he always is.'

There was a long pause. I tried to peer through the banisters and down the hallway to the kitchen, where Aunt Gillian was, the phone cord stretched tight as she moved around the room.

'She hasn't left their room since I arrived. Edward wouldn't say much about it, but I gather she hasn't been speaking to anyone. Poor Tallie, she's the one Edward was worried about. It makes me mad when mothers just abdicate all responsibility like this, it really does. It's just not *normal*, is it?'

I could hear a buzzing sound from the other end of the telephone.

'It's Jack, of course it is. I really wish he'd just stayed away, we were all doing fine. Is that Michael in the background? What's he doing? Put him on then.'

Michael was evidently handed the phone, because her tone changed, and she started threatening not to let him go on a school skiing trip. I waited until her voice got even louder before I slipped into my mother's room.

My mother turned her head when I closed the door softly behind me. I crossed the room to the bed. She was lying on her side, curled up. The duvet was twisted around her legs and there were dark stains underneath her eyes.

'We have to wash you now,' I said. 'I told Aunt Gillian you were washing.'

My mother didn't move, she watched me as I rubbed the soap hard with the sponge. It didn't foam up, but there was a white paste covering it after a few minutes. I put the soap down and looked at my mother. She was wearing a sleeveless cotton nightdress; I decided to start with her arms. The paste smeared onto her skin easily, but then it wouldn't come off.

'Wait a minute,' I said.

I tiptoed out of the room and into the bathroom. I ran the tap and soaked the sponge. I came back to the bedroom and started wiping my mother off, but a lot of water was coming out of the sponge now, and the sheets got wet. My mother started shivering. I got the hairdryer and plugged that in next to the bed and turned it on to maximum heat. My mother dried with white streaks running down her arms; the sheets wouldn't dry. If Aunt Gillian saw this, we'd both be in trouble. I bit my lip.

'Please get up,' I whispered. 'Please, please please.'

She reached her hand out to me and I took it. She looked at me silently for a moment, then pulled me onto the bed with her and wrapped her arms around me. I was so relieved I started crying.

'Sshhh,' my mother said. 'It's alright, Tallie. Sweetheart. It's alright.'

'Are you going to get up now?' I asked her.

She kissed my hair. 'Yes, I'll get up,' she said. We lay there in the wet bed for a while longer then my mother got up and rinsed her arms and put on a jumper and some makeup under her eyes. I sat on the toilet while she rubbed and painted her face and twisted her hair up in a knot. Aunt Gillian didn't say anything when my mother came downstairs; she offered to make tea for everyone and we sat in the kitchen with the garden doors open. Mr Tickles lay outside on the patio, washing his face.

'Lovely weather, isn't it,' Aunt Gillian said. 'I can't believe it's early September.'

We agreed with her. I spooned some sugar into my tea; my mother watched me over the rim of her cup, but she didn't say anything.

'I suppose Tallie will be going to secondary school next year,' Aunt Gillian said.

'Yes,' my mother said. 'Edward wanted her to go to boarding school, but I like to have her here with me.' She smiled at me and I felt my body relax for the first time in weeks.

'Oh, but boarding school is so good for camaraderie,' Aunt Gillian said. She was dipping a biscuit in her tea. 'Vivienne and I went to boarding school and loved it, and Edward, and . . .'

My mother reached across the table and took a biscuit. 'Your children aren't at boarding school are they?' she asked.

'No,' Aunt Gillian said. 'But then there are three of them, and Tallie's by herself. It's so nice to be surrounded by people of the same age,

126

don't you think? And she could even go a year early, they have a middle school that starts from ten. It might give you and Edward some time . . .'

My mother sipped her tea. 'Well, Tallie's staying here,' she said. 'There's a very good school around the corner, and Kathy, a friend from primary, will be going there. We did ask her whether she wanted to go away.'

'I don't want to,' I said quickly.

'You don't have to, sweetheart,' my mother said.

We finished the tea. Aunt Gillian fussed around us with the washing up. 'You've had a rough few weeks,' she said. 'Just let me do this, then I'll get on with the hoovering and then I can start dinner.'

Now that I had my mother back I wanted Aunt Gillian gone. I tugged at my mother's sleeve when Gillian's back was turned. My mother took my hand in hers. 'Gillian,' she said. 'I can't thank you enough. But surely your own family must be missing you. Why don't you go back to them now? Let me do the cleaning and dinner.'

'Well,' Aunt Gillian paused. 'I promised Edward I'd stay.'

'We'll be fine, won't we, Tallie?' my mother said.

I nodded, not too hard, in case Aunt Gillian was offended.

'Michael *is* acting up a little for poor George,' Aunt Gillian said, untying her apron. 'I think he might need a hand.'

She called Uncle George, who came to pick her up. We walked her to the door, and I put her suitcase in the boot. Uncle George didn't get out of the car.

'I'll give you a ring tonight,' Aunt Gillian said, kissing my mother on the cheek. 'Edward will be back in a few days.'

'Of course,' my mother said.

Aunt Gillian hugged me and walked quickly to the car. She carried on waving from the passenger seat until it turned the corner. My mother smiled at me. 'Alone at last,' she said. 'What would you like for dinner? Your choice.'

'Sausages and mash,' I said. 'And mushy peas.'

She put her arm around my shoulder. It smelt of soap still. 'Sausages and mash and mushy peas it is,' she said.

My father came home two days later. If he was surprised to see my mother up and Aunt Gillian gone, he didn't show it.

I stuck close to my mother over the next few days. We made brownies together, my mother's mother's recipe. She plaited my hair while I watched cartoons. We started *Alice Through the Looking-Glass*. We made orange ice-lollies, homemade popcorn, Mr Potato Heads, new cushion covers for the sofa, sock puppets, a soapbox car for my teddies and labels for the autumn jam. My mother spent hours on the phone to Aunt Gillian, who was still calling every day. I tried to teach Mr Tickles to shake paws, without any luck. If I caught my mother staring off into the distance at any point I'd creep away and come back loudly, stomping and yelling her name until she put her hands over her ears and laughed. 'I'm right here,' she said.

'Now can we play cards?'

'You know I love you, don't you, Tallulah?'

We sat down to play cards, but my heart continued to beat double-time all throughout the game.

⋆   ⋆   ⋆

This time it's Aunt Vivienne who calls me. I'm sitting cross-legged in the middle of the bedroom after work, scraping an old coat of hot-pink nail varnish off with the end of a paperclip.

'Hello?'

'Darling,' Aunt Vivienne says. 'You mustn't be so melodramatic.'

I almost laugh. I seem to remember some story about Aunt Vivienne threatening to kill herself after Uncle Jack disappeared. I have an image of her smashing a wine glass against the sink and holding it to her throat, my father calmly telling her to put it down, Aunt Gillian squawking and flapping about in a panic. In my mind I see Aunt Vivienne laughing, her eyes shiny with alcohol, sliding down the kitchen counter and passing out on the floor, the jagged glass rolling out of her hand. I don't know where this picture came from; it's possible I was there.

'I'm not being melodramatic.'

'I suppose running off seems perfectly rational then?'

'It's kind of normal in our family, wouldn't you say?'

She sighs down the line. 'You children, always back-talking. Are you going to come see your father again or not? I have to report back to Gillian, you know.'

'I'm not,' I say. 'I need to work — I need the money.'

'How mercenary of you.'

'We don't all have unlimited funds.'

'Yes,' she says drily. 'I suppose you think you've earned the rights to them too?'

'I don't mean to be rude,' I say, 'but we haven't exactly been best buddies over the years. I don't know why you think I won't just hang up.'

'You'll hurt my feelings.'

'That's a good one.'

'I'm not your enemy, Tallulah.'

'No. You only bother to hate the people you know won't stand up to you.'

She tuts at me.

'I need to go now,' I say. I pick up the paperclip with my toes, raising my leg so I can admire the way they grip it still, after all these years without practising. 'Tell Gillian you did your best.'

'I've got a trick up my sleeve, my darling,' she says, and rings off.

I wonder what she means by that — Starr can't be back from holiday already. I miss her, but even she wouldn't be able to persuade me to go to the hospital again and sit by that bedside, listening to my aunts squabble while I wait for my father to open his eyes and say what exactly — my name? That he wants to rebuild our relationship?

'No fucking way,' I say out loud to myself. 'You can't choose your family,' my grandmother used to say. She probably meant you had to accept them, but it works the other way too. You choose your friends, your lover, you choose whom to spend your time with. When I was a teenager, I spent a lot of time looking for an alternate father figure. I'm sure he would have chosen someone else as his daughter, too.

I leave the flat again late in the afternoon to try to get some fresh air. My skin feels sticky, like it always does after I've been in the café kitchen. I stop off at the newsagents on my way home; I buy cigarettes, a new lighter, some milk and tinned soup. The man behind the counter leers at my tits the whole time I'm counting change into his palm. I hold on to the last pound.

'Hey, you're short.'

'This is for the show,' I tell him. 'You don't get to perv for free.'

'You can't do that.'

'I just did.'

I push my way out of the shop and feel my phone begin to vibrate in my pocket. 'What do you want?'

Starr's voice comes down the line, muffled, like she's speaking through cotton wool. 'Have you been yet? How is he?'

'What? I can't hear you properly.'

'Wait, you're on speakerphone . . . '

I can hear thumps and a crash, as if she's dropped it. Then a man's voice — Ricardo's I imagine — and a slap. 'Get the fuck off me, I'm

131

talking to my cousin.'

'Come on baby, let me kiss your ass. You've got such a beautiful ass.'

'I said I'm talking to my cousin.' She comes back on the line, a little breathless. 'We're flying home in five days' time, a night flight.'

'Hmm?'

'Tal — you there?'

'Okay.' Hearing the two of them reminds me of Toby again, and I'm blushing like an idiot down the telephone.

'So I'll see you next Wednesday, right? Meet you at the Pizza Express on the corner of Baker Street at ten.'

'Did your mum ask you to call?'

'I haven't spoken to her. Why?'

'No reason.'

'She's there too? Jesus — bet she's winding all the nurses up.'

'Uh-huh.'

'But he's okay, right? Has there been any change?'

'Not that I know of,' I say into the phone.

'What? Ric, get off . . . Tal, I have to go. See you soon. And don't let Mum throw her weight around.'

If not Starr, what's Vivienne's trick? Is she here, watching me? I scuttle back to my flat, sleep for a few hours and wake up at seven-thirty. It's still bright and hot outside and I still feel grubby and washed-out. I sit at the kitchen table, smoking, with the window wide open and my feet on the sill. Maybe I'll have a cold shower. I don't want to think about anything particularly, I just want to feel normal again.

At five minutes past eight the buzzer goes. Our lock is stiff, and sometimes I have to let the downstairs neighbour in; I push the button without asking who it is. I can hear heavy footsteps all the way along the hall and up the staircase, but they don't stop at the floor below. Someone knocks on my door. I'm wearing the old, men's t-shirt and running shorts that I use as pyjamas. I open the door a crack and keep my body behind it.

The man must have taken a few steps back after knocking; he's leaning against the banister, and his hat is tipped down, so at first I don't see his face. I see his hands though. They're the same as before, still brown and hairy, with blunt fingertips and nicotine-coloured nails.

'Holy fuck,' I say.

'Hey, doll,' the figure says.

'Hi Malkie.'

I open the door further and he steps forwards and envelops me in a hug. I'm stiff inside his arms and I can feel my heart going double-time. I can't believe this is happening. I can't believe they're all catching up with me at once. I bite my lip, take a gulp of air.

'Your aunt's all shook up about the way you upped and left, you know,' Malkie says.

It takes a few swallows before I have enough saliva in my mouth to get it working properly. 'Oh yeah?'

'Yeah. Now lemme look at you.' He breaks into a grin, holding me at arm's length. 'You're

133

very pretty. Didn't I tell you you'd grow up pretty?'

'Maybe,' I say. 'You want a drink?'

'That would be a pleasure.'

I stand back to let him pass. 'Pull yourself together,' my boss would say. 'Be normal.' I shake myself mentally and go to the fridge and peer inside. 'I have some beers. You want a beer?'

'Sure.'

I don't know how to talk to him now I'm not a kid anymore, and my flat feels suddenly strange, like it's new to me too. Letting in someone from my past, from outside, seems to highlight how closed my world has become recently.

'Sorry about the shittiness here.'

'Doesn't bother me,' he says, looking at the piles of stuff on surfaces and the stains on the walls and table.

'Sit down.'

His giant legs fold beneath him and his crumpled jeans ride up over a larger belly than I remember. He smiles at me; that's the same as before, at least. I put two bottles down in front of him.

'I don't have an opener. Normally I just use the side of the table.' I point to the scuff marks notched into the wood.

'That's okay.' Malkie picks up a bottle and cracks it open in his mouth. 'I've never had a bottle opener neither. Want me to do yours?'

'Yeah, thanks.'

We drink in silence. After a while I start to notice the hum of the fridge, how soothing it is. Then it starts to remind me of the heart monitor attached to my father, back at the hospital.

'Jeez, it's good to see you again.'

I turn the beer bottle slowly in my hands, not saying anything. I can feel my face pulling itself into some sort of grimace. I know what's coming next.

'Pity you gotta be so sulky though. Like I said, your aunt's worried, doll. Why'd you stop going to see your old man?'

'I mean this in the nicest possible way,' I tell him. 'But mind your own business.'

Malkie purses his mouth, but he doesn't say anything.

'So when did you get back?' I ask him.

'Six months, a year, give or take.'

'There's kind of a difference between them, you know.'

'Smart too, huh?'

'Well, I can count.'

He takes a mouthful of beer.

'And you didn't come and find me?' I ask.

'That why you're pissed at me?'

I rub my eyes. 'I'm not *pissed*,' I say. 'I'm tired. It's good to see you too.' I'm lying — I *am* mad at him, but I feel ashamed of it, almost. Malkie's so nice he makes you feel like a criminal for thinking bad things around him. And I've missed him.

'I came to see you a couple of months ago,' he says. 'But your pa said you weren't living with him anymore, and he didn't know where you were. He was kind of short with me, so I guess he wasn't too pleased that I was back. I been asking around and Vivienne's girl told me you

135

were still in London, but she wouldn't say where.'

Nice of Starr to let me know.

'I *had* been writing,' he says. 'Cross my heart. Then my letters started getting sent back to me.'

'Hmm,' I say, but it feels good to know he'd kept his promise. 'So what are you doing here now?'

'This morning Viv calls up, asks me to come and see you. Try to talk you into going back to the hospital.' He fixes me with his gaze. 'So, have I persuaded you yet?'

I take a sip of beer and shrug. We look at each other in silence for a moment.

'You keeping up with the music?' Malkie asks after a while.

'Not so much.'

'You were good, doll.'

'I don't have a piano.'

'What you been up to, then?'

'I left school,' I say. 'I'm working as a waitress. Nothing, really.'

He shakes his head again and stretches out, cracking his knuckles. 'No wonder you had a fight with your old man.'

I finish my beer and stand up, rinse my bottle out and put it on the draining board, keeping my back to Malkie. You have no idea, I want to tell him.

'I hate seeing you cut yourself off from everyone,' I can hear him say.

'I haven't.'

'It sure looks like it from here.'

I turn around and stare at him. I can't believe

he can't tell the truth by looking at me. I want to break something, scream, get his attention somehow. Something happened to me, Malkie. It wasn't my decision.

'Doll, I know that you're angry,' he says. 'But your pa's sick, and he's family. You gotta go see him. Reconcile yourselves.'

'I don't want a reconciliation,' I say. I know I sound petulant, but I can't explain it to him. I could say I was betrayed, and he'd look at me with those sad, brown eyes and tell me that it's better to forgive — for me as well. But it's anger that keeps me going — that allows me to get up, to work and eat. And I've kept this secret for so long I can't physically force it out now.

'Look at it this way,' Malkie says. 'If you go, and he wakes up, and you talk — you'll never regret it. Even if you can't be friends after all.' He stands up. 'But if you don't go, and you never talk again . . . ' He comes over to me, putting his hands on my shoulders. 'You'll regret that, okay? Maybe not for a while, but it'll hit you some day.'

I can feel myself wilting underneath the pressure of his arms; he's staring at me, making me blink. 'Okay,' I say. 'I'll think about it.' Maybe he's right, maybe I would regret it. It's hard to say anymore.

'Good,' he says, and relaxes. He smiles at me. 'I'd better be off. I'd like to come back and do this again though.'

'Yeah, fine,' I say. My flat is small and cold, and I know if he doesn't leave soon I'll try to make him stay, even offer to cook dinner tonight.

'See you later, princess.'

He stoops and gives my forehead a kiss. I wait, hearing him clomping on his way out and the front door slam, then I run into the bedroom and throw the sash open. Malkie's a few metres down the road. 'Hey,' I call to him, waving. 'Sorry for being a dick.'

He looks back, waving too. 'Hey yourself,' he says. 'Take care.'

That night I heat up some soup and chain-smoke over the meal. Seeing Malkie has made my stomach tight, and I can't finish the food in front of me. I pour the soup down the sink and go into the bedroom, undress slowly and climb into my pyjamas.

How is it possible that Malkie's only the second real friend I've seen in years? How can this be my life?

It's still warm outside, even though it's past ten. I grab my cigarettes, a thin cardigan to wear over my pyjamas, and go outside. I sit on the doorstep, barefooted. My downstairs neighbour raps on his window and waves to me. He's wearing a white vest and big headphones; he does a quick burst of shadowboxing as I'm looking at him, maybe to impress me. I hold my cigarette up in a mock salute.

I know what went wrong, really. Or at least, I know where it started to go wrong.

7

We lived in Battersea: No. 1 Kassala Road, the end furthest away from the park. All the houses on the street were the same — Victorian terraced buildings in red and brown brick, with small front gardens enclosed by box hedges, or white picket fences, or low walls. Every house had a bay window on the ground floor, a kitchen extension, a cellar and a loft conversion. The street ran north to south, so the houses were either east-facing, or west-facing. Ours was west-facing, so it got sun in the afternoon, when the day was hottest. There was another house to the right, and to the left there was a narrow strip of grass, leading to the back garden, that I called The Corridor. The Friday before I was meant to be going back to school I was in The Corridor, bouncing a ball against the kitchen wall. A shadow on the front lawn caught my eye. Malkie was standing at the gate.

'Hello, dollface,' he said. 'Your mom in?'

I ran to him, then stopped, not knowing whether he would want a hug or not. He was looking down at me with his mouth twitching. I scuffed my shoes in the grass, and he reached down and squeezed my shoulder. He was wearing a light brown jacket, checked shirt and faded blue jeans.

'She's inside,' I said, and ran back to the house.

My mother came to the front door and beckoned Malkie inside. I followed, slowly. Malkie stopped just inside the hallway. I stopped too, in the doorway. My mother paused; we all shuffled our feet.

'Would you like a drink?'

'A beer would be great.'

'It's only twelve o'clock,' I pointed out.

'Ignore her. Come into the kitchen,' my mother suggested. 'Tallie, go get Malkie a beer from the cellar.'

I loved going to the cellar. I loved the coolness of the air, the smell of wet earth and walls, and the little chinks of light that struggled in through the tiny windows. My father had a stack of beers in the fridge down there, and a rack of wine that ran the length of the room.

Reaching in for a beer, I scraped my arm on the ice that had crystallised in the freezer compartment. When I pulled it out there was a trickle of blood running down from my elbow; a drop or two had fallen onto the ice and spread, pinkly.

On the way back to the kitchen I stopped halfway up the stairs, clutching the bottle to my chest; I could hear muffled voices speaking quickly.

'Why would I want to talk to him?'

'Sorry, Evie. I thought . . . '

'And don't bring him up while Tallulah's here.'

'I won't.'

'No, it's fine. I know you're only trying to do the right thing by your friend. I just *knew* he wouldn't stay away.'

140

By the time I came back upstairs Malkie and my mother were facing each other over the table, Malkie was leaning towards her, his giant body spilling out of his chair. I washed my arm, opened Malkie's bottle for him and fetched a glass from the cupboard. I couldn't believe he was there, in our kitchen. He made everything seem smaller, especially my mother.

'How you doing, doll?' he asked.

'I'm good,' I said. I pulled out a chair next to him, and sat, my face cupped in my hand, looking up at him. He smiled down at me. I smiled back.

'Would you like to have piano lessons?' he asked.

I was surprised. My mother looked surprised too.

'I could teach her,' he said, turning back to my mother.

'It's a very kind offer,' she murmured.

'Can I, then?' I said.

'I'll talk it over with Edward,' she said. 'We'd pay, of course.'

'No you won't,' Malkie said. 'I like spending the time with her. Besides, she'll keep me out of trouble, won't you, Tallie?'

His large hand thumped me playfully on the back, taking my breath away. 'Come on, Evie,' he said. 'It'll be like old times.'

'When you two were friends?' I asked.

'Oh yes,' she said. 'When I was a lot younger, and a lot less wise.'

I held my breath in case Malkie was offended, but now they were smiling at each other and I

141

realised my mother was joking.

'We were the three amigos, plus one I guess,' Malkie said.

'Oh . . . Yeah,' I said, angry with him for bringing Uncle Jack into it.

My mother saw my face. 'I think maybe we should get on with the chores,' she said.

Malkie mussed my hair and pushed himself away from the table. 'Well then, I'd better get,' he said.

'Tallie, why don't you give Malkie some jam to take home?' my mother said.

'What's your favourite fruit?' I asked him.

'That depends,' he said, rubbing his chin. 'Do you do pineapple jam?'

I made a face. 'Maybe I'll pick one out for you.'

'Maybe you should,' he agreed, grinning.

I stood in the pantry, gazing at the shelves. The jars were identical in the dark, but I knew which was which off by heart. I reached up and took one of the apricot jams down. My father liked blackberry, my mother preferred plum, but apricot was the best, I thought.

Malkie took my present with a deep bow. He kissed my mother goodbye, and swung me up into his arms. 'I'll say I tried,' he said quietly, looking at my mother.

'He can come round this afternoon, if he wants,' she said, like she was sad about something.

'Okay.'

'Thanks for stopping by, Malkie.'

He kissed the top of my head, then put me

down. 'Just let me know about the lessons,' he said. 'Bye, princess.'

After he'd gone, my mother stood in the kitchen, holding on to the back of a chair. Something about her face made me not want to ask about who was going to be calling.

'Well,' she said after a while. 'That was a surprise.'

'Are you going back to bed?' I asked. I came to stand next to her, and she put her arm around me.

'No,' she said. 'I wasn't expecting to see Malkie, that's all. He's from a different part of my life, and it can be a bit strange when he appears.'

'Okay,' I said. 'Can I still have piano lessons?'

My mother squeezed me. 'You like him?'

'Yeah.'

'Me too,' she said.

'Why doesn't Uncle George like him?'

'Well, Malkie can be a bit gruff,' she said. 'But he'd never hurt anyone.'

I remembered Malkie's eyes at the party when Uncle George was being rude — he'd definitely hurt Uncle George if he got the chance.

'It's really just that Uncle George has a hard time believing that Malkie has changed,' my mother said.

'Changed from what?'

'Well, sweetheart . . . He was in prison for a while. He hasn't had a very easy life, and he made a few mistakes. But he's a good person.'

'Malkie was in prison?' I asked. Everything felt a little blurry, and I shook my mother's arm off.

143

She turned to face me.

'What did he do?' I asked.

'He was involved in drugs.'

'Like Uncle Jack? He was in prison too, wasn't he?'

She went white. 'Who told you that?'

I didn't say anything, remembering my promise to James.

'Who *told* you?' my mother asked. She was angry, but I wouldn't speak. I shook my head.

'For God's sake,' she said, turning away from me. '*Nothing* is sacred in this bloody family.'

She hugged me when I started crying, and suddenly she wasn't angry anymore.

'I'm not mad at you,' she said. 'I'm not even mad at all really, it's just . . . ' She shrugged her shoulders. 'I'm disappointed in some of the grown-ups. Not with you.'

My insides were hurting now; I'd never worried about being a disappointment before.

'And don't think badly of Malkie,' she said. 'I met him when he'd already realised his mistakes. So you see, it didn't matter to me that he'd done bad things in the past, as long as he tried to be good in the present.' My mother blinked a couple of times and squeezed me harder. 'And Tallulah, we're not going to mention this to your father, okay? It'll just be our little secret that Malkie came to see us.'

I felt my stomach drop when she said that, and I turned away from her. 'Okay.'

Later that afternoon, about an hour or so after Malkie had left, I went downstairs, planning to help my mother in the kitchen. Halfway down I could hear her crying — chopping the carrots up and sobbing quietly.

'Mum?'

She turned around to face me, wiping her eyes quickly with the corner of her apron.

'Tallie, I thought you were upstairs.'

I went to give her a hug, but she'd turned back to the chopping. 'I was going to call you in a bit, you should be outdoors on a day like today.'

I went back to The Corridor and sat propped up against the wall. Mr Tickles was sunning himself on top of the dustbin. I called him to me; he lifted his head and yawned, but didn't get up.

My mother came out after a while, wiping the backs of her hands on her cheeks. 'Kathy got back yesterday, didn't she?'

I shrugged.

'I'm just going to the main road to buy some coconut milk,' she said. 'Why don't we call on Kathy and see if she wants to play?'

'I want to stay here.'

'Well, it'll be easier for me to get on with dinner if I'm not worrying about how bored you are.'

'I'm not bored.'

'Come on, it'll be nice to have the company while I walk.'

'Okay.'

My mother got her purse and we walked the hundred yards up Brynmaer Road to Kathy's house. The pavement was littered with blossoms and the sun was golden on the windscreens of the parked cars; I put my hands over my eyes to stop myself from being blinded and my mother guided me, her hand on my shoulder squeezing me if there was an obstacle in the way, like we used to do when I was five.

She dropped me off at Kathy's house and promised to come and pick me up before dinner. 'Be good now,' she said, and dropped a kiss on my cheek. I threw my arms around her neck and breathed her in. She untangled herself, laughing, and went down the road and out of sight.

Kathy's garden had apple trees and a pond with bright orange fish in it. Kathy's mum collected gnomes, and put them around the pond with little fishing rods. I didn't like them, but Kathy had named them all and took a towel out to dry them if it'd been raining.

We practised our skipping that day, then tried to make a swing out of the skipping rope, a tree branch and a cushion. It wasn't very comfortable, but I sat on it anyway. When Kathy went inside to get a jumper, I stayed out, thinking about Aunt Vivienne at my mother's birthday party. Before leaving with my parents, I'd run across her in the hallway, tugging on Malkie's sleeve. She was asking about Uncle Jack.

'You really don't know where he's gone?'

'Nope.'

'I thought he might come today.'

'Doesn't look like it.'

'I can't believe he just left — he'd tell me where he was going, I know he would.'

'I came home one night and his stuff was all gone, just a bunch of cash to help with bills.'

'Couldn't he stay for me?' She slumped against the wall. 'I'd die for him, you know.'

146

'No one's asking you to, Viv.'

I thought about that especially. I didn't think I'd ever want to die for anyone, except maybe Mr Tickles.

Kathy stuck her head out of an upstairs window and called to me. 'Mum says it's getting cold and you should have a jumper, too.'

I climbed the stairs to her room. Kathy was very neat and all her jumpers were arranged by colour. I stood in front of them, trying to choose.

'Why don't you have the yellow? That's a summery colour.' Kathy knew I was no good at choosing clothes.

'Okay, yellow.' I pulled it on over my head and looked at myself in the mirror. It made me look pale, I thought, and it was baggy everywhere, like I was Kathy's younger sister.

'You don't have any boobies at all,' Kathy said. 'Have you got your period yet?'

'No,' I said, embarrassed.

'I have,' Kathy said. 'I must be nearly ready to have a baby, you know.'

I looked back at my reflection. Last week, I'd stood in front of the mirror in my bedroom, trying to look grown up. I'd put my hands on my hips, like I'd seen Aunt Vivienne do, and pushed one hip out, making a kissing shape with my mouth, and playing with my hair. I looked pretty good, I thought, until my father caught me. Now I felt like more of a child than ever.

'Are you okay?' Kathy asked. 'You look weird.'

I heard footsteps, then Kathy's mum was in the room, looking flustered. 'Your mum's been gone a while, hasn't she?' she said. 'Let me just give her a quick call, see what's happening. I've only just seen the time and we've got to get to a clarinet lesson soon.'

I wandered into the garden with Kathy while she called my mother to come and pick me up. The clouds seemed to be moving too quickly, like someone had them on fast-forward. I lay face-down in the grass for a while; Kathy sat next to me, making a daisy chain. Her mum came out and spoke to me but she sounded muffled. I turned my head to look at her, and her face was creased up with worry.

'What did you say?' I asked.

'I said I can't get through to your house, love. It's been ringing for about ten minutes now.'

'Oh.'

'I think I'd better walk you home.'

'Okay.'

Kathy stood in the hallway with us while her mum decided on shoes and fingered things in her handbag. 'Kathy, stay inside,' she said. 'I'll be five minutes at most.'

'Okay,' Kathy said, calmly. 'See you later, Tallie.'

I leaned my head against the wall. The patch inside the doorway was cool where it had been in the shade all day. Kathy's mum patted my back and I tore myself away from my little spot and followed her down the path.

The sounds are what I remember most when I think of that day — the shuffle of our feet as Kathy's mother walked me home, her gasp when we turned the corner and reached my street and my father came running towards us, his face white and his hands stained a pinkish colour. At the time, I just wondered what he was doing home so early. He kept saying something over and over again, but it wasn't until he shook me by the shoulders, making my brain rattle around inside my head, that I realised what it was he was trying to tell me. 'Go inside. Go inside, Tallulah. Go inside and shut the door.'

Mr Tickles scratching to be let out, and, as if from far away, someone screaming.

★   ★   ★

I'm flicking ash all over myself. A breeze has started ballet-like movements in the trees up and down the street. I'm still sitting on my doorstep, smoking, watching a leaf play aimlessly on the pavement. It's green and juicy-looking, harder to blow around than the dry brown ones that will join it in a few weeks; it's a hopeful-looking leaf, I think, then a passing dog pees on it.

I stretch my legs and wrap my arms around myself; it's cooler now that the breeze has picked up. The elbows of my cardigan are wearing thin and I can see my skin through the material. If my mother were alive she'd have mended it herself, but she doesn't seem to have passed on the gene — my flat is full of broken things.

They buried my mother, killed by a speeding car a few steps from our front door, in a wooden box under six feet of earth. She'll suffocate, I wanted to say, but then she was in the ground and it didn't seem to matter anymore. They told me to be brave and carry on, my father especially. 'We'll have to learn to just be a two, now, Tallulah.' I didn't know how to say that everything had changed. Getting up was different, brushing my teeth, breakfast, playing with Mr Tickles. Only half an hour of the day used up and I was already so angry.

In the weeks following the hit-and-run, I started to have nightmares. Nightmares full of blood, rivers of it. They told us in the hospital that my mother had lost a lot of blood — they were going to try to give her a transfusion. The bleeding wouldn't stop, they said, then, eventually, it did.

The blood that my mother lost was the same blood that had nourished me while I was growing inside her, roughly seven inches below her heart. The blood stopped flowing when the heart stopped beating, and when they buried her all that remained of it was on the road outside our house, a dark purple stain, until a man from the council came and washed it away.

Thinking of this now makes me feel funny. My stomach hurts and I get a prickling sensation behind my eyes. I pull at a loose thread on my cardigan, twisting it around my finger until the tip of the digit goes white. A sudden wind dives at me when I stand up, whipping my hair back. It may have taken another family tragedy, but I think the cobwebs are finally starting to blow away.

PART TWO

Skin

8

Skin functions as a temperature regulator, insulator, the receptor for 'sensation', synthesiser of vitamin D, and protector of vitamin B folates. In humans it is made up of layer upon layer of tissue, and covered with hair follicles.

Skin is actually an organ — although this is not commonly known — and guards the underlying muscles, bones, ligaments and internal organs. It is, in fact, the largest organ of our integumentary system — namely, the one that protects the body from damage. When severely damaged, skin will attempt to heal by forming scar tissue (the name we give areas of fibrotic tissue that have replaced normal skin after an accident, after surgery, after disease). On a protein level, this new fibrotic tissue is the same as the tissue it has replaced. But on a structural level, there are marked differences. Instead of the 'basketweave' formation found in normal skin, you'll find the new tissue runs in a single direction.

The scar above my eyebrow will always be lighter than the skin around it. Even if no one else notices it, it'll always catch my eye, always mark me. Scars are a natural part of the healing process. But sweat glands and hair follicles will not grow back within scar tissue. It is more sensitive to sunlight. Scars are not regeneration. The new tissue is inferior to the old.

The lift doors swish open; no one looks at me twice as I walk down the corridor, familiar by now. I stop at the doorway, knock, and take a few steps in. Aunt Gillian's sitting by the bed, knitting. I don't know whether she's more surprised or I am; her hair's down and she's wearing a frosting of pale, pink lipstick, and sunglasses pushed back into her hairline. She looks relaxed, happy. 'Oh Tallulah,' she says. 'Come and sit next to me.'

I come into the room properly and take the chair she's offering, on the far side of my father's bed.

'How are you feeling?' Aunt Gillian whispers, like she's trying not to let my father hear.

'Fine,' I say. 'How's everything here?'

'Much better now.' She puts her knitting away into a wicker bag at her feet. 'They say he might even wake up soon.'

'Good,' I say, lamely.

'It certainly is,' she says, and smiles at me.

'I'm sorry,' I say. 'I mean, I'm sorry that . . . '

'Forget it,' Aunt Gillian says, waving her hand. 'You're entitled to be scared. We all were.' She brushes a lock of hair away from my father's face. 'But we're over the worst of it, at least.'

He definitely looks healthier — golden, almost, then I realise it's probably the sunlight slanting across his face. He's breathing deeply; a ripple of air comes out of his mouth and tickles the moustache hairs closest by, so they lift a little as in a breeze. He's got a new mole on his neck.

I didn't notice that the other day. I feel a knot inside my chest. If he were to open his eyes, he'd see a stranger, just like he's a stranger to me. But I guess nothing's changed, then.

I pour us some water, and we settle in for the wait. Malkie's right, even though I'm still uncomfortable here, still angry, I'd feel worse if I never came back.

Maybe you don't want to be alone forever then, I tell myself. Except for a few visits from Starr, from time to time. And I can't cherry-pick the family members I stay in touch with. It would be nice to see Georgia again, and Michael and James. But they'd never keep visits a secret from Aunt Gillian; even Starr's been nagging me for months to get in touch with my father. So it's nothing to do with Dad — it's the rest of the family I'm here for.

Aunt Vivienne arrives, carrying a bunch of grapes. They're purple and delicious-looking, nearly bursting out of their skins. 'One must keep up the traditions of the sickbed, darling,' she says to me. She's wearing a navy cape, with a fur collar, and a pillbox hat with netting. I try not to laugh. I suppose with Aunt Gillian becoming more casual, more unfussy, Aunt Vivienne is just redressing the balance. I wonder whether these are clothes from her own wardrobe, or a favourite role. She looks fantastic either way.

Aunt Gillian gives a world-weary sigh and takes out the knitting again.

Aunt Vivienne strips off her outer layers and sits opposite me. From time to time I catch her looking in my direction; she's probably gloating over her little coup. I balance my elbow on the arm of my chair, and rest my head in my hand. I look at my father; when the nurse comes around, I look at her, at her quick, efficient hands. She repeats what they told Aunt Gillian this morning — he'll probably wake up soon. 'He'll be nice and rested,' she says. 'But he might be a bit disorientated, nothing to worry about.'

'Of course,' I say.

I wonder whether my father will remember what happened between us. It might be easier if he doesn't. I don't know if I'll be able to hold my tongue, though. The nurse leaves, and I close my eyes. I'm vaguely aware of Aunt Gillian and Aunt Vivienne talking, then I drift off.

I dream about Toby, it doesn't look like Toby, but it's him. We're up a mountain, or maybe we're in a shopping mall, it keeps changing. He's angry with me, and I feel guilty because I know I did something wrong, I wasn't a very good friend to him, and I buy him a cookie from an old woman, and Toby throws it on the floor and says, '*That's* all you think it takes?', and then Aunt Vivienne's shaking my shoulder. 'Tallulah,' she's saying. 'Wake up. Afternoon hours are over — we have to clear out until this evening.'

'Where are we going?'

'Dinner.'

'I'm not hungry.'

'Look,' Aunt Vivienne says, sitting down again. 'Just come and keep us company.' She looks me over. 'You look like you could do with some food though.'

This is rich, coming from her. Aunt Vivienne has never been more than a size eight.

'Where's Gillian?'

'Bathroom.'

I look down at my father; his face looks even rosier than earlier. It's probably the most peaceful I've ever seen him.

Aunt Gillian appears too. 'He's still asleep,' she says, unnecessarily. She looks at me with a pained expression on her face. 'You must be exhausted, poor thing,' she says.

'Poor thing,' Aunt Vivienne mutters mockingly.

'Where's Georgia?' I ask. 'Wasn't she going to come down today?'

'She's not here, darling,' Aunt Gillian says, again unnecessarily. Aunt Vivienne snorts. Aunt Gillian gives her a dirty look. 'She couldn't make it down today, but hopefully tomorrow . . . ' She looks away.

'What's wrong with her?' Aunt Vivienne asks.

'Oh, you know. Nothing. I'll let her tell you.' She's practically beaming.

'Gillian, has the good husband got Georgia pregnant already?' Vivienne arches her eyebrow.

'Well, it's not really my place to say,' Aunt Gillian says. She's radiating happiness now.

'Congratulations,' I say, feeling sick. Georgia's gone forever, then.

'Gillian, a *grandma*,' Aunt Vivienne coos, unkindly.

'I guess that makes you a great-aunt then,' I say to her, taking some pleasure in her grimace.

'Well, let's go and celebrate,' Aunt Gillian says,

and stops. 'Not celebrate, of course. Not until Edward's fully recovered. Oh, maybe we should save this . . .'

'No,' I say, taking her by the elbow and steering her out of the room. 'Any good news is welcome right now.'

In the restaurant we order a bottle of wine and three pasta dishes. The waitress who brings the drink sidles away from our table quickly, the air between my aunts is palpably thicker than in the rest of the room.

'Georgia's a little young to be having kids, wouldn't you say?' Aunt Vivienne suggests. 'How old is she again?'

'She's twenty-two, as you know,' Aunt Gillian says icily.

Aunt Vivienne swirls the wine around in her glass. 'How old is her husband?'

'Thirty-two.'

'How are the boys?' I ask, hoping to distract the two of them.

Aunt Gillian lets out an exasperated sigh. 'Michael lives in Brazil,' she says. 'He's running a bar out there — he went travelling a few years ago and met some local woman and never came back. James runs a used-car business from home. He buys them, does things to them then sells them on. I would say he's wasting his time but he's made quite a bit of money out of it.'

She looks sad. I wonder whether these were the lives she planned for her children. I wonder whether my father planned for *my* future. I never told him about my nursing dream — would he

158

have encouraged me in that?

I've started playing with my napkin, tearing it into strips.

'What does Georgia do now?' Aunt Vivienne asks.

'What?' Aunt Gillian asks; perhaps she's thinking about James' car menagerie. 'Well, she was — is — training to be a primary school teacher.' She turns to face me. 'She's wanted to work with children for ages, do you remember?'

'Not really,' I say. 'Maybe that was after we used to see each other.'

'Yes, maybe,' Aunt Gillian says. She smiles sadly at me. 'We mustn't lose touch again, Tallie. Family's so important you know.'

Please don't cry, I pray. Aunt Vivienne hisses quietly, but Gillian doesn't hear.

The waitress brings us our pasta and we eat absent-mindedly. I make myself chew slowly — I've suddenly realised how starving I am.

'Could you pass the pepper, please, Tallulah?' Aunt Vivienne's looking at me, hand out-stretched. I give her the grinder. 'Thank you,' she says. She has perfect white teeth, I notice.

'You have really nice teeth,' I say, and something about this stirs a memory.

Aunt Gillian's fork stops halfway to her mouth.

'Thank you,' Aunt Vivienne says, tapping one. 'They're not all real, you know?'

'Oh?' I know what I'm remembering now — Malkie telling me that my grandfather wasn't just violent towards my grandmother. I swallow,

I can't believe that I ever forgot that, but I guess it got buried when I was caught up in my own misery.

'No,' Aunt Vivienne's saying, and I feel a surge of pity for her. She butters a bread roll elegantly. I admire the way her wrist makes the little flicking motions. I can never spread butter; half the time the bread comes apart and sticks to my knife.

'Well anyway, dear. It's nice to have dinner like this, isn't it?' Aunt Gillian interrupts.

'Yeah,' I say. 'How's Paul?'

'Paul? Enjoying the opera, I hope.'

'Is he coming here afterwards?'

'No, dear.' Aunt Gillian shifts uneasily in her chair. 'Hospitals aren't really his scene.'

'Does he think he's getting to the age where they might be necessary?'

'Really, Vivienne. That was horrid.'

'Please do accept my apologies.'

Aunt Gillian sniffs, then pushes her chair back. 'I'll be back in a minute,' she says.

I give Aunt Vivienne a look when Gillian's gone. 'That was pretty mean,' I tell her.

'Was it?' Vivienne gives a little laugh, like we're co-conspirators, and I'm back to not feeling sorry for her anymore. 'You've never lived with her, Tallulah. Not properly, anyway.'

'She's just proud of her daughter. Why can't you let her be happy about it?'

'Happy has nothing to do with it, my dear.'

'What?'

'Think about it,' Aunt Vivienne says. 'Gillian's just relieved her little Georgia's following an

160

acceptable trajectory.' She sneers. 'Marrying her off at some ungodly age to a man practically old enough to be her father. It's hardly the romance of the century. She wanted to make sure her daughter didn't turn into a ruined woman, like me . . . Or you . . . '

Aunt Gillian appears behind her sister as Vivienne says, 'We've been failed by our mothers, Tallulah. But at least no one will be able to say *Gillian* produced a bad seed.'

'Viv . . . ' Gillian says, looking at me.

Aunt Vivienne closes her mouth and bites her lip. Aunt Gillian's doing the same thing. So there are similarities after all.

My mother chewed her fingernails instead. She told me how *her* mother had put bitter aloes on her nails to make sure she wouldn't want to taste them. 'It was awful,' she'd told me. 'People use it as a laxative, so for the first few weeks I had stomach pains all the time.'

I feel my breath catch in my throat when I remember this. 'Well, anyway,' I say. I pull my wallet from my bag and fish out a twenty. 'That should cover me.'

'But we're not finished,' Aunt Gillian says.

'For God's sake, Gillian,' Aunt Vivienne murmurs. 'Let's just pay the bill and go.'

The waitress is only too eager to get rid of us. She brings us our change and I scrape back my chair. I can't bring myself to meet Aunt Vivienne's eye.

I want to know what exactly my mother did to make Vivienne dislike her so much. But at the same time I'm scared to find out.

161

★ ★ ★

I was furious with my father, with myself, with the world, with the driver of the car for taking my mother away. I withdrew. I pretended not to hear my father when he called me for meals, or asked me questions. Eventually he gave up and we ate separately and in silence. I couldn't stop seeing my mother being loaded into the ambulance, covered in tubes and a mask and blankets. Paramedics' hands, holding me back as I tried to climb in after her — 'No, sweetheart, go with this lady here' — and Kathy's mother crying. Kathy, who'd been fetched from her house, in the back with me, saying it'll be alright. Following the stretcher into the hospital, and seeing my mother's arm falling out and dangling there, bumping around as the doctors ran with her to surgery. Then the waiting room and nurses stooping down to talk to me as I lay across three chairs, dry-eyed.

Then I'd see my father, pacing up and down, answering questions the police put to him, wringing his hands. 'It's *my fault*,' he shouted at one of them, the older one, who gave his partner a look. They put their pens away and straightened their faces.

'We'll come back later,' the older one said to my father. 'You've been very helpful.'

I remembered Kathy's mother hugging my father, saying, 'How were you to know she'd run out?'

'They were talking — I should have known, I *did* know.'

162

'Drivers should be more *careful*.'

'I *pushed her away*.'

Then, finally, the white sheet, pulled up over her face, the shape of her body underneath it.

Kathy's dad had turned up halfway through the evening and driven her home, so she hadn't heard my father. 'What do you think he meant?' she asked me, when I confided in her. 'He must be talking about something else. He didn't *actually* push her into the road.'

'How do you know?' I said.

We were brushing the manes of her My Little Pony set, arranged by colour and height. My one had a tangle in the hair somewhere that I wasn't managing to separate successfully with the little plastic brush. Kathy took the pony off me and starting working on the knot. I slumped backwards, propping my head up against her chest of drawers and letting my arms fall to my sides. I'd been feeling heavy all the time, like I was carrying something around inside me, and my eyes felt like they were tiny slits, although, apart from a slight pink rim around them, they looked normal in the mirror.

'Your dad wouldn't do that,' Kathy said.

'Maybe he pushed her and she fell.'

'My mum said it was an accident.' Kathy put the brush down. 'She said your mum just didn't see the car.'

'But she wasn't there.'

'She talked to the police.'

'My mum wouldn't run out into the road,' I said. 'She always made me stand on the kerb and look both ways.'

'Sometimes people forget to look both ways.'

'My mum never forgot,' I said. I was furious with Kathy for suggesting it; I wanted to throw her ponies out of the window. 'It must be my dad's fault. He must have distracted her. Or pushed her.'

'I don't think he pushed her.'

'I don't *care* what you think,' I shouted.

Kathy turned away and started brushing the pony again.

I felt ashamed of myself, but I couldn't say sorry. After a moment of silence I picked up a different pony and showed it to her. 'This one's cool, I like the rainbows on her leg.'

'*His* leg,' Kathy said.

'Oh.'

'He's one of my favourites,' Kathy said after a while, and we went back to brushing.

It was weird to be let back into the house by Kathy's mum. The lights were off, but after she flicked the switch in the hallway my father came out of his study, blinking.

'Oh, Edward, you're home already. I'll just give you these back now,' she said, putting my mum's old set of keys down on the hall table.

'Thank you for looking after Tallulah so often over this . . . period,' my father said.

'Glad to help out. I'd better skedaddle though. Get dinner on for Ted and Kathy.' She bent down and gave me a kiss on the forehead. 'Tallie, you're welcome at ours any time, you know that, right?'

'Thank you,' I said.

'Yes, thanks again,' my father said. He shut the

door after her. 'Now, Tallulah, I think we should have a little chat.' He laid his hand on the top of my head and for a moment I was so shocked at his touching me I didn't say anything.

'I miss your mother too, you know.' He looked at my expression. 'Of course I do. I've been trying to plan the funeral and . . . ' He sighed. 'It's very hard for all of us.'

He didn't even look sad, I thought, just far away. His hand felt hot through my hair and I jerked it off. He stared at the front door, like he could see through it to the road.

'I didn't think it would be this hard,' he said. 'Maybe . . . '

Mr Tickles appeared, crying for food. My father frowned at him and then at me; his eyes looked less cloudy all of a sudden. 'I'm going to need your co-operation, Tallulah. No more tantrums. We can all behave nicely to one other, at least.' He walked back into his study and shut the door, leaving me in the hallway with my heart hammering, although I wasn't sure why.

★ ★ ★

It was at the reception after my mother's funeral that I found out I was going to be joining Starr at boarding school, although not from Starr or Aunt Vivienne, who didn't even come to the funeral.

I was sitting in the boiler room, hiding from everyone, trying to make myself cry. I heard a creaking outside the door, then it opened and my grandmother looked in.

165

'Aren't you getting rather hot?'

'No.'

'Suit yourself,' she said, and closed the door again.

I waited a moment, then scrambled after her. She was sitting on the step opposite, looking straight at me.

I sat down next to her. 'How did you know I was in there?'

'I saw you go in.'

'Oh.'

'A few people seem to be missing today,' she said. 'Don't you find it odd that your uncle and aunt couldn't make it to the funeral?'

'Uncle Jack isn't in the country.'

'Is that what your father told you?'

I nodded.

My grandmother took a cigarette out of a gold case. 'The trouble with stories,' she said, pointing it at me, 'is remembering what's been said to whom.'

'What?'

She put the case away. 'Your father wants to send you to boarding school,' she said. 'You'll go to middle school first then transfer after a year.'

I felt my heart flip inside my chest. 'Why?'

'He thinks he's too busy to be able to take care of you properly, and you're too young to be spending all your time alone.'

'I don't want to go.'

'No one ever does,' my grandmother said, grimly. 'But they say they enjoy it afterwards — when they're older.'

'Do I have to go?'

'That's up to your father.'

'Why are you telling me?'

My grandmother looked at me. 'I didn't think it was a good idea,' she said. 'But I guess we'll see.'

Now the tears came easily enough. I ran upstairs and lay on my bed, face-down in the pillow, not wanting to see anyone.

It felt like hours before my father was standing at the door.

'Tallulah? Why are you lying here in the dark?'

I turned to face him. 'Why are you sending me to boarding school?'

There was a pause. 'I gather Mother told you, then.'

I was silent.

'I'm sorry, Tallulah. It's the only solution I can think of.'

I know it's your fault somehow. I know she's dead because of you.

'Fine,' I said. 'I don't want to stay here anyway.'

In the light of the corridor behind him, I saw my father put his hands in his pockets and look at something on the ceiling. 'I'll give you some time alone,' he said. 'It's been an emotional day for both of us.'

I felt my whole body seething with hate. I tried to keep my voice steady when I spoke. 'When am I going?'

'It's probably best if you start as soon as possible.'

Eventually he left. I heard his shoes squeak as he went downstairs, then I turned to the wall and cried until my face was so swollen, Mr Tickles meowed in fright at the sight of it.

★ ★ ★

Evening visiting hours over, we stand outside the main entrance. Around us, cafés and shops are closing up, everyone gathering up their belongings, ready to journey home.

'I suppose I'll see you both here tomorrow?' Aunt Vivienne says, patting her hair.

'Are you coming back then, Viv?' Aunt Gillian asks, frostily. 'I thought you might be too busy for boring family affairs.'

'*I* know how to stand by my family, Gillian,' Aunt Vivienne says. 'Well — until tomorrow.' She gives me a curt nod and sashays away. Aunt Gillian looks disapproving, but she doesn't say anything.

'Are you getting the 74?' I ask.

'Oh yes, let's get it together,' she says. 'So much nicer to have a travelling companion.'

It means getting two buses instead of one, but I guess I owe her some time together after running away before.

'Sure,' I say. 'Is Paul back soon?'

'Not for another night or two.' She takes my arm. 'But he spends most of his time at his club, anyway. Do you live alone?'

'Yep.'

'And you don't get lonely?'

'Nope.'

'Oh well, it must be me,' Aunt Gillian says. 'I was always a nervous child, apparently. Didn't

168

like to be by myself for too long. I was so pleased when Mother said she'd had another little girl. Edward was a dear, but he was a boy, and not too into playing with dolls.' She smiles at me. 'But then Vivienne was quite horrid, and not at all the playmate I was expecting. I suppose we're not very well suited. And then Vivienne is so good at holding grudges . . . '

'What did you do to her?'

'Oh.' Aunt Gillian shakes her head quickly. '*Everything* I did was wrong.'

The bus pulls up at the stop and Aunt Gillian lets go of me to climb aboard, and then we have to wait while she finds her change purse.

'I'm not used to getting public transport,' she whispers to me as we sit down. 'Georgia used to drive me around until she moved out.'

'When did she move out?'

'Just before the wedding. It made it a little bittersweet, I suppose, letting go of her like that. But I knew she was going to be well taken care of, and that's what you want for your children.' She must remember the conversation at dinner, because she changes the subject hastily. 'Any romantic interest in your life, Tallulah?'

'Not so much.'

'Well now, that must be temporary,' she says, comfortingly. 'You've turned into quite a beautiful young lady. I'm sure you'll find a nice young man soon.' She pats my hand.

'It's okay,' I tell her. 'I'm not that bothered.' That's a lie, Aunt Gillian, it's just that I pushed away the guy I was bothered about and now I'm too gutless to try to get back in touch with him.

'James hasn't found anyone either,' Aunt Gillian says. 'I wish he'd get himself a girlfriend and stop going out all hours of the night.'

'Does he still live at home?'

'He's converted the rooms above the garage into a little flat. We hardly see him.'

'Do you miss Michael?'

'Of course I do,' she says, surprising me. For some reason I never thought the two of them were that close. 'Michael turned out very like his father, in the end.' She smiles, looking softer. 'It's funny, I can't really see John in either of the other two at all. But then, I guess, children aren't always like their parents.'

I catch the No.19 at Hyde Park Corner and I'm back home an hour and half after I boarded the first bus. I'm hungry again — dinner with Gillian and Vivienne feels like ages ago, and I've been burning nervous energy all day. I start to peel a clementine, digging my nails into the orange skin. I like the smell of citrus that will stay under them until I next have a shower. I'm almost too tired to eat though; each day I get through without my father waking up leaves me drained and relieved at the same time. And at the same time, there's the knowledge at the back of my head that the longer he stays under, the less likely he is to ever come round.

If he dies, I'll be an orphan, like my mother was. Like my father is, like all of them are, now — Aunt Gillian, Aunt Vivienne, Uncle Jack.

I've lived like an orphan since I left home. I've been completely alone, not counting the others in the hostel, and it's never bothered me too much until now. Maybe Aunt Gillian's right when she says children aren't always like their parents, or Aunt Vivienne could be right instead, I could be more like my father than I realise. He spent his whole life with his brain switched on, researching, operating, in studies and hospital theatres. He didn't know how to relax with us when he came through the front door; we were probably harder work for him than his patients.

But how could I turn out like him when I tried so hard not to? I guess we both lost my mother, and it changed us, even if he was already drawing away from me before that day.

I eat the clementine. No point in worrying about my father until the hospital staff bring it up. I should be concerned instead that I tried to drop in unannounced on my best-friend-and-maybe-more the other day, after years of radio silence, and now I'm dreaming about him. Am I obsessing? He's been quietly nagging at me, I realise, ever since Starr told me that she ran into him recently. But he'd have every right to be angry as he was in my dream. So now what?

I throw away the peel and crawl into bed.

★   ★   ★

My father drove me to the school. I was in the passenger seat, the first time I'd been up at the front, and I nuzzled against the seatbelt, trying to catch the smell of my mother's soap, or her perfume, tracing patterns with my fingers on the glovebox, imagining they were her fingers.

The journey that day was the same as to my

grandmother's. I could almost predict when we would change lanes, merge with the Ml, when the signs for Watford would appear, then for Birmingham, then Shrewsbury. I stared out at the landscape as it altered gradually, first dusty fields and small villages, and later railways and hills — the green slopes streaked brown with beeches and sweet chestnuts — and market towns, until the houses turned from red brick to grey stone, and iron bridges sprang up over emerald rivers.

My father didn't look at me once during the whole journey. I snuck glances at his profile, trying to work out what he was thinking. Kathy's voice kept coming back to me, 'Sometimes people forget to look both ways.' My mother would never have run out into the road though, I told myself, because that would be dangerous and she would never put herself in danger in case something happened and then I wouldn't have her anymore.

I knew this. I knew it because I knew, for a fact, that my mother never, ever stopped thinking about me.

Kathy was probably right about my father not pushing her, or the police would already have arrested him. But why did he say it was his fault? Why wouldn't he look me in the eye? I tried to work it out while he was driving, and staring at the road, but he might as well have been made of glass.

We ignored the turn for the market town closest to my grandmother, and drove ten minutes in the other direction. The roads were emptier now, and once, turning a corner, we startled a flock of birds who took off flashing orange, brown and white.

'Those were wrynecks,' my father said. It was the first time he'd spoken since we got in the car.

Eventually, he put the handbrake on and turned the engine off. 'We're here.'

The school was exactly as I had pictured boarding school to be: redbrick main buildings and dormitories, green walls in the canteen. The paths around the grounds were gravelled and kept in pristine condition; the gym and swimming pool were modern and tucked away at the back of the grounds, past the boys' dormitories and the playing fields.

My father came on the tour with me, walking a few steps behind. When we got around to the front of the building again, he got my suitcase out of the trunk and handed it to me.

'Be good,' he said. 'You can always telephone, of course.'

'Mm-hmm.'

The teacher showing us around smiled encouragingly at me. 'You won't remember to after a while,' she said. 'Our students love it here.'

My father checked his watch. 'I'd better be off . . . Avoid the traffic. You have everything, don't you?'

I nodded.

He pulled out slowly. It was weird to see him turn left at the gate and disappear behind the wall, like that was the last time I'd see my old life, and for a moment I almost wanted him to turn around and drive back for me. He didn't. The teacher raised her eyebrows and gestured for me to follow her inside.

★ ★ ★

It was a bell that woke me on the first morning, ringing far off somewhere, and then voices much closer, the sounds of doors slamming and footsteps thundering up and down stairs. My bedroom at home was at the back of the house, overlooking the garden, and I was used to waking up to birds, or Mr Tickles yowling to be let in. At the weekends there was the whine of lawnmowers. And always noises in the kitchen directly below me — my mother running the taps or opening the fridge, humming to herself.

I propped myself up on one elbow and blinked away the film of sleep. I could see creamy-yellow walls, thick orange curtains and a brown carpet. There were three small windows and ivy grew like a green fringe on the outside walls, colouring the light that streamed in. There were five other beds, each with a bedside table and lamp. And four other girls, wrapped in towels, bare legs poking out underneath, hopping from one foot to the other like they were trying to keep warm. They seemed much louder than normal people, pushing each other and screaming. One of them saw me awake and nudged the girl nearest her.

'Are you Tallulah?' she asked. She looked older than the others. Her hair was long and perfectly straight, and she had dark blue nail polish on her toes. Two plump mounds spilled over the top of the towel. I'd never seen breasts that big on girls our age and I turned my face away, not wanting to be caught staring.

'Yeah.'

'I'm Cressida. You can have my place next in the queue.'

'Thanks,' I said. I felt embarrassed in my Winnie the Pooh pyjamas, but I didn't want to take them off while everyone was watching. I rooted around in my suitcase for a towel.

The door to the bathroom opened and a girl scurried back in, wet red hair dripping around her shoulders.

'You go,' Cressida said, and pushed me in the right direction.

The bathroom was freezing and smelt mossy. The plastic shower curtain clung to my limbs when I climbed in, and I hadn't brought any soap in with me, so I got myself damp all over and stepped out again, wrapped my towel around myself and went back into the dorm.

I changed quietly in the corner, trying not to draw attention to myself. The red-head sat on her bed, staring at the floor. Her skin was so pale it was almost see-through, except where it was covered by freckles. I vaguely remembered her from the day before. I recognised one of the louder girls too, the one with the blondest hair and a turned-up nose, but I couldn't remember either of their names.

'You can sit with us at breakfast,' Cressida called across the room to me. The red-head didn't look up.

The breakfast hall was in another building,

one long room with a huge ceiling that sloped upwards towards the middle, and tiny, diamond-shaped tiles on the floor. The noise was terrifying; it felt like there were thousands of other children swarming around the room. They all seemed to know each other too. I gripped my tray harder, trying not to panic.

'All Johnston Housers sit here,' Cressida said.

'What's Johnston Houser?'

'Johnston *House*. It's where we sleep,' Cressida said. She tucked her hair behind her ear. 'Daddy wanted me to be in Johnston. He said everyone else was nouveau riche.'

Breakfast was seven-thirty until seven-fifty. We had to be in our form rooms by eight, the girls told me, or we got a Saturday with Ricky Dicks.

'What's that?'

'You have to stay in Saturday night with the Housemistress.'

'She's not married,' Cressida said. 'But she calls herself Mrs Richard Dickson. Everyone knows she's a lesbian.'

The other girls snickered. I didn't say anything. I'd met our Housemistress the day before. She wore lipstick, which had smeared itself into the wrinkles around her mouth. She'd patted me on the head and called me 'poor love'. I thought how, for a lesbian, she looked a lot like any other woman.

I caught a glimpse of Starr as we were leaving the hall and she gave me a wave. I turned my face away from her — if Starr and Aunt Vivienne couldn't be bothered to come to my mother's

176

funeral, I didn't have to bother to be friends now.

'You know her?' Cressida asked me.

'She's my cousin.'

'She's the year above us. That's so cool,' Cressida said. The other girls nodded.

There were even more students in the main school building and I had a sudden urge to cry, although I didn't know if it was because everything was huge and unfamiliar or because it was sinking in that this was going to be my home from now on.

Cressida gave me a hug at my form room door. 'We know about your mum,' she said. She stood back and waited for me to say something.

'Yeah?' I muttered.

'You can be in our gang,' Cressida said, and everyone nodded again. 'We think you're really brave.'

I didn't say anything. My stomach felt cold and I couldn't look at them.

The blonde girl opened the door for me. 'Look after her,' Cressida said, and the blonde girl put her arm around my waist and steered me in.

'Let's sit together,' she said. 'I'm Abi, remember?' She smiled at me and I noticed the whites of her eyes were slightly blue, just tinged that way, and she had a blonde moustache that caught the light.

We walked towards the back of the classroom, and she tossed her plait over her shoulder as we went. 'I'm so glad you're here now. I was stuck in this form all by myself. Cressida tried to get the teachers to swap me, but they said they couldn't.'

'What's wrong with the other kids?'

'Edith — the girl from our dorm — is really geeky.' She lowered her voice. 'Then there's these twins, brother and sister. They're day-schoolers and they always hold each other's hands.' She giggled. 'They have identical packed lunches too. Cressida says they probably share a bed at home, or something.'

Abi kept talking and I zoned out. Slowly the other seats started to fill up, then the teacher arrived and made me come to the front and introduce myself.

'We didn't do this properly yesterday,' she said. 'But this is Tallulah, a new student. Tallulah, why don't you tell us something about yourself.'

Abi smiled encouragingly at me; my mind went blank.

'Like what?' I asked.

'Like your favourite food. Where you live. Anything like that.'

'I'm from London.'

'Okay . . . That's good. Edith's from London too, aren't you Edith?'

'I'm from Kingston,' Edith said.

'Anywhere near you?' the teacher asked.

'I don't know where that is,' I said.

'Oh well, never mind.' She smiled at me. She had big blue eyes and curly blonde hair tied up in a ponytail and away from a high forehead. She looked young, almost younger than Cressida. 'I'm Miss Rochard. I'll be your form tutor for the next year or so, and my favourite colour is gold.' She lowered her voice. 'And Tallulah, if you need to talk to someone, you can come to me anytime.'

I wiped my palms on my skirt. For some reason they were hot and sweaty.

'You can go and sit down now.'

I slunk back to my place.

'Don't worry,' Abi whispered. 'I'll make sure she doesn't try to pair you up with Edith.'

I closed my eyes and tried to shut everything out of my brain. Abi was still whispering next to me. I wished I was in my old school. I wished Kathy was next to me instead of Abi. I wished I had Mr Tickles to curl up on my feet tonight. I wished I could see my mother again.

* * *

The word had spread at school about my mother, and, at first, girls brought me little offerings — lipstick, fizzy cola bottles, chewing gum. The boys ignored me, which was the nicest thing they could think of doing.

A couple of times I heard Starr call out my name when I was in the corridor between classes, but I always pretended I was busy talking to someone else. Once she was coming up the main staircase as I was going down, and I hid behind two girls who had their arms linked together; she didn't see me, and I felt victorious, but also disappointed in a weird way, like I'd actually wanted her to notice me after all.

My teachers were nice to me too. Miss

Rochard was very friendly, although she made me feel uncomfortable — she was always taking my hand in hers, or squeezing my shoulder and saying positive things. I preferred my science teacher, who never bothered me. He had a big white moustache, and wore the same red jumper and green corduroy trousers every day. Then there was Mr Hicks, the head of art. The art studio always smelled like incense, which he burned in little holders. Sometimes during lessons he would give a student some money to run to the tuck shop and get us all chocolate. Mr Hicks was tall; he had good skin and dark hair and brown eyes, and all the female teachers laughed whenever he made a joke, especially Miss Rochard. Once, I saw them standing at the back of the assembly hall together, during a fire safety talk; Mr Hicks was leaning towards her, whispering into her ear and her eyes were even bigger than normal.

From the beginning I found it hard to keep up with lessons. I'd never learned French or German before and I didn't know the difference between a noun and a verb. Mostly I thought about my mother instead. I tried to remember what her favourite colour was, and I realised I'd never known. My favourite colours on her had been pink and peach. When I was younger she'd read a book to me called *Each, Peach, Pear, Plum*, and in my two-year-old mind the two of them had been mixed up, so that I thought my mother was made of fruit, like the flush of peach on her cheeks, or the plum colour she went when she was upset. If you peeled away a layer of her skin, I thought, she'd be sweet and firm underneath, like a peach itself. After the accident though, the few glimpses I'd caught of her had proven me wrong.

'*Ma mère est une professeur,*' we chanted in French. '*Mon père est un avocat.*'

She was wearing dark blue the day she died, a sleeveless dress that always reminded me of sailors because it had a big white collar and a white anchor pattern.

'*Elle est professeur.*'

Somehow, when they buried her, she was wearing a green dress that I hadn't remembered seeing before. I wondered who'd chosen it. No one had asked me.

'*Il est avocat.*'

I thought about my father too, about whether he would send for me. Maybe he would suddenly change his mind and want me around. I didn't think he would.

Some teachers drew me aside to ask me if I was struggling during classes. They went through my homework patiently with me, explaining where I'd gone wrong.

'You really *are* paying attention, aren't you?' Miss Rochard said. 'In all your lessons?'

'Yes,' I lied.

I kept thinking about the accident, instead of listening in class. I wondered if she'd known about the car at the last second, if she'd seen the driver trying to brake, what she'd heard. And if my father hadn't pushed her, had he *not* saved her? Could he have stretched out a hand to pull her back to safety?

'Was it an accident?' I said, once, when I forgot where I was. Abi gave me a weird look, but nothing else happened.

I spoke to my father once in that first term. The Housemistress had to come and find me in my dorm room, so he'd been waiting for a while on the other end by the time I got to the telephone.

'I won't be able to be on much longer,' he said.

'Sorry,' I said. The Housemistress was hovering over me. I turned away, blocking her with my back.

'No, it's not your fault.' He cleared his throat.

I asked about Mr Tickles, clutching at something we could talk about. He asked about the weather and my teachers.

'They're fine.'

'I'm sorry, but I'm going to have to go now — this was just a quick break. You're doing well in class?'

'I guess.'

'Good. Well, I'm sure we'll speak soon.'

'Okay.'

'Bye Tallulah.' He cleared his throat again. 'All my love.'

'That was quick,' the Housemistress said, when I handed the receiver back to her.

I didn't want to go back up to the dorm room straightaway. It felt weird to hear my father use the word 'love'. I couldn't remember him using it for a while, with me or my mother. Now I wondered if he'd ever told us he loved us. Maybe he hadn't, and I only noticed after he got so grumpy. Maybe he didn't think of me as his daughter, and that's why he didn't love me. I didn't look anything like him, but I hadn't looked like my mother, either. I leaned my forehead against the cool of the staircase wall. Which part of me was her, and which part was him? It was hard to believe I'd come from either of them, that I'd grown inside her, even. And now I was left with whatever hidden part of my mother that was in me. Or did it die when she died?

Cressida and Abi tried to ask me about my mother, but it felt wrong to talk about her with them. Sometimes, I wondered if Cressida thought it was romantic that she'd died so young. 'At least your mum will never get old and wrinkly,' she said.

Cressida and the others talked all the time, about boys and lipstick and where they were going skiing over Christmas. I had nothing to add to those conversations. I still wasn't interested in boys, and the way girls fluttered their eyes at them, or found excuses to touch them seemed boring to me. Cressida was obsessed with one boy in particular, Toby Gates, who was two years above us. I'd seen him around school. He had dark hair and green eyes and played rugby. Cressida wrote 'Cressida Gates' all over her school planner and drew up ideas for their wedding, which was going to have white doves and be on a Mexican beach. Cressida liked to plan things. She came up with a secret handshake we all had to practise too, and a password to gain entry to our secret meetings. She wanted to start a relief fund for starving children in Africa, which she said was the most important issue of our time. She said we should memorise facts about all the different countries in Africa and decide which one needed our help the most.

Abi had been bought an encyclopaedia for her birthday, and Cressida made us study it in turn, writing crib sheets on countries she picked for us. Mine were Egypt and Tanzania and Lesotho, which I assumed was pronounced Le-soth-oh. We had to give presentations on our countries and when all the presentations were given, we would vote for our favourite. Abi put a lot of effort into her presentation on Malawi, sticking photos and glitter onto coloured sheets of card, and drawing big red hearts in the margins. I voted for her.

'Are you *sure* you want to vote for Malawi?' Cressida asked me.

'Yeah.'

She turned her face away pointedly. Cressida won with South Africa, and Abi threw her cards away. Even though everyone else had voted for her presentation, Cressida seemed put out. I waited to be told how we were going to help the children of South Africa, but in the end nothing happened.

★   ★   ★

When I'd started at boarding school they'd made me go see the school counsellor, Dr Epstein. He had one long eyebrow hair, like an antennae. 'Tell me what's bothering you the most,' he said.

184

I tried to describe how out of control everything seemed, but he misunderstood. He thought I was saying that my mother had protected me, and now I had to grow up too quickly. But no one was making me feel like I was growing up — not my father, not my teachers; even Cressida told me what to do.

I practised reading his handwriting upside down. After a few sessions I was able to make out the words *disturbed*.

'Are you sleeping?' he asked me.

I nodded.

I woke up every night, my face wet, although I had no tears during the day. A couple of times I'd tried to stay awake all night, because the worst was the morning, just after opening my eyes, before I realised where I was. Sometimes, for a split second, I didn't remember about my mother, or going to boarding school, and then I had a feeling like I'd been punched me in the gut when I saw the other girls, and knew everything again.

When I wasn't sleeping, everything went slowly, when the other girls' heavy breathing meant I couldn't turn a light on and read. My pyjamas and sheets felt sticky after all my tossing and turning, and the ticking of Edith's alarm clock, and the wind slapping the windows were so loud it made me think I'd go crazy.

I'd push my face into my pillow. My mother loved me — that thought was the one thing I could cling to. She used to surprise me after school with little presents that she'd found in junk shops. Little toys or books or trinkets for charm bracelets. Lying in bed, listening to the other girls breathing heavily, and the creak of their beds, I'd think about the times that my mother had stopped me at the front door to our house, her hands behind her back, saying that she'd found something very special for me. I wondered if I'd ever been grateful enough.

I was in pain all the time, but it was a slow pain I'd never felt before. My whole body ached, thinking about my mother. All I wanted was to feel her again, touch her. I wanted her skin pressing against my skin when she hugged me, or her chin resting on my hair. I wanted the pressure of her fingertips on my shoulder, as she held me back at a busy road when I wasn't looking where I was going. I wanted the coldness of her toes. She used to slip her feet underneath my bottom as I sat on the sofa, to warm them up, and I would wriggle away from her. It was these moments that I missed the most; my body was crying out for them. It was like a layer had fallen away from me and left me exposed.

The insomnia was taking its toll. I dragged myself to classes and sat there like a zombie. My head was pounding and my body felt like it was losing power. Everything my brain told it to do, it tried then gave up. I put my head down on my arms and closed my eyes.

Abi woke me up by jabbing a pen into my side. 'You're snoring,' she hissed.

Mr Hicks was standing over us, a half-smile on his face. 'Tallulah, would you mind staying after class?' he said.

He made me stand at his desk while he sat.

'I'm afraid I'm going to have to give you a detention,' he said. He played with his pen, clicking the lid. 'I can't let you get away with sleeping in my lessons, do you see that?'

'Yes.'

'I'm sorry. Are you being kept up by girls in your dorm?'

'No.'

'Well, you look exhausted. You must try to get some sleep. Have you been to the school nurse?'

'I'm seeing the counsellor.'

'Well. We're all here for you, Tallulah.' He tore off a slip of paper. 'You'll have to spend tomorrow lunchtime in here with me, okay?'

'Okay.'

I dragged myself back to my dorm. The girls weren't keeping me up, not directly. I didn't like Cressida; most of the time I didn't want to be around her, but I dreaded being completely alone. It was partly the idea of facing boarding school without anyone on my side that was keeping me up. But my novelty was starting to wear off and I wasn't sure if Cressida still thought I was interesting.

I played out confrontations in my head. I imagined myself telling Cressida what I really thought of her, challenging my father, asking him about the accident, why I had to be here. 'If you couldn't stop it happening, why couldn't you heal her? You're a doctor.' And Uncle Jack, too: 'Why did you come back? You made everything worse. And where are you now if you're not abroad?' In my head, I crushed the three of them with my anger.

9

Aunt Vivienne can't come in the next day after all. I sit with Aunt Gillian at my father's bedside while she continues knitting. I try not to look at him too often — he's so still I can almost forget he's there.

Aunt Gillian is making a jumper for the new baby. 'It's a shame there were no more children after you, dear,' she says. 'I always thought our extended family might be bigger.'

'I guess no one else really pulled their weight.'

'Mm-hmm,' Aunt Gillian says, looking guiltily at my father. She binds off the stitching, shakes the material out and inspects it critically. 'Not really up to scratch,' she says. 'I can give that one to a charity shop, I suppose.' She checks her watch. 'Shall we get something to drink from the cafeteria?'

'Sure.'

As we pass the nurse on duty, Aunt Gillian gives her a detailed account of where we're going, and how long we'll be.

'Georgia asked after you,' she says, as we take the lift. 'She'd love for you to go around sometime.'

'That would be nice.'

I get a coffee and Aunt Gillian has an Earl Grey tea. We sit at a table and drink.

'What's the age difference between all of you?' I ask her.

'Well now,' Aunt Gillian says. 'I'm a year older than Edward, then Vivienne was another three and a half years after him, then Jack came along two years after that.' She purses her mouth when she says his name; it looks almost automatic.

'So you're six and a half years older than Jack?'

'Yes,' she says. 'I suppose it meant I took on the role of second mother, as it were.'

'When Grandma was busy?'

'When she was ill,' Aunt Gillian says, vaguely.

'Who was the easiest to look after?'

'Oh, Edward. He was a darling.'

'Was *he* close to the other two?'

She fidgets in front of me. 'The best way to handle them was to get in their way as little as possible.'

'So they weren't close? Even as kids?'

'Well, no.'

We lapse into silence. I wonder why Jack approached my parents and not Vivienne, if he'd never been close to my father. There was another possibility, of course, but only one person could tell me everything. The other person was dead.

Everything changed after Uncle Jack came back; I wish my mother had had nothing to do with it.

I stand up. 'I've got to make a phone call,' I say.

In the corridor I punch in the number. It rings and rings on the other end; I feel sick. A mechanical voice comes on, telling me to leave a message. I start to speak, my voice shaky.

Then, halfway through, there's a click. 'You

alright, doll?' Malkie says. 'How's your pop?'

'He's okay,' I say. 'He still hasn't woken up and it's been six days.'

'Is that good or bad?'

'It's not good, but it's not bad yet.'

'Mm-hmm. You sure you're okay?'

'Yeah.'

'What can I do for you then?'

'Do you know where Uncle Jack is?'

There's a silence on the other end of the line. 'Malkie?'

'I'm here,' he says; I can almost hear his brow furrowing. 'Why d'you wanna know, doll? If it's okay for me to ask.'

'I wanna talk to him.'

He sighs. 'He's not exactly in great shape.'

'Does that mean you know where he is?'

*   *   *

Autumn was well under way; the leaves that hadn't fallen were the colour of ripe aubergines or rust. Starr came and got me from the Junior Common Room and we walked around the grounds. Our breath rose from our mouths when we talked, like clouds of smoke. I wore a woollen hat with a pom-pom and wellington boots. Starr wore thick grey tights and a diamond-pattern cardigan over her uniform. She was chewing gum, something I knew was forbidden at school.

'They said you needed someone to talk to,' she said. She wasn't looking at me at all, and I suddenly felt shy around her, instead of angry. 'So . . . how you finding it?'

190

'It's okay.'

'Making friends?'

I shrugged.

'Are you mad at me?'

'Why would I be mad at you?'

'I thought you were ignoring me . . . ' She left it hanging there. When I shrugged again she spat her gum into her hand and pressed it quickly onto the underside of a windowsill we were passing. 'So, we're fine, right? I'm sorry if you *are* mad at me, anyway.'

'Fine.'

'How's Uncle Edward?'

'Fine.' I blew into my hands to keep them warm; he'd only called back once more, but I was at Prep and he hadn't left a message. I was pretty much convinced he didn't care about me at all. 'How's your mum?'

'Yeah fine. She forgets about me, then feels guilty. Then she turns up here to take me out as a treat.'

'What do you do?'

'Go to town, get a manicure. Sometimes she takes me to the cinema.' She grimaced. 'Normally she gets drunk. You're lucky your parents are normal . . . Uncle Edward's normal.' Her cheeks were blotchy with red, and she put her hands up to fiddle with her hair, like she was trying to pretend she was busy. I thought of the conversation I'd had with Kathy and stayed silent. Starr would think I was crazy too.

'Did you know I'm on the tennis team? Maybe you could try out.'

'Do you remember our tennis tournaments at

191

Grandma's?' I said.

'Not really. We didn't even have real tennis balls there.'

'Yeah,' I said. 'I guess not.'

'Anyway,' she said, looking at me for the first time, 'you're really fine, right?'

'Yeah,' I said. 'I've gotta go to detention now.'

'Okay,' she said, looking relieved. 'I'll come find you soon. And come to a practice, yeah?'

'Okay,' I said.

For my detention, Mr Hicks got me sorting out the wax crayons into colour groups, and dipping paintbrushes into turpentine with him, while the radio played in the background. He made me laugh while I was working, singing the really high female-voice parts of songs, and cracking cheese-based jokes.

'Which cheese would you use to get a bear out of a tree?'

'I dunno.'

'*Camembert.*'

'Is that a cheese?'

'You shock me, Tallulah, you really do.'

It was almost like spending time with an older cousin, like Michael. Or like a father, who didn't hate me and was less tired and more fun. When I got up to leave, Mr Hicks helped me collect my things. 'Don't keep falling asleep,' he said. 'You'll make me think my lessons are boring.'

'They're not,' I said. 'They're pretty much the only interesting ones.'

Mr Hicks laughed. 'Thank you for the compliment.'

'You're welcome,' I mumbled.

He ruffled my hair, like I'd seen Michael do with Georgia, and I felt my cheeks get hot and prickly.

★ ★ ★

I can't stop thinking about what Malkie's up to. I imagine him picking up the phone, calling old friends, walking to an unknown part of London. Knocking on doors. I don't know what I want after that. What would I ask Uncle Jack? And do I really want the answers?

I can't take it back; don't think about it. Maybe nothing will come of it, anyway.

'What's happening now?' Aunt Gillian asks; another nurse has arrived.

'Nothing yet,' the nurse says. 'Just checking everyone's okay in here.'

'Yep,' I say.

'Good. I'll be back in a little while to move him.'

'Move him where?' Aunt Gillian asks.

'Just onto his other side. Nothing to worry about.'

She leaves. Aunt Gillian turns to me. 'Why do they move him?'

'I dunno.' I think I have an idea, but I don't know why she's looking to me for explanations, like she thinks my father will have passed down a genetic understanding of hospital procedures. It makes me feel weird — it's the fact that my father is part of the medical world that stops me getting into it. Or one of the things that stops me, anyway.

I get up and walk over to the window, looking out onto the red-and-white-brick of the buildings opposite, and the black of the railings on street level. A couple of girls stroll past, wicker bags swinging from their arms. Probably off to the park for a picnic. If things had been different, that could have been me and Edith. Or even me and Toby. 'Isn't it worth talking to him then?' my grandmother would say. She knew how I felt about him. 'I'm sure he misses you too.'

'I'm sure he's been able to replace me,' I argue with her. 'With someone who's not such a head-case.'

I don't want that to be true, but what do I expect? I didn't think about how it would feel for him when I'd gone, about how shitty it would be to be abandoned by the only person who knows all your problems, knows how vulnerable you are. I was a stupid kid who persuaded herself that he wouldn't care; that it was him who abandoned me.

'So go say you're sorry.'

I tip my chin upwards and take in the sky — less azure than the last few days, it reminds me of a shade called Carolina Blue. We used to have tubes of it in the art studio — light blue with a blush of silver, like the sea at sunset. I might even have some back at the flat. Years ago, I went on a splurge, buying stacks of different colours. It was after Toby bought me the paint brush set. I lugged everything back to school with me; I must have wanted him to see me using his present. I try to remember if I packed it all when I left, but I can't.

'Tallulah?' Aunt Gillian says. 'Can you hold the wool for me, love?'

I go back to my chair and take the ball from her, still trying not to look too closely at the sleeping figure in front of us.

'Did you get through to whoever you were calling before?' she asks.

'Yep,' I say. 'Just work.'

★ ★ ★

Christmas was coming, and lessons started to wind down. Teachers wheeled old TVs on tall trolleys into our classrooms and we watched Christmas videos like *Miracle on 34th Street* and *Father Christmas Goes on Holiday*. For days after we watched *Home Alone*, all the boys went around saying 'Keep the change, ya filthy animal' and making machine gun noises. It got dark so early it felt like our lessons were carrying on into the night; we wore slippers and dressing gowns to sit and do prep after dinner. The school choir sang carols at the train station and the shopping centre in town; our year were given elf costumes, and sent out with donation buckets. A few days later, I found a card in my pigeon-hole. Miss Rochard had written in gold glitter: *Dear Tallulah, This Christmas I wish for you to be happy. You're a very special girl and you deserve it! Merry Christmas, Annie (Miss) Rochard xxx*

Aunt Gillian picked me up to spend Christmas at hers then talked all the way home, while I stared out at other cars, other families.

Georgia was waiting by the window when we

195

pulled into the driveway. I climbed out of the car, stretching my legs, and she opened the front door, letting light stream out of the house. '*Tallie*,' she said. 'Oh my God, I can't believe you're *here*.'

Michael carried my stuff up to Georgia's bedroom. 'Welcome to the madhouse,' he said, and left.

I lay on the camp bed they'd made up for me. Georgia lay on her bed, facing me.

'Remember when we were at Grandma's, and we used to nap in the same bed?' she asked me. 'Me, you and Starr?'

'Yeah.'

'I can't believe we ever fit the three of us in a single.'

'We were smaller.'

'Do you see Starr much?'

'Sometimes.'

'What's she like now?'

'Fine.'

'Mummy always says 'poor Starr',' Georgia said. 'But she's so pretty, and she has such a cool name. I always think she's going to do something cool when she's older.'

'What's happening with Mr Tickles?' I asked.

'I think Uncle Edward's bringing him.'

'Can he sleep in here?'

'I'll ask Mummy.'

'Georgia, Tallulah,' Aunt Gillian called. 'Tea's ready.'

There were sausage rolls, smoked salmon on crackers, mince pies, spiced star-shaped biscuits and mini-stollen laid out on the table. All the lights were on; there was a vase of holly and ivy on the sideboard and one white wreath hung on the back of the kitchen door. Taps and the draining board shone. Aunt Gillian beamed. She'd obviously gone to a lot of trouble. 'Help yourself,' she said. 'How's the bed for you, Tallulah?'

'Fine. Thank you.'

'Mummy, can Mr Tickles sleep with us?' Georgia asked, and I felt a glow of affection for her.

'He doesn't have fleas or anything like that, does he dear?' Aunt Gillian said, unenthusiastically.

'No,' I lied.

'Okay then. Now tuck in. I'm making chicken pie for tonight — do you like chicken, Tallulah?'

'Yes,' I said.

'Good.' She turned the oven on. 'I thought I'd check now that Vivienne has become a vegetarian.' She said 'vegetarian' like she'd say 'prostitute', or 'terrorist'. She dipped a brush into some egg yolks and painted the pie crust with it — quick, annoyed brushstrokes.

'Don't worry about Mummy,' Georgia said in a low voice. 'Her and Aunt Vivienne had a big fight about something again.'

I chewed my sausage roll in silence.

'Can we have some apple juice please, Mummy?' Georgia asked.

'Of course.' Aunt Gillian went to the fridge and took the carton out. She poured two glasses and brought them over to the table, all smiles again. 'Did Georgia tell you she won a spelling competition recently? She came top of her age group in the county.'

'Mummy, you're being embarrassing.'

I took a sip of apple juice. 'Congratulations,' I said.

'What about you, Tallulah?' Aunt Gillian asked. 'I remember how hard they work you at that school — the teachers used to say to me, 'If you had half as much brains as your younger brother, you'd be fine'.' She smiled.

'I'm failing most of my subjects,' I said. With two exceptions, my grades were Cs, Ds and below.

'Oh,' Aunt Gillian said, looking embarrassed. 'Well, you mustn't be discouraged, dear. Sometimes it takes a while to discover our strengths. Do you belong to any sports or social clubs?'

'No.'

I looked straight at her, daring her to ask me another question. She stared back at me with her mouth open, then shut it, quickly, and put on a smile. 'I'm sure you're too busy with friends.' She checked her watch. 'I'll just nip down to the cellar to get some wine.'

'Don't worry about school,' Georgia said to me, as soon as Aunt Gillian was out of the room. 'I'm not as clever as Michael either.'

I shrugged. 'What did your mum and Aunt Vivienne fight about?'

'Mummy said Aunt Vivienne should have come to the funeral.'

'What did Aunt Vivienne say?'

'She said Mummy always wanted to sweep

everything under the rug.'

'Were they talking about Uncle Jack?'

'Maybe,' Georgia said. 'Mummy did say when Aunt Vivienne had left that she was kidding herself if she thought Jack was coming back.'

'The trouble with stories is remembering what's been said to whom.' The words quickly came back to me.

I had a sudden urge to see Malkie. I didn't want to tell Georgia that Jack might still be around, or that I thought my father might hold some blame for my mother's death, even if it was only by *not* doing anything. But maybe Malkie would know; maybe he'd be able to explain everything. Like why he'd come by that afternoon, and why my mother had made me leave the house.

'I'm going to the loo,' I said.

Upstairs, I rummaged among my clothes until I got to the photo of my mother I kept at the bottom of my bag. She was smiling, sitting with her knees pressed together, on some steps outside an open front door. It could have been the house she grew up in, the one she lived in with the grandparents I'd never known. I'd found the photo after she died, when my father was throwing out her things, rescuing it and her recipe book from the same box. It was hard to tell how old she was in the picture. Whenever I looked at it, I tried to find some similarity between us, but there was nothing on the surface.

I heard the front door open and male voices, feet stamping; it'd been snowing lightly since we got in. I went to the top of the stairs and crouched out of sight as Aunt Gillian came into the hallway to greet them.

'It's freezing, Mum,' James said.

'How's our notorious guest?' Uncle George said.

'Not doing as well as we hoped.' Aunt Gillian sounded worried. 'She was actually quite difficult earlier. Edward said she wasn't exactly setting the school on fire at her Primary, and we thought maybe the boarding school would be a good influence on her, but she sounds like she's struggling . . . Of course, it's hard to tell how academic Evelyn was, because she had to leave school so early, but . . . '

'Boring. What's for dinner?' James asked. They went into the kitchen and I went back to the bedroom.

★　★　★

My father was due late on Christmas Eve. We were already in our pyjamas, killing time until we could go to bed, and Georgia was fizzing with excitement; she kept hugging me and Michael and her stuffed dog, Humphrey. 'I won't be able to sleep,' she kept saying.

My heart skipped when I heard the doorbell, and then there he was, carrying Mr Tickles in the travelling cage. I let him hug me, quickly, then opened the cage and carefully lifted Mr Tickles out, kissing his ears and stroking his belly.

'I see Gillian got you here in one piece,' my father said.

'Oh shush,' Aunt Gillian said, taking his coat. 'We had a lovely ride over, didn't we, Tallulah?'

'Yeah.'

'Edward, would you like some mulled wine?'

'That would be nice.'

She left us alone in the hall and Mr Tickles struggled out of my arms and padded after her. I inspected my feet, so it seemed like I had something to do.

'Ah. Are you looking forward to tomorrow then, Tallulah?' my father asked.

'Yeah.'

'Good. It's nice of Gillian to let us take over the house, isn't it?'

I didn't understand what he meant. There were only two of us, and my father barely seemed to be there at all. I looked up, he looked back at me, but not like he really saw me. I didn't answer him, and after a moment he walked into the kitchen and I followed, confused. He rubbed his eyes a lot while Aunt Gillian fussed over him, heating up the soup she'd made us all for dinner earlier. He didn't ask me any more questions, or touch me again.

We half-watched TV, then went to our rooms. I climbed under my blanket and Mr Tickles sat on my pillow. He looked thinner and mangier than before and I wondered whether my father was feeding him properly.

Georgia tied her stocking onto the end of her bed, and mine onto the doorknob, then turned the main light off and climbed into bed. I could hear the grown-ups downstairs, the murmur of voices and the chink of glasses and Georgia a few feet away, her breathing getting slower and heavier. I squeezed my eyes shut, but my brain was buzzing and I didn't fall asleep for hours.

Christmas morning was louder than at my house, and later to start, and we were only allowed to open one present each in the morning. Gillian's Christmas pudding was homemade, like my mother's, which she used to start making in February, but it was dry and there were too many pieces of fruit in it. We had to watch the Queen's speech after lunch, while everyone opened the rest of their presents and drew up lists of what they'd got. Michael and James argued over who had the best haul; I pulled a cracker with Georgia and won a wind-up musical toy that annoyed Uncle George no end. In the living-room, in front of the TV, my father sat upright, fingers drumming on the arm of his chair. I'd stared at him over my food earlier, trying to find signs of grief, or guilt, but he looked exactly the same as always. It made it worse that he'd known that I might struggle at boarding school, I thought, because it meant that he'd wanted me out of the way at any cost, even if it meant humiliation for me. Aunt Gillian's words rang in my head the whole time — 'Edward said she wasn't exactly setting the school on fire at her Primary.'

Around six o'clock I escaped to my bedroom. I took the photo of my mother out again and rubbed my thumb across it, over her face. 'Merry Christmas,' I said.

★   ★   ★

I got off to a bad start in 1992. My teachers were losing patience with me. Before, when I got homework or tests back, they wrote comments like *good effort,* or *come and see me and we'll go through it.* Now they wrote *I'm starting to get really worried, Tallulah.* I dreaded seeing the grades circled in red on the bottom of the page. I began forgetting to hand homework in on time, skipping classes and hiding in the toilets, or in the school nurse's waiting area.

'You must have really weak genes, or something,' Cressida said. 'To be ill all the time.'

I didn't say anything. I wondered if maybe my mother had had a weak heart — I knew that was genetic. Maybe that was why *she'd* been ill all the time by the end; maybe that was why she hadn't survived.

'We're going to have to get in touch with your father,' Miss Rochard told me, sadly. 'I'm sorry, Tallulah, but your grades aren't improving at all. It's school policy.'

'Please don't,' I said. 'I'll get better, I promise.'

'Well I'm glad you're willing to work hard,' Miss Rochard said, but she looked worried. Her hair was dirty and scraped back in a bun; she was chewing her nails too, and it wasn't the first time she'd worn the same outfit twice in a row. 'Please try to concentrate,' she said to me. 'For me, please?'

'Okay.'

'I trust you, Tallulah. And you can trust me too — I'm here for you.'

'Okay.'

A week later, Miss Rochard burst into tears

during a sex-education class. The next day, Ms Conrad appeared; Miss Rochard had some personal problems, and they didn't know when she'd be coming back.

Ms Conrad had no time for daydreamers, she told me; either I learn to focus, or spend my lunchtimes going through the lessons by myself.

I glared at her as she walked back to her desk, mad at how smug she looked. Turning, she caught my eye and raised an eyebrow. 'Isn't there something you should be getting on with, Tallulah?' she said.

I stared at the page in front of me, but my heart was pounding so hard that I could feel it in my skull. Please let me leave this school, I begged silently. Please let me go back to my old friends and live in my house and see Mr Tickles. I'll be nice to my father. If he lets me go back, it means he has nothing to hide, anyway.

'Tallulah?' Ms Conrad called. 'I can't see your pen moving.'

'Tallulah, write something,' Abi whispered. 'Or you'll get another detention.'

I met up with Starr every week in my first year, but it wasn't until the summer term that she started talking to me properly. I was trying to blow on a grass stalk like a whistle; she was striding ahead. Starr was nearly a foot taller than me and she had breasts and a gang of friends who did whatever she wanted. I didn't see why Aunt Gillian called her 'poor Starr' either.

'Tallie, I'm sorry I haven't really seen you much,' she said, stopping suddenly. 'And I'm sorry I didn't come and see you when you first got here.'

I threw the stalk away and pulled up another one. 'You have your own friends. Whatever.'

'It's just, Mum was always so weird about you guys. And then I felt guilty for not coming to the funeral . . . '

I stopped listening; I played with my stalk and thought about Aunt Vivienne that summer, how she'd drunk more than usual, laughing hysterically, linking arms with Uncle Jack, and the looks she'd given my mother as she was doing it.

10

My father was busy again over the summer holidays. Aunt Gillian and the cousins were off on a family holiday in Greece for two weeks, so I was sent to my grandmother's this time.

'They'll join you there in August for a bit,' my father said. 'And I'll come down when I can.'

No one picked me up. I caught a bus from town and walked at the other end. The road to my grandmother's was almost a dirt track. I was dragging my suitcase behind me and by the time I arrived I was covered in dust.

I stopped at the bottom of the drive, partly to wriggle my fingers to try to get the blood flowing in them again, and partly to take stock of my surroundings. Looking around, I saw the trees were encroaching onto the path and the grass was high, almost halfway up my calves, and I wondered whether the gardener had left.

My grandmother must have been watching out for me, because the door was thrown open before I had a chance to knock. 'Come in,' she said, 'and may I enquire what on earth is going on with your appearance?'

My hair was pulled back in a ponytail and held there with a rubber band; my fringe was long enough to cover my eyebrows and the tips of my eyelashes. My t-shirt was crumpled and, looking down at my feet, I realised I had odd socks on.

'I . . . ' I started, but she was already walking off.

I followed her into the kitchen. This was the first time I'd been at the house by myself with her, but for some reason I wasn't afraid. A kettle was boiling on the stove; there were fresh chrysanthemums lying on the table, bound with blue string, and a cigarette smouldering in an ashtray on the floor by the open back doors, like she'd been smoking and looking out on the garden.

'Tea?' my grandmother asked. 'I don't drink the stuff, but I know people do.'

'No thanks.'

'Your hair looks like you cut it yourself.'

'I did.'

My grandmother looked away, but I thought she was smiling.

I picked up my suitcase and lugged it up the stairs to my old room. I had a cold shower and changed into a new t-shirt. I tried to do something with my hair, but it was too matted, so I snapped the elastic band back around it and went downstairs. My grandmother was out in the garden, walking around the vegetable patch; it looked like she was squeezing tomatoes, checking them for firmness. 'Tallulah,' she called, 'bring me the spray can from the windowsill.'

I took it out to her, noticing how the sill itself was crumbling under its white paint. The sun was low in the sky, flashing at me through the leaves and branches of the oak trees that grew near the house. My grandmother didn't seem to notice it; she walked between the rows of tomatoes, spritzing them with whatever was in the can. The fat, red fruit, the deep green of the vine leaves, the golden light, the straw hat she was wearing; everything was so vivid and I felt a tug in my chest that my mother would never be able to look at anything as beautiful as this again.

The peace was beautiful too. Except for the birds, and my grandmother's soft tread, there was no noise at all. It was a relief after the confusion of living with hundreds of other kids.

My grandmother turned and walked back towards the house. 'Are you coming?' she called to me. And then, like she'd read my mind, 'No point in catching a cold now you're free.'

★   ★   ★

Before my father came to visit that summer I was left to my own devices, so I had time to roam my grandmother's house and garden. Everywhere I looked seemed to have been touched with neglect. The ornamental pond to the right of the lawns was covered with a fine sheen of algae, the rose garden was withering, the jetty was rotting, the lake clogged with reeds and, beyond the lake, the orchard of apple and cherry trees grew in rows of straggling, twisted wood. Only the vegetable patch near the house had survived. 'What happened to the gardener?' I asked my grandmother.

'The National Trust stole him,' she said, sourly.

Inside the house, the furniture was faring just as badly. Chesterfield sofas were spilling out their stuffing, wooden trunks were splintering, rugs were threadbare and curtains fell off the rods if you pulled too heavily on them. I wandered through the rooms, picking up fluff and dirt as I went, and thinking that my father couldn't have made our house more different to his old one if he'd tried.

★ ★ ★

In the hospital, Aunt Gillian's plumping up my father's pillow. I find myself wondering if it's greasy after being under his head for four days straight. My father would hate that, but maybe they already changed it.

'Open your eyes, Edward,' Aunt Gillian murmurs. 'We're all waiting for you.' She looks around at me. 'Might as well try,' she says.

I force a smile. I want to say: No. I know you're worried, but he can't open his eyes 'til I've got all the answers. Not now I'm doing something about it.

A nurse comes into the room. 'Time to move the patient,' she says.

'Do you have to?' Aunt Gillian says. 'I've just made him comfortable.' She sticks her lower lip out, like an irritable child.

'I'm afraid I do, yes,' the nurse says. 'It's to prevent atelectasis and pneumonia, and bed-sores.'

'What's . . . ' Aunt Gillian begins.

'Need some help?' I ask.

'Go on,' she says. 'But don't let the doctors know I roped you into it.'

We turn my father onto one side. I feel like flinching when I touch him — his skin is so warm and yielding. I have to set my jaw and pretend he's someone else. The other two don't notice.

★   ★   ★

I can probably count on one hand the number of times there was physical contact between me and my father after I went to school. Much like the number of times he called me up. I suppose he called my grandmother about as often.

He called that summer, the night before he arrived, but just to let us know he'd be with us by late afternoon.

My grandmother waited for him downstairs, in front of the Wimbledon final. I lay on my stomach in the first-floor hallway, listening to the muted thwack of tennis balls and excitement from the crowds. When the crunch and spray of gravel came, I drew back from the top of the stairs. A key turned in the front door; I heard footsteps as my grandmother came out of the living-room. 'Edward.'

'Hello, Mother.'

There was a small, dry, kissing sound.

'How are you?'

'Fine. How's Tallulah?'

'Delightful.'

'Where is she?'

'I haven't got a clue.'

'I distinctly remember asking you to keep an eye on her, Mother.'

'Stop fussing, Edward. The girl's not as foolish as she looks.'

I had to hold in a sneeze, and missed most of what my father said back.

' . . . damage. Hardly a candidate for your particular brand of attention.'

'No need to be uncivil, Edward. Come and have a drink. That hideous man is going to win Wimbledon.'

'Agassi?'

Her voice got louder. 'I'm sure Tallulah will be along shortly to say hello.'

I lingered on the top step for a while before going downstairs. My father and grandmother were in the living-room, sitting in their usual spots.

'Hello, Tallulah,' my grandmother said, looking at me over the rim of her glass.

'Hi.'

'How has your summer been so far?' my father asked.

I shrugged.

'I thought we could have a belated birthday celebration for you. Is there anything in particular you'd like to do?'

'Not really.'

'We can ask Cook to make you a cake,' my grandmother said.

'Don't worry about it,' I said. 'I don't want to do anything.'

'You've got to do something,' my father said, impatiently.

'Don't force her to celebrate if she doesn't want to, Edward,' my grandmother said.

211

'You're not helping, Mother.'

'Tallulah doesn't want to have a birthday party. Surely that's all there is to it.'

'Tallulah is still a child.'

'I'm going outside,' I said.

I felt prickles of anger all over my skin as I crossed the lawn to the oak trees and started to climb one. The bark scratched the palms of my hands and my bare legs. I shimmied up to the lowest branch and sat there. I hated grown-ups and the world they ran. My father didn't care about me and none of my teachers cared about me, apart from Mr Hicks. They wanted me to fit in and pretend to be happy as if nothing had happened. Even Malkie hadn't bothered to come and see me. I lay back along the branch, steadying myself with my hands, and kicked my feet against the trunk of the tree. After a while my father came out and stood beneath me. 'I'm sorry, Tallulah,' he said. 'I didn't mean to upset you.'

I looked down at him.

'But these things are important,' he said. 'Evelyn's gone, but we can't give up.'

'How *did* Mum die?' I asked, surprising myself.

My father shook his head. 'I don't think that's an appropriate conversation to have right now.'

'Why not?'

'Because you shouldn't dwell on these things.'

'I should know,' I said. I looked back up through the branches.

He sighed. 'Your mother was hit by a car.'

'But she wasn't dead straight away, was she?'

'No.'

'So how did she actually die? Why couldn't you save her?'

He took a while to answer. I kept staring at the sky. 'She died of an aneurysm, caused by trauma to the skull. There was nothing I could do.'

'Was Uncle Jack there?'

My father's voice changed. 'How did you know about that?' He took a step forward. 'Had he come around before?'

'You answer me first.'

We were silent for a moment, eyeing each other. I put my feet against the trunk and pushed hard. It didn't move, but the strain felt good. I could tell my father didn't want to talk too much about that day in case he revealed something. In my mind, he'd already slipped up by saying there was nothing he could do — my father had always been able to do something. That was why there had been so many missed parties, and dinners, and ballet performances. Because he was needed elsewhere — to save someone.

Eventually he put his hands in his pockets and sighed. 'You don't have to have a birthday party if you don't want to,' he said. 'If there's nothing else, I'll go back inside.'

* * *

I stand back from the bed. I have to stop myself from wiping my hands on my jeans.

'All good for another few hours,' the nurse says to my father. They talk to him like he's listening, like Aunt Gillian does.

'Shouldn't he have woken up by now?' Aunt Gillian asks.

'Recovery times can be different,' the nurse says, soothingly. She looks down at his chart and frowns slightly. 'Although it has been nearly a week — we've rather lost track of time, here, haven't we?' She bends over my father. 'Now, Dr Park. We're very busy and we need this bed.' She winks at me. 'I'll be back in a few hours to turn him again.'

'How did he feel?' Aunt Gillian asks me when she's gone.

'What?'

'When you were moving him.'

'Fine,' I say. 'Like a person.'

'I keep worrying that he'll have gone. And no one will notice.'

'That won't happen.'

'You never know,' she says. 'You hear about patients being forgotten in hospitals all the time.'

'We're here,' I say.

Her face relaxes. 'Yes,' she says. 'At least he has us.'

That's more than he can say for me.

★ ★ ★

I avoided my father for the next few days, making a point of getting up before him and spending all day in the oak tree, reading. And then he left and Aunt Gillian and Uncle George and the kids arrived, and Aunt Gillian tried to rope me into sorting out old boxes with her.

She found one full of my father's books on the

214

top shelf of my wardrobe.

'Look how awful his handwriting was,' she said, holding up a history exercise book. 'Born to be a doctor.'

A medical textbook caught my eye. I pulled it out of the box and flipped it open.

'Oh yes,' Aunt Gillian said. 'Our parents gave him that when he went to university.' She put her hand up to pat her hair. 'He was the only one of us to go, actually. Did you know that? Jack was going to, but didn't . . . ' She looked around after mentioning his name, like it was going to make him appear.

I ran my finger down the contents page. The book seemed to cover every part of the body, every possible complication.

'Better move these somewhere less dusty,' Aunt Gillian said.

I waited until I'd gone to my room that night before I put the textbook safely away in my suitcase. If I understood the medicine behind it, I told myself, I'd know for sure if my father was guilty or not. I didn't believe it was possible that he could save everyone else but not my mother. That couldn't be true.

My grandmother walked me to the bus station when it was time to go back to school. 'Be good,' she said, as I climbed onto the bus.

'Bye,' I said, feeling strangely like crying.

I kept my head pressed against the window as the bus carried me further away from her, trying to think about the cold glass and nothing else. At the other end, I collected my suitcase from the luggage compartment and walked to school. I was the first back, apart from Edith, who came down to help me with my stuff.

'Thanks,' I said, realising that I'd barely spoken to her before.

A couple of weeks later we were filing into assembly, and a girl with a cherry-pink headband stuck her foot out and sent Edith crashing to the floor. A few students in my form stopped, unsure, but quickly started walking again, picking their way around her. I saw Cressida and the others already sitting down, crane their necks to see who'd fallen. Cressida mouthed the word 'Edith' and all of them started to laugh.

I stopped beside Edith and offered her my hand; her cheeks were dark red.

'Get into your seats, girls,' our new form tutor hissed behind us. I felt a flash of anger at her, and everyone else. Edith walked in front of me, her hands dangling at her sides. We passed Cressida, and she said something that made Edith bring her hand up to her face like she'd been slapped. I gave Cressida a cool stare. Her eyes slid away from mine after a moment and she looked uncomfortable.

We were learning about the dangers of drugs that term. Abi was in the States, so I was paired with Edith.

'I wasn't listening last lesson,' I told her.

'I know it,' she said; her head was bent down a couple of inches away from the desk and her hair had fallen over her face like a curtain. 'Don't you care about your grades?'

'Do you?'

'My parents would kill me if I got a 'C'.'

216

'My dad wouldn't,' I said. 'We hardly talk.'

I could see her wince out of the corner of my eye; she must have remembered my mother's accident.

Our teacher set us a quiz. Edith got every question right and we won book vouchers worth five pounds each.

'You can have mine,' I said to her that evening.

'Okay,' she said.

I was starting to realise that she was easier to be around than Cressida, who I avoided even more now. I spent most of my time in the library, poring over my father's book. I was sure I'd find something that could have saved my mother. I started off reading the section about skull fractures, depressed and linear, and then the one on aneurysms. I couldn't really understand more than a few sentences, and reading about the brain made my own thump behind my eyes, reminding me it was there. Maybe aneurysms were genetic. Maybe I would fall and bump my head and die, like my mother had done. I flicked through the pages until I got to the lungs, then the heart. I liked the way the lungs looked like two birdcages; I liked the heart. Unlike its cartoon-shape, it was square-ish and smooth, without the sharp point at the bottom, although there was still a vague arch at the top. I drew doodles on my planner; my heart came out messy and stumpy-looking, with both vena cavas sawn off to give a cross-section.

'That's gross,' Cressida said when she saw the pictures. 'What's your problem, Tallulah?' She tossed her hair and stared at me, her eyes were cold and flat.

My social decline happened almost overnight. Suddenly, whoever I sat next to would find some excuse to move elsewhere, until finally I was placed in the middle of the front row, by myself. I spent lunchtimes alone too, listening to other kids snigger about me. I knew Cressida was making up rumours. I didn't know what she was saying, but I hoped it wasn't about sharing a bed with my twin brother.

I had a growth spurt and shot up almost a foot higher than anyone else in the year, even the boys. I felt gangly and ridiculous. I was given braces; when they took the braces off they gave me a retainer to wear and said I would need it for the rest of my life. I threw it into a bin on the way back to school.

My father was barely in touch. I didn't really want to talk to him, either. I couldn't prove that the accident was his fault, even with what he'd said to the police, or that he should have done anything different after my mother had been hit. But I knew all about *our* relationship.

At least with all the reading I'd picked something up about biology. We started a module on the human body, and I was getting B's, and, one time, a B+. Now that I was off bounds, the only person willing to be my lab partner was Edith. She liked maths and brussels sprouts, I found out, and didn't like art. She wore a necklace with a St Christopher pendant that her great aunt had given to her because epilepsy ran in their family, and he was the patron saint of epileptics.

Edith's father was a banker and her mother was an interior decorator. She had a younger brother, who she hated with a passion, and a girl-gerbil called Zorro who she loved.

'I've got a cat called Mr Tickles,' I said. 'But I haven't seen him for ages.'

Edith started tagging along with me wherever I went. At first, Cressida made snide comments whenever we walked past, but after a while, she went silent. I'd almost forgotten about her by summer term, until we came back into the dorm after a Friday Prep and she was sitting on her bed, looking pissed off. 'Do me a favour,' she said, when we walked in, 'and just hang out somewhere else, yeah?'

'Why don't you?' I asked. 'We sleep here too, remember?'

'I'm grounded,' she said, giving me a dirty look. 'The Housemistress found my cigarettes. Someone must have grassed me up.'

'It wasn't me, I swear,' Edith said.

'Was it you?' Cressida asked me.

'Nope.' I shrugged. 'Maybe one of your sheep stabbed you in the back.'

'It *was* you, wasn't it?' she said, flushing. 'I can tell.'

'Why would I bother?'

'You're jealous.'

'Unlikely.'

'Come on, Tal,' Edith said. 'Let's go downstairs.'

I could feel a bubble of anger inside me that wasn't all about Cressida and her stupid long

219

legs and big tits. If I'd never been sent here I wouldn't be in this situation now, I thought; if my mother had never run out in the road that day, I wouldn't have a huge hole inside me.

'No,' I said. 'I want to stay here.'

'You're jealous that people like me,' Cressida said. ''Cos I'm not a weirdo or a lesbian.'

'Shut. Up.'

'It's not your fault really,' Cressida said. 'You don't have any female role models now your mum's dead. Of course you're gonna dress badly and . . . '

I grabbed a handful of her hair and tugged it until I felt it ripping out of her scalp. She was screaming '*Fucking bitch*,' at the top of her lungs and swinging at me. I dodged her arm, but then she was trying to kick me, and one of them landed. I let go of her hair and got behind her, twisting her arm back.

'*You crazy fucking bitch*,' she screamed. 'You're in *so* much trouble.'

'Whatever,' I said, panting.

The Housemistress was called. I was put on toilet duty for a week.

'See what happens when you try to touch me, lesbian?' Cressida said.

'You want me to break your nose?' I asked.

She backed away from me, covering her face with her hands. 'You're perfect for Edith,' she said. 'You're both freaks.'

I took a step towards her and she fled. If I acted unstable, I realised, people would be more likely to leave me alone.

After that I was definitely stuck with Edith.

220

Starr wasn't too happy about it — she cornered me on the back staircase a few days later and told me I was turning myself into a social pariah. 'It's fine that you beat up Cressida,' she said. 'She's a little snot. But don't be such a weirdo with everyone else — they're not all bad.'

I shrugged.

'I can't protect you, you know.'

'Please just leave me alone.'

'Tal . . . '

'Just fuck off, Starr.'

'Fine,' she said. 'You get your wish.'

* * *

In 1993, someone called Bill Clinton became the President of the United States, getting everyone excited, even in Britain. I wondered briefly what Malkie thought of it, but that just made me sad that I'd never see him again.

Over the next year and a bit, more and more things that I didn't understand seemed to happen in the world. All over school, people were talking about Fred West being arrested and Ayrton Senna's death and other names I'd never heard of. Not that they were talking to me, anyway. By September 1994, the beginning of year nine, I was the most isolated I'd ever been. Starr still avoided me. My teachers had all reached breaking point with me, apart from Mr Hicks and my biology teacher, who thought I was enthusiastic and average. My father had spent a few days with me at my grandmother's that summer, where they both pretty much

221

ignored me, although my grandmother had at least bothered to haul me up for slouching. My father's communication was confined to when we weren't in the same town — brief letters about the hospital and Mr Tickles and the weather in London.

Dear Tallie,

I'm sure you don't need filling in on everything, he wrote, so I'll be quick. They've dug up the street to mend a broken water-pipe and the old sycamore tree outside the house had to go. Kathy and her parents are moving — she said it's a shame she won't get to say goodbye to you — apparently they've accepted an offer and the buyer's quite keen to move in soon. They're going out to Dubai to stay with an aunt until they decide what to do next. I passed on your regards — hope that was alright. I didn't know if you two were still close you haven't seen her much since you left Primary, have you? People move on, I suppose.

Hospital's busy, as usual. The cat is being bullied by another tom. I keep hearing them fighting at night. If they keep it up I might have to start shutting him in — the noise is awful.

Hope everything's going well for you.

Best,

Dad

I started to write a letter for Kathy, then gave up. I hovered between tearing up my father's letter and keeping it as proof of how little he understood or cared about me. I tore it up in the end, and flushed it down the loo. Afterwards, I stood looking at my eyes in the mirror, amazed at how dry they were. No more mother, no more Kathy. My father would probably kill off Mr Tickles next.

In the second week of term I was held back after a textiles class for not having my hair tied up. Edith had had to go in to lunch without me, so I was standing in a queue at the canteen by myself. Groups of older kids were jostling around me, shouting insults and in-jokes above my head. I saw Toby Gates and his friends just in front of me in the queue, flirting with some girls in the year above. The girls were all giggling and tossing their hair around; I tried not to be noticed. Someone behind me stumbled, and pushed me into the group ahead. I caught one of them with my elbow, and held on to someone's shirt to stop myself from falling.

'Watch it,' the girl said. She jerked away from me, making me stumble again.

'Fucking Juniors,' someone else said, and everyone laughed.

'It wasn't my fault,' I said, my face burning.

'Don't speak until you're spoken to,' the first girl said, and pinched my arm. They all laughed again.

'Don't do that,' I said. I glared at the pincher. Out of the corner of my eye I noticed Toby half-turn away, grinning awkwardly.

'She's gonna cry,' one of Toby's friends said. 'Look at her . . . '

'I'm not,' I said, but now that everyone was saying it, I felt like I might. I left the queue. I heard one of the girls call something after me, then more laughter.

I got to my next class hungry and in a bad mood; Edith tried to talk to me when we were sitting down, but I ignored her, and she descended into a hurt silence. Our maths teacher arrived with a mug of coffee and a pile of marked homework sheets. 'My hands are full, so everyone line up at the front to collect your homework,' she said.

I stood up too quickly, catching my foot on the leg of my chair, which clattered backwards, making everyone turn their heads to look at me.

'Tallulah,' the teacher said, frowning. 'Pick up that chair at once.'

I'd been halfway down to pick it up already, but when she told me to do it I stood up again.

'Tallulah, I said pick it up.'

'No,' I said.

The teacher gave me a hard stare; I returned it and she looked away first. 'Fine,' she said. 'If you're going to act like a child you can be treated like a child.' She tore a detention slip from her register and started scribbling on it.

'No,' I said again, and flipped my desk over.

Pens and pieces of paper rained down around me. Someone screamed, then laughed and everyone drew back.

'Jonathan, go and get the Headmaster *immediately*,' my teacher shouted.

'See ya,' I said, strolling towards the door. I watched my hand turn the knob and my feet carry me outside, but my brain wasn't connecting with what was happening.

After a moment, I heard footsteps run after me, and then Edith was at my elbow. 'Tallie, what are you *doing*?'

'They're gonna expel me anyway.'

'They won't,' she said, unconvincingly.

'I'm not going back.' I pushed through the doors of the school entrance and started off down the driveway towards the school gates, my pulse gradually slowing.

'I'm coming with you then,' Edith said. She linked arms with me. 'Where are we going?'

'Who cares,' I said. 'We could join the circus, I guess.'

Edith stopped.

'I think there's one in town,' I said. 'I'll be a trapeze artist, you be one of the clowns.'

'I don't want to be a clown,' Edith said. She was nibbling the pendant of St Christopher nervously.

'Clean up after the elephants then, or something.'

'You're being mean.'

'Sorry, Ed,' I said. 'You can't run away though — your parents would kill you.'

'Your dad will too.'

'He won't even notice.'

Edith started crying. I walked away.

'Tallie please don't go,' she called after me.

'I have to,' I said.

They found me an hour later, sitting by the

side of the road, waiting. There was no point carrying on — I knew Edith would have told them which direction I'd gone in.

* * *

'I'm going to Georgia's for dinner,' Aunt Gillian says. 'I'm sure she'd love to see you too.'

'Maybe next time,' I say. My head's too full of my father and Jack and Toby right now.

We take the lift down together, hug outside the hospital, and she steps into the road, hailing a taxi. 'See you tomorrow, darling.'

'See you.'

As soon as she's out of sight I check my phone, although I already know Malkie hasn't called yet, I would have felt it vibrate. Slow down, I tell myself, he said a couple of days. At least it'll give me time to work out what I'm going to say.

I don't know if he'll want to tell me anything though. I don't even know if he'll show up — the Uncle Jack I remember never seemed to do anyone any favours, he was too angry all the time. Which I guess is how I could have been described back then, too.

* * *

The school wanted to call my father.

'Don't bother,' I told them.

'Who should we call instead?' the school secretary asked. She was standing with a neatly squared fingernail pressed down on the telephone hook, the handset cradled between her chin and shoulder and gold bangles clinking on her wrist. 'We have to call *someone*.'

My grandmother blew into school. From the window I saw her stop the headmaster on his way from the car park to his office; we could all hear snatches of her shouting at him. The headmaster must have realised this, because he tried to steer her inside, taking hold of her elbow. My grandmother shook him off and started thrusting her finger into his chest. The school secretary tutted behind me. 'What on earth does she think she's doing?' she asked.

'He shouldn't have tried to grab her,' I said.

She gave me a dark look.

It was agreed that I could spend some time living with my grandmother, and that she would get a private tutor for me.

'Tallulah's grades have never been very impressive,' Mr Purvis said, flicking through my academic reports. 'She's failing maths and physics, and she's only just scraping by in French. I don't even have a Latin report for her . . . ' He looked at me over the rims of his glasses. 'Tallulah, have you attended Latin at all this year?'

'No,' I said.

He faced me for a moment, then cleared his throat and shot a look at my grandmother. My grandmother stared back at him. 'Moving on then,' he said. 'Just about the only subjects she does okay in are biology and art.'

'Art,' my grandmother snorted.

Mr Purvis stood, came around the front of his desk, and leaned back against it. 'The way things are going . . . ' He rearranged his tie. 'We have an academic reputation to uphold, and she has a lot of catching up to do in these next two years before she sits her exams. Perhaps you can persuade her to apply herself. Now, if you'll excuse me, I have a meeting to get to.' He ushered us out of his office and closed the door.

My grandmother pursed her lips at me, and told the secretary to order us a taxi.

We didn't speak on the ride back to her house. My grandmother hummed something under her breath, I had the window rolled down and the wind blew my hair across my face. Already I felt my shoulders lifting.

When we arrived, I turned left at the top of the staircase out of habit and walked towards my old bedroom. Then I stopped, and went back. I put my suitcase in the room that my parents had always shared, showered in the en-suite then unpacked my clothes into the dresser and went downstairs to find my grandmother.

She was sitting in the living-room, drinking. 'Gin and tonic.' She waved it at me. 'Want one?'

'Alright,' I said. I hadn't drunk gin before. At school we'd had vodka a couple of times, straight, after the lights were out and the Housemistress' footsteps had died away. It had burned my throat and my insides, and the hairs in my nose had felt like they were curling up in protest. My first cigarette had been just as unpleasant, but after a while I'd stopped noticing how harsh the smoke felt and enjoyed the rhythm of the inhale, exhale.

My grandmother poured me a small measure

of gin and a lot of tonic, and dropped two ice cubes and a slice of lemon into the glass. 'For beginners,' she said.

'Thanks.'

I sipped my drink. It tasted much nicer than the vodka, which hadn't even had a label on the bottle. My grandmother was humming again, not looking at me. 'How old are you?' she asked suddenly.

'Thirteen and a half.'

'It's a wonder it took you so long to run off, really.' She took another sip. 'Well, you're here for a few months. See if I can't straighten you out, or something along those lines.'

I took another slurp of my drink. My grandmother raised an eyebrow. 'May I ask, however, why you called me and not your father?'

'Dunno,' I lied.

'Hruh,' she said, looking at her glass. 'I forgot how life for young people is merely a series of spontaneous decisions.'

There was a silence.

'Are you gonna call my father?'

'Don't worry about that,' she said, waving her hand. 'I'll smooth things out with Edward.' She got up and headed for the door. 'You can amuse yourself now.'

★ ★ ★

If I'd found my grandmother's house shabby before, the few years that had passed had turned it into more of a decaying shell. Window panes had fallen out in several bedrooms, plaster was crumbling from the ceiling. Instead of tackling the problems, my grandmother had shut off large areas; in a house of well over twenty rooms, we lived in the kitchen, the living-room, my bedroom and hers. The whole place creaked in the cold. Gusts of wind prised themselves through cracks and vents to hug us as we went about our business indoors. The ceilings were too high, and except for in the hallway, there were no carpets. Every morning, after my shower, I felt steam rise from my skin when I stepped out of the bathtub; no matter how frantically I rubbed myself with my towel, my body was goose-pimpled within seconds. My teeth chattered constantly. My grandmother didn't believe in central heating — she drew the green velvet drapes in the living-room and told me to put another jumper on.

We ate every meal together, and aside from the noises made by the house, we ate in silence. A few days after I'd arrived, I cracked during breakfast. My grandmother had been snapping the pages of the newspaper open and I'd been staring at the ceiling, which was developing a large brown stain, like a dirty tributary across the white.

'Don't you think it's kind of unsafe living like this?' I asked.

'When I want your opinion,' my grandmother said, acidly, 'I'll send you to structural engineering school.'

I bent over my bowl, playing with my cereal, splashing milk around to mask the burning I felt in my cheeks. My grandmother watched me for a moment before saying, 'If you don't want it now, you can finish it for lunch.'

I shoved the bowl in the fridge and stomped upstairs. 'I hope you find something dead in yours,' I said, as soon as I was out of earshot.

I decided to carry out a survey of the rooms. Whatever my grandmother thought, my father and Aunt Gillian would probably agree that some upkeep was needed. That was how I came across the library — most of the rooms I'd seen before, but once, poking at a door I'd previously assumed to lead to a cupboard, I felt it swing open, dislodging a ton of dust. Books covered three of the four walls; the fourth wall had a bay window with red and gold curtains tied up with red velvet ropes, and there was a fireplace with a poker, coal scuttle, shovel and brush arranged neatly in one corner. The air inside smelled odd — maybe mould — but it was in surprisingly good shape in comparison to the other rooms.

A few afternoons later, when the tutor had left for the day, I was flicking through *Gulliver's Travels*. I'd chosen it because it had a cool picture of a ship on the front, half submerged beneath cartoon waves. I was only a couple of chapters in when my grandmother burst into the room, looking thunderous.

'What are you doing in here?'

'Reading. I found it on the shelf.'

'Leave,' she snapped.

'But . . .'

'Get out of here immediately.'

'Aren't I allowed to read?'

She snatched the book away from me.

'You can't do that.'

Her face was red and her eyes were shimmering, as if she was about to cry, but she didn't, and she didn't speak again.

'Sorry,' I said after a moment. 'I didn't know . . .'

After a moment I left. I skulked upstairs for most of the afternoon before going to find her. She was sitting on the sofa in the living-room, her eyes closed and her legs stretched out and crossed at the ankles.

'I'm sorry for doing something I shouldn't,' I said.

'You weren't to know.'

'Are you still angry with me?'

She opened her eyes. 'No, I'm not,' she said, finally. 'But I don't want you snooping around in there.'

'Why?'

'I have my reasons.'

Like — you're crazy? I lingered. 'Can I sit down here with you?'

'I'm going to watch television,' she said. 'You can stay or you can go, but you have to be quiet.'

My grandmother watched *Murder, She Wrote* regularly. She liked Angela Lansbury's perm and disapproving looks. I didn't want to go back to my parents' old room and lie on the bed by myself, so I stayed. We watched as Angela's character, the mystery writer, tramped all around the murder scene, interrupting police, shaking her head and picking up clues. My grandmother waved her drink around and shouted at the screen: 'No, not there . . . Why don't you *think*, woman? It's not going to be the schoolteacher is it?'

When it was over she turned the TV off and leaned back into the sofa, lighting a cigarette. 'What did you think of it?'

'Does that happen every episode?' I asked.

'Does what happen?'

'Does she always find dead bodies?'

'There has to be a murder, doesn't there?' She took a long drag.

'But that's not even realistic,' I said. 'How many episodes have there been? How many dead bodies has she found?'

'There are more dead people in the world now than living,' my grandmother said, blowing out smoke.

'Hhmm.'

'Are you worried you've shacked up with a madwoman?'

'No,' I lied.

'Go on, I know you brats used to make up stories about me,' she said, waving the smoke away.

'No we didn't.'

'I suppose I deserved them. I was always standoffish.'

'I guess you were a little bit.'

She smiled wryly. 'That's better. Your mother always said honesty came naturally to you.'

I blinked, surprised by the mention of my mother.

'I'm going to start on lunch,' my grandmother said. 'Are you coming?'

I looked at the cobwebs drooping from the ceiling, and the dust-streaked windows. My mother had been here; she'd sat underneath the cobwebs, and talked about me to my grandmother, apparently.

'I'm going outside for a bit.'

'As you wish.'

I went out and played badminton in the garden, ducking underneath the net I'd set up between two hawthorn trees the day before, trying to reach the shuttlecock's downward swoop before it hit the ground. Maybe my grandmother was the only person who was actually nice to my mother, then, I thought, although I couldn't really remember them talking, except during the picnic.

I hit a particularly mean overhand, scrambled across, and the shuttlecock sailed over my outstretched racquet and into the water behind me. 'Shit.'

I parted the reeds along the edge of the lake with my racquet; if the shuttlecock was there, I'd never find it. I scuffed my shoe along the cracked wood of the jetty, trailing my racquet in the water. Just beyond the edge of the landing stage, something was glinting in the water, blurred by the ripples. I lay on my stomach and tried to focus on it; it seemed to be round and small and shiny. I tried to scoop it up with my racquet, but the water was already way too deep. I stood up and kicked off my shoes, closing my eyes as I jumped.

The cold made my heart stumble. I opened my eyes — everything was soft and muted, shimmering in the waves I'd created. Below me I saw our rowing boat shift then settle again in the shadows; we'd sunk it a few summers before, trying to drive a mast into it. Something slimy wrapped itself around my wrist and I struggled frantically, until I realised it was just a reed. I doggy-paddled in one spot. I could hear the wood of the jetty groaning, and a faint buzzing that I couldn't identify.

I dived towards the shiny object. Down there, it didn't look so shiny. My fingers closed around it and I swam upwards, kicking until I broke the surface.

Now I could make out what the other noise had been. My grandmother was running down the lawn, her long legs eating up the grass and wisps of grey hair tumbling out of her bun. 'I'm coming,' she was yelling. 'I'm coming.'

I heaved myself up and out of the water and stood there shivering until she reached me.

'What happened? Did you fall?'

'I jumped.'

Her mouth fell open, then she stretched out her hand and gripped me by the upper arm. 'Let's get you inside.'

'What on earth were you doing, diving into the lake at this time of year?' she asked, when I was changed and sitting in the living-room. Just this once, she'd allowed a fire to be lit, hauling logs from the gardening shed into the house. 'Are you ill?' She clamped her hand against my forehead.

'No,' I said, pushing her away. 'I'm fine.' I took a gulp of my tea. 'I thought I saw something.'

'What did you see?'

'Nothing.'

'So help me, my girl, if this is your way of paying me back . . . '

'It's got nothing to do with you,' I said, and I was taken aback to find tears coursing down my face. I opened my palm and showed her the aluminium ring pull I'd dredged up.

My grandmother shook her head at me.

'I thought it was my mum's wedding ring.'

'Why would your mother's wedding ring be in the lake?'

'I don't know, no reason,' I said, sniffing and sipping at my tea. I just wanted it to be, I thought, and then I'd have something of hers for myself.

'Tallulah, you can't dive into the lake in the middle of winter — you could make yourself sick.'

I brushed my cheeks with the heel of my hand. 'I won't do it again.'

'Good.'

'Thanks for not being angry.'

'Of course I'm not angry.'

It's how my father would have dealt with it though.

'Thanks anyway,' I said.

She stroked a lock of hair away from my face. 'Anytime.'

*   *   *

A week later, I was leaning out of my bedroom window, smoking a cigarette I'd stolen from my grandmother, when I heard the doorbell. My grandmother answered the door and a man's voice filled the hallway.

'Tallulah,' she called.

I sprayed deodorant on myself generously then went downstairs, praying it wasn't my father. My heart did a funny dance when I saw Malkie standing in front of the door. We smiled awkwardly at each other.

'What's wrong with the two of you?' my grandmother asked. 'Cat got your tongues?'

'What've you done with your hair, doll?' Malkie asked.

Earlier that day my grandmother had marched me into the bathroom, pushed me onto the toilet lid and taken her scissors to my hair, rapping me on the head when I swore. Now I was fringe-less and sleek locks fell in waves around my face.

I ran my fingers through my new cut. 'It's gone,' I said.

'I can see that,' he said.

'Don't you like it?'

'It's nice. Just makes you look a little . . . older.'

'Hruh,' my grandmother said. 'I think you'll find the word you're searching for, Malcolm, is *feminine*. And Tallulah, don't stand chatting on the stairs. Come down and greet our guest properly.'

'Hi, *Malcolm*,' I said, offering him my hand. 'How do you do?'

'Very well, thank you,' Malkie said, taking my hand in his. I giggled. My grandmother gave us a cold look. 'Malcolm is going to be teaching you piano,' she said. 'Apparently this was a long-standing agreement.' She looked at her watch. 'You know where the piano is, Tallulah.'

I took Malkie through to the dining-room and sat on the piano stool; he drew up a chair next to me. 'First,' he said, 'we gotta get your posture right.' He placed one hand on my shoulder, and the other on my lower back. 'Drop your shoulders,' he said. 'And straighten your back.'

I tried to drop my shoulders. Across the hallway we could hear my grandmother shouting at the TV: 'What's this nonsense about ghosts — come on, woman, it's not going to be a ghost, is it?'

'Why are you really here?' I asked.

'I'm a friendly face, and Matilda thinks you need one right now.' He took a penny out of his pocket. 'So here I am, if you ever need to talk. On the other hand, as we're sitting at the piano, why don't we give it a whirl?'

He took my right hand and placed it on the keys with the penny on top of it. 'Move your fingers,' he said. 'Play some notes.'

I played a few notes. The penny slipped off my hand. Malkie picked it up and put it back. I played again; he caught it this time before it hit the floor.

'The trick,' he said, 'is to move your fingers without moving your hands too much. It should come from your wrists and arms.'

I stared at him. 'How can I move my fingers and wrists without moving my hands?'

'You gotta use gravity.'

'What?'

'It's all about control,' he said. 'You gotta

238

control your fingers, but you gotta let other stuff help you.'

'Riiiiight,' I said.

He poked my back again. 'Don't slouch. Why don't you practise single notes with the penny on your hand? We can start with middle C.'

I took him to the front door when he left. 'Can I ask you a question?'

'Sure.'

'Did you meet Uncle Jack in prison?'

'Nope,' Malkie said. 'And that's not a very polite question to ask, young lady.'

'Sorry,' I said, squirming inside.

'I met him in about 1974,' Malkie said. 'Your aunt too. She was wearing flared trousers back then, and neat little waistcoats.'

I tried to picture Aunt Vivienne in flares and a waistcoat, but I couldn't.

'And your mom — she looked like a blonder Raquel Welch. Jeez she was pretty.'

'Who was that?'

'Look her up, doll.'

I paused. 'Why did you all stop . . . being friends?'

'What makes you say that?'

'I didn't know you when I was younger. Or Uncle Jack.'

Malkie shook his head. 'Life gets in the way.'

'But why?'

'It happens. Make sure you do your practice.'

When the front door closed my grandmother came out into the hallway. 'How was it?' she asked.

'Playing the piano hurts,' I said.

'Hruh,' she said, and went back into the living-room.

*　*　*

My grandmother liked soups, and since the cook had left to run a nearby pub kitchen just before I came to stay, I was drafted in to help. I peeled the vegetables, and she chopped them up, her hands moving fast, like water running out of a tap. We had pea soup, carrot soup, ham and lentil soup, chicken broth and Irish stew, although they all tasted mostly of salt, which my grandmother used liberally.

The night after my first piano lesson, we were making carrot soup. I was peeling the carrots and my grandmother was drumming her fingers on the counter. I never peeled fast enough for her.

'I heard you asking Malkie some questions,' she said.

'Yeah,' I said. 'I wanted to know stuff about my mum.' I scraped my finger with the peeler. 'Shit.'

'If you must swear,' my grandmother said, 'say fuck. No one likes to think about excrement.'

'Fuck,' I said. 'That hurts.'

'You want to know anything else?'

'About Aunt Vivienne and Uncle Jack too, I guess.'

'Ach, those two.' She coughed.

'Why did you say it like that?'

'How exactly did I say it?'

'Like *those two*, like you were annoyed with them.'

'Because they were troublesome when they were younger.'

'Why?'

'It was in their nature I suppose.' She put her hands on her hips. 'Edward and Gillian were quiet, Vivienne and Jack were not. Much like someone else I could mention.'

'But what did they do?'

'All manner of things.'

'Like *what*?'

My grandmother looked at me out of the corner of her eye. 'Albert used to say they were too close,' she said eventually.

I pushed a pile of gleaming-bright carrots towards her; she brought the knife down hard on the first one, slicing off an end, and carried on until they were all done. She swept the carrot slices into the pan. 'Garlic.'

I brought over two cloves from the fridge and she crushed them with the side of her chopping knife. Her fingers picked the waxy yellow pieces out of their wrapping and threw them in the pan with the carrots.

'They spent all their time together. Thick as thieves — that's what their teachers used to call them. Just a euphemism for bullies, as far as I could make out.'

'Who did they bully?'

'Anyone who wasn't in their little twosome. Edward, for one.' She drizzled some olive oil into the pan and started to heat it up. 'You know,' she said, stirring the onions, 'this soup might actually work.'

'What about Dad then?' I asked.

She pointed her wooden spoon at me. 'Well go on — ask.'

'What was he like when he was the same age as me?' Or, why does he have such a problem with me?

'He was a very good boy.'

'Is that it?'

'What do you mean, is that it? That's what he was,' she said. 'He was a very devoted child. Never left my side.'

'That's not very interesting.'

'Don't be such a fool, Tallulah,' my grandmother said. 'You don't have to be bad to be interesting.' She turned the heat down. 'We'll let that simmer for a while.'

We ate in the kitchen that evening as we did every night. It was the only warm room in the house.

My grandmother poured herself a drink, laid the butter out and sliced a loaf of bread. I dipped a thick piece in my soup, weighing up a question in my mind. 'Do you know where Uncle Jack is?' I asked eventually.

'I most certainly do not.'

'You said at Mum's funeral that he was still in the country.'

'Did I?'

'Is he?'

'I don't know, Tallulah. I haven't seen him in years.'

'Because you don't like him?'

'Why on earth would you think that?'

'You don't sound like you do.'

'What people say, and what they mean, are

often two completely different things,' she said, taking a spoonful of soup. 'Pass the salt, please.'

I fetched the salt and pepper from their place next to the cooker. 'Aunt Vivienne never comes to visit by herself, does she?' I asked.

'No,' my grandmother said.

'Don't you miss her?'

'She and I haven't spoken properly since she was sixteen.' Her hand shook a little when she next lifted the spoon to her mouth.

'What happened?'

'She thinks I betrayed her,' she said after a while. 'My children had a tough childhood, I suppose, and Vivienne's never forgiven me for it. I would never have done it on purpose, though. It's a terrible thing to have to do, to let your children walk away.'

'Why does she think you betrayed her?'

'You can't always tell the true intentions behind a person's actions. And you don't always get on with the people who are most similar to yourself.'

'Did you get on with Grandad?' I asked, wondering if that was what she meant by the children having a 'tough childhood'.

My grandmother pursed her lips. 'He was crazy,' she said. 'He used to ride past my mother's farm at six in the morning on his horse and take me off with him.' She looked down at her wedding ring. 'I had to cling on for dear life.'

I couldn't imagine my grandmother clinging on to anybody. 'Do you miss *him*?' I asked.

'It's certainly different around here without him.' She touched her face, just below the eye, and I pictured the children watching as my grandfather hit her there until she was bleeding and half-blind. 'He was so strong-willed, your grandfather, like a hurricane — blowing in and out and taking what he wanted. I'd never met anyone like him.'

'Do my dad and the others miss him? They never talk about him.'

'I really wouldn't know how they feel,' she said, and her voice had gotten harder.

★　★　★

I call my boss to swap shifts the next day. He grumbles, but I don't give him time to say no. When I hang up, I sit in bed for a moment, trying to work up some energy. I'd rather risk looking like a stalker and go back to Gray's Inn than the hospital. But if Toby *does* agree to see me, it'll be better to wait until all this is over.

I sit underneath the open window with my father's old medical textbook propped up in my lap. I run my finger down the index page, and find it — *Atelectasis: where alveoli may collapse or close, with the consequence of reduced or absent gas exchange.* In other words, it becomes difficult to breathe. *If left untreated, atelectasis can be fatal,* I read. *Smokers and the elderly are particularly vulnerable.*

I don't know how my grandmother escaped that particular fate; she was already wheezing heavily a month after I went to live with her. Although after our talk over the soup she started spending more time with me, so maybe I just hadn't noticed it before.

She started to ask me more about my father, and my relationship with him, lecturing me about his responsibility, and how much he needed my support as well. I thought about trying to explain what my father had been like — how he was always away. And how he'd changed after Uncle Jack showed up. And then that day. But I could never tell her that I'd thought he killed my mother. And by that point, the effort of talking for too long made her face turn a weird shade of purple, and something warned me never to get her riled up.

It was a relief sometimes to escape to a different room with my tutor, where she couldn't interrupt, and even more of a relief when Malkie turned up one Saturday morning, car keys jangling in his hand.

'I came to see if you wanted to run an errand with me?' he said. 'I need to go into London, pick up my car from Dennis, my mechanic.'

'What do you want me to do?'

'I'd enjoy the company. I could drive you back this evening.'

'Yeah, cool.'

'Don't you need to ask Matilda?'

My grandmother appeared behind me. 'Ask me what?'

'It's really creepy when you do that,' I told her.

'Thank you, Tallulah, I'll bear that in mind. Ask me what?'

'Can I go to London with Malkie to pick his car up?'

'That depends,' my grandmother said. 'When

will you be back Malkie?'

'Not too late — scout's honour.'

'As if I'd believe you were ever in the scouts,' she said, but she nodded.

'Thanks, Grams,' I said, and kissed her cheek.

We waited thirty minutes for the train. I hooked my fingers over the top of the station sign and swung from it, showing off in front of Malkie.

'Don't break your neck, doll,' he said.

Malkie smoked a cigarette and had a staring contest with one of the cows from the field the other side of the second platform. 'Moo,' he called to her.

We sat in a carriage that was as empty as the station had been. I breathed onto the window and wrote my initials in the condensation. Little towns slid past in grey and green blurs until the rain came and dirtied the windows, obscuring the view.

At Euston, Malkie strode purposefully ahead; I trotted to keep up with him, sidestepping families and backpackers sitting on the plastic green floor of the main hall and the concrete plaza outside. Dennis was in Shepherds Bush, a long Tube-ride away. When we turned up he came out to meet us, wiping his fingers on a towel. Malkie showed me the car. 'See that?' he said, running his hand over the bonnet. 'Isn't she a beauty?'

It was pink and baby blue, with headlamps that looked like frogs' eyes.

'Isn't it a bit . . . girly?' I asked.

'Shows how much you know,' Malkie said, and

pretended to take a swipe at me.

Dennis said he'd be hours yet, so we found a bench in a nearby park to sit on. Malkie rolled another cigarette and lit it; it stuck to his lower lip as he spoke. 'How's it going at Matilda's, doll?'

'She's pretty cool.'

'She's a swell lady,' he said.

'Do you know anything about her and my grandfather?' I asked him.

'What do you mean?'

I wondered if he knew about my grandmother's eye. I didn't want to be the one to spill the beans if not. 'I just . . . don't,' I ended, lamely.

'From what I heard, they had a complicated relationship,' he said, tapping ash onto the ground.

'Who told you that?'

'Jacky.'

'What did he say?'

'Just once, when we were roomin' together after he got out of the joint, Jacky got a fever.' Malkie stubbed his cigarette out. 'He was saying all kinds of crazy things, getting frantic about her being left alone with him. Course, it was gibberish. It was after your grandpa passed away.'

'He said he didn't want Grandma to be left alone with him?'

'That's what I thought at the time.'

I thought about how angry my grandmother had been at finding me in the library. Maybe that was where he'd hurt her. Maybe he'd done more than just damage her cornea. None of the family ever spent time in that room, and maybe that was why. I felt sick.

'Penny for them,' Malkie said.

'Was Uncle Jack *afraid* of Grandad?'

'Well it sounds like your grandpa had a nasty temper.'

'How nasty?'

'I'll tell you a story Viv told me,' he said, lacing his fingers together. 'When she was fourteen she had a fight with her old man. He knocked her out — broke her arm, two ribs and her jaw. They found three teeth in the fireplace.' He coughed. 'So sounds 'bout as nasty as it gets.'

'Oh.'

'You okay, hon? You're looking a little pale.'

'I thought it was just Grandma he hit.' I tried to picture Vivienne as a fourteen-year-old, but I could only see Starr, and I felt something inside me go out to my adolescent aunt. 'I'm glad I never met him.'

'That's 'cos you're smart.'

I made a face at him, but I didn't feel sick anymore.

'Your aunt was a little high when she told me that story,' Malkie said. 'So she could have been confused, I guess. But I got the sense it was true. And my old man knocked us around too — maybe that's why she felt she could talk about it with me.'

'What happened to *your* dad?'

Malkie chuckled. 'One day I realised I was nearly twice his size, and I stopped being scared. Then he died. And I will say this — you remember people differently after they're gone.'

Dennis wasn't finished until ten o'clock that night, and it was nearly eleven by the time we made it onto the motorway.

'Matilda's gonna skin me,' Malkie said, peering through the windshield.

'I'll stick up for you.'

'Thanks, sugar.' He turned the heating up and fiddled with the knob on the glovebox, then slammed his fist against it and it sprang open. 'Here, wanna mint?'

'No thanks.'

'You can go to sleep, if you want.'

'I'm not sleepy,' I said, yawning again. 'Tell me about yourself.'

'What about me?'

'Where do you live?'

'I've got a few places I crash at,' he said. 'Nothing fancy like Matilda's.'

'Where *have* you lived?'

'Canada, obviously,' Malkie said. 'Birmingham. Glasgow. I've lived in Spain — I was there for five years or so. I went there after Paris, and I went to Paris around the time that your mom and Vivienne were moving in together, just after their flat-warming party.' He grinned to himself. 'I seem to remember waking up in the bath.'

'Did my mum and Vivienne . . . suit each other?'

'Sure. Evie was real good at cheering Viv up when she was in one of her moods.'

'Oh.' I thought about teenage, mistreated Vivienne hardening into moody, adult Vivienne, and wondered how my mother had been able to ever cheer her up.

'They were pretty tight. It's a shame they fell out later.'

'Why did they?'

'Dunno, doll. I wasn't around by that point.'

I laid my head against the passenger window and watched colours appear and disappear in the rain drops on the side-door mirror. Malkie switched on the radio and started crooning along to some country classics; within five minutes, I was fast asleep.

★   ★   ★

'They're not all real, you know.'

It's no wonder Aunt Vivienne is temperamental, really.

I flick through a few more pages in the book, reading a paragraph here and there, then shut it. I suppose by definition a medical textbook has to be about all the things that can go wrong with our bodies, but it's bringing back bad memories. Why wouldn't my grandmother trust me enough to tell me about my grandfather — was she ashamed she'd let it happen? Then again, I never told her how I felt about my father. If I'd been open with her, maybe she could have made it better. Or maybe not — she hadn't managed to mend her relationship with Aunt Vivienne, after all.

After a moment of hesitation, I put the textbook on my bedside table and go into the kitchen to turn the shower on.

11

I make my way to the hospital early. It's busier and brighter than yesterday. A young nurse is being shouted at by a doctor as I walk past the Intensive Care desk. I'm comfortable enough to sit alone in my father's room now, reading the notices on the wall — fire safety instructions, a reminder to wash hands regularly and a newspaper clipping pinned directly above my father's bed. I stand up to peer at it more closely and realise it's a clipping about him, some grateful journalist had a relative in my father's hands, and has written about the calm, professional care received by both patient and visiting family. Why was he so strong for everyone else and so utterly useless with me?

It's a relief to go to the bathroom, away from the beeps and the whirring and all the hospital gear; I dawdle in there, rinsing my hands for ages. On the way back, I stop at the open door to another ward. A doctor is doing the rounds with two nurses. One of them must be in training. She looks young and nervous and when the doctor asks her to take blood from one of the patients, I think she's going to faint.

'You've done it before, haven't you?' the doctor asks.

'Yes,' she says.

'Good.' He hands the chart to the older nurse, gives the room another quick scan and walks out, smiling cheerfully at me as he passes.

'Sister?' the patient says. 'One of you's a sister, right?'

The junior nurse is opening the bag with a fresh needle inside; her hands are shaking. The older nurse puts her hand on the younger one's back and leaves it there. 'Are you ready?' she asks.

The younger one pulls herself up and sets her jaw. 'Yes,' she says.

'No,' the patient says, he looks terrified.

'Now,' the older nurse says to him, 'this isn't going to hurt. Nurse Salter is very competent, I promise. Top of her year at uni.'

'Christ,' he says.

Nurse Salter sits next to him. 'Hold your arm out, please,' she says. He looks away as she ties the tourniquet and sterilises the area with an alcohol wipe. 'There'll be a very little sting as the needle goes in,' she says. 'But it'll be over soon.'

He whimpers softly when she inserts the needle, then she's pushing a tube into the hub, filling it, and the needle's out. She puts a cotton pad against the puncture, applying pressure to hold it to the arm, and tape to keep it in place, then discards the needle and labels the tube.

'Very nice work,' the older nurse says. 'Both of you.'

'Thanks,' Nurse Salter says, shakily. She and the patient have both gone grey again.

'We'll get you some water,' the older nurse says.

'What about a whisky?' he asks.

They all laugh, and I'm strangely jealous. I do

a lot of the same jobs as nurses already: listening to complaints, making small jokes, cleaning up puke. But nurses connect with people, they make a difference.

The two leave the room, noticing me like the doctor did earlier.

'You're Dr Park's daughter, aren't you?' the older nurse says.

'Yep.'

'You're on the wrong floor I'm afraid — he's one below us.'

'I know,' I say. 'The toilets down there weren't working.'

'This building,' the older nurse says, clicking her tongue. 'Give your father my love, won't you?'

'Yeah,' I say. 'No problem.'

I walk with them to the lift and then go down one floor. No one else has arrived yet. I take a seat next to my father's bed again; I wonder whether he knows the doctor I saw upstairs, whether he'd approve of his briskness, if that's what people mean when they say calm, professional care. I look down at him, at the blond hairs on the backs of his hands, and the dopey expression people get when they're asleep. You're easier to deal with when you're unconscious, Dad, I tell him silently, then my inner Gillian says, don't think like that in here. Even if I don't want my father in my life, that doesn't mean he deserves to die, or stay comatose permanently. I straighten the hem of my skirt.

'I used to want to work in a hospital, you

know?' I say out loud, feeling stupid. 'That didn't work out, obviously.'

He takes a sudden, shuddering breath, and I'm sure I catch his eyelids flickering.

I cross the room and yank the door open, my heart pounding. 'Can someone come in here please?'

Down the hall the nurse who was being chewed out earlier looks up, sulkily, from her clipboard.

'I think he opened his eyes,' I say. Her expression isn't very encouraging, but I keep talking. 'I think he looked at me.'

'I'll come and check on him,' she says, and starts walking slowly in my direction.

'Are you his nurse?'

'For today.'

'Are there loads of you?'

'Loads of us?'

'I've seen someone different each day.'

'Well . . . we're all very fond of your dad,' she says. She's nearly reached the doorway and she smiles at me for the first time. 'We all wanted to help out.'

'Thanks,' I say, trying to smile back.

She leans in close. 'He's the only doctor that all the staff like, actually.'

'Really?' Really?

'Dr Park's never too busy, doesn't push people if there's a decision to be made.'

'Yeah?'

She nods at him. 'I don't need to tell you what he's like though, do I?'

I smile inwardly. Well yes, you do actually. He

spent all day patiently letting other people make decisions, then came home and refused to let his own daughter do the same.

She goes over to the bed and checks the monitor. 'What did you say happened?'

'He took a deep breath, then I thought he opened his eyes.' My voice kind of squeaks when I say the last bit.

She hums as she checks his chart and peers at his monitor. I wonder if Gillian's on her way.

'His heart rate's gone down,' the nurse says, straightening up. 'I'll get the doctor to come by and have a look.'

'Is he okay?'

'I'm sure everything's fine,' she says, but she looks worried.

I go back to the toilet and lock myself in a cubicle. I sit on the loo, bending forwards so my face is almost touching the knees of my jeans, hands clapped onto either ear; I try to control my breathing. If there's a problem, it'll be my fault. I didn't want him to wake up before Malkie brought Jack round, and now he's getting worse.

Eventually I sit up. I pee, wash my hands and face and pat myself dry with some flimsy blue paper towels. Strange that I was here less than an hour ago; it seems longer now.

★   ★   ★

Malkie's story about my grandfather made me feel weird for a while, but I mostly forgot about it after the bike incident.

255

It was muffled voices that woke me and took me to the top of the stairs. I looked down and saw the bike in the hallway. The door to the living-room was closed and there was a slash of light underneath it. I couldn't hear who was talking, or what they were saying and I wondered about the cyclist. Apart from the tutor and Malkie, no one came to see us at my grandmother's. We were at least a fifteen-minute walk from the village and it was late. A sudden panic took hold of me, and I rushed to my grandmother's room to check whether she was asleep and we were being burgled. Her bed was still made up. I looked at the clock on her bedside table — two in the morning.

I went back to the top of the stairs and called out. The voices paused; a floorboard along the corridor from me creaked and night air rustled through cracks in the walls. I felt all the hairs on my arms stand up, then I heard quick footsteps and light flooded the hallway. Someone was standing framed in the living-room doorway.

'What is it, Tallulah?' my grandmother asked.

'I heard voices.'

'So you decided to get out of bed at two in the morning on a school night?'

'I heard voices,' I said, stubbornly.

'Yes, well now you know — I sleep badly. I'm old. Go back to bed.'

'Who are you talking to?'

There was a pause.

'I'm talking to an old acquaintance. Now go back to bed.'

My bed was cold when I got back into it. I

256

wished I had Mr Tickles there to sleep on my feet. I curled up into a ball and tried to stay awake, listening out for the cyclist leaving, but I fell asleep straight away.

★ ★ ★

Malkie came to teach me once a week. I was picking it up fast, he said. It must be in my blood. 'Your mother was musical,' he said.

'I didn't know that,' I said. There was a small squeezing feeling inside my chest at the thought that I didn't know everything about her. 'What did she play?'

'She played the piano too. Didn't she ever tell you?'

'No.'

Malkie shifted in the seat beside me. 'She wanted to be a concert pianist when I knew her,' he said. 'She was practising loads until she was 'bout twenty-five, then something happened to distract her, or so I hear.'

'She was twenty-five when I was born.'

Malkie grinned. 'Yup.'

I tried to imagine my life in twelve years time. 'Do you think twenty-five is young to have a baby?'

'Depends on the person,' he said. 'Your grandma was twenty when your Aunt Gillian was born.'

'Really?'

'Really. Young and beautiful, or so I hear.'

'My grandma was beautiful?'

'Oh yeah. Good-looking family, the Parks.

Especially your Aunt Vivienne.' He jiggled his eyebrows.

'She's not as beautiful as she thinks she is,' I said, feeling jealous.

'Oh, she is, and more,' Malkie said. 'Don't worry, doll. You'll outshine her one of these days.' He clapped me on the back and checked the clock on the wall. 'Speaking of family — I'll be going back to Canada for a little while. See my mom while she's still up and running.'

I hadn't thought that his mum might still be alive. 'How long will you be gone for?'

'Hopefully not too long. I'll bring you something nice.'

'You won't come and see me.'

He shook his head at me. 'You have a lot of attitude for someone with fancy new hair and clothes.'

'Well, it's true,' I said. 'You never came to see me before.'

He ruffled my hair. 'I'll definitely write — I promise. Now, I better get, you have studying to do.'

I pulled a face.

He stood up and shrugged his jacket on; it was beige, with a white sheepskin lining. He was wearing cowboy boots too, and a woollen hat with ear flaps. He looked like an Eskimo brought up on Clint Eastwood films.

'Malkie,' I said, pulling the black keys of the piano up until they stuck there. 'Did *you* like my mum?'

'Course I did.'

'Why?'

'I dunno — why do you like anyone? 'Cos she was kind and funny.'

'When her and Vivienne fell out,' I said. 'It wasn't . . . '

'Wasn't what?'

'My mum didn't do anything wrong? Vivienne was just being Vivienne, right?'

He started to say something but I cut him off.

'I mean — I get why she'd be angry with Grandma, even if it's not really her fault my grandad was horrible to her. But my mum couldn't have done anything bad to her.'

'No,' Malkie said. 'Your mum would never have done something bad to Viv. She didn't have a bad bone in her body. She was just a sweet kid.'

'She wasn't really a kid.'

'Not a kid then,' Malkie said. 'But there was something about Evie that made you want to look after her. I guess 'cos she'd had to bring herself up, after her parents died. You kind of wanted to give her a break.'

'Oh.'

'You'll grow up, princess,' Malkie said. 'And you'll see we all just want the same things, really.'

When he'd gone I went to find my grandmother in the kitchen.

'When did you grow up?' I asked her.

'Is that a joke, young lady?' She was unscrewing a bottle of arthritis pills and counting them out carefully onto the kitchen table.

'How do you *know* you've grown up, then?'

She carried on counting the pills, heaping them into small neat piles. 'Growing up is just about feeling comfortable in your own skin,' she said. 'Some people never manage it.' She looked up. 'Are you going to bother me, or are you going to do your homework?'

'I'm bothering.'

'Silly question, I suppose.' She put her bottle down and looked at me. 'There's nothing wrong with it. People are just scared of change.'

I eyed her pills. 'I'm not scared,' I said.

'Good girl,' she said. 'Be brave in everything, even things you don't want to do.'

She rested her hand on my forehead. I closed my eyes and concentrated on feeling her fingers as solid, things that wouldn't fall away, but they were as dry and as light as paper.

★ ★ ★

The whole three months I stayed there, the house and grounds felt like they were always on the verge of snow although it didn't in fact arrive until early December. When I finally woke up to see the world covered in a frozen white blanket, I ran outside with boots and an overcoat on, breathing in air that was so crisp it burned my throat on its way down.

Underneath the snow, the garden looked like it rolled on and on forever. I lay on my back and made a snow angel, like my mother had taught me when I was younger, enjoying the feel of my skin go numb then hot again. Eventually I sat up and went to explore the rest of the garden. The lake was solid, and a lonely bird was chirping mournfully in the middle of it, eyes fixed on the food swimming underneath the ice. When he was still there after dinner, I brought him some bread, and left it on the jetty.

My grandmother stopped working in the garden when she slipped on a fine layer of frost and hurt her hip, so I had to do the planting, preparing the beds for onions and digging up the rosemary and winter radishes. My grandmother watched from the living-room and banged on the window if she thought I wasn't treating her vegetables carefully enough.

'What took you so long?' she'd say when I came inside, my fingers swollen and red from the cold and the work. 'When I was younger I had to do this, the washing, the cooking and the scrubbing all in one afternoon. You would never make it.'

'Yeah, but we have technology now,' I said.

'Hruh,' came the reply.

I was planting rhubarb when the first attack came.

I heard the crash and ran indoors, not stopping to take off my muddy shoes.

My grandmother was lying face-down on the rug. Her walking stick was stretched out in one hand; she'd knocked over the bottle of port on the table.

'Grams . . . ' I put my arms around her waist and turned her to face me. Her eyes were wide and her mouth kept falling open.

'I'm going to call an ambulance,' I said. 'I'll be back in one minute.' My tongue felt thick with fear.

My grandmother's eyes narrowed and colour

started to come back into her face. 'Don't . . . ' she said. She closed her eyes and breathed in deeply.

I put my face closer to her to hear better. She opened her eyes wide. 'Don't be ridiculous. Call Edward,' she said. 'And don't move someone who's fallen over — my neck could have been broken.'

'I'll remember,' I said.

'You won't need to,' she grumbled. 'Just call Edward.'

I called my father, my hands shaking as I dialled the number. He came on the line after what seemed like ages. 'Yes?'

'Dad, it's me. Grandma's had an attack, or something.'

'What happened?'

'She fell over, and then her face looked funny. Oh, and her mouth was open.'

'I can hear you, you know,' she called from the other room.

'Tallulah, stay there,' my father said. 'Don't do anything. I'll call an ambulance.'

See, I told my grandmother silently.

'I'll get a train up and be with you in a few hours.'

My grandmother complained about the noise of the siren the whole journey to the hospital.

'Well,' one of the paramedics said, 'the good news is you don't seem to be slurring your words.'

The doctor who looked her over was called Dr Philips and he wore a red polka-dot tie. I sat next to the bed, trying to slow my heartbeat down.

Everything's going to be okay. Everything's going to be okay.

'You seem to have had a mild stroke,' Dr Philips said when he finished. 'But with the right medication, there should be no long-term effects. We'll have to keep you in for a few nights.'

'My son's coming,' my grandmother said, drawing the blanket around her. 'He can take care of me.'

'I wish my mother had the same trust in me,' Dr Philips said, cheerfully. I wondered about his mother — he looked about ninety years old himself.

'Do you want some water?' I asked my grandmother.

'No,' she said. She pushed the blanket away and tried to stand up.

'Now, now, Matilda,' Dr Philips said. 'What's all this? You can't move, you know. You have to stay right here and get our little nurse to look after you.'

'I can't stay in bed all day,' she said. 'Get out of my way.'

Her hand groped for her walking stick; I picked it up and took it outside the ward.

'Tallulah,' she said. 'Bring me my stick at once.'

'No,' I said. I came back in and replaced the blanket. 'You can't go anywhere. Not until Dad gets here at least.'

'She's quite right, you know,' Dr Philips said. 'Just get some rest. Snug as a bug in a rug, that's what you'll be.'

My grandmother looked at him as if he'd farted. 'Are you retarded?' she asked.

'I'll go get you some water,' I said, trying not to laugh.

Dr Philips followed me out.

'Ignore Grandma,' I said. 'She's just mad she can't do things for herself.'

'Of course,' Dr Philips said; he didn't seem especially offended. 'Tell your father I'll be around if he'd like to discuss the patient.'

I found a water cooler and filled a plastic cup. My grandmother drank half of it, then passed it back. 'I'm tired,' she said.

'Do you want me to close the curtains?'

'That would be nice.'

I closed the curtains and brought her an extra blanket from one of the other beds. 'Let me know if you need anything,' I said, perching back on my chair.

'You're a good girl, Tallulah,' she said, turning over. 'And you'd make a good nurse.'

It was already dark when my father arrived. After some wrangling with Dr Philips, my grandmother was told she'd be discharged the next morning.

'Tell the staff to leave me in peace,' she said, and fell back asleep.

I slept too, in the taxi on the way back to the house. My father woke me up at the front door. I climbed out, foggy and aching from being slumped against the window.

'You don't snore anymore,' my father said. 'You used to when you were little, did you know that?'

264

'No.'

The taxi pulled away and left us in the pitch black. My father spent a few minutes trying to locate his key; I shifted awkwardly from one foot to another, aware that this was the first time we'd been alone together since I went to school.

We went straight to bed.

The next morning my grandmother's mood was even worse. She hadn't liked the food or the hospital bed and she didn't like the broken heater in the taxi. My father and the taxi driver helped her upstairs and into her own bed, and I could hear her complaining that now she wouldn't be able to watch her TV programme.

My father paid the driver and came to join me in the kitchen, looking exhausted. 'I'm going to get a district nurse to come in and check on her,' he said, yawning. 'I think that's the safest thing to do. She's ready for some soup now.'

'I'll take it,' I said. I put a tray together, soup, bread, a jug of ice water and an orange. My father watched me expressionlessly.

I stumbled going up the stairs.

'Careful,' my grandmother called, 'I only have good china.'

I placed the tray on the bedside table and sat down at the foot of the bed. 'How are you feeling?' I asked.

'A little foolish,' she said. 'How are you feeling?'

'Scared,' I said.

'Yes,' my grandmother said. She patted my hand. 'Well, you didn't lose your head. That's something to be proud of.'

We smiled at each other.

'Dad says he's going to get a district nurse to come and look in on us.'

My grandmother raised her eyebrows. 'Us?'

'I'm not going to leave now you really need me.'

My grandmother tightened her grip on my hand. 'You're a very loving girl, Tallulah.'

'Let's try this soup,' I said.

I stayed with her until she fell asleep. Her head rolled forwards and she started mumbling,

'Not like that, careful — you'll fall, Albert — put me down — I can't breathe — '

I ran a sink full of hot water in the kitchen and dropped the dirty dishes into it. My father came in. Out of the corner of my eye I could see that he was standing there, hands resting on the back of a chair. 'I haven't perhaps said,' he started, then cleared his throat. 'Thank you for taking care of Mother today. I know it's a lot of responsibility for someone your age.'

I wiped my hands on a dishtowel, and turned to face him. 'Have you told Aunt Gillian or Aunt Vivienne yet?'

'Gillian's coming up tomorrow.'

'What about Aunt Vivienne?'

He shook his head. 'I'll do the dishes.'

I dropped the dishcloth onto the table and went upstairs.

★   ★   ★

I could see Aunt Gillian's suitcase in the hallway. I was sitting halfway up the stairs, listening to her conversation with my father in the kitchen.

'Of course she's not coming,' she said.

'Did you tell her what happened?' my father asked.

'Yes, yes. You know what she's like. She has other 'engagements', Edward. Too busy to see her own mother.'

'Don't be too hard on her, Gillian.'

'*No one's* too hard on her.' Aunt Gillian's voice was rising. 'She likes to play the victim, and you know it.'

I felt a stab of irritation. If Vivienne's story about being knocked out was true, she *was* a victim.

'She has no thought for others,' Aunt Gillian said.

I walked slowly upstairs. My grandmother was sitting up in bed, spooning porridge into her mouth. 'How are you today?' she asked.

'Gillian's here.'

She grimaced. 'I see.'

'How's your porridge?'

'Disgusting, without salt. Salt is the only good thing in this world.'

'Other than gin,' I said, sitting down on the end of her bed.

'Hruh,' she said. 'You'll never settle down with a tongue like that.'

'I don't want to settle down.'

'We all need somebody, my darling.'

'Even you?'

'I have somebody,' she said, nodding her head at me.

'But really, did you need Grandad?'

267

'What's with the questions all the time?' she asked. She flung the bedcovers back. 'Open the window, I need some fresh air.'

'Okay, okay,' I said, getting up quickly. 'I'll do it. You're meant to be resting.'

'I'll rest when I'm dead,' she said, gritting her teeth.

I opened the window, and went back over to the bed. 'Don't use that word.'

'Dead?'

'Don't say it.'

'There's nothing to be afraid of,' she said. 'It's what we're born to do.'

'Can we please not talk about it?' I said, biting the inside of my cheek.

'Tallulah,' my grandmother said gently. 'You have to let go at some point. Look at me — I've buried both parents *and* a husband. Sometimes it helps to talk about it. And sometimes it helps to throw away their things so they're completely invisible everywhere but in here.' She tapped her chest. 'That's what I did with your grandfather.'

'Why?'

'When he died, it was almost as if I died too.' She sighed. 'I went through the house ripping all the telephone cords out of the wall, so I would never have to hear more bad news.'

'So you *did* love him?'

'It's complicated, darling.'

'If dying is so horrible for other people, then why do you want to do it?'

She held her arms out to me. 'But there might come a time when I'm in a lot of pain, sweetheart.' She held up her hand as I turned to leave and I went back to her. She smiled at me and brushed a lock of hair away from my face. 'We won't talk about it then. But I'm not afraid.' I twisted away from her. 'Fine, go downstairs. Tell Gillian I'm ready to receive her now.'

'Yes, Your Majesty.'

'That's my girl.'

★   ★   ★

The next few days Aunt Gillian cooked and cleaned for us while we played cards upstairs on my grandmother's bed. I was in charge of taping *Murder, She Wrote* and looking after the garden. My grandmother watched from her bedroom window now, screaming orders at me from there. She also let me smoke her cigarettes, until Aunt Gillian caught me behind the rose garden. 'What would your father say?' she cried.

'Not much,' I said.

My father had left the day Aunt Gillian arrived, threatening to come back and take me home for Christmas. I tried to make my grandmother let me stay but she sided with him.

'But I don't want to leave you,' I said, frustrated.

'Edward would be lonely if you didn't go,' she said, stroking my arm, and I tried not to look too sceptical.

'*You'll* be lonely if I do.'

'I'll enjoy the peace and quiet.' She saw the look on my face. 'Of course I'll miss you, silly girl. But I'm getting too old to keep an eye on you.'

I rolled my eyes. 'Okay.'

The night before I left, my grandmother showed me where the champagne was kept and I opened a bottle, under her direction, and served it in two glasses that had been chilling in the fridge. I sipped at the drink, not sure about the dry, sharp taste.

'Here's to us,' she said.

The taxi driver taking me to the station the next morning was cheerful, but I didn't want to talk. I still felt guilty for leaving. The district nurse had wheeled my grandmother out to say goodbye, although she'd tried to walk. 'I don't care,' the nurse said, when my grandmother waved her arms indignantly. 'You go in the wheelchair or you don't go at all.'

'Well, then I'll go in the chair,' my grandmother said, disgustedly. 'I suppose you'd like to start breathing for me next, would you?'

The view outside the window of the train seemed to be getting greyer the closer we got to London, matching my thoughts. I wasn't looking forward to Christmas alone with my father. We'd gone to Gillian's every year since my mother's death.

At home, my father opened the front door wearing a dark blue jumper with leather elbow patches; I'd never seen it before. 'Come in,' he said. 'How was the journey?'

'Fine.'

I dragged my suitcase to the foot of the stairs and ran into the kitchen. Mr Tickles was lying underneath the table; he looked even more battered than before. I scooped him up and hugged him. 'Miss me?' I asked him. I stroked him underneath his chin and he started his rattling.

'I'll take your suitcase upstairs,' my father said, appearing behind me.

'No, I'll do it. And I promised I'd phone Grandma.'

'Yes, of course. Fine. How is she?'

'She's probably lonely.'

'Well, Gillian and the children will spend Christmas with her, so you don't have to worry so much.'

I looked down at Mr Tickles who was drooling onto my hand. 'She'll be complaining when I go back then,' I said. 'Gillian fusses too much for her.'

My father frowned. 'You're talking about the Easter holidays, I take it.'

'No,' I said, feeling a flush rising up my neck. 'I'm going back after Christmas to look after her.'

'I'm afraid not, Tallulah. You've spent too long away from school as it is,' he said. 'Your grandmother and I both think you need to rejoin your classmates.'

'Grandma likes having me there.'

'Of course she does.'

'Then please let me stay with her. Just 'til she's better anyway.'

'I don't know how long that'll be.'

'I need to make sure she's okay.'

'That's what the nurses are there for,' he said. 'And I'll be travelling up as often as I can. Too many people will just be in the way. Why don't you try to concentrate on school for now.'

'I'm *not letting it happen again*.'

My father looked taken aback. 'Letting what . . . Ah. I see.' He pinched the bridge of his nose.

Mr Tickles purred loudly in between us.

My father was the one who broke the silence. 'We'll discuss this later,' he said. 'In any case, it's nice to have you back.' He smiled grimly, then went into his study and shut the door.

I went upstairs. Mr Tickles trotted behind me, rubbing his gums on any sharp corners that were easy to reach. The house was hot compared to my grandmother's. I took off my jumper and jeans, unzipped my suitcase and pulled out a dress she'd given me, a black halter neck from the fifties with a full skirt, fitted bodice and red polka dots. She'd made it herself, she said, for a Christmas party one year. My grandfather was only interested in racing and she hadn't always got enough money from him to buy food for the week, let alone clothes. But my grandmother had been a farm girl. She planted a vegetable garden, kept chickens, walked to town to buy fabric cheaply. When my grandfather fell off his horse one winter and broke his leg, she convinced him to set up an account for her and make regular payments into it.

'How did you convince him?' I asked.

'I wouldn't bring him anything to eat or drink until he'd done it,' she said.

I pulled the dress on, smoothing the fabric down and looking in the mirror. I didn't fill the bodice out — my grandmother had warned me about my weight.

'No one likes a skinny girl,' she said.

272

'Why?' I asked.

'You look like you couldn't bear children.'

'I don't think that's what boys my age are looking for.'

★ ★ ★

I telephoned her from my bedroom, sitting on the floor with Mr Tickles passed out in front of me. 'How are you?' I asked her.

'Hungry,' she complained. 'That Nazi woman won't let me have any dinner.'

'Are you sure?'

'Well, she won't let me have what I want.'

'Eat what she makes you, Grams. You can't starve yourself.'

'Don't you start.'

'Eat.'

'Fine,' she said. 'You left a sketchbook here. Would you like me to send it on?'

'No,' I said. 'That's for you.'

I could hear pages rustling on the other end.

'They're very good,' she said. 'Hruh, when did you do that one?'

'Which one?'

'The last one.'

'A few days ago,' I said. 'When you were asleep.' It was a pencil sketch of her, dozing in bed. Her hair had come unpinned and the light coming through the window had made her look fuzzy and transparent.

'It's lovely,' she said. 'I'll frame it.'

'Okay,' I said. 'Grams?'

'Yes?'

'Dad told me I'm not coming back to see you until Easter.'

'He shouldn't have. I was going to do that myself.'

'It's alright.'

'I still want you around, very much.'

'Yeah, I know.'

'Don't be angry with your father.'

'I'm not,' I lied.

'I'd better go,' she said. 'I need to get that Nazi woman to take me to the toilet.'

'I'll call you soon.'

'Goodbye, sweetheart.'

'Bye Grams.'

I hung up and went downstairs. My father was making stew and potatoes in the kitchen.

'I recognise that dress,' he said.

'Grandma gave it to me.'

'You two seem to be very close these days.'

'Yeah.'

'That's good. You certainly seem to have brought her out of her shell.' He was looking down at the pots on the stove; he still seemed angry from our conversation earlier. 'I gather Malkie's been teaching you the piano.'

'Yeah.'

'Have you enjoyed that?'

'Yeah.'

'Maybe we can see about getting you some lessons at school as well.'

'Mm-hmm.'

'I know you don't want to go back,' he said. 'But Mother is really too frail to take care of you any longer.'

'She'll get better.'

'She'll be fine, Tallulah, but she's tired and weak.'

'She'll want someone she knows around the house.'

'It's a nice thought,' my father said. 'But you have to go back to school.'

'It's not just a thought,' I said.

I turned around to leave. My father called my name.

'What?'

'I tried to take some time off work this week, but it wasn't possible.'

I knew Grandma was wrong, I wanted to say. I knew you wouldn't be lonely without me. I knew you'd just be at work anyway.

'I don't care.'

'I'm sure you don't,' he said. 'I just thought I should let you know.'

'Well now I know.'

I slammed the door behind me.

★   ★   ★

I spent the holidays trying to read *Romeo and Juliet*, our set text, although every time I thought about going back to school my spine felt cold.

As far as I could see, the tragedy depended on Friar Lawrence's message not reaching Romeo on time, which seemed pretty unlucky. And Romeo made me feel uneasy, falling in love with Juliet in about a minute. He made me think of my mother and Uncle Jack in fact — now I was older, looking back, I could feel the crackle of tension between them, and I didn't want to think about it.

I bought the Christmas tree myself that year, haggling with the man who was selling them by the side of the road, then dragging it home. I put it up in a giant pot in the living-room and started decorating it. Mr Tickles came to watch, and tried to kill all the baubles.

My father was off work on Christmas Day and up early, sitting at the kitchen table when I came down. I'd spent Christmas Eve alone, watching re-runs of old comedy shows.

'Merry Christmas,' he said, awkwardly.

'Merry Christmas,' I mumbled. The sky was bright outside, but colourless, like salt. My father was already dressed.

'Would you like some pancakes?' he asked.

'Sure.'

He started moving about and opening drawers, hunting for a whisk. I flopped down on a chair. 'What's that noise?'

'I don't know,' my father said, egg in one hand.

We went into the living-room. The tree was swaying in the corner of the room. Purple bows and gold bells were clashing into each other and bouncing across the floor. In the middle of the tree, two big eyes stared out at us.

'That bloody cat,' my father said.

I reached into the branches and pulled Mr Tickles out, kissing his nose. 'What are we going to do with you?' I asked.

My father looked around the living-room. 'Would you like to open your presents now?'

I shrugged. 'Do you want to?'

'For goodness' sake.'

'Alright,' I said. 'Let's open them now.'

We sat by the tree. I had five presents: *Tom Sawyer* from my father — 'it was my favourite when I was a boy,' he said — money from Aunt Vivienne, a fountain pen from Aunt Gillian, a music-box from Georgia and some pearl-drop earrings from my grandmother.

'They're Mother's,' my father said when I opened the box. 'An anniversary gift from my father.'

'I thought Grandad didn't buy Grandma presents.'

'Not often,' he said. 'On very . . . special occasions. I don't know why she's giving them to you.'

'She says they'll suit my hair,' I said, reading the note she'd written. 'What's wrong with me having them?'

'Your ears aren't pierced are they?'

'No, but I could get them pierced.'

'And you're only thirteen.'

'I'm nearly fourteen.' I wondered what he meant by 'special occasions'. Occasions like when my grandfather beat his wife, or her daughter? My father's face was stony; he could have been thinking about those times too. Maybe he'd been afraid for my grandmother like Uncle Jack had been.

He stretched his hand out for the box. I handed it over silently, then gave my father his present. I'd bought him *Birdsong*, by Sebastian Faulks. It was the biggest thing I could find at the bookshop, and the woman at the till had praised my choice. 'It's very moving,' she'd said. 'And sexual.'

Outside, I'd flicked through a couple of pages, but it didn't seem too graphic to me.

My father unwrapped the book slowly. 'Thank you, Tallulah,' he said. 'This will certainly go on the to-read pile.'

'Thanks for my book too,' I said, politely.

'Yes, well,' he said. 'How about those pancakes now?'

We ate for the rest of the day: pancakes, chocolate coins from my father's nursing staff, satsumas, nuts, turkey, roast potatoes, stuffing, carrots, Christmas pudding with brandy cream. I called my grandmother to say thank you for the earrings, but Aunt Gillian answered and told me she was sleeping. After I'd hung up, I curled up on the sofa and watched films. I used to do that with my mother, my head in her lap, one of her hands stroking my hair, the other writing thank you cards. She liked to get them posted off quickly.

During an ad break, I realised that the raised voice I'd been hearing for the past five minutes wasn't the background soundtrack for the film; it was coming from my father's study. He had an extension line in there so calls could come through without disturbing the rest of the house, but this didn't sound like the voice he used for patients. I tiptoed down the hall, avoiding floorboards that I knew creaked or groaned.

'It's really irrelevant now,' he was saying. 'It's not the money. We *have* money . . . I don't see why I should ... I had every right to interfere ...'

I tried to creep closer. Mr Tickles came up behind me and rubbed himself against my ankles, purring loudly. I nudged him away with my foot. 'Meeooooowww,' he said, displeased.

'Of course I didn't trust him,' my father said. 'He wanted to take her away from me. He told me.'

There was a pause — the person on the other end must have started talking.

'I know it could never happen,' my father said, sounding angry. 'But I wanted to avoid any trouble. You of all people should understand.'

Pause.

'Who knows what he would have done if I hadn't? He certainly threatened to ... As I said, it's irrelevant now. What's done is done. I'm quite sure we won't hear from him again. No, don't make excuses for him, Mother, Jack wants to punish me. I don't want to talk about it. And I don't want those earrings in my house. Yes, Merry Christmas. Goodbye.'

I heard the sound of the receiver being replaced and footsteps coming towards the door of the study. I scrambled back to the living-room and lay down quickly on the sofa, my throat pulsing in time with my heartbeat, trying to make sense of what I'd just heard. My grandmother had been right when she implied Uncle Jack was still around, then.

'He wanted to take her away from me.'

I realised something that I must have known all along: Uncle Jack had loved my mother, and he'd wanted her to go away with him.

I concentrated on breathing slowly.

Would she have gone?

Maybe she'd really loved him back. Even if she'd warned him off that time in the rose garden, she could have changed her mind. She'd only got depressed after he left, after all. And my father knew it too.

'I should have known . . . I pushed her away.'

Had he been talking at cross-purposes to Kathy's mum? I'd never considered that he could have been talking about pushing her away emotionally — he certainly did that after Uncle Jack appeared.

He knew that there was something between them. That's why he'd been angry and cold to her. And then he'd come home early and found them talking. He *could* have let her die on purpose.

The footsteps were getting heavier now. The film had started up again and I forced myself to look at the screen. The TV showed the reflection of my father standing in the doorway, looking in at me, but he didn't say anything. He was in bed by the time I switched it off.

12

When 1995 came, my second stint at boarding school came with it. Having had free run of my grandmother's house and garden made me chafe even more against the rules, the curfews, the separation of the girls and boys, the exact measurements specified in the uniform code. But I was determined to make her proud. I'd promised her I wouldn't act up. It was hard, though, when the teachers were unsympathetic, and even Edith was off with me. I was glad to get to my first art class. I arrived early and found Mr Hicks setting up the desks. 'Hey,' I said, feeling shy.

'Hi there, Tallulah,' he said, turning around. He looked like he was going to say something else, but then stopped, and gave a short laugh. 'Wow.'

I flushed.

'You look very different.'

'My hair's shorter.'

'I can see that.'

'My grandma did it.'

'Do you want to help me finish setting up?'

'Okay.'

He looked at me again, then his eyes slid away, then back. 'Sorry, I'm half asleep — here, put a sheet of tracing paper out for everyone.'

'Okay.'

'Thank you,' he said, formally.

He didn't look at me properly for the rest of the afternoon or comment on my work. I wondered if he was annoyed at me for some reason.

I had maths after art. I slunk in and took a place at the back. Cressida sat diagonally in front of me, across the aisle from Edith. Halfway through the class she reached across and poked Edith with her pen. 'I think you might have lost something,' she said, quietly, and brought something out of her school shirt.

'My necklace,' Edith said, sounding like she was going to cry. 'Where did you get that?'

'I found it.' Cressida looked back and smiled at me nastily.

'It's Edith's,' I said.

'I don't see her name on it.'

'It's her St Christopher necklace.'

Cressida smirked. 'Maybe next time she won't keep her valuables underneath her bed like a retard.'

I stood up. 'I think Cressida's confused,' I said, loudly. 'She thinks the necklace she's wearing is hers but it's actually Edith's.'

'We'll discuss this after class,' our maths teacher said.

'*I* think we should discuss it now,' I said, even louder.

'I think we should see what Mr Purvis has to say about your behaviour,' she said, but she looked at Cressida. '*Is* that your necklace, Cressida?'

'It *looks* like it,' Cressida said, simpering. 'I could have picked up the wrong one though.'

'Edith?'

'I probably left it lying around,' Edith said.

'Give it to me,' the teacher said. 'You're not meant to be wearing jewellery anyway. Edith, you can collect it after class.'

I was sent to the Headmaster's office and escorted immediately back by the secretary. 'Tallulah is having some adjustment issues,' she said to my maths teacher. She had pink acrylic nails that day. She spoke in a stage-whisper, so the whole classroom could hear her. 'Herbert feels that she should be allowed to settle back in at her own pace, for now.'

'Who's Herbert?' I asked, and the other students sniggered.

'Mr Purvis, of course,' the secretary said. Her face had gone the same colour as her nails.

'Alright then, thank you for bringing her back, Miss Duvall,' the teacher said. 'Tallulah, work with Edith for now. We've moved on to trigonometry problems. And no more interruptions.'

I slid into a chair next to Edith, who stared at me. 'Thanks,' she said, shyly.

'It's okay,' I said.

★　★　★

I circle the waiting-room while a group of medical students check on my father. I brush past the fronds of overly-green synthetic plants, underneath neon strip-lighting. The air seems stale and I wonder, fleetingly, how my father found the strength to walk through the hospital doors day after day for the last twenty-five years.

The aunts arrive. I tell them what the hospital has told me — he's been in and out of consciousness since his eyes opened, and they're monitoring him closely.

'They say no need to panic,' I say, 'but they'd prefer us in here for now.'

'Of course. Come sit down,' Aunt Gillian says, soothingly, although I think I see her lower lip tremble.

The chairs are hard, plastic, orange versions of the ones you find in schools. I always hated sitting still on them. In summertime, when you stood up, sweat slicks showed where the backs of your thighs and knees had been. Much better to keep moving.

Maybe I never felt comfortable inside my skin. My grandmother would have a lot to say about that.

I flick through the magazines. Someone called Lady Helen Taylor is on the front of *Vogue*, showing a lot of even white teeth and striking greenish-blue eyes. They're the same colour as my mother's; the same colour as Toby's.

My mother would be turning forty-six this month if she'd lived. Uncle Jack, out there somewhere in the world, must be forty-nine, if he's five and a half years younger than my father. Toby was about eighteen the last time I saw him.

My father's birthday is the fifth of May, born three and a half years after the end of the Second World War when my grandmother was still twenty-one. The same age I am now. I don't know how she did it; there's no way I could cope. Clearly my father felt the same way — he was in his early thirties when I came along, but he and my mother must have decided not to have any more children after me. He probably realised he wasn't cut out for fatherhood.

'I haven't seen a soul since we got here,' Aunt Vivienne says, standing up. 'No wonder people die of neglect in these places.'

'Where are you going?' Aunt Gillian asks.

'If you must know, I'm going to the bathroom,' Aunt Vivienne says over her shoulder.

'What if he goes back into a coma?' Aunt Gillian asks, when she's gone. 'How are they going to wake him up?'

'They normally reverse the cause of the coma,' I say. 'Like, they'll give someone a glucose shock if they had low sugar, or medicate them to reduce swelling on the brain, things like that. Sometimes they induce hypothermia for cardiac patients.'

'Isn't that dangerous?'

'Apparently it works,' I say. 'They cool them down to two or three degrees lower than body temperature for about a day, externally or intravascularly.'

'This isn't some experimental treatment they do in the East?'

'I read about it this morning,' I say. 'In a British medical textbook.'

'I still don't like the sound of it,' Aunt Gillian says.

'It's probably to reduce the risk of ischemic injury,' I say.

'That sounds familiar,' Aunt Gillian says; she looks half-placated.

'It's a restriction of blood supply to tissues,' I say. 'After a heart attack, the blood flow's insufficient and . . . '

Someone runs past the waiting-room door, screaming, and we both freeze, but it's just a kid in a Spiderman outfit.

'Mac, get *back* here,' a woman calls after him.

We exchange looks — Aunt Gillian releases her breath and I wipe away the trickle of sweat that's started down my face.

'Now where's Vivienne got to?' Aunt Gillian murmurs.

★   ★   ★

Exams came. I sat in the stuffy room with two hundred and twenty-three other students and stared at the questions in front of me. Someone had left their coffee mug on the original paper, the photocopier reproducing two hundred and twenty-four faint smudgy rings. I bit my lip in frustration, I cursed my private tutor. I tried working on several problems, but gave up halfway through each. I looked at the clock — only fifteen minutes in. We weren't allowed to leave before half an hour was up, but after ten minutes more of tapping my pen on the desk, a teacher came and told me I could go.

After that, Mr Purvis summoned me to his office and told me I was on a final warning. Mr Hicks had volunteered to take over as my personal mentor, he said, and we would meet once a week to work through the assignments I was struggling with most. If I still didn't improve . . . He looked bored, shuffled his papers and I was dismissed.

Mr Hicks was in the corridor outside, chatting to some female students. When he saw me come out of the office he waved me over.

'Walk with me to the studio,' he said.

I carried his register for him and he made small-talk until we were out of earshot.

'Did Mr Purvis tell you the plan?'

'Yep.'

'You're going to have to pull your socks up, you know.'

'I guess.'

'Look, Tallulah, I honestly think you're a talented student.'

I kept quiet, but I felt my skin heat up.

He put his hand on my shoulder. 'Let's say we meet lunchtime every Friday — we can have thirty-minute progress sessions. And, of course I'll be available if you have any problems during the rest of the week. But you'll have to trust me, and work hard even when you don't like the subjects.'

'Okay.'

'Promise?'

'Promise.'

'Friday, then,' he said. 'Come find me in my office.'

★　★　★

When I failed all my exams, Mr Hicks got the teachers to give me extra essays to get me in practice, and catch-up notes for the last term. He was still positive in art class. I was very good at shading and perspective, he said. Edith elbowed me in the ribs.

'You're his favourite,' she said. 'He never says anything about *my* work.'

I looked at her drawing. Bright balls of colour stuck rigidly out of a vase, which was sitting on a perfectly square table.

'That's because you don't have any perspective,' I said, taking her pencil. 'Draw the table like this — the lines should get closer to each other here to show that they're further off in the distance, see? Things nearer your eye are bigger, things further away are smaller.'

'If only you could apply some of that knowledge to your physics homework,' Mr Hicks murmured behind me.

I jumped.

'I'm sorry, I thought you knew I was here.' He winked at me. 'Well carry on with the good work. But don't put me out of a job.' He smiled and strolled off.

'You like him back,' Edith hissed.

'I don't.'

'You do. You've gone red.'

'I don't. I was just surprised,' I said lamely.

'He's cute. He's got dimples.'

'Do you want me to help you or not?'

'Yes, help me. Teacher's Pet.'

My first session with Mr Hicks was scheduled for three weeks into the term, after I was 'settled', he said. I was five minutes late, so I ran; I was out of breath by the time I reached his office.

'Come in,' he called.

I pushed the door open and stopped there. None of us had ever seen the inside — Mr Hicks called it his sanctuary. A rumour had gone around that he'd been seen going into the room with nothing but a towel on once, and a few girls in my year had tried to look through the keyhole after that, but it'd been too dark to make anything out. As far as I could see, the room was basically a cupboard, with shelves lining three of the four walls, and a deep, wooden desk piled high with paper in the middle of the floor. The one unusual item I could see was a futon mattress shoved behind one of the shelving units, and I wondered if Mr Hicks lived here.

'Take a seat,' he said. He was sitting on the other side of the desk, so all I could see of what he was wearing was a white linen shirt, and a dark leather bracelet. He could have had a towel wrapped around him instead of trousers. I blushed when I thought of this.

He put away a cigarette he'd been rolling and smiled at me. 'Look, I know exams seem pointless. But everyone has to do them, so what we'll be discussing here is how you get through them with minimum fuss, okay?'

'Okay.'

'As well as anything else that's been on your mind.' His smile dropped for a moment. 'So, if you don't mind me asking . . . '

'What?'

'Last September,' he said. 'When you went to live with your grandmother. Miss Duvall tells me you asked to telephone her rather than your father.'

'Did she?' I muttered.

'I was just wondering if there was a problem between you and your father?' He smiled encouragingly.

'Like what?'

'I'm sorry,' he said. 'I don't like to pry, but obviously I care about your welfare . . . ' He pulled a face. 'I'm trying to be delicate here, but I'll just come out and ask. Does your father in any way mistreat you?'

I felt myself flushing. 'Like touching me?'

Mr Hicks looked awkward. 'Or put you down, verbally. Or even hit you. They're all forms of abuse.'

'No,' I said, louder than I'd intended.

'I'm sorry, Tallulah. I didn't want to put you on the defensive. I want you to feel that you can talk to me about anything.'

'Yeah, fine.'

He drummed his fingers on the desk. 'We've obviously hit a nerve,' he said. 'Let's start again. How about I tell you something about myself and *my* relationship with my parents, and then you can see I'm not judging you.'

I shrugged.

'Well.' He cleared his throat. 'Take my father, for instance. He had a thing about art being only for girls and homosexuals.'

Mr Hicks wasn't looking in my direction, but I

thought I saw his jaw tighten. 'By the end of my time in that house we only spoke to each other through my mother. And then she died over Christmas, and we haven't spoken since. So you see, I understand completely not getting along with a parent.'

He looked sad, and I wondered how close he'd been to his mum. I wanted to comfort him, but that thought made me blush as well.

'Sorry your mum died.'

He sighed. 'People can't possibly understand until they go through it.'

'Everyone thinks they know best,' I said. 'They either want to forget it, or talk about her. Especially if they didn't know her, they want to talk about her.'

Mr Hicks gave me a half-smile. He'd taken the cigarette out again and was pinching it at both ends. 'I'll take that as a hint. But back to what we were saying. It's stupid, but my father will never change his mind.'

'He sounds like an idiot.'

'Well . . . Some people just can't get along. Does this sound familiar?'

'Yeah, kind of.'

In my head I saw my father's disinterested face. Whenever I thought of him, he did the same thing: he looked blank, then he turned away. I could see him turning away from me in the hall, going into his study, turning away from me and walking back to the car when he dropped me off at school. I pushed the images away.

Mr Hicks nodded. 'It's perfectly normal,' he said. 'And I'm sure your dad's very fond of you, really. But you do deserve to be told how special you are. Which is why you've got me. And now the important thing is to get you to start socialising, showing some team spirit — it'll go down well with Mr Purvis, if nothing else. How about a sport? How are you at netball?'

I was okay at netball it turned out, and my PE teacher said they needed someone tall to stand by the goal and hit the ball away when it came near. It was easy, she said. After the first few games, I started to enjoy it. It *was* easy, and in the summer it was nice to be outside, the sun baking the tarmac.

'I've heard you're practically an Olympian,' my grandmother said during our next telephone conversation.

'What does that mean?'

'That you're doing very well for yourself.'

'Oh.' I wondered who could have mentioned it.

She gave a hacking cough.

'What did the tests show?' I asked.

'Nothing.'

I sighed. 'I know you're keeping things from me.'

'Such as?'

Such as strange visitors in the night.

'Coughing means the nerves leading to your lungs are irritated,' I said. 'It can be a symptom of pneumonia.'

'The tests are fine. You shouldn't worry so much.'

'I can't help it.'

'I know,' she said. Her voice changed. 'You're

as hard as nails, my girl, but you've got a soft centre.'

'I'm not a very good nail, then.'

'You're a perfect granddaughter and that's what counts.' She wheezed slightly as she said it. 'My head's splitting in two. Hruh. Just hope they've invented the cure for everything by the time you're old.'

'Mr Hicks says they already have but the drug companies are holding us to ransom.'

'Well, if Mr Hicks says so. Who is this Mr Hicks anyway?'

'He's my art teacher. He's really nice.'

'Your uncle fractured his leg twice when he was on the hockey team,' she said, from nowhere.

'I didn't know Uncle Jack played hockey.'

'Oh yes, he was very good at sports. He was the school's fastest long-distance runner.'

'Weird,' I said.

'You're your own person,' my grandmother said, as if she could hear my thoughts. 'You're not like Jack, if that's what's worrying you.'

'Yeah.' Although who knows what he's like since you guys never talk about him.

'I have to go, Tallulah. Be careful now.'

'Love you.'

'I love you too.'

* * *

Eventually, 1995 turned into 1996. Russian soldiers and rebel fighters engaged in Chechnya, the O.J. Simpson civil trial started, Dolly the

293

sheep was born, and *Braveheart* won best picture at the Oscars. I stayed on the netball team, I hung out with Edith, I went to my sessions with Mr Hicks. As much as I hated to admit it, I found myself developing a grudging respect for my father's academic ability. But after a few weeks of Mr Hicks' help, I started to get into the routine of schoolwork. Some of our studying must have even got through, because my grades got better, even if I wasn't going to win any awards. I wasn't reading my father's textbook as often, but biology was still easily my best subject apart from art. In others I trudged through weeks of individual assignments that turned into months of class projects; at least in art I was really enjoying myself. I made sketch after sketch of any subject I could find on the school grounds and sent them to my grandmother — a magpie, a discarded prefect's badge, the empty swimming pool early in the morning. When I stayed at hers over the holidays I saw she'd framed all of them and hung them in her bedroom and on the staircase.

'Hruh,' she said, one summer, 'I thought school was to educate and refine you, not turn you into a farmhand.'

'Says the woman who grew up on a farm.'

But it was true. I was toning up from all the netball — my muscles had hardened and the skin covering them had bronzed nicely from being outdoors. My fingers were constantly stained and flaking with paint and I smoked like a chimney.

My grandmother muttered something about

femininity as a lost art and beat me soundly at Monopoly.

Sometimes my father joined me at my grandmother's. He sat in his chair in the living-room, reading medical journals while I spread my homework out on the coffee table. Ever since I'd taken his textbook, I'd wondered whether I should say something. There were questions I wanted to ask him about his work, and how easy he thought it would be to get into the medical world. Not necessarily to be a doctor — my grades weren't good enough for that — but maybe I could be a nurse. Maybe we'd finally be able to break through and have a proper conversation, I thought, or maybe he'd be angry with me for 'borrowing' something of his. Instinctively, I held back each time there was an opportunity to speak about it.

Otherwise I spent my vacation time alone with my grandmother. The rest of the family seemed to have retreated a little too — if Uncle Jack had been the mysterious cyclist, he hadn't shown up for a while, and he wasn't calling my father either, as far as I could tell. I hadn't seen Michael, Georgia or James for ages, although I heard that Michael had aced his A-Levels and had a place at Cambridge to read Italian and French. Aunt Gillian had reported this to my grandmother on one of her rare visits. My grandmother had banned her for a while because she said there was no point paying for home help if Aunt Gillian was going to redo everything herself, and unfortunately she preferred the home help.

Occasionally, I'd hear Starr's name in passing at school, or see her across the canteen. Apparently she'd signed up to the drama group, and was busy breaking the hearts of all the theatrical boys. I envied her easy manner with them. I still hadn't had a real conversation with a boy, unless you counted Stuart — who sat next to me in maths and once left an obscene note in my pencil case — and I didn't. My relationship with Mr Hicks was the closest one I had with a Y chromosome. I thought about it at night, when the lights were out, and wondered if maybe I did have a crush on him. My skin always felt clammy when we were in his office, especially my palms. I lived in fear that he would touch my hands for some reason and discover how disgusting they were, but, at least at first, he wouldn't even leave his side of the desk. He was friendly and entertaining; he acted like I was a little sister, rather than a student, but definitely not like we were equals. In the beginning, he made notes while I was talking; later on he sat making a steeple with his fingers. I started off shy, looking at the floor when I had to describe something I couldn't understand in lessons; after a while, I felt relaxed enough to sprawl in my chair, or rest my elbows on the desk in front of me. He liked using props to demonstrate the answers to maths questions. He made me laugh. He always offered me tea or squash and he always listened carefully to me, and never made me feel like I was being petty or stupid. After the first session, he never pushed me to talk about my parents. A couple of times I mentioned my mother, how she was a pianist, like me, and the stories she used to make up for me when I was younger, how she'd written a few of them out, and illustrated them with pencil drawings of me and my sidekicks in our adventures. Mr Hicks said she sounded like a real artist, and he'd like to see the books if I could find them. I didn't tell him my father had hidden all her stuff away. My father's weird behaviour and indifference didn't seem to matter when I was with Mr Hicks.

After two years, I was turning up a few minutes early to each session, and lingering for a few minutes after the bell for afternoon classes had gone. I really looked forward to Fridays.

* * *

I throw down *Vogue* and pick up *Cosmopolitan*. Sarah Michelle Geller is wearing a red, lacy dress for the 'Hot Issue'. Toby used to have a crush on her, I remember. *Buffy* had just started when I left school, and he watched it religiously. I throw that down too.

Aunt Vivienne comes back in. 'I didn't see any nurses,' she says, 'but I did meet a charming young man who asked after my younger sister.' She sits down. 'I assume he meant you, Tallulah, and not Gillian. He didn't seem to need glasses.'

'Where exactly did you meet this young man?' Aunt Gillian asks, icily. 'In the ladies' toilets?'

'At the café,' Aunt Vivienne says. 'He said he remembered us sitting together the other day.'

'Hmmph,' Aunt Gillian says.

'I told him you were engaged,' Aunt Vivienne

says. 'Cheekbones like yours should not be thrown away on spotty adolescents.'

I stay quiet. It must be because I'd just thought of him, but for a moment I was sure she meant Toby, and my heart is still hammering.

It was the start of my GCSE year when some boys from the Upper Sixth came over to mine and Edith's table in the canteen. Edith was trying to persuade me to come into town with her when she stopped halfway through a sentence; one of the boys who'd been walking past had peeled off from the others and was standing next to us. I turned around and caught his eye.

'I'm Toby,' Toby Gates said to me.

'Hi,' I said.

'You play on the netball team, right?' he said.

'Uh-huh.' Toby Gates had nice eyebrows, I noticed. And good skin.

'I've seen you — you're pretty good.'

'Thanks.'

'Can we sit with you guys?'

'It's a free country.'

The other two came over reluctantly. I recognised them from when they'd come to watch Melinda play netball — she had long blonde hair and big boobs and they got this funny look on their faces every time she ran.

'This is John and Francis,' Toby said.

I could feel Edith shaking beside me. 'This is Edith,' I said.

'Cool to meet you, Edith,' Toby said. The other boys muttered something under their breath.

'We've already met,' Edith said, turning pink. 'In the library. You asked me for a pen.'

'Well, cool to see you again.' Toby turned to me. 'When's your next match?'

'Next week.'

'We're coming along to watch.'

'Okay.'

'What you eating?'

'School dinner.'

'Yeah, but — did you go for the vegetarian or the meat option?'

'Oh. The meat, I guess.' I poked my dinner with a fork; it wasn't giving me any clues.

'Yeah, me too. I like meat.'

'Um, me too.'

'I like chicken,' Edith said.

The boys at the other end rolled their eyes. The one called John mouthed something to the other. He had curly hair and a turned-up nose that made me want to punch it. I glared at him; his friend nudged him and he shut up.

'Anyway,' I said. 'We should go. See you at the match.'

'See you,' Toby said.

Edith lay face-down on the bed for an hour, with her head underneath her pillow.

'Come on,' I said. 'It wasn't that bad.'

'Toby Gates,' she said. '*Toby Gates sat with us.*'

I flopped onto the bed. 'He's just a boy.'

For some reason, the story of how my parents got together was in my head — how she was there with a friend, and how my father appeared out of nowhere.

'He's seventeen,' Edith said, sitting up. 'Do you know what girls in our year would do for a seventeen-year-old boy?'

'Take their clothes off?'

'He's an Adonis,' Edith said. She looked wild.

'You're such a geek,' I said. I rolled over and picked my Discman off the floor. I turned it on and started listening to David Bowie; I could see Edith's lips moving and she looked annoyed. I stood up on the bed and started swaying to the music, pretending to sing into an imaginary microphone. Now she looked horrified and shrank away from me. I took the earphones out.

'You can't do that in front of the boys,' she said. 'Everyone will think you're nuts.'

'What about this?' I asked. I did my best Michael Jackson 'Thriller' impersonation, which wasn't very good.

'I mean it,' Edith said. 'If we sit with them again we have to act grown up.'

'They sound fun,' I said, rolling my eyes.

'Tal, please,' Edith begged. 'I *really* like Toby.'

'Okay, okay.'

'Do you think he thought I was stupid?'

'No.'

'His friends did.'

'His friends are idiots,' I said. 'Who cares what they think?'

'Toby probably does.'

'Then he's an idiot too.'

'Most people care what others think about them,' Edith said. 'It's kind of weird that you don't, you know.'

I picked some dirt out from under my nail and tried to shrug that off.

* * *

Toby stood with Edith at the next match, while his friends sat at the back and threw things at each other.

Mr Hicks was there too. He waved when I looked over, and I nearly missed a ball. Otherwise, I had a good game. By the time the whistle blew, the goal attack I'd been marking was red-faced and out of breath.

'Nicely played,' one of the older girls called after me as I jogged off the court.

Mr Hicks walked over to meet me. I caught a whiff of his smell — sharp and sweet at the same time — and felt suddenly light-headed. 'Good game, Tallulah,' he said. 'You look like you're getting into it now.'

'I'm okay at it,' I said. I wondered, briefly, if I was better than Uncle Jack had been at hockey.

'You're better than okay,' Mr Hicks said, smiling at me. 'I'm really proud of you, you know?'

'Thanks,' I said, feeling like the world could end right then and I'd still have a big grin on my face.

Mr Hicks left when Edith and Toby came over.

'Why was Mr Hicks talking to you?' Toby asked.

'He's my art teacher.'

'Tallulah has a crush on him,' Edith said, batting her eyelashes at Toby.

'Don't you think he's too old for you?' Toby asked.

'What are you, my dad?'

Toby went red. 'I'm just looking out for you.'

'I can look out for myself,' I said. 'And like I said, he's just my art teacher.'

'Fine,' Toby said.

'Don't be angry, Tal,' Edith said. 'We thought you were really good out there today.'

'*Great*,' I said. 'Thanks *so much* for coming to watch.'

Toby was shaking his head. I thought he was going to walk away from us, and I felt a weird prickle of disappointment, but he just looked me in the eye. 'Are you always such a bitch?'

I felt my mouth turning up into a smile, in spite of myself. 'Yes.'

'Good to know,' Toby said. He was grinning back.

Edith was still waiting outside when I finished changing. 'You *do* have a crush on Mr Hicks,' she said. 'Why won't you admit it?'

'Shut up,' I told her.

We walked back to our building in silence. I thought about how Edith always came to cheer me on at matches; I thought about how she never ate her treacle tart whenever it was on the dinner menu so I could have double because it was my favourite pudding, and got a heavy feeling in my stomach. 'Sorry, Ed,' I said. 'You don't have to shut up.'

She gave me a look out of the corner of her eye. 'I tell you whenever I like a boy.'

'Well, I don't like one, so I can't tell you about it.'

She was quiet again for a while. 'I don't think

Toby likes me,' she said, eventually.

'Of course he does.'

'I mean like, like.'

'What's so great about him anyway?'

'He's sooooooooooo good-looking. Can't you tell?'

'He's alright.'

'He's *beautiful*.'

'Fine,' I said, sighing. 'He's beautiful.'

★ ★ ★

My grandmother lost her voice for a week. When I spoke to her afterwards, she sounded deep and raspy.

'It's like talking to a robot,' I said.

'Robots can't talk,' she said.

'They can in *Star Wars*.'

'What's that?'

'A film, or a cultural movement, depending on who you talk to.'

'Hruh,' she said. 'It's quiet here without you.'

'No wild parties?'

'Certainly not now,' my grandmother said.

'Did you *used* to have parties there?'

'A few.'

'What were they like?'

'Champagne, expensive clothes. Boring people. Vivienne invariably made a scene.'

I grinned. 'Have you always been this grumpy?'

'No,' she said. 'Not always.' She was silent for a moment, apart from her breathing.

'How are you feeling?'

'Oh, you know. My feet hurt. You young people. You don't know how good you've got it.'

'Homework's not good.'

'You wait until you get out there in the real world.'

'Are you eating?'

'Yes, yes.'

'And drinking lots of fluids?'

'You're almost as bad as Gillian. Now tell me about school.'

I told her about the netball championships, and the day the boiler had shut down. I told her about my science project — growing tomatoes in different environments — and how Mr Hicks had helped me get my first ever B in maths. I didn't tell her about Toby.

'It's good to keep busy,' she said.

'It's school,' I told her. 'They *make* you do things. How's Dad?'

'Same as always. They work him too hard at that hospital.'

'Uh-huh.'

'It's time for my medication.'

'I'm calling again tomorrow. You have to tell me what happens in *Murder, She Wrote*. And take some hot water and honey for your throat.'

'Yes, yes, stop pestering me,' she said, but she sounded pleased.

A few evenings later, on my way back to my dorm after a late netball practice, I saw Toby and his friends walking ahead. I slowed down. I hadn't told my grandmother about him because I didn't know how to feel anymore. Edith talking about him constantly must have been rubbing off on me; recently I'd caught myself thinking about him during class.

He went into the boys' dorm without seeing me. That night he turned up in my dream. He was wearing his rugby kit and he was muddy and out of breath. He tried to hold my hand and brush my hair away from my face. I woke up feeling restless and couldn't get back to sleep.

13

I cross and re-cross my legs.

'How long have we been here?' Aunt Gillian asks.

'A few hours,' I say.

She fidgets.

Outside, a doctor is talking to the parents of a teenager who has just been admitted. They look like they're in shock — chalk-white, not really saying anything. I wonder if he's telling them the prognosis isn't good, and how often my father had to do that. Whether it ever got any easier. The father has his back to me, but suddenly he turns and I see his profile. For a moment my heart stops; it's Mr Hicks, his black curly hair sticking to his head in damp swirls like he ran here. I'm rooted to my chair although I want to disappear. I can practically smell the cigarette smoke and turpentine on him, and when he opens his mouth, I stare at his teeth to see if they are Hollywood-white, like I remember them. Then I hear his voice. It's not Mr Hicks. Not even close. The man searches for his wife's hand and they hold on to each other like life-buoys.

I remember feeling that close to the real Mr Hicks once, feeling like — apart from my grandmother — he was the only one who supported me. 'You understand everything better than you give yourself credit for,' he said.

'You explain it better,' I said.

'You're very sweet, you know?' he said. 'You can't teach that.'

I feel sick. At how corny I sounded, the way I behaved around him. That was the lesson I asked him for a cigarette, and he looked at me like he was wavering.

'I shouldn't really encourage you — how old are you?'

'I'm sixteen in a month.'

'On your sixteenth birthday then. And not before.'

'What's the difference between now and then?'

'The law, I'm afraid.'

'You sound like my dad.'

'Why?'

'He thinks I'm a kid too.'

'That's ridiculous. No one could mistake you for a child.'

My whole body feels like it's burning up now.

Stupid. What did you talk about then? How your father made all your decisions? How he wouldn't let you look after your grandmother because you were too young? And Mr Hicks looking sympathetic, saying, 'Well I think you're very mature, I really do.'

Aunt Gillian's phone buzzes and for a second I think it's Malkie calling and I jump to my feet. She looks guilty. 'I'll call you back in a minute,' she whispers into the receiver.

I rub my eyes, trying to get rid of the past. That might have been the day we discussed career options, too. The day I first told someone I wanted to be a nurse. He was collecting little clay pots that had been drying on ledges and placing them on a tray, I remember, and he turned around and said that was a great idea. We'd have to work on my maths and chemistry, of course, but my biology was already good.

'Cool,' I'd said.

'Cool,' he'd said, and laughed. 'Okay, good. Good. Nothing else you want to discuss?'

'No,' I said. 'Don't forget my birthday present, though.'

He winked at me. 'I hope you're good at keeping secrets.'

★ ★ ★

'I'm going downstairs,' I say. 'See if the café's still open.'

'Don't be too long,' Aunt Gillian says.

It feels like my life has been a low-budget family drama lately, with only enough money for three sets — hospital, café, home — and my father playing the lead role, even if he's out of sight.

I dial my voicemail number — nothing. I pocket my phone and buy a herbal tea; my nod to being healthy. It's more of a pretence than a nod, and I suddenly want to talk to someone who I've never been able to fool, someone who really knows me. Maybe that's why I've been missing Toby over the last few days.

I cup my hands around the tea and breathe it in: lemon and ginger. It reminds me of a teashop in town Edith and I sometimes hung out in at the weekends. After a while, Toby started joining us, even though it was always full of girls and female teachers and he always looked too big and gangly for the crockery. Some of the teachers would come up and talk to him, laugh at how out of place he looked, and I thought about telling him how I thought the place was twee and ridiculous and that I only went because Edith liked it, but I never did. I kind of liked that he'd take being laughed at so he could hang out with us.

I remember it was easy to find things to talk about, even though we saw each other every day. Toby discovered I barely knew any current TV shows and tried to educate me on *Baywatch* and *Xena*, while I described the joys of *Murder, She Wrote*.

I take my first sip of the lemon and ginger. He even came shopping with us. Every Saturday there was a market in town, mostly, by that point, for the tourists. They came and took photos of the Saxon-era church and the yellow irises along the banks of the canal and the shopkeepers who stood in their doorways wearing aprons, squinting in the sunlight. The old men who sat on the benches in the main square for the rest of the week were swept away, along with the sweet wrappers and coke cans that littered the cobblestones. Instead the place was full of stalls selling tat: antique bowls and oranges and children's books. The three of us would do a slow circuit, and each of us had to name the item we'd least like to own. Then we played rock, paper, scissors, and the loser had to buy their item. That was how I ended up with the hand mirror in the shape of a bear's head, and Edith bought a VHS of *A Nymphoid Barbarian in Dinosaur Hell*. Toby paid three pounds for a jar of buttons.

The other boys wouldn't join us; we used to meet them out on the playing fields instead. After that first lunch, they were okay. John was on the swimming team. Francis was Toby's best friend, they played rugby together. He had four female fans in the first year who turned red whenever he walked into a room; I liked how crinkly his eyes were already, and his big, slow smile. If he'd been older and had longer hair, he might have been Malkie's brother.

The boys scared Edith. She didn't like it when they farted around her, or had arm wrestling matches, but she acted game in front of them so she could spend time with Toby. Lunchtime was the same every day — Toby and Francis messed around, showing off their muscles, and Edith swooned.

One time we agreed to break out at night and meet on the playing fields. Me and Edith climbed out of the window and shimmied down the drainpipe. The boys were waiting for us on the grass, tussling with each other, snorting with laughter. I lit a cigarette and sat watching them, thinking how much fun it looked to be a boy. Edith crouched down next to me.

I pointed up at the stars. 'Check them out. You can't see them in London.'

'That's Ursa Major,' she said, indicating. 'The Great Bear.'

'You know stars?' Toby asked, flopping down onto the grass beside us.

'A little,' Edith said, and I could tell she was turning pink.

'What about star signs?' John asked, joining us.

'That's not the same thing.'

'Course it is. They're all up there. I'm a Scorpio, which means I'm a fantastic fuck.' He waggled his eyebrows.

'John, can you just stop thinking about your dick for one second?' Toby said.

John picked his nose and flicked snot in Toby's direction. 'Can't,' he said. 'It's too big to ignore.'

'Up yours.'

'That's mature,' John said.

'You can talk about being mature when they finally let you finish nursery,' I said.

Toby looked at me. 'What star sign are you?'

'Aries, I think.'

'Stubborn and headstrong,' Edith said.

'Actually, that's kind of a good fit,' Toby said, laughing.

'Shut up,' I said, grinning. I looked at Toby out of the corner of my eye. Everything about him was exactly as it should be, I realised: his eyes, his nose, his eyelashes, which were dark and long, but still not girly. His hands, which were usually rammed in his pockets, were smooth and tanned and long, with blue veins that stood out a little from the surface. His stomach, which I caught a glimpse of when he yawned and stretched in front of me, was completely flat, and there was a dark trail of hair that led from his belly button down to the elastic of his boxer shorts.

'Wanna play catch or something?' I asked.

'What are we, five?' John said.

'We're playing catch,' Toby stage-whispered to Francis, and he bounded over towards us.

'Francis is It,' I said, and ran as fast as I could in the direction of the gym. Out in the middle of the field, the night was black as ink. I jarred my ankle several times where the ground was higher or lower than I expected it to be. I heard footsteps thumping after me, then Francis shoved me and I lost my footing completely, dropping onto my knees.

'You're It,' he said, and I heard footsteps retreating.

I tagged John, who got Toby, who came after me. I tried to run in zig-zags. He chased me around half the field until we were far enough away from the others that I couldn't hear them at all. I couldn't hear anything except the blood in my ears, but I could feel the damp grass and the fresh wind, and everything seemed better than it had for a long time.

Toby lunged at me, his body knocking into mine, and we went down. We were tangled up on the ground, and I could feel the heat of his breath on my neck, and his hands on my shoulder blades, then they were gliding lightly over my skin. I turned onto my back and his hands stopped, fingers splayed at the edge of my ribcage. I was aware of the mud and turf beneath me, and Toby above me, and past him, the sky, which was so far away it almost didn't exist.

We looked at each other and I felt the blood drain from my ears and rush around my body.

'What are you doing?' I asked.

'Nothing,' he said, sliding off quickly. 'I mean — nothing.' He sounded hoarse.

I started to feel stupid, sitting on the ground while he was standing with his hands back in his pockets. I got up slowly, brushing myself off.

'Hurry the fuck up,' John yelled across the field.

'I'm It, I guess,' I said. I felt flat all of a sudden and something made me afraid to catch Toby's eye.

'Yeah,' he said, jogging back towards the rest of them. I followed him, trying not to let my feet drag too much.

'Are we fucking playing or what?' John called, when I was closer.

I tagged Edith, who was only making a half-hearted effort at running away. She went after Toby — I could hear her giggling and panting, while Toby dodged her outstretched hand, then she gave a little scream and fell in a heap.

'Fucking girls,' John said in disgust.

Toby stopped and went back for her and the rest of us moved vaguely in their direction. I felt bad for Edith, falling over in front of her one true love. I started to say something to brush over it, then I got close enough to see her gazing up at him, showing all her teeth in a smile.

'You okay?' Toby asked.

'I think so.'

'Want a hand?'

'Yes please.'

Toby slipped her arm around his shoulders,

then straightened up slowly, bringing her with him. They started limping in my direction. Edith was deliberately hanging off him, letting him take all of her weight, and giggling again. 'You're really strong,' she said.

Francis and John made noises like they were being sick. I felt my stomach twist inside me. It's just Edith being Edith, I told myself. It wasn't like Edith though. She was being girlier than normal, and Toby wasn't even looking at me anymore.

'Can we stop now?' she asked, shivering melodramatically. 'I'm cold.'

Toby took off his jacket and put it around her.

We gave up after that, and lay on the ground, sharing my last cigarette. Edith nearly choked on it when it was her turn, and Francis gave her a hefty whack around her shoulders.

'Ouch,' she said, her eyes streaming. Toby and John hid their grins, and I felt affection for her again.

'It's a really strong one,' I said, and she looked at me gratefully.

★   ★   ★

Thinking about that night must have drawn Aunt Vivienne somehow, because she comes past the café and waves a cigarette in my direction. 'Smoke? I need to do something wicked.'

Outside, I light up and pass Aunt Vivienne my matches. She smokes Gauloises, I notice. I'm sure it fits in with her image of herself.

'It's a filthy habit, you know,' she says.

'I can still quit.'

'The folly of youth.' I can't read her expression. She reaches over and takes my chin in her hand, tipping my face up. Her fingers start to dig in to me, but she just squeezes and lets go. 'Did you ever hear how we met? Me and your mother?'

I shake my head.

'It was Edward who introduced us. He brought her round one evening for dinner. I used to throw very decadent dinner parties.' She makes a face. 'I thought your mother was the most divine being I'd ever seen. She was wearing some hideous floaty nonsense, and her hair was huge. Such a 70s cliché, but absolutely beautiful.'

I stay quiet. She might be trying to make up for what she said at dinner the other night. But even now she can't bring herself to be straightforwardly nice about my mother.

'Eddie had a night shift at the hospital, so he left first.' She pulls on her cigarette. 'We were getting on well — I invited Evie to stay the night. Malkie and Jack and Guillaume were due to stay that night too.' She sees my expression. 'No, not Starr's father.'

'I didn't ask,' I mumble.

'Anyway, that's how your mother became one of the gang.' She inclines her head. 'She fit in very nicely, so we looked after her when your father went off on his little trip to Africa.'

'Dad went to Africa?'

'Oh yes — some tiny country down in the south, somewhere.'

'Lesotho?'

'That's the one.'

I wonder how I didn't know this.

'He was the only doctor in the whole country, from the sounds of it,' Aunt Vivienne says. 'Which suited him just fine, I'm sure.'

'How long was he there for?'

'Oh, a year or so.' She looks amused. 'I don't think Edward thought being on two separate continents necessarily meant they were on a break, but I warned him — girls don't take kindly to being left alone.'

'Don't be such a bitch about it,' I say. It tastes like metal in my mouth, the idea that my mother had been abandoned like that, after she'd lost her parents as well.

'A bitch?'

'Yes,' I say. 'A bitch. Don't be a bitch. I know you can be decent sometimes.'

'Quite the mouth on you, darling.'

I close my eyes and hold my breath, keeping the smoke inside for a moment. I can feel Aunt Vivienne watching me still.

So Dad thought you were going to wait for him, Mum? I'm guessing you didn't, exactly, or Aunt Vivienne wouldn't be telling me this.

I can see the parallels between them and me and Toby already. None of us managed to come out and talk about our feelings properly, avoid any confusion. It makes me feel closer to my father in a strange way, and sorry for him.

'I've never had many female friends,' Aunt Vivienne says. 'But your mother . . . '

I open my eyes, exhaling. 'Can we not, please?'

316

Aunt Vivienne shrugs.

'I wonder if someone's come to see us yet,' I say.

She looks away. 'This place is a shambles,' she says. She brings her cigarette up quickly and pulls hard on it. She doesn't get nervous, I tell myself. You're imagining things now.

I finish my cigarette and stretch, placing my hands on the small of my back and twisting until I hear a crack. I can't get too angry with her. I understand what it's like to be friendless.

'They're not all real, you know . . . '

Was it Grandad who messed you up like this, Aunt Vivienne? Do any of the others have friends? I can't think of any of my father's. He never seemed to want them, but maybe he didn't trust anyone enough.

That's where the damage started, isn't it, with good old Albert Park?

I feel another buzz of adrenalin. 'Let's go back in,' I say.

'Whatever you say,' Aunt Vivienne says, and blows smoke out through her nose.

* * *

Mr Henderson, my fifth-year biology teacher, had a hooked nose and a limp and thinning white hair and reminded me of Mr Tickles.

We were learning about genetic inheritance — dominant and recessive alleles. 'Brown eyes are dominant,' Mr Henderson told us, beaming. 'And blue eyes are recessive. Can you tell me why two blue-eyed parents can't produce a brown-eyed baby . . . Tallulah?'

'You need the alleles to be present in both chromosomes in the pair,' I said. I'd read about this in my father's textbook. It'd confused me at first — my father had blue eyes, and my mother had green, but mine were brown. Hazel was a recessive colour too though, and in certain lights my eyes were hazel.

'Great.' Mr Henderson wrote 'alleles to be present in both' on the board. 'But can two brown-eyed parents produce a blue-eyed child?'

Everyone else looked bored, even Edith.

'Yeah,' I said. 'The parents might have heterozygous chromosomes, where they carry the alleles for both blue and brown eyes.'

'*Exactly right.* That would give these parents a twenty-five percent chance of conceiving a blue-eyed baby.' He sat down heavily behind the desk at the front. 'Fifteen minutes until the bell. First person to finish the multiple-choice questions on page sixty-three gets a prize.'

I sped through the questions and raised my hand. Mr Henderson made a note of my name just before the bell rang, then motioned for me to stay behind.

He rummaged around in his drawers while everyone else filed out, and finally produced a black and grey rectangular object. 'Your prize — a mini, illuminated microscope.'

I went up to his desk and took it from him. 'Thanks.'

'You deserve it,' he said, shutting the drawer again. 'You obviously share your father's love for science.'

I felt a bump of surprise in my stomach. 'You know him?'

'I taught him in my first few years here.' Mr Henderson started rubbing the lesson off the whiteboard. 'Actually, although I never had him as a pupil, I coached the hockey team and came across your Uncle Jack, too.'

'Oh yeah, my grandma said he played.'

'He was our star,' Mr Henderson said, wrinkling his forehead. 'Haven't you seen the photos along the fourth-floor corridor?'

'No.'

'I was very fond of both those boys,' he said. 'Although I can imagine Jack would have been a handful in class. Very bright and interested, your uncle, but only on his own terms.' He shook his head. 'I know your father's in the medical world now, but I rather lost sight of Jack. What exactly did he do after school?'

My mouth felt dry all of a sudden. I put the microscope away in my schoolbag, fumbling with the straps. 'He went away.'

'Well. Pass on my regards to both of them,' Mr Henderson said.

I left the classroom and was walking to my session with Mr Hicks when I heard someone call my name.

'Tallie.'

'Starr?'

She was wearing ripped tights that day, and slinky little fur-lined boots. I noticed, with envy, that she'd put on thick black eye makeup and it made her eyes look huge. When I tried I always ended up looking like I'd been punched.

319

'Tallie, are you hanging around with Toby Gates?' she asked.

'Yeah. Why?'

'Watch yourself.'

'What do you mean?'

'I mean . . . Don't bite my head off again, but one of the girls in my year started a rumour that he only likes you because you're blowing him.'

'What?'

'You know . . . oral sex.'

'I know what it means,' I said, my face flushing. 'I haven't done it.'

'Right,' she said, 'well, she's just jealous. He dumped her and she thinks she's got more right to him because you're so young, blah, blah.' She waved her hand. 'But people talk. Especially about Toby — he's hot, you know? But he's been around. Just don't get too close to him.'

'Why not?'

'You'll get a reputation.'

My heart was thudding angrily. 'I'm meant to be afraid of what people are going to say?' I asked as two girls walking past stared at us. 'You know they used to talk about me all the time, right?'

'You always were a stubborn little brat,' Starr said. 'Just don't say I didn't warn you.'

'Thanks for the warning,' I said. 'It's been fun.'

Starr rolled her eyes and walked off. I watched her go. I felt sick about Toby, that he could have liked other girls before me, maybe more than me. In fact, I didn't even know if he *did* like me.

I barely paid attention to what Mr Hicks was

saying in the session. I finally came around and realised he was waiting for an answer from me.

'What?'

'How's netball?' he repeated. 'I hear we're on course for the gold in the county championships?'

'Yeah, good.'

'I like your top, by the way — green's a good colour on you.'

'Thanks,' I said, confused.

'Are you alright, Tallulah? You seem a little distracted.'

'I'm fine.'

'Are you worried about going home for the holidays?'

'No, my dad's away. I'm staying with my cousins.'

'It probably makes it harder — getting to know each other — if he's not around?'

'I guess.' My father seemed to only use his study and his bedroom now anyway. Days could go by with both of us living there and not running into each other.

'It's difficult, being a teenager,' Mr Hicks said. 'Adults forget that, but it's a real period of change, both within and without. It helps if you have a stable environment.' He pushed his chair back. 'Which is why I'm so pleased that we've been having these mentoring sessions. I really feel like you're coming along. And I hope you feel the same way?'

'Yeah. I like coming here.'

'Good,' he said, rummaging among the papers on his desk. 'I'm going to give you my mobile number. I'm not really supposed to, so best if you don't tell anyone, but I don't want the good influence of these sessions to stop just because you're outside school grounds. Okay?' He handed me a scrap of paper with a number printed carefully onto it. I put it in my pocket, furtively. I could imagine what Edith would say if she found it.

★   ★   ★

I turned up on Aunt Gillian's doorstep, rucksack over one shoulder, a stack of required reading in one hand and a cat-carrier in the other.

'Come in, come in,' Aunt Gillian said. 'Let me take those books off you.' She led the way down the corridor. 'I've put you in Michael's room, he's in Cambridge and they don't get a half-term.'

'Cool.'

'The other two are off next week. I just don't know where the time goes — James in his final year, and you and Georgia doing your GCSEs.' She put the books down, hugged me then stepped back.

'Now,' she said. 'You'll have to excuse me, I'm in the middle of dinner. Make yourself comfortable and come join me in the kitchen whenever you're ready.'

I went upstairs and let Mr Tickles out of the carrier. He shook himself and jumped onto the bed, then curled up and went to sleep.

'Fine,' I said to him, and went downstairs.

Aunt Gillian was pouring glugs of wine into a

pan. The radio was on, a pop station, and she snapped it off when I came in then laughed guiltily. 'Force of habit — George doesn't like me to listen to that kind of music. He says it rots my brain.'

'I don't mind,' I said, sitting down. 'Who's your favourite, then?'

She blushed. 'That nice Australian man, I like him. Very thin, dark hair.'

'Nick Cave?'

'You're laughing at me.' She switched the radio on again. The DJ was talking now about Ireland's recent decision to legalise divorce, and Aunt Gillian pulled a face. 'People are too quick to give up on marriage these days, that's the problem,' she said.

I tried to clear my throat noncommittally. 'Can I help with dinner?'

'Absolutely not.'

'How's Michael?'

'He's doing very well. He'll be living in Rome next year as part of his year abroad.'

'Cool.'

'And how's everything going for you?'

'Yeah, good.'

'Really?'

'Yeah. I guess I'm on track for the exams.'

'Oh, how *wonderful*,' she said, beaming at me. 'You've found your feet, then.' She ground some salt and pepper into the pan. 'I always knew you would. It just takes some of us longer than others.'

'Mm-hmm.'

'And what do you think you'll do after the

exams? Any celebration plans?'

'Dunno. There'll probably be some parties I'll go to with my friends.'

'That sounds *terribly* exciting,' Aunt Gillian said. 'You must be very popular then.' I winced a little at how enthusiastic she seemed to be about my having friends. I must have been almost given up as a lost cause. 'I'm going to take Georgia to Milan for a week on a little shopping trip, a reward. You'd be very welcome to join us. We could make it a real girls' holiday.' She beamed at me again.

'Thanks,' I said. 'I might go see Grandma, though.'

'Oh, you're too nice for your own good, Tallulah. You're allowed to do something for yourself you know.'

'It's a nice offer,' I said, smiling at her.

She came around to give me a hug. 'I'm very proud of you.'

'Thanks.'

'We all are, you know that? Especially Edward. He's *so* proud.'

'I'm . . . ' I started to say, before I heard the front door open.

'Mummy, something smells delicious,' Georgia called out.

'Oh good — they're home,' Aunt Gillian said to me. 'I'm making lamb, sweetheart,' she called to Georgia. 'Come and say hello to your cousin, then set the table.'

Georgia bounded in. She hadn't changed that much, I thought. She was plump and pretty, her uniform straining around her chest, and her shoelaces undone. 'Hi Tallie,' she said, throwing her arms around me.

James came and stood in the doorway behind her. He looked different — he was pale and his nose and chin seemed sharper. 'Hi, Tallie,' he said, his voice was surprisingly low. 'Get me a beer, Mum.'

'Oh, alright then.' She brought over a can of Heineken. 'But not too many before dinner — you must have homework.'

'Whatever.'

Georgia went to the far drawer of the kitchen dresser and took out cutlery and napkins, then sneezed loudly, turning her face away from the things in her hands.

'Are you *still* coming down with something, sweetheart?'

'I think so.'

'Well, you better not touch those, then.'

Aunt Gillian finished setting the table, while Georgia coughed and blew her nose into a handful of tissues and I tried to turn my face away without being rude.

For most of that week, I lurked in the music room, reading, or feeding Mr Tickles leftovers, while Georgia stayed in bed.

The Saturday before I was due back at school, I took the tray up for her. The room was stuffy and Georgia was propped up on about four pillows. She waved and looked glad to see me.

'Dinnertime,' I said, putting the broth down on the bedside table. 'This reminds me of Grandma's.'

Georgia widened her eyes. 'Oh I never asked

— how *was* it? Living with her?'

'I wanted to stay longer, but she got ill.'

'Yeah, Mum was upset about Grandma chucking her out,' Georgia said. She pulled a face. 'She really likes looking after people.'

'How come it was my dad that became the doctor then?'

'Mum doesn't think women should work. Not after having kids, anyway.' She blew her nose and pulled the bedcovers up to her chest.

'What about Vivienne? Is she a secret call-girl or something?'

'Oh,' Georgia giggled, 'Mum says Starr's dad is really rich and famous. And married. I think he sends them money so they stay out the picture. Kind of sordid, right?'

'Yeah,' I said, and I felt sorry for Aunt Vivienne, and for Stan. 'And Uncle Jack — do you know what he did after . . . ?'

'No idea,' Georgia said. 'I'm so sorry I missed your visit.' She plucked at the bedcovers.

'Your mum invited me to Milan.'

'Oh God, you have to come. She's so excited about it, but nothing's going to fit me out there, it'll just be super expensive clothes for skinny Italians.'

'I might.'

'Are you coming back over Easter at least?'

'I'll be at Grandma's. And the boys are in their last year, so I guess they might wanna go on holiday before uni.'

She clutched my wrist. 'You hang out with older boys? How did I not know this?'

'They're exactly the same as boys our age,' I

said, but I could feel my skin warming.

'Tallie, do you have a boyfriend?' Georgia asked, suspiciously.

'No.'

'I can't believe you've been here this whole time and you never said anything.'

'I don't have a boyfriend,' I protested. 'Seriously.'

'Do you *like* a boy, then?'

'I dunno.'

Georgia threw her hands up. 'You're so secretive! You're as bad as Michael.'

'There's nothing to tell.'

'Do you have any good-looking friends?'

'Toby's kind of hot.'

'Who does he look like?'

'Like, have you ever seen *Boy Meets World*?'

'Yeah, you mean like the main guy? The one with curly hair?'

'No, his best friend — the one with the big eyebrows.'

'Oh . . . He's *cute*,' she said.

'I thought he was going to kiss me this one time. But, we haven't done anything.'

'I bet he likes you,' she said. 'Is he nice?'

I didn't meet her eye. 'I don't know — he's cool, yeah.'

'How does he make you feel?'

'Confused,' I said. 'Like I'm tongue-tied, I guess. He's funny, and I can never think of anything funny to say back.' I dug some dirt out from underneath one thumbnail with the other. 'He smells nice, as well. And he can bend his thumbs all the way back to touch his arm.' I tried to show her.

'It sounds like you like him,' Georgia said, lying back in bed. 'But I don't know — Mummy says I'm too young for a boyfriend, anyway. You have to tell me what happens. *Call me.*'

★   ★   ★

A few days after I got back to school, I came down with whatever Georgia had. I was in the San for four days then they moved me back to the dorm when I wasn't infectious any more. Toby brought me pink roses that made me glow inside, until he admitted they were Edith's idea. Being alone with him felt even more confusing than before — I couldn't work out if he was being flirty or shifty. He offered to read *Tom Sawyer* to me, which I'd only gone back to after Aunt Gillian had gone on about how proud of me my father was, but then seemed tongue-tied when Edith arrived with a new hairstyle and plucked eyebrows, and couldn't get out of the room fast enough.

'Did I disturb something?' she asked.

'No.'

'Oh, I nearly forgot, Mr Hicks said to give you this.' She held out a pink card.

I propped myself up on my elbows. There was a quick thumbnail sketch on the front, a girl lying in bed and a doctor checking her chart. Underneath he'd written:

What is it, Doctor?
I'm afraid you have a bad case of nothing

328

much.
Then why are you afraid?
It's contagious.

'I don't get it,' Edith said. 'But don't you think it's cute?'

'Yeah, it's nice. He's nice,' I flopped back onto the pillow. 'I need to sleep.'

She pottered around for a few moments. 'Do you mind if I go find Toby then?'

'Go ahead.'

'Are you sure?'

'Jesus . . .'

'Okay, I'm going.'

She skipped out the door. I tried to sleep, but I kept thinking about how pleased Toby had seemed to see me. I felt sure it was real.

My flu didn't last much longer. When Edith saw me polish off a bowlful of jelly she let the school nurse know I was better.

'Thanks a lot,' I said.

'I can't live with the windows open anymore,' she said apologetically. '*I'm* probably getting ill now.'

I had to go around collecting assignments from all the classes I'd missed. Mr Hicks was the only one to let me off.

'Thanks for the card,' I said, feeling awkward.

'Glad to have you back,' he said, squeezing my shoulder.

I took a detour back from the studio, past the fourth floor. The corridor was lined with framed photos, and eventually, I came to the hockey team, 1971-2. My heart sped up as I looked at it, and at the guy in the middle of the front row. His hair was longer than I remembered, and fell over one eye, but the other eye looked directly at the camera, creased up in a smile. Uncle Jack was happy in the photo, in a way I'd never seen him happy before.

★ ★ ★

April came. My father rang me up early on my birthday to send me his wishes. I could almost see him checking it off in his diary. 'How's everything going over there?' he asked.

'Good. Dad, I can go stay with Grandma this Easter, right?'

'If that's what you want. Will you be coming to London at all?'

'For the first few days.'

'I'll see if I can take the time off,' my father said. 'The cat sends his — hmm — love.'

'Can you put him on the phone?'

There was a short pause, then I could hear a strange metallic rasping on the other end. 'Hi, Mr Tickles,' I said.

'He washed the receiver,' my father said, coming back on.

'I miss him,' I said. 'I'll call about when I'm coming home.'

'Well, happy returns, Tallulah.'

We rang off. I wished Malkie would appear to take me out for the day, but I hadn't heard from him since he left for Canada.

Edith gave me a bracelet while we were standing in the lunch queue. I was touched when

I unwrapped it. I'd seen it in a jewellery shop in the village, and I knew it cost a lot.

'Do you like it?' she asked anxiously.

'Yeah, Ed,' I told her. 'It's beautiful.'

She beamed.

Starr found me in the hallway and gave me a card from Aunt Vivienne and a book voucher. 'Spend it wisely,' she said, and grinned at me. 'Mum's no good at presents, sorry about that.'

I grinned back. 'Thanks. And sorry for . . . '

'No worries.'

'Tell your mum thanks, too.'

'If I must.' She gave me a quick hug and jogged off.

Toby and the guys were waiting on our usual bench when me and Edith took our lunch trays outside. They cheered when they saw us.

'You told them?' I asked her.

'Yeah, come on,' she said, giggling.

I followed her over. 'Guys . . . ' I said, putting my tray down. 'I don't want to make a big fuss.'

'It's not a big fuss,' Toby said.

'Sweet sixteen,' John said. 'Now you can smoke after sex.'

'Cool,' I said. 'I think.'

Toby was sitting next to me and he laid a present down in front of us carefully.

'What is it?' I asked.

'Unwrap it.'

It was a paint brush set, in a black, canvas case, with individual pockets for each brush. The brushes were shiny and clean. I took one out and slipped the protective plastic off, stroking the head across the back of my hand.

'How much was that?' John said suspiciously.

'I thought you'd like them,' Toby said. 'You said you like art class.' I found myself noticing a small brown mole, just beneath his left ear, and then his ears themselves, which were pink and curly like question marks, and then I was looking into his eyes, which really were very green. He looked back at me, and I felt a warmth in my abdomen that spread downwards.

'Thanks,' I said, looking down at the brushes. 'I love them.'

14

If I could freeze my life at a single point and say — this is where I could have been happy, if it'd stayed like this — would I have chosen that moment? Or would I go back much earlier, to before my mother died?

I buy a coffee this time — maybe I really am an addict — and take it to out into the corridor to drink. I lean back against the wall. If I'd never gone to boarding school, I'd never have met Toby. Maybe I'd have met someone else, maybe it would have been more straightforward. But maybe not.

I close my eyes and let my head connect with the wall. You're pathetic, I tell myself. As if your teenage crush was all you needed to be happy. Even if it felt like much more than a teenage crush at the time.

I remember Easter being late that year, so school broke up a few days after my birthday. In the end my father had to work throughout the holiday, so after days of roaming around the house by myself, I invited Toby over.

'Nice place,' he said when I answered the door.

'Thanks.'

We grinned at each other, nervously. I'd been looking forward to meeting up with him, but now that he was on my doorstep, it felt weird to see him outside of school. He looked like he felt the same way; he kept ducking his eyes away from mine. His hands were deep in the pockets of a pair of baggy brown cargo trousers; he wore an orange t-shirt and, over that, an open denim shirt. His trainers were scruffy and suede and wide, making me wonder how big his feet were. I looked down at my outfit — black drainpipe jeans and a cropped lace cardigan.

'This isn't going to work,' I said. 'I went for Michael Jackson and you turn up as Snoop Dogg?'

'I swear I *always* wear sequins and gloves at home.'

'Come in,' I said. 'I'll give you the grand tour.'

I led him into the kitchen and brought some beers up from the cellar. 'I hope you don't need a glass,' I said. 'I haven't been washing up.'

'I can tell.'

'Well, this is the kitchen,' I said. 'We eat here.'

I walked him to the dining-room. 'There's a big table in here for when guests come, except I can't remember when we ever had any . . . and this is the hallway.' We trooped through. 'This is where my dad hangs his hat and coat.'

'Where's he?'

'At the hospital.'

'He works long days?'

'Yeah, pretty much.'

We went through the rest of the house, ending up in my bedroom.

'It's nice,' Toby said. He picked up one of my records. 'Pretty old-school, aren't you?'

'Yeah,' I said. 'Put one on, if you want.'

Toby flicked through them. I shooed Mr

Tickles off the bed, and tried to wipe away all the fur he'd left behind.

'No Nirvana then? No Red Hot Chili Peppers?'

'Why?'

'You always seemed like a grunge chick to me.'

'I'm not sure you can pull off 'chick'.'

'I was hoping you wouldn't notice,' he said. 'What about this one?' He held up a Fleetwood Mac album. 'And who's Evelyn?'

'My mum. They were hers.'

'Oh.'

We sat on the bed together. Halfway through the first track, Toby shifted away.

'Do I stink?' I asked him.

'What?'

'You moved.' I cringed at hearing myself making weird jokes.

'No.' He looked at me again. 'You smell . . . good.'

His face was close to mine. I swallowed, suddenly feeling the need for moisture in my mouth. The needle started skipping and Toby jumped up to fix it.

'Want something to eat?' I asked.

'Yeah.' He sounded relieved.

I made us cheese sandwiches and we sat on the floor to eat them, listening to The Beatles.

'Have you used your paint brushes yet?' Toby asked.

'I will this week.'

'Well,' Toby said. 'When you do, the girl in the shop said they were good for oils, especially.'

I pictured him flirting with her — an

art-student type, tiny and pretty, big-eyed and wearing black — then tried to put it out of my mind. 'Maybe I'll finally get As in art,' I said, 'thanks to you.' I poked him in the ribs, but he wasn't smiling.

'Don't you get As already?' he asked.

'Maybe once.'

'So why's Mr Hicks your mentor?'

'What's your problem with him, anyway?'

'It's not me,' Toby said. 'It's the girls who always get obsessed with him. His last favourite got expelled. Apparently she had a showdown with him in class, asking why he didn't love her.'

I shrugged. 'Well I'm not really the showdown type.'

Afterwards we played snap and pairs and I won both games. I hoped Toby wasn't finding the afternoon lame, but he seemed to be having fun. Mr Tickles came and lay on the cards and Toby stroked him under his chin, which made my toes tingle and Mr Tickles purr in ecstasy.

We made pasta together for dinner. I added everything from the fridge, which was only garlic paste, basil leaves and salami. I left it too long without stirring and everything burnt, so there was a layer of flaky black carbon on the bottom.

'It's *interesting*,' Toby said.

I fed the salami to Mr Tickles, and scraped the rest into the bin. 'I get a lot of takeaway,' I said. 'My mum was a really good cook — guess it's not genetic.'

'How did she . . . ?'

'Hit and run,' I said. 'My dad was there. I wasn't.'

'Shit,' Toby said.

I tried to shrug, but my whole body had stiffened up. Toby came and sat next to me. 'You don't have to talk about it if you don't want,' he said.

'I was at a friend's,' I said, 'and when I got back he was all bloody and stuff. At first I thought he'd killed her . . . You know, beaten her up.'

'Really?'

'Yeah, crazy, huh?'

'Why?'

'Dunno,' I said. 'Maybe I was delirious. And my dad's brother was there, and they don't get on. But then they said she'd been hit by a car. They said she ran out in front of it.'

'Well . . . ' Toby looked uncomfortable. 'At least it wasn't your dad, I guess.'

'He told the police it was his fault.'

Toby's eyebrows shot up. 'Did he mean it?'

'I don't really know.'

He looked at his hands in his lap. 'Tal, I don't know what to say.'

'He was probably in shock too,' I said. Now that I'd started talking about it, I didn't seem able to stop. 'It was horrible, seeing her like that.' I felt sick when I remembered it.

I wandered into the dining-room after that and picked out a few notes on the piano. If Toby had come and put his arms around me then, maybe everything would have been different. I know I wanted him to so badly it felt like I was going to break myself into tiny pieces wishing it.

Instead, he came to the doorway and gave me

a tight smile. 'I better go.'

I shut the piano lid with a bang and walked past him to the front door. I opened it and stood back. So Toby wanted nothing to do with my crazy family, I told myself. Fine by me. I could have told him more — about my mother really being in love with her husband's brother, about my grandfather abusing my grandmother and my aunt. Or how my own dad couldn't look me in the eye. That would really have freaked him out.

'Sorry,' he said, avoiding my eye. 'I just have to get back.'

'I get it.'

'I'll see you when you're back from your grandma's?'

'Yeah.'

He looked at me then and bent down to kiss my cheek. I could feel him trembling. 'See you.'

'See you.'

★ ★ ★

I was clipping Mr Tickles' claws when the phone rang the next day.

'Hi, it's Toby.'

'Yes?'

'Look, I'm sorry about last night. I shouldn't have run away like that.'

I lay back on my bed. 'Don't worry about it.' I tried to make my voice sound dismissive, but it caught halfway through.

'I just . . . freaked out.'

'You think?'

'I'm sorry. It kind of brought back memories

of my brother. He died when I was younger.'

He'd gone quiet, and for a moment I thought I hadn't heard him right. 'I thought you were an only child?'

'I am now.'

'Shit,' I said. Which wasn't exactly the most sympathetic I could have been. 'I'm so, so sorry. What happened?'

'He hanged himself. Apparently I found the body, but I don't remember it at all.'

'*Jesus.*'

'Yeah, no one at school knows about it; it's kind of grim. My parents won't talk about it.'

We didn't speak for a moment while I tried to think of what to say. 'That's awful.'

'Yeah.'

'Did they try to make you see a counsellor?'

'Course. Finding the body — they loved that. I went twice. You?'

'Yeah. For a while.'

'Don't tell anyone. I just wanted you to know.'

'Course I won't.' I felt a sudden thrill inside me — he trusts me — then felt guilty again.

'Anyway,' he said, 'enough family crap. Do you want to come camping with us next week?'

'Who's us?'

'The guys. We go to Broadwater Forest every year.'

'I'll be at my Gran's.'

'Leave early. You're seeing her over the summer.'

'Well . . . ' I rolled onto my stomach and got the phone cord tangled up in my armpit. I unwrapped it from myself in time to hear Toby say, 'We've never asked a girl before — think of it as an honour.'

I felt a smile growing on my face. 'I'm flattered.'

'You should be. So is that a yes?'

'Is Edith coming?'

'I haven't asked her.'

'You going to?'

'Yeah,' he said, 'course.'

'Okay,' I said. 'Gimme details later.'

I gave him my grandmother's telephone number and we hung up.

I thought about Toby a lot over the next few days, when I was packing for my grandmother's, or tidying my room or showering, or doing anything. Maybe that was why we liked each other so much, I thought, because we'd both seen people we'd loved die. Except Toby hadn't seen his brother die — he'd found him already dead. And it must have been worse than I could even imagine if his mind had wiped the image. But he was so together, no one would know. No one *did* know. I felt proud, in a weird way, that he'd been able to handle it so well.

But he must have been supported by his family, too, I told myself. If my father had been more like them, I probably wouldn't be so messed up. If I'd gone to live with my grandmother from the start . . .

On the other hand, I told myself, maybe I would have frozen to death if I'd lived with my grandmother for any longer. The house was only slightly less icy in the spring than in the winter.

'You shouldn't be in the cold, it's not good for

you,' I said, pushing her into the sunshine. She dozed off while I did my homework nearby. Occasionally she woke up and demanded water. 'I'm burning,' she said. 'Are you trying to finish me off?'

I rummaged around in her things until I found a floppy hat for her to wear. 'It's not even that sunny,' I told her. 'You must be cold-blooded or something.'

'I've heard that one before,' she said.

'Who from?' I asked, but she waved the question away. 'So, has Aunt Vivienne come to visit yet?' I asked, casually, arranging the hat on her head.

'You're not as dumb as you look, Tallulah.'

'I'll take that as a compliment.'

She seemed much better now; her cheeks were pinker and her eyes looked clearer. She was impatient being confined to her wheelchair; she followed me around more, poking her nose into everything I did. Toby called every day and it was hard to hide the conversations from her.

'What's with the heavy breathing?' he asked once.

'Shut up, I'm jogging.'

'Now?'

'I'm going to the bottom of the garden.'

'Why?'

'Privacy.'

'Who exactly are you hiding from?'

'My grandma — she's turned into a spy.'

'Where's your dad?'

'London.'

'Sorry — should I not have asked that?'

341

I shrugged.

'Tal?'

'I shrugged.'

'You know I can't see that down the phone, right?'

'It's okay. We can talk about my dad being in London.'

'How often do you see him?'

'Maybe a few weeks a year.'

'You're lucky,' Toby said. 'My dad's around all the time — he took voluntary redundancy a few years ago.'

'What did he do?'

'Construction foreman.' He cleared his throat. 'I got a scholarship.'

'Oh.' I'd never even considered how other people paid their fees. 'So he's used to being in charge?'

'Yeah,' Toby said. 'But he's cool. He kind of wanted Danny — my brother — to get into the business with him, but after he died, Dad said I should do whatever I wanted. He got a t-shirt saying *I'm with Genius* when I got the scholarship.'

'You don't want to be a foreman?'

'I want to make a lot of money so my mum can retire.'

'What does she do?'

'She's a teaching assistant.'

'My mum used to be a waitress,' I said. 'She was good with people.'

'How come you're so terrible, then?'

'Har-dee-har-har.'

'I'll be quiet.'

'She *was* nice,' I said. 'Everyone liked her.' I thought of Aunt Vivienne. 'Nearly everyone. And she was really beautiful.'

'Yeah? Did she look like you?'

'No,' I said, trying not to smirk. 'She had really amazing hair — she used baby shampoo.'

'You sound like you really got on.'

'Yeah,' I said. 'At least I had an amazing mum, right?'

'True.'

'What was your brother like?'

'He was really sweet — the quiet type. He used to look out for me at school.'

'What do you mean?'

'I used to be really tiny, and he was quite big for his age — he used to scare off all the kids who picked on me, even though he'd never have actually done anything.'

'He sounds cool.'

'You'd have liked him. You'd like my dad, too.'

'You'd like my Grandma.'

'Oh yeah?'

'I should go check on her,' I said.

'Talk tomorrow?'

'Talk tomorrow.'

'Who was that?' my grandmother asked when I went back up the lawn.

'I thought you were asleep.'

'Who was it?' she asked again, ignoring me.

'Toby.'

'A boy from school?'

I looked at her; she'd closed her eyes and was smiling to herself.

'Just a friend.'

343

'Of course he is.'

'Can we drop this?'

'If it's bothering you,' she said, still smiling. 'But he's got you mooning all over the place, my girl.'

'I'm *not*.'

'You are.'

I chewed my fingernail for a moment. 'What did you do when you liked a boy?'

'It's been too long for me to remember.'

'How long?'

'I was sixteen when I met your grandfather — towards the end of the war.'

'Did you have a boyfriend before Grandad?'

She gave me a look.

'What?'

'In my day, young women were encouraged not to spread themselves too thinly.'

'So no?'

'No.'

'How did you two meet?'

'He was a pilot,' she said. 'He was a neighbour too, but I'd never really noticed him until a barn dance I went to on my birthday . . . I remember we danced the first dance together, and he wouldn't let me partner anyone else afterwards.'

'Was he handsome?'

'The handsomest.'

'And then what?'

'I let him chase me for two years,' my grandmother said.

'Why?'

'Hruh,' she said. 'I was young, but I knew what marriage meant for women. You think I wanted to cook and iron shirts all day?'

'But you did marry him.'

'He wore me down,' she said. 'He was very persuasive.' I wondered if violence had been part of his persuasion.

'I remember the day I said yes,' she said. 'He disappeared, and came back with a suitcase full of roses. He said if I wanted, he'd bring me roses every day.'

'Did he?'

'Of course not,' she said, putting her hand over mine. 'But don't look so despondent about it, my darling.'

'I don't even know how to spell that.' I leaned over and kissed her cheek.

'My smart-aleck granddaughter.'

★ ★ ★

The next time Toby called, my grandmother made a point of wheeling back and forth past the telephone. After four trips, I grabbed one of the handles of her chair, pulling her up short.

'What?' she asked, trying to look innocent.

'Why are you spying on me?'

'I'm making myself a drink.'

'Go away,' I said. 'Now.'

She gave me another innocent look and wheeled away, stopping just inside the living-room.

'Go further than that,' I called.

'I'm a prisoner in my own home,' she shouted back.

'Sorry,' I said into the receiver. 'She's got

nothing better to do.' I leaned back against the wall and slid down it until I was sitting on the carpet. 'So, how's tricks?'

'Alright. What you up to?'

'Hanging out with Grams.' I wove the fingers of my free hand into the wine-coloured shag-pile. 'I feel bad leaving her.'

'You don't have to come,' Toby said. He cleared his throat. 'I mean, obviously, it would be cool but . . . '

'I want to come,' I said. 'It's just, it's not like my dad will come see how she is, or anything.'

'Don't they get on?'

'I don't know. One of my aunts — the younger one — doesn't speak to her, and *she* doesn't like spending too much time with the other aunt.'

'Is she just an older version of you?'

'And then there's my uncle, who turned up out of the blue, and pissed everyone off for some reason, then disappeared again. Then her and my dad — they don't talk much, but they don't fight either.'

'You have an interesting family,' Toby said.

'You mean weird.'

'I didn't say that.'

I paused; I could feel my stomach knotting up at what I was thinking of saying. 'Uncle Jack was definitely the highest point of weirdness. My dad really changed afterwards.'

'How so?'

'Him and my mum started fighting. I don't remember them fighting before — that could have had something to do with her getting depressed. And he didn't look after her at all, he got my aunt to do it. And he seemed really annoyed with me.'

'With you?'

'Yeah.'

'Why would he be annoyed with you?'

'I dunno,' I said. 'We don't talk either. It got worse after my mum died.'

'What happened?'

'Well — he sent me to boarding school for one thing.'

'My parents sent me, too.'

'But I didn't want to go, and it was only a week or two after it'd happened.' I swallowed, trying not to let any tears out. 'And . . . I can't explain it . . . He looks at me like he doesn't know me. Just after the accident, I felt like . . . ' I suddenly realised exactly how he'd made me feel, something I hadn't been able to admit even to myself. 'I felt like he wished it was me who died.'

Toby was quiet for a moment. I could hear my breathing down the line. I tried to stifle it and made a sobbing sound instead.

'I'm so sorry, Tal,' he said eventually. 'That sounds shit.' He paused again, and I finally got myself under control. 'I'm sure he doesn't feel like that.'

'Maybe not.'

'I wish I was there with you.'

I rubbed my cheek with the heel of my hand. 'We kind of just leave each other alone now.'

'Do you mind?'

'I — ' I stopped. 'We've never even *talked* about it. Other than the medical details — he never asked how I was. Not once.'

'Tallulah,' my grandmother called. 'Are you still on the telephone?'

I took a deep breath. 'Gotta go,' I said.

'Don't.'

'I have to.'

'Are you okay?'

'Yeah.'

'You sure?'

'Yeah, sure. I don't mind telling you these things.'

'I don't mind telling you things either.'

'See you in two days, then.'

★ ★ ★

Edith was hyper-excited about the camping trip, but the day before it was scheduled she got mumps from her younger brother and couldn't come. 'I *hate* him,' she moaned. 'This was my best chance of getting with Toby.'

I made sympathetic noises, but I was secretly pleased about not having to share him. Then I felt guilty and wondered if I should tell Edith that I liked him — but nothing's going to happen anyway, I told myself.

When the train pulled into Worthing platform, Toby was standing alone. He was carrying a backpack, his hat pulled down over his ears. Seeing him there without the others took me by surprise. I waited for a moment, scuffing my shoes before I went over.

'Hey,' he said, looking terrified.

'Hey yourself. Where's everyone else?'

'Francis had to go visit his cousin — new baby or something,' he said. 'And John's on holiday with his folks.'

'So it's just us two?'

'Yeah. Is that okay?'

My mouth was dry. 'Sure, why not?'

The woods the boys had chosen were dense and tangled, with berries growing in splashes of red. They smelled like smoke and wet dog.

'What do you think of it?' Toby asked, gesturing around.

'It's nice.'

He took my hand shyly, brought it up to his mouth and kissed it. 'I wanted to show it to you,' he said. 'It's kind of an escape for me — from home and Danny, and my parents . . . '

I squeezed his hand.

'Come on,' he said.

We walked until we got to a clearing that sloped down to a pond. Two lone ducks circled the edges of the water, calling mournfully to each other. The trees were tall enough to block out most of the light.

We worked silently, driving the pegs into the ground and stretching the material over the poles. Toby surveyed it when we'd finished. 'Not bad for a girl.'

'Watch it.'

We threw our bags inside, then sat down facing each other on two nearby logs.

'Did you bring a sleeping bag?'

'Yeah,' I said. 'But I think it might be kind of moth-eaten.'

'You can share with me if you want?'

'Okay.' I could feel my stomach flutter. Play it cool.

'I've got another blanket too. Oh, and I brought these.' He reached into his pockets and brought out two squashed peanut-butter sandwiches, wrapped in cling-film.

'What do you guys do around here, anyway?' I asked, as we ate.

'Drink,' he said. 'Talk about stuff. Sports mostly.'

'I'll drink.'

Toby grinned. 'I've got beers.' He rummaged around in his bag and pulled out two six-packs. I noticed again how strong and smooth his hands looked.

'If we keep them in the pond they'll be colder,' he said.

'Okay.'

It took three beers each for the sun to go down. We sat, knees touching, playing poker with matches that I'd found in my jacket pocket.

'So a straight flush wins?' I asked.

'Yeah.'

I laid down a jack, and a queen of diamonds, next to the ten, king and nine on the ground.

'You're like a cards fiend,' Toby said, shaking his head.

'Beginner's luck,' I said, trying to not grin from ear to ear.

'I'm going to win those matches back, you know that, right?'

'You can try.'

'How about winner gets both sleeping bags?'

We played a few more hands and Toby took nearly all the matches back off me. I finished my beer and lay back along the log, looking up at the silhouettes of the treetops and beyond, at all the warm, daylight colours that were pooling at the bottom of the sky. There was a loosening inside me, like everything I'd been able to talk to Toby about didn't matter anymore — my father's coldness, losing my mother, worrying about my grandmother. Maybe the woods could be an escape for me too.

I felt a sudden pang over Edith, ill at home. But I hadn't done anything wrong, I reassured myself.

Toby went and fetched us more beers. He passed me one, brushing my hand with his fingertips, and sat beside me on my log.

'I'm cold already,' I said.

'Here, have my jacket.' He wrapped it around me, then huddled closer. 'We should make a fire.'

'We should definitely not do that,' I said, hiccupping. 'You're drunk. *I'm* drunk.'

He put his arm around me, making me jump. 'What do you wanna do, then?'

'I dunno,' I said. Starr's words came back to me. I wondered if he'd done this with other girls, too, the arm pulling them closer as he worked up towards a kiss. I tried to take another swig. Maybe he wasn't going to try to kiss me. Maybe I didn't measure up to the others.

'Truth or dare?' he asked, after a moment or two of silence.

'Alright. You start.'

'Truth.'

'Is . . . it really true you pulled Melissa Albrecht?'

Melissa Albrecht was famous at our school for being bigger than most of the rugby boys.

'Yeah,' Toby said. 'But I was wasted.'

'How was it?'

'Scary.'

'Uh-huh.'

'Your turn.'

'Truth.'

'Okay.' Toby cracked open another can for himself. 'What about you — kissed anyone you shouldn't have?'

'Nope.'

'What d'you mean?'

'I mean nope,' I said. 'I haven't kissed anyone.' I took a long drink, trying to hide my flaming cheeks.

'What, like, ever?'

'I guess there was Tom at primary school,' I said. 'But he slobbered all over me.'

'Wow, really?'

'Really.'

'How did that happen?'

'Isn't it your turn again?'

'I can't believe you've never kissed anyone.'

'Well I haven't. I must be hideous — case solved.'

Toby grinned.

'What?'

'Remember the first time we sat with you guys, and you gave John a dirty look 'cos he was laughing at Edith? You kind of look like that now.'

'Like what?'

'Like you're gonna rip my head off.'

'Yeah, well . . . '

'I like that I can't impress you, which is kind of weird, I guess. But you're actually kind of sweet to other people.' He twisted the ring-pull on his can backwards and forwards until it snapped off. 'Like when you found a clump of hair in your cake in that stupid café, and you didn't tell them because you thought the owner would be embarrassed.'

'And I'm not sweet to you?'

'Not always.' He took my hand in his, drawing circles with his finger on the back of my wrist, and up my arm. 'You've got really soft hands.'

'Mm-hmm.'

'Not really helping with the moment, are you?'

'I don't know what to say.'

'Nice things.'

'Like what?'

'Like — you're so sexy,' Toby said.

'You want me to tell you you're sexy?'

'No *you* are. You're the sexiest person I know.'

'Okay. I mean, thanks. What's so funny?'

'Nothing, it's just . . . I think I'm in love with you,' he said.

I saw his mouth coming towards me; his breath smelled like peanuts. Then his lips were on mine, and I opened my mouth instinctively. My hands were hanging at my side, being useless, and I shifted on the log to find the right position. Toby pulled away, and looked at me with such a weird expression that I almost laughed.

'Is this okay?' he asked.

'I dunno,' I said, feeling my cheeks flare up again. 'I've never been kissed before, remember?'

'I didn't mean that,' he said. 'I meant . . . do you want to keep on kissing?'

'Yeah. It's nice.'

We kissed again, and this time I tried to copy Toby's movements, the way he bit me gently, or ran his tongue along the inside of my lip. He let out a kind of sigh, like he'd been holding himself together, and a tickling feeling ran up my spine and exploded at the base of my brain. I put my arms around him and dug my fingers in, enjoying the heat underneath his clothes, but I still didn't feel close enough, and I pressed myself forwards until there was no space left between us and I was touching him with the whole length of my body. He was cupping his hands around the back of my head, holding me to him as the kisses got harder, almost painful, and I realised I'd wanted this since the moment he came over to my table and sat down next to me.

Toby pulled away again. 'Fuck,' he said. 'I want you.'

I caught my breath.

'Is that too fast?'

I shook my head, not trusting myself to speak. I crawled into the tent ahead of him, feeling the cool material of the sleeping bag beneath my hands in the dark, and the thump of my heart in my chest and my throat. Toby flicked on his torch and tied it to the zip dangling from the ceiling, so a small spotlight bobbed gently in the

354

middle of the space. When he turned around on his knees I could see the bulge in his jeans. I reached out and put my hand against the swelling. I could feel the blood thundering through me. I shook my head to get rid of the buzz in my ears, and everything in front of me slid to one side, then returned to its original place.

He took my jumper off me, and my t-shirt, kissing me the whole time, his lips warm and dry. 'I'm sorry about the other day,' he said, in between kisses. 'I really want to take care of you, you know?'

'Can we not talk about that now?'

A picture of my mother appeared uninvited in my mind, then, even worse, Uncle Jack and my mother that day in the rose garden. I pulled back from Toby, but he didn't seem to notice. 'Hey,' I mumbled.

He was fumbling with the clasps on my bra, swearing under his breath. I felt like I couldn't breathe. I kept hearing Uncle Jack's voice in my head: 'not what nice girls do', and the sound of my mother's hand across his face. I closed my eyes and saw my mother at her birthday party now, white-faced and grieving, Uncle Jack vanished again.

'Stop,' I said. '*Stop.*'

'What's wrong?' he said; he was still trying to unhook my bra.

I felt a bubble of panic rise inside me. 'Fucking *stop*,' I said, twisting away and lashing out. My knuckles cracked against his nose and upper lip and I felt the jolt run up my arm to my shoulder. Toby grabbed at my wrist with one hand and brought the other up to his nose.

'*Jesus*,' he yelled. 'What was that for? That fucking hurt.'

'*Get off me.*' I tried to wrench my wrist away, and it came dangerously close to his face again.

'What's your fucking problem?'

'Don't *touch* me.'

He sat and stared at me. 'Why?'

'Why do I have to explain?'

He looked disgusted. 'Everyone in my year laughs at me, you know. They say I'm your love-sick puppy.'

'I didn't *ask* you to love me.'

'You don't have to treat me like shit, either. If you like me too, you don't have to hide it.'

'I *don't* like you,' I said. 'You follow me around like a fucking creep — I feel sorry for you, that's all.'

Toby recoiled like I'd hit him again. 'Fine,' he said. He sighed loudly. 'We can go to sleep, if you want. Then tomorrow you can go home and you don't have to see me again. How does that sound to you?'

'Why wait until tomorrow?'

'What?'

I grabbed my t-shirt and crawled towards the opening of the tent.

'Where are you going?'

'Don't speak to me like I'm your kid.'

'Don't fucking act like one, then.'

'Fuck you, Toby.'

'That's fine, then. Fuck off.'

I pulled my top on and walked into the woods,

deliberately not putting my hands out to clear a path so by the time I stopped I was covered in scratches. I leant against a tree trunk and lit a cigarette, wrapping my free arm around myself and cupping my shoulder to try to stay warm. Half of me was frustrated that I hadn't been able to go through with it, and the other half was furious with Toby for not understanding why I couldn't. I pulled on the cigarette. If he loved me, then he'd come after me.

I finished two cigarettes, stamping them out in the roots of the tree. There were no stars out up beyond the tree-tops. My heart hurt.

'Fucking fuck you, then,' I said.

I waited for what felt like over an hour before I went back. I was shivering, and my body felt flushed with the cold. I crawled in. Toby was inside his sleeping bag, facing away from me. My sleeping bag was out. I rolled myself up inside it and faced the side of the tent, trying to hold my limbs tight so they stopped convulsing. I could hear Toby's breathing nearby; after about another hour, it became more regular and I knew he was asleep.

The next morning we packed up without a word. Images from the night before kept swimming before me: Toby kissing me, Toby taking my top off, Toby seeing my body. We'd gone so quickly from that intimacy to this heavy silence that I felt ashamed it had happened at all. Every time I remembered the moment I'd punched him, my insides shrivelled in humiliation. In daylight, and hungover, I couldn't be sure I hadn't overreacted.

In London we walked into the underground together.

'Tal, I . . . ' Toby started.

'I've gotta go,' I said.

'I'm sorry. I shouldn't have kissed you.'

'Yeah.' I felt my eyes well up. I looked down at the floor and willed the tears not to spill over. 'I don't think we should tell anyone about it.'

'Bye then,' he said, and left me at the barrier.

I spent the rest of the week clearing out my room. My father left me to it; he didn't ask about the camping trip.

I phoned my grandmother every afternoon. Mr Tickles jumped onto my lap and pawed at me while I spoke to her, asking for affection. Toby called four or five times, but I couldn't face him. The second-to-last time he left a short message, which I deleted, saying he wanted to talk. The last time, he sighed and then hung up.

★　★　★

I take my cup back to the boy on the till.

'Thanks,' he says, uncomfortably, and looks away. Maybe he thinks I'll report him to my 'fiancé' if he talks to me. It's pathetic that when I think of my imaginary fiancé, I think of Toby, isn't it?

I go outside, breathing in the fresh air in big gulps. I check my phone again. Still nothing from Malkie.

'Hurry up,' I say out loud.

The lift on the way back up is packed: two

nurses chatting, an elderly woman in a wheelchair and a porter to push it, and a family with young kids. They all get out before me, the kids dropping crisps everywhere as their mum tries to surreptitiously take the packets back.

Aunt Gillian and Aunt Vivienne are exactly where I left them, both looking off into the distance. Aunt Gillian is rubbing her right thumb back and forth over the fleshy bit between left thumb and left palm. Aunt Vivienne is tapping a pen against the magazine lying open on her lap. If ever I've seen two people trying to keep hold of their anxiety, this is it. I guess it's been a long time since I was told to wait in here; anything could be happening right now.

'Hi,' I say.

They both start.

'A shrub or small tree,' Aunt Vivienne says. 'Anagram of 'camus'.'

'Sumac.'

'I think you're right,' she says, scribbling it down.

'How did you know that, dear?' Aunt Gillian asks.

'Grandma had one.'

'How clever.'

'How was he?' Aunt Vivienne asks.

'Who?'

'The boy in the café.'

'Fine,' I say, sitting down. 'I think I've scared him off for good now.'

It's what I do, guys.

Toby was probably the most persistent, but I was stubborn, and eventually even he gave up.

I'd avoided him for the first week of summer term, but he managed to catch me once, grabbing my shoulder.

'Tal . . . Can you stop running off, please?'

If I hadn't been so dumb, I would have talked to him then. I should have remembered that his childhood trauma was almost worse than mine, that he'd freaked in front of me too, but at the time all I could think was that I couldn't listen to him tell me how much he liked me as a friend, or worse, how he didn't want to be friends anymore because I was damaged and mental.

'Just get out of my way. Please.'

I remember he moved out of the way and sighed again, like I was the most irritating person in the world. 'Off you go then.'

'Whatever,' I said, and walked past him.

Aunt Vivienne's tapping the pen again. It sounds much louder in my brain than it really can be. I start to bite my thumbnail, then think better of it.

If I'd listened to Toby . . .

I hadn't told Edith about what had happened on the camping trip, but she started acting jumpy around me anyway. The day after I ran into Toby, I saw her giving me little looks out of the corner of my eye, until I asked her what was up.

She giggled. 'Nothing really.'

'Please stop staring at me then.'

We were probably going to gym class when we were having the conversation. I remember we were outside. Edith stopped walking suddenly, and said, 'I have to tell you something.'

I heard footsteps behind us, they got faster, then someone tapped me on my right shoulder. 'Hey,' Starr said. She'd dyed her hair blonde, with dark roots, making her look like Debbie Harry. The school had recently voted to scrap uniforms for the sixth-formers and she was wearing a tight striped top, a denim miniskirt and a bomber jacket with the sleeves rolled up. I remember looking down at myself, tugging at the hem of my too-short netball skirt, trying to make it seem less scandalous. Next to Starr, I looked like a child prostitute.

'Hey,' I said.

'Good holiday?'

'Yeah, alright. You?'

'Great. We went sailing for two weeks,' Starr said. She inspected her arm. 'Think the tan's wearing off already. Bloody weather.' I looked down at her beautiful honey-brown colour. 'Look, I've got to run, but I came to tell you about this party the Drama Group's having, for the end of our play. You coming?'

'The play or the party?'

'You don't have to come to the play. It's some weird Russian shit about an albatross or something.'

'*The Seagull*,' Edith said quietly.

'What?' Starr asked.

'It's a play by Chekhov,' Edith said.

'Maybe,' Starr said. 'I just do backstage.'

'Where's the party?' I asked.

'It's at the drama teacher's house, on campus,' Starr said. 'It'll be crazy. She's some weird hippy who makes us call her by her first name.

Apparently she gets really drunk and cries at these things.'

'Oh?'

'It's after the last night; two Fridays from now.'

'Cool.'

'Anyway,' Starr said. 'See you there.' She started to jog in the other direction. Edith stared after her.

'Your cousin's really pretty,' she said.

'What did you have to tell me?'

'Oh — nothing,' she said. 'It can wait.'

I felt a strange sense of relief. Afterwards, I realised I knew all along what she was trying to tell me.

'I hope your boss understands about all of this,' Aunt Gillian's saying.

'What?'

'Wasn't it him you were calling earlier?'

I try not to meet her eye. 'He doesn't really have human emotions,' I say. 'But he hasn't fired me yet.'

'Oh.'

I want to tell her that, actually, I'm trying to get in touch with her errant brother — the one who went to jail and the whole family stopped mentioning. I need to ask him a few questions about my mother, and whether or not they were in love. And whether my father knew and that's why he went so weird.

I stand up and walk around the room once, pretending to be looking for something. No one's even talking about why we're here anymore.

'Last one,' Aunt Vivienne says. 'Six letters, beginning with 'd'. At great cost.'

Another week passed before I saw Toby again. I knew Edith had been hanging out with the boys, but she was vague when I asked her what they'd been up to. Then, on Friday, Toby was waiting outside after my biology class. I felt a half-embarrassed grin spread over my face — I hadn't completely driven him away then. 'Hey,' I said.

'Hey yourself. Where you going now?'

'French.'

'Can I walk with you?'

'Sure.'

'Look — I just wanna say I'm sorry,' he said. 'For what happened. You know, on the trip. That's what I was trying to tell you last time.'

'It's fine. I'm sorry too.'

'Okay, good.' He looked relieved.

We fell into step. Toby was cracking his knuckles. I looked at him properly; he was wearing a white t-shirt that made his eyes seem greener, navy blue shorts that he'd rolled up at the bottom so they stopped just above the knee and grey plimsolls. I tried not to think of his body underneath, how warm it had been when we were kissing.

'What's wrong?'

'What do you mean?' he asked.

'You seem kinda nervous.'

Toby shook his head. 'Tal, we're friends right?' he said. 'Nothing's going to come between us, yeah?'

'Yeah,' I said.

We reached the door of my French class, and he stood in front of it so I couldn't go in. 'Cool,' he said. 'Have lunch with us?'

'Yeah, alright.'

French class felt longer than usual; I ran out of the door when the bell rang, heading to our old spot outside. John and Francis were kicking a football around.

'Hi,' I said, sitting down on the picnic bench. 'You okay?'

'Hey, Tal,' Francis said, coming over. 'You're looking . . . nice.'

'Thanks,' I said, surprised.

'Hey, Tal.' John joined us. 'I didn't expect to see you here.'

'I haven't been kicked out yet.'

'No, I meant, about Toby.'

'What about him?'

Francis shoved John. 'Nothing,' he said.

'I mean about Toby and Edith,' John said.

'What?'

'You didn't know?' John asked.

Francis gave him a dirty look; John smirked. 'Was I not supposed to say anything?' he asked. 'Shame. Oh well, Toby's coming now. You can ask him about it.'

'Yo,' Toby said, dropping his bag on the floor. He saw our faces. 'What happened?'

'John told Tal,' Francis said. He shrugged helplessly. John was still grinning. Toby looked at them and then at me. 'You prick,' he said to John.

★ ★ ★

I called my grandmother, but she was sleeping. The nurse was on her way out.

'It's my afternoon off,' she said. 'I'll wake her up this evening and tell her you called.'

'Can you leave a note at least?'

'Fine.'

I kicked the phone-booth when I hung up.

I went to bed early and lay there staring at the ceiling, wondering if my insomnia was back. I must have fallen asleep though, because I woke in the middle of the night, arms and legs strangely heavy. I heard the telephone ring downstairs in the Housemistress' office, and footsteps shuffling out to answer it; it must have been the phone that woke me.

I got out of bed to pee. On the way back, I stopped at the top of the stairs. The Housemistress was sitting on the bottom step, rabbit-faced slippers on her feet. Normally the sight would have made me laugh, but this time something made me lean over the banister and call down to her quietly. 'Who was that?'

She started and turned to face me. 'Tallulah. How long have you been there?'

'Not long.'

'Oh, goodness. It's so strange that it should be you up.' She seemed flustered.

'What is it?'

She hesitated.

'What?'

'That was your father on the telephone. It's your grandmother.'

I sat down too, on the top step, with my knees pressed together. 'What about her?' I asked, as the Housemistress started climbing up towards me. 'Is she okay?'

'She had a nasty fall,' she said, kneeling in front of me. 'You know, maybe we should get you a hot drink or something.'

I clutched the banister. 'Why?'

'The nursing company just called your father,' she said. 'The nurse found your grandmother when she got back this evening.'

'How is she?' I asked, but even before I asked I knew what was coming next.

'I'm sorry, Tallulah. She's dead.'

★ ★ ★

We hear voices suddenly coming from my father's room. Someone shouts 'Check the monitor', and then footsteps are slapping along the corridor floor, much too heavy for a child this time.

'Doctor,' the voices start up again. 'You're needed.' We're frozen, all turning towards the sounds but none of us daring to go out into the hallway to see what's happening. No one looks shocked. I feel like we knew this was coming.

'Oh fuck,' Aunt Gillian says in a whisper; I think it must be the first time I've heard her swear.

A surgeon comes into the waiting-room, dressed in full operating gear. 'Miss Park?' he says, looking straight at me. 'I'm afraid your father's situation is deteriorating. He's being prepped for surgery now.'

'What happened?'

'He's tamponading — an artery must have been punctured during the PCI. It's not uncommon. We'll do everything we can.'

We follow him into the hallway. They wheel my father out and into the operating room.

'He'll be alright,' Aunt Gillian says, putting her hand on my shoulder. I can feel her shaking.

'Ladies, if you don't mind waiting in the room down the hall,' a nurse says, her arms full of bandages.

'But . . . ' Aunt Gillian starts.

The nurse goes into the theatre, and we catch a glimpse of tubes and instruments and people moving around, with my father in the middle, before the door swings shut.

15

The night before the funeral, we stayed at Aunt Gillian's house, me, my father, Aunt Gillian, Uncle George, Michael and Georgia. James was away on a school trip, and no one was talking about Vivienne. I'd heard Aunt Gillian pleading with her down the telephone. 'Of course we tried. No one knows how to get in touch with him, Viv. Anyway, it's *Mother's funeral*. It's not the time for grudges . . . '

Uncle George had burst in on Aunt Gillian then. He was out of sight, but I'd heard him demanding the telephone, waving aside her objections. 'It's bloody work, Gillian.'

We drove to my grandmother's the next day. The church was just around the corner from the house; it was cold and the minister droned on, without ever saying my grandmother's name. I stared at the back of Uncle George's head in the pew in front of me and noticed how little flecks of white skin kept dropping from his hair onto his shoulders. He seemed even more irritable than normal; halfway through the service he got a phone call and went outside. I heard his voice raising over the minister's from time to time, shouting about 'liability', 'betrayal', and once, 'little shit'.

As soon as we got back to the house, my cousins were sent upstairs to pack my grandmother's things into boxes. Uncle George had brought some over in the boot of the car.

'No sense in wasting time,' he said. 'We'll have to recuperate the cost of the funeral anyway.'

'George,' Aunt Gillian said, looking scandalised.

'Well it's true. You said the old bird was down to her last penny, so that rules out a nice big inheritance.' He looked gloomy.

'This is hardly the time to discuss it.'

'Oh yes, I forgot how close you all were.'

'She was my *mother*.'

'Grow up, Gillian. If you're going to get hormonal maybe I'll go for a walk.'

'Perhaps you should walk off a cliff,' I suggested.

'*Tallulah*,' Aunt Gillian said.

'Sorry, Aunt Gillian. I didn't mean you.'

'This isn't getting us anywhere,' my father said. 'We've all had a stressful morning. Gillian, if you want to put the kettle on, I'll go up and see how the packing is coming along.' He adjusted a shirt cuff.

'You don't seem that broken up, either,' I said. For some reason, looking at my father's blank face made me angrier than looking at Uncle George's red one.

'Why doesn't someone just put her down?' Uncle George said.

'*George.*'

'She's pretty much a wild animal anyway.'

He didn't see the plate leave my hand and fly towards him. It happened so quickly, I wasn't sure I'd seen it either. The sound of his glasses, knocked off his ears and cracking on the floor, woke me up and I turned on my heels and ran.

'You're just proving my point,' he yelled after me. I heard a scuffle, and saw over my shoulder that my father and Aunt Gillian were physically restraining him. 'You need a bloody psychiatrist, girl.'

I went outside and sat in the rose garden, my thoughts even blacker than my dress. I heard Georgia and Michael calling to each other from upstairs, through open windows.

'Look at this spaniel-clock! Isn't it *cute*?'

'It's bloody hideous. Put it in the bin-bag to throw out.'

'I'm keeping it. *I* love it.'

I clenched my fists. I felt a weird hatred for Georgia, claiming things that had belonged to our grandmother when she hadn't even really known her.

My father found me and started trying to give me a lecture, polishing his glasses on his sleeve.

'Save it,' I told him. 'I'm not in the mood.' I went to walk off but he caught my arm.

'Try to think of others, Tallulah,' he said. 'We're all going through this together.'

'Please don't touch me,' I said, shaking him off.

$\star \quad \star \quad \star$

We troop back into the waiting-room. I feel disconnected from my body, and wonder if that's how my father feels too — if he's conscious somehow, but not within himself.

I was so angry with him it's hard to believe.

370

Yesterday, the day before. Most of my life. I left the day after my grandmother's funeral; I couldn't bear to stay in the house if my grandmother wasn't there anymore.

I remember my father already being gone — due back at work — and Michael dropping me off at the station. I remember he gave me a plastic bag and said, 'We found these. Georgia thought you might want them.'

'Thanks. And thanks for the lift.'

'Aren't you going to see what they are?'

'Okay.' Inside the bag was every picture I'd ever drawn or painted for my grandmother.

'They're good,' he'd said. 'Especially that one of the landscape, you know . . . the cliff-top and the beach. That somewhere you've been?'

'It was a photo I found in a magazine. Somewhere in South America.'

I remember him turning the engine off and shifting to face me. He was wearing jeans and a tight red jumper that clung to the muscles on his arms; he looked so much older. 'Smoke?'

'Cheers.'

I slump back into one of the waiting-room chairs. What then? Smoking, stubbing out the cigarette, shaking the plastic bag. 'Thanks for these, again.' Opening the door.

'It was Georgia's idea. She's the sweet one.'

'Say thanks to her too.'

'Yeah. Take care, Tallie.'

Was it really only a few days ago that I got the telephone call about my father? It feels like I've been here forever. But that memory in the car feels like yesterday. I can almost smell the dusty

371

upholstery, Michael, the wet paint of the benches along the station platform. The car fumes as I walked back to our house, mingling with the flowers spilling through the park railings. The windows of the houses I passed were going gold and burnt orange in the setting sun. Then our house, gloomy with all the lights off. I stood outside, wishing my father was dead, wishing I could speak to Toby, or Edith, imagining them together as I stood there, rage building up inside me.

As soon as I opened the door I knew that something was wrong. Same hallway — dark, parquet flooring and deep red runner. Same steady tick of the Great Western Railway clock that hung in my father's study, coming muffled through the wall. There was a smell that I couldn't put my finger on, though. Something musty and sweet at the same time, and I kicked off my shoes, running through the house to look for Mr Tickles, who would normally have been at my feet by now.

I know exactly where I went looking for him. All his favourite places first: sofa, washing-machine, under my bed. Then my wardrobe, calling him, getting more and more frantic.

Did you not notice he was gone, Dad? Were you more shaken by Grandma's death than I realised? At the time I thought you just didn't care.

I rest my face in my hands. Even now it makes my stomach drop, thinking of how I found him, eventually, in my laundry basket. He must have been dead for a while, because his body was stiff and his eyes looked flat. I cradled him to me. I let my tears fall onto his coat, already greasy and matted from old age and showing patches of greyish skin underneath. For a second I thought I saw his chest rise and fall, and I had a sudden crazy thought that my tears had brought him back to life, but it must have been some air escaping, because his heart never started beating again.

★ ★ ★

My sessions with Mr Hicks continued the week after the funeral. He was wearing a green jumper when I opened his office door, and he must have had a shower not long before, because he looked and smelled minty-fresh. Seeing him made my heart-rate jack up.

'How are you doing, Tallulah?' he asked.

'Not so good.'

He pulled a sympathetic face. 'I hope you know I'm here if you want to talk about your grandmother. Anytime.'

It was Toby I really wanted to talk to though, and I felt my throat start to close up.

'Don't cry. Here — have a tissue.' Mr Hicks scrabbled around on the desk and handed me a piece of off-white cloth.

'It's kind of dirty,' I said, holding it between my thumb and forefinger. Mr Hicks spread his arms and grinned ruefully. The cloth smelled like turpentine when I blew my nose in it.

'I like it when you smile, you know?'

'What *is* this?' I asked, scrunching it up.

'A sketch I was working on earlier.'

'Sorry I snotted all over it.'

'I'll take it as a veiled critical reaction.' He picked up the bin and held it out to me. 'Would you like a glass of water?'

'Thanks.'

He went off and came back with a glass. The water in it was warm and cloudy; I took a sip and thought about spitting it back out, but Mr Hicks was leaning against the desk on my side now, right next to me. 'I hope your friends are looking after you properly.'

I tried to make a non-committal noise.

'Well, if you don't mind me asking, how's your relationship with your dad, then? Maybe this is a time for you both to get to know each other.'

'It's alright.'

'Are you sure?'

'It's the same as always.' I put down my glass, trying not to meet his eye.

'Of course, of course,' Mr Hicks said. He put his hand on mine; it felt warm and dry. An image of him holding me, tilting my face upwards, came into my mind, and I blushed so hard it felt like pins and needles. He picked my hand off the table and held it in both of his. I thought of Toby again, and the camping trip, and now Toby and Edith together. Him kissing her instead of me. Edith looking up at him adoringly. I pressed my fingers into the heel of Mr Hicks' palm; I thought I could feel his pulse underneath the skin. I kept looking into his eyes; he didn't flinch, didn't move his hand away. My heart was knocking about in my chest so hard I thought my ribs might break. All I could think about was how much Toby would hate it if I kissed Mr Hicks.

'I really like seeing you,' I said. 'I mean . . . you're cool.'

He kept looking at me; the corners of his mouth twitched. 'You're pretty cool yourself.'

'No I'm not.'

'You're beautiful, you're independent, you're smart. You're not a fake, Tallulah, like a lot of the other girls your age.' He squeezed my hand back, and let go of it. 'Sorry, I shouldn't have said that. You wouldn't see it. You don't have to try to force some semblance of creativity into these useless lumps.' He laughed. 'I'm joking, of course. But you have a special way of looking at things.' He jerked his head in the direction of the door. 'And you're better than them. Especially your friends, from the sounds of it. They should be really taking care of you at this stage, and instead you're being neglected.'

'They're busy.'

'Too busy for grief?'

'I guess.'

He turned my chair so I was facing him head-on, and leaned towards me, looking right into my eyes. 'Well, remember you always have a friend here. Just use discretion. Always consider whether it's in our best interests to draw negative attention to ourselves, especially in your position here, which is . . . ' — he looked like he was searching for the right word — ' . . . tenuous. Does that make sense?'

'Okay,' I said. I could feel the heat of his

breath on my face, and my own was coming too fast. Mr Hicks looked so serious — I didn't know if I was in trouble for what I'd said earlier.

He straightened up and smiled. 'Are you done with the water?'

'Yeah.'

He moved around to the other side of the desk and sat down, looking back to his old self. 'Well — we should talk about your academic progress. How do you feel about the summer exams?'

★ ★ ★

'So, come to the party,' I said. 'My cousin invited me — it's for all the Drama Group and their teacher.'

'Yeah, I've heard about her,' John said. 'Batty.' He nudged Toby with his foot. 'Maybe you'll get lucky. Oh wait — '

'Have you ever even spoken to a girl and not made her throw up?' I asked him.

'Ouch,' John said. 'Just because . . . '

'Shut up, John,' Toby said.

'You haven't even heard what I was going to say.'

'No one wants to hear what you've got to say,' Francis said.

None of us had discussed Toby and Edith's relationship since John had told me. Toby had been avoiding me and Edith was away on a language trip with her German class that wouldn't get back until later that afternoon.

'Anyway,' I said. 'I have to go.' Toby started to say something but I picked up my bag and slung it over my shoulder. 'See you lot later. The party's at nine.'

'See you there,' Francis said.

Edith was back by the time I finished my last class, waiting in the dorm for me. 'Tal,' she said. 'The trip was *amazing*. We drank beer out of a giant mug, although then the teacher caught us and we weren't allowed out of the hostel again at night, but Amy met this German boy and snuck out and then we had to cover for her.'

'I thought you hated Amy,' I said.

'She's not so bad,' Edith said. She was unpacking. 'She was really nice to me the whole time — she thinks Toby's really handsome, she said.'

'Good for her,' I said. I lay down on my bed, and stared up at the ceiling.

'Tal, are you mad at me?' Edith asked. She stopped unpacking and came and sat on the end of my bed. 'Toby said that nothing was happening between you.'

Oh did he? 'Nothing was.'

'Yeah, but,' Edith said. 'I just feel bad that it happened behind your back.'

I shrugged and gritted my teeth.

Edith got up. 'As long as you're okay with it,' she said.

'Whatever. Are you coming to the party?'

'Oh yeah, Toby invited me,' she said.

'No he didn't,' I said. 'I did. After my cousin invited me, remember?'

'Are you *sure* you're not mad at me?' Edith asked.

'Sure,' I said and felt like pushing her down

the stairs. 'I'm gonna have a shower.'

'Okay,' Edith said. 'I'll have one after you. I've got so much to tell you about the trip. And this one thing that Amy did . . . ' She started laughing.

I picked up my towel and left the room.

★ ★ ★

We met the boys behind the gym. The two of us got there first and crouched down by the grey wheelie bin, waiting for the others. I lit a cigarette while Edith fussed with her tights. She stopped and watched me inhale. 'Does your dad know you smoke?' she asked.

'I don't know. Maybe,' I said. I'd had four or five beers before we left the dorm and I could feel the blood starting to build up at the base of my neck; I was going to have a massive headache tomorrow.

Edith was running her fingers through her hair with a worried expression. 'How do I look?' she asked.

'Fine.'

'Really, how do I look?'

I looked at her properly. Her lips were smeared with orange lipstick, and her eyelashes were very long, making her eyes look huge.

'Very pretty,' I said. She did look kind of pretty, in a really messy way.

'Tal, you here?' Francis' voice hissed.

'Yeah.'

We stood and walked around the bin. The boys were huddled together on the other side, looking unsure of themselves.

'What now?' Francis asked. He was carrying cans of lager in his trouser and coat pockets; all of them were, I could hear sloshing and clinking coming from everyone.

'I'll see if I can find my cousin.'

The bungalow was twenty metres or so from the gym. We could hear music coming from inside, and light pooled on the grass by our feet through a chink in the curtains. I walked up to the front door and knocked; a girl in a yellow tutu opened it. She had a plastic cup full of clear liquid in one hand, and a cigarette in the other. I knew her name — Bailey — she was one of the prefects in the A-Level year; last month she'd given a reading at assembly on the dangers of getting into strangers' cars. 'Yeah?' she said. 'What do you want?'

'Is Starr around?'

She bent forwards; her breath was sickly sweet and her makeup was running. 'Come in,' she said. 'I'll try to find her for you.'

I followed her in, leaving the others outside. There was a narrow, packed corridor with five rooms leading off it, two on each side and one at the end. Through the first left-side door, kids were dancing in the living-room. On the right, in the kitchen, more were mixing cocktails. As I looked in, one boy was drinking out of a ladle.

'Not in here,' Bailey said, poking her head into the living-room. 'Let's try the back.'

We picked our way down the corridor. She pointed to the second door on the left. 'Judith's bedroom. It's out of bounds.' She pushed open the door on the right. I could see a small bathroom with yellowish tiles on the walls. A boy was asleep in the bath; another was sitting on the toilet with his hand up the top of the girl in front of him. His face was ecstatic. The girl turned towards us. Her eyes were glassy and she was clutching a bottle of tequila at her side. ''Sup Bailey,' she said.

'Someone's gonna puke,' Bailey whispered to me. We backed out.

'Only one room left,' she said. 'This is where we have workshops sometimes.'

She pushed open the door to a conservatory. The drama teacher was in the middle of the room, playing the bongos. Starr was sitting on the piano, rolling a cigarette. One of her followers was standing next to her, mimicking the drama teacher's eyes-closed, head-back pose. Two boys were flicking through a copy of *Lady Chatterley's Lover*, laughing at something about halfway through.

'Tallulah,' someone called. I turned on my heel and felt sick all of a sudden. Mr Hicks and a tall, horsey woman were standing over by the window, looking at the room with raised eyebrows. He beckoned me over. I thought he was going to tell me to go home, but he just nudged the woman and nodded at me. 'This is one of my art students from year eleven.' He was being normal with me again.

The woman looked me up and down. 'She looks very young.' She wore a large gold cuff on her left wrist and a short red dress that she kept tugging down at the hem. 'Gary.' She put her hand on his arm. 'Do we have to stay here? Watching Judith do her whole ethnic thing is making me feel nauseous.'

'I'm finding it quite amusing,' Mr Hicks said. 'What do you think, Tallulah?'

They both looked at me. I shrugged.

The woman sneered. 'Don't pick on her, Gary, she's just a baby.'

I felt my face heat up. 'Later,' I said, and turned away, catching Starr's eye.

'Tallie, you made it,' she called, waving at me and nearly falling off the piano.

I walked over to her.

'This is my cousin Tallie,' Starr said, nodding towards me. 'This is Melia.'

'Melia?'

'Short for Amelia,' the girl said. She tossed her hair over her shoulder.

'Sorry about that,' I said; Starr took a sip to hide her grin. 'I went to Grandma's funeral,' I told her.

'Bummer,' she said.

'Your mum wasn't there again.'

Starr shrugged. 'Don't look at me — she never explains herself.'

I looked down at the ground, feeling really tired all of a sudden. Starr gave me a gentle prod with her foot. 'Sorry . . . You know,' she said. 'I think she was genuinely shocked, though. Me too. I always thought Grandma would outlive everyone.'

'Thanks.'

'Speaking of family, did you hear about Aunt Gillian and that creep?' she asked.

381

'You mean Uncle George?'

'Yeah. The pervert.' Starr wiggled on the piano, trying to pull her dress down.

'What happened?'

'They're getting a divorce.'

'Oh?'

'Yeah. Big shock, 'cos it's the first in the family or something. My mum's hysterical.'

'She's upset?'

'Are you kidding? She's so happy she nearly soiled herself. Anything that Gillian does wrong makes her feel all warm and fuzzy.' Starr took another sip of her drink.

'Why are they getting divorced?'

'He's a criminal,' Starr said. 'I know — like, duh. But it's just embezzling, or something boring like that. So it's bye bye Georgie.'

'Yeah, I can't see Aunt Gillian visiting him in prison.'

'Maybe for conjugal visits,' Starr said, and snorted. 'Not.'

'So, you here by yourself, Tallie?' Melia interrupted.

'My friends are outside.'

'Who'd you bring?' Starr asked.

'Toby and that lot.'

'Oh God, not that idiot, John too?' Starr pulled a face. 'He's always trying to get into everyone's pants. And what's up with you and Toby?'

'Nothing,' I said, studying my fingernails. 'He's going out with Edith.'

'The ginger?' Starr threw her head back and laughed. Melia copied her. 'Good for her.' She stopped when she saw my face. 'How do you feel about it?'

'I don't own him.'

'That's not how the rumours went.'

'Whatever,' I said. 'They can do what they want. I'm gonna go get them.'

'I'm gonna smoke this,' Starr said. She hopped off the piano and opened a window. 'Help yourself to alcohol. Someone brought vodka — it's in the freezer.'

'Cool,' I said.

'Who opened a window?' the drama teacher asked shrilly. 'It's ruining my concentration.'

I went back outside. The others were standing around awkwardly. It was windy and Edith was only wearing a thin dress — her lips had turned blue and she was shivering, although no one had thought to offer her a jacket, or she'd refused one.

'Come in,' I said. 'There's some vodka in the freezer, apparently.' I held the door open and stepped to the side.

'Dude,' Francis said, coming past me. 'The drama group. They're mental.' I looked at where he was pointing; four boys in the kitchen were shaking salt out onto the counter and snorting it.

'I'm gonna find some girl who's wasted,' John said, pushing his way into the living-room.

Toby and Edith came inside. I shut the door after them. Edith's eyes looked bigger than ever.

'Let's go find this vodka,' I said to her.

The boys in the kitchen made a path for us to walk to the freezer. I opened it and started pulling out drawers. There were two bottles of vodka in the second drawer, and next to them a bag of frozen peas, a pair of boxer shorts and a wooden spoon.

'I put those there,' one of the boys said. 'Nice surprise for Judith tomorrow morning.'

His friends high-fived him.

'Great,' I said. 'You seem really funny.' I took a nearly-empty vodka bottle out and picked two plastic cups off the side. 'Let's go, Ed.'

'Don't you want me, baby?' the boy called after us. His friends laughed and I heard slapping sounds, like they were high-fiving again.

'Jerks,' I said.

'Yeah,' Edith said, quietly.

We found the others in the living-room. John was dancing in the middle of the floor and the other two were sitting in a corner. Some girl was in Francis' lap and he looked at me, embarrassed. I grinned at him.

'Hold these,' I said to Edith. I poured us two half-cups of vodka to finish the bottle. We lifted them up and knocked them together.

'Cheers,' I said. I drank a mouthful; the vodka tasted disgusting, but it was warm on the way down. Edith retched.

'That's so *strong*,' she said.

'I'll find you some juice,' Toby said, getting up and leaving the room.

'Want any?' I asked Francis.

He held his can up.

'Okay,' I said. I drank another mouthful and could feel my stomach heaving already.

'Are you alright?' Francis asked me. The girl in his lap hiccupped.

384

I nodded. My head felt light, it must have been the spirit interacting with the beers. I downed the vodka and jumped up, nearly falling over; someone on my right put a hand out to prop me up.

'I'm getting some more,' I said.

I walked into the kitchen; the back of my head was thumping and the room was spinning.

'Tal,' I heard Toby say. 'You don't look good, you should have some water.'

'I'm fine.'

I couldn't see him until he put his hand out to close the freezer drawer. 'You don't look fine,' he said. 'You should go back to the dorm. I'll take you.'

'I don't think Edith would like that.'

'Listen,' he said. His fingers were digging into my wrist. 'I'm sorry about the camping trip, and I'm sorry that I got with Edith. I know you said you were cool with it but I don't think you are.'

'Get over yourself.'

'Look, if you're *not* cool with it . . . ' He leaned in closer, until our foreheads were almost touching. 'If you're not . . . If you just said that . . . '

'What?'

'I would end it with her.'

'How nice of you,' I said.

He drew back and looked at me. 'I mean it. I would break up with her right now if you asked me to.'

My wrist hurt from where he was squeezing it. I looked at his face, floating in the middle of the fug of alcohol. Him and Edith made no sense, I thought. They were opposites. Does Edith know about your brother? I wanted to ask. I looked at his eyebrows, which were thick and black, and his eyelashes too. They made me want to reach out and tug them. It was strange, I thought, how some people looked so good you wanted to be around them. Like Toby. Like my mother.

'Just go back to your girlfriend,' I said. I could hear myself slurring.

'Fine.' Toby kicked a cupboard door and left the room.

'*He's* not very happy,' someone said and everyone laughed again. This room found everything funny. A boy put his arm around my waist and tried to kiss me. I elbowed him in the stomach, picked up the bottle and left.

I stood in the living-room doorway and poured myself some more alcohol. I saw Toby and Edith kissing in one corner, his hands in her hair. I sat down on the sofa arm, spilling half my drink. Another couple were kissing next to me; I tried to focus on them and realised it was two boys.

Starr was dancing in the middle of the room now with Melia and two other girls. John was hanging around them with his mouth open. One of the girls said something to Starr and pointed at me. They stopped dancing and came over.

'Your cousin looks smashed,' one of them said, giggling.

'Tallie, are you wasted?' Starr asked.

'No,' I said. I drank some more.

Starr eyed me. I belched; the girls made faces and backed away.

'Tallie was never very refined, were you?' Starr said.

'Can't make a silk purse out of a sow's ear,' I said.

'What does that even mean?'

'Dunno,' I said. 'Grams used to say it all the time.' I felt tears building up behind my eyelids. 'She's dead now.'

'Jeez, Tallie, what a downer,' Starr said. She took my shoulders. 'Sort yourself out, go drink some water in the bathroom until you feel better.' She reached for the vodka. 'I'll take this.'

'I'm fine,' I said. I fell backwards onto the two boys, who swore at me and left.

Starr gave me a pitying look and pulled me upright. 'Pace yourself, Cuz. I'm not gonna rub your back while you spew.'

They went back to the dance floor. I stayed on the sofa, drinking and avoiding looking at Toby and Edith.

'Why did you leave?' someone said quietly in my ear. I turned my face upwards. Mr Hicks looked down at me, his head tilted to one side.

'I don't like your friend,' I said.

'Nicola?' he said. 'She's just having a bitchy day.' He sat down next to me.

'Oh yeah?' I said. 'Me too.'

'Why?'

'I don't want to discuss it.'

'If you can't tell your mentor . . . '

'Why don't you just be a guy tonight, and not my mentor?'

He smiled.

'I'd much rather hang out with you than any

387

of these kids here.' I put my hand on his knee. I tried to see out of the corner of my eye if Toby was watching us. Everything was kind of blurred, except Mr Hicks, when I turned back. His face was perfectly neutral.

'Come and talk to me outside, Tallulah.'

I got up and followed him out the room. I thought I saw Toby and Francis exchange looks as I left.

Mr Hicks found a spot in the corridor to lean against the wall. He was drinking orange juice. 'I should report you, you know,' he said. 'Unless that's lemonade you've got in your hand.'

'It's lemonade.'

Mr Hicks put his hand over mine and brought it and the cup up to his face. 'It doesn't smell like lemonade.'

'So, report me,' I said, feeling annoyed at how uptight he was being. I twisted my hand out of his. 'Is that why you brought me out here?'

'You know you're not allowed to drink until you're eighteen,' Mr Hicks said. 'As a matter of fact, I don't believe any of your friends are eighteen yet either.'

I shrugged.

'The boys I'm willing to overlook because they're in the sixth-form and they're not my pupils,' he said, looking at me out of the corner of his eye. 'But I'm your personal tutor. I'm responsible for you. And I'm very fond of you Tallulah, you know.' He took a sip of his orange juice.

My head was too clogged up to follow the conversation, but Mr Hicks was pausing like he expected me to say something.

'Really?' I asked.

'Yes.' He looked at me from under his lashes. 'I'm aware we have a — connection. That's why I agreed to take you on as my personal student. It's why I can't just let you run amok tonight.'

I downed the vodka. 'It's all gone now,' I said. Breathing and talking at the same time was becoming difficult. 'You can just pretend you never saw it.' I threw my empty cup on the floor and put my hand on his chest, partly to keep my balance, partly to feel him. I took a deep breath in and tilted my face up towards him, like I'd imagined in our last session, but he didn't kiss me.

'If I pretended I hadn't seen you,' Mr Hicks said, and put his arm around my shoulders, pulling me towards him. 'If I pretended that, then you would owe me a big favour.'

Someone walked past and he shifted slightly, so that I was leaning into him, like I couldn't stand.

'Stupid kids,' he said to the person passing us.

I looked up. It was the girl from earlier, Bailey. I felt like telling him he didn't need to put on this show, that she was already smashed, but something was wrong, although I couldn't quite work out what it was.

Mr Hicks was squeezing my shoulder. I felt like I was going to be sick. I dropped the vodka bottle I'd been clutching in one hand and he yelled and jumped backwards. I looked down. The lid hadn't been screwed tight and the bottoms of his cream chinos were soaking wet.

'Bloody mess,' he muttered.

'Sorry, sir,' I said. The ceiling started to slide down towards me and the floor slid upwards; I closed my eyes and felt myself falling, but something stopped me. I just wanted to rest my head, which was getting heavy.

'Timber,' someone yelled.

'What's going on out here?' another voice asked; it sounded upset. I felt myself shuffled along, then heard a door click.

'One of the younger students appears to be intoxicated,' a man's voice said.

'Oh dear,' the upset voice said. 'A lower-school student? How did she get in?'

'There isn't exactly a strict door policy,' the man said. 'You know, Judith, I think it's probably best if we don't mention to any of the staff that she was here.'

'Of course, oh dear. Herbert has always been against these parties — oh dear. I never thought anyone *underage* would be drinking.'

'Half these kids are underage.'

I opened my eyes and tried to focus. I was being held upright; my head was hanging down and I could see a pair of shoes and two bare feet. The feet were bony, with freckles all over; the toenails were yellowish at the ends and curling inwards. Looking at them made me start to feel sick again.

'Socks,' I said.

'What did she just say?' the feet asked.

'I can't tell,' the shoes said. They were brown loafers with tassels on.

'Socks,' I said louder.

'Are you alright?' shoes asked me. 'What are you trying to tell us?'

'Perhaps we should take her to the sick bay?' feet suggested.

'Yes, don't worry. I'll do that,' the shoes said. 'You stay here and keep an eye on the rest of them.'

'Oh, thank you so much. You're such a wonderful help.' The feet were fluttering their eyelashes. I felt myself being picked up.

'We'll go out the back way,' shoes said. 'Don't want to draw unnecessary attention here.'

'Of course, of course.' The feet moved in front of us, opening the back door and shooing us out. 'Thank you, again. I knew I could count on you.'

I felt sleep fighting me, trying to make me let go of everything. I didn't have the strength to hold out. I closed my eyes — I couldn't hear anything but buzzing, and a strange panting noise. I couldn't see anything. I couldn't feel anything, not even the sickness anymore.

The shoes were carrying me away from the party. They weren't being very careful with me. I was being bumped and shaken about. We stopped and I heard the scratch of metal on metal, and then a door open.

'Nearly there,' the shoes said. There was a click and I felt a pink burning inside my eyelids. I could smell turpentine. The shoes laid me down on something soft. They were soothing me, stroking my hair and taking my cardigan off. I moaned and tried to turn over. The shoes took my shoulders and pushed me back.

'I'm looking after you now,' they said. 'You're okay.'

I groaned.

'You've been very bad tonight,' they said. 'Drinking, sneaking into parties, answering back. You're a very wild child.'

'No,' I said, but it was muffled.

'Yes,' the shoes said. I felt them undoing the buttons on my shirt. I tried to stop them. I pushed fingers away, struck out wildly in all directions. The fingers came back and caught my wrists, holding them, tightly at first, then softer as I felt my strength flowing out of me. I could hear shushing sounds.

'No,' I said. 'Don't.'

'You want this just as much as I do,' the shoes said. 'You've been playing games with me all year. Pretending you're shy and sweet, watching me in class, blushing when I talk to you. Then swearing you're not the kid everyone thinks you are. And the other day, when you gave me the signal. I knew what you were doing. You're not an innocent, are you, Tallulah? You know how you make me feel.'

'I didn't,' I said. The words felt like they were being dredged up from somewhere deep inside me.

'Oh yes, you've been very bad,' the shoes said. 'Be a good girl now.'

Water gathered beneath my eyelids in frustration. I tried to open my eyes, but it was too much. I felt something scrabbling around at the buckle of my belt and then my jeans being pulled down to my knees.

'No,' I said again. This time I couldn't gather enough breath to speak out loud. A heaviness was on top of me, then I felt something slippery thrust inside my mouth. I coughed and retched. Whatever was on top of me shuddered, making my head rattle and a wave of pain wash over me. I heard grunting noises; they seemed to be coming from inside my mouth, but I wasn't making them. Then the weight lifted off of me, and I could feel hot blasts down near my crotch.

'Pink. Very unexpected,' the shoes said. 'Did you wear these especially?' I heard the sound of someone sniffing, long breaths drawn in. 'I can't tell you how good you smell.'

Then my knickers were being pulled down. I tried to hold on to them, keep them up, but my head was getting heavier and heavier. That was the last thing I knew.

★ ★ ★

'Tallie?' a voice said.

Slowly, light was beginning to come back to me. Shapes shifted in front of my face, blurred at first, then they cleared.

Starr was sitting at the end of my bed. She was rubbing my leg; her eyes were pink and puffy. 'Tallie, are you okay?' she asked.

'Yeah,' I said. Starr leant forwards and I realised I hadn't spoken. 'Yeah,' I tried again. Again my voice wouldn't come out.

'Tallie, what happened?'

I sank back onto my pillows, exhausted.

'Mr Hicks said he tried to take you to the sick

bay,' Starr said. 'But you broke away from him and ran off. We found you a couple of hours later. You had all these cuts and . . .'

I looked down at my body; there were two red marks around my left wrist, and a long scratch on my arm. My jaw felt tender, too. I rubbed it.

'Did you get them from falling over?' Starr asked.

I shrugged — I don't remember.

'Did someone hurt you?' she asked, her voice lowered.

I shrugged again. Images swam messily in front of me.

'Oh, Tallie.' She sounded like she was going to say something more, but then held back.

I tried to drag my voice up to the surface. 'Water,' I finally croaked.

'Of course.' Starr jumped up and went to get me some water. I lay in bed, hands clenching the duvet until they got weak. 'Don't think about it,' I muttered.

'What was that?' Starr came back.

'Nothing.' I sat up, took the glass from her and drained it. I lay back down and rolled over. My whole body ached.

'Are you going to talk to me?' Starr asked.

I closed my eyes, but that made me feel dizzy.

'They're not going to call your father,' Starr said. 'Mr Hicks persuaded the other teachers not to tell Mr Purvis. He said you're under enough stress already, and he'd keep an eye on you.'

I stayed on my side, with my back to her.

'I'll let you sleep,' Starr whispered. 'I'll be in the common room if you need me.'

I got up and showered when Starr left. I went over every inch of my body with the soap, scrubbing between my legs especially hard. When I turned the water on myself, I saw it had gone pink. After I turned off the tap, I stayed in the cubicle for a moment, leaning my head against the wall, eyes closed tightly.

Out of the cubicle I looked at myself in the mirror. I seemed the same — same hair, same face, same breasts, although now there were little purple bruises around my nipples and on my cheek. I wrapped a towel tightly around myself. 'Don't think about it,' I said to my reflection.

'Tal?' Edith called.

She was standing in the middle of our room; Toby was behind her. 'Are you okay?' she asked. 'We were just wondering if you needed anything?'

'Nope,' I said. I forced a smile for them and adjusted my towel.

'Can I talk to Tal alone?' Toby asked Edith.

'Yeah, sure,' Edith said. She turned on her way out and gave me a worried look. 'Tal, you shouldn't *drink* so much.'

'Right,' I said.

Edith left. Toby faced me, hands in his pockets.

'Turn around,' I said. 'I need to put something on.'

He turned away; I saw his face screw up as he did. I went back into the bathroom and took my robe from its hook. I'd never used it. It felt soft, like it had when my grandmother had given it to me the previous year. I pulled it on and tied the belt in a double-knot around the waist.

Toby was facing away from me when I re-entered the dorm. I cleared my throat and he turned; his face was blank now.

'Cigarette?' I asked him.

'Yeah,' he said.

We went back into the bathroom and opened the window. I sat on the toilet cistern and Toby stood in front of me. I lit two cigarettes and passed one to him.

'How did you get in?' I asked.

'Francis and John are distracting the House-mistress,' he said.

'I see,' I said. I crossed my legs; Toby looked away.

'What did you do last night?' he asked me.

I inhaled deeply. 'I went to the party with you guys,' I said. 'I had too much to drink. Then I don't know. I don't remember.'

'Do you really not remember?' Toby asked.

'Really.'

Toby sucked on his cigarette and looked down at the floor.

'I was the one who found you,' he said, eventually. 'You were moaning and you were pretty scratched — you kept saying something over and over again.'

I inhaled again and looked out the window.

'Don't you wanna know what you were saying?' Toby asked.

'No,' I said. My voice shook. 'And I don't want to talk about last night.'

'Why, if you don't remember?' Toby asked.

I hopped off the cistern and stubbed the butt out in the sink. 'I don't want to talk about it,' I said. I opened the toilet lid and dropped the butt down into the water. Toby watched me carefully.

'You're not going to get suspended,' he said. 'You're not even being reported for drinking underage.'

'Yeah, I know,' I said. 'Starr already told me.'

'Mr Hicks sorted that out.'

'I know.'

'Don't you think that's nice of him?' Toby asked. 'He didn't have to go out of his way for you.'

I looked out of the window again. Plump white clouds drifted in the sky; the sun poured itself through the open space.

'I don't want to talk about it,' I said. I reached over and flushed the toilet and watched as my cigarette was sucked out of sight.

PART THREE

Bones

16

There were five weeks left of term after the drama party and the summer was rolling out before us. Windows were left permanently open in the classrooms and from where I sat in English I could see the front lawn. On Fridays, the gardeners cut it, and the smell of fresh grass mixed with the trails of honeysuckle, jasmine and lavender that grew beneath the classroom windows. Ladybirds traipsed across the doodles in my exercise books, legs and wings akimbo, like they were coming apart in the heat. One time I saw a crow with a worm in its beak hopping around on the gravel outside, the worm wriggling desperately like some dull pink ribbon caught in the wind.

Sometimes I felt my eyes fill up for no reason, in the middle of a class. Sometimes I missed my mother so much I hated her.

I stopped hanging out with the others, stopped eating lunch. I showered three or four times a day, and sometimes at night.

'Tallulah, don't you have a private tuition session now?' my maths teacher asked me when I showed up to a lunchtime revision class.

'I don't need them anymore,' I said.

'Right,' she said, and went back to her marking.

One Monday we were called into an emergency assembly. Mr Purvis stood on stage, his face the colour of beetroot. A serious crime had been committed on school property. Mr Hicks' office had been broken into and defiled, he said.

'And to make matters worse, this same student left a threatening note for Mr Hicks. And he tells me this has been going on for *weeks*.' His voice crescendoed; I thought I could see spit forming at the corners of his mouth. 'This school will not tolerate the bullying of its staff by pupils, or *anyone*. I suggest that if you have any information about the perpetrator you come forward with it now. Otherwise, if this behaviour does not stop immediately, we will be forced to question *everyone*.'

Whispers broke out as he swept off the stage. I looked around for Toby. He was sitting two rows behind me with his arm around Edith's shoulder. Her face was white. Toby looked utterly calm.

Edith tried to speak to me after the assembly; I saw her pushing through people and turned away quickly. I didn't feel like talking.

I nicked an apple from the canteen and went to the far side of the playing fields. I took my shoes and socks off and dug my toes into the soil. I could hear someone calling my name in the distance but I ignored it; I lay back, shielding my eyes from the sun with one arm, and bit into the apple.

'Jeez, are you deaf or something?'

Starr flopped down next to me.

'Selectively.'

'Well, thanks for making me run after you like an idiot.'

'I didn't make you run after me.'

I threw my apple core into a bush and lit a cigarette. I tried to make the clouds above me into something interesting, but they just looked like clouds. 'Lack of imagination', my grandmother would have said. I blew smoke rings out above my head.

'What's wrong with you anyway? You've been really quiet recently.'

'When's recently?'

'Don't be annoying,' Starr said. 'I know something's wrong. You can tell me.'

'I'm late.'

I watched her face, waiting for the realisation to hit her. Her mouth dropped open. 'How late?'

'I don't know,' I said, running my fingers through my hair. 'A few weeks, maybe. I was never regular.'

She grabbed my arm. 'Who's the father?'

'Does it matter?'

'Yes,' she said. She looked uneasy. 'Maybe not right now.'

'It's not important.'

'Tallie . . . '

'Yes?'

'You've got to tell him.'

'No way. You know how it is.'

'Tallie, come on,' Starr said. 'Stop being such a fucking hero and ask for help.'

'I'm not being a hero,' I said. I looked back up at the clouds. 'My dad won't want to deal with this.'

'If you don't tell him then I will.'

'You can't,' I said, gripping her hand. 'You can't grass on me.'

'It's not grassing if you need help.'

'You can't tell or it's grassing,' I said.

Starr smacked her forehead with her free hand. 'We're not ten anymore, Tallie,' she said.

'Fuck off, Starr,' I said. 'You can't tell him, and you can't make me either.'

'You can't just ignore it and think it'll go away.'

I stubbed out my cigarette and rested my hands on my lower abdomen. It still felt tight; nothing moved. I drummed my fingers on the skin. 'It's fine,' I said. 'Everything's fine.'

I wiped my nose on the back of my hand. An ant or something was crawling up my back. Sweat trickled from my armpit; time for another shower. I put my shoes and socks back on and jumped up, too fast. Everything started to go grainy for a moment, then black. I reached out and my hand touched hedge. I held on to the branches until my eyes started to clear. 'Help . . . '

'What is it, hon?' Starr asked, jumping up too. That's why I liked her — she forgave everything so easily. 'You changed your mind?'

'No,' I said. 'But I'm gonna go to the nurse. Can you come with me?'

'Yeah, sure,' Starr said. 'Now?'

'I guess,' I said.

'Okay,' she said, and put her arm around my shoulder, then stopped. 'Shoot, I have a careers interview in five minutes. Can we go after that?'

'No, it's okay,' I said. 'I can go by myself.'

'You don't have to do that. Just wait for me. Or I'll cancel.'

'I'll wait,' I said. 'Don't cancel.'

'Are you sure?'

'Yeah. I'll go have a shower first.'

'Okay, come find me afterwards yeah? I'll be in my common room.'

'Yeah.'

'Promise?'

'Promise.'

'I've gotta run,' she said. 'You okay getting back to the dorm by yourself?'

I rolled my eyes. 'Yes.'

'I'm a worrier.' She was grinning and I grinned back. 'See you later, idiot.'

She jogged off and I straightened up and looked around; my hands were itchy from the prickles on the bush. Boys had gathered in the field next to me while I was lying down and a rugby game had started. I saw a group of girls waving handmade flags — Francis must be there.

I tried to follow Starr and jog around the outskirts of the field, keeping away from everyone. It felt harder than normal, like I was seriously out of shape. I hadn't been playing netball recently; my PE teacher had threatened to haul me up before Mr Purvis, but I'd still refused. I couldn't face changing in front of everyone.

I slowed down when I reached my dorm building and went inside. Edith was in our room, making notes from her Latin textbook. 'Oh.' She tried to smile. 'Hi.'

'Hi.'

'You forget something?'

'Nope,' I said. 'This is my room too.'

I shut the door. Edith put her book down.

'Why are you reading in here during lunch?'

'I had a fight with Toby,' she said. 'What have you been doing?'

I shrugged. 'Eating lunch.'

She fidgeted. 'Tal, do you know anything about . . . '

'I didn't do it, if that's what you're asking,' I said. I peeled off my shirt. Edith looked away.

'No, I didn't think you did,' she said. 'That's not what I'm asking.'

'I haven't spoken to anyone about it either,' I said. I felt exposed standing there, with the black of my bra showing through my white vest. Maybe my breasts were bigger, I thought. They felt sore around the nipples and fuller, somehow. I picked up my towel from where I'd left it, draped across my bed.

'Okay, whatever,' Edith said.

'Okay, whatever,' I mimicked.

'You've been really weird recently,' Edith said, frowning. She looked at me closely. 'How many showers have you had today?'

I shrugged.

Edith pursed her mouth. 'You know, sometimes I think you actually have issues, Tal. Like, serious issues.'

'Jesus Edith, pot calling kettle black much?'

She jumped up. 'I'm going to go find Toby.' She paused at the door. 'You know, if you're mad at me for going out with him, it'd be better if you just admitted it.'

'Stick it up your arse,' I replied.

She slammed the door behind her. I uncurled my fists; my hands were shaking.

I padded into the bathroom and turned the light on, looked at myself in the mirror, and turned it back off. I couldn't understand why Edith never said anything about how I looked like a pile of crap — my family certainly would have.

I showered in the dark and dried myself for a few minutes. I felt my breasts; they definitely felt heavier and more fleshy.

'Shit,' I said.

★　★　★

The nurse was temporarily away from her office. The notice said she'd be back in fifteen minutes, but it didn't say when she'd written it. I rested my head on the door, breathed fog onto its glass, then rubbed it off with my sleeve.

'Bloody NHS,' Starr said, sitting down on one of the orange chairs outside the office.

I sat next to her.

'Chewing gum?' she asked, offering me a stick. I took one and put it in my mouth, scrunching the wrapping up and pitching it into the bin on the other side of the corridor.

'I had to come here once,' she said. 'That fucking Melissa Albrecht hit me in the face during a hockey match.' She rubbed her nose like she was remembering the pain. 'I thought she broke it, but the nurse said she couldn't see any difference.'

Starr's nose was as perfect as it always had been.

'Yeah,' I said. 'I think Melissa might have cracked your head at some point, too.'

'Ha-ha. Only two more weeks of school left then.'

'Yep.'

'What are you doing this summer?'

'Dunno.' I chewed my lip. 'I thought I might go away with the boys, but that doesn't seem like a great idea anymore.'

'Hon,' she said, looking sympathetic. 'Do you want me to put a hit out on that Edith girl?'

I grinned.

'Try not to care about guys,' she said. 'If you don't care, you're never disappointed.'

'You're pretty bleak.'

She grinned. 'Mum's homespun wisdom — not mine.'

We were silent for a minute. I wondered if she knew about what our grandfather had done to Aunt Vivienne. Hey, so, funny story . . .

I stretched my legs out, then shifted in my seat; an ache had started down in my pelvis. I felt fuzzy, like I was in pain, but it was too far away to judge properly.

'You look kinda spaced out, you know.'

'I don't feel great,' I said. I rested my head between my legs. 'I think I'm gonna puke.' I felt my stomach contracting and something rushing up inside me, towards my throat and then out of my mouth.

'Holy shit,' Starr said.

I gasped, drawing air in with shaky breaths. I

408

was on my hands and knees, a pool of vomit in front of me. Starr was standing on her chair. 'What the fuck just happened?' she asked.

'I puked, arsehole.'

'Fuck,' Starr said. 'That fucking stinks.'

My throat was burning. I wanted water and my bed. I felt something sticky in my knickers. 'I think I'm gonna lie down,' I said.

'Here?' Starr asked.

'Yes,' I said. 'Right here.' I tried to give her a sarcastic look, but I was finding it hard to focus.

'Okay, okay,' Starr said. She climbed off her chair carefully and took me under the armpits, pulling me slowly to my feet. When I was upright I leant on her shoulder, trying to regain my balance.

'It's okay,' she said. She patted my back. 'I'll take you to the San.'

'No,' I croaked. 'My room.'

'I can't take you there,' she said, her forehead creasing. 'Someone's gotta see you first, check you're okay.'

'I'm okay,' I said, even as everything around me started to go black.

★   ★   ★

When I woke up my father was sitting by the bed. My eyes took a moment to focus on our surroundings: a white room with light-green curtains. It wasn't the San, definitely a hospital ward.

My father had his head cradled in his hands; he jumped when I shifted in the bed, and looked up. 'Tallulah,' he said. He seemed angry. 'You're fine.'

'Oh,' I said. It seemed weird that he was mad at me for being fine. I felt like giggling, but something inside me said it wasn't the time. My mouth felt like I'd been sucking on cotton wool balls. 'Where am I?'

'In the local hospital,' he said, and I wondered vaguely if it was the same one my grandmother had been in after her stroke. 'The school called for an ambulance after you wouldn't stop bleeding.'

'What happened?'

'They think, from the symptoms — and a useful piece of information provided by your cousin — that you may have experienced a miscarriage.'

Thanks for that, Starr.

'You'll have to have a D-and-C, but that's routine.' He stood and started pacing up and down at the end of my bed. 'You're extremely lucky.'

'Okay.'

His anger was almost physical, pinning me down. I felt exhausted already, although I'd only just woken up.

'How could you have done it, Tallulah?'

'What?'

'How could you have kept this to yourself?'

He stopped pacing and gripped the rail at the end of the bed. 'It was *incredibly* dangerous, especially with the symptoms you had. You could have had some serious complications.'

I closed my eyes. 'But I didn't?'

'No.'

'Okay then.'

'It's *not* okay, Tallulah.'

'Can we just forget it?'

'*Forget* it?'

'Please don't do the parenting routine now,' I said, opening my eyes. 'You can pretend you care when we've got witnesses.'

My father shook his head at me, his mouth puckered in disapproval. 'Don't *you* pull the teenage abandonment routine,' he said. 'I sent you to a school where you should have been stimulated and encouraged and kept safe, but it's clearly not worked out that way.'

'She needs rest, Dr Park,' a nurse said from the doorway. 'Perhaps you should wait outside.'

'I'll just be a minute,' my father said. He looked back at me, calmer now. 'What you did was very irresponsible,' he said. 'Frankly, I'm disappointed in you, Tallulah. But I'm more disappointed in the school for not keeping a better eye on you.'

'I guess they didn't want me any more than you did.'

'After all the trouble you've caused you should be grateful they haven't expelled you. That would look much worse on your record.'

'Grateful?'

'Yes, Tallulah, grateful. A lot of people have put themselves out for you over the years; gratitude should be much easier for you than it seems to be.'

I swallowed, and felt the urge to giggle again. I'm losing my mind. Going cuckoo.

411

He sat down, looking tired. 'Nevertheless. It's obviously quite a shock, what you've just been through — that's why I've decided to withdraw you from school and place you in a remedial college.'

'You're joking, right?'

My father frowned. 'No.'

'I don't get a say in this at all?'

'I thought you'd be glad to leave. You always wanted to before.'

'I wanted to go home,' I said. 'To Grandma's or somewhere.' I felt my eyes fill in frustration and I swallowed again. 'I don't want to go to a remedial school.'

'Well, I'm afraid the Headmaster is in agreement with me on this one,' my father said. 'You don't have a choice.' He passed his hand over his eyes. 'I'm taking you home for a week to recuperate. But then you'll be starting at your new college.'

'Can't I just get a tutor?'

'I'm sorry, Tallulah,' he said. 'If you're to have any chance of passing your exams you'll need an intensive learning environment over the next month or two.'

'They're just GCSEs,' I said. 'They don't mean anything.'

'They're important,' he said. 'So we'll see how you do this summer and take it from there.'

'Please,' I said, gripping my blanket.

'You're only sixteen,' he said eventually. 'I know it's hard to understand. I know you think I'm pushing you on this. But it's for the best. It's really the most important thing you can do

— educate yourself.'

'Mum left school at sixteen.'

'Your mother lost both her parents and had no support network.'

'Where's *my* support network?'

'*I'm* here,' my father said. 'Looking out for your welfare, as I always have done. Frankly, I think I deserve to be treated with more respect. I know your mother would have been sad to see you turn out so self-centred.'

I snorted. 'Don't talk about Mum like you knew anything about her.'

'Pardon me?'

'You probably never cared about her either, did you?'

'You're clearly feverish,' my father said, coldly. 'I'll get the nurse to come and take your temperature.'

'Why can't you do it?' I said. My skull felt like someone had it in a clamp. I dug the heel of my palm into my temple. 'You spend all your time at work, looking after other people, but you've never looked after us. I can't work out whether you're a shitty doctor, or just a shitty dad.'

My father was shaking his head. 'I know what you're really talking about here, Tallulah, but you're wrong.'

'How am I wrong?'

'You were a child. And you didn't see how it happened.'

'I heard you talking about it.'

'There was nothing I could do to save her. Believe me, Tallulah, you can be as unpleasant as

413

you want, but it can't make me feel worse than I already do.'

'Because you know it was your fault.'

'Because I couldn't do anything.'

'You didn't want us around, you were so mean to us. I know you were fighting with each other. You could probably have done something and you just pretended you couldn't.'

My father went purple. 'You can't honestly believe that.'

'And as soon as she was dead, you packed me off to boarding school.'

'Tallulah. That isn't funny.'

'And now you pull me out of school and send me to some remedial college where I have *no* friends.'

'I'm taking you out of the extremely expensive and desirable boarding school I sent you to because you're failing at your subjects and you . . . ' He stopped, looking at me.

I wanted to punch him. 'I what?'

'You got yourself into trouble,' he finished, and paused again. 'I thought you were smarter than that.'

'I was *raped.*'

Now he went white. 'You're making it up.'

'You think I'd *lie* about that?'

He jumped up and started pacing again. 'When did it happen?'

'About a month ago.'

'Why would you wait until now to tell me? Why wouldn't you tell the police or the school?'

'Why is it always my fault?'

'I don't understand,' my father was saying. 'I

414

don't understand how that could have happened. It's impossible.' He came forward and gripped my shoulders. 'Tallulah, if you're lying you have to stop it *right now*.'

'I was raped,' I yelled at him. 'Some arsehole raped me and then I was pregnant, and now I've had a miscarriage *and you were never there for me*.' I sat up and tried to swing my legs out of the bed. 'And it wasn't my fault, Dad. It wasn't my fault.'

My heart monitor was bleeping like crazy. I sensed, rather than saw, nurses hurrying in and trying to get me to lie down again. One of them hissed at my father, 'You should know better than to get the patient riled up like this, Doctor.'

'Tallulah,' he said, 'you're trying to pay me back for putting you in the school in the first place, but it won't work, do you understand me? I don't blame you, but . . . '

'*Get him out of here*,' I screamed. I carried on screaming until another of the nurses grabbed my father by the elbow and steered him to the door.

The first one who had looked in was shushing me. 'It's alright, calm down now. This isn't helping matters.'

I looked back at him as he was jostled out of the room, his face still white.

'I don't want to see him,' I shouted. 'Don't let him in.'

'Alright, Tallulah. Just calm down.'

I didn't see him again.

★ ★ ★

415

The nurse who gave me a check-up after the procedure told me briskly that I'd be able to leave that afternoon. 'Who shall we inform?' she asked, clipboard in hand.

'I'm taking a taxi,' I said. 'Back to school. Someone's meeting me there.'

'Your father?'

'No.'

'I see. Is it the young gentleman waiting outside?'

My heart thumped painfully. 'Who's waiting outside?'

'I don't know. He's at reception now.'

'Did he say his name was Toby Gates?'

'I didn't get his name.'

'Tell him I'm asleep,' I said.

'We're going to need the bed soon,' she said, and moved off.

I opened the door to my room a crack and peered down the hall to my left. I could see Toby sitting in a chair opposite the reception desk, his head tilted back. To my right the corridor marched onwards. I could see a sign for toilets and baby changing, and a payphone in the distance. I closed the door and got dressed quickly. I called a cab and then hung up and dialled reception.

'Can you pass on a message to Toby Gates?' I asked. 'He's at reception now. Tell him he needs to call Edith immediately at Honeysuckle House — it's important.'

I opened the door again and saw Toby sit up, like someone was talking to him. He looked in my direction, and pointed towards the pay phone sign. I gave it a minute; when I next looked out, he was gone.

I checked myself out of the hospital and got into the taxi. At school I asked the driver to wait for me. The Housemistress started out of her seat when I walked in, but I called to her, 'My dad's waiting outside. I just need to collect my things.'

She nodded and sat back down, looking awkward.

No one was in the dorm, luckily. I didn't know what I would say to Edith if I saw her, or anyone else. I grabbed my suitcase and shoved my clothes inside, my shoes, towel, the medical textbook, a packet of digestive biscuits I'd been stashing underneath the bed, my wallet, my toothbrush and two framed photographs: one of my mother, the other of my grandmother and me. I left the bracelet Edith had given me and Tom Sawyer — I still hadn't finished it.

I dragged my suitcase down the stairs and waved to the Housemistress. 'Bye.'

'Goodbye, Tallulah,' she said, looking like she was about to burst into tears. 'Don't forget us.'

The driver helped me manoeuvre my case into the taxi, climbed back in and started the meter. 'Where to, love?'

'Shrewsbury train station,' I said. As we drove off I looked straight ahead, but I heard the bell go for lunch break, and out of the corner of my eye, I thought I saw red hair among the heads bobbing between buildings on their way to the canteen.

I moved to a youth hostel in London. I didn't leave a forwarding address.

★ ★ ★

The sky outside the window is angry; the wind's picked up and is chasing dark clouds our way. They're chafing above the hospital, and I can almost feel the thunder building up inside them.

Amid the chaos, the city is winding down; cars choke into life then rumble off, cats spit at each other and people click off light switches and computer screens. I have a sudden craving for chips, fat yellow ones in paper twists with a mountain of salt on top. Malkie bought some like those for me when we came in to London to visit the mechanic. We found a wall somewhere to sit on, with a streetlight nearby, and ate them, picking them up with hands encased in fingerless gloves, letting the vinegar seep through the bottom of the wrapping and onto our jeans. We probably looked like a couple of tramps.

'Tallulah, love, you'll catch a cold like that,' Aunt Gillian says.

I move my forehead from the windowpane.

I wonder, if my mother was right about damaged people, how's it affected Aunt Gillian. I guess she worries too much and that keeps people at a distance. Aunt Vivienne doesn't trust anyone, Uncle Jack went to jail, my father . . .

'Did Grandad ever hit Dad?' I ask.

'Now, really,' Aunt Gillian says. 'Where did that come from?'

Aunt Vivienne gives a short bark. 'He hit all of us,' she says.

'Let's not talk about this now,' Aunt Gillian says.

'Though it was Jack he really had it in for.' Aunt Vivienne inspects her nails.

'Why?'

'Jack was the youngest, the baby. And he was naughty. Our father used to say the beating was to teach him discipline.'

'Jack wasn't just naughty,' Aunt Gillian says. 'You were both naughty. But Jack was *bad*. He was selfish and mean. He stole, Vivienne, and he wouldn't say sorry, ever. No one could handle him. He used to punch us. Bite us. He was *wild*.'

'He was a *little boy*,' Vivienne says, and I think I catch her eyes glistening. 'Not an animal. Don't speak of him like he was that. He's had a shitty life, Gillian, and you know it. The bastard used him as a punching bag and no one ever stepped in to help him. And Jack was the one who provoked Albert if he seemed to be focusing on me, don't forget that.' She wheels around to look at me. 'The last time he came for me, Jack bit through his finger. He left me alone after that.'

I'm stunned. I guess Uncle Jack was nice to one person, at least.

'There's only been one person who ever loved Jack in his entire life,' Aunt Vivienne continues. 'How do you think that must feel?'

'Well, he's difficult to love,' Aunt Gillian snaps.

They glare at each other, then Aunt Gillian throws her hands up in the air. 'For goodness' sake, you'd think we were invisible,' she says.

'Not much chance of that,' Aunt Vivienne says.

'I want to know what they're *doing*.'

'They're probably doing a pericardiocentesis,' I say, mechanically. 'They need to get rid of the fluid that's built up in the sac around the heart, so they put a needle inside and cut open a window to drain it.'

'Oh,' Aunt Gillian says; she looks green, then seems to make an effort to pull herself together. 'You *have* been a mine of information today.'

'I didn't realise we had a second doctor in the family,' Aunt Vivienne says. Her chest is still heaving. 'Pity we're not Jewish.'

'They had to do it for my mum,' I say, looking her in the eye.

'Ah,' she says, and looks away first.

There's a momentary silence.

'I'm going to find someone,' Aunt Gillian says.

Aunt Vivienne shrugs, and we follow her into the corridor.

'No one's around,' Aunt Gillian is saying. 'What kind of hospital is this, anyway?'

'Please,' someone says, and we turn as one. It's the nurse I spoke to this morning. 'We can't have you blocking the hall like this. There might be an emergency.' She looks sympathetic. 'Why don't you all go home for a few hours? Get some rest. I'm sure we won't be able to tell you anything definitive until later this evening. We'll call you as soon as we have any news.'

'I don't see why we have to leave,' Aunt Gillian says, querulously, 'we haven't been causing any trouble.'

'I'm not saying you're a trouble,' the nurse says, gently.

'Why then?' Aunt Gillian asks, but Aunt Vivienne interrupts her — 'Yes, thank you, Nurse. We'll go home and wait for a phone call.'

'I'll call you myself,' she says.

'I'm not going,' Aunt Gillian says, as soon as the nurse is out of earshot.

'You heard what the nice lady said, Gillian.'

'Viv, he's our *brother*. You don't go home when your brother is being operated on.'

'You do when you're told to.'

'Just think how it would look.'

'For God's sake, Gillian. We're not being followed by the national newspapers.'

'I know, I *know*,' Aunt Gillian says. She looks frantic, and I'm not sure she really heard Aunt Vivienne at all. 'There must be somewhere we can be out of the way. He's a *doctor* here for goodness' sake. You'd think they'd bend the rules a little for his family. We're almost one of them.'

Aunt Vivienne looks pointedly at Aunt Gillian's Cartier watch.

'They said they'll call as soon as anything happens,' I say. 'There's nothing else we can do.' I'm tired. I want a smoke and a sandwich and to curl up under my duvet and sort through everything that's going on in my head.

'What about a café in the area?'

'They're *closing*, Gillian.'

'Well, why don't you stay over, Tallulah? That way we can be together when the news comes through.'

'Don't you think he'll make it?' I ask. I feel

dumb for not realising it sooner; there are beads of sweat gathering at the roots of her hair and her mouth looks almost bloodless under the lipstick. Maybe she only gets through things by pretending they're not happening, but now she can't pretend anymore. Or maybe I'm in shock — I vaguely remember being anxious a while ago but now I'm definitely not, a little buzzy, maybe. The other two waver in front of me, like shapes in the desert. It couldn't happen, a voice inside me keeps saying. He couldn't die before I understood everything, not now I've actually started asking questions.

'Oh no,' Aunt Gillian says, hurriedly. 'No, of course that's not it.'

Aunt Vivienne blows air out through her mouth, noisily. 'So we can leave?'

'Yes, I suppose so.'

We gather our things and head over to the lift.

'Will you be going back to yours?' Aunt Gillian asks; she looks like she's trying to be casual.

'I think I should.'

We reach my bus stop.

'I'm going to call a cab,' Aunt Gillian says. 'Would you like me to drop you off?'

'No thanks. I like the bus.'

'I'll get in with you, Gillian,' Aunt Vivienne says.

'Oh, alright,' Aunt Gillian says. She takes my hand in hers and squeezes it. 'I'll see you soon,' she says, uncertainly.

'Soon,' I say.

She kisses me on the cheek and they move off. The bus takes ages to arrive. I smoke two cigarettes and organise my purse, throwing out old ticket stubs and chewing-gum wrappers and a two-pence coin that seems to be growing mould.

When I board the bus I sit at the front of the top deck again, leaning against the yellow rail nearly all the way home. Some man comes and sits next to me, tries to strike up a conversation. He's about twenty years older than me. 'How long have you lived here?' he asks.

'All my life.'

'I love London,' he says. 'So busy, so metropolitan.'

'Sure.'

'I'm from Montreal, originally. Lived in Paris for a few years. Paris is more *chic* than London, but not as lively, don't you think?' His accent is different to Malkie's, but there's something about the way he looks, the way he's slouching forwards in his seat that reminds me of him. I feel like crying.

'I've never been to Paris,' I say.

'It's not possible,' he says in mock horror. 'So close!'

I try to smile at him, but I can feel my eyelids starting to close.

'I'm sorry, am I bothering you?'

'No,' I say. 'I'm just tired. Excuse me.'

I go and sit on the lower deck. I can feel his eyes on my back as I make my way down the stairs, clutching on tightly in case I lose my balance.

It's late when I get home. I pee as soon as I get in, and wash my hands thoroughly, scrubbing underneath my nails. Looking at Aunt Vivienne's perfect manicure all day has made me feel grubby. I let myself into my flat, boil the kettle and scrape my hair back into a ponytail, then try to find a face-wipe to clean away some of the dirt and grease that I've picked up. Now the water's ready, I fancy a beer instead. On the table my phone bleeps pathetically, the battery is almost dead. I have to be available for the hospital, I think. Fucking shit. Maybe Aunt Gillian's right. Maybe I should be more worried. Maybe we shouldn't have left. What if he wakes up and no one's there and he dies of neglect? Or he might never wake up, and I'll never get to see him alive again.

I need to distract myself, do something positive. I grab a beer, get out a notepad and pen and sit on my bed, tallying up my monthly outgoings. I could move to a smaller flat, if that's possible. I could stop eating.

I draw a cat at the bottom of the page, with a collar. I've done the research. I could start off as a healthcare assistant — I don't know how well they get paid, though, or if they get paid at all.

I can cope with the long hours, the heavy lifting, the sadness. As long as it's not my own family. I remember how my father felt in my hands the other day.

I write *Mr Tickles* underneath my doodle and shut the notepad. I take a swig of the beer. I can ask at the hospital about work experience. I don't know if I can stand another vigil in the waiting-room though. Maybe I'll go to work tomorrow — just until I hear about the operation.

I go to bed with my phone plugged into the socket a few feet away; the green charging light makes me feel better.

★   ★   ★

I chose the youth hostel in Kings Cross because of its distance from my family, rather than its standard of hygiene. The bathrooms were windowless, the stairs always smelled like pee, and the tables and chairs in the kitchen were nailed to the floor.

'Charming,' I imagined my grandmother saying, 'but beggars can't be choosers,' I reminded her.

The manager took a week's payment up front and pushed the register across the desk for me to sign. I scribbled something down — the first name I could think of.

'Lauryn Hill,' he read.

'Yep.'

'That's not your real name.'

'Why would you think that?'

'Not my business,' the manager said, deadpan.

I took the key from his outstretched hand.

I sent a letter to my father, telling him not to look for me. I told him I wasn't interested in seeing any of them ever again. I walked halfway across London to post it from a different address, and if he was trying to find me, I didn't hear about it.

Kings Cross in 1997 was supposedly in the middle of a regeneration project, but it looked pretty grotty to me. The building façades were peeling or blackened by pollution; every other shop was a kebab takeaway or a casino, and traffic blared past at all hours of the day and night.

'I thought this was meant to be a red-light district,' one of the backpackers from my dorm said. 'I've only met one prozzy. She had a kid with her and he'd shat all down his leg.'

I was sharing a mixed dormitory with only one other girl. It felt strange after the strictness of school dorms, and I never got used to walking in on boys changing.

Sometimes new faces would appear in the place of old ones, but however enthusiastic they started out, they all ended up lying in bed fully clothed in the middle of the day. Me and the other girl went about our business, both job-hunting, although she was also taking evening classes; seeing her scuttling off at seven in the evening, textbooks clutched to her chest, made me feel ashamed.

I applied for the waitressing job after she showed me the advert. 'Needed: female 16-25 years, good memory, flexible hours.'

'I have fixed hours for lessons,' she said. 'Otherwise I'd apply — it's about twenty minutes on the bus.'

'I'll give it a go,' I said.

I disliked my boss from the beginning. I was wearing black woolly tights, a black, high-waisted cotton skirt and cropped black jumper when I turned up for the interview. He took one look at me and sneered. I felt my stomach drop. I handed him my CV and waited while he flicked his eyes over it.

He gestured to two grubby chairs in the middle of the floor. We sat down. 'How old are you, then?'

'Sixteen.'

'And you went to a fancy school?'

'Yes.'

'Ever waitressed before?'

'Yes,' I lied. 'Private events.' What I mean is I carried a cake out from the kitchen at my mother's birthday party.

He held his hands up. 'Well, I hope we won't be too low-class for you.'

I ground my teeth. 'I hope so too.'

He scowled at me. 'I guess we need someone who can speak the bloody language,' he said. 'Can you start nine a.m. Monday?'

'Yes.'

'You're hired.' He pushed himself up and scratched his giant belly. 'Cash in hand — come fifteen minutes early so I can show you the ropes. After that, it's a rota system.'

I went back to the hostel. One of the boys was in the dorm, reading *On the Road*.

'Hey,' he said.

'Hey.'

'How did your interview go?'

'I got the job.'

'Cool.'

'Not really. The owner's a knob.'

'Fuck the establishment,' he said. 'What's it for, anyway?'

'Waitressing.'

'That's alright, right? Good tips.'

SPECIAL MESSAGE TO READERS

THE ULVERSCROFT FOUNDATION
(registered UK charity number 264873)
was established in 1972 to provide funds for research, diagnosis and treatment of eye diseases. Examples of major projects funded by the Ulverscroft Foundation are:-

- The Children's Eye Unit at Moorfields Eye Hospital, London
- The Ulverscroft Children's Eye Unit at Great Ormond Street Hospital for Sick Children
- Funding research into eye diseases and treatment at the Department of Ophthalmology, University of Leicester
- The Ulverscroft Vision Research Group, Institute of Child Health
- Twin operating theatres at the Western Ophthalmic Hospital, London
- The Chair of Ophthalmology at the Royal Australian College of Ophthalmologists

You can help further the work of the Foundation by making a donation or leaving a legacy. Every contribution is gratefully received. If you would like to help support the Foundation or require further information, please contact:

THE ULVERSCROFT FOUNDATION
The Green, Bradgate Road, Anstey
Leicester LE7 7FU, England
Tel: (0116) 236 4325

website: www.foundation.ulverscroft.com

'I guess.'

'What do you wanna do?'

'I used to wanna be a nurse.'

'Changed your mind?'

'I didn't do my exams.'

'You probably don't need to,' he said. He went back to his book. I lay on my bed for a few hours, trying to work out how I could get into medicine without qualifications. I didn't know if I even wanted to anymore. I couldn't think of anyone in the healthcare profession that seemed nice; the nurses who'd looked after my grandmother hadn't been great. The nurses in the hospital after the miscarriage had been worse. And then my father.

Do I just stay at a café forever, then? I asked myself. I tried to see past next week, but I couldn't.

I steeled myself to the life that followed, although working at the café was worse than I'd thought. My boss didn't bother trying to hide how much I got on his nerves from the start. The work was long and left me with aches in my feet and arms and back and neck. One of the boys in the dorm offered to give me a massage once, and used the opportunity to start kissing me; hot, wet kisses that felt greasy on my skin. I let him do it. I didn't try to stop him when he wanted to go further, even. Afterwards, I gathered my clothes up and took a shower. He was waiting on his bed for me to come to him again, but I went to my own and turned onto my side to face the wall. I could hear him breathing uncertainly, then the springs in his mattress squeaked as he lay back down.

After a few months, I was close to snapping. I joined the public library and checked out all the books I could find on chemistry, biology, medicine, nursing and career opportunities. I read them in the park if it wasn't raining, or on the staircase at the hostel if it was. I took notes. I answered questions and looked up the answers, marking myself like a teacher would have done. I even wrote essays. I thought about taking evening classes; I got as far as walking into the building of the local adult education centre before I realised I wasn't an adult yet. Maybe they'd find it suspicious, how young I was, and turn me in to the police. My palms felt clammy. I turned and pushed my way out the front door again.

I didn't want to present myself at a GP surgery, or the local hospital for the same reason. I couldn't lie my way into work experience there as easily as into being a waitress. Maybe my father could have helped me get work experience — if I'd stayed on, taken the exams. If he hadn't withdrawn me from the school and let me know he blamed me for everything that happened. I convinced myself it was for the best; I didn't want to be like him — I didn't want anything to do with him. At least as a waitress I could pretend I was following in my mother's footsteps instead.

After a while, I took most of the books back. A couple I'd lost in the dorm room, among my other stuff. I paid the fines on those and never went to the library again.

17

Four years or so after I went to live at the hostel, I was unloading my tips into my locker in the hallway of the hostel. Someone grabbed my arm and I shook it off instinctively, my body taut and poised to run.

'*Tallie?*'

I hadn't seen Starr since I'd left school.

'Is it really you?' she asked. 'You're here?' She looked like she was ready to cry.

I felt my stomach flip, and my toes and fingers prick with something. I couldn't work out if it was terror or relief. 'Yeah, it's me,' I said, slamming the locker shut and turning to face her. 'What are you doing here? How did you find me?'

'Nice, that's real nice, Tal.' She looked pissed now. 'No one's heard from you in years and that's the hello I get.'

'I'm sorry,' I said, feeling shamed. 'I didn't expect to see you here, that's all.'

'Dick,' Starr said, but she smiled at me.

'So, what *are* you doing here?'

'I followed you in,' she said. 'I thought I saw you on the street outside but you were too far away to hear me call.' She stepped back and took all of me in.

'I've been working,' I said, suddenly embarrassed by my appearance. 'Gimme a minute to shower, then we can talk.'

Starr sat on my bed while I showered. I came back fully clothed; she was perched on the edge of the mattress, her nose wrinkled up. There was no one else in the dorm. 'Thank fuck for that,' she said when she saw me. 'Let's get out of here.'

We grabbed a six-pack of beer from the fridge and walked with it to a church garden in nearby Islington. It'd been raining, but the sun was out, making little rainbows in the puddles, and in the drops clinging to the poplar trees that grew in the church and the park opposite. I spread my parka out on a bench almost completely hidden by the rose bush behind it.

'So,' Starr said, as soon as we sat down. 'Why'd you run away?'

'I didn't run away.'

'You, like, totally disappeared, Tal.'

'My dad took me out of school anyway, enrolled me in a remedial college. I just left early, before the exams.'

'Don't you think that's a little immature?'

'Look,' I said. 'I've never been good in school. And me and my dad never got on. I don't wanna see him.'

'Well . . . '

'Seriously. I'm not going back.'

She looked at me for a moment, then shrugged. 'Your call. What have you been up to, then?'

'Not much. Working,' I said. I lit a cigarette and took a drag. 'What about you?'

'Yeah, I'm fine, fine,' she said. She tucked her hair back behind her ear, looking around the churchyard. 'Is this where you hang?'

431

'It's not so bad,' I said. 'I generally work at night. I sleep. I don't go out much.'

'What *do* you do?'

'Save my money. I want to get somewhere of my own.'

'Pretty grown up of you, Little Cuz.'

'Yeah, I'm living the dream.'

Across the road we could hear dog owners exchanging pleasantries, and mothers telling their toddlers to be careful on the swings. The churchyard was completely empty except for an old man sweeping autumn leaves off the path a few yards away, and a cat stalking a pigeon.

'What happened to your moggy?' Starr asked, pointing at the cat.

'He died,' I said. I wiped my nose with the sleeve of my jumper; I still got a sinking feeling whenever I thought about Mr Tickles.

'Sorry, man,' Starr said. 'He was like, your best friend, or something lame, wasn't he?'

'What if he was?'

Starr looked at me out of the corner of her eye. 'You almost had me there, you know?'

I grinned, and rammed my hands into my pockets.

'Even *you're* not that much of a loner.'

'Don't be mean about my cat,' I said. 'He was better company than most people.'

'Sucks,' Starr said. She gave me a friendly punch. 'Anyway, enough of being depressing. I've got a riddle for you. Which of our family members is obsessed with The Beatles?'

'I don't know. None of them?'

'Aunt Gillian.' Starr grinned.

'Why?'

''Cos of her husbands.'

'What?'

'Think about it . . . I just picked up on it the other day. John, George, Paul.' She tapped the top of the beer can.

'Who's Paul?'

'The latest one. Oh yeah, of course. He was after your little invisibility trick.'

'Drop it.'

Starr gave me an innocent look. 'Alright, touchy. I was just gonna say Gillian goes out of her way to find the creep-o-lahs.'

'What was John like?'

'Don't remember him, really. I was only two. But, I mean, George — yuck.' She shuddered theatrically.

I wondered about Michael. He must have been five when John died, old enough to remember him. We'd never talked about it though, even after my mother.

Starr was still talking. 'I saw this programme on TV last night . . . Did you know men get boners after they're dead?' She cracked her can open and took a swig. The cat in front of us looked around, hissing at the noise. 'Scat,' Starr said.

The pigeon took off. The cat glared at us then curled up in a nearby flowerbed.

'Yeah,' I said. 'Angel lust.'

'Of course,' Starr said. 'You always knew the weirdest things.'

I opened my can. 'Grandma told me that,' I said.

'You guys talked about sex?' Starr mimed sticking her fingers down her throat. 'I can't think of anything more hideous. Even my mother has more sense.'

'It came up during a programme we were watching.'

'It came up?' She waggled her eyebrows.

'You're not funny,' I told her.

She cackled. The cat opened one eye and glared at us again.

'So what about you?' she said, keeping the can to her mouth. 'Have you . . . since?'

'No.' I took a swig of beer; I'd brought approximately seven guys back to the hostel since I'd been living there.

'Me either then.'

I gave her a look. 'Everyone at school knew about you and Pierre. And you and David, or whatever his name was.'

'It doesn't count if it's less than two minutes.'

'Right,' I said. 'Hope that philosophy works out for you. And the staff at your nearest STI clinic.'

'It does,' Starr said, serenely.

I yawned.

The cat lifted its head and started washing its paw vigorously.

'I need to go back,' I said. 'I'm knackered.'

'Fine,' Starr said. 'I'll walk you.'

In the street she linked her arm through mine and started talking about art college; I concentrated on staying awake. 'One of the maintenance guys is super hot — Ricardo or Rodrigo or something like that. I'm thinking of giving him my number. Anyway, my bus stops here. See you soon, yeah? You're not gonna move again, now I know where you are?'

'Probably not.'

'You're a piece of work, Tal.'

'Love you too.'

★ ★ ★

I hear from the hospital that the operation was successful. My father's under again, though.

Any chance he'll come round before the apocalypse? I want to ask, but I just thank them and hang up.

Work is a bad idea. I've got a headache that won't go away even after two Nurofen, and my boss is in a rotten mood; I'm barely through the door before he's yelling.

'Go take a cold shower,' I mutter, while I'm tying the apron strings behind my back.

He glares at me.

It's almost as bad as the other day. I forget orders, undercharge two tables, snap at the guy who's asking for Dijon mustard.

'Look around,' I tell him. 'Does it look like we've got Dijon mustard?'

'It's not fancy or anything,' he says, hurt. 'It's just not as strong. I can't have anything too strong.'

I feel like throwing my notepad at him. 'I'll see if we have any in the kitchen,' I say.

I push through the kitchen doors. 'Any Dijon mustard in here?' I ask.

Tony, the other chef, doesn't even look at me.

'That's stuff's too expensive for Tight-Wad.'

I sit down on the stool that's shoved up against the wall in between the huge fridge and the dishwasher.

'Please don't make me go back out there,' I say. 'Please don't make me tell Table Four there's no Dijon.'

Now he looks at me; he grins and takes a cigarette out of his pocket. 'Have one on me,' he says.

I take it. 'I'm not due a break for another two hours.'

'I won't tell,' he says. 'Tight-Wad's on the phone — he won't notice.'

'Thanks.'

The cigarette goes a little way towards repairing my frayed nerves, but the headache's worse now. I go back to Table Four with a sorry look on my face. 'No Dijon,' I say.

He sniffs. 'Guess I'll make do. Can you scrape these onions out, too?'

I sigh. I pick up his plate and carry it over to the kitchen. I scrape the onions off the burger into the bin.

'Stop wasting good onions,' my boss yells at me.

'He doesn't want any.'

'Well, he should have said before he ordered. That onion comes out of your pay.'

I put the plate down on the microwave. 'Shut up,' I say.

'What did you just say?' he asks, squinting at me. He's chewing a toothpick and a strand of saliva dangles out of his mouth when he speaks.

'Shut *up*.'

He goes purple. 'Final warning, missy.'

I go to the kitchen door. I look out the porthole and see Table Four tapping his foot. I think about my father, back in his coma, sleeping his life away. 'I can't do this,' I say. 'I quit.'

'You can't fucking quit,' he yells. 'We've got no one else until six p.m.'

'I don't give a shit,' I say. 'Why don't you serve them yourself?'

Tony turns away, delicately; he's still chopping, but I think his shoulders are shaking.

'Rot in fucking hell.'

'Right back at you.'

I tear the apron off and throw it at my boss' feet. He takes the toothpick out and points it at me; for a crazy second, I think he's going to throw it at me, like a mini javelin.

'You'll come crawling back,' he says. 'And just so you know — you'll never get a job here again. Or a fucking reference.'

'Fine by me,' I say. 'You probably can't write anyway.'

He advances towards me, and I slip away and out the back door. I can hear him screaming abuse after me all the way down the alley. Then I'm out on the street and cars are pouring past me. The sky's cloudy and I've got nowhere to be and no money. I should have at least made him pay for my last few shifts. But I don't care, I can't stop grinning. I start out in the direction of the tube.

★　★　★

'So, you're okay for money, right?'

Starr stubbed her cigarette out in the pint glass I'd given her for her orange squash and dropped the butt in the bin behind her.

I ran a hand through my hair and gestured around. 'I'm fine,' I said. 'Check out the palace.'

She wrinkled her nose. Dirty laundry was strewn over every surface and there were dirty dishes piled up in the sink. The posters the last tenants had put up had left darker patches on walls that were sun-bleached around them. The only trouble I took was over the plants growing on the window-sill; I watered them every night, and clipped them like my grandmother had taught me.

'You've been here one month?'

'Yeah.'

'You haven't done much with it.'

'What's wrong with it?'

'It smells weird.'

'Yeah.' I took a drag of my cigarette. 'Something's rotten in the fridge, but I can't find it.'

'Jesus, Tallie.' Starr looked disgusted.

'It's fine,' I said. 'Rent's low. There are no rats this time. The loo flushes.' I shrugged. 'What more do I need? It's better than the hostel, anyway.'

'Yeah, well.' She tugged her skirt down, inching the hem to just above her knees. 'So you're still at the café?'

I took a gulp of coffee — the mug had a crack in it, I noticed. 'Yeah,' I said. 'It's okay. I know the customers — who tips well, that kind of shit.'

'Right.'

Starr let go of the hem of the skirt, and ran her fingers over the front of it, smoothing the leather down. It looked like it had cost her well over a hundred quid, and made me feel even plainer in my denim shorts and oversized grey jumper. Her t-shirt was white, with some sort of punk logo on the front, and her gloves were fingerless and matched her skirt.

'What are you up to then?' I asked her. 'Still with that maintenance guy?'

'Ricardo?' she purred. 'I'm living with him now.' She stretched her improbably long legs and gave me a sly smile. 'Mum's furious.' She opened the handbag slung across the back of her chair and took out some purple lipstick, rolling it around the table in front of her. 'He has a motorbike.' She leaned forward. 'And he's very good with his hands.'

'Yeah, you said.' I dragged on my cigarette again and stubbed it out. 'Probably lucky, given his job.'

'You're such a Park.'

'It's your name too.'

'Not for much longer.' She pulled a face. 'I'm thinking of changing my name — I might marry Ricardo.'

'What would you be then?'

'Garcia.'

'Starr Garcia?'

'Yep.'

'Sounds kinda stupid, don't you think?'

'Not as stupid as Tallulah,' she said, drawing out the looooh syllable.

'Granted.'

'Mum said my name came to her in a dream.' Starr shook her head. 'If I'd been a boy she was going to call me Leopold.'

'Bet you're glad you weren't.'

'Amen.'

I finished my coffee. 'More squash?'

'Nope. I should head soon.' She swung around in her chair to watch me while I got up to boil the kettle. 'Gotta pack — I'm going on holiday to Spain with Ric. It's gonna be heaven.'

'Good for you.'

'What about you? What would your name have been if you'd been a boy?'

'I dunno.'

'Probably something boring like Edward or Jack. Speaking of . . . '

'Yeah, why d'you think he left?' I asked.

'What?'

'Uncle Jack. Why d'you think he left?'

'I wasn't going to talk about Uncle Jack, I was going to talk about Uncle Edward.' Starr leaned forwards, resting her elbows on the tabletop. 'He asked about you recently,' she said.

'And?' I could feel my breath catch in my throat.

'And nothing. I didn't tell him we meet.' She was watching me closely. I turned away and ran the tap, filling the kettle.

'Tallie, are you seriously never gonna go back home?'

'What's the point?'

'Because he misses you,' Starr said. She tapped out a beat with the scuffed toes of her

black Doctor Martins. 'And you're being a little bitch by staying away.'

'You don't know anything about it.'

'I know how he feels,' Starr said. She stood up. Even without heels she was three inches taller than me. I switched the kettle on.

'I don't feel great about lying to Uncle Edward.'

'You lie all the time.'

'Yeah, but he's a nice guy.'

'He doesn't really miss me.'

She shook her head. 'You're wrong.'

'I know him better than you.'

She gave up, throwing her hands in the air. 'So what was it you were asking?'

'Why Uncle Jack left. Do you know?'

'He was on the run, wasn't he?'

'From what?'

'Drug lords, I heard.'

'Don't you think that's a little bit dramatic?'

'What do I know? Why are you so interested, anyway?'

I shrugged. 'I guess I see it more from his perspective now, I guess.'

Starr raised her eyebrows. 'Your situation is totally different, Tal. You have a dad who wants you around. Uncle Jack was a loner already. You're an idiot if you think he's any kind of a role model.'

'Your mum wanted him around.'

Starr screwed her face up like she was remembering something. 'She did try to track him down, I think. But she forgets people pretty quickly.'

441

'I don't think she'd forget him,' I said. 'Do you remember her at my mum's birthday? The one just before she died. Your mum had a fight with Gillian about him.'

'My mum used to pull hissy fits all the time, Tal.' Starr smeared lipstick onto her forefinger and patted it onto her lips. 'I stopped paying them attention when I was, like, seven.'

'Oh.'

She saw the look on my face. 'Don't feel bad for me, doofus. I'm not asking for sympathy. I'm fine, Mum's fine.'

'So she really never talked about Uncle Jack? Did everyone just pretend he'd never been there, or something?'

She gave a world-weary sigh. 'Forget it, chick, that's my advice. If you start thinking about all the weird shit that goes on in this family you'll be here all day.' She checked her reflection in a pocket mirror. 'You ever see any of the old gang?'

'No,' I said.

'Why not?'

'I told you, I haven't spoken to anyone since I left.'

'You know I bumped into Toby the other day?'

My heart gave a thump so hard I felt it in my fingertips. 'How would I know that?'

'Well, I did. He's a lawyer.' She put her lipstick and mirror away. 'I asked about everyone — do you wanna hear?'

'Okay,' I said. Now my heart was beating triple-time.

'Edith's doing some costume design course, can you believe that? The hunky one, Francis,

442

did biology at uni, forget what he's up to now. That little creepy one . . . '

'John?'

'Yeah, him. He's training as an accountant, go figure.'

'Is Toby still with Edith?'

'Nah. She found herself and broke up with him.' Starr shut the clasp on her handbag. 'You should get in touch with him. He's pretty hot stuff. I'd have a crack if I didn't have a psychotic cousin to worry about.'

'And a boyfriend.'

'And a boyfriend. Like you could soon.' She blew me a kiss. 'I should be going.'

★   ★   ★

I see Toby straight away. He's leaning against a bike stand, talking to a leggy blonde girl. She keeps flicking her hair over her shoulder and tipping her head from side to side like a bird. As I get nearer she reaches out and hits him, playfully, saying: 'Stop it.'

Oh come on, I think.

Toby looks up and sees me. 'Jesus,' he says.

It takes me a moment to hear him through the blood pounding in my ears. 'Nope, just me.'

'Tal?'

'Yeah.' Then, because I don't know what to say, and the blonde is giving me a dirty look: 'How are you?'

'How am I? How are *you*? No one's seen you for ages.'

'Well, I've been around.'

The blonde girl giggles. I can't help hating her.

'What are you *doing* here?'

'I was trying to find you.'

'How . . . ' he starts, then stops. 'Sally, this is Tallulah.' He nods at me and the blonde. 'Tal, this is Sally.'

'Hi,' Sally says, sniffing.

'Did you wanna go for a drink?' Toby asks.

'Sure.'

'Now?'

'Sure.'

Sally pouts. 'Tobbeeeee — you promised you'd take *me* for a drink,' she says, linking her arm through his.

'Sorry,' Toby says. 'Another time. I haven't seen Tal in ages.' He disengages himself and comes to stand next to me.

I smirk at her.

The pub is packed and Toby sloshes beer all over himself on the way back to our table. He carefully sets the pints and a packet of crisps down in front of me and inspects his shirt. 'Fucking shit,' he says, under his breath.

'It's just a shirt,' I say, ripping open the crisps. I stuff three in my mouth; I haven't eaten all day and I'm starving.

'Just a shirt that I paid a lot of money for,' Toby says.

'Just a shirt.'

'You're still annoying, I see,' Toby says.

'You're still uptight, I see.'

He sits down and gulps his beer. 'So, what did you want to see me about?' He gives me a quick

once-over. 'You look different.'

'It's been five years.'

'Right, yeah.' He's almost finished the pint. I can't tell if he's nervous. 'So where have you been?'

'Here in London. I lived in a hostel for a while, now I'm renting a bedsit. I hear you're a lawyer these days.'

He shrugs. 'I'm still a junior.'

'Were you always this prickly?'

'What did you expect, Tal? You disappeared off the face of the earth one day. You didn't even say goodbye.'

It's not nerves then. In a weird way, his anger makes me feel better about tracking him down. He cares enough to be pissed at you, I tell myself.

'I wasn't really in the mood for a send-off.'

Toby winces. 'Sorry.'

'It wasn't your fault.'

'No, I know that. I'm just saying I'm sorry.'

'Forget it.'

'I came to the hospital,' he says. 'The nurse said you weren't seeing anyone, but I thought you'd see me. Then I got a phantom phone call from Edith and by the time I got back, you'd vanished.'

'Yeah,' I say. 'I couldn't face you.'

'I thought you hated me.'

'No.'

'I thought that was why you never got in touch.'

We drink our beer in silence. Finally, Toby puts his glass down and sighs. 'Seriously, what made you come back now? There must be some reason.'

'Starr found me about six months ago,' I say, sneaking a look at him; he doesn't blink. 'She visits me occasionally. Last week she said she'd run into you.' I shrug. 'I dunno. It made me think about you guys. I wanted to see you again.'

Toby looks at his hands. 'Well, I'm sorry about being aggro. My feelings were hurt. I thought we were friends.'

'We were.'

'It didn't feel like it, when you ran off. That's all I'm saying.'

'Yeah, well. It didn't feel like it when you secretly got with my best friend.'

'Did you actually care?'

'You're the genius now. What do you think?'

Toby half-grins. 'I've always been a genius,' he says.

'And modest.'

'And good-looking.'

'And shy, and retiring.'

'So why didn't you want me?' His tone's light, but he keeps his eyes on me as I take another gulp of beer.

'It wasn't that easy, Toby.'

'It seemed pretty easy to me.' He takes a sip. 'I was crazy about you. You know that, right?'

'I liked you too,' I say. 'But it felt like everyone I liked died. So no, not that easy for me. And then Edith . . . '

'Yeah,' Toby says. 'We don't really talk anymore.'

'Oh.'

We're silent for a moment. At the table next to us, two men in business suits are laughing hard about something; one of them has the red face that comes with a lack of oxygen. He leans into the wall, slaps it and takes a deep, juddering breath. 'You've got to be *kidding me*,' he says.

'There's another reason I wanted to see you,' I say. My mouth feels dry and my tongue seems to be swollen, so I have to stop and swallow a few times before I carry on. 'My dad's in hospital — he had a heart attack.'

'Oh my God,' Toby says; he scrapes his chair around the table until he's next to me. 'Is he okay?'

'Yeah,' I say, 'maybe, I don't know.'

'What do you mean?'

'He was in a coma,' I say. 'He kind of woke up the other day, but he kept drifting in and out, and then he had to have an emergency operation. They said they'll let us know when he's awake properly.'

'How are you doing?'

'I'm okay,' I say. 'I hadn't seen him since I left school either.'

Toby draws back to look at me. '*What*?'

'I told you — I've been living in a hostel.'

He looks angry again. 'So you went off completely by yourself?'

'Yeah.'

'You *always* shut people out,' he says. 'You should have called me. I would've looked out for you.'

I scratch at the varnish on the table. 'I know,' I say, eventually. 'And I know you were the one

447

who trashed the art room by the way.'

'How?'

I put my hands in my lap. 'I worked it out,' I say.

'Are you pissed off?'

'No.' I should have fucking killed Mr Hicks.

I want to say thank you. I want to tell him how knowing that someone was standing up for me made me feel grateful and ashamed of my own behaviour at the same time. That I should have looked out for him too, instead of leaving him to deal with his brother's death alone.

Tell him everything, inner me says. Tell him you feel guilty and glad and resentful and defiant and vulnerable and he's the only one who can navigate his way around all that.

'I'm really, really sorry,' I say. 'For everything.'

'I'm sorry too,' Toby says. 'The whole time you were away I was thinking about how I made all those mistakes with you, and how I'd make it up to you if I ever saw you again.' He gives me a half-smile. 'I probably should have started with that. And it *is* really good to see you.'

There's another silence, then he drains his beer and stands up. 'I've got an exam coming up — I should go revise.'

'Oh.'

'What's your number?'

I hesitate.

'I'm not letting you disappear again.'

I write the number down on the back of an old receipt I find in my bag and push it towards him. He picks it up and puts it in his pocket without looking at my scrawl. 'See you,' he says. He bends down and kisses me on the lips. It's a long kiss, forceful. At first I feel nothing, then suddenly my whole body is throbbing and my head is buzzing, and I just want to keep on doing this forever. He pulls back, straightens up and walks out of the pub.

I sit and finish my beer, taking time over each sip.

When I leave it's dark and surprisingly chilly for a summer evening. The recent heat has broken, and the streets are slick with the sheen of rain. My phone rings and I fumble in my bag for it; it keeps slipping out of my fingers.

'Fuck exams,' he says. 'Can I come over and see you?'

'No,' I say. 'I have to go to bed.'

'That's not putting me off.'

I find myself grinning.

'What did you say?'

'I didn't say anything. I'm smiling.'

'I can't tell that over the phone, you know.'

'I know.'

'So, can I come over?'

'Yes.'

★ ★ ★

We kiss, we talk. We talk for half the night at each other and over each other. Toby's brought a bottle of whisky around, and we drink that, neat, from plastic cups. We start out in the kitchen, and somehow we end up in the bedroom, although I'm not too clear on how we get there. I take a pillow off the bed and lie on the floor and he sits next to me, his hand in my hair.

'What are you thinking?' he asks.

'I'm thinking about something I read earlier,' I say.

'Oh good.'

'Shut up, it's interesting. There's this thing in physiology called 'Dead Space', where a third or so of every resting breath is exhaled unchanged.'

'Come again?'

'It means the oxygen hasn't been diffused in the alveoli from the alveolar gas into the blood passing by in the lung capillaries. That's the Dead Space — the portion of air where no useful transaction has taken place.'

He strokes my face with his free hand. 'You sound like a doctor.'

'Maybe a nurse.'

He tells me about his law conversion, and uni, and travelling around Europe for three months. I feel sad that I never did any of this, and he says, 'You're still young', and then I laugh at him again for looking so serious, like twenty-three is old and he grins and says his family are worried he might turn into a prick, and I think I might have loved him all this time, or maybe it's the whisky.

Then we're kissing again, and I'm not scared this time. He takes his clothes off first, and then mine; each time he takes a layer off his hands tremble. When we're completely naked he lies on top of me, very gently, just skin-on-skin. I finally feel comfortable in mine, maybe it's being next to his. He's hard, underneath me, and I want him. I move my hips up and then it's happening and, this time, it's right.

Afterwards, he talks some more. I half-see him get up to open the window then come over to me and I feel him gently shaking my shoulder.

'I'm not asleep,' I say, 'I'm listening. I heard everything you said.'

'Sure,' he says. 'You've been snoring for half an hour.'

'I was in a sex coma,' I say. I wrap myself around him, not minding the stickiness from earlier. He bends his head down to kiss my collarbone, then my neck, then my chin, my mouth, and we start again.

18

Bones are made up of marrow, nerves, blood vessels, epithelium and various tissues. When there is a break in the continuity of the bone, it is called a bone fracture, or more colloquially, a broken bone. Fractures are mostly commonly caused when the bone comes into contact with another body (such as the ground, a wall, even another person) and the force of this contact is too high, but sometimes they can happen after a period of accumulated trauma to a particular area (such as the legs if you run too much); these fractures are known as *stress fractures*. On average, you will suffer two fractures in your lifetime.

The development of the human skeleton can be said to start at the end of the third month after conception, when your bones begin to calcify inside your mother's womb. When we are born, we have over two hundred and seventy of them, but as we grow some fuse together, and the tissue hardens.

It takes twenty years to fully grow, one year less than the age I am today. As I dream next to Toby, I have two hundred and six bones, and they're as strong as they'll ever be.

★   ★   ★

Toby leaves early the next morning to pick up clean clothes before work.

'Call me,' he mumbles into my ear, and I roll over and grab his chin.

'Stay,' I say, eyes still closed.

'How about I come round tonight? I get the feeling you're not a morning person anyway.'

'Less talk, more sleep.'

I vaguely hear the click of the door being closed, then it's four hours later and I'm sitting up blurrily, not quite sure if what happened really happened.

I shower and stand in front of the mirror, running my fingers through my hair. I should get a cut — a proper one. I've been butchering it myself for the last few years and it shows. I crack my joints, knuckles, neck, shoulders, lower back. I text Aunt Gillian, checking in. I read. I go out and buy tea bags and lemons and make myself some iced tea. I do almost anything other than think about my father, and how worried I should be right now.

On the table my phone beeps angrily at me.

Princess — found Jack. Coming round this afternoon about three o'clock. Malkie.

I check my watch. Two fifteen p.m.

I put on a lacy white dress, then take it off; it makes me look like I'm taking my Holy Communion. I put on a white, sleeveless, v-necked shirt instead, and bright green shorts. I tie my hair back and dab the skin under my eyes with concealer — don't want Malkie to notice how tired I look. And maybe Uncle Jack?

At five to three the buzzer goes; he's early.

'Oh God,' I whisper to myself. 'Oh fuck oh

453

God.' I don't know if I'm ready to see him now. I still haven't decided what to ask him, got things straight in my head.

I let him in and he clomps up the stairs. I leave my front door open and put some glasses in the freezer to chill so we can have iced tea.

'Hey.'

I turn around. 'Hey yourself.'

He comes in and hugs me.

'Want a drink?'

'No thanks. You sure you want to see him?'

I try to swallow.

'You sounded pretty urgent the other day, doll.'

'I am,' I say. 'It is.'

'I don't know what you want with him,' Malkie says. 'But like I said before, you gotta be prepared for him to be changed, okay?'

'Yeah,' I say. 'I'm fine.'

Malkie sighs. He looks at the clock on the oven and gestures to the door. 'Shall we?'

My heart's in my mouth. I grab my purse and lead him out of the flat, double-locking the door behind us.

'So where are we going?' I ask.

'You know a pub called The North Star on New North Road?'

'Yeah.'

'Okay. We're going there.'

What if it turns out it wasn't an accident, after all? What then? I try to distract myself with thinking about Toby.

'Tallulah, you okay?'

'Yeah.'

'You just looked a little flushed. You got a fever?'

'No, I'm fine.'

We cut through the estates, and then the nice residential roads, with cute three-storey houses and windowboxes and well-mannered teenagers learning to drive in quiet squares.

The dry-cleaners comes into sight, and the Golden Jade — Chinese food and fish & chips — and then we're opposite the pub. There are a few bollards in front of the building; someone's leaning against one now, smoking and coughing a lot, bending over to spit into the gutter.

A drunk, I think, until Malkie crosses the road and stops in front of him. 'Here we are,' he says. I don't know who he's addressing; the man in front of us is still bent over. I look at him properly and feel like I've been punched in the stomach.

'Uncle Jack?'

He looks up and grimaces at me, coughing some more. Even standing straight up he looks bent over. His arms are hanging loosely by his sides. He's lost weight and his hair is dirty. 'Hi, kiddo,' he says. 'Malk said you wanted to see me.'

Beside me, Malkie shifts uncomfortably again. 'I thought maybe it would be better to meet out here — neutral ground.'

'Okay,' I say. I can hear my voice, a pitch or so higher than normal. I'm looking at Uncle Jack's eyes — they're bloodshot and dead flat. 'Is he alright?'

'Jacky's not going to cause any trouble, are you?'

455

'Nope,' Uncle Jack croaks. 'Cross my heart and hope to die.' He grins at me.

Malkie's looking even more worried than before. 'You *sure* you're ready for this?' he asks.

'Yes,' I say, at the same time as Uncle Jack.

Malkie hugs me and steps backwards. 'I'll be on my way then,' he says. 'But you have my number now. Call me if there's any problem. Any problem at all.'

Uncle Jack pulls a face.

We watch Malkie shamble off; when he reaches the corner he turns around and raises his hand to me. I wave back at him. *Call me*, he mouths and vanishes from sight.

'You've got even friendlier since we first met,' Uncle Jack says.

'I'm in shock,' I say. 'I didn't think Malkie would find you. You disappeared, remember?'

'Yeah, I guess I did.'

I bite my lip. 'How *did* he find you?'

'He knew where to look for me.'

I remember Starr saying that Aunt Vivienne tried to track Jack down too, and wonder, briefly, how she went about it. And why she didn't try harder.

'It's funny, actually — you think we're so different when we're really the same person. Guess Malk's just cuddlier.' He coughs again, retching at the end of this fit.

I dig out a bottle of water from my bag and hand it to him, silently. He drinks thirstily, spilling half around his mouth and chin, then tries to give it back.

'You keep it.'

456

'What did you want to talk about?'

He's shivering uncontrollably. The afternoon's as cloudy as the morning, and I can feel goosebumps starting. I wrap my arms around myself. I don't want to be alone with Uncle Jack, but I can't take him into the pub. He's clearly in a bad shape, and the last thing I need is a public drama.

'Look,' I say. 'We can go to my flat. But no funny business.'

'What do you think of me?' Uncle Jack asks, then holds up his hand. 'Don't answer that.'

We walk back together without speaking, Uncle Jack coughing next to me. The noise reminds me of my grandmother and I wish she was there with us. 'Be brave,' I hear her saying.

Inside, I throw the keys on the kitchen table and turn to Uncle Jack. 'Does anyone else know you're around?' I ask.

'Nope.'

'Didn't you ever want to see them? Vivienne at least?'

Uncle Jack shrugs. 'Maybe it was best I stayed away,' he says. He looks sick and clammy. 'So?'

'I asked Malkie to find you,' I say, 'because I want to know some stuff.'

'Yes?'

Breathe, then launch. 'About my mum. About when I was younger. Lots of shit happened that I don't really understand, and I feel like you were the reason it happened.'

'Always the villain with you, huh?' He sits down in a chair, letting his head fall forwards until I can't see his face anymore. 'I haven't slept

457

since she died you know.'

'Who?'

'Who do you think?'

I shake my head, although I know what's coming.

'Evie,' he says. 'I haven't slept since Evie died.'

Hearing my mother's name is exactly like that feeling on a rollercoaster; the feeling of my insides plummeting. 'You haven't slept for eleven years?' I say.

'You know what I mean. Were you always this pedantic, Tallulah?'

'Pretty much.'

Uncle Jack laughs and shrugs his shoulders. There are dark circles around his eyes and his cheekbones jut out like little cliffs overhanging the dark fleshy pool of his mouth. Outside I'd thought that he was just unhealthy, but now I recognise the look from people at the hostel.

'You on heroin?' I ask.

'There — that's my smart little niece,' he says, rubbing the back of his hand against his cheek. Skin rasps against beard and sets my teeth on edge. Uncle Jack laughs again; he's starting to annoy me. 'So what did you want to ask me about your mum?'

'Do you know what happened the day she died?'

'No,' he says. 'I left when Eddie came home early.'

'Oh.' I feel deflated suddenly, like I've been waiting for his answer for a really long time, and now it's never coming.

'Sorry I can't help,' he says. He does look

sorry, or at least that's what I think his face is doing. He squints at me. 'Why are you asking now, anyway?'

'Dunno,' I say. 'I guess when Starr was the only person I saw, it didn't seem as important.' I shrug. I don't know how to explain what I've been thinking — how suddenly it felt like the right time to clear up unanswered questions, confront things from the past that I've never understood.

Dear Uncle Jack, if you hadn't shown up, my mother might still be alive. Then I might have finished school and gone to university. But I think I've let that possible life stop me from living this one.

I cross over to the sink and lean back against it, facing him again. 'What *can* you tell me about my mum, then?'

He looks sly. 'What do you mean?'

'Why was she so upset when you turned up?'

'She obviously didn't want to see me, wouldn't you say?'

I think back to the conversation in the rose garden, remembering what my mother had said: 'Don't you dare say anything. I've worked so hard to build a life for my family. I won't — I won't let you come between us, you hear me?'

'What did you have over her?'

Uncle Jack slams his fist down onto the table. 'You were always so strong, weren't you, Tallulah?' he says. 'So unable to forgive weaknesses in anyone else, huh? You had it so fucking *easy*, that's why.'

My heart's going a million miles a minute, but

459

I keep my voice steady when I answer him. 'Apart from everyone dying, I guess I had it okay.'

I start clearing up the crockery from the draining board, shoving bowls and mugs into cupboards, rattling and slamming, half to get away from him, half to let myself calm down. Uncle Jack comes to stand next to me, holding his hands up in mock surrender. 'Sorry,' he says. 'This isn't going well, is it?' He leans back against the counter. 'Has anyone ever told you you look nothing like your mother?'

'I've got eyes don't I?'

'You're too defensive, kid.'

'Don't call me kid. Or kiddo.'

'Here.' He pulls an envelope from the inside pocket of his jacket. 'I put this together after Malkie got in touch. This is for you. Don't say I didn't try to look out for you.'

He's baring his teeth in the wolf smile I remember from our first meeting. I take the envelope; it feels heavy. I slide the flap open and look at, then run my finger over the giant wad of notes inside. They're dirty and creased, lined up neatly in order of value. Fives, tens, twenties.

'Is this drug money?'

'So suspicious.'

'Can you blame me?'

He pulls a face.

'Excuse me for not falling at your feet,' I say. 'I thought junkies were pretty tight.'

'Don't you worry about me,' he says. 'I've got my own little stash.'

'I don't worry about you,' I say. 'I don't want

your money, either.' I put the envelope down next to the sink, between us. Uncle Jack licks his lips.

'It's yours,' he says. 'Take it.'

'Nope.'

I walk to the fridge and open the door, pulling out milk and a packet of coffee.

'I'm not taking the money back,' Uncle Jack says. 'I mean, Christ . . . ' He runs his fingers through his hair. 'I'm trying to do the right thing, here, ki — Tallulah. Can you just let me, for once?'

'I don't want to be mixed up in something dodgy.'

'It's not dodgy.'

'How can I believe that?'

'It's not,' he says, trying to look sincere. 'It's from Edward. A more upright man than my brother has yet to be born.'

At the mention of my father's name I feel a pang; I haven't thought about him once since Malkie turned up, even though he's the reason I needed to work all this out. I haven't even mentioned his condition to Uncle Jack, although I can't be sure he'd care.

'Why would you have my dad's money?'

'A coffee would be good,' Uncle Jack says.

'Tell me about the money first.'

'Edward gave it to me.'

'So you said. Why would my dad give you money?'

'Your dad didn't give it to me. Not exactly.'

'So you stole it off him?'

'No.'

461

I roll my eyes. 'I think your brain's been fried by all those drugs. Did he give it to you or not?'

'Yes, Edward gave me the money.' He looks up then, trying to catch my eye. 'But not your *dad*.'

'What?'

'My brother,' Uncle Jack pauses, 'is not your dad. I am.'

For a moment I feel like I'm falling, not my stomach this time, but my brain. I put a hand out to steady myself. 'I'm sorry?' I croak.

'I'm your father.'

'You can't be.'

'I know, I know; it was a surprise to me too. But Evie wouldn't have done the dirty on me.' He sees my expression. 'I'm sorry, I didn't mean that. That was low.' He bites his lip. 'What I was trying to say was — we were an item. We were in *love*, for fuck's sake.'

'You and my mum?'

'Now don't tell me you hadn't guessed that.'

'I knew something had happened,' I say, even though a voice inside is saying you did. You always knew. Even if there had never been that weirdness going on, you look exactly the same as Uncle Jack. ' . . . She was always so scared of you.'

Uncle Jack laughs again. 'That's a good one.'

'When did you get together? Where was my d — where was Edward?'

'Away in Africa.' He tugs at his earlobe. 'I'd worshipped her from the moment I met her. And then, one night, I walked her home — this is before she lived with Viv — and she asked me to come up.' He spreads his hands in a shrug. 'I didn't need asking twice.'

Please, no more, I think, but he's carrying on.

'She was so gorgeous, your mother. And we were happy, you know, really fucking happy. We spent all our time together, didn't need anyone else. I remember when she told me she was pregnant — I couldn't stop kissing her.'

I shift from one foot to the other; it feels strange, jarring, to hear myself mentioned like that.

'Is this why she had the fight with Vivienne?' I ask.

Uncle Jack smiles his wolf smile again. 'My sister can be a tad possessive,' he says. 'She said Evie was just using me while Ed was away. That she didn't love me as much as I loved her.'

'Nice friend.'

He laughs.

I clear a space on the sofa and sit down. A million questions are crowding my brain, but I can't work out which are the important ones right now. 'Then what happened — how come she ended back up with Edward?'

For a second I think I chose the wrong question — he looks angry again, really angry, and I don't understand what he says next. 'I'd have given my life for Evie, you know? And you too. I *did* give my life.'

'What are you talking about?'

'Protecting you.'

'What do you mean?'

'Why do you *think* me and Evie didn't work out?'

'Drugs?'

463

'Nope.'

'You went to jail?'

'I did.' He has his arms wrapped around his body, hugging himself. 'And she waited a whole three months before moving in with my brother.'

There's something else in the room now, something big. Uncle Jack's blinking at the floor. I feel my voice sitting at the bottom of my stomach, and I have to clear my throat twice before I can get the next question out. 'Why?'

'Because I killed him,' he says. 'I killed my father.'

PART FOUR

Blood

19

'What?'

Nothing I ask seems enough of a reaction. 'How? Why?'

We look at each other properly for the first time.

'My father was a bully,' Uncle Jack says. 'Everyone in the village was scared of him. His kids walked around with black eyes, permanently, and no one said anything.' He scratches his face; if not for the tremor in his hand, I'd assume he was completely calm right now. 'He never liked Evie because she had no money. When he found out we were going to have a baby he lost it, told me he'd disinherit me before he let me squander the family savings on some gold-digging whore.'

'What did he do?'

'We'd gone to see Mother. Albert was meant to be away that weekend — meeting someone who was trying to sell him a horse. Our flat in London was pretty dingy, and Evie ended up looking after Starr more than Viv did. She needed a break. You were nearly due and she used to fall asleep all the time.'

'Was he there?'

'I'd gone to the pub. Mother was upstairs, reading. Evie was in the library, just sitting, thinking about you, apparently. She liked doing that.' He takes a deep, ragged breath. 'We found out afterwards the meeting hadn't gone as planned. The man was asking too much for the horse, and Albert didn't like to be taken for a ride. He came home early. When he walked in on Evie, he was three sheets to the wind and in a foul mood. He started on her, saying she'd never get a penny out of him. Accusing her of lying about who the father was.' Uncle Jack looks at me quickly, then away again. 'She stood up to him, and then he got violent.'

I feel faint.

'That's the scene I came home to, my father pushing Evelyn around.' He splays his fingers open. 'He put his hand on her face, like this, and shoved her backwards onto the floor. She was crying, she was alone and scared and the bastard could have killed her. Or you. Then, when I come in, he starts on me. Shouting about how worthless I am.'

'What did you do?'

'I hit him.'

'That's it?'

He shakes his head. 'He fell over and cut his face pretty bad — he was lying there bleeding and I couldn't stop.' He gives me a funny smile. 'I hit him enough for his heart to give out.'

'Then what?'

'Your mother was horrified — couldn't understand that the man had had it coming.' He's working himself up into a rage, and now he points a shaky finger in my direction. 'After everything he'd done to me.'

For a moment I feel trapped. If he'd wanted to hurt you, he would have done it by now, I tell myself. He wants you to understand him, that's all. I focus on breathing slowly. 'So. You went to prison.'

'Yes I went to prison.'

'And?'

'For manslaughter. Twelve years. Out in ten.' He laughs. 'That's when I started taking heroin — I'd only ever done cannabis before, believe it or not.' He looks at the floor. 'There was a mix-up. I asked for gear, but it was a heroin-tobacco blend. They said it would be less likely to show up on drug tests. And the rest is history.'

I let myself fall backwards on the sofa. The tap is dripping onto the dirty mugs and empty beer bottles in the kitchen sink; it's easy to let myself get distracted by the noise. Drip, *your father killed your grandfather*, drip, *your mother never told you*, drip, *and then she married his brother* . . . drip, *while your real father turned into a junkie.*

'Why,' I start, and then I don't know where to go with the question. 'Why . . . didn't you stay in touch? Why didn't I know you existed?'

Uncle Jack lets out a sigh. 'I *killed* him, Tallulah,' he says. 'As much as I hated the bastard, I'd crossed a line even he'd never crossed. And your mother wouldn't look at me anymore, let me touch her.'

'So she wouldn't come and see you?'

'She did — once or twice. She felt guilty, like it was her fault we'd been at Mother's in the first place. But she didn't want to visit, I could tell.'

'Then?'

469

'I stopped coming out of my cell. I just wanted to smoke H. Visitors can't get in if you don't want them. That's the one thing you have control over.'

'And my mum?'

'Edward told me he found her in a hostel.'

I feel my heart give a little thud. My father — Edward — my uncle. I think of him in surgery, surrounded by tubes and green gowns and shiny instruments, and somehow he seems even more vulnerable now I know the truth. If he'd died on the table, there'd be nothing left, I think. When my mother died, I was proof that she'd existed, but he doesn't even have that.

'I don't blame her for going back to him,' Uncle Jack is saying. 'Not really. She was scared and alone, and, out of all of us, Eddie's the nicest. And maybe Viv was right, maybe she never stopped loving him anyway, the whole time we were together.' He stops and takes a cigarette out. 'And then she watched me . . . ' He's trying to light the cigarette but he's shaking again. 'Sorry, kiddo,' he says. 'Guess I'm not as hard as I look. I just . . . ' He closes his eyes and a tear squeezes out. 'I fucking adored her. And you. Or at least, the idea of you. I just keep thinking it was going to be so different. That's all I think about, really. How my life was meant to be so different.'

He takes a long, harsh breath, then he's quiet and all I can hear is a hum in my ears.

'I wanted to tell you a long time ago, but . . . ' He gestures to himself. ' . . . Evie told me I'd

470

ruin it for you two, then Eddie said he wanted to look after you, he said I'd do a shitty job. They gave me the money to disappear, and I guess I couldn't really say no, the state I was in.'

I feel a rush of conflicting feelings when he says this — so Edward actively chose to keep me, after all, even if he did a terrible job of making me *feel* wanted.

Uncle Jack wipes his cheek with the back of his hand. And he wanted me too. 'But Malkie . . . When he said he knew where you were . . . He said you wanted to see me . . . '

'Jack,' I say, and then I can't go on.

★   ★   ★

I can hear Toby running up the stairs as soon as I've buzzed him in, then he's pounding on the flat door. I open it so suddenly he falls in, then has to grab me to stop me from falling too.

'What happened?' he asks. His face is inches from mine; I feel calmer suddenly, in the face of his panic. My dad is not my real dad, I tell him, and watch him try to process it.

'*What?*'

'Yep.'

'Is this . . . The one who had a heart attack?'

'He's my uncle,' I say, 'but he was actually with my mum before she and my other uncle — my real dad — went out.'

'Wait,' Toby says. He sits down at the kitchen table and pulls me in front of him. 'Start again.'

'I just saw him.'

'Your . . . ?'

'Uncle Jack. My real dad.'

'Where's he now?'

'I told him I had to go to work, I couldn't deal with any more revelations. And then I texted you.'

'It's a pretty big fucking revelation.' He circles his arms around me. 'How are you feeling? Do you think you've taken it in yet?'

'Wait, it gets better.' I can feel myself grinning, stupidly. Don't fall apart now. 'I *also* found out that Uncle Jack got into a fight with my grandad and my grandad had a heart attack and died and Uncle Jack — my dad — went to prison for manslaughter.' I drop my face into my hands. He's going to run away if you tell him any more of this shit, I think. 'It's just a fucking mess,' I say, and then I start crying.

'Tal,' Toby says, softly. He pulls me onto his knee. I press my face into his chest, letting the sobs break and subside. The cotton of his shirt is sucked away from his skin and towards my mouth with every deep breath inwards; I can hear his heartbeat.

'No wonder you're so fucking crazy,' he mumbles into my hair.

'*Hey.*'

'I'm joking.'

I blow my nose on a napkin. 'Sorry, I got mascara all over your shirt.'

'I really need to stop wearing them around you,' he says, and I grin for real. 'So, do you wanna talk about it?'

'Where do I start?'

'Wherever you want.'

472

I blow my nose again. 'What do I say to him now I know? If he wakes up. Do I bring it up? Do I wait for him to tell me?'

'Bring it up.'

'But he clearly didn't *want* me to find out.'

'Well maybe it was your mum's idea to keep it a secret.'

'Maybe.' I dunno how I feel about that, either.

'And this was why your dad was weird with you when you were younger — is that what you think?'

'Yeah,' I say. 'Actually, he *was* fine until Jack showed up.'

'And then what?'

'Maybe when Uncle Jack turned up, he thought my mum was going to leave with him and he was so scared of losing us he was horrible to us. Or maybe he was angry . . . I don't know.'

He pushed us away, I think, like he told Kathy's mum. But he must have loved my mother a lot. He took her back even though it meant raising me; he must have really adored her.

Toby's frowning. 'Did your mum still like Jack then?'

I lean my head against his shoulder. 'There was definitely something between them. Even I could tell and I was ten.'

'Okay.'

'*God*,' I say. I wipe my eyes and take a deep breath. 'I feel bad for all of them. I mean — one guy kills his abusive father and goes to prison, loses his girlfriend and daughter, and the other one's stuck bringing up his brother's child, wondering if his wife is pining away for the father-killer.'

Toby shakes his head. 'When you put it like that . . . '

'I *know*.'

We catch each other's eye, and suddenly we're both laughing. I feel weirdly better already, I feel my mind and body stretching forwards, unfurling themselves. I feel hopeful, I think.

Toby squeezes me. 'What are you going to do now?' he asks.

'I guess I'll see him again,' I say, and I have a sudden tug of sadness again. 'I should hear more about it, I *want* to hear more about it. He's just . . . I'm not sure I can do it straight away.'

'Understandable.'

Maybe I'll get Malkie to keep an eye on Jack, make sure everything's okay. I give a silent prayer of thanks that he came back from Canada.

Another thought strikes me, and I sit up again. 'I just can't believe all the adults knew what Jack did,' I say. 'When he first turned up at my grandma's, I thought everyone was tense because he hadn't told them he was coming.'

'How did your grandma react?' Toby asks.

'She didn't really.'

Why not, Grandma? Did you feel responsible? For the first time since I went to live with her, I can't imagine what she'd say in this situation. I remember Vivienne, that summer back in 1991, saying 'she did what she always did, nothing.' Maybe my grandmother was so worn down she could only go along with her circumstances. Not act for herself, not make decisions. She couldn't have been so crazy for my grandfather she sacrificed her kids for him, I try to tell myself, not when she was so loving to me.

I realise Toby's been talking. 'What was that?'

'Could I wash myself in your kitchen?' He nods at the shower. 'I ran all the way from the station.'

'Sure,' I say. I try to pull myself together; I look at him like I'm seeing him for the first time, run my finger along his jawline. 'You don't have a beard.'

'Nope.'

'But you've got more manly-looking since I knew you.'

'I should hope so.'

'You were so cute back then,' I say. 'What happened?'

I lean forwards for a kiss, then we're interrupted by the telephone. It sounds shriller than normal, and louder, and it brings me back to what's going on around me. I'm up and across the floor before it rings for a third time, the receiver in my hand.

'Miss Park?'

'Yes.'

'I'm calling from the hospital.' Down the line she clears her throat. I look at Toby, we both seem frozen exactly as we are. Outside, the evening is still, hanging perfectly in the air.

'He's awake,' she says.

★ ★ ★

Aunt Gillian and Aunt Vivienne are in the reception area when I arrive. They're both in

475

yellow, strangely — Aunt Vivienne in a Grace Kelly-style lemon dress with a nipped-in waist, and Aunt Gillian in an apricot chiffon shirt and black trousers.

'There you are,' Aunt Gillian says. 'What took you so long?'

'Taxi got stuck in traffic,' I say, peeling my jacket off. I left Toby at the flat when I went out to hail one; it feels nice to know I'll be going home to someone tonight.

We file into my father's room. He's staring at something on the ceiling and doesn't seem to hear us.

'Don't get him too excited,' the nurse says. She looks suspiciously at Aunt Vivienne, who looks back at her, all innocence.

We stand over him. Aunt Gillian is crying already and Aunt Vivienne looks wary.

'Hi Dad,' I say.

My father tears his eyes very slowly away from the ceiling. 'Who's that?' he asks.

'It's me, Tallulah.'

'Tallulah?' My father seems to think about the name for a minute.

'Your *daughter*,' Aunt Gillian bursts out. 'And Gillian and Viv. Your sisters.'

'Sisters?' my father asks.

'Oh *God*,' Aunt Gillian wails.

We stand awkwardly in front of him, not knowing what to say next. I look at Aunt Vivienne; she shrugs.

My father sighs. His face looks funny, unfocused. I lean closer so he can take a look at me. My throat is pulsing in time with my heartbeat.

476

'Evelyn,' he says, very quietly.

'No, it's Tallulah,' I say. 'Mum was Evelyn.'

My father's face clears. It hits me, now that our eyes are locked, how there are little flecks of gold in his irises.

'It's Tallulah,' I say again.

'I know,' my father says. 'Tallulah.'

★ ★ ★

The technical term for bleeding is 'hæmorrhaging', meaning the loss or leaking of blood either outwardly, such as through an orifice or break (cut) in the skin, or inwardly, when the blood escapes from blood vessels within the body.

As an adult in good health, you can lose up to twenty percent of your total blood volume with no long-term damage done. After that your skin might become clammy, your fingernails and lips bluish, your head dizzy. After a loss of forty percent, your body goes into shock, and immediate treatment becomes critical. However, if incompatible blood is transfused the new cells are perceived as 'foreign invaders' and the body's immune system will attack them, causing shock, kidney failure and even death.

It is the red blood cells that determine the blood type for each person. These contain a variety of antigens (substances that trigger the production of antibodies), which divides them into types: A, B, AB and O. Each child inherits one antigen from the mother and one from the father, which is why it is common for children to have the same blood type as at least one parent.

I've always known my blood type, it's the same as my father's: O negative, the universal donor. Anyone can receive a transfusion of our blood, but we can only receive from another O negative individual. If I start hæmorrhaging, it will be my father who can save me.

★　★　★

'Edward,' Aunt Gillian says, dabbing at her eyes with a handkerchief. 'You gave us such a fright.'

'How are you feeling?' I ask my father.

'I've been better,' he says.

'Yeah, probably,' I say, and I try to smile.

'How have *you* been?' he asks, looking at me. His face is as blank as it always was, except that now his eyes are bigger, and purplish underneath.

'Okay,' I say. 'Worried about you.'

'I didn't mean that,' he says.

'I know.'

'Don't talk in code, you two,' Aunt Gillian says, automatically. 'It's rude.'

I'm looking at my father, drinking him in. I guess he does look a little bit like Omar Sharif — not the smiley, horse-betting, card-playing Omar Sharif in real life, more like his character in *Doctor Zhivago*, the tortured, honourable medic.

'Always enjoy sticking your nose in, don't you?' Aunt Vivienne's saying now. 'People don't need to tell you absolutely *everything* that's going on, Gillian.'

'Oh for goodness' sake, Vivienne,' Aunt Gillian

says. 'Would it really hurt so much to be civil?'

My father closes his eyes.

'Both of you shut up,' I say. 'Dad's awake, so let's try and get on for half an hour. Just half a fucking hour.'

I see my father smile quickly; just a flash, then it's gone.

'I swear,' Aunt Vivienne says grimly. '*Someone* in this room is going to die of high blood pressure, and it might just be me.'

20

Aunt Vivienne comes to stand next to me by the window. We watch Gillian plump my father's pillow for him.

'My daughter's been updating me on your whereabouts, your health, you know,' she says. 'Little details like that.'

'I thought so,' I say. 'It feels funny.'

She folds her arms. 'I'm not a mind-reader, Tallulah.'

'Knowing that you two were thinking about me, I mean.' I rock back on my heels, resting my hands against the windowsill behind me. 'I always assumed that everyone just went on with their lives without me.'

'Well, we did struggle on,' Aunt Vivienne says; her mouth twitches. 'But you don't forget family. Even when they seem to have forgotten you.' She cocks her head at me. 'Why did you come back?'

I chew my lip. 'My mum said something when I was younger,' I say. 'About damaged people.'

'Yes, well,' Aunt Vivienne says. 'If anyone knows damaged people it would be this family.'

'But not just that they're damaged.'

'No?'

'She said it's a cycle. So when you're damaged, you're damaged for life.'

Aunt Gillian looks up from my father's side. 'Tallulah, darling. Must you talk about that here?'

'She can talk about whatever she pleases,' Aunt Vivienne says. 'It's one of the great things about our democratic society.'

'This is not a democracy, this is a hospital,' Aunt Gillian says, but she turns back to my father.

'And what was the conclusion?' Aunt Vivienne asks.

I shrug. 'She was saying that when you're damaged, you damage others, and you put yourself in situations where you're going to be damaged again because it's the only way you know how to be.' I shrug again. 'But I didn't get it. And then I was so angry that she left me . . . ' I stop. She wasn't just talking about the Parks, I realise. She needed security because she'd lost it after her parents died. And then when my father went away too she needed reassurance, and she turned to Uncle Jack. She just fell for him harder than she expected. But that was why she blamed herself — she thought that her neediness had caused all the trouble.

Aunt Vivienne looks impatient. 'And now you want to prove her wrong?'

'I guess.'

'Your mother was very smart, you know,' she says. 'I wasn't her biggest fan, obviously, but she was no ball of fluff.'

'I know you don't hate us as much as you pretend to,' I say, and she smiles at me. I think about telling her that Jack is back — that I know everything. That I understand now why she might have felt my mother betrayed her brothers, why she resented her. It wasn't her fault though,

481

Aunt Vivienne. That was the way she was damaged.

I squeeze my eyes shut and think of Jack as he was in my flat, half strung-out and high, and I can't bring myself to say any of it. Aunt Vivienne loves Jack I know, really loves him, and it'll be much worse for her to see him in that condition than it was for me. He knew that too — that's why he wouldn't let her visit him in prison.

'Starr's flying home tonight,' I say. 'She said she'll come visit.'

'As long as she doesn't bring that ape with her.'

'Have you met him?'

'You know Starr — she never brings them home if she likes them. She's afraid I'll scare them off.'

'He's probably really nice,' I say. 'She wouldn't like him otherwise.'

'I did something right, then,' Aunt Vivienne says. 'It's a terrible bore loving men who don't give a hoot for you.'

I think of a fourteen-year-old Vivienne, unconscious with her teeth in the fireplace; I think of Uncle Jack trying to rile my grandfather himself so Vivienne would be left alone. I think of the scene between her and Malkie after my mother's party — 'I'd die for him, you know.' I think of Aunt Vivienne at the prison, being turned away by the guards, sitting in her car in case Uncle Jack changed his mind. Waiting for hours, then driving home and checking the calendar to see when the next visitation day was.

I lean in quickly to kiss her cheek. She puts

her hand up to the spot I've just pecked, blushing; it makes her look like a little girl.

'What was that for?'

'For being you,' I say.

She blushes deeper, then calls over to Aunt Gillian, 'Gillian, just be quiet for a minute, will you? Let's leave these two alone.'

'We've only just got here,' Aunt Gillian says, but Aunt Vivienne takes her by the elbow.

'You owe me,' she says over her shoulder.

I sit next to my father again when they've gone, leaning forwards and resting my hands on the bed. 'I'm sorry,' I say.

'You've nothing to be sorry about.' He coughs. It sounds like a smoker's cough — a proper hacking noise, with plenty of phlegm behind it.

'I thought you were going to die.'

My father leans back onto his pillows. He pats my hand. I take his in mine; it's very cold.

'I went over what you said for a very long time,' he says, slowly. 'I suppose I was in denial. I didn't want to face up to the guilt of having put you in that situation. I tried to talk to the school about it and have action taken against the person who . . . But without you there, and I didn't even know if it was a teacher or a student.' He grips his bedsheets.

'It was a teacher.'

I think I see his eyes glisten. 'I'm so sorry that it happened to you.'

'It's fine,' I say. 'I mean, it's not fine, but it's in the past.'

He looks guilty. 'And I suppose I did seem cold when you were younger, but that wasn't

483

because I didn't love you . . . Don't love you.' He trails off.

'Dad . . . '

'And as for your mother . . . '

'Dad, it's okay. We can talk about this later.'

'No,' he says. 'I want to talk about it now, while we still have time.'

'Okay.'

'I loved your mother.'

'Of course.'

'It's important for you to know that although she . . . she probably married me to secure a future for you,' he says, 'that doesn't mean you should think less of her.'

'She didn't . . . ' I start, but he holds his hand up to stop me.

'She never did a single thing without thinking of you first.' He squeezes my hand tightly. 'Your mother loved you very, very much, Tallulah. Don't think that she didn't love you more than anyone has ever loved anyone, because she did.'

'I know,' I say. 'And I'm sorry I blamed you for her dying.' I clear my throat. 'I saw Jack earlier. I know . . . ' I try to figure out how to phrase it delicately. 'Everything, I guess.'

'He told you about your mother?'

'Yeah.'

'Did he explain?'

'Grandad? Yeah. And he gave me some money — he said he got it from you.'

'Ah.' My father passes his free hand over his face. He's silent for a moment. 'I have to admit, I didn't give him enough credit. I thought he just wanted to come between me and your mother, to punish us. But he said he still loved her. And you.'

'What happened at Grandma's that time? Why were him and Mum fighting?'

'He'd threatened to tell you everything.'

'Oh.' And then what? Was she scared I'd think badly of her? Is that why she got depressed? Or did she still feel guilty for everything that happened?

'So we paid him to go away.' My father coughs again. 'I thought he'd take the money and run.'

'He did.'

'But he came back again, after Evie died, with some idea about claiming his own back. He said he'd take me to court.' He frowns. 'I know — legally speaking — he had no leg to stand on, but by then it was too important for you not to find out. You were so devastated about your mother, I was afraid.'

I have a sudden flashback to the telephone conversation I'd overheard that Christmas — so it was me Uncle Jack had tried to get back, not my mother.

'And you paid him off again?'

My father bites his lip. 'I did. I'm sorry. I know it was wrong of me. Mother said I shouldn't interfere with someone trying to right the wrongs they did their children. And she was . . . ' This time the coughing fit wipes out the end of the sentence.

'Take it easy, Dad.'

'I truly believed,' my father says, hand to his mouth, 'he couldn't give you a stable, loving home. And I managed to persuade him, finally.'

485

I lean back in my chair. 'I always thought Mum was keeping a secret from you,' I say. 'That *that* was why she was scared when he turned up.'

'She was nearly eight months pregnant when she moved in with me,' my father says. 'It would have been quite hard to keep that a secret, believe me, even without my medical training.'

I can't hold back my laugh, in spite of the situation.

He shakes his head. 'Your mother did keep secrets,' he says, slowly. 'But not very well. I could tell she still had feelings for Jack. And then he called that afternoon — he said she'd told him to. I didn't know they were speaking behind my back. It made me realise that perhaps she still wanted to be with him. Confirmed my fears, I suppose I should say. But I should never have confronted her.' He stares at the ceiling.

'Hey,' I say. 'You didn't know what was going to happen.'

I've been blaming him for the wrong thing, I realise. It wasn't his fault my mother died — he didn't push her, he couldn't have fixed her. It was his fault I felt abandoned afterwards, but then he was traumatised too.

'I'm sure you'll have plenty of time to get to know Jack better now?'

'I don't know.'

'I know we had a falling out,' he says, letting out a pent-up breath. 'And you seem to have done a pretty good job of growing up without me — but I'd like to spend some father-daughter time together, if you'll let me call it that. Getting to know each other again.'

I hesitate. I still have questions.

Then again — maybe she did still have feelings for Jack, after everything, but I think my mother loved my father too. He was the stable, caring one. He's who she chose to raise her child with. That means something to me.

'What do you think?' my father asks; he looks anxious.

'I'd like that too,' I say.

'Good,' he says.

'But slowly.'

'I really am so sorry, Tallulah.'

'Dad,' I say. 'Just concentrate on getting better. We can talk about everything else later, okay?'

'Okay.'

'Good.'

He smiles weakly, then puts a hand up to his face, and pats his right eye.

'Something wrong?'

'It's twitching,' he says. 'Just a little annoying.' He coughs again.

'Do you want some water?'

He nods.

Another nurse comes in. 'I'm afraid visiting hours are over,' she says.

'Let me get him a drink,' I say. I pour him a cup, and stand next to him while he sips at it.

'I'll come back tomorrow,' I say.

He looks up. 'That would be nice.'

I bend down and kiss him on the forehead and he puts his hand up, catching my hair, tugging it.

'It took a heart attack to bring you back,' he says.

'No,' I say. 'It wasn't that.' I want to shake my head, but he seems to be using my hair as support.

'Good,' he says. 'Because I don't think I could survive another one.'

The nurse gives me a sympathetic smile as I leave the room.

'They're all a bit groggy for a while after they wake up,' she whispers to me. 'He'll get better, don't worry.'

'He's fine already,' I say.

She gives me one of those pitying looks they keep for relatives in denial, and closes the door behind me. Outside my father's room a cleaner is mopping the floor. My shoes squeak as I pick my way around the bucket, and everything smells waxy, fresh and new.

PART FIVE

Heart Again

21

Did you know the heart is the only organ not completely in thrall to the brain? Specialised pacemaker cells at the entrance to the right atrium are myogenic, meaning they will contract without an outside influence — such as the electrical impulse coming from the central nervous system. In fact your heart forms two weeks after fertilisation, and beats in the fifth week of the gestation period, before it is first fed by this impulse.

In other words, if you cut your heart out it could — in theory — continue beating.

★   ★   ★

When I was younger we went on a day trip to the museum. I don't know which museum; it was dark and had waxwork figures re-enacting scenes from Anglo-Saxon life. Men carrying shields and spears, women stirring huge cauldrons. My mother held my hand around the exhibitions and let me have an ice-cream in the café afterwards.

I remember sitting in the museum grounds with my face turned up towards the sun, my mother and father opposite me. My father wasn't wearing a tie that day, and he took his shoes and socks off to feel the grass with his bare feet. The two of them exchanged looks and laughed when I asked about the sandy hair growing on his toes.

Years later, I realised that we must have looked like an odd little trio, the two full-bodied, blond parents with their skinny, dark-haired daughter.

I remember it being a national holiday, or something like that, because the place was crowded with people. Some boys — they must have been teenagers, although at the time they seemed old to me, and I hid behind my mother's legs when they came near — were kicking a football around, and my father kicked it back at them when it landed on our picnic blanket. He kicked it quite hard, and one of the boys, the closest one, clapped him and said something complimentary. My mother raised her eyebrows, 'I didn't know you played football,' she said, and my father laughed again.

We must have gone somewhere else, although I don't remember that, because it was late when we came home, my mother carrying me in her aims. I fell asleep up there, my cheek nestled in the crook of her neck, my father walking next to her on the kerb side. Just before I dropped off I felt his hand reach up and ruffle my hair. I heard him murmur something, and a car whoosh past. Then my mother's heartbeat pumping blood around her body, warm and safe and full of love for me.

Acknowledgements

There are countless people I would like to thank, but I should start with Ruth Salter and Jenny Slattery (two friends who happen to be great nurses). During my MA I practically lived at their flat and the week before I had to hand in my first piece of writing they were talking about the heart; this started me thinking about the metaphorical possibilities inherent in medicine, and the novel took off from there. I'm also eternally grateful for the existence of Wikipedia, and Orijit Banerji, another friend and a brilliant doctor, who kindly read through the medical sections for accuracy.

My agents, Natalie Butlin and Christine Green at Christine Green Authors' Agent, have been wonderful, working tirelessly on the manuscript and still finding time to prepare delicious lunches for me. Also Claire Anderson-Wheeler, who gave me my first invaluable feedback on the novel before jetting off to New York. I will definitely be taking you up on your offer of a drink out there someday.

My editor, Lauren Parsons, and the rest of the brilliant staff at Legend Press. Having someone fall in love with your book and get behind it as they have done has been the most incredible feeling.

My tutors, Fiona Stafford, Annie Sutherland and Philip West at Somerville College, who were fascinating and encouraging and made Austen, *Beowulf* and Shakespeare even more enjoyable, if that's possible.

I owe a huge debt to Susanna Jones at Royal Holloway, who always believed in this book, and Andrew Motion, who led me gently to the conclusion that I would make a terrible master criminal.

John Robertson and Charles Milnes, two of the nicest, most understanding bosses I could have hoped for.

For their patience and for all the drinks, the following writers: Emma Chapman; Liz Gifford; Carolina Gonzalez-Carvajal; Lucy Hounsom; Liza Klaussmann; and Rebecca Lloyd-James. No one makes gin more fun.

My amazing friends, whose excitement about my becoming an author has been so moving. My favourite family, Janet, Alex and Hannah Gordon; Tallie might be a lot like me, but they made sure our lives were completely different. And my favourite cats, Daisy, Lucky and Maggie.

And last but not least, my boyfriend Tom Feltham. You're almost as brilliant a writer and editor as you are terrible at cleaning kitchen surfaces, and I love you very much.

We do hope that you have enjoyed reading this large print book.

Did you know that all of our titles are available for purchase?

We publish a wide range of high quality large print books including:
Romances, Mysteries, Classics
General Fiction
Non Fiction and Westerns

Special interest titles available in large print are:
The Little Oxford Dictionary
Music Book
Song Book
Hymn Book
Service Book

Also available from us courtesy of Oxford University Press:
Young Readers' Dictionary
(large print edition)
Young Readers' Thesaurus
(large print edition)

For further information or a free brochure, please contact us at:
Ulverscroft Large Print Books Ltd.,
The Green, Bradgate Road, Anstey,
Leicester, LE7 7FU, England.
Tel: (00 44) 0116 236 4325
Fax: (00 44) 0116 234 0205